SPLENDID ISOLATION?

Also by John Charmley

Duff Cooper: The Authorised Biography
Lord Lloyd and the Decline of the British Empire
Descent to Suez:
The Diaries of Sir Evelyn Shuckburgh 1951–6 (Ed)
Chamberlain and the Lost Peace
Churchill: The End of Glory
Churchill's Grand Alliance
A History of Conservative Politics 1900–1996

Splendid Isolation?

*Britain, the Balance of Power
and the Origins of the First World War*

John Charmley

Hodder & Stoughton

To Lorraine

Copyright © 1999 by John Charmley

First published in Great Britain in 1999 by Hodder and Stoughton
A division of Hodder Headline PLC

The right of John Charmley to be identified as the Author
of the Work has been asserted by him in accordance
with the Copyright, Designs and Patents Act 1988.

10 9 8 7 6 5 4 3 2 1

All right reserved. No part of this publication may be reproduced,
stored in a retrieval system, or transmitted, in any form or by
any means without the prior written permission of the publisher,
nor be otherwise circulated in any form of binding or cover other
than that in which it is published and without a similar condition being
imposed on the subsequent purchaser.

British Library Cataloguing in Publication Data

A CIP catalogue record for this title
is available from the British Library

ISBN 0 340 65790 1

Typeset by Hewer Text Ltd, Edinburgh
Printed and bound in Great Britain by
Clays, Ltd, St Ives PLC

Hodder and Stoughton
A division of Hodder Headline PLC
338 Euston Road
London NW1 3BH

Contents

Illustrations	vii
Acknowledgments	ix
Introduction	1

PART ONE: High Politics

1 Disraeli, Derby and the Eastern Question	11
2 Disraeli *Contra Mundum*	29
3 An End to Palmerstonianism?	45
4 Reading the Russian Sphinx	61
5 Lies, Intrigue and Politics	77
6 Low Politics	95
7 Resignation	113
8 Derby's Last Victory	129
9 Disraeli's Triumph	145

PART TWO: Isolation

10 Beaconsfieldism Falters	165
11 'A Great Many Mistakes'	181
12 Salisbury	195
13 Navigating the Rapids	211
14 Isolation	227

15 Assaulted by Asses' Jaw-bones 245
16 Blackmail 261
17 The German Alliance Mirage 277
18 Alliances and Understandings 295
19 The Myth of 'Continuity' 313

PART THREE: Balance of Power
20 Grey and the Balance of Power 331
21 Unbalancing Europe 347
22 Responsibility without Power 363
23 'Measurable distance of Armageddon' 379

Conclusion 397
Notes 403
Bibliography 491
Index 507

List of Illustrations

Disraeli
Salisbury
The Fifteenth Earl of Derby
Mary, Countess of Derby
Count Peter Shuvalov
The Fourth Earl of Carnarvon
Bismarck at his zenith
Gorchakov at Berlin
Andrassy as seen by *Vanity Fair*
The Second Earl Granville
Joseph Chamberlain at the Colonial Office
Arthur James Balfour
The Fifth Marquess of Lansdowne in old age
Paul Cambon
Royalty at play – King Edward VII, the Duke of Connaught and Kaiser Wilhelm II
Bernhard von Bülow
Sir Edward Grey

Acknowledgements

It will be evident to anyone familiar with the period how immense my debt is to a legion of scholars; no one can write in such an over-crowded field without acknowledging the work of others. The bibliography must serve as a thank you to the wider historical community, but on a more personal level there are a number of debts to be mentioned. My colleague and friend Professor Edward Acton, despite protesting his ignorance of British history, went through what I thought was the final draft of the book and improved it greatly; I am profoundly grateful to him for his efforts and owe much to his acuity as a critic. I am also grateful to Geoff Searle, for yet again (the seventh time, I think) taking time off from his research to read the fruits of mine. He is a constructive and searching critic, and I am grateful as ever, for his time, patience and comradeship. Other debts owed to colleagues at UEA are of a more general nature, but I should like to thank both Colin Davis and Michael John for many instances of moral support during the long slog which this book has involved; combining authorship with a heavy teaching and administrative load is only possible with such supportive colleagues. I would like to extend particular thanks to Professor John Vincent of Bristol for answering my questions about Lady Derby and for adding much invaluable material to my knowledge of the period.

I am grateful to my old friend and publisher, John Curtis, for his continued support, as well as to my new publisher, Roland Philipps. I should also like to thank Linda Osband who, as ever, copy-edited the book with skill and tact.

On a more personal level I would like to acknowledge, again, the great moral support provided by my wife Lorraine, who creates the conditions in which I can combine writing, researching, teaching and administration, and who keeps me reasonably sane. I also want to thank my sons, Gervase, Gerard and Kit, who tolerate my occupation of the laptop computer at inconvenient times; Gerard may even get some benefit from this book as he works away at Aberystwyth, and both he and Gervase will, I suspect, agree with the conclusions I reach here about Britain and Europe.

I would like to thank the following for permission to quote from papers: the National Trust (Beaconsfield papers); the Marquess of Salisbury (Salisbury papers); the Earl of Derby (Derby papers); Trustees of the British Museum (Carnarvon papers, Lansdowne papers). If I have inadvertently failed to acknowledge anyone's copyright I would be grateful if they would contact me at my publishers so that the oversight can be corrected. I am particularly grateful to Malcolm Howard who, once again managed to turn my collection of photographs into something my publishers could use.

Introduction

As we approach the end of the twentieth century, the place of the Great War in determining its shape looms as large as ever. The British have a special relationship with the two World Wars. They ended up on the winning side twice, yet the rewards for so doing have hardly seemed commensurate with the sacrifices involved. One result of this has been to take as an article of faith the utter necessity of becoming involved in the wars; this way the lack of anything to show for the sacrifices can be ignored in the warm glow of self-satisfaction which usually follows British evocations of the wars.

One strand in the 'inevitability' argument is the belief that Britain had a role to play in maintaining the balance of power in Europe and that this 'traditional' policy was being fulfilled in 1914 and 1939. Neville Chamberlain is assaulted for not following this tradition. Yet where was this 'tradition' between 1815 and 1914, or between 1714 and 1793 for that matter?

This book dissents from the view that there was such a traditional foreign policy, and therefore from the opinion that the British involvement in the war of 1914 was inevitable; it dissents, by implication, from the view that British participation was desirable. Just before this book begins in 1874, the Germans had defeated the French. The skies had not fallen in and civilisation had not ended; nor would it have done in 1914 had the Germans once more defeated the French.

So why did the British Government in 1914 feel that it ought to go to war? Statesmen are the prisoners of their assumptions, which, in turn, derive from their experiences and their reading of events. This book attempts to delineate the experiences and events which shaped the consciousness of British policy-makers in 1914.

For that generation, as for the previous one, the formative event had been the creation of Bismarck's German empire, so the book begins with the Disraelian attempt to regain for Britain the prestige which he felt had been lost under Gladstone and the Liberals. Disraeli, the first, last and only Earl of Beaconsfield, has generally been credited with reviving the fortunes of Queen Victoria and of the Conservative Party, making the one an Empress and the other the party of Empire; even the revisionist view that there was more style than substance to all this has been trumped by a more modern perspective which can admire a politician who denied that 'politics and government were a primarily ratiocinative activity'. Disraeli's mastery of 'image', and his sense of 'the direction in which the nation and the party ought to be travelling', are sufficient to win admiration in an era of 'spin doctors'. To have 'more or less single-handedly hewed out the central image of his party's platform for a century by creating the image of the Conservatives as the national party'[1] can now be recognised as having been of more significance than pushing through a legislative programme, the details of which have long ceased to be of interest. He was an imperialist who added little to the Empire; an advocate of aristocratic rule who ushered in democracy and made it Tory. It was not what Disraeli did, but what he said, and even more importantly the way he said it, which mattered; substance fades, image remains and, in time, is everything.

Historians who wrote in an era when achievement was measured in terms of legislative impact tended to dismiss Disraeli's odd ideas on foreign policy as part of his 'fondness for the bizarre and the fantastic',[2] and as lacking any 'compensating flair for diagnosing the trends of the time, or discerning the future trend of events'.[3] The Whig statesman, Lord Clarendon, summed up the popular view when he called Disraeli a 'political acrobat'.[4] But in an era of rapid change, a talent for acrobatics can be useful. Disraeli recognised that the unification of Germany was 'a greater political event' than the French Revolution, and that 'not a single principle in the management of our foreign affairs, accepted by all statesmen for guidance up to six months ago, any longer exists'; the balance of power had been 'entirely destroyed', much to England's disadvantage.[5] George Canning had declared as long ago as 1826 that the 'balance of power' was 'a standard perpetually varying, as civilization advances and as new nations spring up';[6] upon his return to office in 1874, Disraeli would attempt to readjust it in Britain's favour. His methods and actions would create a crisis within the Conservative Party, controversy in the country, and set the tone expected from British governments for the next fifty years.

One of the book's underlying themes is the relationship of British politicians to the notion of 'the balance of power', so it might be as well to define what contemporaries meant when they spoke of it. When the House of Commons had debated the declaration of the Crimean War against Russia on 27 March 1854, Lord John Russell, the Leader of the Commons, referred to it as the 'maxim which, since the time of William III, has governed and actuated the councils of this country', namely that of denying 'preponderance' to any one Power by throwing Britain's weight 'into the scale'; he declared that war was necessary in order to maintain the 'balance of power'.[7] That a scion of the great Whig dynasty of Russell should have favoured a 'maxim' which had enabled his own kind to enrich themselves was only natural. It was equally natural that from the other end of the Liberal coalition the concept should have been questioned. The Radical Liberal, John Bright, asked what it meant to say that the war was necessary in order to maintain the balance of power, and professed himself unable to see what British interests would be served by the sacrifice of blood and treasure which would be entailed.[8] Like his friend Richard Cobden, Bright believed that diplomacy was a 'gigantic system of outrelief for the aristocracy', and saw no reason why a rational and liberal polity should engage in warfare. Lord Palmerston, the Home Secretary and darling of the patriotic press, declined to 'explain the meaning of the expression "the balance of power" ', to an obviously ignorant middle-class manufacturer from northern parts who would, he suggested, 'give his vote against going to war for the liberties and independence of the country, rather than bear his share in the expenditure which it would entail'. He declared, *de haut en bas*, that the term was 'one that has been familiar to the minds of all mankind from the earliest ages in all parts of the globe'; it meant 'that a number of weaker States may unite to prevent a stronger one from acquiring a position which should be dangerous to them, and which should overthrow their independence, their liberty, and their freedom of action'.[9]

Palmerston got his war in 1854, but a decade later Bright had his revenge. Despite declarations that Denmark would not stand alone if she defied Bismarck's Prussia in 1864 in the Schleswig-Holstein affair, that was precisely what occurred. Bright allowed himself to gloat over the downfall of the balance of power, describing it as a 'foul idol' which had loaded the country with debts, taxes and the cost of hundreds of thousands of lives; there was, he rejoiced, 'one superstition less which has its hold upon the minds of English statesmen and English people'.[10] Certainly during the next decade, whilst the map of Europe changed dramatically, Britain stayed on the sidelines. Lord Stanley, Foreign Secretary in 1866, declared of the war which decided the struggle for mastery in Germany that 'there never was a great European war in which the direct national interests of England were less concerned'.[11]

In a sense then Disraeli's foreign policy after 1874 amounted to a reassertion of the importance of the balance of power and of the need for Britain to actively readjust it in her favour. But his reaction was not shared by many even in his own Party. Lord Stanley, who succeeded as the fifteenth Earl of Derby in 1869, remained unmoved by Disraeli's fears. To those who argued that Britain should increase her spending on armaments, he replied: 'France and Germany have their hands full now, and will be exhausted when peace is made; the US have cut down their navy to the lowest point and disbanded their army. . . . Where is the enemy?' He could understand Radicals and Liberals wanting to help the new republican France and advocating intervention in the Franco-Prussian war, 'but for Conservatives and generally for those who have anything to lose, it seems suicidal'.[12] This was a line very different from that of his leader, but it was not the product of Stanley's personal oddities; rather it was a manifestation of a type of thinking with a long and distinguished lineage in the Conservative Party.

Gladstone (who, unlike Disraeli, had been a member of it) described 'the old Tory party' as following 'essentially a Peace policy' in foreign affairs.[13] The longest-serving (if least successful) Conservative leader, the fourteenth Earl of Derby (father of Disraeli's Foreign Secretary) reminded their Lordships in 1866 that it was not true that a Conservative Government was necessarily a warlike one, since the Conservative Party 'consists, in a great measure, of men who have the greatest interest and the largest stake in the country; they are the men upon whom the consequences of a war would fall most heavily'. The duty of a Conservative Government was 'to keep itself upon terms of goodwill with all surrounding nations, but not to entangle itself with any single or monopolizing alliance with any one of them; above all to endeavour not to interfere needlessly and vexatiously with the internal affairs of any foreign country'.[14] This was a doctrine from which neither the Tories of the seventeenth century under Sir Edward Seymour, nor their eighteenth-and nineteenth-century successors, would have dissented. It was certainly the line taken in 1876 by Derby's son and heir.

The first part of the book focuses upon the realities of Disraelian diplomacy rather than the 'realities behind diplomacy'. It concurs with Marx that men do not make their history 'just as they please', but do so 'under circumstances directly encountered, given and transmitted from the past'. But men 'make their own history' nonetheless,[15] which means that their thoughts and actions are an essential part of any 'reality' and not simply an epiphenomenon. More than some aspects of history, that of diplomacy depends upon the contingent and the accidental. Late-Victorian foreign policy was conducted by about three dozen people ranging from the Queen through to individual diplomats; they did not operate in a solipsism, but nor were they the puppets of some hidden reality. The duel between Disraeli and Derby did not have a preordained outcome – as the narrative makes plain. The realities of diplomacy matter as much as those 'behind' it; they are just messier to deal with because they exist outside historians' attempts to tidy up history and include everything from a crucial despatch not being delivered in time because a clerk was having his Sunday afternoon constitutional,[16] through to allegations that the Foreign Secretary's wife was giving Cabinet secrets to the Russian Ambassador.[17]

But for all its showiness, Disraeli's triumph in 1878 may have been less impressive than it seemed; at least that is the suggestion in Part Two, where Lord Salisbury's diplomacy is examined. In place of the simplicities of the 'balance of power' and 'traditional British foreign policy', we see something more flexible and sensitive to the international situation. Salisbury retained a free hand for British diplomacy; so, it will be argued, did the underrated and neglected Lord Lansdowne, whose diplomacy is given its fullest examination to date. The assertion that if there was 'continuity' in British policy it was between Salisbury and Lansdowne, not the latter and Sir Edward Grey, is at the heart of the last part of the book. If there was a 'turning-point', it was in 1906 when the electorate put into office a Liberal Government.

It was not the electorate's fault that Grey was a cold warrior in a warm climate, or that he soon succeeded in hotting things up. Maybe Germany was the great danger to the balance of power in Europe; did that matter to an island Empire? The question arises as to the extent to which Grey's policies contributed to the origins of the war, not as part of an understandable and even laudable

British response to German malignity, but as part of the upsetting of the balance of power at its geopolitical epicentre.

Grey's victory in 1914 is not without its relevance to the larger story of 'British decline' which has preoccupied modern historians. Some historians have argued that Britain has been a Power in decline for a good long time.[18] In this version of events, the two World Wars were, at most, catalysts which speeded up trends already well under way; at worst, they did no more than validate those trends. One of the implications of the version of events offered here is that participation in the wars was a cause of British decline. By deciding to abandon the realities of the old Conservative tradition for the garish purple of Disraeli's imperial destiny and its Liberal variant, Britain's policy-makers forced her to punch above her weight in a global conflict from which she could only emerge severely weakened.

Part One

High Politics

'We ought not to allow the matter simply to drift. We ought to have a policy.'

*Sir Stafford Northcote
to Lord Beaconsfield, 21 April 1877*

1

Disraeli, Derby and the Eastern Question

The British general election of 1874 saw an upset in the domestic political balance of power which was, in its own way, as significant as the more momentous change in the European balance noted by Disraeli in 1871. For the first time since 1841 the Conservatives had won power, and for the first time in his career their leader, Benjamin Disraeli, would have a parliamentary majority to carry out his wishes. This was not a prospect which brought pleasure even to some Conservatives.

Of all the leaders of the British Conservative Party, Disraeli was by far the most improbable. Jewish by birth and ancestry, he had not passed through the 'staff colleges' of public school and Oxbridge which had helped other outsiders such as Peel and Gladstone to assimilate into the British ruling elite. A novelist and a dandy, with manners and morals to match, Disraeli always lacked that *gravitas* which the solemn English prefer to talent in their statesmen. Politicians are expected to conform to a number of stereotypes and to be amenable to being judged as a whole; Disraeli confounded the former and defied the latter. The paradoxes, the epigrams, the prevalent sense of a mocking irony tinged with a Romanticism leavened by cynicism, made him at once an object of fascination and distrust. It was not altogether surprising that some prominent Conservatives were not keen to join a government led by such a man.

There was, however, no doubt about the identity of the new Foreign Secretary. Edward Henry Stanley, fifteenth Earl of Derby and son of Disraeli's former leader, was a long-standing friend of the new Prime Minister and held a prescriptive right to the Foreign Office, having occupied it before. Derby has not received much in the way of posthumous recognition from historians, who have largely taken at face value the criticisms later made of him by Disraeli and Salisbury, and who have seen in his vacillating foreign policy a reflection of his own personality quirks.[1] This is a conspicuous example of history as written by the victors. Disraeli and Salisbury have both left a great name in the history of the Tory Party, Derby has not.

Upon his father's death in 1869, Lord Stanley succeeded to the earldom with its vast acres and great wealth; but the fourteenth Earl was a difficult act to follow. He had been a superb natural orator, whose 'knowledge of the science of parliamentary defence' resembled, according to Macaulay, 'an instinct'.[2] Tall, dashingly handsome and intellectually able, Edward Geoffrey Stanley had followed a political odyssey which took him from Grey's Reform Bill Cabinet in 1832, through Peel's Cabinet from 1841 to 1845, and from thence to a long period as leader of the Protectionists. In 1851, he had become Prime Minister, and such was his experience and his colleagues' lack of it that he called them his 'babies'.[3] He had served twice more as premier, from 1858 to 1859, and again from 1866 until his retirement in 1867. His talents as a classical scholar were such that he found fame as the author of a noted translation of the *Iliad*, and he was not only Chancellor of the University of Oxford, but also a notable figure in Racing circles, and he was to be found at Newmarket as often as at the Palace of Westminster.

The Spectator drew an unflattering comparison between this dazzling figure and the new Earl in 1875, when it noted that: 'The late Lord Derby was a spirited statesman, who rather approved of one-sided enthusiasm. The present Lord Derby . . . prefers . . .

"cultivated apathy" . . . to anything like earnestness of the one-sided sort.'[4] The new Earl cut a rather commonplace and slightly rotund figure, but nevertheless enjoyed the sort of reputation for soundness which in England usually accompanies aristocratic wealth unencumbered by anything in the way of flair. Palmerston had thought well enough of him to offer him a post in his Government, but filial reverence had kept him in the Conservative Party.[5]

Palmerston's offer came only a few years after Stanley had proposed to Disraeli that they ought to make efforts to win him for the Conservative Party.[6] He quite lacked the visceral pessimism of his father's creed, and found his desire 'to keep things as they are & impede "progress" ', too bleak for his taste. He relied upon Disraeli to save the Conservatives from a 'reactionary course of opposition',[7] and noticed in himself a 'distaste for hot partisanship'.[8] That he should have looked to Disraeli rather than his father for support was not surprising, since he was his oldest and closest political friend and had 'No pleasanter recollection than that of our walks in the backwoods about Wycombe' which had been 'my chief political education'.[9] The thirty-year friendship between the flamboyant, extrovert, spendthrift Jew and the quiet, introverted, millionaire Englishman was the mainstay of the new Government. But by 1874 the new Foreign Secretary had a relationship which meant even more to him than his long connection with Disraeli – his marriage to the dowager second Marchioness of Salisbury.

In 1847, the widower second Marquess of Salisbury had married the twenty-three-year-old daughter of the fifth Earl of Delawarr, Lady Mary Sackville-West, who thereby became the stepmother of the future third Marquess, who was only seven years her junior. The elder Salisbury wanted a mother for the sickly offspring of his first marriage, and a wife who would produce another brood of Cecils; Lady Mary provided both. She also provided Hatfield House with a chatelaine who drew to it a glittering array of personalities, from Wellington to Palmerston, and from Disraeli to Clarendon. Through family connections (one of her sisters married into the prolific Russell clan, whilst her husband's niece was the daughter of Wellington's brother, the prominent diplomat, Lord Cowley), Lady Mary's network spread into the world of diplomacy, and through her salon at Hatfield all the great figures of the day passed.[10]

At some point in the mid-1850s, possibly in August or September 1855, Lady Mary's relationship with one of her visitors, Lord Stanley, became more intimate. The exact nature of the intimacy can only be guessed at. Some of the Cecil family came to regard Stanley as a black-hearted adulterer, but he did his best to try to persuade the second Marquess to approve of his son, Lord Robert's marriage to the daughter of a distinguished, but middle-class lawyer, which is not an obvious role for an adulterous lover to have assumed. Lady Mary referred to Stanley as '*le bien aimé*', which, to modern ears, suggests more than a close social acquaintanceship, but Victorian ears were attuned to other cadences.[11] She was not 'really beautiful to the eye, with her plain weatherbeaten skin and big feet', but according to her friend, the Queen of Holland, she had 'beautiful eyes, brown and shining, perfect teeth and a very good figure'; however, what was most striking about her was 'her intelligence' and her 'clear, almost masculine intellect'. The Dutch Queen did not believe that Lady Mary was Stanley's 'lover', but noted that 'she totally dominates him intellectually' and thought that she would marry him 'as soon as the old trembling Lord Salisbury passes away'.[12] So it proved. The deaths of James Salisbury in early 1868, and of the fourteenth Earl of Derby the following year, left the way open for Lady Mary to become the Countess of Derby in July 1870.

Mary Derby provided her new husband with great emotional and intellectual support, but there would be no reassembling of the glittering salon of her Hatfield days; Edward Stanley liked to live quietly. She did, however, provide Disraeli with a channel through which he could approach one of the great Conservative dissidents in 1874.

Disraeli could have formed his Government without the third Marquess of Salisbury, but it went against his grain to leave out a figure who could be a formidable opponent. As Lord Robert Cecil, Salisbury had been one of Disraeli's severest critics, and although he had graciously consented to join the Derby Government in 1866, he had resigned the following year and later excoriated Disraeli as a rootless Jew-adventurer at whose behest the country gentlemen of England had opened the high-road to democracy. But Disraeli bore no ill-will – indeed, he could never afford to do that – and he did want the impetuous, brilliant and sea-green incorruptible Marquess in his administration; and since he was hardly on speaking terms with Salisbury, he used Mary Derby as an intermediary – with some success, eventually.

Salisbury, who thought that good government depended 'upon the respect which the Chief's intellect or power in the country is held', thought that a Prime Minister would be 'respected if his mental powers are such as to inspire respect, or if he is so strong with the country that he can insist upon his opinions being respected'; Derby fitted this bill better than Disraeli.[13] He told Lady Derby that 'if Lord Derby were prime minister I should feel no difficulty in accepting office without emphasis as to prospective policy: for I think I know his mind' – but no one knew Disraeli's.[14] Lord Carnarvon, who had resigned with Salisbury in 1867, also urged him to join the Cabinet, but in order to help contain the Prime Minister.[15] Both men took office, but more to keep a weather-eye on the captain of the ship than with any expectation of serving out the full voyage.[16] As early as August 1874, Lady Derby was describing Salisbury to Disraeli as 'the wild man of your team'.[17] It would have seemed incredible to have suggested that before the end of the administration Derby would have split irrevocably from Disraeli, who would have formed a crucial political axis with Salisbury; yet that is what happened.

Disraeli 'always regarded foreign policy as the most important and fascinating task of the statesman'.[18] To his mind, 'political questions' seldom presented 'clear-cut moral issues, so that you can definitely say that one course is morally right, the other morally wrong', and Disraeli took 'the common-sense view that in politics it is generally a question merely of the more expedient course'. For him, 'the prime duty of a British statesman' was to look out for 'British honour and promote British welfare'.[19] Surveying the diplomatic scene, Disraeli agreed with Gladstone's Foreign Secretary, Lord Clarendon, that the 'selfishness that dictates our present system of isolation has reduced our importance, and therefore our influence, on the Continent to zero'.[20] He deplored the fact that 'our just influence in the councils of Europe has been lowered', but his objections went deeper than wounded *amour propre*.[21]

Disraeli's vision of England went beyond the fog-shrouded Atlantic archipelago. In 1866, he had declared that 'England is no longer a mere European Power; she is the metropolis of a great maritime Empire, extending to the boundaries of the furthest ocean.'[22] Disraeli agreed with his colleague Lord Sandon that the 'tendency of the day was in favour of large nationalities and the day of small nations was past'.[23] The day was coming 'when the question of the balance of power cannot be confined to Europe alone'. Britain would have to compete on a global scale not only with Russian expansionism in Asia, but with the rise of American and German power; and to do so with success meant using the Empire to Britain's advantage.[24] But imperial governance implied an ability to take a broad geopolitical perspective; Britain had a 'greater sphere of action than any other European Power', yet she could not 'look with indifference upon what takes place on the Continent'.[25]

Disraeli was well aware of how difficult it would be to get his fellow countrymen to take such a broad view. Even to utter the phrase 'foreign affairs' made 'an Englishman convinced that I am about to treat of subjects with which he has no concern'. However, leadership involved more than pandering to the wishes of an uninformed electorate; it had an educative function. Disraeli knew that 'upon . . . foreign affairs' matters as 'diverse as the levels of taxation and the health of industry depended'. He called not for a 'turbulent and aggressive diplomacy', but for a restoration of England to her rightful place in Europe and in the world.[26] But this was as much a domestic political as it was a geopolitical imperative.

Disraeli and the Conservatives had long suffered from Palmerston's ability to harness popular opinion behind his assertive foreign policy, and Disraeli had seen the damage which the abandonment of this line by Gladstone had done to the Liberals. Disraeli's own sense of the theatrical and taste for the meretricious, combined with his cynicism about human nature, meant that he recognised the importance of symbolism and rhetoric in winning public support. This combination of geopolitical awareness and populism was evident from the start of Disraeli's administration. His famed acquisition of the Suez Canal in 1875 could be criticised as an expensive gimmick which actually only gave Britain the reversion of the Khedive's shares, but from Disraeli's twin perspectives it gave Britain a stake in a vital artery of imperial trade and security, and symbolised her determination to assert her interests in regions of the world where they were under threat. Something similar could be said of his other controversial action in 1875 in making Victoria 'Empress of India'. To Gladstone and other Liberals, it was needlessly to degrade the ancient and honourable title of King and Queen for a flashy new bauble, but in a world where the Russians, Germans and Austrians were all ruled by men holding the imperial title, it was sending out an important signal. Disraeli recognised that the 'majesty of power' was a 'genuine element in the world'.[27] His actions staked out his vision of Britain as a great Asiatic empire. Derby, who admired the 'complete political success' of the purchase of the Canal shares, was nonetheless rendered uneasy by the revelation of 'the intense desire for action abroad that pervades the public mind'.[28]

By this time, however, Disraeli's imagination had been inflamed by even greater prospects which might lie before him. Writing to his confidante, Lady Bradford, on 3 November 1875, he commented that: 'I really believe "the Eastern Question" that has haunted Europe for a century, and which I thought the Crimean War had adjourned for half another, will fall to my lot to encounter – dare I say – to settle?'[29] It went without saying that Disraeli would indeed 'dare' to try to settle the Eastern

Question, which appealed both to his Romantic instincts and to his vision of Britain's place in the world.

From the terrace of the Topkapi Palace in Constantinople the Sultan could look upwards in the direction of the Bosphorus, and down to the Sea of Marmora towards the far Dardanelles, and see that he possessed the finest strategic position in the world. But the days of Turkish power were passing, and from the pillars of Hercules in the west, to the Persian Gulf in the east, the Ottoman Empire presented a spectacle of decay which offered its rivals tempting opportunities. For the British, at least from the late eighteenth century, it became an essential point of policy to prevent the Russians from seizing the key to the eastern Mediterranean at Constantinople.[30] Pitt's disciple, George Canning, had in 1807 made the integrity of Turkey an object of British foreign policy,[31] and it was his self-proclaimed successor, Viscount Palmerston, who had made the most vigorous efforts to prevent any dissolution of the Ottoman Empire,[32] which served two functions from the point of view of British geopolitics: it guarded the Straits at the Bosphorus and the Dardanelles; and it acted as a buffer state against Russian expansionism elsewhere.

On the eastern marches of Ottoman territory lay the crumbling Persian Empire as well as the Central Asian Khanates, which had been the subject of Russian aggrandisement throughout the century.[33] Persia and Turkey were 'barrier Powers to British India' and 'the destruction of either by a European Power would endanger India in so far as it would expose it to the early invasion of such a Power'. It had been British policy since the days of Bonaparte to 'aid and support those states'.[34] Britain had attempted to bolster the Persian Empire and to use it as a buffer zone to isolate India from the struggle for the balance of power in Europe; her attempts to prevent it going the way of the Central Asian Khanates had been attended with success.[35]

As Secretary of State for India, Salisbury concurred in the widely held view that 'Russia is slowly gaining hold of Persia', although he doubted the efficacy of the traditional British policy of opposing the advance towards the frontiers of India by gaining influence in Afghanistan: 'If ever we quarrel with Russia we shall have to fight her ourselves. No present setting of our neighbours will induce them to do it for us.'[36] Disraeli, who lacked Salisbury's pessimism, was 'quite prepared for acting with energy & promptitude' if the Russians advanced towards Afghanistan, but he preferred to stick with the traditional policy of getting others to keep the Russians out.[37] Disraeli saw the continued existence of the Ottoman Empire as a vital bulwark against Russian expansionism.[38]

Disraeli's interest in the Eastern Question was thus purely geopolitical. When revolts broke out in Bosnia-Herzegovina in early 1875, he cared nothing for Turkish misrule which was claimed to have provoked them, and much for the chance which the disorder offered Russia to intervene in the affairs of the Ottoman Empire. He did not want to see Russian power expand, and he did not wish to lend Britain's assistance to any plot organised by the *Dreikaiserbund* (the League of Three Emperors). In these things he differed from Derby, who saw the Eastern Question as one of equal concern to 'the Cabinets of Europe', and doubted the prospect of a 'final solution'; for him, it was enough to try to discover 'temporary expedients to meet the emergency of the time'.[39] But even that prospect raised the question of co-operating with the other Powers with a direct interest in the fate of the Ottoman Empire, Russia and Austria-Hungary; and that, since 1873, also involved dealing with the German Chancellor, Otto von Bismarck, who had sponsored the *Dreikaiserbund* as a means of isolating France and making Berlin the pivot around which Austro-Russian relations revolved.[40]

Derby thoroughly mistrusted Bismarck, who he thought suffered from 'the disease of despotism. Not only can he bear no opposition . . . [but] Nothing must be done in Europe in which he does not at least seem to take the lead.'[41] He had been happy enough to co-operate with the Russian Chancellor, Prince Alexsandr Gorchakov, in clipping Bismarck's wings in May 1875 during the co-called 'Is War in Sight?' crisis. German menaces towards France were met with warnings from the British and the

Russians.[42] Derby found 'something comic' in the slanging match between Bismarck and Gorchakov which followed, but he was happy to have put a spoke in the wheel of the former.[43] He distrusted any notion of solving the Eastern Question through co-operation with Bismarck alone.

Bismarck had not been best pleased at, in effect, being 'bound over to keep the peace by Russia', and sought his revenge with the recrudescence of the Eastern Question by seeking to re-create the old 'Crimean coalition' of 1854.[44] Disraeli saw in this rift an opportunity to disrupt the *Dreikaiserbund* and fashion a solution to the crisis in the east which would accord with his vision of British interests.[45]

In Bismarck's diplomatic universe everything was in flux and nothing – save anxiety – was permanent. Diplomacy was 'a series of manoeuvres on constantly shifting terrain where any combination was theoretically possible'.[46] He was haunted by a 'nightmare of coalitions' which might follow the breakdown of the *Dreikaiserbund*: 'the Western Powers' might be joined by Austria; or Russia, Austria and France might combine. A close *rapprochement* 'between any two of these may be taken advantage of by the third, to exercise grievous pressure on us'.[47] This dictated the nature of his diplomacy. All politics could be reduced to the formula: 'try to be one of three so long as the world is governed by the unstable equilibrium of five great powers'.[48] But the irreconcilable nature of Austrian and Russian interests in the Balkans threatened to put a mine under the Bismarckian system. If the Ottoman Empire collapsed, Austria would seize Bosnia and Herzegovina, and she would certainly want to prevent Russia from expanding her influence in the Balkans.[49] However, ever since the reign of Catherine the Great, the Russians had seen themselves as the champions of the oppressed Orthodox Christians inside the Ottoman Empire,[50] and with the rise of 'Pan-Slavism' in the 1860s and 1870s there was considerable pressure upon Alexander II to offer 'aid' to the victims of Turkish violence.[51] Indeed, the trouble in the Balkans had been partly stirred up by the activities of Russian Pan-Slavists and Austrian expansionists,[52] and their respective

Governments might be tempted into taking advantage of the situation thus created. Bismarck was also worried lest the Russians should bring the French into the diplomatic equation and, at a stroke, gain an ally and deprive Germany of her leading position.[53] These fears led him to toy with the idea of a British connection.

The question of whether Britain should co-operate with the other European Powers in pressing the Porte (the name commonly given to the Turkish Government) to reform its treatment of its Christian subjects was one fraught with problems. What sort of co-operation was required, and on what terms? Exactly who would Britain be collaborating with, and to what end? There was an argument on moral grounds for co-operation in admonishing the Sultan, but would it stop there? These dilemmas required facing when, in late December 1875, the Austro-Hungarian Foreign Minister, Count Julius Andrassy, proposed that a Note demanding reforms should be presented to the Porte and acted upon by all the Great Powers.[54]

Derby, who thought that the reforms were 'moderate and reasonable enough in the main', was inclined to co-operate with the Note, not wanting to be 'responsible for the failure of what is at least a promising attempt at conciliation'. If Britain rejected the Note and the Turks accepted it, Derby warned that 'we stand in the foolish position of being more Turkish than the Turks'. The idea of taking a stand on the 'independence and integrity' of the Ottoman Empire struck Derby as futile: 'a sovereign who can neither keep the peace at home nor pay his debts must expect to submit to some disagreeable consequences.' He acknowledged the danger that 'we may be dupes', but he thought it unlikely that Austria and Russia had agreed among themselves on anything resembling a partition of the Ottoman Empire.[55] He did not rule out the idea that the Note might be a prelude to Austrian plans to dismember the Ottoman Empire, but doubted that was the case.[56] Derby was sure that 'to stand alone is . . . out of the question'.[57]

Disraeli's basic instincts ran exactly counter to Derby's. He was convinced that a plot was afoot to carve up the Ottoman Empire and deny Britain her share, and far from being fearful of acting alone, he gloried in the prominence it would accord his Government in the eyes of British opinion.[58] Eventually, at the Sultan's request (he wanted one friendly Power on the commission which was going to look into reforming the Turkish system of rule), Disraeli did eventually adhere to the Note, but only because British public opinion would not allow the Government to take unilateral action to sustain the Porte.[59] Unlike Derby, Disraeli was interested in the prospect of coming to some arrangement with Bismarck.[60]

Bismarck quite failed to understand Derby's 'extraordinary' attitude of quiescence in the face of an offer which would, he thought, allow the British to teach the Russians a lesson, whilst relieving him of the burden of having to choose between his two allies.[61] On 2 January 1876, in a conversation with the British Ambassador, Lord Odo Russell, Bismarck exhorted the British to take a greater part in European matters, to co-operate with Germany and to draw closer to France. He even went so far as to suggest that if there should be a partition of the Ottoman Empire, the British might take Egypt as their share.[62] But in seeking to draw Derby into a speculative enterprise, Bismarck had mistaken his man.

'When in doubt, do nothing', was Derby's basic diplomatic tenet. Sir Phillip Currie, who worked under Derby at the Foreign Office in the 1870s, commented on his tendency 'to take no action unless it was forced upon him',[63] whilst *The Spectator* thought that his principal 'weakness as a statesman' was his radical timidity.[64] Even Lady Derby admitted that 'his peculiar character irritated certain of his colleagues . . . and his exaggeration of common sense tended to stimulate the antagonism of imagination and eccentricity of the Prime Minister'.[65] Derby certainly lacked self-confidence,[66] and he was also inclined against acting on instinct, but his rejection of Bismarck's initiative, like his difference of opinion with Disraeli over the Andrassy Note, should not be written off merely as a personal quirk; they owed as much to the political tradition to which he belonged as they did to his personality.

Under Canning and Lord Aberdeen, the Conservatives had maintained something of their seventeenth-century reputation as the 'Country Party'. Both men had been ill-disposed towards too great an intervention in European affairs and had tried to avoid expensive commitments abroad. Derby's foreign policy was fully in accord with this tradition. Despite his reputation for liberal sympathies, he had no time for the 'Manchester School' and had 'never thought Cobden an oracle'. John Bright and Richard Cobden had argued that 'the example of England would be to bring about free trade all over the world' and that 'great wars could never be made again being incompatible with the ideas of an industrial age'. This was all good, optimistic liberal stuff, but when Derby looked about him he saw that 'Europe is showing more protectionist tendencies than twenty years ago . . . and all the world is armed to the teeth.'[67] But whilst this was 'not precisely an ideal condition of civilization', Derby did not believe that just 'because these forces are there' they would necessarily be used.[68] When Disraeli told him in June 1875 that the Duke of Cambridge, Commander-in-Chief of the British army, was 'alarmed by the state of our armaments', Derby responded laconically that 'I should have been more impressed . . . if I could remember a time when . . . [he] had not been seriously alarmed.' The Continent was 'arming', but 'with Germany and France watching one another both are more likely to be civil to us than if they were on good terms'. Then there was the question of 'how long these enormous armaments will be endured by the masses who are compelled to serve'. Britain should not, he thought, go down the Continental road. He was willing to spend £300,000 or £400,000 more a year because that was 'inevitable. Beyond that we cannot go.'[69] Derby was not willing to yield to the 'howls and screams' of public opinion in the way that he thought Disraeli was.[70] What was at issue between the two men was how Conservatives should manage imperial foreign policy in a way which both carried public support and protected Britain's geopolitical interests; the great Eastern crisis revealed the extent to which the two men differed from each other on both subjects.

Derby preferred to try to keep popular opinion at arm's length and to work with the *Dreikaiserbund* over the Andrassy Note in order to contain the Eastern Question, whereas Disraeli wanted a more prominent role for Britain and was prepared to work with Bismarck by himself, but not Bismarck as part of the *Dreikaiserbund*. Disraeli's instincts were supported by the Queen. Although she thought Bismarck 'so overbearing, violent, grasping and unprincipled that no one can stand it',[71] she felt that 'the importance of establishing a link between the two countries cannot be overstated' and wanted to 'accept the proferred aid of Germany . . . whose interests are the same as ours'.[72] However, Derby suspected that Bismarck's 'object was to embroil us with Russia',[73] and was sure that there would be strings attached to any Anglo-German collaboration.[74] Odo Russell thought that Bismarck's motives were the obvious ones – he did not want Austria and Russia to fall out.[75] In his view, 'an ambitious, irresponsible, unaccountable genius with a million of soldiers at his back' was 'a friend worth having'.[76] But Derby was not disposed to become Bismarck's catspaw and let the matter drop, after replying anodynely that he was, of course, willing in general to co-operate with Germany.[77] Disraeli was not best pleased with Derby's 'chilling' attitude: 'You have to deal with a man who is dangerous, but who is sincere; and who will act straightforwardly with an English Minister whose sense of honor he appreciates.'[78]

Derby watched the 'dead lock' in the East without any great concern. It was, he thought, for 'the Powers which initiated the policy of the Andrassy Note to suggest now a way out of the difficulties'.[79] They did just that in May 1876 with what became known as the Berlin Memorandum. Its text arrived in the Foreign Office late on the evening of Saturday, 14 May, but when Disraeli tried to find out further details on Sunday at one o'clock, he was told that the Resident Clerk was not 'in residence', and to his fury he did not get the details until late on Sunday.[80] The result was a rocket to Derby and to the Foreign Office,[81] where the shame-faced Resident Clerk, Philip Currie, explained that he had been taking his constitutional after lunch.[82]

If the circumstances in which the Berlin Memorandum were received threw some light upon the inadequate staffing of the Foreign Office, the contents threatened to embarrass the Government still more: the dilemma which Derby and Disraeli had faced over the Andrassy Note was back but this time writ large. Should Britain co-operate with the European Powers in urging reforms on the Porte or not? The Memorandum demanded a two-month armistice between the Turks and the Serbs and called for the Turks to make restitution, as well as proposing a commission composed of consuls of the Great Powers to supervise reforms. The sting in the tale was a provision for 'efficacious' measures to follow if the Turks failed to comply.

All Disraeli's instincts were against becoming involved. He not only objected to being treated as though Britain were Belgium, by being asked to adhere to a note which she had played no part in composing, but he suspected that 'we are being drawn step by step, into participating in a scheme, which must end very soon in the disintegration of Turkey'. For the Powers to claim to want to act in 'Concert', and then to consult Britain only after the fact, was to make a 'mockery' of the term. Disraeli did not believe that the Porte would be able to meet the terms of the Memorandum and did not feel that Britain should 'take a leap in the dark' by supporting it.[83] The Cabinet accepted Disraeli's arguments, and Britain refused to give her adherence to the Berlin Memorandum.[84]

It was a crucial decision. At the time the Queen complained about a decision being taken before she had had time to comment on it, and she feared that the Cabinet's refusal 'may have a serious effect and may lead the Porte to expect us to support Turkey in her difficulties'; it might also lead to allegations that Britain had created difficulties by refusing to co-operate in an attempt to make the Turks reform their treatment of their Christian subjects.[85] She was absolutely right. Throughout the ensuing crisis Gladstone and other Liberal commentators would argue that there was 'no possible doubt that it was the British refusal of co-operation, and still more the failure to put forward any concrete alternative, that made joint action by Europe impossible and actually precipitated events in eastern Europe'.[86] Disraeli not only failed to 'do something', he prevented others from acting. As Gladstone put it, 'Turkey had broken her pledges to Europe, and we had the clearest moral obligations towards her victims.'[87] Even some of Disraeli's own colleagues would argue that the refusal to co-operate with the other Powers had helped create the crisis which followed.[88]

But Disraeli's eyes were, as usual, on geopolitics rather than morality. It was all very well to call for the coercion of the Sultan, but Disraeli recalled that when Britain and Russia had co-operated against the Turks in 1827, the result had been the destruction of the Turkish fleet; who could tell what might happen this time?[89] There was also the impact of Pan-Slavism to be taken into account before deciding that the poor oppressed Balkan peoples needed helping. Disraeli had a somewhat histrionic tendency to see international relations in terms of secret societies and conspiracies; when it came to the Balkans, there was some justification for this. There were many varieties of Pan-Slavism ranging from the deeply mystical belief in the spiritual unity of all Slav peoples, all the way to thinly disguised Pan-Russianism;[90] either variety threatened to promote Russian aims in the Balkans. To those Russians who wished to see the boundaries of their empire expand, Pan-Slavism was a welcome instrument; chief among these was Count Nikolai Pavlovich Ignatyev. As director of the Asiatic department from 1861 to 1864 and then Ambassador in Constantinople from 1867 to 1877, Ignatyev had acquired two reputations: the first as the pre-eminent champion of Pan-Slavism; the second as 'an inordinate liar'.[91]

Ignatyev's view was that Russia would have to fight Austria for predominance in the Balkans as part of her bid for the leadership of Slavdom. Where Foreign Minister Gorchakov wished to see Austria and Russia combine to prevent the situation in the Balkans deteriorating, Ignatyev looked towards exploiting any crisis to secure Russian dominance at Constantinople, even at the risk of a war with Austria.[92] Where Gorchakov would have been happy to have allowed Austria a sphere of influence so long as she recognised Russian supremacy in the Balkans, Ignatyev saw no need for this. He believed that Turkey was 'rotten to the core' and that Austria would not fight without allies.[93] Since 1867, Ignatyev had been encouraging the ambitions of Prince Milan of Serbia to throw off Turkish suzerainty, not from any concern for the Serbs, but as a means of extending Russian influence by stealth.[94] The Russians also showed themselves willing to support the activities of the other Balkan prince who sought to play a leading role in encouraging nationalist revolts against the Turks, Nicholas of Montenegro.[95] It was the activities of these men, and of Russian consuls in the Bosnian provinces, which had encouraged the revolt against the Turks; now Ignatyev sought to profit from it.

To see Disraeli's rejection of the Berlin Memorandum as simply an act of pique, or a return to an outmoded Palmerstonian policy, is to miss the geopolitical element in the Prime Minister's thought. He was correct to think that the Russians welcomed the nationalist revolts, and that Russian imperialism stood to gain most from any further weakening of Ottoman power. He was acutely aware that to act with the Bismarckian Concert was to run the risk of having to coerce the Porte, and to court the certainty of being seen to act as a Power of the second rank; British national interests, as well as those of the Conservative Party, pointed in the direction of rejecting the Memorandum. It was a sign of the acuity of Disraeli's instincts that Derby should have recorded that 'the general attitude assumed by England has been a success. We are more respected & consulted than has been common of late years.'[96]

2

Disraeli *Contra Mundum*

Disraeli enjoyed the excitement of *haut politique* and thought that there was 'no gambling like politics', especially when 'you have to deal only with Emperors and High Chancellors, and Empires';[1] after long years in the political galleys, he finally had 'politics worth managing'.[2] It was such comments and the manner which accompanied them which led Disraeli's opponents to accuse him of flippancy, and even to identify his policy as 'un-English'.[3] The Russian Ambassador, Count Shuvalov, like later commentators interpreted the rejection of the Berlin Memorandum as the result of '*l'orgueil blessé* [wounded pride]';[4] there was certainly an element of truth in this, but it was not the whole story.

A more telling criticism of Disraeli's policy is not that it was opportunistic and frivolous in character,[5] but that its premises were unthinking, old-fashioned Palmerstonianism, and that 'Disraeli knew there was a great problem but did not think it through. When things came to the point he relied instead on solving matters by applying what he thought of as the "traditional policy of England", trusting that all would come well of it.'[6] This is a line which takes seriously the Salisburian criticisms that Disraeli was a 'clear-sighted' but 'short-sighted' politician, and that 'the traditional Palmerston policy' was 'at an end' in 1876.[7] But to see

Disraeli as being stuck in a 'Palmerstonian mode mainly as a matter of habit'[8] is to ignore the differences between a liberal and a conservative sensibility. Palmerston genuinely thought that the Ottoman Empire could be reformed and that the improvement of the lot of the Christian subjects of the Grand Turk should be an object of British policy. Disraeli thought no such things. He had indeed promised the electorate a new assertiveness in British diplomacy, and in that sense alone was he a Palmerstonian. It was central to Disraeli's strategy that Britain should be seen to be respected by the other European Powers and not consulted as a sort of afterthought; along with the Memorandum, Disraeli was rejecting 'Gladstonism' and its pious belief in the European 'Concert';[9] but that did not mean that he adopted the old Palmerstonian position. Tactical flexibility is often mistaken for indistinctness of aim or even for aimlessness, but it can also mask a willingness to achieve ends by whatever means are available. Salisbury took it as axiomatic that in foreign affairs 'the choice of a policy is as a rule of less importance than the methods by which it is pursued', and his main criticism of Disraeli would be that he pursued not only the wrong policy, but did so with insufficient vigour.[10] This critique is, of course, having it both ways: damning Disraeli for being wrong and for not being forceful enough in wrong-doing. But Salisbury had yet to discover the truth which Disraeli knew from long experience, that a politician does not make his fate as he wishes it in circumstances he controls. The argument pursued here is that Disraeli's policy was dictated not by Palmerstonian echoes, but by his geopolitical sensitivities; and if it lacked vigour, that was due in some small measure to Salisbury himself. In fashioning an Eastern policy, Disraeli had to reckon with a Cabinet which made up in moral sensibility for what it lacked in geopolitical perspectives; and, of course, he had to deal with something even less predictable than the whims of his own Ministers – the march of events abroad.

The Queen, the diplomats and Derby all feared that the 'isolation' in which Britain now found herself would have 'serious consequences',[11] although Odo Russell in Berlin swiftly changed his tune when it became clear that Bismarck had been impressed by Disraeli's actions.[12] Disraeli reassured the Queen and Derby that a policy of 'determination and conciliation' would rescue Britain from isolation without her having to play a 'secondary part' to Germany or Russia.[13] The decision to despatch the fleet to Besika Bay off the Dardanelles, and to issue a warning to Europe that existing treaties must be respected, established that British interests must be observed if there was to be a resolution to the crisis.

But Disraeli's expectations of an early result were dashed for three reasons: in the first place, he miscalculated the chances of enlisting Bismarck's aid; in the second, he overestimated his success in extinguishing the 'tripartite confederacy' of the *Dreikaiserbund*;[14] and finally, his concentration on the geopolitics of the Eastern Question left him vulnerable to the charge that his diplomacy was immoral.

The *Dreikaiserbund* was, in part, an attempt by Bismarck to confine the forces of nationalism by harnessing them to the dictates of dynastic diplomacy, and to limit those of republicanism by isolating France,[15] and he would not easily allow it to fall apart. Bismarck once commented that he had 'wasted several years of his political life by the belief that Britain was a great nation'.[16] Being of a vindictive nature, Bismarck had not forgiven Gorchakov for the humiliation of the 'War in Sight' crisis and, according to Odo Russell, he took a malicious delight in seeing Gorchakov snubbed by the British.[17] He was 'in high spirits and rare good humour' at the discomfiture of the Russian Chancellor and told Russell that 'the independent attitude of England suited him to perfection'; the 'old coxcomb' had been warned off Pan-Slavist adventures without Germany having to do anything.[18]

Disraeli and Derby were quite willing to co-operate with Bismarck, but neither of them trusted him very far, and they preferred to see whether he would follow up his words with action.[19] But the likelihood of this was remote. As Bismarck warned Russell on 10 June when asked why he was not openly supporting Andrassy against Russian ambitions, 'his policy was hampered by the Russian sympathies of the emperor William who cared nothing for Austria and everything for his nephew the Czar'.[20] Bismarck still hankered after Britain resuming her 'Crimean policy' of organising resistance to Russian aggrandisement in order to save him from having to take sides in the Balkans, which meant that he would do nothing to help Disraeli.[21]

Historically British statesmen had pursued one of two options in seeking to restrain Russian expansionism: Disraeli had tried the first, finding allies to deter Russia; now he attempted the second – restraining Russia by co-operating with her, as Canning had in 1827 and Palmerston in 1839. This variant of the Palmerstonian legacy is one not often stressed when Disraeli is charged with mindlessly following his predecessor's Eastern policy; there was, after all, no one simple Palmerstonian policy on the Eastern Question.

Disraeli broached the prospect of Anglo-Russian co-operation to Shuvalov in early June, telling him that neither he nor his Government distrusted a 'Great Power which is governed by wise men on conservative principles'. The message was clear: if Russia's objectives did not conflict with Britain's interests, the two states could do business. Disraeli's only caveat was that the Russians should 'do nothing which could react on Afghanistan'. He told Shuvalov that he was prepared to believe that Russia did not wish to precipitate the break up of the Ottoman Empire, but he argued that it was unwise to keep Ignatyev at Constantinople because he was stirring up the Slav Christians. Disraeli had no faith in projects for reforming the Ottoman domination. The Balkan Christians wanted independence, not reforms, so it would be better for all concerned if Serbia and Montenegro went ahead and declared war on the Porte; if the Christians won, 'we shall only have to register accomplished facts: if Turkey crushes the Christians and the repression becomes tyrannous, it will be the turn of all the Great Powers to interpose in the name of humanity'. Shuvalov was unsure what to make of all this: was it to be taken at face value, or was it an attempt to break up the *Dreikaiserbund*? On the whole he was inclined to think that it represented Disraeli's real thoughts. It would, after all, allow him to reap the fruits of his dramatic action *and* solve the Eastern Question;[22] but Gorchakov was more sceptical[23] and asked for firm British proposals about the future status of Serbia and Montenegro after a war against the Porte.[24] Disraeli had no wish to get into conversations about carving off bits of the Ottoman Empire, and when war between Turkey and Serbia and Montenegro broke out in late June, it removed the need for immediate action by the British. Disraeli was sure that the Slavs would be defeated, and equally certain that the Russians would have to intervene to stop them from being exterminated. Austria and Germany would not, he thought, permit unilateral Russian action, so there would have to be a European Congress; Britain could make her voice heard there.[25] What he failed to appreciate were the forces in favour of an Austro-Russian agreement to liquidate the Eastern Question to their mutual satisfaction, which would have left Britain in the cold.

Trying to divine Russian policy, Disraeli could not quite decide whether they were behaving with 'great duplicity' or whether it was simply that thanks to 'administrative weakness' there was no single Russian policy; either way there was 'no acting with people when you cannot feel sure they are telling the truth'.[26] But Russian policy was genuinely torn between the old impulses of dynastic diplomacy and the new dynamics of Pan-Slavism.[27] Alexander II was broadly sympathetic to the ideas of the Pan-Slavs, but having come to the throne during the Crimean War he was mindful of the danger of resuscitating the 'Crimean Coalition' by pursuing an aggressive foreign policy; his mood fluctuated according to events and his own geographical location. In the 'European' surroundings of St Petersburg, he favoured the *Dreikaiserbund*; at his Crimean retreat, surrounded by Slavic influences, he found it difficult to resist the impulse to become the liberator of the Balkans.[28] Turning Constantinople into 'Tsargrad' would make Alexander's name echo in history, but the attempt might lead to a repetition of the humiliation of the Crimean War.[29] As Baron Alexander Jomini, the senior counsellor at the Foreign Office, noted: '*malheuresement les gros écus et les gros canons ne sont pas de notre côté* [unfortunately the big bucks and the big guns aren't on our side]'.[30]

If the conflicting impulses to which Tsarist foreign policy was subject made it difficult to fathom, the character of the man charged with conducting it did nothing to help matters. Prince Gorchakov's diplomatic experience went back to the early 1820s and he had been Foreign Minister since 1856, but the Russian political system allowed him no position of independence from the Tsar. The impression he made on the Earl of Kimberley, the British Minister to St Petersburg in the late 1850s, was typical of the way he struck foreign observers: 'a man of unquestionable ability, but irritable, hasty, & devoured by a ridiculous and insatiable vanity'.[31] His vanity was especially piqued where Bismarck was concerned; that a man he had known as a junior figure at Frankfurt in the 1850s should now be the arbiter of Europe was more than he knew how to bear, and he was always fearful of the '*perfidies de Bismarck*'.[32] Even at his peak Gorchakov had been 'an immense talker, vain and indiscreet, with a great deal of cleverness';[33] in decline, only the first two characteristics seemed to remain unimpaired.[34]

Gorchakov's rivalry with Bismarck was particularly acute since they shared a common 'short term view of diplomacy' and regarded 'any combination' of Powers as 'theoretically possible'.[35] Gorchakov had been happy to rebuke Bismarck during the 'War in Sight' crisis, and although Russia was a member of the *Dreikaiserbund*, he was willing to seek a solution to the Eastern Question which did not involve Germany. Even as Ignatyev looked to harness the new forces of Pan-Slavism, Gorchakov, as befitted his age, looked backwards; in rejecting Disraeli's suggestion for a repeat of the Anglo-Russian co-operation of 1827 and 1839, Gorchakov was hoping for a resurrection of the Romanov–Habsburg dynastic axis which had provided a conservative dominance for Central and Eastern Europe between 1833 and 1854. Nor were these hopes entirely in vain.

There were those in power in Austria who shared Gorchakov's

hankering for the old dynastic alliance and the glory days of the Metternichean conservative alliance. The Habsburg Emperor, Franz Joseph, still remembered the defeat by Prussia in 1866 with some soreness, and saw co-operation with the Russians in the Balkans as a means of recouping his losses in Italy and Germany.[36] The leading Russophile at Court was Franz Joseph's cousin, the Archduke Albrecht, who, apart from being the richest man in the Empire, was a talented and intelligent soldier who remained grateful for the part the Russians had played in putting down the revolutions of 1848.[37] The main obstacle to a bilateral agreement between Vienna and St Petersburg lay in the ambitions of the main beneficiaries of the Austro-Russian estrangement, the Hungarians, who had taken advantage of the disasters of 1866 to negotiate themselves a joint partnership with the Germans in ruling the Empire. Magyar privileges were enshrined in the 1867 *Ausgleich*, or constitutional 'Compromise', and they were unlikely to welcome anything which raised the prestige of the dynasty.[38] This famous 'Compromise' between Habsburg and Magyar was, after all, based on the principle 'You look after your Slavs and we'll look after ours.'[39] The Empire's Foreign Minister, Andrassy, was a 'true Hungarian' and like all such wished to 'keep the Slavs in their place and to maintain the Magyar supremacy over them'.[40]

Andrassy was the third major European figure with whom Disraeli had to deal as he sought to gain some purchase on the crisis caused by the war in the Balkans. There were, as his biographer noted in suitably melodramatic style, similarities between Andrassy and the British Prime Minister: 'bohemian artists, political geniuses of the first order who astounded the universe by their cleverness. Both relied upon their Empress-Queens.'[41] But he was a difficult man with whom to deal; as one British Ambassador noted: 'I never yet had to do with a public man whose language was so little clear and precise.'[42] But there were good reasons why Andrassy should have tried to avoid being pinned down, particularly about the Eastern Question.

As a Magyar, Andrassy had one set of prejudices and priorities; but as Habsburg Foreign Minister, he was subject to those of others which pushed him in a different direction. His ideal policy would have been to 'preserve the Turkish Empire in alcohol to prevent its decomposition'.[43] But the war which began in June 1876 suggested that this was no longer possible, which posed a cruel dilemma for him. He had no wish to see the Habsburgs gain in prestige from a carve-up of the Empire; but he had equally little wish to see the Russians take the initiative and make great gains for Slavdom, which would leave Austria-Hungary as 'the sick man of Europe' after the end of the Ottomans.[44] He neither wanted to see a greater Serbia on Austria's southern border, nor yet to see Russia aggrandised by Serbian successes.[45] He would have been willing to run the risk of war with Russia to prevent this, but the Emperor was unwilling to agree, which meant that Andrassy had to acquiesce in his preference for an agreement with Russia.[46] When the two Emperors met at Reichstadt in early July 1876, it was a last attempt to show that dynastic diplomacy could contain the forces of nationalism without resorting to the dangerous expedients of Bismarck. On 8 July, they concluded an agreement which sought to prevent their mutual rivalry in the Balkans leading to war.[47]

If the Reichstadt policy had worked, then Disraeli's Eastern policy would have been at an end; agreement between Austria and Russia on partitioning the Balkans would have left Britain isolated. Fortunately for Disraeli's hopes, the treaty was fatally flawed by a basic misunderstanding between Russia and Austria. Both sides agreed to remain neutral during the course of the Balkan war, and both of them assumed that it would end in a victory for the Serbs; but after that accounts differed. Austrian and Russian records agreed that there would be no '*grand état slave*', but Andrassy thought that the Russians had said that they would allow Austria to have most of Bosnia-Herzegovina in return for concessions to Serbia, whilst Gorchakov went away with the impression that Serbia and Montenegro would both gain territory in Bosnia and Herzegovina respectively, with Austria obtaining only some of the border regions of Bosnia.[48] The most likely explanation for this discrepancy was that Gorchakov, whose ignorance of the geography of the Balkans was as great as his vanity, simply misunderstood what had been agreed;[49] but deliberate obfuscation on Andrassy's part cannot be ruled out.[50] The two Powers decided to keep the agreement secret, but did accept that at some future date it might be necessary to involve the other Powers in a final settlement.[51]

If the Serbs and Montenegrins had won their campaigns against the Turks, then the gap between the Russian and Austrian interpretations of Reichstadt might have remained concealed. Had that happened then Disraeli, bereft of support from Germany or Austria, and facing a Russia guarded by Reichstadt from the threat of a Crimean coalition, would not have been able to make much headway in protecting British interests, and his policy of awaiting the outcome of the Slav–Turkish conflict would have been in vain. But the forces of a resurgent Islam saved Disraeli from this fate. Following the deposition of the Sultan in May, the new Turkish Government made determined and successful efforts to suppress both the local rebellions and the Serb and Montenegrin revolts.[52] Instead of the Russians profiting from Serb successes, it began to appear as though they might be pushed into unilateral action to save their Slavic brethren from extermination. Under pressure from the Pan-Slavs and the march of events, even Gorchakov became militant.[53] Turkish military success may have saved Disraeli from the consequences of his misjudgment of the likely reactions of Bismarck, Gorchakov and Andrassy, but it was to cost him dear.

Disraeli's concentration during the Eastern Crisis was upon its geopolitical aspects: how could the Ottoman Empire be protected from partition; and if it could not be, how could Britain ensure that her interests at the Straits and the Persian Gulf were protected? As his comments to Shuvalov reveal, he was quite oblivious to the moral dimension to the crisis represented by the fate of the Balkan peoples; this was to prove a serious chink in his armour.

In late June when the *Daily News* first published reports of massacres by the Turks in Bulgaria, Disraeli asked Derby for information, only to receive assurances that nothing out of the ordinary had happened. He was thus quite happy to dismiss as 'coffee-house babble' the accounts appearing in the newspapers.[54] One of Disraeli's besetting sins in the eyes of his more sober-sided opponents was his fondness for frivolous rhetorical asides, and this time the habit led him into trouble. He admitted that 'proceedings of an atrocious character' had taken place, but he denied that there had been any torture: 'Oriental people seldom resort to torture but generally terminate their connexion with their culprits in a more expeditious manner.'[55] He who lives by the aphorism must, according to the inexorable rule of Fate, die thereby.

Disraeli was apt to blame the inefficiency and incompetence of the Foreign Office for keeping him in ignorance of events in the Balkans,[56] but according to the Permanent Under-Secretary, Lord Tenterden, the problem lay in Disraeli's own failure to draw a distinction between the denial of knowledge of the specific allegations made in the *Daily News* and the acknowledgment that there had been atrocities committed on both sides.[57] Both Disraeli and Salisbury were apt to throw the blame for his ignorance of the real state of affairs on the Turcophilia of the British Ambassador to the Porte, Sir Henry Elliot. 'Elliot's stupidity' had, Salisbury later commented, 'brought us into the position, most unjustly, of being thought to connive' at the massacres; he had, in short, 'contrived to change the bent of opinion in England on the Eastern Question'.[58] But this did Elliot too much honour. Any change in British opinion owed more to the outraged moral sensibilities of the high Victorian era.[59]

A generation ago Professor Shannon pointed to the spontaneous nature of the 'Atrocitarian' agitation and noted its roots in a tradition of public protest in Victorian England, as well as its significance in exposing the intellectual fault-lines which were to characterise the last quarter of the nineteenth century.[60] He wrote that the moral outrage which followed the news of the massacres in Bulgaria was 'the most convincing demonstration of the susceptibility of the High Victorian public conscience'.[61] More recently it has been pointed out that the propensity to blame the

Turks for the massacres and to ignore the fact that (as in more recent times) atrocities were committed on both sides was symptomatic of the way in which 'stereotyped views of Islam and the Turks affected political debate'.[62] The Turks were assumed to be decadent, licentious and barbarous, so they were obviously guilty of any heinous crimes charged to their account. This was certainly the case with the Bulgarian atrocities.

The distinction between *Realpolitik* and *Idealpolitik* was unusually clear as the hurricane of public opinion gathered force. In the first camp were those who agreed with Elliot and Disraeli that 'feelings of revolted humanity' should not make people forget 'the capital interests involved in the question', as well as those like Derby who thought that the stories in the *Daily News* 'were put about for a purpose'.[63] To those who thought like this, the 'necessity' of preventing changes detrimental to Britain's interests taking place in the Turkish Empire was 'not affected by the question whether it was 10,000 or 20,000 persons who perished in the suppression';[64] nor yet by outcries from the Queen, Cabinet Ministers or anyone else. As Disraeli put it in his last speech in the Commons on 11 August, 'our duty at this critical moment is to maintain the Empire of England';[65] geopolitics was all. In the opposite camp were those who felt that the Turkish massacres raised a moral issue which transcended narrow national interests.

Disraeli, who hoped that the outcry would end with the parliamentary session, took that opportunity to translate himself to the Upper House as the first Earl of Beaconsfield. His old friend, the former Foreign Secretary, Lord Malmesbury, commented on 8 June, 'of all the privileges you possess above us all not the least envied is your power of rallying your physique as well as your party',[66] but by the summer of 1876, racked by gout and afflicted by asthma and chronic bronchitis, Disraeli could only continue in this vein by retiring to the Lords. He was, he famously remarked, 'dead, dead but in the Elysian fields'. Derby agreed to be his sponsor there, accepting 'that office of friendship' with 'real pleasure' after 'nearly thirty years' of 'pulling together'.[67] But circumstances would soon make that seem a nostalgic memory.

Demonstrations throughout the summer showed that public feeling was too strong for any British threat to help the Turks to be credible. Had it not been for Elliot and the 'atrocities', Disraeli thought that 'we should have settled a peace very honourable to England, and satisfactory to Europe';[68] but the Chancellor of the Exchequer, Sir Stafford Northcote, was right when he noted that 'the stupid brutality of the Turks has gone far to justify the Servian attack in the eyes of the world, and has made it difficult for us to say a word in their favour'.[69] Derby regarded the great demonstrations with the disdain of a man charged with the execution of policy: 'It is not clear what the promoters of these meetings expected that the British govt. should have done.' But he was realistic enough to see that it was 'natural that popular feeling should be strong' and that its existence 'greatly complicates the situation'.[70] Disraeli had to warn the Turks in August that if their failure to grant the Serbs an armistice led to war with Russia, Britain would 'find it practically impossible to interfere'.[71] Derby's view was equally bleak: the 'remarkable' change in British opinion 'weakens our hands abroad, & strengthens those of the Russians'.[72] He thought that the paralysis which now gripped British diplomacy made the Balkan situation even more dangerous by giving the Russians the impression that 'they may do what they please'.[73] Disraeli could only wait for the country to recover from its 'mad' fit,[74] and hope for 'a great reaction' once Russia's predatory intentions became clear.[75] But in the meantime from the Queen and the Cabinet came demands for immediate reforms from the Porte.[76]

Lord Chancellor Cairns told Disraeli at the end of August that they were 'at the most critical point in our foreign policy' and that they should support Russian and Austrian attempts to get the Turks and the Serbs to negotiate with each other: 'we should use absolute pressure – in fact everything short of compulsion – to make the Porte come into liberal & *un*vindictive terms of peace.'[77] Lord Carnarvon, who thought that the Turks were 'mere barbarians',[78] argued that unless the Government took 'urgent action', 'we shall be at variance with Europe, and, which is worse, with

England'.[79] He told Disraeli that 'public feeling' was 'extremely strong' and that unless the Government 'reassure the public mind as to our real attitude towards Turkey', it would 'either drive us into some precipitate and undignified course or will end in serious catastrophe'.[80] Northcote, who was not only Chancellor of the Exchequer but also a sensitive barometer of the public mood, thought that it was essential 'that we should make some demonstration on the affair', and that it might be necessary to go so far as to intervene with the other Powers to make matters in Turkey 'a little better' than before.[81]

Disraeli, wishing that 'all the Turks' were 'in the Propontis', nevertheless determined not to make any concessions to the agitation. As he told Derby on 6 September, there was nothing to be gained from acting 'as if you were under the control of popular opinion. If so, you may do what they like, but they won't respect you for doing it.'[82] Derby's own view was that any raising of the question of partition entailed a great risk of a general war 'for all the Powers will want something, and the division of the spoil is not likely to be made in an amicable manner'.[83] Throughout this most trying stage of the crisis Disraeli's 'great object' was never to 'admit that we have changed our policy';[84] but Gladstone's dramatic irruption onto the scene on 6 September with his pamphlet, *The Bulgarian Horrors and the Question of the East*, made Disraeli's task even more difficult.

In retirement after his defeat in 1874, Gladstone was now galvanised into action by the realisation that there still existed the means to pursue a politics based upon Christian moral precepts.[85] Granville, who led the Liberals in the Lords, did his best to dissuade his old chief from any hasty or extreme action, but he was too elliptical in his advice and too much in awe of his predecessor to do so with any force.[86] Gladstone detested everything Disraeli represented in public life.[87] As he told Granville:

> Palmerston certainly had something of a weak side with respect to brag. It was the supposed glory of Conser-

vatives of his time to resist and denounce him for it. But during the last eight months the present Govt. have enormously outdone whatever in him was open to exception, and without his redeeming qualities, for he was a lover of liberty all over the world and was entirely above flattering as these people have done (with great effect) the most vulgar appetites & propensities of the people.[88]

He blamed Disraeli for this development.[89] Mixed in with the moral outrage and the high-minded liberal critique was an anti-Semitism which to modern Western sensibilities is at least as distasteful as Disraeli's levity about the fate of the Bulgars. Gladstone's obsession that 'Dizzy's crypto-Judaism' was dictating his policy[90] was matched and even out-done by the vituperative comment of the historian E.A. Freeman that 'even the Jew in his drunken insolence' would 'think twice before he goes to war in our teeth';[91] nor were such comments untypical.[92] Gladstone's view that the atrocitarian movement represented a 'virtuous passion' in politics[93] reflected the naïve faith of the nineteenth-century Liberal in 'the people'. The irruption into the political and diplomatic arena of the forces of democracy could unleash passions which were far from virtuous.

Gladstone's famous pamphlet on the atrocities was, in classic liberal vein, long on heated rhetoric but short on practical suggestions. The Turks were denounced as 'the one great anti-human specimen of humanity', a piece of illogic quite up to the standard of his declaration that although the Serbs had had 'no stateable cause for war', there were 'states of affairs, in which human sympathy refuses to be confined by the rules, necessarily limited and conventional, of international law'. Disraeli's verdict on the whole production had much to be said for it: 'The document is passionate and not strong; vindictive and ill-written – that of course. Indeed, in that respect, of all the Bulgarian horrors, perhaps the greatest.'[94]

SPLENDID ISOLATION?

Disraeli's vituperative reaction stemmed from his instinctive distaste for this sort of pious moralising, with its self-righteous instant moral absolutism which pronounced itself capable of solving complex political and diplomatic problems by the application of simplistic notions of right and wrong. This may have held, and did hold, an appeal to the nonconformist conscience and to Radicals, but most Conservatives felt instinctively uncomfortable with it, as did Whigs like Granville and Hartington (joint leaders of the Liberal Party); in that sense Gladstone's pamphlet may actually have helped Disraeli in dealing with his own Party. Even those Ministers with some sympathy for the plight of the Bulgarians could deplore Gladstone's 'very wicked' attacks and feel under an obligation to support their own Government.[95]

The problem which Disraeli had to face was not the moral absolutism of Gladstone's universe of black and white, but the very real difficulty of upholding Britain's geopolitical interests in the Near East. Disraeli wanted to maintain his position of being able to protect the Porte from overt Russian aggression and partition by the *Dreikaiserbund*, but it was clear that the state of public opinion would not allow him to do so.

If Disraeli and Derby resisted the pressure from Cairns, Carnarvon and Northcote to try to rival Gladstone's mastery of the politics of windy rhetoric and empty gestures, they did try to make some headway against it. Derby attempted to apply some plain English 'commonsense' to the agitation when he addressed a delegation of working men on 11 September. It was, he told them, as untrue and unfair to say that the Government did not care about the massacres as it was to allege that it had caused them. There seemed to be, he commented in a rare moment of lightness, 'a great many people in England who fancy Lord Beaconsfield is the Sultan and that I am the Grand Vizier', when, in fact, Britain had no more influence than any other Power on the actions of an independent state. He reminded the delegation that 'The last word of the Eastern Question is this: "who is to have Constantinople?" No Great Power would be willing to see it in the hands of any other Great Power. No small Power could hold it at all'; this eternal interest was not, he said in best *Realpolitik* vein, 'in any way affected by the insanity of a Sultan ... or by the crimes committed by Turkish troops'.[96] All this was sound reasoning, but, as Cairns commented, it was 'too negative and too destitute of sentiment or suggestion for the present gale of public opinion'. Gladstone's rhetoric was destitute of practical suggestions 'but the public don't see this', and Cairns was correct to perceive that 'the result is to paralyze us at Constantinople and make Russia mistress of the situation'.[97] It was this, and not a bankrupt Palmerstonianism, which had stymied Disraeli's attempt to pursue a *Realpolitik* line based upon geopolitics; the British public wanted sentiment, not sense.

3

An End to Palmerstoniansm?

Sir Stafford Northcote, the Tory leader in the Commons, regarded the new parliamentary session with some trepidation, and told Carnarvon that he had no idea how he was going to defend the Government's Eastern policy since he had no idea what it was: 'at present we seem to be living from hand to mouth, with no true conception of our own, or any other Power's policy'.[1] His defeated rival for the leadership of the Commons, Gathorne-Hardy, felt 'uncomfortable and dissatisfied at not knowing what is going on', whilst Cairns, the Lord Chancellor, thought that they had better press the Turks to make a 'liberal peace'.[2] If the lineaments of Disraeli's policy seemed obscure, it was because he lacked the means to see how it could be pursued successfully through the Scylla of moral concern at home and the Charybdis of the *Dreikaiserbund* abroad.

Disraeli's first preference remained for Bismarck to pluck British chestnuts out of the fire by convening a European congress or conference to sort out the Eastern Question.[3] But Bismarck had no intention of convening a conference or congress (he attached 'no importance to the distinction between these two indefinite ideas') on the future of the Ottoman Empire; in his view, 'the whole movement [for congresses] is but a fresh proof how greatly a statesman's conscientiousness may be injured by a temptation to pose before Europe'.[4] Any conference would expose the gap between Austria and Russia, and thus place him in the position of having to choose between them. Indeed, quite as much as Disraeli himself, but for different reasons, Bismarck laboured hard over the summer to avoid having to make a declaration of German policy,[5] using one of the remaining resources of the old dynastic diplomatic style to help him.

Bismarck, who preferred biddable soldiers to the 'ponderous specialists' who made diplomacy their profession[6] (a predilection shared by the Kaiser),[7] was happy to take advantage of the private link which the Kaiser kept through special military plenipotentiaries to his fellow monarchs in the *Dreikaiserbund*.[8] The Kaiser, who was worried by the pressure under which his nephew Alexander found himself from the Pan-Slavs,[9] allowed Bismarck to give him assurances of German friendship through this private channel. On 2 September, the Kaiser's military aide, General Manteuffel, was sent to Warsaw, ostensibly to observe army manoeuvres, but in reality to assure the Tsar of Germany's continued friendship.

This informal approach allowed Bismarck scope to do things which the 'usual channels' would not permit. Manteuffel raised the prospect of full German backing through 'thick and thin' ('*durch dick und dünn*') if Russia would guarantee Alsace-Lorraine. This was a risk-free manoeuvre. If the Russians took up the offer, then Bismarck would be comfortably placed; if they did not, he would have given the impression of a willingness to commit Germany to a full-scale alliance, without having done so, and in circumstances which would allow him room for recrimination if he later had to take action against Russia. If the whole business became public, Bismarck could simply deny that any formal diplomatic approach had been made.[10]

With Bismarck unavailable as a mediator, and with Andrassy refusing to let his fears about Russia take him as far as co-operating with Britain, Disraeli was, by early September, beginning to wonder whether he might not have to take the Palmerstonian path of 1839 and co-operate with the Russians – but this time in the 'solution of the Eastern question' by partitioning the Turkish Empire;[11] it was, Disraeli told Derby, a 'false assumption' that his policy was one of 'upholding Turkey'.[12] Despite warnings from Andrassy,[13] Disraeli was happy to see Derby open negotiations with the Russians about possible armistice terms to be put to the Turks. As Shuvalov told Gorchakov, Disraeli had no alternative given that British public opinion would not allow him to support the Sultan.[14] The Russians were so 'enchanted' with the armistice terms which Derby put forward that on 11 September they joined with the British in presenting them to the Porte.[15] It was proposed that Bosnia-Herzegovina would receive autonomy, whilst the *status quo* would be maintained in Montenegro; as a sop to the Turks, they would be allowed to retain their garrisons in their Serbian fortresses.[16] Andrassy immediately expressed his opposition to the phrase 'autonomy' and was relieved when Derby reassured him that this meant nothing more than parochial self-government.[17] But there was one Minister who favoured going much further.

Salisbury was clearly among those with the mistaken assumption that Disraeli was fixated on maintaining Turkish integrity, and he wrote to him on 23 September urging him to abandon 'the traditional Palmerstonian policy' in favour of an Anglo-Russian deal at the expense of Turkey and, if necessary, Austria, whose 'vocation in Europe is gone'.[18] But in spite of his obsession with ending Palmerstoniansm and his love of a clear policy, Salisbury himself was not a consistent advocate of the Russian option, for, as he acknowledged in another letter written on the same day as his advice to Disraeli, to 'throw ourselves into the arms of Russia and ignore the rest of Europe' would be 'attended with very great risk'.[19] Derby, who found Salisbury's radical proposals 'large and new', doubted whether a new constitution for the Ottoman Empire would be workable.[20]

Disraeli was not unsympathetic, as he had told Derby in early September, to a radical solution of the Eastern Question, but the problem, as he now told Salisbury, was that 'all depends upon

Russia, and Russia cannot be trusted'.[21] With the Tsar at his summer retreat at Livadia in the Crimea, Pan-Slav influences were particularly strong, and even Gorchakov was said to be 'highly militant in mood'.[22] Derby protested at the thousands of Russians who were joining the Serbs in their war, but Gorchakov responded that there was nothing he could do to stop them. To Disraeli, it began to look as though the 'dualism' which had marked Russian policy was indistinguishable from duplicity. Gorchakov was co-operating in the diplomatic efforts, but he was demanding a prolonged armistice of at least six months to give the Serbs a breathing-space. When the Serbs recommenced the fighting on 27 September, doubts about Russia's intentions intensified. As Derby told the Queen on 29 September:

> It is necessary at present to act as if we trusted Russia, for the present state of popular feeling makes all action in an anti-Russian sense practically impossible; but everything points to the probability that the Russian Government, while ostensibly promoting peace, are by indirect means making it impossible.[23]

This suspicion was increased by Shuvalov's 'startling proposition' that 'in the event of the Porte's refusal to accept the terms proposed, Austrian troops should march into Bosnia, Russian troops into Bulgaria, and the united fleets come up to Constantinople'.[24] Disraeli determined that in the event of a general war Britain would occupy Constantinople, and he asked his Minister of War, Gathorne-Hardy, for details of its fortifications and the size of the force needed for this task.[25] He had always thought that the 'English people will come to their senses', and was convinced that with any Russian threat to Constantinople the focus could switch back to the geopolitical aspects of the Eastern Question.[26] Now that moment seemed to have come.

On the home front the high tide of the 'Atrocitarian' agitation seemed to have receded. From Wakefield Northcote reported on 28 September on a 'wonderful anti-Atrocitarian demonstration' with more than 12,000 people 'rapturously' cheering every mention of Derby's name, and ferociously jeering Gladstone and the Liberal Russophile MP, Robert Lowe.[27] But everything depended upon the dynamics of the *Dreikaiserbund*. If Russia and Austria could agree on a programme of action which Bismarck approved, then England would be cut out of the Eastern Question; fortunately for Disraeli, this proved impossible.

In late September, the Tsar tried to develop the Reichstadt accord by proposing that Russian and Austrian troops should make simultaneous entry into Bulgaria and Bosnia respectively, accompanied by a demonstration by the fleets of the Great Powers in the Bosphorus.[28] Because any such action could lead to complications, Alexander wanted assurances of German support, much to the discomfiture of Bismarck, who was holed up on his estate at Varzin complaining about his 'nerves'.[29] On 1 October, Alexander asked Wilhelm whether, in the event of hostilities between Russia and Turkey pulling in Austria, Germany would imitate Russia in 1870 and remain benevolently neutral.[30] 'It lay', Bismarck recalled in his memoirs, 'even beyond Russian usages, for the German military plenipotentiary at the Russian Court to place before us ... by order of the Russian Emperor, a political question of far-reaching importance in the categorical style of a telegram.'[31] Bismarck shared Frederick the Great's opinion that 'of all the neighbours of Prussia, Russia demands the most attention as being the most dangerous'.[32] He had no intention of being 'a party to hostile or merely diplomatic manoeuvres against Russia',[33] but equally little desire to give the Tsar *carte blanche* to act in the Balkans. He suspected the hand of Gorchakov in the Tsar's initiative: 'If we answer "no", he will use it to prejudice Tsar Alexander against us; if we answer "yes", he will use it in Vienna.'[34]

Bismarck prevaricated, but Wilhelm insisted that honour bound him to answer the question.[35] Bismarck ensured that the answer was as Delphic as possible: 'We could endure indeed that our friends should lose or win battles against each other, but not that one of the two should be so severely wounded and injured that its position as an independent Great Power taking its part in the councils of Europe would be endangered.'[36] Bismarck had returned a similar answer to Austria when her Ambassador, Baron Münch, had enquired about Germany's intentions in the event of a breakdown in relations between Austria and Russia. Bismarck told the Austrian what he had told the Russians – which was that a conflict between the two states had to be avoided. In a piece of evasion which doubled as a fine piece of cheek, Bismarck announced that, 'In general he no longer considered it wise to form an alliance for future eventualities' – although he did encourage the Austrians to occupy Bosnia.[37]

Bismarck's sphinx-like attitude enabled Andrassy to prevail against the Russophiles in Vienna who wanted to take up Alexander's offer. In early October, Franz Joseph agreed to participate in naval operations, but declined to join in any military moves in Bulgaria and Bosnia. Had the decision gone the other way, the consequences could have been fateful. Austro-Russian co-operation at this point would have averted the later Balkan rivalry which led to the Great War, and some historians have seen in Andrassy's refusal a 'turning point which did not turn'.[38]

Disraeli scented the shift in the wind, and seized the occasion of a dinner on the eve of the by-election in his old constituency of Aylesbury to renew Britain's claim to a major say in the future of the Eastern Question.[39] For Disraeli, any Russian occupation of Turkish territory would have been the 'real Bulgarian atrocity', and he now hoped that the revelation of Russian ambitions would swing opinion back behind a policy of using sea power to deter Russia. He told Shuvalov that if there was going to be any naval presence at Constantinople, it would be a purely British one, and sent him 'off with a flea in his ear'.[40] At Cabinet on 4 October, it was decided to reject the Russian proposals and to insist on an armistice in the Serb-Turkish war to be followed by a conference. Disraeli, who was convinced by the diplomatic intelligence and his own reading of the situation that the Russians intended to occupy

Constantinople, insisted that Britain should occupy it first if need be; but since Derby dissented from such a bold course of action, and since no one disagreed with the rejection of the Russian terms, a desultory discussion petered out into waiting upon news of Russia's reaction.[41] Disraeli refused to put pressure on the Turks to agree to Russia's demand, but he did allow it to be known at the Porte that in existing circumstances it was unlikely that Britain would be able to help Turkey. On 12 October, the Turks decided to agree to a six-month armistice, but the Russians had wanted a much shorter one – six weeks – and so rejected the Turkish offer. Bismarck declined British requests to press the Russians to agree to the Turkish proposal.[42]

Disraeli correctly divined that the dynastic link between Hohenzollern and Romanov was an obstacle to securing German agreement to a 'treaty . . . to maintain the present *status quo* generally' – hence his wish that the aged Wilhelm 'were in the same cave as Friedrich Barbarossa'; but he still thought that he might be able to win Bismarck over.[43] The Queen thoroughly approved of Disraeli's idea of an 'understanding with Germany' and hoped that it would be pursued vigorously.[44] But there were, as ever, obstacles in Disraeli's way; in this instance they were twofold: the distrust Derby and Salisbury felt for Bismarck; and, as ever, Bismarck's own desire to avoid committing himself in a situation where he could hope to gain little and lose much.

Bismarck was 'silent and impenetrable'.[45] Derby still did not believe that he could be trusted and thought that he would 'probably not be sorry to see England and Russia quarrel'.[46] The likelihood of this seemed to be increasing with Russia insisting that the Turks should agree to a short armistice. Shuvalov told Lady Derby in mid-October that 'a week ago he would have said the Czar wanted peace but now he did not know what to think of it', which was, Derby thought, 'pretty strong language from an ambassador'.[47] Bismarck remained uncommunicative,[48] and Salisbury, who shared Derby's distrust of him, urged Disraeli to make sure that any 'engagements' with him 'should only bind us to respect the *status quo* as a whole: & should not bind us whenever, if ever, it ceases to exist'.[49] Salisbury did not want Bismarck coming up with an Anglo-German treaty as an excuse to deprive Britain of her spoils if the empire did collapse. Derby would go no further than a cautious enquiry in Berlin to see whether Bismarck would convene a conference.[50]

Bismarck's attitude towards the situation in the Balkans was governed solely by considerations of *Realpolitik*. Repulsing all requests for German intervention, on the general ground that it was 'an error' to 'suppose . . . that the wisdom of statesmen can discover a magic recipe for the maintenance of peace' which lay beyond the ken of the interested parties, he saw no reason for Germany to involve herself in the crisis: 'All Turkey, in which I include the various races inhabiting it, is not so valuable an institution, as to justify the civilized peoples of Europe in ruining themselves and each other in a great war for her sake.'[51] His own fantasy scenario (*Phantasie-gemälde*) was that peace could be preserved at Turkey's expense, with Russia taking Bessarabia, Austria Bosnia, Britain Egypt and France Syria, with Constantinople remaining under Ottoman rule. He told the British that he 'failed to understand what interest England had in risking a second time to dissolve the European Concert for the sake of the Turkish Empire. . . . He was the first to acknowledge the vital interest of England in Egypt, Asia and India . . . but he failed to see what interest England had to defend north of the Balkans.'[52]

Disraeli's interest remained the denial of Constantinople to the Russians. He was convinced that if they seized the Turkish capital, they could 'at any time march their Army through Syria to the mouth of the Nile, and then what would be the use of our holding Egypt? . . . Constantinople is the key of India.' It was upon this point that his eye remained. He was sure that in the end 'Germany will eventually go against Russia', but in the meantime he wanted to make sure that Britain would be able to secure her interests at the Straits.[53] His suggestion at Cabinet on 19 October for occupying Constantinople also encompassed the idea of taking up some other fortified position, perhaps on the Dardanelles or at some other eastern Mediterranean version of 'Malta or Gibraltar'.[54]

Derby was uneasy both at Disraeli's ideas and the urgency with which he pressed them. He had no objection to checking out the sea defences of Constantinople, but doubted whether the Russians were 'in the state of readiness' Disraeli assumed, or that they would really take the risk of trying to occupy the city.[55] Derby feared that any Disraelian precautionary moves might actually precipitate the eventuality they were designed to avoid.[56] At Cabinet on 23 October, Disraeli proposed to send the fleet to Constantinople and to issue a warning to Russia about the consequences of occupying Bulgaria. But Derby told the First Lord of the Admiralty that 'the step of sending the British fleet to pass the Dardanelles' without the consent of the Porte was 'not to be taken off-hand, nor without the fullest consideration'.[57]

Derby denied that he had 'ignored the decision of the Cabinet',[58] and prevaricated before sending a much watered-down version of the message which Disraeli had wanted to send to St Petersburg.[59] Disraeli, unable to shake his stubborn subordinate, had already turned to Salisbury and the Viceroy of India, Lord Lytton, asking whether Russia could be attacked through Central Asia. Salisbury had warned that 'a Mahommedan rising in India is a real danger if the Turkish Government in Constantinople should be overthrown',[60] and Lytton, delighted to have an opportunity of meeting such a challenge directly, responded with enthusiasm to Disraeli's query.[61]

Derby belonged firmly to Gladstone's 'old Conservative school' which had believed in 'economy, peace . . . [and] sound and strict finance',[62] but he recognised that to Disraeli, 'the main thing is to please and surprise the public by bold strokes and unexpected moves'. He thought that Disraeli 'would rather run serious national risks than hear his policy called feeble or commonplace'; his own 'first object' was 'to keep England out of trouble, so long as it can be done consistently with honour and good faith'. He began to realise that under the pressure of a prolonged crisis there was 'the probability, or at least the chance, of a breach between us'.[63] But the immediate prospect of this vanished with Russia's ultimatum to the Porte at the end of October demanding an armistice and a reply within forty-eight hours.

Disraeli could not decide whether this meant war or not, but he pressed the Turks to agree to an armistice followed by a conference all the same.[64] Gorchakov proposed to Derby that he should organise a conference of the Powers to discuss the terms of a peace settlement.[65] Derby saw this as the longed-for signal for closer co-operation, and told Disraeli on 7 November that they could probably get over the difficulty of Russian objections to Britain's insistence upon Turkey's 'territorial integrity'.[66] On 10 November, the Russians accepted the proposal for a conference.[67] For Gorchakov, this prevented any immediate entanglement with England, which in view of the belligerent noises being made by Disraeli was a good idea;[68] it also allowed Russia to try to continue to 'seek a mandate from Europe' to take action. Gorchakov saw no alternative to a military occupation when it came to forcing reforms upon the Turks, but he knew that would arouse British distrust, and he had not yet cleared the decks with Vienna and Berlin, so the conference gave him time to do this, an opportunity to see if he could arrive at *'une entente générale des Grandes Puissances'*, without ruling out unilateral action in the spring when the snows in the Balkan mountains had melted.[69] But Gorchakov, like everyone else, was taken by surprise by the news that Britain's representative at the Constantinople conference would be Salisbury.

The suggestion had been Disraeli's own, and he had passed Salisbury a note in Cabinet which read: 'I want you to go. That is my idea – a great enterprize & would not take much time.'[70] Salisbury thought the matter over before accepting the commission. He was 'not so anxious for perfect freedom'[71] that he was prepared to go unless the Cabinet decided upon its policy.[72] Gladstone approved of the choice of Salisbury: 'he is very remarkably clever, of unsure judgement, but is above everything that is mean: has no Disraelite prejudices, keeps a conscience and has plenty of manhood and character';[73] so did Derby, who thought that Salisbury had the merit of 'not being supposed to be Turkish' in his sympathies, which would satisfy the public in Britain, whilst his Indian experience had endowed him with enough knowledge to be aware that 'the Russians are not exactly the self-sacrificing apostles of a new civilization which our Liberals seem inclined to consider them'. As a Minister he would have the rank to talk with authority, whilst Elliot could hardly complain at having to play second fiddle to such a senior figure.[74] Neither Gladstone nor Derby were exactly at one with Disraeli's views, and in view of the long history of disagreements between Salisbury and Disraeli, it was a risky and surprising choice.[75]

Salisbury's impatience with the old Palmerstonian policy, as well as his High Anglican sympathy with the plight of the Orthodox Christians, made him an unlikely exponent of Disraeli's line. Lady Derby, who carried on a correspondence with the Russian Ambassador, Shuvalov, who had told her that the Russians had no designs on Constantinople,[76] offered to put her former step-son in touch with him, but Salisbury declined, saying that 'I don't think anything is to be gained talking politics to "Shou" just now. I am afraid Shou's master is being run away with.'[77] But he did make it clear that he wanted to be able to threaten to coerce the Turks if they did not agree to the reforms proposed by the Great Powers, a line which received support from Cairns and Northcote, as well as his old friend Carnarvon.[78] Disraeli was viscerally opposed to any such line, and recalled the unhappy precedent of Canning's policy in 1827 which had led to Navarino and a Russo-Turkish war, the results of which had taken decades to reverse. The most he would agree to was diplomatic coercion. To Salisbury's questioning of what he should do if the Turks declined this, he replied airily: 'Oh, they won't refuse'.[79]

If Salisbury was not the obvious choice for the mission, he was not very enthusiastic about it either, accepting it with no great expectations or, indeed, with any pleasure; it was, he thought, 'an awful nuisance – not at all in my line – involving sea-sickness, much French and failure'.[80] He doubted 'the possibility now of Russia being content with any terms to which Turkey can reasonably submit', and remained dubious about representing a Cabinet which seemed to have no clear policy.[81]

Disraeli went out of his way to make the mission as attractive as possible to Salisbury, telling him that it would be a 'momentous period in your life & career', and that if 'all goes well you will have achieved a European reputation & position which will immensely assist and strengthen your future course'. Disraeli told him that it would be a good thing that he 'should personally know the men who are governing the world' and that he should meet them 'under circumstances which allow you to gauge their character, their strength & their infirmities'.[82] Even allowing for Disraeli's habitual flattery, the implication that Salisbury was being groomed for greater things was impossible to miss, and it may have been that Disraeli was trying to drive a wedge between him and Derby, as well as trying to win over the ambitious young Marquess.

In fact, Disraeli had little to lose by sending Salisbury to Constantinople. He had already told Shuvalov as far back as June that he would be willing to co-operate with Russia on the basis of both sides restraining their ambitions. Since Derby and other members of the Cabinet doubted his diagnosis that Russian ambitions were in fact unlimited, and since they wanted to explore the possibilities of co-operation with Gorchakov, Disraeli lost nothing by sending a sceptical proponent of such a policy to Constantinople. It was possible that Salisbury would succumb to Russian blandishments, but with public opinion already shifting back towards a policy of resisting Russian ambitions at the Straits, and with even the Cabinet declining to countenance the coercion of Turkey by mid-December,[83] Disraeli could be fairly confident of his position. Should Salisbury really concede too much, he would damage himself; should the Russians, as Disraeli expected, demand too much, then Salisbury would have had a useful lesson in the realities of diplomacy, and no one would be able to accuse the Prime Minister of not having done his best to co-operate with St Petersburg.

Salisbury's mission to Constantinople would have been an ideal subject for a Victorian triptych: the first panel would have been entitled 'The young Saint is tempted by the great Satan', with the neophyte diplomatist sharing centre-stage with the imposing bulk of a sinister Bismarck; the second, and most lurid, would have figured the grave young Anglican alongside the vivacious and flirtatious figure of Mme Ignatyev, with the title 'Christian is tempted by the wiles of the Russian Eve'; whilst the final picture would have featured a weary and travel-stained Salisbury arriving back in London with the caption 'A sadder but wiser man'.

The first temptation came in the form of Bismarck right enough, and it is a shame that we do not have a fuller record of what the two men said when they met on 22 November. The Chancellor expressed himself conventionally enough afterwards, pronouncing himself 'impressed by [Salisbury's] agreeable and trust-inspiring personality' and considering him to be both 'a shrewd and careful politician'.[84] For all that, he tempted Salisbury with nothing more than the bait he had held out so often to Disraeli and Derby.[85] The Chancellor renewed his declaration that 'Germany had but little personal interest in the fate of Turkey, but a very great one in her enduring friendship with England, Russia and Austria'. He professed scepticism about the Constantinople conference, but counselled strongly against the British taking unilateral action against Russia: 'in England they believed too much, and in his opinion wrongly, in a cut and dried plan of Russia's, which she was pursuing relentlessly'. He floated the prospect of preserving peace at Turkey's expense by a partition – with Constantinople falling into the British sphere.

That was what Bismarck said, but was it what he meant and could he be trusted? Derby, whose distrust of him went deep, thought that Bismarck 'probably wishes for a war more than he has thought fit to acknowledge. Russia crippled (as, whoever wins, Russia will be for some time) puts an end to the danger he most fears, that of a Franco-Russian coalition.'[86] Salisbury also suspected that Bismarck would welcome a war, but he thought that the intended victims were 'Russia and Turkey'.[87] In fact, as so often, both views of Bismarck's intentions were right. Bismarck was certainly not averse to Gorchakov being taught a lesson; he had not forgiven him for the 'War in Sight' debacle and regarded his flirting with republican France as a dangerous portent.[88] Bismarck did not think that the Turks would simply collapse if attacked, and so doubted whether war would bring Russia easy gains.[89] But what he did not want was a repetition of the Crimean War, which would bring France out of diplomatic purdah and force him to choose between Russia and Austria.[90] What he wanted least of all was to see Austria collapse.[91] As he told Prince Hohenloe in September 1876: 'If Austria is defeated by Russia, we could, of course, annex the Germans – but we would not know what to do with the South Slavs and the Hungarians. The ruin of Austria would make Russia dangerous for us. With Austria we can hold Russia in check.'[92] It was little wonder that Salisbury should have found Andrassy's views identical with those of Bismarck, even if he found the Hungarian himself less than impressive.[93] He came away from his first encounter with the arbiter of Europe convinced that Derby was wrong to suspect him of wanting an Anglo-Russian war.[94]

Disraeli did not think that a Russo–Turkish war would necessarily involve Britain; that would depend upon Russia's progress and upon the fate of Constantinople. It was, he told Salisbury in late November, 'a most critical moment in European politics'. Disraeli warned of the dystopia which might follow the fall of the Ottoman Empire: 'If Russia is not checked, the Holy Alliance will be revived in aggravated form and force. Germany will have Holland, and France Belgium, and England will be in a position I trust I shall never live to witness'.[95]

The fact that Salisbury's instructions had been drawn up with some haste reflected not the dilatoriness of the Foreign Office under Derby, but the difficulty the Cabinet had in arriving at a consensus over how to proceed. Everyone, more or less, could agree that the Turks ought to grant something called autonomy to the insurgent provinces, but the questions of what guarantees should be exacted, and what to do if Turkey refused the proposals, were ones which placed wedges into the fissure lines of the

Cabinet. The Russians spoke vaguely of autonomy for 'Bulgaria'; but what should the frontiers of such a state be, who should decide them, and what should be its relationship to Turkey? Derby and Disraeli both half expected the Russians to put forward demands as the patron of 'Bulgaria' which would be impossible for the Turks to meet, but which it would be impossible for Britain to refuse as they would be linked to better treatment for the Christians in the Turkish Empire.[96] It was thus with some concern that soon after Salisbury's arrival in Constantinople on 5 December, Disraeli found that he seemed to be 'more Russian than Ignatieff' when it came to accepting the terms that were to be put to the Porte.[97]

4

Reading the Russian Sphinx

For diplomats of the old school, like the former Ambassador in Paris, Lord Cowley, there was something 'not dignified' in the notion that a 'Cabinet Minister should wander all over Europe to see what support he can get', especially when he was told 'by every visit when he knocks on the door that they intend to let Russia have her own way'.[1] It took between five and nine days for letters to get from Constantinople to London,[2] which left plenty of time for 'discontent in the Cabinet' to manifest itself after Salisbury's departure.[3] Disraeli thought that 'we shall win, if we clearly know what object we aim at, and then are becomingly firm';[4] but Salisbury's views were not Disraeli's. He pressed for 'full power to squeeze the Turks', finding the Russian terms 'as good . . . as we could fairly expect', and fearing that if Turkey continued to resist them there would be a war which 'will be the opening of a terrible European chapter'.[5] It was this, and not Mme Ignatyev's outrageous flirting,[6] or her husband's wiles,[7] which induced Salisbury to accept Russian proposals for the creation of a semi-autonomous Bulgaria.

Ignatyev was a 'hawk' when it came to dealing with Turkey,[8] and was regarded by Derby as the 'most audacious and the most plausible' of 'all the untruthtellers that have walked this earth'.

But Salisbury had spotted this, and was amused rather than scandalised when, having pointed out to Ignatyev that he had altered the line of a frontier which had been agreed at a previous meeting, he had responded good-naturedly: '*M. le Marquis est si fin, – on peut rein lui cacher* [Your lordship is so quick, one can hide nothing from you].'[9] Salisbury liked his politics 'free of sentimental humbug',[10] and preferred such candour to the behind-the-scenes intrigue indulged in by the British Ambassador, Elliot, who put it about that it was he, and not Salisbury, who represented the real views of the British Government.[11]

Northcote, who wanted Disraeli to call a Cabinet meeting to discuss the proposals tabled by the Russians, favoured taking them at face value, but wanted to replace the purely Russian gendarmerie by a Belgian force with English officers. The most important thing for him was that by moving away from supporting a corrupt and blood-stained regime, 'we should liberate our own souls, and should get a better standpoint for this country'. He thought it ought to be possible to unite the 'Two Englands' around a policy of constructive reforms for the Porte.[12] But the crucial question remained what to do if the Porte rejected the plans of the Great Powers;[13] and here the Cabinet showed itself more united and less liable to sentiment than it had in the autumn.

Derby and Disraeli were determined not to accept any part in coercing the Turks and were resolved to resign rather than lose their 'self-respect' if the Cabinet decided otherwise.[14] But there was no dissent from colleagues when Derby declared this position on 18 December: everyone agreed that Russia could coerce the Porte, but that Britain would not join her.[15] On 22 December, Ministers confirmed their decision, but decided not to offer the Turks any help if this resulted in war with Russia; if the conference broke down then Salisbury would return home, but diplomatic relations with the Turks would be maintained. Only Carnarvon seemed disposed to disagree, but his argument, that by breaking with Turkey they could not be held responsible for Turkish mistreatment of her subjects, was so odd that no one supported it.[16]

The aggrieved Carnarvon spent a cheerless Christmas Day penning a long epistle to his old friend in Constantinople. Suspicion of Disraeli, whose mind was 'full of strange projects', suffused every line in the letter. Carnarvon felt 'uneasy as to what he intends and what he may be able to do before there is time or knowledge enough to stop him'; he suspected that 'as far as it depends on him [he] intends us to take part in the war and on behalf of Turkey', and that had Disraeli been 'ten years younger' he might well have broken up the Cabinet rather than have agreed to putting any pressure on the Porte. The language employed outside the Cabinet room by Disraeli was, Carnarvon warned, more bellicose than that he allowed himself inside it,[17] and he feared the influence which he seemed to be able to exercise over Derby, whose 'mental position' he 'hardly' understood.

Derby's position was not that hard to comprehend; it was made up in equal parts of his views on the crisis in the East and his opinions about its domestic political ramifications; the problem was that these pulled him in different directions. He shared some of Carnarvon's concerns about Disraeli's language and his propensity to want to take dramatic action, but because he was closer to the Prime Minister, he reacted differently to them. After nearly three years in office, Derby felt tired and out of sorts, and there were few ties binding him to public life. But one of those was his long friendship with Disraeli, 'whom I will not desert while he continues a Minister'.[18] It could not be long before Disraeli's health forced him to retire, and when that happened Derby, who felt no ambition to be Prime Minister, and who had insufficient interest 'in the questions which most Conservatives have at heart to fight well upon them', would be quite content to follow him.[19] The two men were still close together when it came to the line of policy Britain should adopt towards the Eastern Question. Derby would have gone with Disraeli had their colleagues not backed the policy of refraining from coercing the Sultan, and he calmed the Prime Minister's fears about the public perception that Salisbury was 'more Russian than we are', by saying that as the conference was going to fail, that did not matter: 'what was of most importance was to take from Salisbury's special partisans the possibility of saying that he had failed because thwarted at home'. If not even Salisbury could find a way of working with the Russians, then even the most severe critics of the Government would have to admit that it had been right to reject the Berlin Memorandum. What mattered to both men was establishing, one way or the other, Russian *bona fides*.[20]

Salisbury's own diplomatic priorities were those of his hero, Castlereagh: 'he cared for nationality not at all; for the theoretic perfection of political institutions very little; for the realities of freedom a great deal; and for the peace, and social order and freedom from the manifold curses of disturbance, which can alone give to the humbler masses of mankind any chance of tasting their scanty share of human joys . . . he was quite willing to forego all the rest'.[21] He thought that in defining the 'national interest' statesmen should take a clear-sighted view and avoid both the excesses of moralising and the temptation to bully and bluster.[22] Ignatyev might be a rogue, but Salisbury thought that it was in Russia's interests as much as Britain's to avoid a war in the Balkans. He wanted a radical break with the Palmerstonian policy,[23] and during the conference he became more and more 'convinced of the deplorable folly of the Crimean War',[24] concluding that it was impossible 'that we should spend more blood sustaining the Turkish Empire'. He wanted to devise 'some other means of securing the road to India'.[25] He was not uninfluenced by the fact that fellow Christians were being oppressed by Moslems,[26] but he was more influenced by the decay of Ottoman power. He doubted whether, after two depositions, the Sultan possessed the moral authority to get the 'oligarchy of place-hunters' by whom he was surrounded to accept the reforms which the ambassadors were pressing upon him, and was convinced that the Empire was on its last legs.[27] Elliot's 'restless', 'vicious' and 'open' opposition to Salisbury's mission[28] simply muddied the waters and made matters worse.[29] Lady Salisbury thought that 'it would be everything' to get him 'away *at once*',[30] but, as Disraeli explained, matters were not so simple; the

Russians also wanted him removed and, 'if this gets out, and everything does at Constantinople, and Elliot withdraws, we shall be turned out the first day of the session by our own men'.[31] Shuvalov denied making any such demands, and when told of Disraeli's comment by Lady Derby, described it as *'un nouveau mensonge de Lord Beaconsfield'*;[32] but it served its purpose – Elliot stayed.

Salisbury accepted Ignatyev's proposals for an armed gendarmerie to oversee the implementation of the internal reforms insisted upon by the Great Powers, and for Bulgaria to be divided into two provinces, with the westernmost one having almost complete autonomy.[33] Disraeli's later claim to have sent Salisbury to Constantinople because he was *'L'homme le plus favorable à l'entente avec la Russie'*,[34] was belied by his hostile reaction to his agreement with Ignatyev. He told Derby that Salisbury should remember that he had not been sent out to 'create an ideal existence for Turkish X[Christ]ians'.[35] The feeling in the London Clubs also ran 'against Lord Salisbury', who was supposed 'to have given himself over to Ignatieff body and soul'. But the 'Tadpoles' and 'Tapers' of the Tory Party warned Disraeli to remember that 'things are now much changed and that it is not the opinion of the Clubs that influences public opinion. The real voting power of the country is several degrees lower.' Like it or not, it appeared that 'the tradesman class and people in the country' would probably prefer 'pressure and bullying even if done in alliance with Russia' than leaving the Porte to carry on in its traditional manner.[36] But Derby's suspicions that the Turks would refuse the proffered reforms proved correct.[37]

It is characteristic of European attitudes towards the Ottoman Empire that most commentators should have supposed that Turkish unwillingness to be coerced by the Great Powers should have been inspired either by secret British diplomacy or by expectations that the Russians would be unable to carry out their threats.[38] The revolt which had brought Abdülhamid to power and stiffened the sinews of war against the Slavs was a sign of Islamic resurgence; it was the outrage at the infringement of

Turkish sovereignty which prompted the Turks to pre-empt the conference by promulgating a new constitution on its very first day (23 December).[39] Even had Abdülhamid wanted to bow to pressure from the Great Powers, it is unlikely that he would have been allowed to; the rejection of the proposals at the end of December satisfied all shades of Turkish opinion.[40]

The European Ambassadors at Constantinople were all 'exceedingly angry and disposed to look upon it [the Turkish proposal] as a deliberate insult', but Salisbury persuaded them to put to the Sultan those points in their own proposals which had been ignored in the Turkish Counter-Project.[41] There followed a fortnight of negotiation in which the Powers watered down their proposals in a vain effort to secure concessions from the Turks. As Salisbury told Derby, there were only three alternatives: coercing Turkey – which 'you will not do'; 'allowing Russia to do her worst' and then trying to 'regulate her demands when peace is talked of'; or coming to terms with Andrassy and Gorchakov for 'a regulated occupation of Bulgaria and Bosnia'.[42]

A fourth option presented itself courtesy of Bismarck once the conference had failed. Initially Bismarck had tried to stay out of the diplomacy at Constantinople. When questioned as to what Germany wanted, he declared: '*Es fiele ihm nichts ein* [I can think of nothing]';[43] he could see 'no interest for Germany which would be worth the healthy bones of a single Pomeranian musketeer'.[44] But with the Russians blaming him for the failure of the Turks to accept their proposals,[45] and the fear that 'influential people' in Russia 'would rather go against Germany together with the Paris Government, than fight for the Eastern Christians in Turkey',[46] Bismarck realised that inaction might be dangerous. When Gorchakov asked the Powers to assent to a list of demands to be put to the Porte following the failure of the conference,[47] Bismarck hoped that Britain would continue to refuse to coerce the Turks; he also made it clear to Russell that Germany would support such a line. But he went further than this, asking whether Germany could 'reckon on the benevolent neutrality or moral support of England for the maintenance of peace if a coalition were formed by France, Russia and other powers against Germany'.[48] The Chancellor's main worry was that a Russo-Turkish war might be avoided at his own expense, with Austria and Russia reverting to dynastic diplomacy and dividing up the Balkans, leaving Germany isolated.[49] It was for this reason that he was willing to offer an 'offensive and defensive' alliance to the British, and to make similar suggestions to Andrassy.[50]

Bismarck's fears about an Austro-Russian deal were not without foundation. Despite Andrassy assuring the British that Austria had no secret agreements with Russia,[51] he was actually busy augmenting the Reichstadt Agreement with a supplementary Convention signed at Budapest on 15 January,[52] which guaranteed Austrian neutrality in the event of a Russo-Turkish war. In return, the Russians agreed to let Austria occupy Bosnia-Herzegovina at a time of her own choosing. Andrassy followed this up in March with a political agreement which was antedated to 15 January, and which sanctioned the annexation of Bosnia-Herzegovina; it also provided for the recovery of southern Bessarabia by Russia. The Convention also bound the two Powers to support each other if the territorial changes produced by the war were subjected to the 'collective deliberation' of the other Powers.[53] It was little wonder that Andrassy declined both British and German overtures.

Derby was 'rather amused' by the suspicions which were entertained abroad about Britain's intentions, and by the Machiavellian manoeuvres to which they gave rise. As he told Odo Russell in Berlin, 'these fellows make us act as they would act in our place, they can neither deal straightforwardly themselves, nor give anybody else credit for doing so'.[54] If the Secretary of State for War, Gathorne-Hardy, wondered 'how far' Bismarck's offer was 'sincere',[55] his superiors had no doubts. Derby remained convinced that Bismarck probably wanted 'Russia to be involved in a Turkish war'[56] – a view which Disraeli now shared.[57] They also feared that Bismarck might seize the opportunity afforded by such a war to settle scores with France.[58] Their mistrust of the German Chancellor was shared by the Queen and by Salisbury.[59]

Derby thought that even if the British parliamentary system had made such an alliance possible, 'I do not think Bismarck a person with whom it would be safe to enter into a political partnership.'[60] Salisbury was 'happy' that Bismarck's overtures received a negative response.[61] British policy remained one of 'watchfulness'. With Turkey having rejected Britain's advice to accept the international reform, there was, Northcote told Derby, 'no immediate occasion for our acting';[62] as Derby put it, 'We shall wait, say little, and pledge ourselves to nothing.'[63]

Northcote thought that there 'seems to be a great opportunity now for the initiation of a sounder policy with regard to Turkey than has obtained of late years'. By rejecting the proposals of the Great Powers, she had 'taken on herself a great responsibility' and must be 'carefully watched'.[64] The Home Secretary, Richard Cross, who reminded Northcote that they were backed by 'the first really Conservative House of Commons for more years than I care to name',[65] thought that 'if we are careful and stick together . . . the country will be entirely with us'.[66] Speaking in the Lords on 8 February, Disraeli declared that: 'What was at stake was not the "mere amelioration" of the lot of the Christians – but "the existence of Empires".'[67] In a further uncompromising speech on 20 February, he acknowledged that the 'people of this country' were 'deeply interested in the humanitarian and philanthropic considerations' involved in the Eastern Question, but went on to say: 'I am very mistaken if there be not a yet deeper sentiment on the part of the people of this country . . . the determination to maintain the Empire of England.'[68]

Disraeli's performance was all the more remarkable given the state of his health. The 'gout' which had plagued him the previous year had flared up again, and his bronchitis was made all the more severe by the rigours of a London winter and the medical mistreatment he was receiving. Indeed, there had been times when it had seemed that the ageing Premier would not be able to carry on.[69] What rallied him was 'the prospect of having defeated Governments and bluffed Bismarck and secured European peace'; but his greatest feat was 'keeping the Cabinet together'.[70]

SPLENDID ISOLATION?

As so often with Disraeli, the high line which he had taken in public allowed him to explore softer ones in private. A war between Russia and Turkey would inflame British opinion, strain Cabinet unity and might even lead to Britain becoming involved, so before it happened Disraeli wanted to see whether he could avert it by providing a 'golden bridge' over which the Russians could retreat.[71] When he saw Shuvalov on 20 February, he disclaimed any 'hostile or belligerent intentions' towards Russia. Referring back to his proposals for co-operation of the previous summer, he reiterated what he had said then, that the days of the Ottoman Empire were numbered; but he emphasised that the time was not ripe for its disintegration. The European Powers must first make their dispositions in order to ensure that war did not follow the demise of the Grand Turk. For this time was needed, and the Turks must be allowed to see whether their reforms could be implemented. If the Russians would show the necessary restraint, then Britain and Russia could co-operate; there would not be merely a 'golden bridge', but one of 'diamonds and rubies'.[72]

It has been cogently argued that the correspondence between Gorchakov, Ignatyev and Shuvalov leaves 'no possible room for doubt as to the pacific intentions of the Tsar and his Government', and that Disraeli's policy was therefore wrong-headed.[73] But, of course, Disraeli did not have access to this correspondence; and even had this been the case, it is by no means clear that Russian policy was fully represented by Gorchakov and Shuvalov. When Ignatyev asked Gorchakov on 26 November 1876 whether, if the conference did not succeed, the War Ministry preferred a rupture 'in December, January, or towards the spring',[74] this did not mean that he was planning on a war; but it did show that he had not ruled one out, either. By the end of the year, there were about 190,000 Russian troops mobilised for action.[75] The Russian willingness to negotiate came partly from a fear of the financial consequences of a war,[76] and partly from the feeling that they could not depend upon the *Dreikaiserbund*, which, in Shuvalov's withering phrase, offered them all the 'inconveniences of an alliance' without any of its advantages.[77] But, as the Tsar told his Ministers in February 1877: 'In the life of states, just as in that of private individuals, there are moments when one must forget all but the defence of his honor.'[78] In such circumstances, the pacific intentions of Gorchakov would count for little.

Lady Derby, who wanted closer co-operation with Russia, saw an irony in Disraeli's offer of a 'bridge of diamonds and rubies' to Shuvalov: 'The Chief and those who went with him, have now utterly forgotten that they ever had a Turkish sympathy, that they are not only Russian now, but are under a profound impression that they have never been anything else.'[79] She encouraged Salisbury to press his line that 'England's traditional policy' should be abandoned in favour of one of partition, and showed him letters from Shuvalov which protested Russia's peaceful intentions. But Salisbury was convinced by this stage that Disraeli would not accept his policy,[80] and whilst he accepted her argument that a failure to reach agreement would lead to a war between Turkey and Russia, but thought that 'little – very little – chance is left. I doubt if either we or Shouvaloff have now any hold over events – the fatal resolution has been taken at St. Petersburg', he promised to 'destroy' the 'compromising document' which she had sent him.[81] Any effects which Shuvalov had been able to have in presenting Russian policy in a more favourable light were compromised by the Tsar's decision to send Ignatyev to London in early March to try to obtain an Anglo-Russian *entente*; what had been denied the suave and subtle Shuvalov would certainly not be yielded to the distrusted Ignatyev; and in so far as Gorchakov's proposals to the Turks now became identified with Ignatyev, the visit may actually have done harm.[82]

When the Cabinet met on 13 March to consider whether to support Gorchakov's demands for reforms from the Porte, there were nearly as many strands of opinion as there were Ministers, but only three mattered:[83] Salisbury's view, that if they did not accept the Russian Protocol they would find themselves isolated whilst Russia coerced the Porte as Europe's mandatory Power;[84]

Derby's, which advocated accepting a modified version of the Protocol which committed neither Britain nor Turkey to specific reforms which might have to be implemented by the other Powers;[85] and Disraeli's, that it was time to prepare the public for the possibility of war with Russia, and that by taking a tough stance in public the Russians might be warned off. There was general agreement with the principle of finding the Russians a viable line of retreat by urging reforms on the Porte, but not on the subject of how far that 'urging' should go. Disraeli irritated Derby by 'talking in his swaggering vein about the deference paid to English opinion, and the change in that respect since the Berlin Memorandum'; but the Foreign Secretary was inclined to dismiss such 'vanity' as a personal foible which 'cannot be helped'. The important point was that the Cabinet agreed to follow his policy of accepting the principle of the reforms and of letting him discuss the details with Shuvalov.[86]

On 23 March, in what Disraeli called 'the most important meeting of the Cabinet which has yet been holden',[87] he pushed as far as he dared for his own policy. Salisbury, who was disappointed that Russia appeared to be backing away from her support for the 'oppressed races', argued that Britain should formally abandon the policy of supporting Turkey. Disraeli dismissed this 'sentimental eccentricity' as 'the policy of crusade', and argued that there must be 'unanimity' on the policy to be followed.[88] This seems to have 'alarmed' some Ministers,[89] and Carnarvon came away with the impression that Disraeli was trying to drive himself and Salisbury from the Cabinet.[90] Salisbury, disclaiming the title of 'crusader', dissented from Disraeli's policy of imposing conditions on the Russian proposals, but like Carnarvon agreed to be bound by the views of the majority. It was agreed that the Porte would be asked to implement reforms and to disarm, but only if Russia disarmed and agreed that the Porte would not be actively coerced.

For Disraeli, it was another triumph over the forces of Gladstonism, this time within his own Cabinet.[91] For Carnarvon, it was another sign of how dangerous the Prime Minister was. The

Queen was 'ready for war', and he was sure that Disraeli was pressing in the same direction. He reminded Salisbury of the parallels with the 'same suspicions, anxieties and intrigues' and the 'open struggles' of ten years before, and wondered whether he was not going to try to force them to resign as he had a decade earlier: 'This may seem improbable, but you must remember the character of the man. Unlike Derby he has plenty of courage.'[92] Salisbury was less alarmist. He did not think that Disraeli would just dismiss them; apart from the lack of precedent for such a course, it would be tantamount to saying that he intended to declare war on Russia. Their best course would be to 'be cautious till the crisis comes'.[93] As he later lamented to Lytton: 'English policy is to float lazily downstream occasionally putting out a diplomatic boat-hook to avoid collisions.'[94]

The London Protocol was signed on 31 March and presented to the Porte on 6 April. It was as anodyne a document as could be imagined. It asked the Porte to put into operation all 'necessary' reforms, but these were defined as those announced by the Turks on 6 February rather than those of the Constantinople conference. The Turks were asked to demobilise, except for troops needed to keep order, with the implication that Russia would follow suit. They were also asked to 'ameliorate' the condition of the Balkan Christians, but there was no threat of reprisals if they failed to do so – merely a reference to the need for the Great Powers to consult together in that eventuality.[95] On 9 April, the Protocol was rejected.[96] On 24 April, the Russians declared war on Turkey, and the debate inside the British Cabinet moved into a fresh phase.

From a distance and with hindsight, the main feature of the next year is the estrangement and extrusion of Derby;[97] but this is to oversimplify terribly. Through the contemporary chiaroscuro of light and shade, the gap between Derby and Disraeli assumes a significance beyond the purely personal, and the simple verities of Northcote's dichotomy between a 'war' and a 'peace' party give way to a more complex reality.[98]

Northcote told Disraeli at the end of April that 'We ought not to allow the matter simply to drift. We ought to have a policy';[99] in this he was expressing only part of what came to preoccupy so many Ministers. Northcote was undoubtedly genuinely afraid that they would find themselves 'entangled in a war policy, without allies, without any clear knowledge of the views or intentions of any other Power, and perhaps without even a distinct conception of what to do ourselves and how we are to do it'.[100] He wanted – and even offered – a policy; but it had to be one which would keep the Cabinet together. As Cross told Lady Derby at the end of April, 'I do feel at present very strongly the absolute necessity of the Cabinet remaining united. It is absolutely necessary not for the Government but for Europe.'[101] Cabinet unity mattered to Ministers quite as much as (if not more than) the solution to the Eastern Question, which is why they could embrace policies regarded elsewhere as mutually exclusive. They accepted Derby's line that Britain needed to cultivate an Austrian connection in order to find a diplomatic partner and possible ally, but they also went along with Disraeli's conviction that Britain needed to seize a base on Turkish territory. Northcote was happy to warn Russia away from Constantinople, whilst accepting that Britain might take the Suez Canal; it was inconsistent diplomatically, but politically it made perfect sense.[102]

From this point of view the very act of defining Britain's interests in the Near East helped Cabinet unity. It was agreed on 5 May that Britain's vital concerns were: the Suez Canal, the Persian Gulf and the Bosphorus; it was also agreed that this should be communicated through Derby to Shuvalov.[103] But the question of how those interests should be defended was one which continually threatened to undermine unity. At this early stage the debate was over the character of the message to be given to the Russians. Was it a warning or a friendly word of advice, and did it imply any threat of the abandonment of neutrality *in extremis*? Or was it to be delivered in tones which implied that in a tight corner there could be accommodation? Beyond that lay the even more divisive issue of what action should be taken to reinforce the message; here the forces of disunity were at their most intense.

Northcote wanted to occupy the Suez Canal as a British base, Cairns preferred the Gallipoli Peninsula. This was a Disraelian shibboleth. Cairns thought that if the Commons refused permission, they should 'lay down the emblems of a power we are not allowed to use'.[104] At the extreme limit of this end of the spectrum lay the Queen, who threatened to abdicate rather than acquiesce in a Russian occupation of Constantinople and Egypt; she wanted the Russians to be given a firm and public warning of Britain's disapproval of the war and of her determination to safeguard her own interests.[105] But 'occupation' and firm public warnings, however agreeable to the pride of the new Empress, were not the watchwords of political unity; those whose objectives lay along that line searched to find a way of accommodating the Queen's noisy bellicosity to Derby's quiet diplomacy.

When Derby informed Shuvalov of the British interests and of the Cabinet's views on 8 May, the Russian replied that he was 'well satisfied' with the terms of the British Note, and that Derby could be 'free of apprehension' on all three points. He warned that there was 'a party in Russia which was desirous of getting rid of the restrictions on the navigation of the Bosphorus and the Dardanelles, and he could not tell whether, or how far, his Government might be disposed to adopt this view'.[106] Derby was happy enough with the assurances and preferred not to accentuate the possible problem. His contribution to unity was to suggest to Disraeli that there was little point in holding Cabinets to 'talk . . . over things when no action is possible. Men only work each other up into a state of agitation, and are then ready to risk anything to relieve it.'[107]

This would have kept Northcote and the rest of the Cabinet quiet, barring some dramatic development in the war. But Disraeli, whose nature was always to anticipate the dramatic, wanted to send a stronger message to the Tsar than Derby's diplomatic formulaics allowed.[108] This would have pleased the Queen and Cairns, but it would have posed a threat to Cabinet unity, so instead of acting, which would have disrupted the Cabinet, refuge was taken in arguing about the circumstances in which it might be necessary to do so. The lack of any dramatic developments in the Russo-Turkish War allowed matters in Cabinet to remain at this level of talk for longer than anyone anticipated, but it did not prevent Derby and Disraeli from beginning to move into opposite camps. The process would be slow, personal history and political interest would ensure that; but their very different interpretations of the way to conduct British foreign policy would ensure that it happened.

5

Lies, Intrigue and Politics

If concerns about Cabinet unity explained the direction (or lack thereof) of British policy during the rest of 1877, then much of the politics of the period is to be explained in terms of the dynamics of the relationships between Disraeli, Derby and Salisbury. The latter owed their main personal connection to Lady Derby. What effect (if any) the rumours of an adulterous relationship between Stanley and his stepmother may have had upon Salisbury's attitude towards Derby in 1877 can only be guessed at;[1] certainly Disraeli sought to use the rumours of Mary Derby's connection with Shuvalov to win the Marquess over to his side in December. The two men were never close, but that could well have been the result of Derby's intense dislike of Salisbury's 'sacerdotal' politics. Salisbury would have been happier serving under Derby in 1874 than he felt taking office under Disraeli, and he was on good enough terms with his former stepmother (whom he called 'Lady Salisbury' in a slip of the pen as late as 1876).[2] Carnarvon came to suspect that Salisbury's change of front was motivated by personal ambition, and it would certainly have been odd had that acute intelligence failed to note the likely consequences of Derby's removal from the line of succession to the ailing Disraeli.

If the Derby–Salisbury relationship defies the definition its importance demands, that between Derby and Disraeli is more amenable to analysis, even if it too has its dark corners. Their friendship went back to the late 1840s and was the most intimate political connection formed by either man. Derby would later persuade himself that Disraeli had been plotting against him from 1874,[3] but there is no evidence that he thought so at the time. However, there were political tensions dating back at least to 1872, when Derby had disliked Disraeli using Manchester, his own bailiwick, for one of his great speeches; there were also rumours that Disraeli resented the fact that in 1868 and again in 1872, there were sections of the Party who thought that Derby would have made a more suitable leader. Certainly Disraeli had gone out of his way in May 1876 to complain about the sloppiness of the organisation of the Foreign Office at the time of the fracas over the Berlin Memorandum. The two men had visited each other regularly before 1870, but after Derby's marriage in that year this stopped.[4] Derby himself thought that 'questions of peace or war must override all merely personal considerations',[5] but his reluctance to push his own views against Disraeli's owed much to his reluctance to break with his old friend; this feeling was not reciprocated.

There was little sign during 1877 that Disraeli's move in sending Salisbury to Constantinople had done anything to remove the latter's hostility. Salisbury thought that Disraeli was the victim of the 'commonest error in politics', that of 'sticking to the carcasses of dead policies'; the Ottoman Empire was, in his view, finished.[6] Neither did he share Disraeli's fear of the Russians: 'their naval history simply does not exist. Their finances, never good, are now desperate; their social condition is a prolonged crisis threatening at any moment of weakness, socialist revolution. Their people are unwarlike.'[7] To those like the Viceroy, Lytton, who argued that Russia's frontier in Central Asia was rapidly approaching that of British India, he recommended the use of a 'larger map', where he would find that 'the distance between Russia and British India is not to be measured by a finger and thumb'.[8] He condemned the 'emasculate, purposeless vacillation' that passed for British policy,[9] and by June was complaining that it 'lacked a bold initiative and a settled plan'.[10]

If Salisbury had not shifted his position, there was no prospect that Disraeli would give way either. His objections to the partition of the Ottoman Empire remained what they had been when Bismarck had proposed it: the acquisition of Egypt would lead to problems with France; Russian control of Constantinople would lead to trouble at home, with public opinion ejecting neck and crop any Government which allowed it.[11] But as long as both Derby and Salisbury refused to go along with him, he would remain unable to secure his own policy. He first tried to win over Derby, as being the more obviously amenable figure; but when a mixture of cajolery and bullying failed, he switched to Salisbury, who had begun to seem less inflexible. After their triumph, Disraeli and Salisbury fostered what might be called a 'black legend', which portrayed Derby as an increasingly lonely figure, undermined by his wife's treachery and by the effects of drink and over-work.[12] The success which this version of events has enjoyed is to be explained in terms of the fact that whereas Disraeli and Salisbury both made assiduous attempts to spread it, and were aided by their official biographers, Derby remained silent and had no official biography.

Yet Derby's position was one with which many of his colleagues sympathised. Derby knew that it might, one day, be necessary to keep the Russians from Constantinople, but he could neither understand nor stomach Disraeli's anxiety never to be seen playing a 'secondary part': as 'long as our own interests are not touched, why should not foreigners settle their own affairs in their own way?'[13] This was a classic statement of the Country Party view, and Disraeli's 'state of mind' during the summer and autumn of 1877 began to make Derby 'uneasy'; Disraeli evidently thought that 'for England to look at a war, without interfering, even for a limited time, is a humiliating position'. Derby not only did not feel this, but he was far more concerned with the 'injury to finance and industry' which would occur if Britain mobilised every time there was a risk of Russia occupying Constantinople.

Disraeli's attempts to invoke 'public opinion' failed to shift Derby. The fact that the Court, the military and a 'noisy but small' section of the public were backing Disraeli[14] made no difference to Derby, who told him on 24 May that he was 'quite sure that in the middle class at least the feeling is so strong against war that you would lose more support by asking for money for an expedition than you could gain by the seizure of an important military position'.[15] He was aware that the 'feeling out-of-doors' was growing 'more & more anti-Russian', but that was neither a reason for changing his mind, nor for resigning; rather it was one for staying put and applying soothing poultices to the Premier's fevered brow. In his own mind, Derby represented a normative Conservatism. In practice, this translated into an impulse for inaction which conflicted with Disraeli's attacks of St Vitus's dance.

There was also a prudential diplomatic element in Derby's opposition to schemes for seizing Turkish territory; what Britain could do in the name of protecting the Porte, others might do in imitation and anticipation, which would make such a move the 'signal for a general scramble'. Derby did not rule out taking any action. If events made it necessary, 'we might at any time make a naval demonstration, which was an easy matter costing next to nothing'; but a 'land expedition' was another matter entirely. Derby saw himself as the voice of traditional Conservative common sense in a Cabinet given over to mad enthusiasms: on the one side was Disraeli with his penchant for grand gestures to satisfy the public and frighten the Russians; on the other were Salisbury with his radical ideas and Carnarvon with his concern for suffering Christians; in the middle was Derby. The idea that in practice this might put him 'on the side of Salisbury & Co. against Disraeli' struck him as singularly ironic, but failed to deflect him from his course.[16] Derby was 'quite alive to the risk of Cabinet differences' and he promised Disraeli in late May to 'do all in my power to avert them', which was why he deprecated too many Cabinet meetings as 'useless, and . . . certainly mischievous'.[17]

Derby may have perceived himself as the still centre of the

raging storm, but to Disraeli and the Queen he was an obstacle to action who was to be wooed and won over or else circumvented. Disraeli was attracted by the notion of landing a force on the Gallipoli Peninsula to secure the rear of a British fleet invited to Constantinople by the Porte, and he privately pressed this on the new British Ambassador, Sir Henry Layard.[18] The Queen, who was thoroughly alarmed by Odo Russell's accounts of the 'extreme readiness of the Russians and of the dangers of letting them go on', complained to Disraeli on 7 June about the 'extreme imperturbability of Lord Derby', who 'must be <u>made</u> to move'.[19] She made the mistake of writing to Derby in this vein, warning him that England risked 'humiliation' and that 'delay <u>now</u> will be most disastrous'.[20] An appeal to the Divine Rights of Kings would have had as little appeal to Derby as this evocation of the *vox populi*. He responded with a firm statement of traditional Conservative foreign policy: 'a war not absolutely forced upon us by necessity and self-defence would be unpopular'. Public opinion was by its nature fickle and unreliable, and he pointedly reminded her of the Crimean War, when he had 'never seen so near an approach to really revolutionary conditions of public feeling as after the first failures and disasters of that struggle'.[21] The Queen told Disraeli petulantly that 'another Sov[ereig]n must be got to carry out Lord Derby's policy'.[22]

The question Ministers had to answer was clear: 'shall we do nothing, or something, to prepare for the possibility of having to act in the event of the Russians marching into Constantinople?' But when the Cabinet discussed it on 16 June, there were almost as many variations of opinion as there were Ministers. The Russians had promised not to annex Constantinople and to respect British interests as defined in Derby's note of 8 May;[23] but nothing had been said about not occupying Constantinople temporarily, or about any time limit on such an occupation. Moreover, the terms of peace being offered by the Russians, which included territorial losses to Russia and to Serbia and Montenegro, as well as a loss of full sovereignty over Bulgaria and Bosnia, were unlikely to be accepted, which meant that the war was likely to continue. Disraeli, supported by Gathorne-Hardy, Cairns, the Duke of Richmond, Ward Hunt and Sir Michael Hicks Beach, wanted to take steps which would allow Britain to send an expedition to protect her interests if necessary; Cross and Northcote 'did not altogether dissent'. Derby's view was that 'the Russians would be at Constantinople if nothing were done, & that once in it would not be easy to get them out'. This all failed to move Salisbury, who said that he did not think that a Russian occupation of Constantinople would do 'any harm'; he preferred the Bismarckian option of seizing Egypt.[24]

Disraeli's mastery of the politics of the personal was shown by his immediate attempt to use Salisbury's stance to win Derby to his side. Referring back to Salisbury's alignment with Ignatyev at Constantinople, and to his High Church sympathies, Disraeli told Derby that he was quite willing to see Salisbury depart – if he had a united Cabinet behind him: 'your course, on this occasion, is not that of an ordinary colleague. My heart is as much concerned in it as my intellect, and I wish not to conceal how grievous would be to me the blow that severed our long connection and faithful friendship.' If Derby would just agree to support a vote of credit in the Commons, he would be guided by 'your particular sanction' and the 'general approval' of the Cabinet. Disraeli only wanted to 'reassure the country, that is alarmed and perplexed'.[25] Derby was not tempted by the prospect of getting rid of Salisbury and replied that he did not 'think we shall have any difficulty in agreeing, at least at the present stage of the affair. It seems to me that the vital question is not yet raised; and I hardly anticipate a disruption until it is raised.' He added, for good measure, that he did not think that Salisbury had made up his mind in the way Disraeli thought, and concluded on a note of pathos: 'I need not add that a political separation between us two would be as painful to me as it could possibly be to you.'[26] Derby was right to think that the 'real difficulty' would come 'later when we have to consider whether these preparations will be used or not'.[27] When Ministers agreed on 20 June to ask the Commons for a vote of £2 million, it was on the understanding that it 'pledged us to nothing farther'.[28]

But if Disraeli could not get the Cabinet to go further than that, he knew someone who could try – the Queen, who was the archetype of the Society 'Jingo'. Indeed, so indignant was she at any slight to England's honour that she bombarded Disraeli with letters and telegrams every time her over-active imagination received a fresh stimulus. Her scarcely legible letters may have generated more heat than light, but Disraeli was sensitive to her all the same, as Derby noticed.[29] On 25 June, with a startling lack of political *nous*, she suggested that Disraeli should replace Derby with the Ambassador in Paris, Lord Lyons; she also thought that both Derby and Salisbury should be allowed to go, once the present crisis was over.[30] Disraeli knew that he could hardly hold the Government together if that happened, and told her that there was no question of either peer going 'at present'.[31] Victoria's suggestion that Disraeli should gather 'all your followers' in order to tell them that 'they should rally round their Sovereign and country. . . . And only say Russia shall not go farther and she will stop',[32] spoke equally eloquently of her lack of knowledge of her own political system. Disraeli had to explain patiently that War Estimates needed parliamentary sanction, which would not be given whilst the Government was committed to a policy of neutrality; even supposing Britain had the men and the money, troops could not pass through the Straits without the permission of the Porte. It was true that 'all these difficulties would be removed, if we declared war against Russia: but there are not three men in the Cabinet, who are prepared to advise that step'.[33]

Perhaps it was the constant flow of hysteria emanating from Windsor, or maybe it was just the burdens of ill-health, but Derby was much struck at this juncture by Disraeli's 'pale and ghastly' appearance, which made him look like 'a dying man'.[34] Had his old friend died or retired, Derby had made up his mind 'to go too'. He disliked the 'clerical' politics of Salisbury and Carnarvon, and had very little desire to stay on. He had already begun to make this fact known to his colleagues and relied upon it to help him get his way in the diplomatic crisis.[35] It was, however, intimations of political immortality rather than physical mortality which occupied Disraeli's thoughts.

From the days of his early political novels through to the Reform Act triumph of 1867, Disraeli had liked to make rhetorical play with the notion of an alliance between the upper classes and the lower orders, and he did so now in late June, pointing out to his colleagues that they 'were united against Russia'. Derby's contending view, that the 'middle classes would always be against a war', was dismissed by Disraeli with the comment that 'fortunately the middle classes did not now govern'; Derby was correct to see this as 'significant'.[36] Derby, whose position as a Lancashire magnate gave him a broader contact with 'the people' than that possessed by Disraeli, thought that 'London society does not represent the views of the constituencies' and that 'those who never really feel the pressure of war taxes are not the best judges of the burdens which a war imposes'. Derby recalled 'many instances in which the majority of our class wished to interfere in European quarrels but no instance in which the nation agreed with them'. He did not 'believe the majority of the public wants war with Russia, so long as it is honourably possible to keep out of one'.[37] Here, side by side, were the old Tory tradition and the lineaments of what would supplant it. Disraeli was a 'social imperialist' long before anyone had invented the phrase.

But dissent was still on the level of abstract principle, which allowed opportunity for agreement on practical measures. The Cabinet on 30 June had no difficulty in deciding to formalise an arrangement for mutual support with Austria and to send the fleet to Besika Bay.[38] Derby was happy to agree with his colleagues on 11 July that in order to avoid the parliamentary difficulties which would be caused by asking for a vote of credit, they should send the same message to the Russians by strengthening the garrisons at Malta and Gibraltar;[39] but he remained immune to Disraeli's conviction that if the Russians got to Constantinople, 'there would be an outbreak of popular feeling against us, the bulk of the Conservatives would desert us, the Whigs would join . . . [and] the ministry would be upset . . . with ignominy'. Disraeli wanted to make this into a *casus belli*, and was even willing to see Salisbury and Carnarvon go, if necessary. Derby would 'go to any length in the way of warning' Shuvalov, as 'I had done already', of the danger of approaching Constantinople – 'but . . . not go to the length of pledging the country to war in such an event'. Derby was happy to embody this in a formal note, but saw no need to go any further.[40] In his eyes, the excited state of public opinion was a temporary phenomenon rather than a reason for decisive action.[41]

Private persuasion having failed to move Derby far enough, Disraeli now tried to get the Cabinet to help him. When Lord John Manners, Disraeli's oldest political friend, proposed on 14 July that the occupation of Constantinople should be made a *casus belli*, it needed no great political acumen to see whence the idea had originated. But if Disraeli was behind the move, he had miscalculated; Manners carried no political weight and Ministers felt quite happy to reject his proposals in a way they could not have done had they come from Disraeli directly. Cairns and Northcote argued that since the Austrians had said they would support Britain in the event of a permanent Russian occupation of Constantinople, it was unnecessary to go as far as Manners wanted; this carried the rest of the Cabinet. Only Disraeli spoke in defence of Manners. A firm warning was despatched to Russia about the dangers of occupying Constantinople, but it contained no threats. The Queen, despairing of Derby, became positively hysterical, telling Disraeli that if they allowed the occupation of Constantinople, England would 'no longer exist as a Great Power' and the Government which had permitted this 'could not exist!'[42] Disraeli was reduced to explaining that he could not prevail in Cabinet with no real support.[43]

It may, of course, have been entirely coincidental and accidental that it was at this moment when he found himself stymied by Derby that Disraeli should have chosen to raise with him the delicate question of breaches of Cabinet secrecy. Every Minister knew that Derby took notes of what was said in Cabinet, and Disraeli now complained that these must be the source of the Cabinet leakages which had been worrying him for some time.

Derby hotly, and then more formally, denied that this could be so: 'anyone professing to have seen notes of mine . . . is either saying what he must know not to be true, or has been hoaxed by somebody else'. The only people who ever saw his notes were his private secretary, Thomas Sanderson, and his own wife, both of whom were above suspicion.[44] Derby may have been confident in his wife, but it would become plain before long that the Prime Minister, and others, were not.

Derby tried to explain to Shuvalov that Disraeli did not actually want a war with Russia, but could not dissent from the Russian's shrewd observation that he was 'anxious for the glory of a spirited policy, and wished to take the credit of having prevented Russia from doing many things which she never meant to do'. All Derby could do was to deliver his own warning, which was that 'our most popular Ministers, Pitt, Palmerston etc.' were those who had 'gratified' the 'strength of the war-feeling in England'. Derby confessed that this was hard to explain since peace was England's 'strongest interest', but advised Shuvalov simply to take his word for it.[45]

Disraeli's political antennae had, however, picked up signs that whilst Salisbury and Derby disagreed with him, they did not necessarily agree with each other, and that Salisbury might be susceptible to arguments in favour of taking a strong line against Russia in certain eventualities. Disraeli asked him in late July: 'What are we to do, and how are we to assert our position if the Russians succeed in getting to Constantinople?' Salisbury's response was as gratifying as it was simple: 'declare war'.[46] At Cabinet on 21 July, when Manners threatened to resign if action was not taken to discourage the Russians, Salisbury and Cross declared that Britain was under an obligation to ensure that any Russian occupation of the city should be purely temporary; to Derby's 'surprise', the former added that he would be 'ready to send the fleet up, if the Porte invited us, and that Russia could not be allowed to fortify the position'.[47] Gathorne-Hardy, however, joined Derby in opposing action. But Disraeli telegraphed triumphantly to Windsor that there had been 'unanimous agreement' that if Russia occupied Constantinople, war should be declared on Russia.[48] Disraeli thought that the die in favour of war had been cast, and told the Queen that Russia would be attacked in Asia: 'We have a good instrument for this purpose in Lord Lytton, and indeed he was placed there with that in view.'[49]

Carnarvon noted that Salisbury's 'marvellous conversion' revived the 'drooping spirits of the Turkish section of the Cabinet',[50] and that the pressure in the Cabinet 'that for the sake of appearances something should be done'[51] was now too great even for Derby to resist. After a highly disorderly meeting on 28 July, the Cabinet decided to ask the Porte what terms of peace it would accept, and to enquire about the status and future of the fortifications at Gallipoli. The Russians were to be told that Britain wanted peace, but that in the event of 'disturbances' at Constantinople, the fleet would go to the Golden Horn. Derby agreed to this, but with the caveat that he was not committing himself to follow that policy should it become necessary. He thought that Salisbury was succumbing to 'the war fever' which was 'clearly getting hold of my colleagues'; for the first time since the crisis had begun the possibility had arisen that Derby might be the 'sole seceder'.[52]

It is not easy to account for Salisbury's change of mind. His explanation to Carnarvon, that 'war was necessary to blow up the whole unsound foreign policy of this country',[53] may be part of the truth, but Salisbury was never averse to clothing his thought in clear language designed to shock others.[54] Salisbury's new alignment began to change 'the balance of parties' within the Cabinet and, according to Carnarvon, led 'directly to the important changes in the composition of the Government which subsequently followed';[55] that, however, was in the longer term. But it did indicate to Disraeli that if Derby remained immovable, Salisbury might prove more amenable.

Derby remained convinced that although it was 'loud and active', the 'war party' was 'small in numbers', and that 'the great bulk of the nation desires nothing so much . . . as the maintenance of peace';[56] but even he had to acknowledge that 'war fever' was very strong within the Party and in the Commons generally.[57] It was clear to him that if the Cabinet was 'more pugnacious than it was a few weeks ago', it was down to the fact that 'feeling out-of-doors had changed in the same direction'.[58] But it was antipathetic to Derby's notion of statesmanship to allow a temporary ebullition of public feeling to affect the course of British diplomacy, and although it took a great effort, he was determined to ensure that no message would go from London to the Porte which could be read as a sign that Britain would abandon the conditional neutrality outlined in his Note of 8 May.

Derby had to spend his political capital heavily on 31 July when Disraeli attempted to get the Cabinet to take a more bellicose line over the subject of a possible Russian occupation of Constantinople. Gathorne-Hardy, who found Derby's attitude 'strange', noted that he seemed to 'shrink from any action, diplomatic or other'.[59] For Derby, it was the 'sharpest struggle' which he had 'ever had on any political question'. He did not actually say he would resign unless he carried his point ('thinking menaces of that kind to be in bad taste'), but he did make it plain that he 'did not mean to be overruled in my department'. Derby succeeded in toning down the message which would be delivered to the Porte, in order to avoid giving the impression that sending the fleet to the Straits would mean an end to British neutrality.[60] Significantly, Salisbury took the radical view that they should simply send the fleet through the Straits regardless – which would have meant making war 'without declaring it'. But Derby gained the day, and his message was sent, omitting all references to possible seizures of Turkish forts on the Dardanelles and emphasising that there was no change in Britain's neutrality. It was not a grand heroic triumph, but it was one all the same.

Disraeli was determined that the Russians would get the warning he wanted them to have about the dangers of occupying Constantinople, and if he could not do so through the usual channels because of Derby, he was not averse to finding some unusual ones. He possessed a perfect instrument for his purposes in the person of the British Military Attaché at St Petersburg,

Colonel the Hon. Frederick Wellesley. Those historians who have happily relied upon Wellesley as the chief source for the gossip about Lady Derby's relations with Shuvalov might have done so with less confidence had they looked behind the title and the Wellesley name to the man himself.

Despite his impressive rank, Fred Wellesley was a colonel of very recent date, and he owed his appointment, if not his rank, to Lady Derby's influence. As a young woman Lady Salisbury, as she then was, had been a great friend of the Duke of Wellington, and she was also close to his nephew, the second Lord Cowley, who was also the step-son of her niece by marriage, Lady Georgiana Cecil.[61] Cowley, whose most notable post was as Ambassador in Paris during the Second Empire, was Mary Derby's most devoted correspondent, and after Lord Derby's appointment as Foreign Secretary he pressed her several times to see if she could get a job for his somewhat scapegrace soldier son,[62] Fred.[63] This she duly did, and young Fred's sudden preferment as Military Attaché to St Petersburg aroused the jealousy of some of his fellow officers, especially when he suddenly became a full colonel and an aide-de-camp to the Queen in January 1877.[64]

Fred Wellesley was an engaging rogue, and he offered to return to London without permission in the summer of 1877 in order to act as an unofficial channel of communication between the Russians and Disraeli.[65] Disraeli was quite prepared to use him for the same purpose. The Queen wanted Disraeli to warn Wellesley 'about Lord Derby's views', and thought that the latter should be kept in ignorance of the mission.[66] What she wanted was for Wellesley, who would be charged officially with a mission, to give a confidential and oral warning to the Tsar about the dangers of occupying Constantinople; although she worried that Gorchakov would inform Shuvalov, who, in turn, would tell Lady Derby.[67] This last prospect worried Fred Wellesley a good deal, and he told the Queen's private secretary, Sir Henry Ponsonby, that it would not be 'loyal' to go behind Derby's back. She arranged for Wellesley to see Disraeli. There is no record of their conversation,[68] but Wellesley's minute of his instructions stated that the correspondence and conversations which had taken place between him, the Queen and Disraeli were 'to be considered secret and on no account to be mentioned at the Foreign Office'; nor did he mention what had happened to Derby when he returned to England.[69] Under cover of an official mission, Wellesley was to stress to the Tsar that there was no dissension in the Cabinet, which was 'led by one mind and has the entire support of the Government'.[70] Even Disraeli's admiring biographer thought this a 'questionable procedure' and defended it by reference to Derby's 'attitude and language';[71] this was one way of describing a deliberate attempt to substitute his own policy for that agreed by the Cabinet.

Disraeli tried very hard to get his colleagues behind the position which Wellesley would put to the Tsar. On 14 August, he once more 'held language that alarmed [Derby]', and reasserted his view that 'We should be disgraced ... if we did not interfere effectually to prevent a second campaign. England would not keep her position in Europe, if she did not take a leading part in the settlement.' Derby could now see the real difference between his traditional Conservatism and the line favoured by Disraeli, who 'sincerely and really believes that it will be better for us to risk a great war, & to spend £100,000,000 upon it, than not to appear to have had a large share in the decision come to when peace is made'. Derby thought that 'most continental statesmen would agree with him, & a considerable section of the English public', but he did 'not think *prestige* worth buying so dear' and felt 'sure that the majority are on that side'.[72] However, as Derby had to acknowledge, public opinion was fickle: 'howling and screaming' for war at one moment, and blowing cold the next; in his eyes this meant that no respectable Tory could rely upon it as a guide to action.[73] This was not Disraeli's view – but then he was never respectable.

Disraeli's instinct that public opinion would move to support the Turks as victims of Russian aggression proved correct, and the defence of the fortress of Plevna by Osman Pasha gave the newspapers a new hero to boost; he was sure that if peace and

British honour became incompatible, the public would prefer to go to war for the latter.[74] Wellesley's mission allowed him to warn the Russians of the dangers of a second campaign, and with that, and with the tide of opinion out of doors running his way, Disraeli preferred, as he told the Queen on 8 October, not to 'make any communication to Lord Derby' about Wellesley's reports.[75] It was better to avoid committing the Cabinet to the policy they had announced to the Tsar until it became plain that there would actually be a second Russian campaign.[76] Shuvalov had already dropped hints that during the winter Russia would be receptive to the idea of a European Congress to settle the Eastern Question.[77]

But Disraeli had no intention of waiting upon events, and as Carnarvon warned Lady Derby in early September before the political season got under way again, 'we shall have a tussle or two during the autumn'.[78] Derby himself was worried by Disraeli's exultant mood (without knowing anything about Wellesley's mission), and feared that, egged on by the Queen, he might 'very possibly break up the Cabinet' in an attempt to get his way.[79] Disraeli was, however, too conscious of the fragility of Cabinet support to run the risk of a split until he was certain he would win. He talked to Gathorne-Hardy, and got the Queen to do the same to Cross;[80] they received the same message from Northcote and Salisbury – namely the need for a policy which would place them 'in a clear and intelligible position and would disembarrass them of all the difficulties which hampered them last session'.[81] Naturally enough this policy was 'no second campaign', combined with an honourable peace for Russia which would give her Bessarabia but keep Bulgaria within the boundaries which had been agreed back in May. Should the Russians refuse, they would be told that Britain would 'depart from our present position of neutrality' and afford Turkey 'material assistance' if Constantinople was threatened. Disraeli even tried to square Derby by asking him to present these proposals to the Cabinet on 5 October.[82] This, Derby thought, was 'characteristic of him . . . knowing that the scheme is utterly opposed to my ideas'.[83] Although he was prepared to mediate between the Turks and the Russians, Derby would not threaten the use of force;[84] he was confident that 'the country believes that as a government, we are not in favour of a policy of adventures'.[85]

Derby's view of what his colleagues would agree to was, as so often, more accurate than Disraeli's. Northcote, who was always a good weather-vane, wrote to Disraeli before the Cabinet, deprecating a second Russian campaign, but disliking still more Britain getting herself into a position of 'selfish isolation' by acting precipitately;[86] others took the same view. Although Disraeli gave the Cabinet the benefit of a full rehearsal of his views on 5 October, his colleagues were unconvinced either by his arguments, or by his proposal that they should seek to mediate between the Russians and the Turks, putting terms agreeable to the latter to the former, with the threat that in case of their being refused Britain would defend Constantinople. As Disraeli telegraphed disgustedly to the Queen afterwards, they seemed 'indisposed to mix up the question of mediation with anything like a threat'.[87] Derby asked Gathorne-Hardy after the meeting 'whether the Cabinet or Turkish Empire would last the longest as each seems shaky'.[88] Derby approved of the idea of mediation, but his argument that the time was not yet opportune, and that Russia might well come seeking it, carried the day; Carnarvon and Salisbury stood firm behind him.[89]

Lady Derby told Carnarvon on 8 October that it was not 'quite certain that even a majority of the Cabinet' could prevail 'against you and Cranborne and Lord Derby'; but even into her confident frame of mind, a worm of doubt had entered. Reluctant to criticise her husband openly, she told Carnarvon that he was 'quite as strong as you are against the proposal [to warn Russia from Constantinople]' and hoped that 'a kind of dogged resistance will prevail against the wonderful chief'; but as an afterthought she added, 'Cranborne [Salisbury] will not make any sudden changes of front, will he . . . ?'[90] Carnarvon also recognised the importance of 'Derby, Salisbury and myself' continuing to 'sail on in the same boat – and on this question of the Turkish alliance I imagine we are all three entirely agreed'.

SPLENDID ISOLATION?

He knew that they were 'in a decided minority', but did not 'believe that Disraeli would dare to sacrifice us all three'; but like Lady Derby, he worried lest Disraeli would find some way of driving a wedge between them.[91]

6

Low Politics

Disraeli would go to great lengths over the next few months to undermine Derby's position, and one of his weapons would be the notion that he was the ultimate source of those Cabinet leaks which were common knowledge in Society. The most obvious 'leaker' was the garrulous Prime Minister himself, who, after going to so much trouble to tell the Tsar that the Cabinet was of 'one mind', entertained his fellow guests at Woburn in October (including Lady Derby, Lord Lyons and Lord Odo Russell) with a droll account of the 'six parties' inside the Cabinet.[1] He gave a similar account to the Queen in early November, but by then there were 'seven parties'. Both accounts were broadly similar: Manners, Gathorne-Hardy and Hicks Beach were the 'war party pure and simple'; Cross, W.H. Smith and Cairns were 'for declaring war' if Constantinople was occupied; Salisbury was a party by himself, holding the view that if the Russians did not withdraw from Constantinople there should be war; Carnarvon too was held up to ridicule in both versions as 'the party . . . for having Christian service in St. Sophia'. In both versions only Derby was in the 'peace at any price party'. The interesting variation was that in his more private account to the Queen, Disraeli lampooned Northcote, who was left out of the Woburn version, as belonging to the 'party which disapproves of any policy avowedly resting on what are called "British interests" . . . they approach silliness'. The sixth or seventh party was, of course, 'that of your Majesty, and which will be introduced, and enforced, by your Prime Minister'. That entailed deciding upon a 'notification to Russia that the present state of British neutrality cannot be depended upon for another campaign' without a 'written engagement from Russia, that under no circumstances will she occupy Constantinople or the Dardanelles'.[2]

Both Lyons and Russell argued strongly at Woburn that it was 'too late to act', and for all Disraeli's anxiety that '*Something must be done*',[3] most Ministers preferred to find an ally first. But with Derby now certain that Andrassy had lied when he denied having an agreement with the Russians, and with Bismarck assumed to be both malevolent and Russian in his sympathies, it was not easy to see where an ally would be found.[4] Shuvalov confirmed Derby's suspicions that Bismarck would welcome a war between Britain and Russia,[5] and even Disraeli, who did not think that Bismarck 'wishes to destroy our Empire', thought that by depriving 'us of all influence', he would end up doing so.[6]

Derby was not unduly worried, however, since he did not believe that Constantinople was in any real danger.[7] A despondent Monty Corry, Disraeli's private secretary, told Disraeli a few days before the Cabinet met on 5 November: 'I gather from my Lady Derby that our friend is as resolute as ever to keep his hands in his pocket. And I am told that an insistence on a bold policy will lead to the secession of certainly four Secretaries of State.'[8] Disraeli tried to persuade Derby that 'we should promise to Russia continued neutrality on condition that she gives us a pledge that she will not occupy Constantinople';[9] that, he claimed, was 'the policy for which the country [gave] him credit'.[10] Derby was worried that concentrating on Constantinople might lead the Russians to think that they could occupy other points such as Gallipoli; he was also concerned about acting separately from Austria. But the policy seemed 'reasonable enough',[11] and since it gave 'a better chance of keeping the Cabinet together than any scheme I have heard of',[12] Derby supported it in Cabinet on 5 November, despite Carnarvon's dissent.[13]

As long as Derby was at the Foreign Office, there would be a 'plentiful douche of cold water' for those advocating 'a bold course', and he took his time about drafting the message to Russia.[14] This drove the Queen into an epistolary fury directed at Disraeli: 'When will you communicate to the Emperor of Russia the decision of England about Constantinople?' She warned that unless it was done at once, 'We shall be too late! . . . Pray do insist on action, or the Russians will crow over us'.[15] Derby denied deliberately obstructing the Cabinet decision and told Disraeli on 19 November that it was 'a very awkward paper to draw'. He did not believe that the Russians would go further than Adrianople, where they had stopped in 1828 and where 'they are near enough to overawe the capital without threatening it. We shall have to take care that we do not seem to give them more freedom of action than we desire.'[16]

On 24 November, Disraeli drafted a warning to Russia to stay away from Constantinople, but omitted to mention that Britain remained neutral. Derby refused to despatch it, calling it 'either a threat or nothing . . . we ask something and offer nothing'.[17] He accused Disraeli of trying to alter policy without consulting the Cabinet.[18] After talking to Cairns, Disraeli responded that he had only been abiding by Cabinet policy.[19] The situation was, as Lady Derby noted, 'anything but a pleasant one'.[20]

When the Cabinet met again on 4 December, although Derby recorded 'no substantial difference of opinion among us', only Carnarvon supported his interpretation that the warning to the Russians had to be accompanied by a restatement of British neutrality,[21] and he agreed to draw up a new note along this line;[22] but as on previous occasions he entered a verbal caveat. Disraeli understood him to have said that whilst an actual Russian occupation of Constantinople would amount to a *casus belli*, the mere threat of one would not – a position which the Prime Minister thought was untenable.[23] He told the Queen triumphantly on 4 December that despite 'some opposition from Lord

Derby', it had been agreed to 'combine an offer of mediation with the note to Russia'.[24]

Derby attributed Disraeli's growing desire for action to the influence of public opinion, and noted that in 'society', the army and 'among the mob' war would be 'popular', but that 'the middle-class is almost to a man on the other side'; but 'unfortunately the Prime Minister neither understands nor likes the middle-class'.[25] He would not have dissented from Salisbury's view that since public Russophobia 'no-where rises nearly to Income Tax point',[26] Disraeli's bellicose instincts would have to be curbed. But the march of events – and the Russian army – soon put a question-mark against this assumption. In late November, Derby noted a new 'swagger' in Shuvalov's language. He put it down to a desire to 'impress, if not to frighten', and thought that it meant that 'he wanted to lead or drive us into pressing the Porte to give way at once, and that he feared a desperate resistance'.[27]

On 11 December, the news reached London of the fall of Plevna; the road to Constantinople was open. In London the floodgates of what became known as 'Jingoism' were opened. The spectre of Russia descending upon Constantinople allowed popular Russophobia to reassert itself, and the music halls rang to the 'Great Macdermott' singing 'We don't want to fight, but by Jingo if we do, we've got the men, we've got the ships and we've got the money too . . . the Russians shall not have Constantinople!'. Finally, Disraeli appeared to have the popular outcry he needed to drive the Cabinet in his direction.

Derby differed from Disraeli only with the greatest of 'regret, for we are very old friends, & he is about the only man in public life for whom I have a personal feeling of friendship'.[28] But that friendship now came under intolerable strain. On 7 December, the Queen wrote to Disraeli renewing her complaints that Cabinet secrecy was not being maintained and blaming Lady Derby for this;[29] historians have tended to repeat this line, usually adding a coy reference to the 'intimate' contacts which Lady Derby had with Shuvalov.[30] Disraeli passed the letter on to Salisbury, asking for his advice.[31] The family connection perhaps made Salisbury the obvious man to consult, but in doing this Disraeli at once altered the relations between himself and Salisbury, as well as those between him and Derby. Salisbury advised against raising the matter in Cabinet, partly because Derby would not want such a delicate matter mentioned in front of his social inferiors like Cross and Smith; he thought that Disraeli ought to raise it privately. However, Derby himself referred to it in Cabinet, and it was agreed that secrecy must be maintained.[32]

The fall of Plevna brought numerous alarmist telegrams from Layard in Constantinople, including an appeal for British mediation from the Sultan. Disraeli's response was to propose to recall Parliament in order to get a special grant of £5 million towards preparing the armed services; he also wanted a declaration that Britain was willing to act as mediator between the warring parties.[33] The Queen had told him before the crucial Cabinet on 14 December, 'most emphatically' to be 'very firm' even if it meant accepting Derby's resignation. 'England', she warned, 'will never stand (not to speak of her Sovereign) to become subservient to Russia, for then she would fall down from her high position and become a second-rate Power!!'[34]

However, the Cabinet was still relatively insulated from the Jingoism which infected Windsor, and only Manners was fully behind the three proposals – although Cross, Smith, Northcote, Gathorne-Hardy, Cairns and Richmond 'all more or less agreed'.[35] Salisbury had no objection in principle, but was not willing to have a formal alliance with Turkey. Carnarvon stuck to his usual position. Derby heard his colleagues out before intervening himself. When he did so, it was 'at some length, and with unusual fire'.[36] He argued that summoning the House would create an unnecessary sense of panic at home and tension abroad. Britain had just communicated her wishes to Russia; she should await a response. To couple an increase in armaments with a proposal for mediation was, he thought, 'a new policy, which I had not sanctioned, & did not agree in'.[37] Faced with Derby's opposition, Disraeli staged a tactical withdrawal and agreed to consider matters again after a weekend of reflection.

Lady Derby told Carnarvon on 15 December that 'Lord D[erby] holds the key of the position'. She told him in confidence that 'Northcote had written most strictly confidentially (so much so I scarcely ought to tell you) saying that he and others will defer to Lord D if he will make a counter proposal.'[38] That there was indeed a willingness to follow Derby if he gave a lead is confirmed by a letter which Northcote sent to Salisbury written the same day, saying that if Derby would 'rouse himself to take a lead or give us a line of his own', he would 'find a good backing in the Cabinet'; but it was impossible to go on 'without a policy or with nothing but a *non possumus*'.[39]

Salisbury agreed with Northcote that the '*non possumus* is leading to very bleak results', but thought that 'this remedy is worse than the disease'. He told the Chancellor that 'an active policy is only possible under one of two conditions – that you shall help the Turks, or coerce them'; but that since he could not follow the former, and Disraeli and the Queen would not agree to the latter, it was not easy to see the way forward. He opposed the idea of summoning Parliament early and asking for a vote of credit because, 'The infernal newspapers, who dog our footsteps, pretending to belong to us, and howling for blood, will from the first moment place the most belligerent interpretation on [it].' Disraeli's proposals were, he thought, designed to 'place us on the steep slope which leads to war', and he could see no justification for one in terms of 'danger to "British interests" '. The Russians had not yet crossed the Balkan mountains, and Austria had pledged to help if Constantinople was really endangered: 'I hold therefore that Constantinople is in no real danger and that a call to arms, hasty and urgent, may have the effect, and probably proceed from the wish of involving us in a war to uphold Turkey.' This, in itself, would be 'difficult enough to swallow', but if it also entailed the resignation of Derby, then the results would be 'still more serious'. It would cause 'the utmost consternation' and not only unite 'all sections of the Opposition and throw into great discouragement the non-warlike portion of our own Party', but it would also 'divide the nation into two camps – those who are for aiding the Turks and those who are for leaving them to their fate'. This could even lead to a re-run of the 'Atrocitarian' movement, with the latter attacking the Government 'furiously, by every weapon which popular agitation or parliamentary forms can furnish'. In the ensuing 'bitter fight', there would be 'no room for "half opinions" ' and 'all nice distinctions will be crushed out'; that was not Salisbury's idea of politics. In the heat of such a political fight, the 'Cabinet will surrender itself to the war party, and any advocates of peace who may have stayed behind Derby will not be in a pleasant position'.[40] This hardly suggested that Salisbury was about to ally himself with Disraeli.

As a signal mark of support for her beleaguered favourite, the Queen came down to Hughenden, Disraeli's country house, on 15 December. The gesture was unmistakable and much resented by Disraeli's opponents, one of whom, the historian E.A. Freeman, wrote of the Queen going to 'dine with the Jew in his ghetto'.[41] Monday, 17 December, would be the judgment day for the Cabinet, if Derby asserted himself. It was no wonder that the mood was tense when Ministers assembled. Derby described the discussions which followed as 'the most anxious and difficult . . . we have had yet'.[42]

Disraeli had twisted, he had turned, he had cajoled and used all the arts of persuasion of which he was the master, and yet against him the hereditary nobility of England sat unmoved, and in full Cabinet there could be no attempt to divide and rule. But no one had ever questioned his political courage, and even Derby, his severest critic, thought his opening remarks were 'excellent in taste and judgement'. Disraeli appealed for a 'decided policy', arguing that if Russia was acting in good faith, the actions being proposed would strengthen the case for mediation; if she was not, they would be necessary to defend Britain's interests. There was a 'golden opportunity of asserting the position of England', and to remain inactive was to risk personal discredit and public disaster: 'We sh[oul]d end as the Ministry of L[or]d Aberdeen ended.' He went on to say that his own ambition 'was satisfied' and that he 'remained in his present post only because he thought the party wished it'. In case anyone had missed the implication, Disraeli added that: 'He had led a great party for longer than anyone in English history: he thought he knew public feeling: & he did not wish again in his life to undergo the pain of parliamentary condemnation'; he had given everyone liberty to state their views, and he had never tried to impose his own on them, 'but he shrank from the results of remaining in our present position'. This was an eloquent appeal to personal, political and national interests, mixed with judicious hints of resignation if his colleagues did not agree to his demand for an early recall of Parliament. It was a call for the Conservative Party to distinguish itself from that Gladstonian lack of national assertiveness which Disraeli had criticised in Opposition. By defending Britain's geopolitical interests, the Tories could secure their own political future. Instead of gratefully accepting the stacked deck of cards they were being offered, Conservative Ministers all but threw them back at Disraeli.

Gathorne-Hardy and Manners agreed with the Prime Minister, as did Cairns and the Duke of Richmond, but neither in numbers nor weight could they balance the forces on the other side. It is in the nature of Conservatives to be susceptible to appeals for caution. It is not usual to become a Conservative to promote radical change. Conservatives prefer 'soundness' to 'brilliance'. These atavistic instincts, Disraeli's most formidable political opponents, once more threatened to bring him down.

It was, therefore, entirely appropriate that it should have been Northcote who began the process of checking the Prime Minister. He was the very essence of Conservative common sense and saw every side to every argument, which he was willing to expound at length; but he was a 'sound' fellow, and his opposition was subtle, flexible and deadly. He did not object to British mediation, or even to asking Parliament for money, but he argued against summoning it back early, because it would cause 'sensation, alarm, & surprise', which would lead to a 'dangerous & protracted' opposition in the House: 'England would be weakened by the spectacle of our division' and 'we should not get the money we wanted any sooner'. These were arguments which Salisbury had used, and this, along with the fact that Northcote immediately asked Derby to speak, made Disraeli suspect that he had been 'got hold of' by 'the conspirators'.

This was Derby's opportunity to take the lead. Had he given vent to the dangers of pursuing a policy of 'prestige', then he might have begun to sketch the lineaments of a Conservative policy to rival Disraeli's; but that would have required challenging Disraeli and being willing to replace him – which Derby would not do. He did not want to be Prime Minister and preferred to continue his line of reining Disraeli in; he thus confined himself to Northcote's arguments, trying to lessen the tension by referring to the warmth of 'our personal feeling for the Premier'. Salisbury agreed with Derby, right down to the proposition that they might summon Parliament towards the end of January, which would be earlier than usual but should not provoke alarm. But this drift towards a compromise was halted by the newest member of the Cabinet, W.H. Smith. As First Lord of the Admiralty he was concerned about sending the fleet to Constantinople, and so, raising a point his political superiors had all steered clear of, Smith said that whilst he would be prepared to turf the Russians out if they got there, he was not prepared to send an expedition to anticipate this event. The First Lord had steered the ship straight on to the rocks.

Disraeli's earlier mood gave way to a more passionate one. The 'present negotiations', he declared, 'were illusory, the object was to keep Russia from going to Constantinople', which was why they needed 'a large increase in forces' to be ready to 'send out an expedition'. He wanted 'the Porte to put its case in our hands that we should arrange the terms of peace, & press them on Russia. That would be a decided policy. If we were to let the Russians do what they liked, it would be better to have a Liberal gov[ernmen]t in power.' In the ensuing melée two things became clear: Salisbury, Carnarvon and Derby would not agree to such a policy, and Disraeli would resign if it was rejected; rather than break up the

Government, Ministers dispersed scarcely knowing if they would meet again.

The Queen was horrified at the notion of losing her Prime Minister, but the weary Disraeli reassured her that whilst he might resign she could always ask him to form a new administration.[43] This was the strongest card in his hand. A determined opponent would have called him and exposed his bluff, but Disraeli's colleagues were men who had grown used to having this strange, exotic and unaccountable genius at the head of their Party; they respected his uncanny instinct for what public opinion wanted, and they did not want to break up the Government. Such, at least, was the burden of Northcote's rather shame-faced letter to Disraeli after the Cabinet. He explained his actions by saying that the consideration which had weighed 'most heavily' with him was the old shibboleth of 'unity': if they had adopted Disraeli's proposals, Derby would have resigned and 'it is certain that Salisbury and Carnarvon would follow him'.[44]

But why should the three peers stick together? It was already plain to Disraeli that Salisbury's position differed from that of the other two, and that he was more amenable to persuasion. He had already entrusted him with the secret of Lady Derby's indiscretions and thus driven a peg into the cracks between Hatfield and Knowsley; now he despatched Cairns to Hertfordshire to work further on Salisbury.[45] He needed no intermediary with Derby, whom he asked to see before the Cabinet met again.[46]

The two old friends met just after eleven o'clock on 18 December for a discussion Derby called 'friendly & frank'; even then this phrase was euphemistic. The two men 'did not conceal from each other that disagreement existed', and Derby again noted that Disraeli 'sees things in a way which is not intelligible to me'. He thought that for Russia and Turkey to arrive at a settlement without British intervention would be 'disgraceful to us'. To Derby, this was 'the foreign view, which treats prestige as the one thing needful in politics'. He accepted Disraeli's assurances that he did not want a war, but doubted that he would resist it if the 'temptation comes his way'.[47] The two men left for

Cabinet at midday without any agreed compromise. Derby had, however, evinced a willingness to compromise on the date at which Parliament would be summoned if that would help avert a rupture. Fresh from Hatfield, Cairns reported a similar willingness on Salisbury's part. After the *sturm und drang* of the previous day, Disraeli (or rather Cairns on his behalf) now made an appeal to those atavisms which he had ignored the previous day. He was willing to compromise over the date at which Parliament should be summoned, proposing the 17th rather than as previously the 7th of January. No sensible man could want to upset the Cabinet over a matter of ten days; all Conservative Cabinet Ministers were sensible men, therefore everyone concurred. Derby hoped that the 'narrowness of our escape from a break-up may induce caution on all sides: but at bottom we are far from agreement'.[48]

Just how far Derby was from agreeing with Disraeli was clear from a letter he wrote to Salisbury on 23 December. Relying upon the unspoken assumptions of a common Conservative attitude towards foreign affairs, Derby told Salisbury that Disraeli 'believes thoroughly in "prestige" – as all foreigners do'. He would be willing to spend '£200 millions on a war if the result was to make foreign States think more highly of us as a military power'; these were 'intelligible' ideas, 'but they are not mine, nor yours'.[49] Nor were they. But even as Derby was recalling Salisbury back to traditional Toryism, Disraeli was writing with a request that was bound to drive a wedge between the two peers.

In a letter written on Christmas Eve, Disraeli tried to win Salisbury's understanding, and once more attempted to enlist his sympathy and support. Trying to soothe the suspicions that his policy was one of war, Disraeli revealed the story of Wellesley's mission to the Tsar in the summer; his policy, he explained, was one of facing the Russians down: 'a firm front shown by England would terminate the war without material injury to our interests. I think I could persuade you of this, but I will not dwell on the matter here.' What he chose to dwell on was an enclosed letter from Wellesley which referred to the damage being done to this policy by the fact that Shuvalov seemed well-informed about divisions in the Cabinet: 'What I wish to show you is that if the present system of the Cabinet is persisted in, and every resolution of every council is regularly reported . . . it seems inevitable that our very endeavours to secure peace will land us in the reverse.' He congratulated Salisbury on the news that Lady Salisbury had 'socially expressed her sentiments to the great culprit'. He told Salisbury that 'you and I must go together into the depth of the affair and settle what we are prepared to do. I dare say we shall not differ when we talk the matter over as becomes public men with so great a responsibility.'[50] Disraeli had now made Salisbury privy to two pieces of information kept from the rest of the Cabinet: Wellesley's mission and Lady Derby's supposed betrayal of Cabinet secrets; by so doing, he had made plain his desire for a more intimate co-operation, and his willingness to lean on the advice and support of the younger man.

Salisbury was not insensible to the compliment which the Prime Minister was paying him, and could not but deplore the 'leaking out' of Cabinet secrets, but that did not mean he was ready to throw over the natural sympathies he felt for the principles which Derby had expressed to him. He was certainly not ready to listen to Wellesley's palpably unsound advice 'to fight Russia now': Turkey would be no use as an ally, Austria had been 'seduced' by Russia, and the Indian army was not ready to fight. 'The national feeling here, though strongly partial to the Turk, shrinks from war; and I think with a true instinct.' He acknowledged that events might push them into a war, 'but it will be unpopular and unprofitable'.[51] For all the later comments by Disraeli's biographer that it was now that Salisbury 'began to range himself more and more by Beaconsfield's side',[52] and despite Carnarvon's opinion to the same effect,[53] the contemporary reality was more complex. Lady Gwendolen Cecil's view that her father was trying to keep the Government together during this period[54] had something to be said for it, but even that disguises the fact that he was doing this by leaning towards Derby's arguments rather than Disraeli's blandishments. He was gravely concerned at how 'affairs are likely to be conducted in a Cabinet in which the Queen's & the Prime Minister's wishes are no longer balanced by Lord Derby's well-known aversion to war'.[55]

If Lady Salisbury did upbraid Lady Derby with her supposed treachery, it could not have conduced to Christmas harmony between Hatfield and Knowsley, but it did not mean that the master of the former was prepared to back Disraeli; nor did it mean that the stories Disraeli was peddling were true. There is no reliable evidence to impugn Lady Derby's honour. Lady Derby had described Wellesley as 'obsolete' and his information as 'useless', when writing to Lord Halifax in August,[56] and as the editor of Derby's diaries comments, delation by him was not something 'one would wish to hang a dog on'.[57]

Wellesley's brother, the Dean of Windsor, wrote to Lady Derby on 27 December bringing the charges to her attention.[58] She received the letter whilst she was at Knowsley for Christmas; on the evening of 27 December Shuvalov joined her.[59] There is, in Lady Derby's papers, a tantalising fragment of text written in a kind of 'franglais'; it is not in her hand, or that of Shuvalov, yet the fact that it is partly in French (which she spoke well and in which Shuvalov always wrote to her) suggests that it may have been written for, or even with, him. Lady Derby suffered from problems with her sight and sometimes used an amanuensis, but given the intimate content of the notes, it appears unlikely that she dictated it: perhaps her handwriting was distorted by emotion, as some of it may be in her hand. The notes are a mystery, but they show how traumatic Dean Wellesley's letter was, as they begin with the statement, '*Je me refuse d'être warned (ou je proteste contre le mot warned*'; one could only be 'warned' if one was culpable, and Lady Derby denied that categorically. She could not, and did not, deny that she often spoke to '*le Ct. Shouv.*', but everyone knew that; it was no secret and she had never tried to hide it. She knew that he wrote to Gorchakov about the dangers of a break with England, and that there were those in Russia who accused him of being intimidated by the British, so it was ludicrous to accuse her of giving him false assurances that Britain would never go to war. She talked politics with all the ambassadors, which was what the wife of the Foreign Secretary was supposed to do; but she did no more than she had to. But towards the end of the final page, a note of despair crept in: '*Qu[e] vous devoir je?* [What do you want me to do?][60] What Lady Derby did was to write back indignantly to Dean Wellesley, calling his rumours the sort of thing which circulated in the scurrilous press. She was 'vexed and annoyed and hardly able to believe the amount of *malveillance* which could get them round to the Queen in such a form as to deem them worthy of attention'. She added that had she done what was alleged, she would 'have been guilty of a degree of imprudence and bad taste which I shudder to imagine, or I should be open to the still graver charge of betraying Her Majesty's Government or indeed my country'.[61]

There is no evidence that Lady Derby and Shuvalov were lovers. His letters to her indicate no more closeness than do those of the German Ambassador, Count Münster. Such rumours are easy to spread and next to impossible to disprove; the truth is now unknowable, but the context in which the rumours circulated does suggest that they were put about with ulterior motives. Derby certainly had no anxiety on that score, and relations remained close between the Derbys and Shuvlov until he left London in the 1880s.[62]

Corry told Derby's private secretary, Sanderson, that Shuvalov had been giving the Tsar detailed accounts of Cabinet meetings, but Sanderson told him that the leakages had not come from Derby.[63] The Permanent Under-Secretary at the Foreign Office, Lord Tenterden, objected to the special and unrecorded conversations between Derby and Shuvalov,[64] but Derby's only indiscretion seems to have been the revelation that Disraeli was looking towards Vienna for an anti-Russian alliance[65] – which could hardly have surprised the Russian, and was designed to make him think again before dismissing the possibility that Britain would find an ally. Derby, like Shuvalov, suspected that leaks of information came through Disraeli's contacts with the Rothschilds.[66] Another possible source of leakages was the unfortunate practice of some Ministers of discussing confidential dispatches at dinners at which non-Cabinet member were present.[67]

However, the more salacious version of events is obviously more exciting, and historians have adopted it uncritically, with one American biographer embellishing matters to the point at which Derby, who was 'drinking heavily . . . recognized his disloyalty', but found the 'enticements of his wife were overwhelming';[68] there is no proof for any of this, but why spoil a good story? Lady Derby was undoubtedly correct in her comment to Carnarvon that an alliance between him, Derby and Salisbury might 'make all safe against a trick';[69] but as the allegations against her showed, Disraeli was not short of a 'trick' or two.

The suspicion that the timing of the manoeuvre against the Derbys was part of a campaign of 'divide and rule' by Disraeli against his opponents is strengthened, at least circumstantially, by the fact that he chose this period to launch a drive against the weakest link in the chain against him – Carnarvon. The Colonial Secretary made a speech on 2 January 1878 in which he said that Britain must avoid another 'insanity' like the Crimean War.[70] At worst, this deserved no more than Derby's description of it as 'imprudent and inopportune', but Disraeli chose to use it as the occasion for a full-scale attack on Carnarvon at Cabinet on 3 January. He was normally careful of his temper, and the intemperate way he tore into the Colonial Secretary suggested to Derby that there was more to it than simple annoyance.[71] Carnarvon thought that unless Disraeli withdrew his insulting comments, his own position would be 'false, and not even, I think creditable', and he threatened to resign.[72] Wearily, Northcote rolled into action as the Cabinet conciliator, telling Salisbury: 'Here we are on the rocks again, & I am afraid we shall have some difficulty in getting off.'[73] Salisbury told Carnarvon that he ought not to go at such a time except upon a general point of principle, and urged him not to resign 'on account of a rude phrase by a man whose insolence is proverbial'.[74] Derby pressed similar advice on him: 'Don't strengthen the war party by secession.'[75] In the face of this solidarity, Disraeli pretended to believe Carnarvon's assurance that he had not been speaking for the Government, whilst Carnarvon affected to believe that Disraeli had not been rude;[76] no one was deceived.

The alliance between the three peers was still, to outward appearances, intact. The relationship between Carnarvon and Salisbury was a close one, 'founded on the unrestrained intimacy of many years'. Carnarvon later came to suspect that Disraeli had begun to woo Salisbury as far back as the Constantinople conference, and recalled that from the summer of 1877 he noted a 'distinct change in Salisbury's relations' with the Prime Minister; he later concluded that Salisbury had probably 'already formed his projects with regard to the Foreign Office'.[77] This goes further than the evidence allows, although Disraeli's attempts to cultivate an intimacy with Salisbury at this time are striking. But there was no tripartite alliance between the three men. Derby may have helped persuade Carnarvon to stay in the Cabinet, but he considered him a 'weak, vain' and 'fussy' man, and supported him because it was 'essential that he should not be driven out at this moment'.[78]

The main axis against Disraeli was that formed by what Derby assumed to be the distrust which he and Salisbury shared of Disraeli's opportunism. Salisbury had criticised it often enough, and Derby thought that Disraeli's acuteness in seeing 'what is most convenient for the moment' was combined with 'apparent indifference to what is to come of it in the long run'. He doubted whether Disraeli actually wanted war, but thought that 'he fears above all things the reproach of weak or commonplace policy'. Derby assumed that it was his Society intimates and the Queen who encouraged Disraeli to think that the 'public feeling [is] much more warlike than it really is'. The idea that he might compromise the 'future of the country by reckless finance' was, like 'distant results of any kind', foreign to Disraeli's way of thinking. This was an 'unpleasant and dangerous' state of affairs – with a divided Cabinet, no Continental ally and a public which expected 'to have the results of victory without the sacrifices of war'.[79] Derby expected this critique to unite him with Salisbury; and so it did – for a little while yet.

SPLENDID ISOLATION?

The draft Queen's speech prepared by Disraeli was so bellicose in tone that even Derby was willing to set aside his personal fastidiousness about organising cabals. He wrote to Carnarvon, who communicated his reservations to Salisbury, and by the time the Cabinet met on 9 January, they had agreed that the speech must be toned down.[80] When Derby attacked the draft as too anti-Russian, he was joined by Carnarvon and Salisbury. To his 'concealed consternation', Disraeli was once again almost isolated in his own Cabinet: Cross 'gave a faint note and dwelt on the depression of trade'; Gathorne-Hardy 'touched only on some technical military points, but gave no assistance on the great issue'; and even the faithful Cairns thought that what was being proposed was 'intervention and not neutrality'; he voiced doubts, shared by others, about whether the national finances could stand a war with Russia. Only the faithful Manners and the 'able' Northcote were 'true'.[81] Disraeli did not try to hide his resentment from the Queen.[82] The Turcophile and Russophobic elements in the speech were duly toned down, and Disraeli had to save face with the Queen by pointing out that the Cabinet was still agreed upon an early summons of Parliament, an increase in armaments and mediation in the Russo-Turkish War.[83]

If Disraeli was isolated and furious, Derby was relieved. Had he not won the day, he would have resigned, 'not out of pique, but because it would have been impossible for me to defend in parl[iamen]t ideas which are contrary to mine'.[84] Carnarvon called it a 'real victory', recalling it as the 'last occasion upon which Salisbury acted with Derby and myself'.[85] The connection between the two phenomena does not need labouring.

The Queen, by contrast, was 'really distressed at the low tone which this country is inclined to hold', and wanted Disraeli to take 'every opportunity' to 'show them that the Empire and even their low sordid love of gain will suffer permanently if this goes on'. It was, she declared, Lord Derby who was 'the real misfortune; another Foreign Secretary who felt as he ought, would support the Prime Minister'.[86]

7

Resignation

Derby's line of restraining Disraeli was sensible and cogent, but it suffered from two problems: it made him look as though he had no policy of his own; and Disraeli refused to sit still and be restrained. He seized every opportunity to press for action, and they came swiftly in January, with Layard telegraphing almost hourly warning of the dangers of the Russians taking Constantinople, and passing on an appeal from the Sultan on 10 January. The Queen sent an urgent telegram to Disraeli: 'Hope Admiral is ordered back at once. I think we may await to hear Adrianople is taken and Constantinople threatened. And then England may kiss Russia's feet.'[1] Before the Cabinet met on 12 January, she exhorted: 'We must take strong decided line or England no longer mistress of the sea and East. Decided instructions must be given to Mr. Layard.'[2] And when it did meet, Disraeli was able to preface his call for the occupation of the Gallipoli Peninsula with a long diatribe from the Queen which argued that the 'state of the Eastern Question' was now so serious and events moving with such speed that 'what was decided even two or three days ago seems no longer of much avail', and which went on to say that if they did not take steps to deny Constantinople to Russia, 'England must abdicate her position and retire from having any longer any voice in the Councils of Europe and sink down to a third-rate power!'[3]

Gladstone was wrong to describe the Cabinet as nothing more than an expression of Disraeli's will.[4] Derby assumed that although Shuvalov was not telling the whole truth, he was correct in advising him that Russia would not push things to extremes: that made him less inclined to panic or to believe coffee-house babble; he assumed that the function of the Conservative Party in foreign affairs was to prevent cosmopolitan notions of 'prestige' or plebeian Russophobia pushing the country into a war which the country squires would have to pay for for the next half century in the form of increased taxation; he assumed that enough of his colleagues shared these unspoken and half-spoken assumptions to rein in the Prime Minister; and he also assumed that the Queen was suffering from the sort of hereditary loopiness which had afflicted her grandfather and some of her uncles. These assumptions governed Derby's response to the Queen's message to the Cabinet on 12 January, even as they did his reaction to Disraeli's desire to steal a march on Russia's evil intentions. Immune to the high Romanticism of the Prime Minister, he insisted on pointing out that sending the fleet up through the Straits, or landing troops at Gallipoli, would amount to 'intervention' and would be a breach of neutrality. The result was a 'Cabinet of three hours: most stormy'.[5]

For nearly an hour Derby and Carnarvon bitterly opposed the Prime Minister. Salisbury tried to break the deadlock by proposing to ask the Sultan's permission for the British fleet 'to anchor in the Straits' and demand from the Russians an 'assurance' that they would not occupy Gallipoli. But 'after long reflection & extreme stubbornness [Derby] . . . rose from his seat & said that he c[oul]d not sanction any projects of the kind & that he must retire from the Ministry'. Salisbury said that 'if Lord Derby retired, he must retire too, as he felt that the differences of opinion in the Cabinet were insurmountable'; he had only suggested his compromise 'to keep them, if possible together at this moment, as he felt it would be disastrous to the Queen's service to break up now'. Cairns asked what Derby proposed they should tell Layard to do, but in Disraeli's exasperated phrase, 'as usual Lord Derby had nothing to propose. He opposes everything, proposes nothing.'[6] According to Carnarvon, Disraeli said that 'it was plain that the Government could no longer be carried on' and that Parliament would have to be prorogued. Derby 'said he was sorry, but there was no choice', and Salisbury 'made a curious and complimentary speech to Disraeli in the sense of a leave-taking'.[7] For 'nearly an hour', Derby assumed that he 'had ceased to be a Minister',[8] and Gathorne-Hardy thought that the Cabinet would 'break up'.[9] With the Cabinet hovering on the brink of dissolution, Derby decided that he could accept Salisbury's compromise after all, although Carnarvon 'had the impertinence of violently protesting against it, even after that'.[10] But although Derby agreed to ask the Porte whether 'an application to allow our fleet to go up into the Dardanelles would be favourably received', it was with the caveat that this did not 'imply consent to send the fleet up under present circ[umstance]s'. It was also agreed to ask the Russians for guarantees about not occupying Gallipoli, and to tell the Porte that 'we intended to have a voice in the final settlement'.[11]

It was at this point that Derby inadvertently committed his greatest error; the first rule of politics is to be in the Cabinet room, and Derby now transgressed it by falling seriously ill. He had been feeling 'unwell and weak'[12] for almost a week, and by Monday, 14 January, he was suffering 'so severely' that he was unable either to work or to go to bed.[13] This is the origin of the stories about his 'breakdown', which led to lurid rumours about his drinking and which were used later to imply that he lacked moral fibre.[14] He wrote to Disraeli on 15 January saying that it was 'vexatious in every way to be helpless in a crisis'.[15] For the next three days he did not leave home, and it was a week before he was again ready to conduct business.[16] But that did not mean that his voice was stilled.

If Derby was vexed by being ill, the Queen was even more vexed by what he had done before going sick. After reading the telegrams despatched to Constantinople and to St Petersburg, she told Disraeli that Derby's way of phrasing the Cabinet decision was a 'disgrace', and that she hoped it would 'not bind us in any way <u>not to</u> send forces if we later decide it. I could not consent to that.'[17] But her own attempt to get an assurance from Alexander II simply produced a 'very unpleasant' and 'rude' response saying that his commanders knew the terms for an armistice.[18] This just heated up the coals she poured on to Disraeli: 'Indecision and half measures <u>now</u> would be ruin to this country. <u>You must</u> be decided. The reverse will ruin us forever and not conciliate those who wish us to do nothing.'[19] She urged Disraeli to accept Derby's resignation and become his own Foreign Secretary: 'Lord D. will <u>do nothing, originate nothing</u>, and besides is indiscreet & leaves our Ambassadors <u>abroad</u> without instructions. . . . What can be the <u>cause</u> of Lord Derby's incredible conduct?'[20]

Derby was too ill to attend the Cabinet or even to agree to the suggestion that it should meet on 15 January at his London house.[21] But from his sick-bed he dictated a letter telling Disraeli that the 'more I think of the Dardanelles business, the less I like it'. Derby thought that the fact that negotiations were now in train between the Porte and the Russians obviated the need to send warships through the Straits.[22]

When the Cabinet met without Derby at six o'clock, there was yet another new circumstance to take into account: the Sultan had rejected the British request to send the fleet up through the Straits. Under the International Treaties of 1841 and 1856 he had every right to do this, and this should have settled the matter, but Salisbury, who was 'worn out' (according to Gathorne-Hardy) by 'Russian duplicity', argued strongly that since the Porte was obviously acting under fear of Russia, its opinion could be ignored and the fleet despatched accordingly.[23] It was agreed to postpone any telegram to Admiral Hornby until the Austrians had been sounded out about joining a naval demonstration, but Carnarvon would not consent to the policy and threatened to resign.[24] Gathorne-Hardy, who had been 'much struck by Salisbury's resolution', did not expect to see Carnarvon in the Cabinet again.[25]

Carnarvon stomped off to disturb Derby's rest immediately the Cabinet was over. He said that he disliked the idea of sending the fleet through the Dardanelles so much that he had decided to resign; but with his eye fixed on the need for allies in Cabinet, Derby advised him not to go.[26] Typically, Carnarvon still sent in a letter of resignation, but told Disraeli that he would not actually go until the order had been given to the fleet, and that in order 'to prevent the circulation of any rumours' he would attend the Cabinet on the morrow for a short while.[27]

Although Derby's doctor advised him against going to Cabinet on 16 January,[28] he was able to dictate a note of what he 'should have liked to be able to say' to Sanderson, who delivered it to Disraeli. Derby had six 'objections ... to the sending up of the fleet': the Porte would not agree whilst Britain remained neutral; to defy the Porte and send the fleet would break the Treaties of 1841 and 1856, as well as placing the fleet in danger; nor was it clear what the fleet would do if the Russians did not go to Constantinople; if the Russians did get there, there would be an 'imminent risk of a collision'; finally, Derby saw no need to act while talks were under way between the Russians and the Turks. He feared that Disraeli's proposals were designed to 'irritate rather than to conciliate' and were 'useless' if not actually 'dangerous in a military point of view'.[29] The Russians were now prepared to give assurances that they would not occupy Gallipoli unless the Turks forced them to.[30]

The prospect of Derby's resignation was enough to prompt Smith to urge Northcote to hold back the fleet: 'the delay of a few hours is important, but the loss of Lord Derby would be a greater evil'.[31] By the time the Cabinet met to consider Derby's memorandum, the panic had subsided.[32] Thus, when Disraeli opened the Cabinet on 16 January with Derby's advice against sending the fleet through the Straits, it was the prelude to consensus rather than to a further argument. The only rift in the lute came from Carnarvon, who, hurt by Disraeli's attitude, insisted upon mentioning his letter of resignation.[33] Disraeli wanted to let the whole business drop,[34] but Carnarvon persisted, writing on 18 January that he did not want to resign, but asking for guarantees against armed action at the Straits.[35] Disraeli, who regarded 'Twitters' as an ineffectual dilettante,[36] refused to give him either a guarantee or the satisfaction of accepting his resignation: 'These are not times when statesmen should be too susceptible.'[37]

Parliament finally opened on 17 January, which gave the Opposition a chance to taunt the Government with 'vacillation' and 'indecision', and Disraeli an opportunity to quiz them with neglecting British interests. But the sensation of the day came with Salisbury's speech. After a repetition of the old theme of the plight of the subject races of the Ottoman Empire, he switched into a cutting and ironic denunciation of what he called the Liberals' 'new gospel ... that it is our business for the sake of any populations whatever to disregard the trust which the people of this country and our Sovereign have reposed in our hands'.[38] It was the authentic voice of *Realpolitik* and an 'open challenge to Mr. Gladstone'.[39] It was little wonder that Disraeli commented in particular on the 'vigorous, loyal and uncompromising support' which he had received from Salisbury.[40]

The alternative Foreign Secretary had now revealed himself, and the Queen was in no doubt that Disraeli ought to 'let Lord Derby and Lord Carnarvon go' as a prelude to the longed-for policy of 'firmness'. She offered Disraeli the Garter along with her usual advice; he declined the former whilst deciding to take the latter.[41] Her son, Prince Leopold, told Corry that she considered Derby and Carnarvon to be 'traitors'.[42] But Disraeli was now in a strong enough position to push for the policy which he wanted: without Salisbury, Carnarvon counted for little, and he had been weakened still further by his gaffe about the Crimean War; without Salisbury, Derby would have to choose whether to go or stay, but he would be doing so in a political climate made febrile by wild rumours from Constantinople and might damage himself more than the Government.

Fortified by rumours that the Russians were advancing on Constantinople, and that Andrassy might, given a subsidy, finally be willing to act with the British, Disraeli made another play for a policy of action. On 21 January, he proposed that they should offer the Austrians an alliance and 'pecuniary aid' if they would mobilise a 'sufficient force' and join Britain in a note of warning to Russia. As an earnest of British sincerity, 'Our fleet, of course [would] . . . go up to Constantinople.' Derby did not believe that Parliament would sanction either the alliance or the loan that would be needed to cover the cost of the 'aid' to Austria; and he had the liveliest doubts whether Andrassy was a reliable partner.[43] The discussion was 'fiery', with Derby arguing 'fiercely' and Carnarvon 'feebly'.[44] Gathorne-Hardy was less impressed than Disraeli by Derby's manner, which he described rather inconsistently as 'so timid & irresolute that all the rest of the Cabinet cannot move him'.[45] But since he did not think that Andrassy would agree to proposals for an alliance, Derby eventually acted on his belief and sent the request as a way of flushing the Hungarian out. Derby despatched the telegram with the air of a man who did not expect to be in office much longer.[46] But it was Salisbury himself who drafted the terms of the Identic Note, which stated that the 'continued occupation of Bulgaria by foreign troops, or of any part of the shores of the Bosphorous, the Sea of Marmara and Dardanelles, or any alteration of the rules affecting the navigation thereof are to be deemed inadmissible without the consent of Austria and England'.[47]

One of the best examples of the way in which a quick filter through preconceptions could alter the realities of diplomacy was provided by Disraeli's reaction to the Austrian response. Andrassy, who like most foreigners found the parliamentary debates as confusing as anything that was happening at Constantinople, expressed disappointment that the British had not sent up the fleet, asked Parliament for more money or yet occupied Gallipoli. But Disraeli took this as a sign that if he took those steps, the Austrians would then assent to the alliance, and so used the reply as a further spur for action.[48] Naturally there were also yet more alarming telegrams from Layard to support Disraeli's conclusion that circumstances had now changed sufficiently to demand immediate action,[49] but there was something more. With the

Queen, Salisbury, Layard and even Andrassy called in to move the waverers, there was lacking from Disraeli's armoury only the weapon of public opinion; fortuitously this deficiency was made up by a report from the Chief Whip, Sir William Hart-Dyke, which just happened to back Disraeli's line. Even before the Cabinet met, Disraeli was anticipating that Derby and Carnarvon would resign, and he solicited the Queen's permission to accept their resignations on the spot.[50]

With the deck nicely marked, Disraeli summoned the Cabinet at short notice,[51] for three o'clock on 23 January. He began with Hart-Dyke's memorandum, which made it plain that immediate action against Russia, even at the risk of war, would win the support of a 'united Party', many Liberal MPs and the mass of public opinion; but that if Russia was allowed to 'advance to a position from whence she can dictate her terms', then 'nothing but disaster' would follow. A divided Party would lead to 'a feeling of disgust among our supporters in the country, which must prove disastrous at every Election'. Only 'one thing . . . can injure the Tory Party of the Future – namely if it can be hinted either in Public or Private that in a great historical emergency, of two courses open, it's [sic] Leaders forsook the brave one & preferred the timid'.[52] The message was clear: if patriotism was not sufficient, if intellect did not lead you to share Disraeli's world-view, then self-survival should be enough; rely on Disraeli, the people's Premier. Against this the lachrymose protestations of Carnarvon and the rather more restrained but firmer protests of Derby availed them naught. The Cabinet agreed to give the order to send the fleet through the Straits and to sanction an increase in the Estimates.

Derby doubted every word Disraeli said: none of his six arguments against sending the fleet had been controverted; he did not believe that Andrassy would co-operate and took his words at face value; nor was he terribly convinced that things at Constantinople were as bad as Layard made out. The problem was that he could not prove that any of his preconceptions were true, and those of Disraeli seemed more cogent because of Hart-

Dyke's assurance that they would win popular support. If Hart-Dyke was correct, and no one challenged him, then the view that Russophobia had not risen to 'income tax level' was wrong, and a failure to act would lead to political disaster. Derby thought that he was right, but his cards all appeared to have been trumped.

Carnarvon was all for resigning in a huff at once, but Derby's cautious instincts told him to play for time, and he persuaded him to wait until the morrow.[53] So much of what had been decided was based upon rumours – telegrams flowed in by the hour – and no one could tell what the morning would bring. But Derby still wrote out his own letter of resignation that evening, and Disraeli was so confident of his going that he noted him as having resigned on 23 January.[54] On the morning of 24 January, two letters of resignation were despatched: Carnarvon's formal and barely polite, Derby's 'manly and touching'.[55]

Derby made it clear that he had to go; he could not defend the decision to call the fleet up to Constantinople since he thought it neither 'safe nor wise'. He 'deeply and sincerely' regretted having to resign, but took comfort from the fact that 'you will get on better with a thoroughly harmonious Cabinet'. On a personal level Derby feared that resignation would end his long friendship with the Prime Minister, whose 'way of looking at politics is always a personal one, and it is not easy for him to understand objections founded solely on public considerations'.[56] He told Disraeli on 24 January that he had 'no wish to make explanations at any time' and thought that he had best stay away from the Lords.[57] The Queen expressed her deep satisfaction to Disraeli and authorised him to offer the vacant post to Salisbury.[58] There was, however, one formality which had not been completed; Derby reminded Disraeli on 25 January that he had had no formal acknowledgment of his resignation.[59] This was because Disraeli had just discovered that he had been wrong in the assumptions which had allowed him to let Derby go. In the first place, the Austrians did not respond positively to the British overture; in the second, the Russians finally stopped playing 'hide the thimble' with the terms they were asking from the Porte; and finally, the remote fears of future electoral failure predicted by Hart-Dyke added to the panic engendered by the near-certainty that Derby's resignation would entail an election at a very near date.

According to most accounts, Lady Derby told Shuvalov about the Cabinet's decision to send up the fleet, which prompted him to telegraph Gorchakov that 'immediate rupture' with England was imminent; this finally produced some information about what Russia wanted from the Turks.[60] When Shuvalov saw Derby on 24 January, he tried to reassure him that the Russian terms of peace would not be too severe; but the 'bombshell' which hit Ministers and prompted them to recall the fleet was the news from Layard that among the bases of peace was a provision that the question of the Straits should be settled between 'the Congress and the Emperor of Russia'.[61] The moment Northcote received the news, he and Smith dashed over to see Disraeli. Their suggestion that the order to Hornby should be countermanded was supported by another new circumstance: the Sultan would not give formal permission for the British fleet to pass because he was afraid of the Russian reaction.[62] It is an index of how on edge everyone was that this mixture of rumour and unconfirmed half-facts was enough to prompt a message to Hornby at 7.23 p.m. ordering him back to Besika Bay.[63]

So the grand old British fleet had sailed right up to the Straits and had turned right back again. This meant that when the news came through on 25 January that the Straits issue was actually to be settled between the Sultan and the Emperor, not even Disraeli felt that they could countermand the original order; as Layard reported, Britain was a 'laughing stock' at Constantinople.[64] The Government was not doing much better at home.

It was impossible to hide the fact that Carnarvon had gone, and the reassembled Parliament was alive with rumours that Derby had joined him. Disraeli had asked Derby on 24 January not to make his resignation public,[65] and Derby had complied, taking the view that 'the less said at the moment the better';[66] but his failure to appear in the Lords that afternoon could not but have given rise to speculation. When he heard the news that the fleet had been recalled, he noted laconically: 'In that case all this trouble of the last few days has been taken for nothing.'[67] He wrote to Disraeli reminding him that he had not yet had a formal acceptance of his resignation;[68] the queue of people flocking to his door was some intimation that he was not going to get one.

Hart-Dyke had prophesied doom if the Cabinet did nothing, but circumstances had changed since the distant date of two days earlier; now another doom appeared closer to hand, and men will always accept a remote chance of death in preference to an immediate certainty of it. Northcote wrote anxiously to Disraeli on 25 January, telling him about 'alarming accounts of the effect which Derby's resignation might produce, especially on our Lancashire and Cheshire members'; according to the Chief Whip, 'the feeling was much worse than he believed it to be when he spoke to you'. Evidently the subject of Derby coming back had already been canvassed between the two men, since Northcote went on to say that he feared Derby would take no post save the Foreign Office, and then only if things 'all went right'; but in that event, 'we should not want him back and the objections you spoke of would I suppose continue'. Northcote thought that they could not change policy simply to get Derby back and that they 'must face the chance of a bad division and be prepared for a possible overthrow', but he told Disraeli that he had arranged for Cross to call on Lady Derby, whilst he was going to see Derby himself.[69] However by this time they had, thanks to Layard's telegram, already changed policy, so Derby's brother, Frederick, who was Financial Secretary at the Treasury, was sent to see whether he would, after all, come back, preferably not to the Foreign Office. Derby suspected that Northcote had sent him and found the suggestion that he should, on grounds of health, take some other office, unacceptable. His view was that 'I had offered to retire, and any proposal to me to withdraw the offer must come from the other side'.[70]

With the fleet back in Besika Bay, it was becoming essential to get the Foreign Secretary back before anyone noticed he had gone. Hart-Dyke wrote to Disraeli on 25 January, confirming Northcote's line and adding that he had 'heard much to confirm my opinion that he [Derby] should at this moment be retained if possible in the Cabinet'; the 'commercial element' was, he reported, 'thoroughly alarmed'.[71] The Government would have looked remarkably silly, or rather even sillier than it already did, had it become known that the Foreign Secretary had gone for protesting against a policy which had later been abandoned; arguing that it had been dropped on the wrong grounds would probably not have sounded well in mitigation. With Disraeli trying to keep clear of the whole mess created by his miscalculations, it fell to poor old Northcote to pick up the pieces.

Northcote went round to see Derby on the morning of 26 January to try to persuade him to accept either Salisbury's place at the India Office, or Carnarvon's at the Colonies; but Derby stuck to his determination to have the Foreign Office or nothing.[72] After lunch, at Derby's request, Northcote went back for a second, and more fruitful, conversation. Northcote assured Derby that nothing more would be done about sending the fleet through the Straits, and that although they would have to proceed with the vote for the supplementary Estimates because it had already been announced, only about £1 million of it would be spent, and that if negotiations succeeded then even that might be dropped. Derby was still tempted to go, but proved susceptible to Northcote's argument that if he did, then foreign policy would be entirely in the hands of Disraeli and the Queen, and the country might find itself at war before Parliament could stop it. The argument that in the event of the Government collapsing an election would produce either a 'radical' government or one dominated by the 'war party', was also a persuasive one. Derby noted: 'As matters are, I am a check on the Prime Minister, and though I do not put much faith in them, I have the assurances of several of my colleagues that they will support me in resisting a war policy.' The only reasons for going were personal ones, and Derby was not so constituted that he could let them prevail over his sense of 'public duty'.[73] Northcote told Disraeli that he thought Derby would come back.[74]

SPLENDID ISOLATION?

It also fell to Northcote to explain to the Queen why she was getting her least favourite carbuncle back on her neck. He was lavish with political excuses: it was Lancashire; it was the Tory Party; it was the fact that both Parties respected Derby; it was the need to stop him bolting to the Liberals, a prospect not to be 'contemplated with equanimity';[75] what he did not say was that it was, above all, a loss of nerve. Disraeli's version of events, so convincing on 23 January, was no longer so two days later, so Derby would have to pretend that nothing had happened.

The problem, as evidenced by the fact that it was Northcote who had conducted the negotiations, was that quite a lot had happened and that most of it would not be forgotten, particularly the fact that Disraeli had backed down. Derby did not reach his decision easily and spent most of 26 January wrestling with his conscience.[76] But finally he wrote a stiff letter to Northcote agreeing to stay on 'reluctantly and doubtfully'; he made his unease clear and implied that he might not stay for very long.[77] Lady Derby told Carnarvon, who did not withdraw his resignation, that the 'struggle has been dreadful', but she believed that 'it is right'.[78]

It only remained for Disraeli to write his 'Madam and most beloved Sovereign' a letter which he feared she would 'never pardon me for writing'; political necessity seemed to demand Derby's retention; the only comfort he could offer her was that he would be 'powerfully controlled by the Cabinet'.[79] Salisbury, who gracefully declined the Foreign Office, told Disraeli that he was glad that Derby was back since 'at this juncture his secession would have exposed us to all kinds of wild suspicions, and would have added to the difficulties which, in any case, the country will have to face'.[80] Derby went to the Cabinet meeting on 27 January; however, he did not take his usual seat next to Disraeli, 'but sat far apart, in the vacant seat of Lord Carnarvon. This was very marked. He is evidently in a dark temper', but, as Disraeli told the Queen, 'all must be borne at this moment'.[81]

The impression was created later that the episode had been a sad lapse of firmness by Disraeli caused by 'electoral alarmism',[82] but that it did not really matter because henceforth Derby's time at the Foreign Office was a sort of life-after-death experience. Lord Blake has described how the 'Prime Minister himself openly conducted the Eastern Policy of the country in Cabinet',[83] following straight in the footsteps of Salisbury's biographer, who wrote about 'an experiment which was probably unique in the history of Cabinets', in which Disraeli, Cairns and Salisbury acted as an 'inner Cabinet', with Derby as a glorified office boy.[84] This account in turn owed its existence to Cairns telling Salisbury's nephew, Arthur Balfour, that 'all that Derby did was done at the point of the bayonet!', and to Salisbury's own description of Derby 'in a condition of utter moral prostration, doing as little as possible' and then only 'under compulsion'.[85] It is not a pretty story, and without the help of Cairns and Salisbury it might never have been noticed, since the evidence points to a different conclusion. It certainly excuses the lapse in letting Derby back; it was certainly meant to do that. But was it true?

Disraeli's attitude is not as straightforward as his withdrawal from the negotiations and his comments to the Queen suggest. He evidently wrote a conciliatory letter to Derby, which he asked Derby to burn, expressing his sorrow at the rupture in their association. Derby, who complied with the wish, responded that there was inevitably 'a certain awkwardness in the renewal of interrupted official relations'; that could be seen by the fact that for the first and only time in their long correspondence Derby began the letter without any superscription whatsoever. That, he explained, was why he had decided to see him first in Cabinet, so that they could get over the initial awkwardness in public. The problem was that 'the question now dividing the whole political world is one which cuts across the existing division of parties'. He had, he assured Disraeli, destroyed his note without showing it even to Lady Derby; he advised Disraeli to do the same with his letter 'so that no record may exist of personal unpleasantness between us'.[86] This does not quite square with the version which Salisbury and Cairns sponsored, but then nor does the fact that Derby came back. He came back to continue doing what he had been doing ever since late 1876, that is to balance Disraeli's preconceptions with his own; there would have been no need for him to have stayed had he been relegated to the periphery of decision-making. If we accept the Cairns/Salisbury version, it is difficult to explain why Derby did stay; if we accept Derby's account and the contemporaneous record, this problem vanishes. Derby stayed because he was Foreign Secretary in fact as well as in name – which meant that the struggle went on.

8

Derby's Last Victory

Derby's return was a mistake for Disraeli, as it was, from a personal point of view, for Derby himself; but in so far as it allowed him to continue to restrain Disraeli, and to work his relationship with Shuvalov towards that end, then on the political level it was a success.

It is hard not to feel that Derby was right in predicting that 'Disraeli and I shall never be on the same terms again: his way of looking at politics is always a personal one, and it is not easy for him to understand objections founded solely on public considerations.'[1] The most striking change was not the effacement of Derby which Salisbury and Cairns later described, but the disappearance of Disraeli; from being in almost hourly contact with the Queen and his colleagues, Disraeli suddenly went quiet. If Cairns and Salisbury stood in for anyone, it was for Disraeli.

The care with which Ministers had to handle the presence in the same Cabinet of a sulky Disraeli and an unrepentant Derby can be seen from Northcote's handling of the job of getting Derby back. In his letter to Disraeli on 25 January, Northcote showed a proper recognition of the fact that Derby was the sole obstacle to a forward policy; whilst in his conversation with Derby the following day, he stressed the need to unite to restrain Disraeli. There is no use asking the real Sir Stafford Northcote to stand up and be identified; both Northcotes were real in their own way. Disraeli was meant to feel that Northcote sympathised with him, so was Derby; this was the only way political life could be carried on. But Derby's refusal to take the lead in challenging Disraeli's leadership meant that even his sympathisers were forced into a painful dilemma.

On the one hand there was the Eastern crisis itself. No one could tell how that would pan out. The Russians were at the gates of Constantinople, the Queen and the press on the verge of hysteria, and Disraeli wanted action. On the other hand, there was the more familiar world of politics. Derby's importance had just been demonstrated. Whatever Hart-Dyke's little report had said before the event, the news of Derby's possible departure had provoked such a reaction in the Party that there had been an abrupt about-turn. Had Derby tried to use this opportunity to replace Disraeli, his colleagues would have faced a dilemma. But he did not, so they faced one of another sort. Disraeli was clearly not going to give way on the Eastern Question. As the first Conservative leader since Peel to win a general election, and as the man who had led them in the Commons during the lean years between 1846 and 1874, Disraeli had claims on both the loyalty and gratitude of his Cabinet colleagues. As an ailing and ageing Party leader, he was the object of other, less noble sentiments. Derby would not push his line, and it would not satisfy the inflamed state of public feeling; the way to the Conservative succession clearly did not lie down that road. In fact, Derby's destruction of his own prospects of the leadership opened, for the first time in a generation, the possibility of that post going to somewhere other than Knowsley or Hughenden; 1878 offered the rare sight of ambitious men looking towards the setting sun.

It was at this level that Salisbury's public emergence as the muscular champion of Disraeli's position on 17 January was of immense significance. Disraeli had always been willing to hold out his hand to Salisbury; now, instead of feeding off it, Salisbury was prepared to take it. Carnarvon saw it as base opportunism and betrayal; Salisbury presented it as politically necessary if the Government was to have a policy. Although his general attitude towards foreign affairs was closer to Derby's Country Party position than it was to Disraeli's Jingoism, on the specifics of the crisis at issue Salisbury's position differed from both Disraeli's and Derby's. This, of course, could have cut either way. Salisbury wanted a break from Palmerstonianism, and he was not going to get it from Disraeli (even though Disraeli was not a Palmerstonian in Salisbury's definition of the term); but he was not going to get it from Derby either; and he was not going to get the Foreign Secretaryship, or if it came to that the premiership, from Derby.

On this last point much now depended upon whether Derby was right in his estimation of Russia's policy. Because Shuvalov's accounts of their conversations have been available for half a century longer than Derby's, it has been easy for historians to read them at face value. But it is clear that like many diplomats, Shuvalov was not averse to composing his dispatches in a way which reflected most credit upon himself. Derby was far from the nodding donkey he appears as in Shuvalov's accounts. Lord Blake's view of Shuvalov and Derby as a pair of cosmopolitan aristocrats trying to rise above popular Jingoism is a tempting one, but it gets Derby wrong. He was no cosmopolitan; he was a deeply insular figure, with roots sunk in his Lancashire background. He wanted to avoid an unnecessary war if that was at all possible, and if Shuvalov was right then war was unnecessary. What weakened Derby's position in the weeks after his return was the growing perception that Shuvalov's views were not those of his Government. Even Derby had to admit that the march on Constantinople was 'bad policy, for it confirms the popular idea of Russian trickery and deceit'.[2]

If the Russians were increasingly unhelpful, then the decision of the Opposition to move an amendment against the Government's motion for Supply was also unfortunate from Derby's point of view, since it polarised the political situation. William Forster, who opened for the Liberals, accused the Government of wanting to wage war and of neglecting the interests of the

Christian subjects of the Porte.[3] Out of doors things got even hotter, with Macaulay's biographer, G.O. Trevelyan, father of the historian, accusing Disraeli of a 'desire to plunge the nation into war', a suggestion described by Gathorne-Hardy during the debate in the Commons as evidence of 'a criminal state of mind'.[4] Speaking at Oxford on 30 January, Gladstone put all the blame for the crisis on Disraeli.[5] Although Disraeli condemned this privately as showing that Gladstone was no more than a 'vindictive fiend',[6] his remarks cannot have been altogether unwelcome. There is nothing like being assaulted from the moral high ground by Liberal rhetoric to induce in Conservatives a common feeling of nausea. Speaking in the Lords on 31 January, even Derby admitted that there were circumstances in which sending the fleet through the Straits might be justifiable.[7] Shuvalov warned Gorchakov that this signified that Russophobia in Britain had reached a level at which the fleet would, in fact, be sent to Constantinople.[8]

The accuracy of this estimate was shown by the reaction to the rumours which began to emerge about the armistice terms which the Russians had exacted from the Turks. The terms of the settlement were not known in London until late on 7 February, and the secrecy surrounding them stimulated the forces of Russophobia greatly, but the Foreign Office analysis of what could be gleaned from Constantinople suggested that it was 'little more than an armed truce' which would 'leave behind it the smouldering embers of war'.[9] The terms seemed to mark a victory for the 'war party' in Russia, providing as they did for the creation of a large, autonomous Bulgaria; independence and territorial aggrandisement for Montenegro, Romania and Serbia; autonomy for Bosnia and Herzegovina; the payment by the Turks of a large indemnity, or, in its default, the cession of further territory to Russia; and, in addition to all of this, the Sultan would have to confer with the Tsar to safeguard Russia's rights with regard to the Straits.[10] When the Turkish plenipotentiaries finally accepted these terms on 30 January, they declared that 'Turkey is lost.'[11] Disraeli told Derby on 1 February that Shuvalov was 'tricking us' and should be asked to leave the country. Derby thought it would be 'absurd' to send Shuvalov home, but he could hardly doubt that Disraeli might be correct about Russia's policy;[12] public opinion had no doubt at all.

On 31 January, there were demonstrations at the Guildhall, followed by larger and noisier ones at Peckham and Bermondsey on 2 February; there was a great meeting of 20,000 people in Manchester that same evening. The message was the same: 'the Russians shall not have Constantinople!'[13] The great Jingo at Osborne deluged Disraeli with telegrams on 1 February: in mid-afternoon she demanded to know what he 'proposed to do' about the Russian terms;[14] by the evening she was 'much shocked' at the proposal to make peace at Constantinople which would be a 'cruel insult to the fallen foe' and was bound to lead to disorder;[15] by nightfall she wanted 'one or two ships' to be sent through the Straits with a view to protecting the safety of British subjects.[16]

However Jingoes, whether on the streets of Peckham or the purlieus of Osborne House, were not in control of British policy – yet. Despite making positive noises, Andrassy's responses to British questions about the Austrian reaction to a Russian occupation of Constantinople did not suggest that he could be relied upon unequivocally.[17] But from Berlin,[18] Vienna[19] and Rome[20] came demands for a European conference to discuss those parts of the Russo-Turkish settlement which concerned other Powers. Thus, when the Cabinet met on 2 February, it was a simple task to agree that Britain should respond favourably to these initiatives and see whether Andrassy would convene a conference.[21] On 4 February, Derby confirmed that Britain would attend a conference; Germany, Italy and France also made positive noises. If, as Shuvalov indicated, Russia was prepared to let such a conference discuss at least the European parts of the peace settlement, then Derby hoped to avoid the prospect of a war.[22]

But a combination of events proceeded to whip up a tide of Jingoism which would swamp Derby. Disraeli did his best to get him to move voluntarily, passing on to Derby a copy of a letter from Crown Princess Victoria saying that, according to reports in Berlin, the Russians were 'pushing to Constantinople as fast as they can wishing to imitate the Germans at Paris',[23] but Derby, who put this down to Bismarck's desire to stir up trouble between Britain and Russia, was unimpressed.[24] Then the telegraph lines from Constantinople went down, and on 6 February the rumour swept London that the Russians were advancing on Constantinople; the *Morning Post* reported on 7 February that Constantinople had fallen. Huge crowds gathered in the vicinity of Parliament, and the police had to be called out to keep order.[25] Salisbury had no doubt that the Government had to act. He wrote to Disraeli on the morning of 7 February that 'the mere fact that our ambassador is cut off, and that the Russians are still advancing, seems to require the presence of the fleet at Constantinople'.[26] Disraeli told Derby that if they did not take such action, then there would be French and even Italian squadrons at Constantinople before Britain had any ships there: 'This won't look well. I believe you will see a burst of indignation in this country that has not been equalled since '32';[27] in 1832, the mob had burned down the centre of Bristol and set fire to Nottingham Castle. The Queen added her voice to the shrieks for action. Even Derby realised that sending the fleet through the Straits could not now be avoided.[28]

With the noise of the crowds audible in the Cabinet room, Ministers agreed to Salisbury's suggestion that the fleet should be sent up 'at once';[29] it was also decided to ask the French to join in, and to find out what the Austrians would do.[30]

By the time Disraeli reached the House, he could hardly get out of his carriage, so fierce was the press of people. Inside the Chamber there were equally remarkable events: Forster and the Liberals agreed to an immediate grant of Supply of £6 million. But Derby's contacts with Shuvalov enabled him to remain a voice of sanity in a Westminster given over to war-fever. Speaking in the Lords he read out a hastily delivered communication from Shuvalov confirming that the movement of the Russian armies was in accord with the terms of their armistice with the Turks,[31] news which he immediately passed down to the Lower House, where Northcote read out its text: 'The order has been given to our military commanders to cease hostilities. . . . There is not a word of truth in the rumours which have reached you.'[32] The question now posed was whether to send the fleet up the Straits after all; the answers were predictable.

The Queen told Disraeli that she could not believe that any of her Ministers would 'sacrifice' Britain's honour or safety; Constantinople had been defined as a vital British interest and should therefore be protected by whatever means available.[33] Northcote told Salisbury on 8 February that 'we shall do no good by confidential communications and shall only make ourselves contemptible. A bold move . . . is really the safest, for Russia cannot with any decency object'; he wanted to send the fleet up to Constantinople on the excuse of saving British lives, and, at the same time, invite the other maritime Powers to do likewise; he also wanted to announce the fact to the House that same evening.[34]

Derby, whose faith in Shuvalov seemed to have been justified, remained immune to the popular outcries. With a favourable reply from France to the idea of sending ships through the Straits, discussion at Cabinet on 8 February allowed Derby to suggest that there was no need for immediate action, and that perhaps only part of the fleet should go since this looked less like a 'menacing' military demonstration. It was a sign of Northcote's ability to vacillate that in the face of Derby's arguments he sided with him against Salisbury and Manners, who would have preferred to send the whole fleet up; in the end, Derby had his way.[35] He told the Queen that this should go 'far to satisfy those who complained of government inaction';[36] she knew otherwise – she was one of those, and she was far from satisfied when Disraeli told her of the decision.[37] In a letter marked by constant underlinings and exclamation marks, she fulminated that 'thanks to the <u>cowardly</u> conduct of Lord Derby and Lord Carnarvon',[38] she felt 'deeply humiliated'; her own 'first impulse would be to throw everything up, and to lay down the thorny crown, which she feels little satisfaction in retaining if the position of this country is to remain as it is now'. She stressed, the '<u>absolute necessity</u> of this country's interests' being secured in the conference, and their being '<u>defended by force</u> if <u>necessary</u>. This the Queen <u>does insist on</u>, and does <u>expect</u> . . . We must see our <u>rights secured</u>.' Disraeli could only apologise in his most courtier-like manner; but he made it clear that between the Atrocitarians, the want of allies and the lack of Cabinet unity, he could hardly be blamed for what had happened. The vote of money from the House provided the means for preparing for war, he reminded her, so the present situation was 'not a conclusion, or a catastrophe'; it was, he wrote (in a phrase which would be made more famous by one of his successors), 'not the beginning of the end; it is the end of the beginning'. She could, of course, always dismiss him and appoint a new government – from the Opposition.[39] There was no more talk of abdication from the Widow of Windsor.

The Queen's opprobrious view of Derby reflected what had now become a widespread gossip campaign of great scurrility directed at both him and Lady Derby: their character, patriotism and honour were assailed in both the lower organs of the press and the higher reaches of Society.[40] Rumours spread rapidly, as the foundations of the 'black legend' were laid: Derby was supposed to have had a 'breakdown' and was drinking to excess; 'ribald verses' about Lady Derby and Shuvalov circulated in the London Clubs; no rumour was so preposterous that it failed to find an airing.[41] This was an atmosphere in which political reputations built up over decades could be corroded in days; Derby's never recovered from his inability to share the popular hysteria.[42] Shuvalov told Gorchakov on 14 February that the Clubs were 'signing petitions' for Derby's dismissal: 'they cry loudly that if England's humiliation should last a few days longer, they would hang Lord Derby on the first tree of Hyde Park.' He noted, with some justice, that 'at great crises nations need expiatory victims' and that Derby had been chosen for the role.[43]

The struggle to prevent an Anglo-Russian war from breaking out now narrowed down to the question of whether or not to order Hornby's squadron through the Straits to Constantinople. By 10 February, it was clear that Abdülhamid dared not give his permission because the Russians would probably retaliate by occupying Constantinople. Salisbury told Disraeli that day they had reached the 'critical moment', and that if the fleet did not go through the Straits, 'our position will be utterly ridiculous. We shall disgust our friends in the country and lose all weight in Europe'; he urged him to order Hornby through the Straits.[44] Derby found Disraeli 'excited and inclined to swagger', when he saw him on 11 February; he was 'saying war was unavoidable' and that although it would last 'three years it would be a glorious and successful war for England'. Derby was 'disgusted with his reckless way of talking, and evident enjoyment of an exciting episode in history, with which his name was to be joined';[45] this was the antithesis of Conservative statesmanship.

Derby agreed that if the Russians occupied Constantinople, the 'anti-Russian feeling here will go beyond all control', but he still feared that sending Hornby through the Straits was more, rather than less, likely to produce that result.[46] He told Disraeli on 10 February that Shuvalov had shown him a telegram from his Government saying that the Russians would not pass through the Dardanelles without provocation;[47] sending Hornby's fleet to Constantinople would be offering that provocation – and it would break international law. The Cabinet reached a classic compromise when they discussed the issue on 11 February: Hornby would be told that he could pass through the Straits, but time would be given for Layard to reduce the risk of war with Russia by getting the permission of the Sultan.[48] It was clear that if the Russians occupied Gallipoli and Constantinople after the British fleet had passed through the Straits, it would be at great risk,[49] but Ministers now seemed willing to accept the possibility of war.

Derby tried to secure Turkish assent to the British proposal by stressing that there was no war-like intent.[50] He also attempted to reassure Shuvalov, but received a warning that his Government had sent a circular to the Chancelleries of Europe stating that it might become necessary to occupy the Turkish capital.[51] Noticing the public mood (something his post-bag made impossible to miss), Derby thought: 'We never needed coolness more, and there is not much of it in the Cabinet.' He explained to Shuvalov how unwise Russia's action in concealing the terms of the armistice had been; public feeling had made inaction impossible.[52] But Shuvalov was under pressure from the Tsar and the Commander-in-Chief to Constantinople. He assured Derby on 13 February that such an occupation would only be temporary, and, as with the despatch of the British fleet, solely in order to protect public order in Constantinople. Derby responded that there was no parallel between the two moves, and told Shuvalov that he could 'not answer for the consequences' if the Russians went ahead; he also asked for reassurances that the Russians would not move troops to Gallipoli or otherwise threaten the 'communications of the English fleet'.[53] When Layard reported that the Sultan wanted to know what answer he should give to the Russian request to allow troops to enter his capital, Derby checked with Disraeli before returning the only possible one: the Russians should not enter Constantinople.[54] Shuvalov warned Gorchakov that unless they gave that assurance, Derby would fall and there would be war – in a given number of hours.[55]

Disraeli was certainly preparing for war. At Cabinet on 14 February he proposed that Britain should have some permanent base in the eastern Mediterranean which could act as a *point d'appui* for the Ottoman Empire: 'if we could combine with it the presence of an English fleet in the Bosphorus, and a British army corps at Gallipoli', then Britain could maintain the Ottoman Empire as 'an independent and vigorous' Power, if not a first-class one.[56] Other Ministers were seized with the idea, and there was 'wild, excited talk' about which island to occupy. Derby, who deprecated this sort of expensive commitment as delivering little more than a publicity coup at great expense to the public purse, 'resisted the various schemes suggested to the best of my power'; but he went back to the Foreign Office 'ill-pleased and despondent'.[57] Conservative Ministers no longer seemed disposed to act on what he considered Conservative principles.

At the Carlton Club they passed a motion of no confidence in Derby; in the press, they poured vitriol over him; even historians have interpreted Shuvalov's praise for his cool nerve as 'an almost complete loss of control rather than an effort of will and determination'.[58] In fact, Shuvalov was, for once, reporting no more than the plain truth; it was Derby's cool head, along with his own strenuous efforts, which helped prevent Britain and Russia stumbling into an unnecessary war. Alexander II took the passage of Hornby's squadron as a personal insult, as well as a violation of international law, and told the Grand Duke Nicholas on 10 February to arrange for a Russian entry into Constantinople to protect the Christians; should the Porte object, 'we must be prepared to occupy Constantinople by force'. Although Gorchakov managed to persuade him to make a Russian occupation dependent upon a British landing at Constantinople, the Tsar actually sent both telegrams. As an added complication, the Grand Duke received the second one first — and that was three days later.[59]

On 15 February, the Cabinet approved the terms of the note to be given to Shuvalov warning the Russians from occupying Gallipoli; it was also agreed that the fleet should be pulled back from Constantinople itself. Derby thought that although this still carried the risk of war, it at least left the Russians knowing what they had to do to avoid it; and he still thought that they could avoid it. Ironically, it was the two Service Ministers, Gathorne-Hardy and Smith, who were now also in favour of a cautious line; Salisbury was not.[60] Derby added weight to the warning by telling Shuvalov on 16 February that Austria would certainly join England's side if Constantinople was occupied; a warning which he passed straight on to Gorchakov.[61]

Contrary to the suppositions of those who assume that he was now 'out of the loop',[62] Derby was well aware of Disraeli's so-called 'secret negotiations' with the Austrians. This was the one part of Disraeli's policy of which Derby heartily approved: 'with Austria as an ally, the risk of war appears to me almost none'.[63] 'Real control' of British foreign policy was not 'in the hands of a secret, unofficial committee' with Derby 'virtually never consulted'.[64] Derby knew what was going to happen if the Russians occupied Constantinople or the Gallipoli Peninsula, and he was not being daring, or indiscreet, in telling Shuvalov that such actions would cause a war; he wanted him to know that the Russians had run out of options: it was war or compromise. Shuvalov was not intriguing or gambling when he warned Gorchakov; he was telling the truth. Like Derby, his career did not benefit from his efforts; and unlike Derby, he probably took less comfort from the knowledge that he had acted in the public good.[65] He told Gorchakov on 17 February that he had done his best to prevent *'une explosion de la part des Ministers anglais'*, and that 'Lord Derby's attitude' and the 'personal *rapprochement* which has come about between him and me in these last grave circumstances, are the sole means of which I dispose'. With a pardonable degree of hyperbole (knowing how unpopular his line was in St Petersburg), he described himself as raising Derby's 'fallen courage' and sustaining his 'force of resistance when almost exhausted'.[66]

At 4.30 on the afternoon of 16 February, Derby sent a circular to all British ambassadors, asking them to inform the Government to which they were accredited that Britain thought that 'the assembling of the Conference' seemed the only way out of the 'present political complications', and to urge all neutral countries to press this solution upon Russia 'forthwith'.[67] Derby spent Sunday quietly at home, enjoying the first intimations of spring; Disraeli spent it preparing for war, writing to Gathorne-Hardy to ensure that everything was ready militarily for the despatch of the Expeditionary Force: 'There is no time to be lost, much depends upon the power to act, when we do, with promptness.'[68]

At Cabinet on Monday afternoon, Ministers began discussing arrangements for military action, but news arrived that telegrams had been received from Gorchakov; although they had not all been deciphered, their 'general contents were satisfactory'.[69] Later on Shuvalov brought the texts of the official replies: Russia would not advance to the Bulair Lines on the Gallipoli Peninsula provided the British did not land troops. It was, Derby noted, 'a fair offer, as matters stand'.[70] There was no mention of Constantinople or the conference, but it was hardly an answer which required the Expeditionary Force to leave; indeed, quite the opposite. Derby had, as it turned out, spent his Sunday more profitably than Disraeli.

When Andrassy had first suggested a conference at the end of January, Bismarck had been less than happy with the idea. He feared the creation of an Anglo-Austrian 'Crimean' coalition against Russia which would leave France as the 'second strongest military power in Europe' and increase the chance 'she would attack us at the earliest possible opportunity'.[71] The Russians wanted him to put pressure on Andrassy to keep him away from the British, but Bismarck feared that this might lead to the Hungarian's fall from power, an event which might end the pro-German orientation of Austria's foreign policy. The Crown Princess, hardly known for her partisanship of the Chancellor, reassured her mother that Bismarck had 'no wish whatever to see "everyone quarrelling", he must not quarrel with Russia but can only regret any thing that strengthened her or weakens England's position. This is self evident and needs no explanation: he would be a madman to wish anything else.'[72] Since the Russians were willing to attend a conference to discuss the peace terms, Bismarck supported the idea, even acceding to the request that it should be in Berlin.[73] In the Reichstag on 19 February, Bismarck declared that Germany's role would be that of 'an honest broker who really wants to do business'.[74] Derby thought the speech 'cynical' and suspected that Bismarck would welcome an Anglo-Russian war.[75]

When the Cabinet met on 19 February, Ministers were grudgingly satisfied with the Russian assurance that they would not send troops to Gallipoli provided the British did not do so. On the issue of the conference, Derby strongly pressed the 'absolute impossibility of my going'; the likes of Andrassy and Gorchakov could go to such events since they only had to implement the orders of their Emperors, but an English Foreign Secretary who stayed at a conference for a month or so 'simply abdicates his place as a member of a Cabinet. He cannot settle European questions on his own account.'[76]

It was too much, in the fevered climate engendered by events at Constantinople, to expect that matters would move smoothly towards a conference. On the evening of 20 February, the news came in that the Russians were demanding the cession of the whole Turkish fleet, and that they had despatched 30,000 troops to occupy Constantinople.[77] However, when the Cabinet met to discuss the situation on the 21st, there had been no developments. It was plain that for Hornby's squadron to try to resist any transfer of the Turkish fleet would be tantamount to a declaration of war, and so that was ruled out; nor, given Russia's promises about Gallipoli, could the Expeditionary Force be landed. It was decided that Derby should prepare a note for Shuvalov declaring that in the event of Russian troops occupying Constantinople without the consent of the Sultan, Britain would withdraw her Ambassador, Lord Augustus Loftus, from St Petersburg and 'decline to go into Conference while the occupation lasts'. This went further than the Government had yet gone, but, as Derby noted, it stopped short of either a declaration of war or even a threat to make it; it would apply only if the Sultan did not consent to a Russian occupation; and no one could imagine having a conference whilst Russian troops remained in Constantinople.[78]

This was all a considerable triumph for Derby's cautious diplomacy – much to the disgust of the more bellicose sections of the press, whose mood was expressed by *Punch* in a parody of the great patriotic song: 'We don't want to go to war; for, by jingo if we do, we may lose our ships, and lose our men, and what's worse our money too.' Much of what was objected to was laid down to Derby's account; but not, of course, in a complimentary manner.[79] Baulked of Russian blood, the great Jingo public settled for Derby's reputation.

In the absence of any dramatic developments, Ministers could only watch and wait. The Austrian alliance continued to be a chimera, with Andrassy offering 'neither cooperation, nor security' and yet wanting subsidies which 'no House of Commons would grant'.[80] The one point which continued to worry Derby was the recrudescence at Cabinet on 23 February of the idea of seizing a Turkish island: 'I could not well make out what the island is wanted for, or what the possession of it is to do for us: still less what right we are supposed to have there.' Derby confined himself, in the vague state of the discussion, to indicating his disagreement with the idea.[81]

From Constantinople came the word that peace was about to be signed between Turkey and Russia at a place called San Stefano; there was no demand for a surrender of the Turkish fleet and Constantinople remained unoccupied. Derby continued to tread the thin line he had set himself. The Russians were in receipt of warnings from Britain, but Derby wanted some public reassurance for them that if they abided by them, there would be no war. Speaking in the Lords on 25 February, he said that there were only three policies open to Britain: co-operation with Russia, which was impossible; neutrality; or to maintain the Treaties of 1856 and 1871 by war. Since, however, 'the great majority of the nation held that adherence to the policy which led to the Crimean War was no longer desirable', only the second policy was practicable. This was brave talk; that same day crowds smashed Gladstone's windows and there was a riot in Hyde Park.[82] Derby was unmoved by such things, and did not greatly notice the hostility which his name now aroused. There was, he noted in his diary on 27 February, 'no difference of opinion, so far as present action is concerned, between my colleagues and myself'.[83] To miss the slings and arrows of criticism was one thing; to miss the growing distance between him and his colleagues was a different matter. The first sort of blindness had enabled him to keep his head and to remain calm at the heart of the storm, thus helping to avoid war; the second cost him his career.

9

Disraeli's Triumph

The Liverpool middle classes with whom Derby had most contact were 'in favour of peace if possible', for much the same reasons which animated his own Country Party Conservatism.[1] When he told the Lords on 25 February that the 'great majority of the nation held that adherence to the policy which led to the Crimean War was no longer desirable',[2] he was speaking with confidence of the sensible portion of the political nation. But Lord Sandon, President of the Board of Education, and a Lancashire neighbour of Derby's, noted that 'the bulk of our party ... as far as the leading men are concerned, are thoroughly at one with the "firm policy" of the Government. Descending in the social scale the feeling is almost unanimous for firmness and determined attitude.'[3] This union between Society and the music hall would outflank Derby.

Disraeli's schemes to deliver a great public triumph for his Tory Jingoism entailed an inevitable clash with Derby, who first began to get some notion of what was afoot on 27 February. Ministers agreed at Cabinet that Russia should be asked for details of the peace settlement with Turkey, but Salisbury argued that since the 'balance of power in south-east Europe' would be affected, Britain should 'secure some position to give us back the influence which we had' by seizing an island somewhere. Derby thought little of the idea and later drafted a telegram for Loftus embodying what he had told Shuvalov, who had raised the question the previous day: namely that the notion was a dangerous one which might well lead the Russians to abandon their pledges about not occupying Constantinople and Gallipoli. The flurry of protests from his colleagues revealed not only the gap which had opened up between him and them, but also one of the ways in which secrets leaked out.[4]

Northcote wrote to Derby and to Disraeli that evening saying that he and seven other Cabinet Ministers had perused the draft over dinner at the Duke of Cambridge's and that 'all our eight heads of hair stood upright' at Derby's words, which they did not think 'expressed the policy of the Government'.[5] Derby did not take kindly to Northcote's letter, telling him that if important drafts were circulated 'at dinners where necessarily others besides our colleagues are present . . . it is easy to understand how so little of what we do or say is left secret'. He reiterated his view that it would not be 'unreasonable' of the Russians to react to such a 'violent' British action by treating it as absolving them from their pledges.[6] But the draft was not sent. Philip Currie, who only eighteen months before had been grateful to Derby for defending him from Disraeli's wrath over the mix-up over the Berlin Memorandum, wrote to Layard in Constantinople that there was a 'very strong feeling against Lord Derby who is denounced on his own side as a traitor. . . . He will be thrown overboard by his colleagues if he gives them a chance.'[7]

Signs that this was so were abundant. Cairns complained to Disraeli on 28 February about the terms in which Derby had couched a telegram enquiring about the peace terms which had just been signed at San Stefano between Russia and Turkey: 'I own I cannot feel comfortable in appearing in the present crisis to be sending the Russians a civil message.'[8] Disraeli passed the complaint on, warning Derby that 'the uneasiness and dissatisfaction of the country on this head are great'.[9] Derby responded sharply that he had pressed Shuvalov 'as strongly as courtesy allowed': 'we cannot demand as a right' the details of a treaty 'not yet negotiated'. With heavy sarcasm, Derby commented that he had not been aware that 'it was the desire of the Cabinet to shape their enquiry so as to bring about a refusal to answer it; nor does this seem to me to be good diplomacy'.[10]

When the issue of seizing a Turkish island came up at Cabinet on 2 March, Derby put his objections at length. If Turkey refused her consent, then Britain would be breaking international law, and to what effect when she already possessed Malta? Such an act of 'spoliation' might encourage other Powers to follow Britain's example, and the Russians to abandon their pledges about occupying Gallipoli and Constantinople. That made him wonder whether this was what Disraeli wanted – namely to 'bring about a collision in such a way that most of the blame will be thrown on Russia'. It would also, Derby suspected, mean that the idea of a conference would be 'knocked on the head'. When the Cabinet authorised a study of the idea, Derby noted that he had 'laid the ground for my resignation'.[11]

In Disraeli's mind, the Turkish island gambit was only part of a grander design to secure Britain's position in the eastern Mediterranean by means of a League of Mediterranean Powers, with France, Austria, Italy and Greece.[12] This would have meant a revolution in British foreign policy. A Mediterranean League, had it come off then, would have freed Britain from the need for German mediation, released France from isolation, pushed Italy into Britain's sphere of influence and confined Russia without the need for a war; it might also have provided a way of finally getting Andrassy to commit himself, and have drawn out the Italians who had been indicating their anxiety about Russia's intentions.[13] Disraeli's 'secret of secrets' involved a 'considerable number of points', as he told the Queen, and its success depended on 'inviolable confidence', which meant that it had to be managed 'by private communication with colleagues, & not be brought, at least at present, before the entire Cabinet'.[14]

Disraeli tried to insinuate the first part of the scheme past Derby on 6 March, when he suggested that they should respond to

Abdülhamid's request to withdraw their fleet by asking to occupy an island base. But Derby would not agree, fearing that if the Russians followed suit it would precipitate rather than prevent conflict. He dismissed the notion as driven by Disraeli's 'wish to do something that would please the public here'.[15] This was entirely correct, but Disraeli was bent on his triumph and now prepared to see Derby go.[16]

Disraeli obtained the excuse he needed to act when news of the terms of the Treaty of San Stefano became known on 4 March. It was pure Pan-Slavism, depriving Turkey of vast tracts of territory and creating a 'Big Bulgaria' with a Mediterranean coastline. The Tsar had been thoroughly irritated by the British, and had responded to the warning that Loftus might be removed by saying, 'L'Angleterre fera ce qu'elle voudra [England can do as she pleases].' The fact that the final settlement was cast in the form of a treaty rather than a protocol (the details of which might be settled later) marked a victory for Ignatyev over Gorchakov.[17]

Despite the outcry in the London press, there was still support for Derby, at least in Cabinet, on the question of the occupation of a Turkish island.[18] On 6 March, both Gathorne-Hardy and Northcote 'wavered and showed a disposition to revoke their opinion' in favour of the scheme, and it was Salisbury and Disraeli who both 'laid stress on the argument that unless we do something decided, we shall not be treated with respect, or believed to be in earnest when the conference meets'. The projected League also came under criticism from Tenterden and Lyons as well as Derby, Gathorne-Hardy and Northcote.[19] Despite Disraeli's confident report to the Queen afterwards that his policy had been backed, and that whether Derby 'resigns or not' the Cabinet had 'taken the management of the FO into its own hands',[20] the truth was more prosaic.

That Salisbury should have been the most ardent advocate of the plan to seize an island was, to Derby, evidence in favour of the rumours that 'he wishes to be in my place'. He certainly took a most Disraelian line when Derby argued that any occupation was unnecessary and contrary to international law, responding that it was necessary to satisfy public opinion; he 'treated scruples of this kind with marked contempt, saying truly enough, that if our ancestors had cared for the rights of other people, the British Empire would not have been made'.[21] In the end, Derby acquiesced in Cairns's lawyerly proposal that in the event of the peace treaty or the proposed conference proving insufficiently respectful of Britain's interests, 'a new naval station in the east of the Mediterranean must be obtained, and if necessary by force'.[22] Disraeli thought that Derby would go; Derby saw no immediate need for resignation over such a hypothetical possibility.[23]

Thus it was that he was able to maintain some influence over the presentation of government policy. When he told the Lords that evening that they had accepted the proposal to hold a conference in Berlin, he said that they wanted a 'European' rather than a 'Russian' settlement, but he added that Britain's obligations to Turkey under the 1856 Peace of Paris did not extend to making war on her behalf.[24] His words were not those which Disraeli or Salisbury would have used, and they did little to increase his popularity with those who were thirsting for action.

Shuvalov described conditions in England as defying 'all logical appreciation; it has latterly become no longer political, but psychological, dependent not upon events but on the temperament of the English and . . . public opinion'.[25] But Russian evasiveness about whether they would be willing to submit the whole San Stefano Treaty to the proposed European conference played 'only too well the game of those who want to prevent an understanding being come to'.[26] There were certainly plenty of those about.

On 18 March, the Cabinet agreed to repeat the warning to the Russians not to occupy any point on the Bosphorus or at Gallipoli.[27] Derby had no objection to a friendly repetition of a warning already given, and although worried by Salisbury's 'violent' tone, readily gave his assent and conveyed the message to Shuvalov. However, the following morning the newspapers were full of the story that a *fresh* warning had been given to Russia. Derby's protest to Disraeli showed his conviction that this was no accident.[28] The whole purpose of deciding to keep the renewal of the warning secret was in order that it might retain the character of a friendly warning, and not assume that of a public defiance: 'I wish I could think that the disclosure was the result of accident or indiscretion. But the facts point to a different conclusion'; 'What can one infer' from the fact that information which was bound to increase tension between Russia and England had been leaked to a newspaper which was known to be in favour of Disraeli's bellicose line? He warned that he would bring the matter up in Cabinet.[29] Disraeli passed Derby's complaint on to Salisbury, who jocularly remarked that he knew no *Telegraph* journalists by sight and could not think how the secret had slipped out; he wondered whether it might have had something to do with Derby's famous 'notes' on Cabinet discussions.[30]

When Derby saw Shuvalov on 20 March, he urged on him the importance of a Russian answer to the British conditions. Shuvalov did not tell Derby that Gorchakov had already said that the British fleet had no business to be in the Sea of Marmora and that he would not agree to the British conditions.[31] Instead, he urged Derby to delay any provocative action on the British side whilst he strove to find ground for a compromise. Derby told Shuvalov the following day that the Cabinet's view was there was no restriction implied in the condition that Russia should lay the whole Treaty before the Congress; this was not a view shared in St Petersburg.[32] The following day the terms of the San Stefano Treaty were finally published in the British press. Disraeli noted with some satisfaction that 'People are very alarmed and think war instantaneous. I do not.' San Stefano appeared to justify everything Disraeli had said about Russian ambitions knowing no limits; it was time for action.[33]

The arrival on 25 March of Russia's rejection of Britain's conditions completed Derby's discomfiture. With the news of the Russian response being confirmed on 26 March, Disraeli told the Queen that he had summoned a Cabinet for the morrow which would recommend the immediate calling up of the Reserves, the despatch of troops from India and the occupation of 'two important points in the Levant'.[34] He told Gathorne-Hardy that the 'critical time has come' and that only a 'bold' and 'determined' policy could 'secure' peace.

By this time the long campaign against Derby had damaged his reputation sufficiently to make his loss less serious than it would have seemed earlier, and now Disraeli had the support of Gathorne-Hardy, Salisbury, Cairns and Northcote before the Cabinet met on 27 March.[35] Disraeli stated bluntly: 'All our attempts to be moderate and neutral, and avoid collision with Russia, have lessened our influence with Russia, and caused it to be thought that we had no power'; now Russia had imposed a settlement on Turkey which was far from moderate and which she was refusing to submit to a Congress: 'a bold policy will secure peace: one of conciliation will end in war'. He proposed the various measures that had been agreed on, and, with the exception of Derby, there was unanimity. Derby did agree with Salisbury's comment that 'no compromise was possible', and told his colleagues that they had come 'to the point where the two roads diverge'; he could not agree to Disraeli's proposals 'and it was understood that my resignation was to follow'.[36] Disraeli wanted the Cabinet's decision and Derby's resignation to be kept secret until the next day.

Derby saw Shuvalov after the meeting and gave him 'in confidence a hint as to what is going on'.[37] In fact, Derby's opening comment, that this would be their 'last conversation', was so gnomic that Shuvalov assumed that he meant that war had been decided upon.[38] Derby told him that he was going to resign, and did one last service to his country by adding that he was sure that his colleagues did not want war, and by suggesting that a Russian proposal for direct negotiations, which allowed Britain to have a naval station in the region, might provide a way forward. On the afternoon of 28 March, following the announcement by Disraeli that the Reserves had been called up, Derby resigned. Considerations of national security and confidentiality precluded his revealing the rest of the decisions reached by the Cabinet, which only strengthened the impression that he had gone because of a want of courage.[39]

Derby's speech was a dignified and honourable one. He paid

tribute to the Prime Minister and his colleagues: 'No man would willingly break, even for a time, political and personal ties of long standing; and in the public life of the present day there are few political and personal ties closer, or of older date than those which unite me with my noble friend.' This time there was no letter to Disraeli, but Derby wrote to the Queen saying that 'nothing but a strong conviction of duty to the State could have made him break off from colleagues whom he respected and regarded . . . especially his old friend Lord Beaconsfield from whom it is a real pain to be separated';[40] the Queen thought it 'a very good and proper letter'.[41] Only a few days before, Derby had noted the views of the Duke of Bedford that 'family life and political life' were incompatible. Such a view would, he thought, 'be fatal to the existence of a governing class'.[42] Derby had tried to act on the principles which informed the Toryism of that old governing class, but he had not been willing to confront directly Disraeli's subversion of them.

Disraeli responded in kind to Derby's comments and privately offered to put his name forward for the vacant Garter. It may be doubted whether the Queen, who was delighted at Derby's departure, would have consented to such an action, but Derby spared everyone the trouble of making the attempt by declining it.[43] It would have been out of character for him to have done anything else; showy decorations, like showy foreign policies, were not in his line. He told Northcote that he wanted to 'rest for the present, and take no more part in public business than is forced upon me'. There seems to have been no question in his mind that the breach of 'political ties of long-standing' would be 'temporary';[44] this was not to be the case.

The strategic objectives of Disraeli's policy marked a break with mid-Victorian practice and the assumptions which had governed it. Derby suspected that Disraeli's ultimate object was to 'change the map of Europe'.[45] When he heard Disraeli and Salisbury insist that 'unless we do something decided, we shall not be treated with respect, or believed to be in earnest when the conference meets,'[46] he did not readily understand what they meant. The notion that the essential thing in diplomacy was not to 'lose popular favour' was not one to which he could subscribe; the Conservative Party was there to act as a brake on ill-considered enthusiasms, not to promote them.[47] In 1864, scornful of Palmerston's 'portentous mixture of baseness and bounce', Lord Salisbury had censured his foreign policy for giving in to the public desire for 'cheap war';[48] Salisbury may no longer have held to that criticism by 1878, but Derby did. In retrospect, Salisbury was inclined to think that the crisis inside the Government had lasted so long because of Disraeli's defects as a leader; his 'want of firmness' and concern that 'the party must on no account be broken up' made him 'shrink from exercising coercion on any of his subordinates'.[49] But it had been more complicated than that. Had Derby taken the lead in December 1877, then Salisbury might have backed him; Derby's failure to do so left Salisbury following the only man who would take that lead – Disraeli; that it brought him the Foreign Secretaryship, and appreciably closer to the premiership, were no doubt incentives.

Traditionally, historians have burst into whatever their version of applause is when dealing with the advent of Salisbury to the Foreign Office. It has been said of his famous circular of 1 April that it 'at last broke the deadlock, allowing an exhausted Russia to give ground without loss of face'; this illustrates the dangers of the broad perspective in diplomatic history.[50] The international tension actually continued for more than another month, and to some extent the removal of the Derby–Shuvalov link actually increased the chances of a war.[51] The only place that tension disappeared was the British Cabinet, and henceforth it becomes possible to write about a single British policy. Disraeli himself discerned something of this after Derby made a speech in the Lords on 8 April defending himself. Disraeli, although furious at the revelation of Cabinet disunity, told the Queen that Derby's speech 'has benefited Your Majesty's Government abroad. It marks still more decidedly the difference between the late & the present policies of Your Majesty's advisers.' He added that all that he had 'devised and contemplated will now be carried into effect, and England already occupies a leading, and soon a commanding position' on the European stage.[52]

This was not quite true, but then it was not meant to be. The Mediterranean League crumbled into dust as not even the Italians would respond to the idea.[53] Salisbury's circular certainly drew a distinction between those parts of San Stefano which were open to negotiation, and those, such as Bulgaria's frontiers, which were intolerable,[54] and as such constituted an invitation to the Russians to negotiate; the announcement on 17 April of the calling up of the Reserves and the despatch of Sepoys to the Mediterranean was an indication of what might happen if there was no negotiation, but the invitation was accepted because Russia's *Dreikaiserbund* allies had found the San Stefano Treaty as hard to swallow as had British public opinion,[55] and Salisbury was able to rely on Bismarck's good offices as mediator.[56]

In St Petersburg, there was something approaching chaos. Gorchakov was too sick to direct affairs, but not so sick that he would cede their direction to others. Ignatyev, 'the one-eyed among the blind', used his detailed knowledge to argue against Shuvalov's idea of negotiating with the British, but his own line of policy had produced no success, and with the Russian army before Constantinople decimated by disease, and the Minister of War, Milyutin, warning that the national finances could not stand the strain of another campaign, Alexander II declared that it was a matter of indifference to him how many Bulgarias there were.[57]

Salisbury knew that Bismarck shared his view that 'a Congress would be of little value unless an understanding had previously been come to on the chief points at issue'.[58] It was Salisbury who formulated a list of British objections to San Stefano:[59] 'it admits a new naval Power [Bulgaria] to the coasts of the Ægean'; 'it threatens with extinction the non-Slav populations of the Balkan peninsula'; and it rendered the Porte dependent upon Russia.[60] The Russians proved willing to concede upon the Aegean coast, and to let the Balkan mountains delimit the southern border of an autonomous Bulgaria. But the Tsar was not willing to let the Turks keep troops in the part of Bulgaria south of the mountains, and he wanted compensation for Montenegro in the form of territory and independence. The Russians also wanted to have Bessarabia and parts of Asia such as Kars and Batoum.[61] Salisbury persuaded Disraeli to agree to these terms, but only at the price of conceding his demand for an Anglo-Turkish alliance to secure the future position of the Porte. Salisbury was 'not a believer in the possibility of setting the Turkish Government on its legs again, as a genuinely reliable Power',[62] but since Disraeli appeared to be, he consented to the alliance, and to the acquisition of Cyprus as a base from which England could help the Turks.[63] Disraeli exulted to Queen Victoria: 'If this policy be carried into effect . . . your Majesty need fear no coalition of Emperors. It will weld together your Majesty's Indian Empire and Great Britain.'[64] On 30 May, an Anglo-Russian protocol was signed, and the way clear for the Congress to meet in Berlin on 13 June.

Bismarck once said that 'the foreign policy of a great country cannot be put at the disposal of a parliamentary majority without getting onto a false track'.[65] Salisbury was inclined to agree that a country like Britain, 'which is popularly governed', could not be counted on 'to act in any uniform or consistent system of policy', and would therefore 'probably abandon the task of resisting any further Russian advance to the Southward in Asia, if nothing but speculative arguments can be advanced in favour of action'; but he was convinced that it would 'cling to any military post occupied by England as tenaciously as it has clung by Gibraltar'.[66] From that point of view the acquisition of Cyprus was a sop to democracy.

The Berlin Congress was consecrated to power-politics,[67] but it resembled a home for geriatric invalids. Bismarck had spent most of the year at his estates complaining of his nerves and digestion – usually before devouring a massive evening meal washed down with copious draughts of champagne and stout, after which he would settle down and smoke too many cigars. He loathed Berlin in the summer, and when he arrived there he was all but unrecognisable, hidden behind a great silver beard.[68] Disraeli, who had not met Bismarck for sixteen years, was astonished by the change in him: 'Then, he was a very tall man with black hair, a puggish nose and a pallid face and a waist like a wasp. Now he is a giant, his face ruddy, his locks and head silvery-white; on the whole, however, a very effective appearance.'[69]

At the age of seventy-three and a martyr to bronchitis and asthma (no doubt worsened by his smoking with Bismarck, but business exacted its price), Disraeli was advised to stay at home for the good of his health; but neither his infirmities nor the threat of assassination[70] would keep him from his hour of triumph. He assured the Queen that he would 'attend the first meetings of the Congress, and exhibit his full powers, and then return to England, leaving Lord Salisbury to complete all the details of which he is consummate master'.[71] A new doctor ameliorated the worst effects of his illness with the use of homeopathic medicines,[72] but it was sheer willpower which enabled him stay in Berlin for the whole Congress. When he had risen to make his maiden-speech in the Commons those many years ago, resplendent in lovelocks, ruffles and lace, he had been jeered and heckled, and had resumed his seat muttering that the 'time will come when you will listen to me'; now it had. The Congress would be his apotheosis. The remnants of the lovelocks were still there, reminding the young German diplomat, Bernhard von Bülow, of a 'Galician Jew', but the Regency finery had long ago given way to more sober, yet elegant garb: he was 'always very smartly dressed, in the latest fashion, a true British gentleman'. However 'foreign' his appearance, 'English interests only, English wishes and advantage inspired his acts'. Bismarck, who had started the proceedings with a prejudice against Disraeli, 'soon fell under his spell'.[73]

If their first meeting at the Congress inspired mutual admiration between the old Jew and the *Reichsgründer*, there was no such outcome to the renewal of the Bismarck–Gorchakov relationship. The ageing Russian saw the Congress as his chance to bid a grand farewell to the European diplomatic scene of which he had been an ornament for half a century; as he put it to one of his assistants: '*Je ne veux pas m'en aller comme une lampe qui file, mais comme un astre qui se couche* [I don't want to go out like a spluttering lamp, but rather like a falling star].'[74] He used this argument to prevail

SPLENDID ISOLATION?

against the Tsar's wish that he should not attend the Congress. So, at the age of nearly eighty, 'much enfeebled' and in a wheelchair, Prince Gorchakov attended his last diplomatic function.[75] Salisbury, who was meeting him for the first time, described him as a 'little insignificant old man' whose 'presence materially complicates matters'.[76] His vanity and self-regard profoundly irritated Bismarck. Gorchakov missed the first session of the Congress through illness, but made up for his absence at its second meeting. Supported by two stout lackeys, he declaimed in perfect French that his remarks were, as always, 'inspired by his love of truth and of his country'. He then blamed Shuvalov and the Ambassador to Berlin, Paul Oubril, for making more concessions than he would have done in their position. Still, he went on in the grand style, 'Russia only made such sacrifices because of her love of peace, just as she had waged the whole war to help the Near Eastern Christians. Russia was pursuing no selfish or no secret ends.' Now she would 'show the world that she willingly exchanged laurels of victory gained at the cost of so much precious blood, for the palm of peace'.[77] Whilst this orotund and self-regarding oration proceeded, Bismarck, visibly impatient, jotted down the words 'pompos, pompo, pomp, po', which summed up his view of the man he called a 'clown'.

If Bismarck dominated proceedings, it was upon Disraeli that most attention fell. The British Prime Minister was a poor linguist, and one of Lord Odo Russell's main achievements was to persuade him not to speak to the Congress in its official language, French. The task was not easy, since Disraeli, like most poor linguists, was sensitive on this point. But Russell proved himself a master diplomat. He told Disraeli that the *corps diplomatique* were dismayed to hear that he was going to speak French, and before the Prime Minister could take offence, Russell added that they had been looking forward to hearing 'the greatest living master of English oratory' address the Congress in his own tongue. Disraeli either 'took the hint or accepted the compliment'.[78] But like another great orator and Prime Minister whose French was somewhat idiosyncratic,

Disraeli had no difficulty in conveying his meaning by his manner.

Salisbury and Shuvalov had prepared the ground well, and the Anglo-Turkish Convention ensured that even if the Congress collapsed, England would have her stronghold in the eastern Mediterranean. It was little wonder that Disraeli took a hard line – indeed, it was on occasion so hard that Salisbury wondered whether his leader was fully appraised of the pre-Congress deal with Shuvalov.[79] But it was necessary for Disraeli to provide British public opinion with a clear triumph.

When news of the Salisbury–Shuvalov deal of 30 May had been broken by *The Globe* the following day, Salisbury had turned aside anger at the cession of Bessarabia and Batoum by claiming that it was 'wholly unauthentic'; but on 14 June, *The Globe* published the full text, which showed that the two areas had indeed been ceded. Disraeli and Salisbury shrugged this aside publicly,[80] but warned Shuvalov and Bismarck that they could not afford to be seen to make any more concessions. Anglo-Russian arguments over the Bulgarian frontiers went on right up until the final session of the Congress. The impasse produced one of the most dramatic moments of the Congress.[81] Disraeli let Bismarck know that he had ordered a special train to take him from Berlin should the Russians refuse Britain's terms.[82] Historians have, as is their wont, ruined a good story by pointing out that the Tsar's order to yield on the salient points must have been given before all of Disraeli's dramatic gestures, but the Prime Minister's firmness certainly impressed his German hosts.[83] The Russians conceded the essential point of leaving Turkish authority over Eastern Rumelia intact and effective – or at least as effective as the Porte proved able to make it. From Disraeli's point of view, 'Turkey-in-Europe' was saved.[84] Gorchakov stayed sulkily in his quarters, whilst Bismarck celebrated by shaving off his beard and inviting Disraeli to dinner! In response to Turkish protests that they had not been consulted, Bismarck told them to accept what they were given.[85]

The struggle over the Asiatic portion of the Treaty of San

Stefano was more difficult to pursue to a successful conclusion. As Salisbury had foreseen, no one save the English and the Turks much cared what obscure parts of Asia the Russians chose to annex. Salisbury much preferred to negotiate *á deux* and at one remove, with responsibility lying in his own hands, but at Berlin he had to do the former in plenary session – and cope with Disraeli, who, with his 'deafness, ignorance of French, and Bismarck's extraordinary mode of speech', often had the 'dimmest idea of what is going on'.[86] Salisbury failed to impress in the way Disraeli did: the Germans found him too preoccupied with detail; and the Russians thought that his frequent appeals to humanitarian considerations (when it suited English interests) were hypocritical; had they won more of their points, they might have found him more charming.[87]

If it was Salisbury who did the hardest work, it was Disraeli, as Salisbury recognised, who was the key figure on the British side: 'the Jingoes', he told Northcote, 'require to be calmed in their own language', and only Disraeli 'speaks it fluently'.[88] When Andrassy tried to go into depth on the question of Bulgaria's southern frontier, Disraeli declared that 'common persons understand what the line of the Balkans means', and that to indulge Andrassy's 'little interests and obscure influences' would only 'convey an impression that we were surrendering something intelligible and substantial'.[89] He described himself as speaking 'thunder' to Gorchakov about Eastern Rumelia.[90] He was, he told Northcote, 'brought forward as the man of war on all occasions' in order 'to speak like Mars'.[91] He would have made a good headline writer, and, in one sense, that is exactly what he did at Berlin. In terms easily intelligible to the 'popular opinion' which had supported him, he presented a British triumph over cunning foreigners. It is significant in this respect that the revelation of the Salisbury–Shuvalov agreement, in itself a perfectly sensible diplomatic arrangement, should in the opinion of the editor of the *Daily Telegraph* have made the Government more unpopular than it had ever been.[92] The news of the Cyprus Convention, which so outraged Liberals, was, by contrast, 'very well received by the Press and our [Conservative] party generally'.[93]

Salisbury's task with regard to the Asiatic part of the Congress was rendered all the more difficult by the 'extravagant nonsense talked at home about Batoum'.[94] The port, on the north-west coast of Turkey, was, in Salisbury's eyes, of little value to the Russians, but the press had seized on the notion that its cession would threaten the future of Turkey. So in between negotiating on European matters, attending balls organised by the Crown Princess, and trying to keep Disraeli on the straight-and-narrow path when it came to detail, the over-worked Salisbury found himself arguing with Shuvalov over what he considered an entirely unnecessary detail; it was little wonder that his patience began to fray.[95] He found the anxiety expressed by Northcote on the subject of Batoum puzzling, and put it down to 'the hot weather' and 'some violent revulsion of feeling in our party'; he told Disraeli on 2 July that he would 'try to frighten Shou[valoff]'.[96] In the final analysis, the agreement was to prove less satisfactory than the British had hoped; lack of attention to fine detail by Salisbury and some sharp practice by the Russians gave them more than had been thought.[97] But such minutiae were overshadowed by the announcement on 8 July of the Cyprus Convention. It was, the Crown Princess told her delighted mother, 'such a _great_ event. . . . Lord Beaconsfield has . . . restored to his country the prestige of power & dignity it had lost on the Continent.'[98]

The 'achievement of Beaconsfield and Salisbury' has been described as 'a masterpiece of diplomacy for all time'[99] – an opinion endorsed by a delighted Queen Victoria, who awarded them both the Garter. From 10 Downing Street, Disraeli declared that he had returned from Berlin bringing 'Peace with honour', thus setting a precedent which would have but one successor.[100] The acclaim for Disraeli was nationwide and intense; it was the greatest moment of his career. He had set out to do three things: to break up what he thought was a new 'Holy Alliance'; to prevent Russian expansionism in Asia; and to raise the prestige and international standing of Great Britain; in all three areas he had enjoyed a considerable measure of success.[101]

In a speech at a banquet in Knightsbridge, Salisbury claimed that he and Disraeli had simply been picking up the 'broken thread of England's old imperial position'.[102] Had it been left to the likes of Derby, Britain would not have had an Indian Empire. For him, the real question was 'whether we should have given a guarantee of Asiatic Turkey'; not to have done so would have been an evasion of responsibility – in which event 'we ought to renounce Empire'. The loyalty of the peoples of the east was given to those who possessed power, and what chance was there of retaining that of the Indians 'if they know Russia is to be dominant on the Tigris and the Euphrates'?[103]

Derby was less than convinced by the apotheosis of Lord Beaconsfield. Speaking in the Lords on 8 April, he had delivered a cutting attack on the notion of letting public opinion influence diplomacy. When a policy of defending the Turkish Empire had been practicable in 1875 and 1876, the great British public had opposed it in an atmosphere of some hysteria; now people had changed their minds: 'how can they expect to have a foreign policy – I do not say far-sighted, but even consistent and intelligent – if within eighteen months the great majority of them are found asking for things which are directly contradictory?'[104] It was an excellent question, and little wonder that neither Disraeli nor Salisbury addressed it.[105] The *Pall Mall Gazette*, which called this 'the very philosophy of political despair', used it as the occasion to pronounce against 'that terror of the multitude which is visibly overcoming all English public life', and praised Disraeli for holding to his own opinion throughout.[106]

As one contemporary commentator noted, 'Disraeli-Toryism' had 'nothing to do with the Conservatism which is founded on a bias in favour of extreme caution';[107] it represented an 'alliance between "society", the music-halls and Lord Beaconsfield'.[108] That was not an alliance which Derby could possibly have joined. His old private secretary and confidant, Sanderson, wrote that when Derby was a Conservative, he 'always represented the

Liberal, and when a Liberal the Conservative wing' of his Party.[109]

Disraeli's victory required Derby's extrusion. But that was a personal rather than a political caesura. At the time of his resignation, Derby had taken comfort in the reflection that 'where . . . both sides act from strongly-held convictions, there need be, and there is no break of private friendship';[110] but he had been wrong. After a correspondence and friendship going back to 1847, no more letters would be added to the thousands exchanged between him and Disraeli. Derby had 'made a sacrifice of . . . his own personal feelings to a sense of public duty'; but as Lord Halifax wrote to Mary Derby in April 1880 after the defeat of 'Beaconsfieldism', 'it is not often that such conduct is appreciated as it deserves'.[111]

Part Two

Isolation

'We know that we shall maintain against all comers that which we possess, and we know, in spite of the jargon about isolation, that we are amply competent to do so.'

Lord Salisbury, 4 May 1898

10

Beaconsfieldism Falters

Disraeli's apotheosis at Berlin was a triumph for Beaconsfieldism – the respectable name for Jingoism. But the *Pall Mall Gazette* had been correct to comment that 'Nobody can create habits of excitement in a nation with impunity.'[1] Disraeli knew that the Jingo opinion to which he had so successfully appealed would require further sustenance. He told Salisbury in October 1879 that the twin themes of Conservative foreign policy were the 'maintenance of our Empire, and hostility towards Russia'. Despite 'the general depression, a fear of Russia, as the power that will ultimately strike at the roots of our Empire' was, he thought, 'singularly prevalent and is felt even by those who do not publicly or loudly, express it'.[2] Disraeli reminded Salisbury in September that: 'So long as the country thought they had obtained "Peace with Honour", the conduct of HM Government was popular, but if the country finds there is no peace, they will be apt also to conclude there is no honour'; Disraeli saw 'strong symptoms of this feeling becoming very prevalent, & by no means confined to our party'. He had always 'deplored "masterly inactivity" which was certain to bring us to the state of affairs we have now to encounter, but it is not too late to put it all right'.[3]

But the task of satisfying the popular taste for cheap successes abroad was to elude Disraeli as it had Palmerston before him. Disraeli looked towards Afghanistan as the area where he might satisfy popular Russophobia and win further laurels.[4] For the previous half-century, the Russian advance through Central Asia towards the frontiers of India had been a cause of concern to British opinion; the arrival of a Russian mission in Afghanistan in the summer of 1878 seemed, at least to those like Lytton and Disraeli who were apt to see matters in such a way, evidence that a dangerous situation was developing on the North-West Frontier.[5] Disraeli approved of Lytton's idea to press the Emir of Afghanistan to get rid of the Russian mission in Kabul; if that was achieved, Russia would have to 'draw in her horns in every way, if, while very conciliatory in Europe, we are firm'.[6]

But Salisbury was worried about Lytton. He warned Disraeli that his successor at the India Office, Gathorne-Hardy, newly ennobled as Lord Cranbrook, did not 'realise sufficiently the gaudy & theatrical ambition which is the Viceroy's leading passion'.[7] Salisbury had certainly had plenty of experience of this side of Lytton's character. Disraeli's request back in 1876 about the measures which Lytton might be able to take against Russia had filled his mind with 'warlike dreams', and Salisbury had had to telegraph back hastily 'to prevent the immediate annexation of Central Asia'.[8] Salisbury had had to warn Derby the following year that 'Lytton is burning with anxiety to distinguish himself in a great war'.[9] The idea of a 'forward policy' in Afghanistan was one which held few charms for Salisbury. He had warned Disraeli in June 1877 that Lytton seemed to want to 'plunge Affghanistan [sic] into war in order to turn the edge of its sword from us', which, as far as he was concerned, was a 'new policy' which carried great risks. It might work if they were content to see the Emir 'defeated and his kingdom partitioned', but if 'we are not content to let him go, we are exposing ourselves, for a very inadequate object, to the risk of having to undertake costly and difficult operations' north of the Hind-Kush, which would 'tax our resources to the utmost'. Salisbury thought that 'war with Russia along the whole line is an intelligible policy, though I do not think circumstances justify it now. . . . India, for better for worse, must be content to take the English foreign policy of the moment, & work upon it.'[10]

Lytton, however, had his own ideas about British foreign policy. In October 1877, he produced a pamphlet which alleged that British policy was to ally with Russia and France against Germany. Derby characterised it as 'either the result of insanity or intrigue';[11] it suggested, to his mind, 'grave doubts as to the fitness of the man for the place!'[12] But Disraeli, who liked a bit of bluster and brag, kept Lytton on, only to discover, once Salisbury's restraining hand was removed, that Derby had been right.

Lytton, who had long wanted to extend Britain's influence northwards, saw the Russian mission as providing the occasion for 'some new and radical assertion' of British influence in Afghanistan;[13] he demanded the right to send his own mission to Kabul. From London came instructions to send it via Kandahar, but he despatched it through the Khyber Pass, where it was held by Afghan forces; instead of waiting until he received orders to send the mission on, he chose to take responsibility for doing so on his own initiative, which exposed him to a snub from the Emir.[14] Salisbury deprecated being hustled by Lytton into taking precipitate action, and at Cabinet on 25 October 'spoke with great bitterness of the conduct of the Viceroy, and said that, unless curbed, he would bring about some terrible disaster'.[15] But as so often, Salisbury's toughness stopped with talk, and he accepted Cranbrook's decision that Lytton must be supported, even at the risk of war.[16]

Lytton saw himself as implementing a policy which the Cabinet desired but hesitated to approve because of the limitations of 'democracy' – and 'that deformed and abortive offspring of perennial political fornication, the present British constitution'.[17] Lytton thought that 'England is fast losing the instinct and the tact of Empire'.[18] Just as Salisbury combatted Derby's arguments about Cyprus with the rejoinder that there would have been no British Empire at all if his precepts had been followed, so Lytton used the argument of the primacy of imperial interests to buttress his own predispositions. As *The Times* commented on 28 October:

'It is rather late in the day to appeal to Grotius, after we have annexed nearly the whole of India in defiance of his artificial precepts.'[19]

In his speech to the Lord Mayor's Banquet at the Guildhall on 9 November, Disraeli seemed publicly to commit the Government to an annexation of Afghan territory when he spoke about the 'rectification' of India's North-West Frontier.[20] In the ensuing conflict, British arms were victorious and the Government enjoyed a great popular success, with Disraeli taunting the Liberals as being in favour of the 'deleterious doctrine' of 'peace at any price'.[21] In the Lords on 13 February, he declared: 'We have secured that object for which the expedition was undertaken. We have secured that frontier which will, I hope, render our Indian Empire invulnerable.'[22] In early 1879, the Viceroy concluded treaties with the new Emir, Yakub Khan, which seemed to consolidate British influence in Kabul. It seemed as though Lytton's disobedience had, in the grand tradition of British imperial expansion, brought another area under British domination.

But proconsular daring and the assertion of imperial interests did not always deliver the cheap and easy success which seemed to have been won in Afghanistan. Indeed, even whilst the Government was basking in the glow of popular esteem, there came, on 11 February 1879, the news of the massacre of British troops at Isandhlwana, where 13,000 soldiers were killed by the Zulus. This was the bitter fruit of Carnarvon's policy of trying to create a South African federation. Following the annexation of the Boer republics of the Transvaal and the Orange Free State in April 1877, the High Commissioner for South Africa, Sir Bartle Frere, was anxious to push on with plans to create a federation and, without authority from London, insisted on pursuing a forward policy; in this case it meant taking on the main threat to the Boer republics, the Zulus. The hope was that British military successes would reconcile the Boers to rule from Cape Town; the reality was a bloody war with the Zulus which resulted in the fiasco at Isandhlwana. The blow to the Government's prestige was immense, and not even Disraeli's mastery of the black arts of politics could make anything from the disaster.[23]

Of course, had Frere's disregard of instructions not to provoke a war ended in a military victory instead of a disaster, all would have been forgiven, but the first lesson of imperialism is that disobedience had better succeed. Further campaigns in the summer rectified the situation in South Africa, but at a cost of more than £5 million; 'prestige' had, as Derby had predicted, proved an expensive commodity to purchase. In fact, if the cost of the mobilisation of the fleet during the Eastern crisis and that of the Afghan war were taken into account, the amount came to nearly £12 million.[24] That stern guardian of the public finances, Mr Gladstone, condemned the Government both for its profligacy and for its constant resort to what should have been the extraordinary expedient of Supplementary Estimates.[25] But even such expenditure could not guarantee success. On 3 September, the British mission in Kabul was massacred and all the gains from the first Afghan campaign were lost. For once there was no Disraelian hyperbole when he told Salisbury, 'This is a shaker, and it is difficult at the first breath, to recognise all the consequences of such a disaster.'[26] Disraeli despaired of both Lytton and the Indian army, but once more it was the indefatigable General Roberts, victor of the first Afghan campaign, who saved the day, executing a brilliant forced march to Kabul and deposing the treacherous Yakub Khan. The cost in blood and treasure was high, and the episode was to figure prominently in the indictment of Beaconsfieldism which Gladstone was concocting.

To the Liberal Mind, the 'main element in Lord Beaconsfield's foreign policy was brag, bluster and strong jingoism';[27] and his idea of politics was 'a game where the boldest adventurer will win'.[28] At the height of the Eastern crisis the Radical MP, Joseph Chamberlain, accused him of harbouring ambitions for 'personal government', and of using the device of a 'forward' foreign policy to help achieve it.[29] Had Liberal opinion been privy to the diplomatic initiatives of late September 1879, it would have gone even further in its condemnation of Beaconsfieldism.

Quite who took the initiative in proposing an Anglo-German alliance is uncertain: Disraeli's account attributes it to Bismarck and Münster, whilst Münster's says that it came from Disraeli; both men had reason to want an alliance, and both had a motive for making it appear that the overture came from the other. German historians have found Bismarck's excuses quite as convincing as British historians have those of Disraeli, but what is of interest in the context of this study is Disraeli's eagerness to use an Anglo-German alliance to consolidate the position he had won at Berlin.[30]

According to Disraeli, it was Münster who referred to German worries about Russian hostility as providing the motive for an alliance with England, whilst Münster has Disraeli using hostility towards Russia as Britain's motive. Münster's record of Disraeli saying that he could answer for 'his Party's support' so long as British policy pursued a firm course hostile to Russia, certainly has the ring of truth, as does the statement that: 'politically speaking, the Tories were the Party of action and wished to uphold the influence of England in Europe and to resist that of Russia, which alone they regarded as injurious'.[31] But for all his welcome of the idea, there was no particular reason why Disraeli should have raised this issue at this point, and there was every reason for Bismarck to have done so. With negotiations with the Austrians for the Dual Alliance at a crucial stage, and with Russian hostility still manifest, Bismarck had every motive for checking out the British position, just as he had every motive for keeping the initiative unofficial. Certainly Disraeli's reaction to his conversation with Münster suggests that whilst welcoming it, he had not taken the initiative.[32]

Writing to Salisbury on 1 October, Disraeli did not 'venture to say' exactly 'what Bismarck's game may . . . be', but 'no doubt, he is a man who, if he have cards in his hand, will play them'; the 'question is, whether, at this moment, his game is not ours'. The fact was that the 'preponderant impression' at home was that 'the general policy of our Government may be good but that we have been unskilful or unfortunate in managing its details'; an alliance such as the one proposed by Bismarck would be a major political event. It offered the opportunity of completing their spell in office as the 'representatives of a strong and intelligent policy, and the advantages of this will be felt by the Tory Party hereafter'.[33]

Salisbury was sceptical. He was startled by what Münster had said, but it was plain enough that tension between Germany and Russia was increasing. The question was whether this was another of Bismarck's efforts as diplomatic *agent provocateur*; was Russia 'really seeking a quarrel', or was Bismarck 'forcing the offensive on her' as he had done on Denmark, Austria and France? Like Disraeli, Salisbury was concerned about the French reaction to any Anglo-German treaty, but he acknowledged that if there was an attack by Russia on Austria, it would be 'very difficult for us not to go to Austria's assistance'.[34] But what neither of them could decide was whether Münster's proposal was an actual attempt to obtain an alliance, or simply to test the water. That it was the latter soon became clear.

When Salisbury saw Münster on 13 October, the German 'never advanced beyond vague generalities & expressions of "tendency": & there was nothing positive which I could reply to, or analyze'. It was evident that Germany and Austria were forming an alliance, although Münster was careful to emphasise that it was 'purely defensive'.[35] Disraeli thought that Bismarck had probably been disappointed 'at my not more completely accepting his proposal', and had therefore not 'wanted to get involved in a long and fruitless negotiation'.[36] In fact, if Bismarck had taken the initiative on the alliance issue, he now had every reason to draw back, having concluded the Dual Alliance with Austria on 7 October 1879.

Bismarck's motives here have been open to a number of interpretations, not all of them mutually exclusive. Some historians have seen the proposed alliance as part of a continuum with his domestic policy, and thus as a move in a Conservative direction;[37] others have seen it as part of a complicated attempt to provide Germany with security against a hostile Russia;[38] and there are those who have seen in it a gambit to drive Russia back to the negotiating table.[39] Bismarck's own explanation, that he had had the idea in mind since 1866, should not be rejected out of hand, but needs to be taken if not with a pinch of salt, then at least with caution.[40] As one historian reminds us, 'It will not do to accept any one of Bismarck's statements as the true exposition of his policy. What he aimed at was rather a system of checks and balances. Germany desired peace, because she had nothing to gain from war.'[41]

Disraeli was not as cool towards the idea as he appeared to be. He told Salisbury on 14 October to take it up with Münster and to blame him for any 'mix up': 'We gain nothing', he told Salisbury, 'by reserve.' Disraeli wanted Bismarck to see that 'in the event of European complications', it was 'our determination . . . not to be neutral and non-interfering, but to act, and to act with allies'.[42] However, when Salisbury saw Münster on 15 October, it was evident that 'there had been a slight change of mind: and that B[ismarck] [wa]s not so keen now as then'.[43] But Disraeli had not given up all hope.[44]

An alliance with Germany would have given a decisive twist to British foreign policy and have meant that the Berlin Congress would have been, as Disraeli wanted it to be, the first step towards a more active diplomacy. He told Münster that the 'Liberals, the Manchester School . . . who had been in power under Gladstone' would 'never again establish a firm footing in England', and saw the eclipse of Cobdenite foreign policy proceeding apace with the extinction of his Free Trade ideas.[45] But Disraeli was premature in predicting that 'the people' would 'permit no alteration as far as Foreign Policy was concerned'.

The Eastern crisis had given Disraeli a chance to assert his vision of Britain's world role, but he had not been able to build upon the achievement. Indeed, far from destroying the ideas of the 'Manchester School', Disraeli had given them a fillip by the amorality of his *Realpolitik*. One of the fiercest objections of the Liberal Mind to Disraeli's policies was that they amounted to 'nothing less than the assertion of England's freedom to act untrammelled by any moral considerations whatever'.[46] This was repugnant to the Liberal vision of Britain's world role, which Gladstone reasserted in 1879 and 1880, as Beaconsfieldism ran out of momentum and into trouble. For Gladstone, Britain was subject to two important constraints on her action in world affairs: Christian morality and the law of the European Concert. For Britain to act in defiance of either would be to fall below the level of events; for her to flout both was to 'degrade' and 'debase' the 'great name of England'.[47] In what became known as his Midlothian Campaign, on 27 November 1879 at West Calder Gladstone called for a reassertion of the 'right principles' which should govern British foreign policy.[48]

The first of these 'principles' was 'to foster the strength of the Empire . . . and to reserve . . . [it] for great and worthy occasions'; this would be attained by 'just legislation and economy at home', which would produce the 'two great elements of national power – namely wealth, which is a physical element, and union and contentment which are moral elements'. The second was 'to preserve to the nations . . . the blessings of peace – especially were it but for shame, when we recollect the sacred name we bear as Christians, for the Christian nations'. The third was at the heart of Gladstonism: 'To strive to cultivate and maintain, ay, to the very uttermost, what is called the Concert of Europe', because by so doing 'you neutralize and fetter and bind up the selfish aims of each.' Gladstone's fourth principle was 'to avoid needless and entangling engagements'. The fifth was to acknowledge that 'all nations were equal' and the sixth that no one should declare a 'pharisaical' superiority over another. British foreign policy should 'always be inspired by the love of freedom' as it had been in the days of Canning, Palmerston and Russell.

This powerful speech was reactionary in two senses: it was clearly a reaction against Disraeli's foreign policy; but it also harked back to a world of 'lost content'.[49] Gladstone contradicted Salisbury's 'preposterous pretence to be simply following the traditions of former Ministries save one', by pointing out that 'from 1830 to the happy reign of Dizzy', the Tories had been '*the pacific party*'.[50] This was so, and it helps to explain the adherence of Derby to the Liberal Party. He wrote to Lord Sefton on 12 March 1880 explaining that the 'present position of parties and the avowed policy of the Conservative leader in reference to foreign relations gives me no choice'.[51] Derby thought that the Liberal Party was the best vehicle for the foreign policy of mid-Victorian Britain; but his 'strong personal feeling'[52] blinded him to the limitations of Beaconsfieldism.

Salisbury commented that Gladstone's 'great quality is eloquent indistinctness of expression. It decides the electorate full easily: but of course it breaks down when the draughtsman has to translate it into clauses';[53] this was certainly true of his foreign policy after the election victory of 1880.

In early May 1880, Gladstone, now Prime Minister, and his Foreign Secretary, Granville, tried to put his concept of the 'Concert' into operation almost at once, proposing that the Powers should act together to put pressure on the Turks to implement the terms of the Berlin settlement as they concerned Greece and Montenegro.[54] By late July, Granville was able to tell the Queen that 'this has been done (not without much trouble)',[55] and Odo Russell in Berlin could congratulate Granville on having established a 'European Concert' which would be 'a guarantee against surprizes in the East'.[56] But this mistook a temporary conjunction of self-interests for a community of ideas which was entirely lacking.

Bismarck, Gorchakov and company did not share Gladstone's Liberal prejudices, and their own ran directly counter to them and actually inculcated hostility to them. Bismarck regarded the 'notion of conducting diplomacy through the Concert of Europe as an elaborate nonsense'.[57] He told the Russian Ambassador in Berlin, Count Saburov, that 'in politics one cannot be guided by presumptions alone'. Political life was 'just as if one were in a wood filled with suspicious characters, where one feels oneself instinctively on the defensive'.[58] For Bismarck, the whole idea of defining diplomatic objectives in terms of abstract principles was absurd. His diplomacy was driven by 'an effort to limit the range of the possible anti-German coalitions' in order to retain the gains won before 1871.[59] His scornful aphorism that '*Qui parle a Europe est tort: notion geographique* [He who speaks of Europe is wrong, it is simply a geographical expression]' was shared by Saburov, who thought it 'only the dream of idealists'.[60] For there to be a 'Europe', there would have had to have been 'a Confederation obeying a single will'; instead, there were five 'wills'. The Russians thought that to align themselves with Gladstone would have been to 'cling to the shadow' whilst giving up the substance; they were willing to 'make use of' the Concert idea to 'arrive at some practical result in connection with the pending questions which interest us in the East';[61] that was why they were prepared to join with Britain in coercing the Porte.

Lord Odo Russell who, like his Liberal masters, attached a great deal of importance to the notion, was convinced that Bismarck would lend his 'moral support' to the idea that Britain should coerce the Turks as Europe's mandatory.[62] But Russell's view that Bismarck would do so because he valued England's 'great moral influence'[63] was just another example of the unfitness of even the finest of Liberal minds to deal with Bismarck. He cared everything for German security and nothing for 'moral influence' unless it brought concrete benefits. It was 'no part of the policy of the German Empire to lend her subjects, to expend her blood and treasure, for the purpose of realising the designs of a neighbour Power'.[64] As far as he was concerned, Germany had 'no direct interest whatsoever in Eastern affairs'[65] and would not 'sacrifice the life of a Pomeranian Soldier or the value of a "Pfennig" to settle the Turkish question'.[66] Bismarck had no intention of doing anything which fostered Anglo-Russian co-operation in the Balkans; not only did it suit his purposes to keep those two Powers apart,[67] but he did not want his Austrian ally thrown on the defensive.[68] Indeed, if Gladstone's invocation of the 'Concert' had any effect on Bismarck apart from irritation, it prompted him to mend fences with Russia.

Bismarck told Saburov in January 1880 that it was important to be 'one of *three* on the European chess-board',[69] and having secured the Dual Alliance, Bismarck was quite willing to seek closer ties with Russia. Whilst Disraeli had been in power, Bismarck had been able to rely on British hostility to Russia as a means of containing her; he could do so no longer. The coincidence of this desire with Alexander II's conclusion that Pan-Slavism needed playing down in favour of an assertion of Russian imperial interests at the Straits, and that Germany was, after all, Russia's natural ally,[70] led towards a Russo-German *rapprochement*.[71]

The central problem with Gladstone's 'Concert' was that not only did it not exist in the form he imagined, but that his actions stimulated Bismarck to resurrect a conservative version of it based upon the idea of national self-interest. The second major difficulty was one of moral absolutism. As A.J.P. Taylor commented, pressed to its logical conclusion, Gladstone's doctrine was one of 'universal interference'.[72] Unlike Bismarck's *Realpolitik*, Gladstone's policies might well involve the loss of 'precious blood and treasure' in pursuit of 'moral' objectives. Granville, whose Whiggish instincts recoiled from the implications of Gladstone's doctrine, presumed that if the 'Concert' broke up, 'we shall not consent to act as a policeman to enforce general European objects', but would rather 'say we will attend with all our firmness to our own special interests'.[73] Gladstone himself admitted that 'our ideas are not recondite, nor are they developed except in proportion to what is immediate or at least not remote'; if the Concert broke up, then 'two duties will remain, one to let it be known who has broken it, the other to see whether enough remains to be sufficient for the end in view'. This was not particularly enlightening, but then, as Gladstone acknowledged, this was 'the part of our creed which has as yet been least opened out, and which might be developed with utility from time to time'.[74]

When the Porte conceded the demands of the Powers in October, Gladstone declared, in characteristic fashion: 'Praise to the Holiest in the Height', adding that it had been 'the working of the European Concert for purposes of justice, peace and liberty. . . . This has always been the ideal of my life in Foreign Policy'; he looked forward to the 'shabbier Powers' being shamed into joining 'us'.[75] But this was to misread the light of the oncoming train for that at the end of the tunnel.

The Russians were quite willing to use British naval power in the Adriatic, but they looked forward to Gladstone resuming his 'insular policy' and to being able 'to take courteous leave of one another'. As Saburov put it, 'Let us take from the European Concert whatever is useful to us now, but not throw aside the real for the shadow.'[76] The 'real' was not the pursuit of 'justice, peace and liberty', but rather of Russian interests, which were neither so widely nor so vaguely defined. For 'nearly a century the friendship of Prussia' had done Russia 'the incalculable service of covering our most important frontier', thus saving her 'milliards' of roubles. Friendship with Gladstone might allow the Russians to pursue a 'Slav' policy in the Balkans at the risk of conflict with Austria-Hungary and Germany, but the objectives which might be achieved were not commensurate with the dangers such a policy would encounter. A return to the old 'Prussian' policy would place Russia 'in the privileged position of being the only Power in Europe which need fear no attack'; it would also allow her to pursue a 'Russian' policy in Central Asia and at the Straits.[77]

The main obstacle in the way of a revival of the *Dreikaiserbund* had been Austrian reluctance to become involved in talks with the Russians. Andrassy's successor at the *Ballhausplatz*, Heinrich, Baron Haymerle, a professional diplomat, imitated his predecessor's policy vis-à-vis Russia, and even hoped that Britain would provide Austria with an ally.[78] But Gladstone's willingness to co-operate with Russia, his hostility towards Austria, and the prospect of a carve-up of the Ottoman Empire by such an alliance, along with improved Russo-German relations, raised the spectre of Austrian diplomatic isolation. In September 1880, Haymerle visited Bismarck at his estate in Freidrichsruh and intimated that his old opposition to a link with Russia was no longer as strong as it had been.[79] Gladstone's diplomacy had created the conditions in which Bismarck could reconstitute the League which Disraeli had destroyed during the Great Eastern crisis.

Bismarck was 'at a loss to understand the great . . . interest England took in the future of Turkey'; the notion of acting to achieve 'purely moral and philanthropic ends' struck him as a sign of softening of the brain. He dangled before Granville and Gladstone, as he had before Derby and Disraeli, the prospect of a settlement of the Eastern Question which would take care of Britain's only 'real material interest' – Egypt.[80] But the Liberals showed as little interest in a partition of the Turkish Empire as Disraeli had.

Indeed, Gladstone's policy towards Turkey brought the worst of all possible worlds. Although bitterly critical of the Cyprus Convention, the Liberals retained the island but renounced the obligations Disraeli had undertaken to secure internal reform in Turkey through the use of consuls and Turkish officials.[81] This further alienated the Sultan without in any way securing Britain's interests.[82] Odo Russell was right to predict that 'Bismarck's policy will henceforward be to preserve Turkey in status quo for his neighbours, and to promote the collapse of the Concert, in which he apprehends a troublesome Rival to his present exclusive influence in Europe.'[83]

Russell's only mistake was the characteristically British one of supposing that Bismarck had to 'promote the collapse of the Concert'; it would first have had to exist outside the Liberal Mind. Saburov had been right to think that 'under the appearance of general agreement' which the 'Concert' action against Turkey had seemed to present, there was concealed a 'lack of real alliance'; the 'seeming Concert only serves as a transition to groupings as yet unknown'.[84] That grouping turned out to be a revived *Dreikaiserbund*.

The *Dreikaiserbund* was the only 'system' which, in Bismarck's opinion, offered 'the maximum stability for the peace of Europe'.[85] It offered 'more guarantees' than any other alignment of Powers 'for the maintenance of all the conservative elements of modern societies'.[86] Far from marking the beginning of a new 'Concert of Europe', the years 1878–9 might be considered as 'marking the end of *laissez-faire* liberalism and the beginning of the new conservative trend'.[87] In October 1879, Russell had commented that 'the Conservative-protectionist reaction all over Europe is very significant and instructive', and he had wondered 'how it will affect us all in the long-run'.[88] With the formation of Bismarck's alliance system, he was about to find out the answer to his question.

Gladstone was fighting against 'ideas and practices neither Liberal nor Conservative'.[89] He thought that 'there never has been a period when the differences between the two parties were more broadly pronounced'.[90] Disraeli's Conservatism, with its geopolitical preoccupations and its ability to reach those parts of the electorate immune to Gladstonian high-mindedness, laid itself open to the moralistic assault it received from Gladstone in 1879 and 1880. By always defining 'British interests' in terms of Britain's role as a great military and Asiatic Power, it laid itself open to the charges that it was immoral, dishonourable – and expensive. It was a policy fit for a World Power willing to act on *Realpolitik* principles, but the British were only fitfully willing to assume that burden and they preferred their self-interest to be decently veiled. Gladstone's definition of British interests was neither narrow nor amoral; but in Bismarck's Europe, Gladstone's 'Concert' was still-born.

11

'A Great Many Mistakes'

Gladstone's 'mission' to unravel gradually the 'tangled knots of the foreign and imperial policy' of Disraeli[1] quickly ran into trouble; the nostrums which had seemed so beguilingly simple when 'on the stump', were less so in office; he was neither the first nor the last Liberal to discover that an ethical foreign policy is easier to preach than to practise.

Gladstone had condemned Disraeli's annexation of the Transvaal and his aggressive policy in Afghanistan,[2] but in neither area did he manage to make a difference – at least for the better. In the process, he inflicted political damage upon his own Government and left Britain with serious problems abroad. The central irony of Gladstone's second administration was that it managed to out-do anything Disraeli had done in the way of territorial acquisitions by occupying Egypt; but this was done in a way which maximised the problems which Disraeli had always thought would attend on such a project, without securing any advantages to Britain.

Gladstone's rhetoric raised expectations which an administration headed by the Archangel Gabriel might have found difficult to realise. The South African Boers assumed that Gladstone would revoke Disraeli's annexation of the Transvaal, and when he did not they rose in revolt. Gladstone's attempt to suppress it ended in the annihilation of a small British force at Majuba Hill in February 1881, after which he negotiated the Convention of Pretoria, which conceded the substance of the Boer demands, with an ill-defined British 'suzerainty' being the only face-saving feature of the treaty from Gladstone's point of view.[3] That may have satisfied Gladstone's rather sophistical imagination, but it did not please the Jingoes; Disraeli may have got into a scrape in South Africa, but at least he had come out of it with some success.

Gladstone's unintended achievement in providing the impetus for the renewal of the *Dreikaiserbund* left Britain in a position of potentially dangerous diplomatic isolation. This was something his hero Canning had had to face in the 1820s, but he had not had, as Palmerston had after him, a liberal France as a possible partner; Gladstone had that advantage in 1881; by 1882 he had thrown it away, and done so in a manner which left Britain permanently vulnerable to the ill-will of Bismarck.

The Liberals deprecated attempts to hive off parts of the Ottoman Empire, but they did so in vain. In April 1881, Granville told Lyons to inform the French that any seizure of Tunis without the consent of Turkey and the permission of the other Powers 'cannot be allowed'.[4] But, as Lyons's biographer observed acidly, 'it is not of the slightest use to employ such language if merely moral suasion is contemplated'.[5] Granville claimed that he disliked 'barking without biting',[6] but having warned the French, he did nothing to prevent them from taking over Tunis. France was encouraged by Bismarck, who saw in it a dual benefit for himself: it would simultaneously turn France's gaze from the blue line of the Vosges and give her '*gloire*' elsewhere as compensation; and by irritating the Italians, it might drive them into his camp.[7] Lyons called the Treaty of Bardo, 12 May 1881, between France and the Sultan, 'so like' a 'protectorate' that it 'would be difficult to point out a difference'. It was a 'very bad augury' since 'there are not wanting all over the globe places and questions in which the French might make themselves very inconvenient and disagreeable to us, and might, if encouraged by Bismarck, come at last to a downright quarrel with us'.[8] But Gladstone proved quite capable of encouraging Anglo-French rivalry without any encouragement from Bismarck.

Egypt was the most sensitive point in Anglo-French relations, and as such it required delicate handling; Gladstone and Granville brought to it the touch of a bull in a china shop. Since the bankruptcy of the Khedive in 1877, Egypt's finances had been managed by the *Caisse de la dette publique*, a body organised by, and representing the interests of, the Great Powers; the country had, in effect, been under joint Anglo-French control. This inherently unstable situation was made worse by the incapacity of the new Khedive, Tewfiq, and by the nationalist movement which his toleration of European control helped to foster in Egypt. From January 1881, there were disturbances in Cairo and Alexandria, encouraged by Egyptian army officers.

Gladstone could never quite make up his mind what he wanted to do about the unrest. He thought that there were 'strong objections' to 'all single-handed action by us on Egyptian ... territory',[9] and wanted to co-operate with the French. Being of a Liberal and legalistic frame of mind, he took the view that this should be done through the medium of the Porte, which was still the nominal sovereign power in Egypt.[10] The fact that that 'one great anti-human specimen of humanity', as Gladstone had called the Turks, might not want to co-operate with the British and the French appears not to have occurred to him. Lyons warned that an appeal to the Turks would be both useless and an affront to the French; on both points he was correct.[11] But that did not stop Gladstone. Granville, who worried that Lyons might be right, wanted to try to secure Bismarck's co-operation in putting pressure on the Porte.[12] But like Lyons, Odo Russell, newly ennobled as Lord Ampthill, feared that 'having once succeeded in leading France into trouble, he [Bismarck] may be tempted to do so again, by shewing her the road to glory in Egypt, and thereby get rid, during his own lifetime, of a threatening neighbour, who stands between him and his rest'.[13] Ampthill had begun to appreciate the Bismarckian interpretation of the European 'Concert'.

When the Khedive attempted to head off Colonel Arabi and the nationalists by summoning a 'Chamber of Notables', it might have been expected that Gladstone would have rejoiced at this sign of constitutionalism, since ' "Egypt for the Egyptians" ' was 'the sentiment to which I should wish to give scope: and could it prevail it would I think be the best, the only good solution of the "Egyptian Question" ';[14] but in practice, he opposed the Chamber since its ambitions threatened to encroach upon the financial affairs of Egypt. In late 1881, Léon Gambetta, the new French Prime Minister, proposed that the two Powers should present a note offering support to the Khedive against encroachments upon his powers.[15] Gladstone, pained at the idea of getting in the way of a 'national movement', but conscious of the interests of the Egyptian bondholders (of whom he was one),[16] agreed to this policy; but both he and Granville seem to have been hoping that the crisis would pass over before any action needed to be taken.[17]

From Berlin, Ampthill continued to preach his old doctrine that 'confidence in Bismarck' was the 'means to success in foreign policy'.[18] 'We are', he told Granville on 18 November 1881, 'on excellent terms with Bismarck' and 'can at any given moment be on the very best if required.' He did not think that Bismarck's disapproval of 'Parliamentary Government, liberal principles and free trade for Germany', or his want of sympathy for the Liberal administration, would 'prevent his acting cordially with H.M. Govt. for the promotion of peace in Europe, when invited to do so'.[19] This was a highly dubious diagnosis. Rumours that Bismarck was encouraging the Sultan's apprehensions about British designs on Egypt had been current since early October 1881,[20] but it was not until February that the Chancellor made his move. On 2 February, identical notes were issued by the *Dreikaiserbund* Powers and by Italy to the Sultan, reassuring him that no change could take place in the status of Egypt without negotiations between him and the Powers; the 'Concert' had united – against Britain.[21]

Gladstone wanted to find a way of working with this 'Concert',[22] but Lyons warned that it would have disastrous effects: it would alienate the French and it would undermine Britain's position at the Porte by making her actions there dependent upon the machinations of the other Powers.[23] Granville admitted that it was not 'easy to find an answer to all your powerful arguments',[24] so he and the Prime Minister did not attempt it. The fact was that the Government, heavily embroiled in Irish problems, had no real policy and so fell back on its own natural impulses; in Granville's case, this meant a sort of invertebrate dithering tempered by Lyons's good advice; in Gladstone's, it meant a futile harking after a 'Concert' which was little more than a figment of his imagination, fostered by Ampthill's misreading of Bismarck's motives and likely actions.

On 11 June, there were violent riots in Alexandria. Upon hearing that the French Chamber had passed military credits, Granville consoled himself with the thought that 'we have avoided a rupture with France, a rupture with Europe, and a possible war';[25] as usual this was too optimistic by far. Gladstone was now confronted with a dilemma. On the surface there was little difference between his professed aims in Egypt and those of Arabi and the Egyptian nationalists,[26] yet his own Party was split about what course to take. That Hartington, the leading Whig, should have been in favour of intervention was hardly surprising, but that the Radical Joseph Chamberlain should have been 'almost the greatest Jingo', was. Bright, the elderly representative of mid-Victorian Radicalism, was, 'of course, the most peaceable'.[27] The French, despite the gesture of voting military credits, did nothing, and Bismarck, when consulted, replied irritably, 'Let the Powers interested settle it as they please, but don't ask me *how*, for I neither know nor care.'[28]

Gladstone's hankering after an international solution to the crisis proved all but impervious to the dawning reality that no one else was going to pull Britain's chestnuts out of an Egyptian fire which the British themselves had helped light. As late as 21 June he still thought that something might be had from intervention at Constantinople.[29] Although he reserved the right to act unilaterally if the Suez Canal was threatened,[30] Gladstone continued to shy away from accepting unilateral responsibility. Without even consulting the Cabinet, he rejected a proposal from the Sultan to transfer exclusive administrative and military control to the British.[31] He stood out against any one Power having a 'preponderant interest' and in favour of the *status quo*.[32] Gladstone carried on hoping that he would be able to avoid taking any action,[33] and on 5 July, two days after the British admiral had been given orders to fire on Alexandria unless work was stopped on fortifications,[34] Gladstone was still maintaining that Britain had no 'separate rights which justify the adoption of military measure'.[35] Yet at Cabinet he agreed to troops being despatched. Bright resigned in disgust[36] and later denounced the subsequent military action as 'simply damnable' and 'worse than anything ever perpetrated by Dizzie'.[37]

Gladstone continued to hope that the approval of military action would render its implementation unnecessary, and counselled caution even as the British fleet bombarded Alexandria on 11 July. Thereafter, he justified the action because it had brought peace in Egypt a 'good deal' nearer.[38] Even allowing for the fact that this argument was used in a letter to Bright, it was hardly very convincing. Gladstone's protests that the increased disorder which followed the British bombardment was the fault of the 'wanton wickedness of the Arabs' was curiously obtuse for a man negotiating with the leaders of lawlessness in Ireland; but one set of rules obtained when dealing with Europeans, and quite a different set when it came to 'orientals'.[39]

From Berlin, Ampthill congratulated Granville on escaping the 'inextricable complications of "entangling alliances" ' in 'the independent prosecution of a truly British national policy'; but he spoke too soon.[40] Gladstone's faith in an international settlement of the crisis remained undimmed. He wanted to pursue a policy of 'non-interference' in Egypt – much to the displeasure of the Queen, who assumed that the bombardment of Alexandria had meant that Britain was interfering;[41] her robust common sense failed to grasp the complexities of the Liberal Mind in search of an escape hatch.

Throughout July, Gladstone grasped at whatever straws he could devise: action with the Turks and the Italians; action with the French; action with the approval of the Constantinople conference; all these phantasms teased his overactive imagination.[42] When Granville attempted to bring him down to earth by positing unilateral British action,[43] Gladstone did not reject it, but responded that he could not 'travel quite at the pace you propose'; he first wanted to see the 'exhaustion of every effort to procure collective or joint action'. Only then should they 'not be deterred by any apprehension as to the magnitude of the enterprise, or the amount of force required, if the way be clear in point of principle'.[44] The policy which followed was as convoluted as the thought-processes which gave rise to it.

On 30 July, the Sultan was informed that Britain 'considered herself invested with the duty of restoring order in Egypt, and maintaining the safety of the Suez Canal'.[45] On the 31st, two days after the collapse of the Freycinet Government rendered the chances of French intervention negligible, Sir Garnet Wolseley was sent instructions to 'put down Arabi and establish the Khedive's power'.[46] On 7 August, with the approval of the Khedive, Granville sent a circular to the Great Powers informing them of the instructions sent to Wolseley.

By this time Gladstone's anxieties to exonerate himself and his Government of any charges of selfishness were acute.[47] When the international conference at Constantinople adjourned on 14 August having been productive of nothing save delay, Gladstone had already announced in the House that Britain was intervening in Egypt for 'purposes admitted to be material in the general interest'.[48] He convinced himself that 'we are discharging single-handedly a European duty'.[49] If no one else would nominate the British as Europe's mandatory, then Gladstone would do it himself. He saw Britain's eventual position in Egypt as being analogous to that of Russia in Bulgaria, 'not the result of stipulation, but of effort & sacrifice crowned by success'.[50] On 13 September, British troops under Wolseley won the battle of Tel-el-kebir, bringing to a close the shortest war in history.

Gladstone ordered the guns to be fired in Whitehall – hoping that they would 'crash all the windows'.[51]

Whilst Gladstone was thanking 'God Almighty, who has prospered us in what I feel & know to be an honest undertaking',[52] the question of the future status of Egypt had to be considered. Gladstone's own view was that Britain should withdraw her troops 'as early as possible' once order had been re-established,[53] and that 'apart from the Canal' Britain had 'no interest in Egypt which could warrant intervention'.[54] Now the moment had come to decide between 'more intervention and less'; Gladstone was firmly in the latter camp.[55] The Queen was furious at the very idea: 'Short of annexation we must obtain a firm hold and power in Egypt for the future. . . . If you bind yourself beforehand you will be hampered as you were by the Conference and the Convention. We shall be laughed at and despised by all Europe if we do not maintain a high tone.'[56]

To some extent the Egyptian Question *was* an international one; the Great Powers had lent money to the Khedive, as had individual investors, and these loans and investments were guaranteed by half the country's revenue being pledged to their repayment. By undertaking to reform Egypt's finances, the British manoeuvred themselves into a situation where they needed the approval of the other Powers. Thus Ampthill's exultation that 'You have got the Great Powers well in hand'[57] was precisely the opposite of the truth. Bismarck would have had no objection to a British annexation of Egypt, although he advised against it on the grounds that it would provoke a permanent breach with the French.[58] In this there may have been a little Bismarckian malice, since the French were already in high dudgeon, and there was little, save evacuation, that the British could do to assuage their feelings. But Bismarck need not have worried. Gladstone had no intention of dealing with Egypt in a manner which would have left Britain open to the censure of the 'Concert'.

'Dual control' had obviously broken down, and on 3 January 1883 Granville announced that in future the country would be occupied by Britain, but only 'for the preservation of public tranquillity'; forces would be withdrawn 'as soon as the state of the country ... will admit of it'.[59] Negotiations over the next two years failed to produce an early British withdrawal, and by 1884 even Gladstone was having to admit that 'we are an Egyptian Government'.[60] But this was wide of the mark. Gladstone's refusal to annex the country left any British efforts to reform its finances dependent upon the agreement of the Powers on the *Caisse de la dette*. Since the French erected non-cooperation with the British in Egypt to the status almost of a doctrine, it was left to Bismarck, with his influence upon Russia and Austria, to decide whether British plans went ahead or not; and he was not slow to wield his '*baton Egyptienne*'.

Bismarck's sudden interest in the acquisition of colonies in 1884 has given rise to a great deal of speculation. Was it an act of 'social-imperialism' (i.e. an attempt to distract the electorate from trouble at home by a bold imperial policy)? Was it designed to provoke a quarrel with the British just at the moment when the Anglophile Crown Prince might find himself on the throne? Or was it a manoeuvre designed to improve Franco-German relations by highlighting their common concern with overweening British imperialism?[61] At any rate, no one seems to entertain the opinion that Bismarck was genuinely converted to a desire for African colonies. There were certainly electoral reasons why Bismarck might have moved as he did in 1884, but he would not have done so 'if the international situation during 1883–1885 had not permitted their acquisition without serious harm to Germany's foreign relations in Europe'.[62] For this Bismarck had Gladstone to thank. Austria and Russia were already bound to Germany, as was Italy after 1881; thanks to events in Egypt, the old liberal *entente* between Britain and France was dead. With Britain needing German support in Egypt, Bismarck was in an ideal position to demand payment for his favours. It was, as Salisbury later put it, what in a humbler walk of life would have been called '*chantage*', or even blackmail[63] – but Gladstone had put himself in a position where he would have to pay.

That the execution of the Egyptian policy was maladroit and

unconvincing is obvious, but these defects derived as much from the shortcomings of Midlothianism as from those of Gladstone and Granville as executive politicians. Gladstone had not only effectively isolated Britain by alienating the French, but he had done so in a manner which left Britain dependent upon Bismarck. Bismarck's charmless and ungracious son Herbert summed up his position: 'Our policy will avail itself of this most favourable moment to squash Gladstone against the wall, so that he can yap no more . . . he must ride the English deeper into the mire so that his prestige will vanish even among the masses of the stupid English electorate.'[64] The vein of cruelty and bullying which was so close to the surface in Bismarck's nature certainly came through strongly in what followed.

Gladstone and Granville were not well-equipped to deal with, or even to understand, Bismarck's policy and the motives which drove it. Granville's policy towards Germany had been to show Bismarck that 'he had our earnest support, and that I do not wish to put my finger in the pie, excepting when and as much as he desires it'.[65] He had accepted Ampthill's reassurances that his own kindness to Herbert Bismarck had 'softened the fierce fond Father and taught him that Liberals are not as bad as he thought',[66] which made all the greater his surprise when Herbert came on a special mission to Britain in June 1884.

A conference to settle the Egyptian Question had been convened for 18 June, and Granville was expecting Bismarck's support. Herbert made it clear that this could not be taken for granted and that it would be linked to Bismarck's being able to 'give some satisfaction' to 'German public opinion' on 'colonial questions'.[67] Although Herbert claimed that there was 'no question of bargain', that was precisely what there was. Puzzled by this sudden efflorescence of German colonial claims, the Cabinet agreed that Granville should 'see Herbert Bismarck & ask him what it is the German Gov[ernmen]t want'.[68] Ampthill, who had been watching developments in Germany and prophesying since 1883 that a 'graceful and speedy settlement' of German claims in Fiji would 'save further trouble',[69] had warned that Bismarck was likely to raise colonial questions.[70] Now he did so, in the form of part of West Africa, Angra Pequena.[71]

The Germans had first raised the issue in 1883, asking whether a factory established by a German merchant, Adolf Lüderitz, could expect British protection. Lord Derby, who had joined the Liberal Government as Colonial Secretary, was dilatory in his response, and by May, Lüderitz was able to announce that he had acquired by treaty 215 square miles of land in West Africa. Following an outcry in the Cape Colony and complaints by the British press, the Germans had asked the British whether they had any claims on the territory, and, if so, what was their foundation.[72] Granville's response might well have been calculated to exhibit British arrogance at its most pronounced and indefensible. It acknowledged that sovereignty had only been proclaimed 'at certain points', but announced grandly that the whole area was a British 'sphere of influence'.[73] Bismarck enquired further as to the nature of any British claims, but despite Ampthill's warnings, Derby, who thought that Germany was uninterested in colonial acquisitions, decided upon a course of leisurely consultation with the Cape as to whether Britain should establish her claims over the territory.

Liberal Ministers were remarkably slow to divine the drift of German policy. In April, Bismarck had pressed for British recognition of the 'well-established interests of German subjects in the Fiji Islands', and Granville had responded favourably.[74] This was followed up in May by enquiries as to whether Britain would be willing to cede Heligoland to Germany. Granville asked whether 'it was not an awkward moment to open such a subject, when it might be supposed we wished to secure the assistance of Germany on another matter'.[75] Despite Ambassador Münster's polite disclaimer, the Germans were, as Herbert Bismarck's *démarche* made plain, looking for colonial concessions as the price for any support for Britain in Egypt.[76]

The announcement by the Cape Government in early June that it would consider the annexation of Angra Pequena provided Bismarck with the opportunity to wield the 'Egyptian baton' on the heads of the hapless Liberals. He was able to adopt a tone of high outrage at the notion of Germany being treated to an example of 'naïve egotism' by the British, who, he claimed, were attempting to treat Germany as though she were not a Great Power.[77] Granville's reaction to Herbert Bismarck's abruptness was pure appeasement: on 22 June, German sovereignty over Angra Pequena was accepted; four days later, an Anglo-Portuguese treaty which the Germans objected to was abandoned; in July, a commission of inquiry was appointed to examine German claims in Fiji. It was little wonder that Ampthill reported on 28 June that 'Bismarck is very grateful to you for your final settlement of the question which has produced the most excellent impression throughout Germany and has really done immense good.'[78] It had certainly done Bismarck 'immense good'; the same could hardly be said for British prestige and interests. Nor was Ampthill correct in thinking that Bismarck was satisfied. Münster did not support the British at the conference over Egypt, which broke up in failure as a result.[79] It was, Gladstone concluded, a 'return slap for Angra Pequena'.[80] Ampthill was reduced to hoping that 'this anti-English mania may not last longer'.[81]

Gladstone feared that 'some of the Foreign Governments have the same notion of me that [Tsar] Nicholas [I] was supposed to have of Lord Aberdeen', which showed that he recognised the ease with which foreigners could mistake liberalism for pacifism. But he declared that 'there is no one in the Cabinet less disposed than I am to knuckle down to them in this Egyptian matter about which they except Italy behave so ill, *some* of them without excuse'. He was willing to give Bismarck every satisfaction about his colonial matters, 'but about Egypt we ought not to be kept dangling in the air as is now the case'.[82] Gladstone wanted to re-establish Egypt's finances and thought it reasonable that the bondholders should accept a slightly lower return on their money; the French objected to the idea because it would make Britain's life easier, and Bismarck because it would deprive him of a stick with which to beat Gladstone; this the latter seemed not to be able to appreciate. The more Whiggish element in the Cabinet wished to cut the Gordian knot by treating Egypt as 'Tunis', but Gladstone would not follow this route.[83]

In return for the concessions made to Bismarck, the British press – and the Colonial Office – wanted 'compensation', something Gladstone deplored.[84] But it was futile of him to protest against 'annexationism'. British action in Egypt and the German claims in West Africa had precipitated a land-grab, and Gladstone, acknowledging that 'close co-operation' with Germany was of 'immense importance',[85] had to agree to Bismarck's demands for a conference in Berlin to discuss colonial affairs. Granville thought that there was a 'wild and irrational spirit abroad'.[86] Isolated in Europe, faced with Bismarck's European alliance system, dependent upon Germany for support in Egypt, Gladstone's divided and distracted Government went along with one manifestation of the 'Concert' which was most certainly not in Britain's interest – the partition of Africa at the Berlin Colonial Conference.

For most of the century Britain had been able to exercise a sort of 'Monroe Doctrine' over the African Continent, which had been open to trade and exploration, without the expense and responsibility of direct rule. In future, Britain would have to compete for territory and influence with the other Powers.

Gladstone's 'temporary' intervention in Egypt for 'no selfish aims'[87] had turned into an open-ended commitment which had ruined Anglo-French relations and left Britain exposed to the whims of Bismarck's ill-will. The dangers to be apprehended from her diplomatic isolation became apparent as Anglo-Russian relations deteriorated over encroachments by the latter in Afghanistan in the course of 1885. Even the usually optimistic Granville thought that the prospect before them was 'too dreadful, jumping from one nightmare into another. Once at war with Russia we shall be obliged to toady Germany, France and Turkey.'[88] He was not alone in failing to see how Britain could 'effectively' carry on a land war against Russia.

The crisis caused by Russian encroachments into Afghanistan in 1885 revealed the damage done to Britain's position by

Gladstone's diplomacy. Because the Government had just 'lost' General Gordon at Khartoum, its prestige was at a nadir, and the public wanted strong action. However, with the Cabinet split every possible way over Ireland, and with Hartington threatening to resign, this was hardly likely. The comment of the British Ambassador in Vienna, Sir Augustus Paget, that 'England had no friend on the Continent', was very much to the point.[89] The Emperor Franz Joseph expressed his 'astonishment at the compliant attitude of the British Cabinet', and could 'hardly have thought it possible that he [Gladstone] would allow British policy to play so lamentable a part'.[90] When Gladstone's private secretary, Edward Hamilton, commented: 'I can't help thinking great mistakes have been made by the Government',[91] he was putting it mildly.

The Liberal vision of the role of England in foreign affairs was not an ignoble one, but it had had disastrous results. Gladstone saw England as one of the Great Powers of Europe, acknowledging as the proper criterion of her conduct international law and Christian morality; it was for its offence against these standards that he had castigated Beaconsfieldism and that he had recalled the country to its higher destiny. This was all a far cry from the fractured and fractious Government which resigned on 8 June 1885. After Gladstone's first administration it had been written that there was a 'vague impression that the Liberals would put up with anything rather than go to war, and that foreign affairs was not their *forte*'.[92] By 1885 this last impression was, if anything, stronger, and given the situation in Afghanistan it seemed possible that, having 'put up with anything', the country would still find itself at war. The record of the previous five years hardly commended Midlothianism as a future template for British foreign policy; would the advent of another Conservative Government see a revival of Beaconsfieldism?

12

Salisbury

Salisbury's foreign policy, like Disraeli's before it, was in part a reaction to the legacy left by Gladstone's moralism; but it was not a continuation of Beaconsfieldism and quite lacked the Jingo element which had marked Disraeli's diplomacy. In objective and tone it was similar to Derby's Conservative diplomacy: it wanted to avoid war; it abhorred taking risks; it did little to try to stir up popular excitement behind a policy of asserting British prestige. But it could not be identical with Derby's diplomacy; it was a post-lapsarian version of it. Salisbury had witnessed the skill with which Disraeli had harnessed the mob to achieve his imperialist objectives; he had also seen how swiftly that opinion could turn on its masters, and he had experienced its sharp revulsion in the face of Gladstonian impotence and humiliation. Moreover, unlike Derby's Country Party view of Britain's role in the world, with its insular and English orientation, Salisbury's world-view acknowledged the burdens of Empire – even if it sought to make them more bearable.

On balance, Salisbury's diplomacy marked an adaptation of the old Conservative tradition to changed circumstances, not a continuation of the Disraelian policy of prestige; but unlike Derby, Salisbury could not try to act as though public opinion could be ignored, and he doubted whether it could be effectively educated. At best, diplomacy could be kept out of its ken, and the avoidance of disaster and humiliation would do this; it could also be placated. At worst, it could, in the hands of unscrupulous demagogues, drive foreign policy off course. But it always hovered in the background, a far from nameless shadow which constricted, constrained and confined the work of the aristocratic diplomatist. Perhaps after him would come the deluge, but given the Fallen Nature of Man, avoiding that during his time would, in itself, be sufficient.

Salisbury's diplomatic style and objectives were also shaped by the circumstances in which he came to, and retained, office. He became Premier because Gladstone had resigned, not because he had won an election. He was continuing the long mid-Victorian example of the fourteenth Earl of Derby, by providing a stop-gap administration until the Liberal coalition could decide to bury its hatchets; precedent suggested that the back of the Tory Party would be the place where this would happen. Salisbury also arrived in office in the middle of a crisis with Russia over Afghanistan which could easily have led to a war for which Britain was neither militarily nor diplomatically prepared. As he surveyed the state of Britain's relations with the European Powers, Salisbury could only seek refuge in his mordant wit: 'The Liberal government have at least achieved their long desired "Concert of Europe". . . . They have succeeded in uniting the continent of Europe – against England.'[1] The nature of the circumstances facing Salisbury as he took office exercised a great influence over his diplomacy.

Salisbury enjoyed none of the advantages which Disraeli had at home and abroad. Disraeli had been the first Conservative to win a general election since 1841, which gave him great prestige and untrammelled control over the choice of his own Cabinet; none of these things was true of Salisbury in 1885. Had the new electoral registers needed after the 1884 Reform Act been ready, there would have been an election, but since they were not, there had to be a Conservative Government. Salisbury had become Prime

Minister by the Queen's favour, and there were those who felt that post ought to have gone to them, and who, accordingly, bore Salisbury little in the way of either loyalty or goodwill. In fact, Salisbury would have preferred not to have taken office, but Gladstone left him with no choice.[2] Many Prime Ministers have acted as though they were also Foreign Secretary, but Salisbury was the first to take this to the logical conclusion;[3] telling the Queen that 'none of his colleagues was well acquainted with foreign affairs', Salisbury took the post himself.[4]

The omens were not good. Salisbury's dislike of removing 'older men in favour of rising talent'[5] ensured that there were plenty of familiar faces from Disraeli's Cabinet. But Northcote, along with the Duke of Richmond, Carnarvon, Cross, Cranbrook, W.H. Smith and Fred Stanley, were all past their best (which had not been saying much in some cases); the fact that Lord John Manners had been in every Tory Government since the 1850s seemed the only explanation of his reappearance in this one, but his inclusion hardly suggested that the Party was overflowing with new talent. The one startling exception to this dominance of the 'old gang' was Lord Randolph Churchill, who hated them so much that he wanted to pack Northcote (whom he despised) off to the Lords,[6] and to veto Cross;[7] indeed, his demands threatened to prevent a government being formed at all.[8] It required a great deal of persuasion by Salisbury, and the grant of a peerage by the Queen, before Northcote agreed to become First Lord of the Treasury in the Upper House as the Earl of Iddesleigh.[9] The Churchill–Iddesleigh feud weakened an already feeble administration, and Salisbury's leadership failed to compensate sufficiently for this.

Salisbury had said of Disraeli that 'as the head of a Cabinet his fault was one of firmness. The chiefs of departments got their way too much – the Cabinet as a whole got it too little.' This, he said, 'necessarily followed from having at the head of affairs a statesman whose only fixed principle was that the party must on no account be broken up'.[10] Yet much the same criticisms were to be levelled at Salisbury himself, with Hicks Beach recalling that, as Prime

Minister, 'he did not exercise the control over his colleagues, either in or out of the Cabinet, that Lord Beaconsfield did . . . [he] frequently allowed important matters to be decided by a small minority of votes'.[11] Salisbury adhered to the view that as Prime Minister he was only *primus inter pares*. Because he was also Foreign Secretary he could deal with diplomacy without always having to trouble the Cabinet, but when, as in 1886 and again after 1896, there were powerful figures in the Cabinet with views of their own on foreign affairs, Salisbury had difficulty getting his own way.

But the most formidable restriction upon Salisbury's freedom as Foreign Secretary was 'our absolute sovereign . . . the people of this country'.[12] Defending himself in May 1885 from Granville's imputation that he had been unpatriotic by criticising the Government's handling of the Afghan crisis, and refuting the allegation that such criticism was unhelpful to the process of diplomacy, Salisbury said that it was only natural that he should have made his criticisms public: 'You have a form of Government which is in many points purely democratic, and you must take with it the incidents which naturally adhere to it, and one of these incidents is publicity of deliberation.' The Cabinet continued to take its decisions in private, but 'the authority to which you must appeal from the Cabinet is the people, and their deliberations are conducted in the open field'. This fact inevitably hampered any British Foreign Secretary, especially when dealing with autocratic Powers; it made British diplomacy more transparent than that of, say, Germany, whilst at the same time making it less consistent.

One of the things which made Bismarck distrust British diplomacy so much was its 'democratic nature'; he loathed the 'Blue Books' published by the Government to explain its foreign policy, and he doubted whether any reliance could be placed on Britain as a diplomatic partner when her policy was so exposed to the influences of popular prejudice.[13] Salisbury found this reaction entirely intelligible. His oft-repeated statement that engagements involving a *casus belli* were incompatible with the British

Parliamentary system was certainly a useful excuse for avoiding binding commitments, but it was more than that; he genuinely believed that because a decision for war would depend on the Parliament of the day, no British Minister could promise in advance that Britain would go to war in a given set of circumstances.[14] Disraeli had harnessed public opinion to his chariot, but he had also been overthrown by it; an intelligent Sorcerer's apprentice could learn from such a lesson – and no one doubted Salisbury's intellect. By temperament Salisbury was unfitted to bend the bow of Ulysses, and his spiritual home lay close to the Derbyite tradition; moreover, circumstances alone would have precluded an aggressive policy of 'prestige'.

Salisbury stared into the 'abyss of isolation'.[15] Gladstone had alienated Turkey and Austria by his moralising at their expense in 1880; he had provided the catalyst to the renewal of the *Dreikaiserbund*; his occupation of Egypt had aroused lasting and bitter French enmity, whilst creating conditions in which Bismarck had been able to blackmail Britain; and his final decision to resist Russian incursions into Afghanistan threatened Britain with a war on the North-West Frontier of India. In these circumstances, Derbyite 'masterly inactivity' was not an option. Salisbury needed German help.

Only two days after accepting the premiership, Salisbury told Münster that 'a leading principle of the Conservative Party would be to reach and maintain a good understanding with Germany'.[16] On 2 July, he wrote privately to Bismarck recalling their former co-operation and stressing his intention to 'restore the good understanding' between Britain and Germany, and emphasising his desire for peace in Afghanistan.[17] The message was clear: would Germany help mediate a settlement? And if not, would she at least use her good offices to help ease Anglo-Russian tension? Much of Bismarck's animus had been against Gladstone and Derby, who, as Lord Lyons's biographer commented sympathetically, must 'from the Bismarckian point of view [have] represented a singularly futile type of statesman'.[18] Derby's behaviour as Foreign Secretary had been neither forgiven nor forgotten, and as Colonial Secretary he was regarded as both dilatory and anti-German.[19] As for Gladstone, the most printable of Bismarck's comments on him was that 'he was a man who had no knowledge of foreign affairs and with whom it was impossible to do business'.[20] But though Bismarck later came to regard Salisbury's friendship as 'worth more than twenty marshy colonies in Africa',[21] at this stage he still tended to think of him as an 'obstinate and clumsy lay clergyman'.[22]

It was not Salisbury's way to rush his fences. Unlike Gladstone, he was no great believer in action for its own sake. Where the 'Grand Old Man' had poured energy into great legislative feats, Salisbury believed that little good came from such ventures. His view of the functions of government was not a high one: 'I reckon myself as no higher in the scale of things than a policeman – whose utility would be gone if the workers of mischief disappeared'.[23] Given his diplomatic inheritance, Salisbury expected that 'England will remain comparatively isolated and her word will weigh less in Europe than it did twenty years ago'.[24]

In addition to his formal approach to Bismarck, Salisbury also used more informal methods. His private secretary, Sir Philip Currie, now long recovered from his *faux pas* over the Berlin Memorandum, visited Hamburg in early August and sounded out Herbert Bismarck about the diplomatic situation.[25] Young Bismarck explained that much though his father wanted 'a close alliance between England and Germany', the 'irritating policy of the late Cabinet had been impossible to understand'. However, when it came to persuading the Russians to give the Zulficar Pass back to the Emir of Afghanistan in return for Penjdeh, Bismarck was unwilling to become involved. In response to Salisbury's fears that there might be a 'complete rupture between England & Russia',[26] Herbert thought it unlikely that the Russians would agree to arbitration about the issue of the frontier, but nor did he think that war was inevitable – unless British public opinion refused to abide by the results of arbitration on other issues at stake. But when it came to influencing his father, the young man confessed that 'no one has any influence with [him]'.[27]

Bismarck professed himself 'flattered' by the British approach, saying that he would be 'glad to do what he could to promote good relations and peace between England & Russia', but he could not 'undertake arbitration unless it was also proposed by Russia in concert with England'. He was 'most anxious to please Lord Salisbury personally and . . . desired strongly to comply with his request, but . . . the interests of Germany did not allow him to do so, and . . . Lord Salisbury as a patriotic statesman, would understand that they must be his first care'.[28] Bismarck could not be sure that Gladstone's 'peculiar deviations' from 'traditional British policy' would not be repeated,[29] and was not willing to risk Russia's wrath by arbitrating in the Afghan dispute; if Russian troops were employed in Asia, they were no danger to him in Europe.[30] So Salisbury had to make his own way with regard to Russia.

Salisbury inherited the traditional mistrust of Russian imperialism, but his answer to it was more Derbyite than Disraelian. Gorchakov's old comment that 'one of Russia's main objects in drawing near to us in India was to make her Asiatic politics react on our European politics',[31] touched one of Salisbury's deepest concerns. He told the new British Ambassador in St Petersburg, Sir Robert Morier, that although it was 'very difficult to come to any satisfactory conclusion as to the real objects of Russian policy', he was 'inclined to believe that there are none, that the Emperor is really his own Minister, & so bad a Minister that no consequent or coherent policy is possible'. However, 'if Russia satisfies us that there is not room in Asia for herself & us also, our policy to her must be one of a very intensive, & probably also, of a very effective character'. Russia's only weak point was her 'financial embarrassment', and 'if we become her chronic enemy it is to that weak point that our efforts must be addressed. We must lead her into all the expense we can' in the hope that 'a few steps further must push her into the revolution over which she seems constantly to be hanging.' But he was not sure that Britain would have 'the tenacity to pursue such a policy'. Russia was 'really invulnerable to military attack', which was 'all the more reason to avoid, if we can, a crisis which must lead to such terrible calamities'.[32]

The crisis was avoided on this occasion because the Russians themselves, aware of the dangers of provoking a conflict with a government which might well force the Straits, had already decided to seek a peaceful solution to the Pendjeh crisis.[33] On 10 September, the British and the Russians signed a preliminary agreement which removed the immediate prospect of war. But Salisbury suspected that the Russians might be preparing 'for immediate war' in the event of the Conservatives remaining in office after the general election in December.[34] The firm line over Afghanistan was continued when, a few days later on 18 September, the Eastern Question entered a new phase with the announcement by the ruler of Bulgaria, Prince Alexander of Battenberg, of a union between his country and Eastern Rumelia.

This was in direct breach of the treaty agreed at the Congress of Berlin, but Salisbury's attempt to co-ordinate a protest against this action met with no success. Austria and Germany took the view that if the Porte, as the nominal sovereign of Eastern Rumelia, had not objected, it was hardly up to them to do so. Salisbury himself had to admit that Turkey's refusal to act 'proves that Turkey is dead', and he feared that they might be 'at the beginning of the end'.[35] But the eventual opposition of Russia to the union of the two Bulgarias convinced him that there was something to be said for it; the question was how to keep Alexander in place and to prevent the Russians replacing him with a 'Russian Prince' under cover of acting for the 'Concert'.[36] Salisbury's refusal to agree to the German proposal that there should be a return to the *status quo ante* in Bulgaria risked, in the words of the Russian Foreign Minister, Nikolai Giers, 'lighting a conflagration in the East which could finish off the Ottoman Empire and set fire to Europe'.[37] For the man who had helped engineer the division of the two Bulgarias to have thus resisted attempts to keep them together might have appeared inconsistent, but it was not. Salisbury had opposed a 'Big Bulgaria' when he thought it would be a Russian tool; he now approved of it because under Alexander it had turned out not to be so.[38]

In the face of opposition from the other Powers and from his own Secretary of State for India, Lord Randolph Churchill, Salisbury stood firm.[39] As long as the Bulgarian issue was alive, a wedge was driven into Bismarck's *Dreikaiserbund*: Austria would look to England for support; Bismarck would not dare choose between his two allies; and Salisbury would gain some freedom of manoeuvre. There was always a possibility that the Turks would try to put down the revolt, but a Pan-Slavist like the new Tsar, Alexander III, could hardly sit by and watch that happen; and if the Bulgarians fought back, as they would, Alexander's dilemma would become acute.[40] So, with an election imminent in England, Salisbury enjoyed the rare luxury of being able to win the approval of the Turcophobes and the Russophobes.

On 14 November, the Serbs declared war on Bulgaria in search of 'compensation'. On 19 November, they suffered a crushing defeat at the hands of the Bulgarians at the battle of Slivnitza. Salisbury's comment to the Queen was apposite: 'if Prince Alexander continues to fight as well as he has hitherto done, it will be impossible for Russia to separate the Bulgarias'.[41] So it proved. First the French and then the Italians withdrew from support for the conditions of the Berlin settlement. Bismarck, alarmed by the prospect of his two allies in the *Dreikaiserbund* quarrelling by proxy through Serbia and Bulgaria, was anxious to bring the affair to a settlement. Salisbury's solution was to maintain the fiction of Turkish sovereignty by prevailing upon Alexander to ask for recognition of the union from the Sultan; once this had been conceded, the Russians could hardly fail to acquiesce.[42]

The Queen could be pardoned for writing about the 'admirable manner' in which Salisbury had 'conducted public affairs'. The 'triumphant success of his conduct . . . has in seven months raised Great Britain to the position she ought to hold in the world'.[43] His triumph had certainly owed something to luck, but he had put himself in the way of riding it. Prestige counts as a weapon in international affairs. When Salisbury came to the Foreign Office, he had to act without it; by the time he left it, he had acquired it. Salisbury had established himself as a skilful and resourceful diplomatist and had made it as plain as Disraeli had done that Britain would not hesitate to act, if need be alone, in defence of her vital interests. Unsurprisingly, Bismarck's 'cordiality grew substantially'.[44]

Salisbury's certainty that even under a new Liberal Government there would be 'continuity of policy' puzzled his daughter, who assumed that it was an 'audacious kind' of 'bluff' used to persuade Bismarck that he could rely on Britain;[45] that may have been the case, but other explanations are possible. The failures of Midlothianism had damaged the Liberals, and by the time Gladstone left office it had been abandoned in practice – as the Penjdeh crisis showed. Given the political situation, it was not likely that the Liberals would win the sort of majority which would give Gladstone a mandate to revisit Midlothianism even if he wanted to. Finally, the electoral situation was not likely to produce a strong Liberal Government with a common focus on foreign affairs. Nor did it. The election left the Irish Nationalists holding the balance. Thrice in Gladstone's lifetime the Conservatives had passed measures which they had formerly opposed: 1829, with Catholic Emancipation; 1846, with the repeal of the Corn Laws; and 1867, with the Second Reform Act. On the first two occasions the Party had split irrevocably, dooming itself to a long period of political impotence; Salisbury refused to repeat the trick for Gladstone's benefit. So Gladstone came out for Home Rule and the Liberals split. The Government Gladstone formed in January lacked Hartington and most of the Whigs, and he was too preoccupied with Ireland, and latterly by the defection of Chamberlain and his followers, to take much interest in foreign policy. In this situation, as Salisbury had surmised, there was little room for a distinctly Liberal foreign policy; what there was was reduced to vanishing-point by the replacement of Granville at the Foreign Office. Ailing though he was, Granville would have been glad to have returned there, but partly through the offices of the

Queen, he was replaced by the rising star of the Liberal Party, the Earl of Rosebery.

Rosebery represented a younger generation of Liberals. Even during the Great Eastern Crisis of 1876–8 he had declared that the Liberals were as proud of the Empire as any Tory, and would maintain it 'with their blood' if necessary.[46] He had disliked Gladstone's Egyptian policy and shared the view of Hartington that until a stable government had been established and British interests safeguarded, there should be no evacuation.[47] He also shared Salisbury's view of the Bulgarian crisis and made clear his determination to continue his policy. But unlike Salisbury, who had used rhetoric about 'freedom' for his own ends, Rosebery genuinely believed that Britain should promote the cause of the Balkan people.[48] Perhaps fortunately for his reputation, he had little chance to show the difference between himself and Salisbury before the Liberal Government fell in July.

From the point of view of domestic politics the flight of the Whig earls was a welcome development for Salisbury. He had long regarded their presence in Gladstone's increasingly radical Cabinets as an anomaly. In early 1885, he wrote to Northcote: 'They are perpetually trying to solve Chamberlain's question as to how much ransom they should pay for their property, and the ransom they pay is the support they give to the radicals.'[49] But the smoothness of any realignment of Whigs with Conservatives to form a party of vested interests was disrupted by the flight of the Chamberlainite Radicals. In terms of foreign affairs, however, it presaged a period of minority government which might damage Britain's standing in the world still further.

The election of July 1886 produced, as Salisbury had feared, a situation in which no one party had a majority in the Commons, but since Gladstone declined to take office with an anti-Home Rule majority against him, the Queen sent for Salisbury. The Tories were at least twenty seats short of a Commons majority and would have to look to the Liberal Unionists under Hartington and Chamberlain for support.[50] Salisbury's initial thought was to cement the anti-Home Rule forces by offering to serve under

Hartington, but the latter declined the offer because he did not want to accept the implication that the Liberal split was permanent.[51] This left Salisbury to cope with trying to put together a Tory Cabinet to form a minority government.[52]

It was not simply distaste for all that went with the job of forming a government which made Salisbury willing to pass that burden to Hartington; it would have solved the problem of the Foreign Secretaryship. In Derby's view, no one 'except Lytton' was 'fit for the place'.[53] In a Hartington Cabinet, Salisbury could have gone to the Foreign Office; now he could not. He did not think that he could 'with any hope of carrying it through successfully, repeat the experiment of last summer by uniting the Foreign Secretaryship with the Premiership', and offered the post to the vastly experienced Ambassador in Paris, Lord Lyons.[54] But at the age of sixty-nine, in indifferent health (he was to die within the year) and lacking parliamentary experience, Lyons was not eager to change his comfortable existence. Salisbury then turned to Lord Cranbrook, but he felt 'so terribly my incapacity as a linguist' that he declined the offer.[55] This allowed Salisbury to offer the Foreign Office to Iddesleigh.[56]

The appointment was not a happy one. It was not just that Iddesleigh was ailing, but that he remained the butt of Lord Randolph's hostility. Churchill, whose oratorical and political skills had enabled him to demand, and receive, the Exchequer, liked to proclaim himself as the heir to Disraeli's 'Tory Democracy', although the suspicion that this was 'mostly opportunism' was never far from the minds of his critics. But in foreign affairs he turned out to be something quite different. As Chancellor it was not surprising that he should have favoured a pacific foreign policy, such is the habit of most holders of that office, but he combined parsimony with a scepticism towards the carcasses of dead policies which out-matched even that of the author of that phrase.

Lord Salisbury once compared Churchill to the Mahdi, saying that where the latter pretended to be mad but was in fact sane, the position was the reverse with Churchill. Salisbury's irritation was understandable. Fundamental to his policy during the Great Eastern Crisis, and the more recent fracas in Bulgaria, had been the linkage between Russian expansionism in the Balkans and Central Asia. He had sent Sir Henry Drummond-Wolff on a mission to Constantinople in late 1885 to try to restore the old relationship with Turkey, which had been so damaged by Gladstone's attitude and actions in Egypt. He still looked towards a lessening of Anglo-French tensions over Egypt and the consequent possibility of a renewing of the old 'liberal *entente*' which would restore to Britain that freedom of manoeuvre she had possessed in the 1870s. Both these objectives were threatened by Churchill, who took the view that the possession of Cyprus and Egypt made the Straits a matter of indifference to Britain. He thought that India should be defended on the North-West Frontier. This was a point of view with which Salisbury disagreed, but, given the instability of his administration and the important position held in it by Churchill, it was difficult for him to combat it.

If domestic circumstances and the continuing effects of the Liberal inheritance constituted two of the restrictions upon Salisbury's diplomacy throughout the next two decades, a third one made itself felt almost at once upon his return to office. In July 1886, the Russians kidnapped Prince Alexander and forced him to abdicate. The Queen, as ever, was in favour of forceful action, but as Salisbury pointed out:

> As land forces go in these days, we have no army capable of meeting even a second-class Continental Power; that is we could never spare force enough at any one point to do so. The result is that, in all places at a distance from the sea, our diplomatists can only exhort, they cannot threaten; and this circumstance often deprives their words of any weight.[57]

This triad – problems in the Cabinet; the *damnosa hereditas* of Egypt; and the want of sufficient armed forces – would dog Salisbury throughout the next decade and a half. He would make occasional headway with the first, but the second two proved more intractable.

Churchill's opposition first manifested itself in Cabinet on 7 September, when Salisbury and Iddesleigh argued for the retention of Prince Alexander; to his surprise, 'a section of the Cabinet showed a strong inclination to depart from the traditional policy . . . of resisting the designs of Russia upon the Balkan Peninsula'. He feared that this might produce 'serious' difficulties 'at any moment'.[58] Churchill's view was that there was nothing that could be done for Prince Alexander and therefore England should stay out of the affair; he doubted whether her interests would be much affected even if Constantinople fell.[59] Salisbury did not concur in Churchill's disregard for the fate of Constantinople: '[it would] be an awkward piece of news for the Minister who receives it. The prestige effect on the Asiatic populations will be enormous, and I pity the English party that has this item on its record. They will share the fate of Lord North's party.'[60] As he told Churchill, who made much of the constituency opposition to any policy which might be held to favour Turkey: 'My belief is that the main strength of the Tory party, both in the richer and poorer classes, lies in its association with the honour of the country.'[61] He had learnt Disraeli's lesson well. The problem was that Churchill was popular in the constituencies, and Salisbury was ill-equipped to deal with fractious opposition.

Churchill, in pursuit of his objective of a German alliance, wanted Britain to act in the Balkans only with German and Austrian support.[62] Although Salisbury was prepared to agree that nothing could be done about Prince Alexander, he was not prepared to restrict British action in the Balkans, and still less was he prepared to abandon his attempt to come to terms with the French over Egypt by announcing that Britain was going to stay there. As worrying as Lord Randolph's ideas on diplomacy was his desire to cut back the Defence Estimates. This presented Salisbury with the unalluring prospect of having to align himself permanently with Bismarck, without any alternative, and without the possession of sufficient military weight for Britain to be able to act alone.[63] Churchill's policy was hopelessly crude. Salisbury knew that he had to work with Bismarck, but he wanted to leave himself room not to be exploited; indeed, if necessary, he would be prepared to look again at some of the interests which needed defending rather than leave the initiative wholly to the Germans.[64]

Lord Cranbrook wrote to Salisbury on 23 November, urging him to abandon his attitude of 'self-renunciation' and assert his leadership.[65] Salisbury explained that his attitude arose from the 'peculiarities of Churchill'. Although Churchill and the rest of the Cabinet were out of sympathy on many issues, the former was a crucial figure for the Government's survival.[66] When the Government had been formed, Salisbury had worried about the 'lamentably weak' state of the Front Bench in the Commons,[67] and he did not think it could survive losing Churchill. He tried fresh negotiations with Hartington as a way of strengthening the Government's position, but his escape from the incubus of Lord Randolph came courtesy of the latter's overestimate of his importance. As Christmas loomed, so did a crisis over the Estimates. On 23 December Lord Randolph offered his resignation if he failed to get his way; Salisbury jumped at the resignation 'like a dog at a bone'. In the resulting reshuffle, Iddesleigh was moved from the Foreign Office; he reacted by dying in Salisbury's antechamber. There could only be one replacement – Salisbury himself.

Churchill's personality, policy preferences and prejudices were all unpalatable to Salisbury, who viewed his departure in the same light as might a man who has had a carbuncle removed from his neck. Impetuous, impulsive and self-willed, Lord Randolph would have allied Britain with the Triple Alliance, let the Russians have Constantinople and cut defence spending; he relied upon his own demagoguery to sell this interesting variant on Beaconsfieldism to the 'people'.[68] But in Salisbury's eyes relations with the Triple Alliance needed more skilful handling, whilst letting the

Russians have Constantinople would remove one of the few reasons why Austria and Italy might need British support, as well as damaging the Government in the eyes of the country; it would also provide little likelihood that the 'crypto-belligerency' between Russia and Britain would come to an end.[69] As for defence spending, that needed to be carefully tailored to a conservative definition of Britain's national interests. With Churchill gone, Salisbury could return to the task of sweeping up the china broken by Gladstone.

13

Navigating the Rapids

Salisbury's maxim that 'whatever happens will be for the worse', and that it was therefore 'in our interest that as little should happen as possible', applied to foreign as well as domestic affairs. The whole of his politics was suffused with the tension between his instincts and the realities of change. Salisbury had to deal with the international legacy of the shift from Beaconsfieldism to Midlothianism, their failures, and the impression they had given of a 'shifting foreign policy'; he had to adapt 'our foreign policy to the views of a Cabinet . . . usually ignorant of it'; and it was always his destiny to be 'making bricks without straw'. Without 'money, without any strong land force, with an insecure tenure of power, and with an ineffective agency', Salisbury had to 'counterwork the efforts of three Empires, who labour under none of these disadvantages'.[1] With Britain 'torn in two by a controversy which almost threatens her existence', she could not 'interfere with any decisive action abroad'.[2]

From this litany it is easy to see why Salisbury's policy came to be labelled one of 'splendid isolation'; this was a sadly reductionist way of describing a nuanced and subtle diplomacy which rescued Britain from the dangerous isolation of 1885. The 'isolationism' for which he was criticised in the late 1890s was the product of the diplomatic revolution of the post-Bismarckian period, and was certainly absent from his diplomacy in the late 1880s, when his primary object was to escape from isolation. Here Salisbury agreed with Iddesleigh's comment in 1886: 'Prince Bismarck is cold and sarcastic, but he is our best hope, and I want very much to get on something like friendly terms with him.'[3] Salisbury needed to work with the grain of Bismarck's conservatism, to guard against the two 'restless' Powers of France and Russia; but he did not want to go as far as Disraeli had in 1879, or as Churchill wanted in 1885. Alignment with Bismarck, *not* alliance, was his slogan. The Achilles' heel of the Bismarckian system was the Balkan rivalry between Austria and Russia: 'The dam which [Bismarck] had built up between them burst on the average once a year, and then he had, like a bricklayer, to patch it up.'[4] It was certainly 'somewhat cool' of Bismarck to 'expect that we are to pull the sting of the showerbath', by intervening in the Balkans when he was unwilling so to do,[5] but that very fact gave Britain a utility in Bismarck's system.

The maintenance of the *status quo* in the eastern Mediterranean was not only a British interest, it was an Austrian and even an Italian one; an alignment with them would be one, at a remove, with Bismarck, who desired neither Russian expansionism there, nor to prevent it. Since Britain did want to prevent that expansion, Austrian and Italian support would ensure that she did not do so alone; this was the key to Salisbury's success.

Salisbury entirely disbelieved in Churchill's idea of an agreement between Britain and Russia: 'You can have an *entente* with a man or a Government: but no-one except Canute's Courtiers ever tried to have it with a tide.' Salisbury saw the Russian advance as remorseless, 'moved by the forces which cause vast, rude populations to overthrow their borders'. 'Russia craved Constantinople for religious and military reasons': alongside the desire to 'put the cross on top of St. Sophia' was the 'constant appetite for gain and distinction which animates the officers of a vast military organization'. Because the 'British Philistine' would not fight 'except in self-preservation', the Russians might well be able to seize Constantinople and Afghanistan before public feeling was roused, and then war would be inevitable. The best policy he could pursue was a 'Fabian' one: 'Let her take as long on the road to C[onstanti-no]ple as we can possibly contrive. We have everything to gain, and nothing to lose by the delay.' Time and chance might provide the answer to the Russian problem, either in the form of revolution, Islamic revival or war against Germany, and Britain should not try to anticipate them by throwing herself in the path of the juggernaut. Salisbury was not worried about an Anglo-Russian war for its own sake – geography ensured that the two could inflict little direct harm on each other – but he feared the collateral damage; it might offer France the occasion for revenge, and an Anglo-French war would be extremely serious.[6]

Salisbury hoped to use Austrian fears of Russia as a key to the alignment he wanted, but the statesmen in Vienna had not forgiven Gladstone's disobliging comments in 1880. Bismarck told Currie in 1885, the 'feeling in Austria was that no reliance could be placed on the support of England'.[7] In October 1886, Salisbury made overtures to Austria about co-operation over the Bulgarian question,[8] and in his speech at the Lord Mayor's Banquet at the Guildhall on 9 November 1886, he stated that 'Austria's policy' towards Bulgaria would 'to a great extent govern that of England'.[9] Austria remained cautious.[10]

At the same time as Salisbury was struggling to overcome the Gladstonian legacy in Vienna, he was endeavouring to do the same with regard to France. He 'heartily' wished that 'we had never gone into Egypt. Had we not done so, we could snap our fingers at all the world'; but with the national or 'acquisitional' feeling 'roused', Britain could not just pull out.[11] The need for international co-operation in dealing with Egypt's finances placed Britain a 'great deal at the mercy of the German Powers', who had only to 'guarantee France from interference on their part to cause us a formidable amount of trouble'.[12] In addition to costing 'us a packet of bothers in various parts of the world',[13] French hostility had left Britain vulnerable to Bismarck's *chantage*, or blackmail.[14]

In November 1886, Salisbury publicly stated that no date could be set for the evacuation of Egypt, which could be decided only by internal circumstances and not external pressure. This created an obstacle to any negotiation with Freycinet, the French Premier who had been responsible for policy in 1882, and was 'anxious to improve his own position in the Chambers and in the country by obtaining our withdrawal'.[15] It is a sign of the importance Salisbury attached to getting back on good terms with the French that he should have assured them privately that he would be willing to negotiate directly about the terms for a British withdrawal.[16] But the unstable politics of the Third Republic brought in a new administration in December, whose Prime Minister, René Goblet, and Foreign Minister, Emile-Léopold Flourens, seemed to know 'nothing about foreign affairs'.[17] In January 1887, Drummond-Wolff was sent back to Constantinople to continue with negotiations about the future of Egypt, and Salisbury hoped that 'slow . . . hazy and ambiguous' negotiations with the French might produce the desired result.[18]

Without support from Vienna or Paris, Salisbury depended on Bismarck's Germany, whose 'political morality diverges considerably from ours on many points'.[19] But since Bismarck was not anxious to help his Italian and Austrian allies in areas which might involve a conflict of interests with Russia, he needed British co-operation, and so when the Italians approached Salisbury in January 1887 with a request for an alliance to maintain the *status quo* in the Mediterranean area, it was with the German Chancellor's full support.[20]

Italy was not well regarded by the other Great Powers, who tended to treat her as though she were one of them only by courtesy. On hearing that the Italians were demanding compensation for changes in the Balkans, Bismarck asked laconically whether they had lost yet another battle, commenting that their large appetite was accompanied by poor teeth. But with the anti-German feeling stirred up by the French War Minister, General Boulanger, creating tension between Berlin and Paris, Bismarck could neither afford to lose his Italian ally, nor to worsen relations with France by helping her. During the last few months of 1886, the Italians had been indicating to the British that they were available for diplomatic business in Egypt and elsewhere; frustrated at Salisbury's unwillingness to take their hints, they decided to make their proposal.[21]

Salisbury thought that the Italian proposal for an 'offensive and defensive' alliance against the French was against 'our traditions',[22] but that since it would also preclude an *entente* with France without providing security against Russia, it also ran counter to common sense. As it stood, the proposal was 'grave and impossible to accept'. Such an alliance would have to be approved by Parliament, but, as Cranbrook noted, 'publicity would be ruinous'.[23] On the other hand, it was clear that Bismarck favoured the idea, and it might therefore provide both a line to Vienna and a means of winning Germany's favour. Salisbury's response committed Britain to nothing, but left the door open for further talks.[24]

The situation required both diplomatic finesse and strong nerves. Italy was reported to be rearming heavily.[25] If this presaged an attempt to seize Tripoli as compensation for the French occupation of Tunis in 1881, it might also precipitate a general land-grab directed at the Ottoman Empire, as well as upsetting the French. But Salisbury was finding the French quite 'inexplicable'. Their relations with Germany were strained, and he was offering them a settlement in Egypt. He had thought they would have leapt at the opportunity. Instead, they seized one of the islands in the New Hebrides to which Britain had a claim,[26] and then raised the old question of the use of the Newfoundland shore which had been rumbling on since 1713.[27] As Salisbury expostulated to Lyons, France seemed 'bent upon aggravating the patient beast of burden that lives here by every insult and worry her ingenuity can devise'.[28] But despite his frustrations, Salisbury had not despaired of results from Drummond-Wolff's mission, and he had no intention of throwing away the chance of an *entente* with France by accepting Italy's offer as it stood.

But neither could Salisbury afford to pass up the chance of

escaping from isolation. A report on Britain's 'military and naval condition' was 'not agreeable reading'.[29] As Salisbury told the Queen on 10 February when presenting her with the results of his negotiations with the Italians, along with a plan to conciliate the French in Egypt: 'If, in the present grouping of nations, which Prince Bismarck tells us is now taking place, England was left out in isolation, it might well happen that the adversaries, who are coming against each other on the Continent, might treat the English Empire as divisible booty, by which their differences might be adjusted.' The risk and the cost of defending England in such a situation would be 'fearful', and given the congruence of interests between Italy and Britain, it made sense to come to an agreement with her. If there could also be a settlement of the Egyptian issue with France, which Salisbury doubted, then Britain would find herself in calm diplomatic water.[30]

The agreement with Italy was signed on 12 February.[31] Salisbury thought that whilst falling short of a pledge of 'material cooperation', it 'undoubtedly carries very far the *relations plus intimes* which have been urged upon us'. It was, he told the Queen, 'as close to an alliance as the Parliamentary character of our institutions will permit'.[32] But it was not only the immediate benefit of an agreement with the Italians which had prompted Salisbury to act; he looked towards Germany for diplomatic support 'elsewhere' in return for agreeing to the 'grouping' with Italy.[33] Bismarck's promise of assistance in Egypt helped sell the agreement to the Cabinet, and later that month the Austrians entered into discussions which resulted in Vienna adhering to the Anglo-Italian agreement.[34]

The terms of the First Mediterranean Agreement were deliberately vague. All the parties could decide what was meant by 'cooperation' if circumstances arose which made it necessary. No one could foretell what might happen, but if the Russians did attempt an adventurous policy at the Straits or in Bulgaria, it was certain that both Austria and Britain would seek each other's co-operation; Italy's adhesion was a useful makeweight. Given the 'rapidity with which the sight of armed men moving across the frontier of one of the allies of England' had transformed the 'fierce philanthropic fever' of 1876 into the 'equally violent' imperialist 'fever' of 1878, Salisbury was quietly confident that if it came to war, popular Russophobia would approve the Austrian alignment; as he told Morier, the Russians should be reminded that 'it is never safe to trust in the apparent apathy of the British people'.[35]

Salisbury was happy to co-operate with the 'Central European Powers – that has always been our policy', but there were times when Bismarck pushed his luck, such as when he argued that Britain ought to remain in Egypt to protect German trading interests. As Salisbury commented, 'when he wants us – as he evidently does – to quarrel with France downright over Egypt, I think he is driving too hard a bargain'. Gladstone's 'disastrous inheritance' allowed Bismarck to make 'unreasonable' demands not as the price for his support, 'but of his refusal to join a coalition against us'.[36] Unfortunately, there was no escape from this 'very inconvenient and somewhat humiliating relation'.[37] By the end of May 1887, Drummond-Wolff had drawn up a Convention to give effect to Salisbury's plans, and had even agreed to the Turkish request to evacuate after three years. But it was to no avail; the French and Russians put pressure on the Sultan not to sign it. Salisbury's exasperation at seeing a chance to restore some freedom of movement to his diplomacy vanish prompted him to exclaim to Lyons: 'Can you wonder that there is, to my eyes, a silver lining even to the great black cloud of a Franco-German War?'[38] But there was 'nothing for it but to sit still and drift awhile: a little further on in the history of Europe the conditions may be changed';[39] that would not happen in Salisbury's lifetime.

Salisbury was forced to the conclusion that 'for the present the enemy is France'.[40] Despite this, in October he was willing to put up with a great deal of public criticism in order to sign a convention with the French in which they agreed not to annex the New Hebrides in return for Britain consenting to the neutralisation of the Suez Canal: 'Do not be surprised', he told his Chancellor, George Goschen, 'if you see a good deal of bad language from the Jingoes.'[41] In spite of his siding with Disraeli in 1878, and despite the wary respect which he had for public opinion, Salisbury was never a Jingo. He always retained a Derbyite willingness to see the other person's point of view, and the sense to know that it is sometimes worth giving a little in order to oil the wheels of diplomacy: 'some people', he complained, 'seem to think that no negotiation is worth having unless the other side is very sore'.[42]

Salisbury was willing to come to an agreement with Russia over a specific issue like Afghanistan, as he did in July 1887, but any wider arrangement was ruled out by his own interpretation of the nature of Russian expansionism.[43] However, if France had to be regarded as inveterately hostile, it was at least worth thinking about whether Russia might be open to conciliation. One of Salisbury's habits as a diplomatist was to think aloud before coming to conclusions, and he now started to ask whether it was really worth supporting an Ottoman Empire which was too invertebrate to hold on to Bulgaria or to resist pressure from France and Russia. If war did break out between France and Germany, Salisbury was certain the latter would buy the Russians off at Turkey's expense. It would no doubt be a 'terrible blow to lose Constantinople', but, he wondered, 'have we not lost it already?'[44] Talking with Count Paul Hatzfeldt, the German Ambassador in London, on 2 August, Salisbury referred to Churchill's notion that 'England possessed no ... essential interest in the Bosphorus'; once concede that idea, and a *nouveau départ* in British foreign policy could be conceived. Whilst securing Austrian interests in the Balkans, it might be possible to do some sort of deal with the Russians at Turkey's expense. Salisbury's language was, even for one of his picaresque monologues, difficult for Hatzfeldt to comprehend, but the general tenor seemed plain enough.[45]

The idea of an Anglo-Russian *rapprochement* was not at all to Bismarck's taste. But he could hardly say that he would much prefer it if Britain and Russia remained at daggers drawn across the Hindu-Kush, so he professed to welcome such a development between two Powers who were Germany's friends; he simply asked whether Salisbury had considered what price he would have to pay for it. In a wonderfully Bismarckian move, he suggested that instead of a general agreement, the British might like to come to a specific one, such as giving in to Russian desires in Bulgaria.[46] Bismarck was well aware that if he had 'discouraged it, the idea would become a means to bring pressure on us'.[47] If it could not be used in this way, the notion lost its attractions for Salisbury, but he neatly returned the Bismarckian lob, saying that as he did not think a Franco-German war was likely, there was no urgency about the situation; in any case, he was anxious not to drive Italy into France's arms. Bismarck thought this unlikely, and was rather irritated that Salisbury was using his responses as excuses for doing nothing.[48] The Chancellor had met his diplomatic match. Salisbury had probed him and withdrawn delicately without ever actually having made any formal proposal which Bismarck could later misrepresent.

Bismarck and Hatzfeldt continued to take Salisbury's musings with more seriousness than they probably deserved. Hatzfeldt told Bismarck in late August that he was contemplating some 'diplomatic action' to 'stem the process of disintegration, which was becoming evident in the British Empire, and the lack of cohesion in political parties'. Should Salisbury be contemplating a spot of what historians would call social-imperialism, Bismarck kindly offered to back the summoning of a conference on Bulgaria in London. But again, Salisbury returned the ball. He still had no intention of letting the Germans encourage him to take Russia's chestnuts out of the fire in Bulgaria, but he was as adept as Bismarck in delivering his message in code. He told Hatzfeldt that he was 'honestly grateful to Prince Bismarck for his sympathetic offer', but that because the 'exercise of England's sovereignty is now in the hands of the uneducated masses', who 'neither care for nor understand foreign politics', he could not take it up: 'the British Empire is, to my deep regret, not able to make its voice heard in the Concert of Europe as strongly as her position as a Great Power ought to make possible.'[49]

It is tempting to conclude that Salisbury just used 'the nature of insular democracy' as an excuse to evade commitments he did not want, but there was more to it than that. As his comments in 1885 about the 'absolute sovereignty' of the people revealed, the question of how to deploy British power in a 'democratic' age was one which exercised him greatly. The occupation of Cyprus had been undertaken, at least in part, because of his feeling that whatever the British people thought about the 'balance of power' and Turkey, they would not stand for an eastern Mediterranean version of Gibraltar being threatened by Russia. He had only been happy to accept the commitment of the Mediterranean Agreement because he felt that public opinion would respond positively to any threat from Russia. The constraints imposed on diplomacy by 'democracy' constituted one of the greatest limitations on Salisbury's freedom of action. But having acknowledged that, Salisbury played his hand most skilfully. He remained, however, suspicious of Bismarck's taste for *chantage*, and looked with some scepticism at an approach from him in October which suggested that the Mediterranean Agreement should be expanded to include Turkey.

The Italians and Austrians had their own reasons for suggesting that Turkey should join the Mediterranean Agreement: the former feared growing Franco-Russian influence at Constantinople; the latter noted with anxiety Bismarck's tendency to support the Russians in Bulgaria following his Reinsurance treaty with them in June; an infusion of power into the Mediterranean Agreement might help combat these unfavourable developments. Bismarck's agreement to use his good offices in London helped him shore up the Triple Alliance, but it also aroused Salisbury's suspicions.[50]

The Austrian draft agreement, which Hatzfeldt presented to Salisbury in October, did not impress him. He told the Queen on 27 October that it was 'rather for the advantage of Germany than of the three other Powers'. It was 'impossible not to notice that Prince Bismarck is urging the three Powers to lift a weight which he will not touch with one of his fingers'. In addition to safeguarding the *status quo* in the Mediterranean, the new agreement proposed both to assist the Sultan in resisting pressure to delegate his suzerainty over Bulgaria, and to take naval action to prevent him from so doing. In Salisbury's phrase, it amounted to telling Turkey that, 'if she resists Russia, she will be supported, but that if she makes herself Russia's vassal she will be invaded'.[51] But despite these reservations, Salisbury was too much of a realist not to conclude that 'some adhesion on our part may be expedient as a lesser evil than breaking up the present understanding'.[52] Salisbury saw Bismarck's motives with a Bismarckian eye: 'If he can establish a South-Eastern raw, the Russian bear must perforce forget the Western raw on his huge carcase.' If Bismarck could 'get up a nice little fight between Russia and the three Powers, he will have the leisure to make France a harmless neighbour for some time to come'. It went against the grain 'to be one of the Powers in that unscrupulous game', but a 'thorough understanding with Austria and Italy is so important to us that I do not like the idea of breaking it up on account of risks which *may* turn out to be imaginary'.[53]

Moreover, this time circumstances enabled Salisbury to get more out of Bismarck than the latter wanted to concede. The Franco-Russian *rapprochement* at Constantinople worried all three members of the Triple Alliance, and Salisbury knew that without British support for Italy and Austria, Bismarck would have to make some invidious choices. Bismarck had remained aloof from the first set of negotiations; now Salisbury insisted on ringing him in: he wanted to know exactly what Germany's commitments to Austria were; and even more importantly, he wanted Bismarck to reveal which of his *Dreikaiserbund* allies he would support in the final resort. It is a sign of the strength of Salisbury's hand that he was able to force these concessions from the secretive Chancellor.[54]

Bismarck's responses showed the weaknesses which were beginning to undermine his once impregnable position.[55] With only a nonagenarian emperor and a mortally stricken heir standing between the twenty-three-year-old Prince Wilhelm and the throne, Salisbury was looking for assurances which might go beyond even the political lifetime of the seventy-three-year-old

Bismarck. These the Chancellor was happy to provide, in a twenty-page letter designed to reassure him that German foreign policy would remain dominated by the spirit of his diplomacy: dynastic politics had had their day, and no monarch could wrench German policy in another direction. German policy was pacific, and nothing save a direct act of aggression against Germany's frontiers could change that fact. If Austria were to vanish from the map, then Germany would be isolated facing France and Russia: '*ll est de notre intérêt d'empêcher même par les armes que pareil état de chose puisse s'établir* [It is in our interest to prevent, even by force of arms, such a state of affairs coming about].' Austria, Germany and Britain were conservative Powers who benefited from the *status quo* and who could only suffer if it were to be changed; France and Russia, by contrast, were Powers seeking their own advantage. An *entente* between Austria, Britain and Italy would help to prevent such a combination, or to keep it in check should it occur. Of course, when it came to the 'Orient', Germany lacked sufficient interests to play an active part, but no German Emperor could afford to see those Powers friendly to Germany weakened.[56]

This told Salisbury what he needed to know: Bismarck's system really was designed to preserve the *status quo*; and in the final resort, he would choose Austria and conservatism over Russia. This provided him with a guarantee that in the event of a Franco-German war, Russia would not be able to threaten Austria and make gains in the Balkans by relying upon Austrian helplessness in areas British sea power could not reach. He was quite prepared to enter a grouping of states which would be 'an effective barrier against any possible aggression of Russia'. Moreover, he was able to insist that the Triple Alliance Powers should extend the agreement to cover the defence of Turkey in Asia Minor.[57] On 12 December 1887, the Second Mediterranean Agreement between England, Austria-Hungary and Italy was signed. Its aim was the 'maintenance of peace' and the present state of affairs 'in the East', including the 'independence of Turkey' and the 'freedom of the Straits' to be 'independent of all foreign preponderating influence'.[58] Salisbury had secured his barricade against

Russian expansionism, and he had done so without any sacrifice of British interests; nor had he been forced to accept obligations towards others which were not necessarily consonant with those interests.

Cobden and Bright had believed that the 'absolute sovereignty of the people' in foreign affairs would bring about an end to aggression and diplomacy; Salisbury's observations led him to conclusions which were diametrically opposite. At the Guildhall on 9 November 1887, he said that, 'If there is any possible danger in the future, it rather arises . . . from possible gusts of passionate and ill-informed feeling arising from great masses of population.'[59] He had seen what public opinion could do to diplomatic continuity, and had discovered the truth of Derby's bitter observation that it was inimical to a stable foreign policy. Disraeli had been prepared to manipulate and channel popular Russophobia towards his own imperial ends. Salisbury, whose ends were a good deal less grandiose, was anxious not to stir the sleeping giant of public opinion.

On 11 January 1889, Bismarck proposed 'a Treaty between England and Germany, binding both Powers for a limited period to combined resistance against a French attack';[60] Herbert Bismarck pressed the matter further in March. Salisbury agreed that an alliance would be the 'best tonic for both countries', but regretted that the parliamentary situation made it impossible: 'We live no longer, alas, in Pitt's times . . . the aristocracy governed then and we were able to form an active policy, which made England after the Congress of Vienna the richest and most respected Power in Europe. Now democracy is on top', which brought with it 'the personal and party system, which reduces every British Government to absolute dependence on the *aura popularis*. This generation can only be taught by events.'[61]

Public opinion, like the old placemen and Whigs of the seventeenth and early eighteenth centuries, could afford, literally, to be irresponsible; the burden of paying for foreign wars and for the defence policy to support them would fall elsewhere. Salisbury's Country Party Toryism was reinforced by his sense that the ruling elite of which he was a part was suffering under unprecedented pressures. At a time when the political pressure to displace England's traditional rulers was increasing, the economic prosperity which was the necessary precondition for allowing them to give unpaid public service was faltering. Derby's comment in 1887 that he doubted that 'democratic politics will have many attractions for cultivated men in the next generation',[62] seemed very much to the point. In this situation sensible aristocrats would shy away from wars which would unleash 'tremendous' powers of 'destruction'. It was little wonder that Salisbury had come round to Derby's way of thinking, that it was worth paying a price in terms of 'prestige' if it avoided an unnecessary war.

When Salisbury declined the German alliance proposal, he told Hatzfeldt: '*Nous sommes des Poissons* [We are fish].'[63] Country Party Tories had always abhorred standing armies and preferred instead to rely upon sea power, which was cheaper and more effective in protecting British interests; Salisbury shared these preferences and the desire to keep defence spending under control.[64] The great American naval historian, Arthur Marder, wrote that the 'most important factor in stimulating the English interest in their navy was the appearance of Mahan's truly epoch-making sea power volumes in 1890 and 1892';[65] that may have been true of public opinion, but Tories like Salisbury did not require lessons in the importance of sea power from American sea captains. If the Mediterranean Agreements were going to be effective, and if the *rapprochement* at Constantinople between Russia and France was to be resisted, then Salisbury was well aware that Britain needed to modernise her naval forces.[66] Salisbury's response to popular anxiety about Britain's ability to hold her position in the world was to ask the Commons for £21.5 million and to pass the Naval Defence Act of 1889. Its aim was to establish the 'Two-Power Standard',[67] which, although more a term of art than science, did the job of quieting public concern. Over the next five years Britain committed herself to building ten battleships, forty-two cruisers and eighteen torpedo boats.[68] It was the largest naval building programme ever undertaken in peace time, but its defensive and conservative aims chimed perfectly with those of Salisburian diplomacy.

Salisbury's diplomacy had rescued Britain from isolation, but without limiting her freedom of manoeuvre. His defence policy, traditional and conservative, chimed with the instincts which inspired his diplomacy. Derby himself could not have asked for a policy more in line with traditional conservatism. But Salisbury could not entrench his policy, which remained at risk from the weakness of his parliamentary situation and the unpredictable pressures of public opinion. It was clear from the fuss over his arrangements with France over the New Hebrides that popular opinion did not like what the newspapers and the colonial interest groups presented as 'concessions' to foreign imperialism. This provided a limitation on the extent to which Salisbury could employ his favourite device of using colonial issues as bargaining counters in his wider diplomatic scheme of things. Salisbury had never seen any problem with German imperialism; indeed, to the extent that it directed Germany's ambitions away from Europe and distracted her with the burdens of Empire and the problems it brought with other Powers, he had always welcomed it;[69] but the different perspectives of others limited Salisbury's freedom. As Herbert Bismarck warned his father in 1889, Ministers feared that concessions to Germany in East Africa would lead to such a loss of support in the Commons that the administration would collapse. Salisbury had always held out for co-operation with Germany in the wider British interest, but it was questionable how much longer he could do so.[70] The obvious way out was a general settlement, but Salisbury, wary of his own Jingoes, was not sure that he could make the concessions which would be necessary to secure it.[71]

It was one of the preconditions of Salisbury's success that Germany should continue along the conservative path prescribed by Bismarck. The Chancellor refused to give any priority to those like Carl Peters who had grandiose African ambitions: 'England is more important to us than Zanzibar and East Africa'.[72] Where, as in East Africa, colonial disputes became severe enough to threaten to cause real problems, bilateral negotiations could usually sort things out. In the case of Zanzibar, this came about through the exchange of German interests in the region for the British concession of Heligoland. The Queen, despite having acquired so much territory during her reign, was reluctant to give up a small island, but Salisbury knew that the imperialists would happily agree to this in return for an even larger area of the map which could be coloured in red. It was a classic move, with Britain able to make fewer concessions in East Africa and the Germans able to explain away those they had made by reference to their gains.[73] Germany was 'freed from the danger that England might join with France and Russia',[74] whilst Britain was able to avoid enmity with Germany which might have forced Salisbury to 'change our system of alliances in Europe'.[75] However, with Bismarck's downfall in early 1890, the circumstances which had enabled Salisbury's policy to work so successfully began to change; and change was the great enemy of conservatism abroad as well as at home.

14

Isolation

After 1887 the 'key of the present situation in Europe', as far as Salisbury was concerned, was 'our position towards Italy, and through Italy to the Triple Alliance'.[1] But with Bismarck's fall, new directors of German foreign policy wanted clearer lines of definition in their diplomacy. The young Wilhelm II accepted Holstein's view that the Reinsurance treaty with Russia was incompatible with the Austrian alliance, and let it lapse; he also wanted more clarity in Britain's relationship with the Triple Alliance. He tried to get Salisbury to provide the Italians with a 'written guarantee' that France would not be allowed to have Tripoli,[2] as well as pressing for the Mediterranean Agreements to be extended to cover Italian interests in the west.[3] Salisbury feared that statements from Berlin and Rome during 1891 were giving the impression that 'we are more "Tripliste" than people thought'.[4]

Salisbury was right to be worried. France and Russia both feared that Britain's entry into the Triple Alliance was imminent, if it had not already occurred, and this helped push the two Powers towards a military *entente* in 1892, which grew into an alliance by 1894. The spectacle of Britain's two major imperial rivals coming together was one which convinced the Kaiser that it could only be a matter of time before bitter necessity drove the British into his arms;[5] it had a similar effect on some in Britain.

Wilhelm II lacked the ability and the appetite for concentrated work which would have let him direct German diplomacy in the way he desired,[6] but the political system allowed him enough power to push Germany along a diplomatic course which appealed to so many different interest groups. A man who could state publicly that Bismarck was a mere 'servant' and a 'pygmy', who had followed the orders of the omniscient Wilhelm I,[7] was clearly more than usually susceptible to the megalomaniac tendencies to which monarchs are subject. His conviction that Germany needed to command respect abroad, and that she needed to be a 'world power', led him into competition with the British.

This German restlessness, combined with the Franco-Russian *rapprochement*, changed the context in which British foreign policy had to operate. The full effects of this only became clear after Salisbury had left office in 1892, but since his two Liberal successors, Rosebery and Kimberley, ran a foreign policy along Salisburian lines, there is no reason to suppose that he would not have faced the same problems which hamstrung them; indeed, when he returned to office in 1896, this was precisely what happened.

Because the Germans wanted an end to what they saw as Britain's free ride on the coat-tails of the Triple Alliance, and because the Dual Alliance of Russia and France posed a threat to British imperial interests, Rosebery and Kimberley found themselves singularly vulnerable to an unprecedented concatenation of crises in the period 1893 to 1895. As the influential editor of the *Navy League Gazette*, H.W. Wilson, complained in March 1896: 'It is clear that we have no certain ally in Europe or in the world.'[8] In 1893, a Franco-Russian combination over a dispute in Siam forced Gladstone and Rosebery into a compromise favourable to Paris.[9] The following year a Franco-German alignment made the British resile on a treaty with King Leopold of the Congo (and Belgium).[10] Later that year Germany had joined with France and Russia to force the Japanese to disgorge the gains they had made at the end of their war with China at the Treaty of Shimonoseki. Rosebery had assumed that the Franco-Russian alliance was directed against Germany; it now appeared that it was aimed at Britain.[11] A new Eastern Question had now been opened up, 'pregnant with possibilities of a disastrous kind, and it might indeed result in an Armageddon between the European Powers struggling for the ruins of the Chinese Empire'.[12] Isolation in the Far East might compel the British to seek the assistance of the Triple Alliance – and even to join it.[13] This was, indeed, the aim of the Kaiser and his Foreign Minister, Baron Marschall,[14] although in joining the Far Eastern *triplice* they were also trying to renew links with Russia.[15]

Rosebery's response was in the best Salisburian tradition: taking the view that 'our only sure policy is to strengthen our fleet',[16] he went ahead with the Spencer programme designed to do just that; then, on the principle that 'our hands must be free', he sought an opportunity to show the Germans that he could co-operate with the Dual Alliance Powers.[17] Thus when the Eastern Question flared up again with Turkish massacres of Armenians in 1895, Rosebery formed a *triplice* with the Dual Alliance Powers with a view to imposing reforms upon Abdülhamid.[18] It was in the midst of this that his Government collapsed. Much though Salisbury would lament the inheritance he had been left, it was the result of the changes in Great Power diplomacy, not, for once, of Liberal insufficiency; no one could accuse Rosebery of having tried to run a Liberal foreign policy.

Salisbury had agreed with the Liberal Unionists beforehand that they would form a coalition government, and this time there was no offer to stand down in favour of Hartington, who had now become the Duke of Devonshire; although he was offered, and declined, the Foreign Office. The other Liberal Unionist leader, Joseph Chamberlain, surprised Salisbury by refusing the Exchequer and taking instead the Colonial Office.[19] The first act of the new Government was to call an election for July, which proceeded to give the Conservatives only their third majority in the Commons since 1841. With over 340 seats, and with seventy Liberal

Unionists on his side, Salisbury could look forward, for the first time in his career, to working from a position of strength.[20] But far from inaugurating a period of Salisburian control, what followed was a struggle for mastery over British foreign policy, at the heart of which were two different perceptions of how to react to the new circumstances facing Britain. Salisbury's chief antagonist was Joseph Chamberlain.

Chamberlain, like Churchill and Disraeli, saw himself as a man capable of moulding and directing public opinion. He was a man of decided opinions and of great energy, who was more than willing to play the Disraelian role of rallying public opinion to the cry that 'British Interests' required defending by a spirited and enterprising foreign policy; his own perception of Britain's deteriorating international position added an edge and an urgency to his actions, which made him a permanent thorn in Salisbury's side. Salisbury was bad at dealing with determined opponents: Churchill had provided his own answer to the problems he caused by removing himself; Chamberlain would not be so obliging. His position as the leading Liberal Unionist made it impossible for Salisbury to sack him. The fact that his *fin de siècle* anxieties chimed with those of the press made his words strike a chord with the public; and as the most controversial and dynamic politician of the day, he was a formidable figure. Salisbury's diplomacy, like Derby's, was incapable of providing the thrill and sensationalism upon which popular opinion thrived. Chamberlain's taste for showy triumphs was shared by the people who looked to him to provide an answer to the problems which the 1890s brought. Chamberlain shared Disraeli's penchant for judging diplomatic success by the deference which other countries paid to Britain's opinions; this went down well with large parts of the press and with popular opinion, who saw in it an affirmation of British superiority. In a conflict for public support, 'Jack Cade' had an obvious advantage over the reclusive aristocrat at Hatfield.

Salisbury's disdain for 'democracy' was practically unlimited: 'First-rate men', he once said, 'will not canvass mobs; and if they did, the mobs would not elect the first-rate men.'[21] He referred with contempt to the 'great democracy we all have to obey', with its 'ill-informed and unbridled impulses'.[22] Salisbury suspected that what passed for 'public opinion' was an artefact manufactured by 'the journalists, the literary men, the professor, the advanced thinker of the day',[23] who all used it to their own ends. But it existed all the same, and a political system which gave the vote to those of rudimentary education was only too vulnerable to 'gusts' of 'ill-considered' and unpredictable public opinion. Salisbury never forgot that in the final resort 'the British people and not the Cabinet were the arbiters of foreign policy'.[24] When Sir Philip Currie asked him in 1900 what he should tell the Italians about Britain's conduct in case of a Mediterranean conflict, he responded: 'we cannot predict our policy in the event of a war, unless we can see what the *casus belli* will be. The public opinion here will be guided by the causes of the quarrel; and in questions of peace and war, the action of the Government is entirely dependent on that opinion.'[25] He was well aware of how triumphalism in the newspapers could inflame Britain's relations with France and Germany and was determined 'not to allow the fruits of his diplomacy to be imperilled by unwary popular comment'. On one occasion, upon being told that the papers were 'full' of his latest diplomatic triumph, his only comment was, 'I hope to goodness there's no trumpeting! I have done my best to prevent it.'[26] This was not the way to combat 'pushful Joe'.

This preference for quiet diplomacy, like Salisbury's determination to adhere to his old lines of policy in a changed world, could, and eventually did, strike others as nothing less than 'polite appeasement'.[27] Although many of his colleagues would approximate tentatively to this conclusion, it came to be held most firmly by Chamberlain, to whom the word 'tentative' meant as little as the words 'tact' and 'diplomacy'. This cleavage between Salisbury and his colleagues has been attributed in part to a generational difference – 'Edwardian' pessimism being pitted against 'Victorian' optimism[28] – but this can only be wholly sustained by following Henry Kissinger in misdating Chamberlain's birth by a generation.[29] In fact, although temperamentally Salisbury was as much a pessimist as Chamberlain was an optimist, in the realm of foreign affairs they may be said to have exchanged characters. Salisbury's conviction that things would always change made him less inclined to view Britain's current problems as more permanent than anything else; Chamberlain's inability to resist trying to find solutions to every problem made him anxious about their seeming intractability.

Salisbury's priorities remained what they had been: he wanted to get on good terms with France and Russia, but until that proved possible he would lean towards the old conservative alignment with the Triple Alliance.[30] But here he encountered two problems which seemed to undermine his whole strategy: concessions to France and Russia failed to work;[31] and the Germans wanted a firm commitment to join their alliance system. The more the former state of affairs prevailed, the more tempting the latter option became to those who deplored what they saw as Salisbury's inactivity. For those of an activist frame of mind, it seemed as though everywhere they looked Britain's position was crumbling: in Africa; in the Near East and in the Far East, the challenges were mounting, and an isolated Britain under Salisbury's impassive leadership appeared to have no strategy for dealing with the situation.

The French Ambassador, Geoffrey de Courcel, reported that Salisbury had a tendency to see the world in terms of a multitude of 'sick men';[32] of these the sickest was the Ottoman Empire. The success of the Bulgarian revolts and the sympathy of the Great Powers for the Christian inhabitants of the Ottoman Empire had encouraged unrest in parts of the Sultan's domains, and nowhere more so than in the eastern vilayets where there were substantial numbers of Armenians. Those who wished to see the creation of an Armenian state had seized the opportunity of a return to power by the Liberals to create a situation in which, as they hoped, the British and the other Powers would be able to intervene. Unrest in 1894 was met with the usual Turkish response, which was followed by the usual European demands for reforms.[33] It was this situation which Salisbury inherited. He thought that Rosebery and Kimberley had left him a 'very bad hand to play and doubted his winning any tricks'.[34]

The question of how Salisbury played that hand goes to the heart of the debate over his diplomacy.[35] The Germans[36] and the Russians[37] both came to believe that Salisbury was interested in abandoning the old British position at the Porte and that he was willing to partition the Ottoman Empire. Some historians have seen this reversal of policy as being accompanied by a fresh determination to hold on to Egypt, despite the risk of a clash with France. There are, however, grounds for thinking that this is to attribute too much clarity to a policy which was marked by more caution than boldness.

Three external changes made a simple continuation of the old Palmerstonian policy impossible: British actions at and since Berlin in 1878 had convinced Abdülhamid that the 'traditional old friendship' of England for Turkey had given way to 'outspoken enmity';[38] as a consequence, he was now more willing to listen to the Russians, who, disappointed by the ingratitude of the Bulgarians, had ceased offering pressing 'reforms' on him; finally from Salisbury's point of view, the possibility of action was constrained by the Dual Alliance. Even before he had left office in 1892, the Admiralty was warning of the dangers to the position at the Straits to be apprehended from a Franco-Russian alliance;[39] by the time he returned, it had not changed its mind.

These external facts impinged upon a consciousness which, as we have seen, had already played with the idea that the Crimean policy was a 'dead carcase'. It would, therefore, have been surprising had Salisbury not meditated over his options. On the other hand, he severely rebuked Lord Kimberley in March 1897 for saying that his Party could no longer support the old policy. Salisbury declared that abandoning Turkey would be to 'disregard the solemn signature of England with regard to one of the most important treaties of the century'.[40]

The conflicting evidence can be reconciled if the nature of Salisbury's diplomacy is appreciated. Historians and commentators at the time searched for consistency and clarity, but where circumstances made consistency problematical, clarity was not always desirable. Committed by the Liberals to a reform project drawn up in May, Salisbury was bound to see whether the Russians would support it; his own public opinion demanded as much. Once the Russians had made their refusal to coerce the Porte plain, he was also bound to consider other options. But the problem of defining what British interests were at stake now in the Eastern Question had become a formidable one. Salisbury was puzzled that 'two psychological climates can exist side by side so utterly different as those of England and Continental Europe'. He doubted whether anyone on the Continent cared 'whether the Armenians are exterminated or not. Here the sympathy for them . . . approaches to frenzy.'[41] With fresh massacres of Armenians in September 1895, the public demands for action grew louder. Salisbury would have been quite happy to have considered unilateral British action, but his naval advisers were unanimously of the opinion that in the new circumstances created by the Dual Alliance, Britain should not take the risk of forcing the Straits alone.[42] Moreover, Russia might react by attacking India, which would be a 'war, not of battles, but of devastation'.[43] With his admirals treating their ships as though they were made of porcelain, and his soldiers fantasising about Russians coming through the Khyber Pass, Salisbury had to face the fact that Britain could do nothing.

Salisbury would have responded to Austrian requests in October for a renewal of the old Mediterranean Agreements, but the Austrians showed themselves unwilling to cross the Russians; what Salisbury did not know was that the Austrian reluctance derived in part from German pressure. Prince Chlodwig Hohenloe-Schillingfurst and Baron Friedrich von Holstein of the German Foreign Office did not want the British to be able to use the Austrians and the Italians unless they joined the Triple Alliance.[44]

It was this inability to act unilaterally, and the search for partners with whom to act, that imparted opaqueness to Salisbury's diplomacy. It is easy to see why he would have objected to Kimberley's remarks. Salisbury was well aware of the fact that foreigners would take them to mean that when the next Liberal Government came in, Turkey would be abandoned. Even if Salisbury was being driven towards that conclusion, to announce it would have meant losing all influence at the Porte immediately; it would also have broken the line to Vienna and shown the Russians the cards in his hand. Salisbury sought to pursue the old policy to see if it was still viable; it kept his lines open to Vienna and Rome, and it prevented him having to decide to maintain Britain's interests in the eastern Mediterranean by making the occupation of Egypt permanent. But he was always open to the possibility that it might be time to liquidate the Eastern Question, which is why he sounded out the Germans and the Russians about their respective attitudes.[45]

Hatzfeldt's reports of Salisbury's comments about the possible fate of the Turkish Empire were interpreted in Berlin as signs that he wished to 'hasten the process' of Turkey's dissolution 'in the hope that England might be able to hold aloof from the struggles on the Continent resulting from it'.[46] But Hatzfeldt, more acute in his perceptions of Salisbury's motives, was prepared to accept his assurances that his policy had not changed.[47] He warned Holstein that Salisbury still thought of the preservation of Turkey as a 'significant British interest', but that 'he is too practical a statesman not to reckon with the consequences, no matter how undesirable he might find them, that would result'.[48] But nothing could shake Holstein and company from their tendency to read every British action as confirmation of their view that the British were becoming desperate for German assistance; or of their determination to extract a price for it.

The Kaiser used the opportunity of a visit to Cowes in August 1895 to raise the subject with Salisbury; he later claimed that his 'distrust of British policy under Lord Salisbury's administration' was to 'a great extent' the product of this meeting.[49] He seems to have furnished Salisbury with his own plans for the possible partition of the Turkish Empire,[50] but when the Prime Minister failed to turn up as promised for a second meeting, Wilhelm felt snubbed; as he did when there was no reaction to his scheme. The

Kaiser claimed that Salisbury's remarks could 'only be interpreted as a prelude to the dismemberment of Turkey', adding that his interpretation must have been the correct one because Salisbury had said as much to Hatzfeldt earlier.[51] But according to Salisbury's Permanent Under-Secretary, Sir Thomas Sanderson, there was 'nothing in Lord Salisbury's official utterances which shows that he seriously contemplated a speedy partition – rather the reverse'. He thought that the misunderstanding arose through Salisbury's characteristically subtle way of parrying Hatzfeldt's loaded questions. Hatzfeldt had pressed Salisbury to do something to help the Italians in Abyssinia, but he diverted the conversation to a discussion of the 'eventual share of Italy in the Turkish possessions in Tripoli and Albania'. Salisbury was sure that this would get back to Constantinople, where it might have a 'wholesome effect'; if the Sultan thought that he was on the verge of losing British support, then he might be induced to implement a reform programme.[52] But such subtlety was far beyond the comprehension of the Kaiser.[53]

Wilhelm warned the British Military Attaché in Berlin, Colonel Swaine, that 'England could only escape from her present total isolation, which was the result of her "policy of selfishness and bullying" by uncompromisingly siding openly with the Triple Alliance or against it.'[54] He certainly shared his English grandmother's fondness for holding fiercely to the few ideas which managed to effect a lodgement in his mind. He was to remain convinced that the English statesman would have to come to heel. Events towards the end of the year reinforced this notion, and seemed, at least to Wilhelm, to require some action from him to convince the British of their plight.

The first sign of the crisis which was to threaten to engulf Salisbury's policy came on 17 December, when President Cleveland of the United States addressed a special message to Congress in which he said that although it was grievous to contemplate conflict between the 'two great English-speaking peoples of the world', he was prepared to risk this rather than to compromise American honour.[55] This warning was prompted by Britain's failure to respond to a despatch sent back in August protesting about Britain's attitude to the border dispute between British Guiana and Venezuela.

The British had acquired Guiana from the Dutch in 1814 at the end of the Napoleonic Wars.[56] The exact boundary between British and Venezuelan territory had been a matter of dispute for much of the century, with the latter making, ever and anon, claims which the former always regarded as exorbitant.[57] When the issue flared up in the 1890s, the Venezuelans looked to the Cleveland administration for support – and they were not disappointed. Secretary of State Richard Olney's despatch had claimed that the Monroe Doctrine applied to Venezuela, and he demanded that the British should refer the dispute to arbitration, stating that: 'today the United States is practically sovereign on this continent, and its fiat is law upon the subjects to which it confines its interposition'. The 'infinite resources' of the United States, 'combined with its isolated position render it master of the situation and practically invulnerable as against any and all powers'.[58] To some extent Olney was responding to pressure from the press and American public opinion. Cecil Spring-Rice, a minister at the British Embassy in Washington and an Americanophile, took the view that it was not the 'slightest good trying to conciliate the U.S. You might as well conciliate a jackal or, let us say, a tiger. The jealousy of England is so acute that nothing we can do will do the slightest good.'[59] Salisbury's instincts pointed him in the same direction, and when he did respond, on 26 November, he rejected Olney's interpretation of the Monroe Doctrine.[60] The American diplomat Henry White, whom Olney sent to London in early 1896 to sort out the imbroglio, regarded the 'famous' message as 'another proof' of Cleveland's 'ignorance of diplomacy. I don't think he had realized the international tempest which the message would occasion.'[61] White was correct in this supposition, as in the view that the British had 'miscalculated the force of American public opinion on the Monroe Doctrine'. Salisbury himself was unworried by the American bluster, but a few days later worse was to come.

Even as Salisbury and Chamberlain were digesting the implications of Cleveland's message, Dr Starr Jameson was preparing for the raid which he launched into the Transvaal from Rhodesia on New Year's Eve 1896. His object was to precipitate an uprising among the British miners in Johannesburg, but instead he achieved only ignominy, being captured by the Boers on 2 January. If the Raid was an act of stupidity, it paled in significance to Kaiser Wilhelm II's response to it.

The Germans were well aware of the sensitivity of the British to intervention in southern Africa. In January 1895, the President of the Transvaal, Paul Kruger, had toasted the Kaiser and spoken of the need for a closer relationship between the Boer republics and Germany. The British Ambassador in Berlin, Sir Edward Malet, had warned the German Government not to give the Boers the impression they could rely on German support; he had also made it clear that good relations between England and Germany would depend, to a large extent, on this issue.[62] According to the Kaiser, Malet 'had gone so far as to mention the word "war" '. Wilhelm was furious that 'for a few square miles full of niggers and palm trees England had threatened her one true friend'.[63] Salisbury strongly denied that Malet had had any instructions to use such words, but Wilhelm thought that they might be able to 'make capital' out of it by demanding an increase for the navy.[64] Holstein came up with the idea of a Continental League as a way of convincing the British that they had better join the Triple Alliance while they still could.[65] The Kaiser told the British Military Attaché on 20 December that 'if England wants allies or aid, she must abandon her non-committal policy'.[66] The German Foreign Minister, Marschall, told the British Ambassador, Sir Frank Lascelles, that Germany must insist upon the independence of the Transvaal, and that a coalition of the Continental Powers might look to the British Empire 'for objects of compensation'.[67]

The Kaiser reacted to the Jameson Raid with a 'transport of fury',[68] and wanted to declare an immediate German protectorate over the Transvaal, mobilise the marines and send troops there.[69]

Marschall persuaded him not to send the telegram he had originally composed to Kruger, but what he sent was bad enough. On 3 January 1896, Wilhelm congratulated the Boer leader on the fact 'that without calling on the aid of friendly Powers, you and your people, by your own energy against the armed bands which have broken into your country as disturbers of the peace, have succeeded in re-establishing peace and defending the independence of the country against attacks from without'.[70]

The Times spoke for the rest of the press when it described the telegram 'as deadly and unprovoked an insult as was ever offered by the head of a European nation to one of equal rank'.[71] The windows of German shops were broken and Germans were boycotted in the clubs of London,[72] whilst Hatzfeldt reported an 'entirely changed situation' which had stirred up such depths of public bitterness that 'if the Government had lost its head or had wished for war for any reason, it would have had the whole of public opinion behind it'.[73] As one authority puts it: 'Probably no single act in the years before 1914 did more to inflame British and German public opinions against each other than the sending of the Kruger telegram.'[74]

The German hopes that the telegram would impress upon the British that their 'independence' led only to 'isolation and that isolation can be dangerous',[75] were not altogether without foundation, as reactions to the concatenation of crises showed.

On the Cleveland issue Salisbury wished to stand firm, telling his colleagues on 11 January that 'if we were to yield unconditionally to American threats another Prime Minister would have to be found'.[76] But when Chamberlain responded to the Kruger telegram by arguing that 'I think what is called an "Act of Vigour" is required to soothe the wounded vanity of the nation. It does not matter which of our numerous foes we defy, but we ought to defy someone',[77] he revealed the chasm which divided his attitude from Salisbury's. Chamberlain was thinking only of satisfying public opinion; Salisbury was not.

In the aftermath of the Cleveland message and the Kruger

telegram, the press in Britain and Germany was full of comment about Britain's 'isolation'. This impression was not confined to the public prints. When Salisbury saw Hatzfeldt on 11 January 1896, the German Ambassador stressed the advantages which a formal connection with the Triple Alliance would have for Britain in view of her 'isolation'. Salisbury saw straight through the flimsy gauze of German diplomacy, and he told the Queen that this confirmed his own suspicion that 'the Emperor has really been trying, during the last six months, to frighten England into joining the Triple Alliance'. Queen Victoria, who as ever in these matters managed to represent the views of the average man, did feel that Britain's isolation was 'dangerous' and was inclined to take Hatzfeldt's words to heart; but Salisbury would not be moved.[78]

The Prime Minister now found himself under assault from what he would later call 'Jingo critics',[79] and a line of attack opened which lasted for the rest of his time in office. Chamberlain had been affronted by Gladstone's diplomatic humiliations in the early 1880s when he had been a member of his Cabinet. He had thought that Derby's and Granville's policies at the Colonial and Foreign Offices had been criminal in their aimlessness and drift, and he now thought that he discerned these same tendencies in Salisbury's policy.[80] The Secretary of State for India, Lord George Hamilton, thought that the policy of 'the German alliance and safeguarding Constantinople' had failed, producing only a 'consolidated friendship between Russia and France' as well as 'kicks from Germany and enmity from other nations'. Feeling that Chamberlain and Devonshire would both be behind a change in policy, he wanted Arthur Balfour to put together a memorandum which could be used as a lever with Salisbury. Hamilton wanted to 'spare' Salisbury's feelings in order to avoid a 'rupture in the Cabinet' which might lead to his resignation, but it was essential to 'alter our action'.[81] Although Balfour declined to follow this suggestion, it showed that a substantial section of the Cabinet was susceptible to the argument that Britain was 'isolated' and that 'something must be done' about it.

On this occasion Salisbury did act – in characteristic fashion – with a naval initiative and an attempt to reduce the number of potential opponents. On 9 January 1896, he announced that a 'Flying Squadron' of five extra cruisers would be constructed, so that 'whether we be isolated or not', Britain could rely on her fleet for her own safety.[82] On 11 January, despite his own inclination to out-bluff the Americans, Salisbury authorised the opening of negotiations with Olney. By the end of the week there was even an agreement with France regulating spheres of influence in Siam.[83]

But the fault-line in the Cabinet resembled that which had opened in Disraeli's Government in 1876. Once more those who interpreted Britain's role in imperial terms, and who wanted a forward policy which would both protect British interests and win the backing of the public, found themselves being blocked by those who took a more traditional conservative line: the irony was that it was now Salisbury who was the immovable object. His general view was that there was 'no such thing as a fixed policy, because policy like all organic entities is always in the making'. Politics was 'a matter of business: our allies should be those who are most likely to help or not to hinder . . . [our] interests'. The Triple Alliance Powers fell into this category, whilst France seemed to fall into the category of an implacable foe; in these circumstances, it was important to avoid conflict with the other member of the Dual Alliance, Russia.[84]

Ideally Salisbury would like to have continued with the old policy of 'leaning to the Triple Alliance without belonging to it',[85] but he was well aware that Germany wanted something more. He explained to the Austrian Ambassador, Count Deym, in January 1896 that he was perfectly willing to renew the Mediterranean Agreements with the Austrians, but that it was quite unreasonable of Hohenloe to expect him to join the Triple Alliance; it was a far greater obligation than he could accept, particularly given the current British view of Germany.[86] In order to avoid the 'danger of being without allies', Salisbury would have been happy with the old Mediterranean Agreements, but he could not go as far as a guarantee to defend Constantinople. He made it clear that he thought that if the Russians did menace the city, then British public opinion would probably change as it had in 1878;[87] but that was not enough for the Austrians.

Salisbury valued the Austrian connection, not only because he thought that the two Powers had a common interest in maintaining the *status quo* in the eastern Mediterranean, but also because her continued existence was vital to the peace and stability of Europe itself.[88] Without British support at the Straits, the Austrians might cut a deal with the Russians, which might see the reconstitution of the *Dreikaiserbund*.[89] On the other hand, if, as seemed to be the case, the Austrians were acting at the behest of Berlin and wanted Britain to forge closer links with the Triple Alliance, then much as he wanted to be 'good friends with Germany', he could go no further.[90]

It was significant that Salisbury offered to renew the agreement of March 1887, which expressed a general desire for co-operation, rather than the wider one of December which bound the parties to support Turkish independence.[91] Salisbury saw the commitment to the maintenance of the integrity of the Ottoman Empire as a dead-weight which might lead to an unwanted war with Russia,[92] but it was enshrined in treaty form and there was no escaping from it.[93] However, although the independence of Turkey was 'written in the public law of Europe', it was 'a very special kind of independence; it is independence which exists by agreement of the other Powers'.[94] It therefore followed that if the Powers decided not to maintain that independence, all that remained to be done was to discuss the terms upon which the 'traditional British policy' should be liquidated. Until he knew how Russia would react to this idea, Salisbury had to keep his lines to Vienna open.[95]

Abandoning the old policy of supporting Turkey sounded easy enough, until you came to discuss it. As Tsar Nicholas II told Salisbury in September 1896, the collapse of Turkish power might lead to 'European war'. Salisbury saw the need for Austria and Britain to receive compensation for the disturbance to the balance of power which would follow Russia gaining control over the Straits, but even speaking in this way might give the Russians the wrong idea and precipitate what was better postponed.[96] However, Salisbury's conservative instinct to put off the evil day here, and elsewhere, was not widely shared by his own Cabinet.

15

Assaulted by Asses' Jaw-bones

'The bias which rendered public opinion so ready to respond to the cry of "British Interests" was one towards an aggressive, or at least a spirited and enterprising foreign policy':[1] that was as true in 1896 as it had been twenty years earlier. Of course, for much of the time public opinion did not think about foreign policy, but when events thrust it to the fore, the bias was towards 'a strong, passing into a high-handed foreign policy'. As in 1878 there was one politician pre-eminently who sought to profit from this Jingoism: then it had been Disraeli; now it was Chamberlain. Of course, in both cases, the motives were the usual mixture of personal ambition and partisan advantage, but there was also an important element of principle at stake. Both men were imperial visionaries who saw the Empire as vital to Britain's future.

Chamberlain had taken the Unionist victory in 1895 as showing the 'good sense' of the 'deep-seated patriotism of the masses'.[2] He felt that the electorate wanted the Government to 'maintain the honour and obligations of this country',[3] and he was inclined to complain when Salisbury failed to do this. In particular, he condemned what he called the 'craven and poor-spirited' policy of buying off France and Russia with concessions.[4] George Curzon, one of the rising stars of the Party, and Salisbury's own Under-Secretary, held the same view. The youthful Winston Churchill winced at the 'tactless' blunders which led Salisbury to follow the 'idiotic' Crimean policy of supporting the Turks, and lamented that he had 'irritated or offended' nearly 'every section of the Union party & nearly every Cabinet in Europe'.[5] When Salisbury said that like the Philistine he was assaulted by the jaw-bone of an ass, it is easy to see which asses' jaw-bones he had in mind.

It was left to that acute observer of the diplomatic scene, Hatzfeldt, to divine the secret of Salisbury's diplomacy, when he commented that he 'has no political sympathies whatever and in this respect is as cold as a dog's nose. He cares . . . exclusively for English interests'.[6] If 'isolation' was dangerous, then so was connection with one of the European alliance systems. The real key to diplomatic flexibility was Russia. It might not be possible for Britain to return to the relationship she had had with Russia before the Crimean War, 'but it is an object to be wished for and approached as opportunity offers'.[7] Over the next few years Salisbury not only lost no opportunity to co-operate with Russia, he actively sought them out. He followed up his conversations with Nicholas II about the future of Turkey in September 1896 with a calculated bid for *détente*. Speaking at the Guildhall on 9 November, Salisbury declared that it was a 'superstition of antiquated diplomacy that there is any necessary antagonism between Russia and Great Britain'.[8] He went still further in January 1897, when he blamed Britain for rejecting Nicholas I's overtures in 1853, and stated that he and Disraeli had 'put all our money on the wrong horse'.[9]

If the Russians had responded to these initiatives positively with more than words, Salisbury would have had something with which to ward off those critics who thought that he was simply appeasing the unappeasable; but they did not. Although St Petersburg did not spurn Salisbury's approaches, neither did it show signs of wanting a real agreement. If tension in the Balkans decreased after 1897, it was more to do with the fact that Russia's ambitions were now directed towards the Far East. In 1897,

SPLENDID ISOLATION?

Russia and Austria agreed to maintain the *status quo* in the Balkans with the signature of the Mürsteg agreement;[10] however, this was the prelude not to a period of stability in European diplomacy, but to one of extreme turbulence. Curzon, who had criticised the Guildhall speech as 'bad' not only in delivery, but in substance because of its undue subservience to the 'Concert',[11] spoke for many Unionists in finding Salisbury's diplomacy too feeble by half.

Despite the failure to make any headway with France during his last administration, Salisbury was determined to continue his attempts to improve Anglo-French relations. Liquidation of the British occupation of Egypt, the main French demand, was now more unlikely than ever. With the Ottoman Empire being circled by the vultures, it made no sense to give up a firm base from which Britain could defend her interests in the eastern Mediterranean. But that made Salisbury all the more anxious not to give needless offence to the French, and he was quite happy to offer them compensation elsewhere in Africa, where redrawing 'lines on maps' could give them vast tracts of land at no cost to Britain. He defended the agreement of 15 January 1896 (which provided for Britain's abandonment of the buffer state on the upper Mekong in return for a French undertaking to respect the independence of Siam) on the ground that it was a 'good bargain' because he had surrendered 'only worthless territory' to get it.[12] Salisbury once commented, not wholly frivolously, that 'Africa was created to be the plague for Foreign Offices'.[13] He saw no harm in making concessions of 'paper empires' in Africa if it helped Britain's relations with France.

This inevitably brought Salisbury into conflict with Chamberlain, who had not gone to the Colonial Office to appease the French and accused the Prime Minister of throwing away 'all our cards'.[14] Chamberlain wanted to meet French pretensions with firm British resolve, so that they would realise 'that they must give way or take the consequences'.[15] In pursuit of this aim, Chamberlain encouraged the formation of a West Africa Frontier force in order 'to keep the hinterland for the Gold Coast, Lagos and the

Niger territories' – even at the risk of provoking war with France.[16] To Salisbury this was an absurd idea. To risk war with France over lines on maps of Africa was a ludicrous inversion of priorities. Chamberlain, he told the Queen, 'hardly sees the other side of the question', and was 'too warlike' by half.[17]

The division between Jingo Joe and Salisbury was obvious enough to foreign observers, some of whom shared the view of the French Ambassador, Courcel, that Chamberlain would get his way because Salisbury was *'affaibli par l'âge et la maladie'*.[18] The French did their best to achieve just that result, because despite Salisbury's attempts to get a deal over Egypt, they would not negotiate.[19] Hatzfeldt did not share Courcel's views about Salisbury's weakness and had a clearer understanding of his diplomacy. He told Holstein that Salisbury was trying to 'break off the spearhead of the threatened coalition between France and Russia', and that he was not going to bid for Germany's friendship.[20] He also counselled against supposing that Salisbury's policy was one of 'splendid isolation': he 'does not lose sight of the possibility that England and Germany may one day come together over the bridge Austria-Italy'.[21]

At the same time as he was looking to improve relations with the Dual Alliance, Salisbury was also not keeping his lines open to the other members of the Triple Alliance. He never made the mistake of his Liberal successors in assuming that that Alliance was some sort of monolithic expression of German willpower. Requests for help from the Italians in early 1896, following their humiliating defeat at the hands of the Abyssinians at Adowa, resulted in a decision to restore order in the neighbouring Sudan.[22] This allowed Salisbury to 'kill two birds with one stone, and to use the same military effort to plant the foot of Egypt rather further up the Nile'.[23] By helping Italy, Salisbury was steering close to the Triple Alliance; but he was also helping himself.[24] The Germans, who saw the dual motive, were quite happy; as Holstein put it, 'foreign policy is certainly made *easier* for us if Egypt is *not* abandoned'.[25]

Chamberlain was impatient with such subtle alignments and

wanted a thorough revision of British foreign policy; like Churchill before him, he sought a German alliance. Chamberlain's timing could hardly have been worse, since far from looking for a British alliance, Germany was embarking upon a 'world policy' which bade fair to make her another rival to Britain's global position. To some, *Weltpolitik* was 'a red herring of the ruling classes to distract the middle and working classes from social and political problems at home';[26] to others, it was the product of the ambition of the Kaiser and of some of the military leadership.[27] The twin architects of the new German policy, apart from the Kaiser himself, were Admiral Alfred von Tirpitz, State Secretary of the Naval Office, who inspired and directed Germany's *flottenpolitik*, and Bernhard von Bülow, the new Foreign Minister. If Tirpitz's naval ambitions ensured that Anglo-German relations would come under strain, it was Bülow's diplomacy which would really squander the Bismarckian diplomatic inheritance.

The son of Bismarck's Secretary of State, Bülow had had a long diplomatic career by the time he became State Secretary. Conscious of his place in history, he strove in his posthumously published four volumes of memoirs to cast himself as Bismarck's worthy successor; he also sought to avoid responsibility for what happened in 1914. Dismissed as 'vain, inaccurate and vague',[28] the volumes demonstrated only Bülow's irresponsibility and prompted the remark that he was 'the only man to commit suicide after his death'.[29] His courtier-like language when addressing the vain and unstable Kaiser did little to efface such an impression,[30] and prompted Tirpitz's scathing comment that, 'An oiled eel is a leech compared with Bülow.'[31] Attempts have been made to argue that as Chancellor after 1900 he had a strategic plan,[32] but they have not been convincing.[33] However, since with one or two exceptions most recent historians of Germany have generally preferred the study of perversity and peasantry to *Große Politik*, an authoritative account of his diplomacy is still lacking.[34]

Reading the significance and purpose of *Weltmachtpolitik* was no easier for contemporaries than it has proved to be for historians. There were those, then and later, who regarded it as a

German bid for world domination. The eminent German scholar, Fritz Fischer, has interpreted it in exactly this way, seeing the naval build-up in conjunction with ambitions for a *Mittelafrika* and *Mitteleuropa* programme as evidence of a '*Griff Nach der Weltmacht*', or grab for world power.[35] Like most revisionism, this was a return to a contemporary view that Germany was 'consciously aiming at the establishment of a German hegemony, at first in Europe, and eventually in the world'.[36] This comment, made by the British diplomat Eyre Crowe, in 1907, was later used as an example of foresight, and in order to boost the views popularly associated with one of his successors in the 1930s, Lord Vansittart, that the Germans could never be trusted. But Crowe did offer another explanation of German policy which is less well-remembered because it did not fit in with later interpretations, namely that 'the great German design is in reality no more than the expression of a vague, confused, and unpractical statesmanship, not fully realizing its own drift'.[37]

Weltpolitik has been difficult to decipher because it was the antithesis of *Realpolitik*, in substituting grandiose and ill-defined aims for limited, definable gains. Crowe got as close to the truth as we are likely to get with his later comment that: 'It is the openly avowed policy of Germany to make herself so strong that in all matters in which she considers German interests to be involved, she will have her own way. The ambition is not deserving of moral censure. It inspires the policy of every Great Power worthy of the name, to a certain degree.'[38] This seems preferable by way of explanation to arguments which place responsibility for Germany's plight on her 'exposed geostrategic position' and the 'alliance mechanisms'.[39] Where Bismarck had played chess, Bülow and the Kaiser played poker – and badly.[40]

In fact, the Kaiser and company had no need to try to impress upon others how powerful Germany was; ironically it was the recognition of this fact by other Powers which made Germany's erratic and blustering diplomacy such a destabilising factor in international relations. Where Salisbury had been able to rely on Bismarck's conservatism to keep Europe on an even keel, the

Kaiser's fidgety interventionism could be relied upon only to have the opposite result.

Bülow's intuitions were usually a good deal more acute than his attempts to put them into practice. He saw the damage done to Germany by the loss of the Russian alliance, and wanted to reconstruct that relationship, with the Russians keeping the French 'from being stupid' whilst the Germans did the same with the Austrians; a general war would, after all, threaten both the Hohenzollern and the Romanov dynasties.[41] He supported the *rapprochement* which followed the Kaiser's visit to St Petersburg in 1897 and generally strove to improve relations between the two countries. But he either failed to see, or did not care about, the effect this had on Anglo-German relations, which can be summed up in the words of one junior British diplomat: 'the sum of the whole tendency here is . . . [to] organize a continental alliance against England'. With the passage of a Naval Bill through the Reichstag in November 1897, it seemed to some in Britain that Germany might become a potentially dangerous imperial rival.[42] Bülow seems to have hoped that *Weltpolitik* would help push the British towards joining the Triple Alliance on Germany's terms, but in doing so he made the same mistake as others, which was to suppose that Germany occupied as high a place in Britain's priorities as Britain did in Germany's. However, that is not to say that Bülow's policy did not sharpen the debate between Salisbury and Chamberlain over the future direction of British policy.

Bülow's first major initiative came in the Far East, where it helped to precipitate what looked like a 'scramble for China'. Sergei Witte, the powerful Russian Finance Minister, had warned the Germans that any move to seize a Chinese port would force the Russians to 'occupy some more northerly port', which might lead to the partition of China itself;[43] but Bülow went ahead regardless and occupied Kiaochow in November 1897.[44] The Kaiser, jubilant at this assertion of German virility, declared that 'the whole German nation will be delighted that its Government has done a manly act'.[45] Salisbury, who could have done without yet another imperial trouble-spot, objected more to the 'mode in which the purpose of Germany had been attained ... than the purpose itself'.[46] Other members of his Cabinet were less philosophical.

The authors of *Weltpolitik* thought it better to 'range ourselves on the side of the opponents of England at every opportunity' in the hope of persuading the English to 'grow mellower'.[47] Since this was the product of over-heated fantasies about the effects of 'isolation', it is not altogether surprising that it met with a response from those in Britain of like minds. To a man of 'Chamberlain's nature a course of drift, even when philosophically adopted as the lesser evil, was little endurable'.[48] In the aftermath of Kiaochow, he feared 'grave trouble for the Government' if 'we do not adopt a more decided attitude', and he thought that Salisbury's passivity gave the impression that 'England is going to the dogs'.[49] Chamberlain was convinced that only his own particular brand of dynamism could retrieve the political situation.[50]

Salisbury's conservatism was based upon quite different premises. As far as he was concerned Britain's only interest in China was economic, and his main objective was to prevent a carve-up which would close her ports to British trade. But he knew his electorate well enough to fear that ' "the public" will require some territorial or cartographic consolation in China. . . . It will not be useful and will be expensive; but as a matter of pure sentiment we shall have to do it.'[51] That did not stop him from trying to avoid a partition of China. He tried to impart more urgency to the negotiations which were already in train with the Russians for a general settlement of their mutual concerns in the Far East.[52] He also sought to secure trade concessions on the Yangtze from the Chinese as one of the conditions of a British loan.[53] By these means he sought to halt any 'scramble for China', which, he feared, was bound to follow if the British demanded territorial compensation for Kiaochow. But the Russians not only showed no willingness to come to a deal with the British, they put pressure on the Chinese to drop negotiations for the British loan.[54] With

Chamberlain pressing for action, Salisbury went ahead and extracted the trading concessions from the Chinese without any loan in return.[55] Although the Russians declared a willingness to continue negotiations, Salisbury thought that they were 'insincere'.[56] His scepticism was well-founded. The Russians continued to press for the concession of Port Arthur and Talienwan – with promises to the British that they would remain open to foreign trade.[57] The failure of Salisbury's diplomacy, combined with his absence from the Cabinet through ill-health, left the road open to Chamberlain.

Where Salisbury's policy had been based upon a conservative reading of British interests – trade rather than territory, economic activity rather than occupation – Chamberlain's was based upon an imperialist reading. Britain could not afford to lose face, or her position in the imperial struggle. Nations which did not 'keep up', fell behind. Britain's position as a Great Power, and the demands of the electorate, both pointed towards her securing proper compensation for what the Germans had done and what the Russians might do next. Salisbury had sought to defuse tension with Russia; Chamberlain sought to cope with it in his own way. If the Russians cut up rough in the Far East, he would find allies to help him. Germany and America were the obvious partners.[58] But the Americans, preoccupied by their own concerns in the Spanish-American War, declined to co-operate,[59] which left only the Germans. Chamberlain, as ever, was driven by the thought that action was urgently needed.

On 20 February 1898, the Russians formally demanded from the Chinese leases on Port Arthur and Talienwan.[60] On 1 March, the Chinese signed a loan agreement with an Anglo-German syndicate, which prompted the Russians finally to break off negotiations for an Anglo-Russian understanding.[61] The British Ambassador in St Petersburg, Nicolas O'Conor, could now only suggest that Britain herself should insist upon the cession of a port, even though this was 'tantamount . . . to accepting spheres of influence' which actually ran counter to previous British policy.[62] Salisbury could see no alternative:[63] America and Germany would not co-operate; the French, with whom the British were negotiating over the future of West Africa,[64] were thought to be 'a standing danger and menace to Europe';[65] and the Government was under daily attack from 'slashing' articles in *The Times* because of its inactivity.[66] In public Salisbury tried to stick to the line that there was no danger to British interests in China, which were purely economic in nature. But the press and public were neither impressed nor conciliated. The Cabinet faced the difficulty of changing tack without looking as though it was a capitulation to public pressure.[67]

Curzon's fury at Salisbury's inactivity almost overflowed the boundaries of ministerial propriety. He regarded the Foreign Office as criminal in its 'apathy' and took advantage of Salisbury's absence, and his own attendance at Cabinet, to press for the acquisition of the port of Wei-hai-Wei. Balfour, who was acting Foreign Secretary and deputising for Salisbury as Prime Minister, was convinced by Curzon, and after a three-and-a-half-hour debate on 25 March, the decision to occupy was taken.[68] The news was broken to the Commons in the course of a debate on China on 5 April. Salisbury told Curzon to be careful to emphasise that 'we only abstained from raising the question of Wei-hai-wei until we knew the attitude of Russia with respect to Port Arthur & that it was not taken up at the last moment under pressure from the Jingo press'.[69] But as Balfour acknowledged, much later, 'The policy . . . had *no* commercial side at all. It was a strategic reply to Russia's strategic action.'[70]

This was clear from Balfour's own statement to the House on 5 April, in which he said that 'British interests and German interests are absolutely identical', and expressed his hope that the two countries could 'work hand in hand' towards 'carrying out' their 'general commercial objectives'.[71] This assumption, itself dubious, was even more so when made the basis for a German alliance, as it was by Chamberlain, who saw it as the solution to Britain's problems. According to Hatzfeldt, Chamberlain spoke to him in March about wanting to 'abandon the traditional policy of isolation' because of anxieties about Russia in the Far East and

France in Africa, and said that Germany was Britain's natural ally because the two countries had no conflict of interests. Chamberlain's own account denied going quite this far, and had him saying that: 'it is possible that the policy of the United Kingdom may be changed by circumstances which are too strong for us to resist.' According to him, he talked only about an Anglo-German agreement over China rather than a full-blown alliance.[72] But Hatzfeldt's version sounded well enough in Berlin, where it chimed with Bülow's view that Britain would come to realise that she needed German support.

Bülow's diplomatic career had never taken him to Great Britain.[73] Holstein thought that his youthful experience of seeing the family's Danish properties sacrificed thanks to Britain's betrayal of 1864 had left him convinced that 'anyone who has dealings with England comes to rue it later'.[74] Since the Kaiser was contemplating a Continental coalition against England, Bülow was hardly keen to follow Chamberlain's advice.[75] He thought that an Anglo-Russian 'collision' was an inevitability, which, from Germany's point of view, was to be 'most fervently desired',[76] and he had no desire to save the British from their fate. He also thought that the Navy Bill, which was going through the Reichstag, was irreconcilable with 'a really honest and trustworthy Anglo-German alliance'.[77] Whether these thoughts are to be read as part of a long-term plan to secure Germany's 'place in the sun' by the elimination of British power,[78] or as a reluctance to consider an alliance except on Germany's terms, they led in the same direction.

Bülow used the nature of Britain's parliamentary institutions as an excuse not to take up Chamberlain's offer. In best Dutch uncle fashion, he proferred his own advice on how to conduct British diplomacy: Britain should not quarrel with both members of the Dual Alliance, but should, instead, settle with Russia; Germany and Italy would remain neutral in any Franco-British conflict.[79] Since this was a more or less accurate description of Salisbury's own policy preferences, it made no appeal to 'Joe'. Chamberlain was baffled that the Germans did not share his view that an alliance between their two countries was the most natural thing in the diplomatic world. When he saw Hatzfeldt again on 1 April, he repudiated the notion that a British commitment could not be relied upon because of public opinion, and stressed the need for an Anglo-German agreement in China.[80]

Holstein, always inclined to attribute to others the Machiavellianism which others claimed to see in him, was thoroughly suspicious of the 'clever and unscrupulous' Chamberlain. He saw the bid for an alliance as a manoeuvre designed to compromise Germany in Russia's eyes, fearing that the British would reveal the fact that Germany had sought an alliance in London.[81] Hatzfeldt tried to persuade him that such subtle calculations greatly overrated Chamberlain's 'diplomatic virtuosity', and that he would pay a high price for a German alliance.[82] But since Bülow was convinced that 'in the long run England could not escape the fight for her life', at which point she would pay any price for an alliance, he preferred to carry on stressing the problem of Britain's parliamentary institutions.[83]

When Hatzfeldt informed Balfour of Bülow's reaction on 5 April, he found him happy to proceed more slowly than Chamberlain wanted; he correctly divined that the House of Cecil took some satisfaction from Chamberlain's discomfiture.[84] Salisbury's mordant comment to Balfour showed an ability to divine the Kaiser's intentions which Chamberlain quite lacked: 'the one object of the German Emperor since he has been on the throne has been to get us in a war with France. I can never make up my mind whether this is part of Chamberlain's object or not'; he was quite certain that in the event of a conflict with France, 'Germany will blackmail us heavily'.[85] Balfour may have been better disposed towards the idea of a German alliance, but he had no desire to pay too much for it, and he was 'amused' at the revelation that German diplomacy seemed predicated on the notion of trouble between Britain and the Dual Alliance.[86] Hatzfeldt, aware of these suspicions, warned Bülow that it was necessary to exercise 'the greatest caution' when mentioning such matters to the British.[87]

Chamberlain's clumsy diplomacy had fed all the German

misconceptions about Britain's position. In his excited marginalia, the Kaiser exclaimed that the 'Jubilee swindle' (Queen Victoria's Diamond Jubilee) was already over and that England was looking to join the Triple Alliance.[88] Bülow advised trusting in Balfour's methods rather than in Chamberlain's 'theoretical and vague fantasies'.[89] The misapprehension that the British were getting desperate for a German alliance received further reinforcement from the amateur diplomacy of Baron Eckardstein, who was married to the daughter of the English furniture magnate Sir Blundell Maple, and liked to think that he cut a fine figure in English Society; he also had ambitions to succeed Hatzfeldt at the Court of St James's. Grandees like Salisbury and Balfour hardly regarded Maple as a social equal,[90] whilst professional diplomats like Bülow never thought of Eckardstein as a serious contender to succeed Hatzfeldt, whom Bismarck himself had described as the 'best horse in my stable'.[91]

Bülow and Holstein wanted Hatzfeldt to keep the lines to London open against the day that the British were ready to pay their price.[92] Eckardstein's misrepresentations led them to think that that day was not far removed; and yet no definite proposal for an alliance came. Bülow would have done better to have listened to Hatzfeldt. He counselled that Chamberlain was behind 'the bitter decision to seek the alliance of Germany and her friends', and therefore if it failed he would turn towards the Dual Alliance. He entirely dismissed any notion that Britain would fight the French over an African squabble, and warned that 'we must keep the more or less remote possibility of an Anglo-French *rapprochement*' in mind.[93] Hatzfeldt's long association with Salisbury gave him a keener insight into the workings of that subtle mind than Bülow had. But the perception that the thrusting and dynamic Chamberlain was the man of the future counted for more in Berlin.

The slight chance that Bülow and company would have paid heed to any of this was removed by Eckardstein's meddling, which reinforced their impression that Chamberlain was prepared to run after the Germans. On 22 April, Eckardstein told Chamberlain that the Kaiser was 'most anxious' that 'an agreement should be come to' immediately by which Britain and Germany would each guarantee the possessions of the other.[94] Balfour suspected that Eckardstein was acting without Hatzfeldt's knowledge, but given the unconventional habits of the German autocrat, it seemed probable that Wilhelm II was behind the initiative; no one imagined that Eckardstein was simply lying. Chamberlain thus accepted an invitation to dine at the German Embassy; Eckardstein told Hatzfeldt that the Colonial Secretary had invited himself to dinner.[95]

Bülow was delighted to hear that Chamberlain had not given up the notion of an alliance, but was still anxious to avoid committing Germany; he was prepared to offer the British benevolent neutrality in return for colonial compensation.[96] Chamberlain, secure in the knowledge that the Germans had invited *him* to dinner, acted as though they had overstepped the mark, telling Hatzfeldt that compensation would only be possible as part of a wider agreement between their two nations; he warned that the moment for such a thing might yet pass. Hatzfeldt took this to mean that Britain could arrive at an understanding with France and Russia if Germany refused an alliance, but failed to realise why Chamberlain had made the comment.[97]

The Kaiser wondered 'what was eating' Chamberlain and rejected outright the notion of any alliance designed to stop Russia in the Far East: 'the deeper the Russians get involved in Asia, the quieter they will be in Europe!' Nor was he impressed by Hatzfeldt's report of Chamberlain's assertion that Britain might reach agreements with Russia and France. For him, the kernel of the matter was that the British found themselves in a very uncomfortable position in the Far East, having occupied Wei-hai-Wei in a fit of temper and shaken their fist in Russia's face. Thus far Russia had not responded, but he thought it was beginning to dawn on John Bull that this was bound to happen and that he now wanted 'somebody to help him out of his predicament'; Wilhelm was not going to do that 'merely on Chamberlain's promises. . . . We shall see what may happen later on.'[98] Berlin was now, thanks to Eckardstein, firmly under the impression that the British were desperate for a German alliance. Eckardstein meanwhile told Chamberlain that he could not understand why Hatzfeldt had not been more forthcoming, and assured him that the Kaiser still wanted an alliance.[99] By this time, however, the Prime Minister had returned from sick-leave.

Although Chamberlain was beginning to suspect that everything was not quite as it should be, he still thought that 'the country would support us in a Treaty with Germany';[100] but Salisbury would have none of it. When he saw Salisbury on 2 May, Hatzfeldt acted on his instructions and professed a desire for good relations whilst playing down the notion of an alliance. Salisbury told Chamberlain later that: 'I quite agree with you that under the circumstances a closer relation with Germany would be very desirable; but can we get it?'[101] This was the prelude to a reassertion by Salisbury of his position and priorities.

In a speech at the Albert Hall on 4 May 1898 to the Primrose League, he asserted that the nations of the world could be divided into the 'living' and the 'dying', and showed which category he thought Britain came into by declaring: 'We know that we shall maintain against all comers that which we possess, and we know, in spite of the jargon about isolation, that we are amply competent to do so.'[102] It was a public affirmation of British power, but it was also a warning to Chamberlain and those who thought like him. Nor was Salisbury's assertiveness confined to the political platform. When the Russian Ambassador protested against Britain's objection to the occupation of Port Arthur and questioned her need for Wei-hai-Wei, the Prime Minister simply shrugged his shoulders and said that the 'Cabinet was pushed by public opinion' into doing something – and Wei-hai-Wei had seemed the lesser of many evils.[103]

Salisbury followed this up by making it clear to Hatzfeldt that he had no intention of allowing Germany to blackmail him in the way that Bismarck had Gladstone in 1884. In private conversation on 4 May, after the German had mentioned the possibility of Britain making colonial concessions to secure German goodwill,

Salisbury told him: 'You demand too much for your friendship.'[104] A few days later he commented pointedly that one side could not always be giving and the other always taking.[105] Salisbury did not agree that Britain had 'an excessive share of the advantages which might be derived from the less civilized portions of the world', and should therefore buy Germany's friendship by colonial concessions. Aware that only a Eurocentric alliance would be of use to Germany, Salisbury knew that there was nothing in this for Britain. On the crucial subject of the Ottoman Empire, Salisbury admitted that the two Powers might be able to co-operate – but only when the Germans had made their position plain.[106]

But Chamberlain was not so easily squashed.

16

Blackmail

The differences between Salisbury's conception of British priorities and Chamberlain's soon became a matter of public comment.

On 12 May, at the annual dinner of the Bankers' Association, Salisbury spoke of the need to make financial sacrifices to keep the army and the navy up to the task of maintaining British power, making it plain that Britain would hold her own against all comers if need be. This caused a panic on the French *Bourse* thanks to rumours that it portended the breakdown of Anglo-French talks over West Africa. France's diplomats were more adept at reading Salisbury's words than her bankers, and Courcel assured the Quai d'Orsay that the Prime Minister was simply asserting himself against Chamberlain.[1] If the Ambassadors of Spain and Portugal turned up at the Foreign Office to enquire whether Salisbury had been referring to their Empires in his 'dying nations' speech, Chamberlain was under no illusion as to its main target. He responded on 13 May in characteristic fashion with a speech at Birmingham Town Hall.[2]

Where Salisbury's speech had reflected his belief in the verities of the traditional conservative approach, Chamberlain bluntly declared that there was 'no longer any room for the mysteries and reticence of the diplomacy of fifty years ago'. He wanted to abandon the 'policy of strict isolation' because of the rise of two European Alliance systems and the vulnerability of the British Empire to 'a combination of Great Powers'.[3] Referring to the failure of the attempts to come to an arrangement with Russia in the Far East, he commented: 'Who sups with the devil must have a very long spoon.' His preferred allies were America and Germany. He proclaimed his support for an 'Anglo-Saxon Alliance', and spoke glowingly of the common heritage of Britain and America in a way which would later become common amongst British politicians.[4]

These ideas were so at variance with those of Salisbury that foreign observers were unsure what to make of the speech: Courcel thought it a sign of Chamberlain's overweening ambition;[5] Baron G.G. de Staal, the Russian Ambassador, puzzled by the eccentricities of the parliamentary system, thought that Chamberlain must have been speaking in a private capacity;[6] even Hatzfeldt, who understood the British political system rather better, could not believe that Chamberlain had spoken without the tacit approval of Salisbury and his colleagues.[7] Chamberlain's speech upset the Russians and the Irish-Americans quite as much as it upset the Spanish.[8] Challenged about it in the Lords by the former Liberal Foreign Secretary, Kimberley, Salisbury took refuge in the excuse that he did not have a copy of it with him and so could not comment upon it.[9] Kimberley admired the 'craftiness' of Salisbury's response, but thought it was 'plain enough ... that he did not share C[hamberlain]'s opinion'. But the coincidence of the timing of Chamberlain's attack with the death of Gladstone prevented a fractious Liberal opposition from making much of the divisions in the ruling coalition.[10] Hatzfeldt read all this as a sign that the British had not quite given up on the idea of a German alliance, but warned that once they did so, 'we can in my opinion no longer either expect or ask for concessions or favours here'.[11]

But the consistent refusal of Bülow and the Kaiser to listen to Hatzfeldt's warnings, and to follow instead the will-o'-the-wisp of

Disraeli – the Queen's favourite photograph: 'the great Asiatic mystery' incarnate

Salisbury – Bismarck's 'obstinate lay clergyman' making his point

Above left: The fifteenth earl of Derby – 'cultivated apathy'

Above: Mary, Countess of Derby – 'beautiful eyes and a good figure'

Count Peter Shuvalov – 'the third man' whom rumour attached to Lady Derby

The fourth earl of Carnarvon – 'Twitters' to his intimates and a nuisance to Disraeli

Bismarck at his zenith – a signed photograph given to Disraeli at Berlin

Gorchakov at Berlin – a 'spluttering candle' about to go out

Below: Andrassy as seen by 'Vanity Fair' – more Coco the clown than European statesman

Below right: The second earl Granville – 'are you being served?'

Joseph Chamberlain at the Colonial Office – 'a dynamic force' at work

Arthur James Balfour – 'the nephew also rises'

The fifth marquess of Lansdowne in old age – 'the very last of the Whigs'

Paul Cambon – the quintessential diplomat and 'architect of the entente'

Royalty at play – (l to r) King Edward VII, the Duke of Connaught and Kaiser Wilhelm II

Bernhard von Bülow – 'the courtier as statesman' – at least in his own eyes

Sir Edward Grey – 'the preux chevalier'

their own imaginings, led to further attempts to blackmail the British into concessions. The Kaiser let the British Ambassador in Berlin, Sir Frank Lascelles, know in late May that he was not unsympathetic to an alliance, but that he did not think that the time was ripe.[12] He wanted 'compensation' in Borneo, the Philippines, Samoa and the Caroline Islands as the minimum price for Germany's assistance.[13] Wilhelm thought that the English only wanted an alliance because they were worried about the new German fleet, and he preferred to try for Russia's friendship,[14] using the British 'alliance request' to blackmail Nicholas II.[15] Even Holstein thought that this was going rather far, whilst Hatzfeldt thought it 'beyond human calculation what effect will be created here'.[16] In fact, the Tsar simply trumped his cousin's supposed ace by revealing Salisbury's earlier approaches to Russia.[17] The letter did no damage in London either, because Salisbury, who did not want a general alliance, remained willing to make limited agreements with Germany on specific matters.[18] Obsessed with their own diagnosis of Britain's position, the Germans continued to demand a high price for their co-operation, and in the process simply confirmed Salisbury's suspicions that there was no common ground for a wider alliance.

The news that Britain intended to lend the Portuguese money and to take as collateral their colonial empire aroused in Berlin the twin emotions of envy and avarice.[19] Bülow interpreted it as a sign that the British had designs on the Portuguese Empire, and Hatzfeldt made it plain that the Germans expected 'compensation'.[20] Hatzfeldt asked whether the British would join Germany in 'common action', and Salisbury opened discussions over the future of the Portuguese colonies.[21] Salisbury was not keen on the idea of effectively partitioning Portuguese territory, given Britain's many diplomatic commitments to her oldest ally,[22] but as the Germans wanted to discuss the matter, he felt that he had little choice. Salisbury consistently told the Germans throughout June 1898 that he wanted to preserve rather than partition the Portuguese Empire.[23] The Kaiser simply regarded this as further evidence of how 'false and unreliable' he was. 'This', he noted on one of Hatzfeldt's despatches, 'is not the way to lure us into an alliance. God preserve us!'[24] When Hatzfeldt obliquely hinted that Germany's past services to the British Empire warranted some 'consideration', Salisbury rather wickedly 'pressed him to specify these incidents, which my memory did not enable me to recall'.[25]

If the Germans remained the prisoners of their own preconceptions, they had the excuse that Chamberlain consistently gave out signals which were consonant with them. He pressed for the negotiations over the Portuguese Empire, partly because of the strategic value of South-West Africa, but also as the prelude to an Anglo-German agreement.[26] Germany's valuation of her fee was a steep one: British territories in West Africa such as Walfish Bay; the Volta triangle of the Gold Coast; Blantyre and parts of Nyasaland; and the Portuguese half of the island of Timor.[27] Chamberlain thought this 'extravagant' and tried to bargain for more reasonable terms;[28] but, as he told Balfour, the consequence of failure would be 'the assurance of Germany's further interference in Delagoa Bay and the Transvaal'. This amounted to paying 'Blackmail to Germany to induce her not to interfere where she has no right of interference'. However, Chamberlain thought, 'it is worth while to pay Blackmail sometimes'.[29] To allow Delagoa Bay to fall into the hands of any other Power, or to allow it to seem as though Britain had no interest in its future, 'would be regarded throughout South Africa as the sign of the abdication by us of our position of paramount power', which would make a war with the Transvaal 'eventually inevitable'.[30] Moreover, if such a war did come about, then it was worth paying a price to avoid any repetition of the 'Kruger telegram'.[31] Finally, if this was the entrance fee to a German alliance, then Chamberlain was certainly willing to pay.

On 11 June, Lascelles told Bülow that Chamberlain's earlier desire for a German alliance was genuine enough, which prompted him to enquire to what extent Germany could rely on Britain if she were attacked by the Dual Alliance.[32] Lascelles discussed this question the following week at a meeting held at

Chamberlain's town house on 18 June, at which neither Salisbury nor Balfour were present.[33] Lascelles appears to have said nothing to the Kaiser about the matter until August, but in the meantime the Dowager Empress Frederick emphasised to her mother that 'any definite advance on the part of Lord Salisbury would be very well received by Wilhelm'.[34] With the Queen firmly in the ranks of those who saw a German alliance as the escape from isolation, Salisbury had to respond carefully. He told her on 4 August, with some exaggeration, that although he was no less keen than Chamberlain on a German alliance, 'it would be impossible to do what the German Emperor desires without incurring the reproach of deserting British interests and making undue concessions'.[35] Even Chamberlain was unwilling to concede quite as much as the Germans wanted,[36] to the indignation of those in the Wilhelmstrasse who took the view that abandoning the Boers was a concession for which the British should pay handsomely.[37]

The negotiations over the Portuguese Empire certainly provided the opportunity for a further appearance of the idea of a German alliance, but the outcome was not what the Queen and the Empress Frederick wanted.[38] In late August, Wilhelm complained to the British Ambassador that 'all his proposals had been rejected in a manner which he would most certainly have strongly resented if any other Power than England had treated him with such scant consideration', and demanded 'some document to go upon' to show that the British were serious about an alliance. Lascelles (according to the Kaiser's account) told him about the meeting on 18 June, and said that Chamberlain wanted an alliance based upon the principle of mutual assistance if either Power were to be attacked by two others. Wilhelm approved of this idea and indicated that he considered it a satisfactory basis for negotiations.[39]

The Anglo-German Treaty concerning the future of the Portuguese Colonies was signed on 30 August and provided for partition only in the event of the Lisbon Government defaulting on its loan.[40] Balfour, who had been its chief protagonist, argued that it contained nothing which, if made public, 'would be discreditable to the diplomacy of this country or give just cause of offence to Portugal'. He still took great care to get it signed before Salisbury returned, telling him that, 'for good or for evil, I am afraid that you and my colleagues will have to take the responsibility of my handiwork'.[41] Salisbury, who did not much like the agreement, suspected that Germany would wish to 'force the pace of destiny' to get her share of the Portuguese possessions and generally doubted its utility,[42] but he had good reasons by this time not to arouse German antagonism needlessly.

If Salisbury's return put an end to Chamberlain's attempts to prepare the ground for an alliance with Germany, Bülow served much the same purpose with regard to the Kaiser. Bülow pointed out that Germany could not afford to take sides in an Anglo-Russian conflict and argued that the agreement over the Portuguese colonies was as far as they could go.[43]

The growing tension between Britain and the Dual Alliance Powers confirmed Holstein in his belief that Britain was drifting into serious trouble. He saw Salisbury as a declining force hampered by his own weakness from taking firm action.[44] This diagnosis was shared by those like Chamberlain and Curzon who criticised his attempts to get on terms with France and Russia as no more than 'throwing bones to keep the various dogs quiet'.[45] But Hatzfeldt disagreed with the view that Salisbury 'would be incapable of energetic action no matter what the circumstances, particularly if it were clear to him that he would thereby lose touch with the country or the majority of his colleagues'.[46] Acutely aware of the inter-relationship of British diplomacy on a global scale, Salisbury's vision was more incisive than that of most of his colleagues. The possibility that Britain might clash with France in Africa made him wary of quarrelling with Russia in the Far East,[47] and he agreed with the view of Alfred Milner, the British High Commissioner in South Africa, that it was 'perfectly vain ... to try & set artificial barriers to the advance of other Powers in quarters where they are strong & we are weak'.[48] The price of dependency on Germany was all too clear, and it was not one which he was willing to pay. He had spoken of Britain's ability to hold her own without allies, and when the French finally sprang their challenge to British domination in Egypt, Salisbury showed that he had meant what he had said.

The mission of Captain Marchand to Fashoda on the Upper Nile was part of a harebrained French scheme to force the British to make concessions to them in Egypt.[49] Fortunately for Marchand, he and his party arrived after Kitchener's army had defeated the Dervishes at Omdurman; but that was the end of his good fortune.

Egypt and the Nile Valley were considered vital British interests, and there was no possibility of the French being thrown any 'bones' there. Indeed, as the French Chargé d'Affaires in London, Geoffray, told the new French Foreign Minister, Théophile Delcassé, on 9 August, there existed *'dans une partie considérable du public'* a *'sentiment d'hostilité'* towards France. The general view seemed to be that France was Britain's 'natural' enemy who had always tried to stand in her way, and Geoffray feared that although there was no desire to start a war with her, there would be no reluctance to prosecute one if France started it.[50] Geoffray's assumption that Salisbury was the main bulwark against Jingoism was correct; which is why it was unwise of Delcassé to place him in a position where he had no alternative but to back what the Jingoes wanted.

Had the Russians or the Germans been willing to assist France at Fashoda, matters might have turned out differently. But since the French had not helped the Russians over Port Arthur, St Petersburg now returned the favour.[51] Bülow had only flirted with the French to alarm the British.[52] So Delcassé discovered that France was isolated. The British had made it clear in 1895 that the Nile Valley was a purely British sphere of influence. Kitchener acted on that policy from the moment he encountered Marchand in September 1898.[53]

At first Delcassé sought to hold out for British concessions by arguing that the only alternative was a complete rupture in Anglo-French relations leading to war.[54] He was endlessly fertile in alternatives to French humiliation: he held out the prospect of a

Franco-British alliance as an inducement to compromise; he raised the threat of Russia standing by France if it came to war; he pleaded for Britain not to ask him to 'do the impossible', citing the 'dangerous' state of French public opinion; he wheedled, threatened blustered and cajoled – but to little avail.[55]

Salisbury was mindful of the argument that French public opinion might push France into war, but as ever he was even more aware of his own public. He would have been willing to make minor concessions to cover Marchand's retreat, but the Jingoes in the Cabinet would not go even that far; they wanted unconditional withdrawal.[56] Despite warnings from the British Ambassador in Paris, Sir Edmund Monson, that 'France can count on more than moral support on the part of Russia in the event of a rupture with England',[57] the Cabinet decided on 27 October that 'we are unable to discuss questions of frontier between Egypt and the French Congo so long as the French flag remains at Fashoda'.[58]

Monson was being alarmist. Delcassé was getting no support from Russia, and he feared that the agreement over the Portuguese colonies meant that the Germans had given the British *carte blanche* in Egypt.[59] As early as 3 October, he had decided that Fashoda was not worth a war, but he retained the hope of getting territorial concessions on the Upper Nile.[60] From Paris, Monson advised Salisbury to build a 'golden bridge' across which Delcassé could retreat.[61] But when Salisbury did not oblige,[62] the French came in with such large claims that it would have been impossible to have conceded them.[63] British public opinion seemed to be almost eager for a war with France, and even the Liberals were backing the hard line being taken by the Government.[64] As the Russian Ambassador noted, all fears that Salisbury was too disposed to make concessions had vanished, and his 'firm attitude' had won over popular opinion.[65] On 2 November, Delcassé ordered Marchand to withdraw from Fashoda.[66]

The aggressive instincts of the *Parti Colonial*, which had brought France to this pass, now discredited its adherents.[67] This did not mean that the French had given up all hope of ending British rule in Egypt,[68] but it did mean the abandonment of a high-risk strategy for doing so. When the new French Ambassador to Great Britain, Paul Cambon, arrived in London, it was with instructions to try to reach agreement with the English on all outstanding points.[69]

Fashoda was a resounding public success of the sort Salisbury had always deprecated. It had not only left him with the job of repairing relations with France, but it had aroused the appetite of the British public for an annexation of Egypt. In his annual speech at the Guildhall in November 1898, Salisbury disappointed the Jingoes by failing to announce this. In the course of his remarks, he once more referred to 'nations who are decaying, whose Government is so bad that they can neither maintain the power of self-defence nor the affection of their subjects' and who fell victim to the greed or the philanthropy of their neighbours; this, he declared, was 'the cause of war'.[70]

One of the main problems facing Salisbury was the fact that his own common sense and wide perspective were not shared by more excitable souls, whose more lurid vision of Britain as a great imperial Power was more attractive to the public mind than his own. The dangers into which the imperial passion could lead was shown in the autumn of 1898, when just as the Fashoda crisis was developing, Chamberlain and the Germans managed to work themselves up into a lather about the Samoan Islands.[71] Despite the fact that during the earlier stages of the crisis Britain might at any moment have found herself at war with France over Fashoda, Chamberlain insisted upon acting as though the islands were a vital national interest, even though he talked about the islands as 'trumpery affairs not worth twopence to either of us'.[72] The Germans, who acknowledged that the Samoan Islands were not worth the cost of the telegrams generated by the crisis over them, also insisted upon seeing them as an issue where the British could make concessions to prove their goodwill.

Salisbury found it very difficult to get worked up about an insignificant set of islands on the other side of the globe. He did not doubt that Wilhelm wanted to be on better terms with Britain, but he also noted that 'he did not wish that we should be so with other countries and in particular Russia, whom he was always trying to set us against'.[73] When Hatzfeldt attempted to use the continuing crisis in Samoa as the peg on which to hang talks for a more general alliance, Salisbury remarked coolly that 'the time' for such alliances 'was past', adding that 'there could only be rapprochements between States with common or non-contradictory interests'. To Hatzfeldt's warning that France was thinking of an alliance with Germany, Salisbury responded by saying that he would have thought that the Germans would prefer a Russian connection. In the face of this studied lack of interest, Hatzfeldt could only warn that this too might happen if the British let it. Hatzfeldt once more suggested that it might be a 'good move to warn him quietly and calmly that if this goes on, we might secure our interests by other means to the injury of England'.[74] Holstein wondered whether they should try to put pressure on imperialists like Chamberlain, or even Cecil Rhodes, who was due in Berlin soon.[75]

In Samoa itself, events seemed to conspire to bring Britain and America into alliance against Germany. After the death of King Malietoa in August, the exiled Pretender, Mataafa, had returned to the islands and had himself elected King by a majority of the Chiefs. He received the backing of the German consuls, but the Americans and the British refused to recognise him. The Americans despatched a squadron to the islands, and on 11 March 1899 its commander declared Mataafa and his Government illegal. When the Germans protested, their Consulate was occupied by British and American marines. On 15 March, British and American ships bombarded Apia and damaged the German Consulate there.[76]

The absurdity and dangers of *Weltpolitik* were now exposed. Bülow candidly acknowledged in private that 'the whole group of islands was of very small value' and were certainly not worth poisoning Germany's relations with Britain and America for; but *Weltpolitik* had given the German public the impression that 'they were of importance to Germany'.[77] Bülow and Tirpitz needed support for their naval bills, and the Kaiser was incandescent with rage at the insult to his country,[78] so Bülow had little choice other than to tell Hatzfeldt to warn the British that their 'further behaviour in the Samoa matter will be of decisive and far-reaching importance for the political relations' between the two countries.[79] Bülow suggested to the Kaiser that Hatzfeldt should secure from the British a declaration that they would 'not make fresh arrangements in Samoa except with Germany's consent'; if they would not do this, then Hatzfeldt should be withdrawn. It was, he told Wilhelm, further proof if any were needed that 'an overseas policy can only be carried on with a sufficiently powerful navy'.[80]

Lascelles, infected by the heightened atmosphere in Berlin, particularly after the Americans apologised for shelling the Consulate, tried to alert his masters in London to the gravity with which the Germans were viewing the situation, and argued that Britain should also send an apology and agree to a commission of enquiry.[81] Salisbury declined to do either, confining himself to assuring the Germans that he would abide by the 1889 Treaty, and reciprocating what he called Bülow's 'remarkable frankness' by commenting that 'an impression exists in England that Germany has been attempting to force America and England out of Samoa'.[82] For the best part of the next two weeks the Germans piled on the pressure in London for the British to agree to a commission which would be able to act only by unanimous decision. On 12 April, Bülow told Hatzfeldt that he should use his judgment whether or not to break off relations with the British.[83] In the end, Salisbury rather wearily conceded the case for the sort of commission which the Germans wanted; he thought that the 'tone of menace' adopted by the Germans was 'very much out of place'.[84]

So upset had the Germans become at what they took to be Salisbury's deliberately insulting way of dealing with the crisis, that the Kaiser took the extraordinary step of penning a bitter complaint to his grandmother at the end of May, accusing the Prime Minister of 'despising' the German race and treating Germany as though she were 'Portugal, Chile or the Patagonians'. He wrote of his own 'shame and pain' at the blocking of all his personal efforts to bring about good Anglo-German relations: 'Lord Salisbury's Government must learn to respect and treat us as equals; as long as he cannot be brought to do that, people over here will remain distrustful.'[85]

Salisbury had not troubled himself too much over the Samoan crisis because he 'always declined to regard the question as having any serious importance or requiring any great hurry'.[86] He agreed with the Queen that the Kaiser's letter was 'not a desirable innovation', and thought that much of his spleen could be explained away by the fact that far from quarrelling with France, Britain had recently reached agreements with her concerning West Africa colonial boundaries.[87] In Samoa matters dragged on until November 1899, when the islands were finally partitioned between Germany, Britain and America.[88] Rumours that the Kaiser was 'looking round for allies' left Salisbury's withers unwrung since 'he cannot get any on what he considers to be reasonable terms'.[89]

Negotiating with Germany, whether over the Portuguese Empire or Samoa, simply confirmed Salisbury in his belief that there were not only no grounds for an alliance, but that Berlin would use any sign that Britain wanted one as an opportunity to engage in a little extortion and blackmail. But the Germans could not convince themselves of this, or of the fact that Salisbury still controlled British policy. When Hatzfeldt reported in May 1899 that Chamberlain still hankered after an alliance, Bülow told him to keep in touch with him: 'Owing to his outstanding cleverness he is more susceptible to rational arguments than many other British statesmen.'[90] This did not mean that Bülow wanted an immediate alliance; it simply meant that he saw an opportunity to extract concessions from the British over Samoa in return for benefits that Germany might decide to confer later.[91]

Hatzfeldt realised the foolishness of a policy which insisted on linking better Anglo-German relations to continuous concessions by Britain, almost as though the latter were on probation. If, as Bülow and Holstein seemed to want, conversations upon matters of mutual interest such as the future of Morocco were kept back until the British had apologised and made reparation for the shelling of the Consulate in Samoa, 'we would run the greatest risk of getting neither'. Hatzfeldt warned that with Salisbury's prestige waning, he simply could not afford to offend British opinion by making further concessions. The Prime Minister was also growing more feeble, and was depressed both by the ill-health of his wife and the state of Britain's relations with the Transvaal.[92] But Bülow's feeling that the British needed Germany more than she needed them was increased by the consequences of Chamberlain's policy in South Africa.

If Salisbury was able to check the results of Chamberlain's diplomatic style in his own field of expertise, he proved quite unable to do so in the Colonial Secretary's own bailiwick. In South Africa, Chamberlain wanted to force the Boers into acknowledging British suzerainty over the Transvaal and the Orange Free State, and he ignored those who warned that a hard line would simply drive them into a corner and lead to war. Salisbury was always willing to use threats, but when dealing with those who were unreasonable, he thought that there was 'no need to act on it'.[93] But Chamberlain saw South Africa as an area in which he could alert the electorate to the vital importance of Empire, a view shared by Milner, the British High Commissioner in South Africa.[94] Between them, Milner and Chamberlain drove the Boer leader, Kruger, into a corner from which he could only emerge fighting. The Boer War was thus the finest flowering of the *Furor Consularis*, which was at once the characteristic vice and the Nemesis of the new imperialism.

Lord George Hamilton, the Secretary of State for India, expressed a common view when he told Balfour in December that he expected that Russia would try to 'take advantage of our entanglement in South Africa: whether she squeezes us in Persia or Afghanistan remains to be seen'.[95] Stories of a 'Continental League' were not long in coming.[96] In October 1899, rumours reached Salisbury that the Russian Foreign Minister, Count Michael Muraviev, was peddling the idea in Madrid and Paris.[97] Salisbury never believed that such a League would be formed, and regarded Muraviev's evocation of it 'as a threat or warning to make us comply with some demands he means to make'.[98] The fate of the proposal showed that Salisbury was correct to doubt whether it really was practical politics. Delcassé was interested in the idea, but wanted to be assured that the Germans would support it.[99] On 18 October, Bülow told the French Ambassador, Geoffrey Noailles, that except for the small area covered by the Anglo-German agreement over the Portuguese colonies, French and German interests in Africa were 'absolutely the same'.[100] On 27 October, the Kaiser, who was in a high state of excitement because of Britain's refusal to come across with the 'blackmail' for Samoa, vented his spleen to Noailles: 'The English no longer make war except for money.' He described English Society as 'gangrenous and utterly corrupt'.[101] But when Muraviev raised the question of a League with the Kaiser in November, the lack of German response showed that whilst they were willing to use the spectre to frighten the British into making concessions on Samoa, they were not prepared to join with the Dual Alliance against her.[102]

However, as usual, Chamberlain's more excitable temperament left him open to the sort of pressure which the Germans hoped would lead the British into their alliance system. When the Kaiser and Bülow visited London in November 1899, Chamberlain proposed an Anglo-German alliance which 'would control the world' by relegating 'barbaric Russia to her proper bounds and compel turbulent France to keep the peace'.[103] Bülow claimed that he parried this by suggesting that Chamberlain might mention the idea publicly first.[104] Had he possessed any diplomatic 'feel', Chamberlain would have realised that with Britain entering a war in South Africa, the Germans would feel under no pressure to conclude an alliance; instead, he assumed that he had the green light to speak about it.[105]

In a well-reported speech at Leicester on 30 November, Chamberlain referred with enthusiasm to the prospect of an Anglo-American alliance in the future. After making further reference to the dangers of isolation, he went on to say that 'the natural alliance is between ourselves and the great German Empire'. Bitterly criticising the 'gross and obscene' caricatures of the Queen in the French press, he spoke of a 'new Triple Alliance' between 'the Teutonic race and the two great branches of the Anglo-Saxon race'.[106] Afterwards Chamberlain expressed the hope that his speech had not been 'unsatisfactory' to Bülow and the Germans;[107] it had, in fact, caused the most acute embarrassment.[108]

There were rumours in the British and German press that the speech had been prompted by the recent talks between Bülow and Chamberlain, and that it showed that they had done more than exchange pleasantries about the weather.[109] Bülow wanted to 'gradually improve' relations with Britain,[110] but with the Navy Bill before the Reichstag, the last thing he could afford was any impression that an alliance with England was in the offing. Significantly he chose to respond to Chamberlain on 12 December during a debate on the Navy Bill, when he said that Germany was 'quite ready to live in peace and harmony with her [England] on the basis of full reciprocity and mutual consideration'; but he told the German people that they must seize this favourable opportunity 'in order to secure ourselves for the future', which included building a 'fleet strong enough to prevent an attack'.[111] Holstein, who had suspected Bülow of wanting to wait until Germany was stronger at sea before inaugurating 'an irresponsible and aggressive anti-English policy',[112] was shocked by the vehemence of his comments.[113] Hatzfeldt had hoped that Bülow would give Chamberlain grounds for continuing to expect that 'we will eventually allow ourselves to meet his wishes about an alliance or an intimate understanding', since that would encourage him to 'show us consideration in the colonial questions that will probably arise'.[114] Bülow's remarks had precisely the opposite effect.

Chamberlain was mortally offended by Bülow's comments.[115] He told Lascelles that he felt 'rather as if I had been made to pull the chestnuts out of the fire for him'[116] – and reacted accordingly. He told Eckardstein coldly that it was 'advisable to drop every kind of further negotiations on the Alliance question', which was 'just not to be'.[117] As for the famed Continental League, Chamberlain declared that he 'did not care a twopenny damn if the whole gang combined against us, and that in that case we and the United States would give them such a lesson as they would never forget'.[118] He now took the view that England, which had 'faced with good fortune a European coalition before now', did not need an alliance.[119]

Although Chamberlain's outburst did not signal the end of his hopes for a German alliance, it ought to have suggested to Berlin that Hatzfeldt's warning about his impatience ought to be heeded. Instead, the Kaiser continued with his attempts to frighten the British into an alliance. In March 1900, he told the Prince of Wales about Muraviev's invitation to 'take part in a Collective Action with France and Russia against England for the enforcing of Peace and the help of the Boers'.[120] But Salisbury's scepticism remained undisturbed: 'there lingers', he told the Queen on 10 April, 'a doubt whether the proposal for a combination against England was ever really made by France and Russia to Germany'.[121] In this, Salisbury was wrong, but his assumption that the Continental League would come to naught was well-founded.

For all Germany's bluster, her real interest in a League was limited to the prospect of it frightening Britain; the Germans had no interest in providing the Dual Alliance with a victory over the British, or in paying the price which the French wanted for it. Nor would the French pay the German price for any joint initiative, which was a mutual guarantee by the three Powers of each others' European possessions; in short, a second ratification of the Treaty of Frankfurt.[122] Not even for the pyramids would the French abandon their claims to Alsace-Lorraine.

But if Salisbury's instincts were correct in telling him that Britain's potential enemies would be unable to present a united front, that did not prevent them from taking advantage of Britain's South African preoccupations *seriatim*.

17

The German Alliance Mirage

The failure of a Continental League to materialise immediately did nothing to soften the asperities of Salisbury's critics. The outbreak of the 'Boxer' rebellion in China in the summer of 1900 saw the European Powers co-operate against an insurgent Chinese nationalism.[1] Salisbury's handling of the crisis became another item in the indictment made by his critics, with Curzon fulminating that the 'Chinese policy of HMG' was a 'riddle insoluble to man';[2] he described Salisbury himself as a 'strange, powerful, inscrutable, brilliant, obstructive deadweight'.[3] The cause of his anger was Salisbury's unwillingness to follow up German hints that they might be disposed to co-operate with Britain in the Far East – and elsewhere.[4] At the end of August, Bülow asked with some impatience for a response to the Kaiser's 'overtures' and suggested 'a practical understanding on the question of the Yangtze'.[5] Salisbury responded that he had not been 'aware' that the Germans had made any overture.[6] This was too much for those of his colleagues who thought that Salisbury was becoming a liability. The First Lord of the Admiralty, Goschen, suggested to Chamberlain that they should get together with other Ministers to put pressure on him. The difficulty, he told Chamberlain, 'lies not in any one step which we might jointly persuade Salisbury to take, but in his whole attitude'.[7]

The Germans, who were worried about Russian intentions, were interested in guaranteeing the continuation of the 'Open Door' policy, especially in the Yangtze Valley.[8] Suggestions that an Anglo-German agreement there might be the precursor to an alliance aroused Chamberlain's interest, and despite Salisbury's scepticism he pushed ahead with the idea.[9] He set out his reasoning in a memorandum written on 10 September.[10] He took it for granted that China was doomed, and his objective was to get Germany to 'throw herself across the path of Russia'. An agreement with Germany would not only scotch the idea of a Franco-German agreement, it would 'emphasize the breach between Russia and Germany and Russia and Japan'. Chamberlain seemed to imagine that an alliance could be had for the price of Britain agreeing to keep her troops in Peking as part of the multi-national army there to maintain order.

Salisbury, who attached far less importance to the Far East than did Chamberlain, was correspondingly sceptical of the notion that Germany would save Britain's face there: 'She is in mortal terror on account of that long undefended frontier of hers on the Russian side. She will therefore never stand by us against Russia.'[11] Salisbury was sure that Germany would exact a 'considerable price' for recognising any British sphere of influence in the Yangtze Valley, and he doubted whether she would allow herself to be used as a 'catspaw' against Russia.[12] But once again, Salisbury let himself be overruled by his colleagues and allowed negotiations to be opened.

Much to German displeasure, Salisbury negotiated slowly and doggedly.[13] The final treaty was signed on 16 October and provided for both countries to uphold freedom of trade, 'as far as they can exercise influence', and to try to 'maintain undiminished the territorial condition of the Chinese Empire'.[14] Chamberlain was delighted, and took the view that 'events are slowly tending to draw us closer and to separate Germany from Russia'.[15] Salisbury was less enchanted and suspected that the agreement signified nothing very much once the Germans had entered caveats to make it less objectionable to Russia,[16] but by this stage he had finally surrendered his tenure of, if not his hold on, the Foreign Office.

In September, with the Boer War seemingly won, Salisbury had called and won a general election. His health provided a convenient excuse for raising the question of his continuance at the Foreign Office. He had been in office so long that many considered him 'the only Foreign Minister', and it was thought that his resignation 'would be disastrous' abroad, especially if he were to be succeeded by Chamberlain.[17] On the other hand, the work was arduous, and his colleagues were anxious for him to go.[18] A Cabinet reshuffle was arranged, in which Salisbury remained as Prime Minister, taking the office of Lord Privy Seal – which saw the departure of the only other survivor from Disraeli's administration, Lord Cross.[19] The new Foreign Secretary was Lord Lansdowne.

Chateaubriand's dictum, 'Men generally rise to office through their mediocrity and remain there through their superiority. This conjunction of antagonistic elements is the rarest thing, and it is for that reason that there are so few statesmen',[20] might have been coined for Lansdowne. A former Liberal who had defected from Gladstone as early as 1880, Lansdowne had served both as Governor-General of Canada and Viceroy of India before joining the Salisbury Cabinet. A fluent French linguist, with the blood of Talleyrand flowing in his veins, Charles Henry Keith Petty-Fitzmaurice, fifth Marquess of Lansdowne, remains the least studied of twentieth-century British Foreign Secretaries.[21] He has generally been regarded either as a postscript to Salisbury or the ante-chamber to Sir Edward Grey, and either way has been overshadowed. It has generally been held that under him British policy changed direction.[22]

Lansdowne has been portrayed as being in favour of a dramatically different policy towards Germany than Salisbury would have preferred, mainly on the basis of the so-called 'alliance project' which he drew up in early March 1901.[23] It is easy to see why this idea got abroad. He told Lascelles in November that he came to his office without 'too many preconceived ideas', but he pleaded 'guilty to one: the idea that we should make every effort to maintain, and, if we can, to strengthen the good relations which at present exist' between Britain and Germany.[24] It has been assumed, usually in the light of Chamberlain's abortive talks, that Lansdowne was committed to resurrecting the idea of an Anglo-German alliance, and that this occupied an important place in his priorities.[25] But this too readily assumes that Salisbury ceased to influence British foreign policy, when in fact Lansdowne kept in constant touch with him and usually waited for his approval before taking action; indeed, on some occasions the two men would exchange letters three times a day on the same topic, so close was the contact between them.[26] Lansdowne's policy was a continuation of Salisbury's in different circumstances. He was anxious, above all, to limit Britain's liabilities. He shared Salisbury's desire to improve relations with the Dual Alliance Powers; but given the situation in the Far East, it seemed easier to try to solve Britain's problems by strengthening the German connection. Lansdowne took a resolutely Salisburian line on the question of the terms for any agreement with Germany, arguing against 'our making any concessions for which we do not receive a completely adequate compensation'.[27]

An Anglo-German alliance continued to be the King Charles' Head of Chamberlain and the Germans. Holstein's view in December 1900 was that a 'grouping of England and the Triple Alliance would easily obtain every just objective', and that if 'England fails us now' it would show that 'no combinations could be based on her'.[28] Hatzfeldt warned him that English 'difficulties' had not been 'great enough' for them to want to join the Triple Alliance, and if that was what Germany wanted, she had better be prepared to wait until events convinced them of 'the value of this arrangement'; he thought that there was little utility in taking it up 'at this time'.[29] Hatzfeldt's complaints to Lansdowne about Britain's reluctance to take on far-reaching commitments met with little sympathy from Salisbury, who told his successor: 'My answer always was that England never gives assurances of unconditional support (unless under existing treaties). Our conduct in any future war will depend largely on the *casus belli*. As that cannot be foreseen – so neither can our action be foreseen.'[30]

Because Holstein and company thought that the British were still desperately seeking Germany's friendship, they had no difficulty believing Eckardstein when he reported that on 16 January 1901 Chamberlain had reopened the subject of an Anglo-German alliance.[31] The Kaiser declared: 'So "they're coming" it seems, which is what we've been waiting for.'[32] Anxious to pour cold water upon his master's ebullience without actually upsetting him, Bülow told the Kaiser that he was correct to think that the English 'must now come to us', but he warned against a premature commitment: 'England's troubles will increase in the coming months, and with them will rise the price which we shall be able to demand.'[33] Holstein took a similar view, ridiculing Chamberlain's notion of an Anglo-French or an Anglo-Russia agreement. Such appeasement would, at best, postpone for a few years Britain's 'final fight for existence', and at worst make it even more certain by revealing Britain's weakness to her enemies: 'We can wait. Time is on our side.'[34] But the British showed no immediate interest in a German alliance.[35]

It was Russian expansionism in the Far East that forced to the fore the question of what the October agreement (to which the Japanese had adhered) actually meant: the different answers given by Germany, Britain and Japan would determine the nature of future diplomatic alignments in the Far East. On 12 and 15 January, Count Hayashi, the Japanese Minister in London, asked whether the British would join them in protesting to St Petersburg against Russian attempts to establish a privileged position in China.[36] Lansdowne and Salisbury were not inclined to be 'fussy' about reports that the Russians had concluded a secret treaty with the Chinese, but they were anxious about railway sidings which the Russians had just seized from the British.[37] Lansdowne asked Lascelles to find out whether the Germans would be willing to join in representations to the Russians.[38] The Germans were evasive.

The problem for the Germans was that any attempt to establish just what it was they were willing to do in the Far East risked exposing the contradictions inherent in *Weltpolitik*. The Kaiser would consider identical British and German *démarches* in St Petersburg,[39] but Holstein, who thought that the October treaty did not apply to the recent Russian concessions, was against even that unless the British made greater commitments to Germany. Bülow was willing to co-operate with the British in the Far East – provided it cost Germany nothing.[40] Holstein stressed that any agreement would have to be very favourable to them to be acceptable to German opinion;[41] it was 'self-evident that we should not run after the English with proposals for a rapprochement'. If Russia proved troublesome, then 'Anglo-Japanese pressure' should be enough to deter her: 'We can wait', was Holstein's verdict.[42] He remained deeply distrustful of Salisbury, whom he described as a 'confidence trickster' determined to ruin Russo-German relations.[43] Eckardstein was specifically told 'on no account' to raise the subject of an Anglo-German alliance.[44] The Kaiser accepted the view that the British request went further than the October treaty, but warned that Germany could not be forever swinging between the Russians and the British.[45]

On 1 March, Lansdowne told the Cabinet that despite Russian assurances, it seemed as though they were 'endeavouring to force upon China a permanent treaty which will virtually establish a protectorate . . . over . . . the whole of Manchuria, as well as Mongolia and Chinese Turkestan'.[46] The Cabinet authorised him to deliver a protest to the Russians and to ask for the text of the treaty.[47] It was against this prospect of having to confront the Russians that the October agreement had been made, but Salisbury had been right to predict that the Germans would not act against Russia. Bülow told the Reichstag that 'Germany must not pull chestnuts out of the fire for England'.[48]

On 9 March, Hayashi asked Lansdowne whether the Germans could be relied upon to remain neutral in the event of a Russo-Japanese war, and whether the British would help them if they had to 'approach Russia';[49] he was vague about whether Japan was contemplating military or diplomatic action.[50] Salisbury told the new King, Edward VII, on 13 March that there were 'several members of the Cabinet' who were 'disposed to agree that England and Germany should join in undertaking to join Japan'.[51] One of these was Lansdowne, who had drawn up a 'draft declaration' which bound both Powers to neutrality in the event of a Russo-Japanese war, but which committed them to provide naval assistance if Japan were to face two other Powers.[52] This was the famous 'draft alliance' which was supposed to mark off his policy from that of Salisbury.

Bülow's words to the Reichstag on 15 March gave the British the answer to the question about the German interpretation of the October agreement: 'there were no German interests of importance in Manchuria', and its fate was 'a matter of absolute indifference' to Germany.[53] Baron von Richthofen thought it 'rather hard that the German Government should be asked to declare their attitude' whilst the British 'declined to give any indication of the line they intended to pursue'.[54] Lansdowne explained that this was because Britain was 'sincerely desirous of keeping in step so far as we are able', and because her 'South African entanglements' made it 'impossible for us to commit ourselves to a policy which might involve us in war, unless we can assure ourselves that any obligation which we might incur would be shared by another Power'. Lansdowne had correctly anticipated that 'Germany was not prepared to "keep a ring" for Russia and Japan', and now even Eckardstein, who had been urging him to 'egg on Japan to fight', was holding rather more modest language about a 'defensive alliance, limited in duration to . . . 5 years between Germany and England against Russia and France'. Lansdowne doubted that 'much will come of this'.

Lansdowne saw clearly the danger that an alliance would 'oblige us to adopt in all our foreign relations a policy which would no longer be British but Anglo-German', and he was so suspicious about Eckardstein's claims that Wilhelm supported the notion that he asked Lascelles to investigate.[55] Lascelles had not seen the Kaiser and could only offer 'conjecture'.[56] But he doubted whether Eckardstein 'would have suggested an alliance without authority'.[57] This obliged Lansdowne to treat the proposal which came from Eckardstein on 18 March with due seriousness, but his response was entirely in the Salisburian tradition.

Eckardstein put forward 'the idea of an understanding of a more durable and extended character' with England, which, with her 'scattered and vulnerable possessions all over the world, was more likely to require help than Germany'. Lansdowne's response was that 'the proximity of Russia to Germany along so extensive a frontier made the situation of Germany quite as vulnerable as ours'. He called Eckardstein's 'project' a 'novel and very far-reaching one, which would require careful examination, and which obviously I could not encourage without reference to my colleagues'.[58] This was not the language of a man making a proposal which 'marked a decisive breach with Britain's traditional diplomacy of concluding no alliances in time of peace'.[59] Thinking that the Germans were going to take the initiative with the text of an alliance, Lansdowne told Eckardstein on 22 March that provided means could be found to 'remove the difficulties due to the peculiarities of British parliamentary feeling with regard to long-term agreements', Salisbury was in favour of a 'strictly defined defensive alliance'. Eckardstein told Lansdowne that only an agreement approved by Parliament would be acceptable, and that Germany would prefer Britain to join the Triple Alliance.[60]

When the portly Baron mentioned the alliance again at the end of March, Lansdowne was still sceptical; but still thinking that the idea came from the Kaiser, he thought that he ought to 'treat it with all possible deference'.[61] Eckardstein had told Berlin that it had been the British who had raised the question of an alliance on 18 March,[62] and deliberately omitted to send any account of Lansdowne's comment on 29 March that he was not keen on the idea of any 'far-reaching' arrangement.[63] He asked Holstein for instructions about the reply he should make if Lansdowne came forward with specific proposals, clearly in the hope of being able to present any text to the British as though it were a German initiative.[64] But Holstein's suspicions of Salisbury denied Eckardstein the document he wanted. Holstein responded that the British should open negotiations in Vienna with a view to joining the Triple Alliance.[65] Bülow, who was frustrated at the 'academic' way the British had raised the question of the alliance, also thought that Britain ought to adhere to the Triple Alliance.[66]

Eckardstein now risked finding himself stranded, since neither his own Government nor the British would give him the text of an alliance which he could pass off to the other as an official initiative. He did raise with the Austrians the idea that they might like to approach the British, but got little joy. When he saw Lansdowne on 29 March, there was equally little pleasure to be had, since the Foreign Secretary made plain the reservations of his colleagues and the impossibility of making progress because of Salisbury's illness.[67] It may, of course, have been entirely accidental that two days later Eckardstein handed in his resignation, offering as a last piece of 'inside' information the prophecy that Salisbury would soon be succeeded as Prime Minister by Devonshire.[68] Unfortunately his offer was declined, and his misrepresentations remained unexposed.

Lansdowne invested little hope in a German alliance, but encouraged by Eckardstein's lies, he kept the lines to Berlin open; however, he would have been just as happy to have achieved the objective of restraining Russia by more direct means. Although the Russians were behaving 'abominably in China',[69] Lansdowne was not disposed to be 'pedantic about Manchuria. We have already recognized its "gravitation" for Railway purposes, and we should not fall foul of any reasonable arrangement of the conditions under which the Russian troops might be withdrawn'; with a 'little *bonne volonté* and mutual confidence the whole affair might be capable of settlement'.[70] On 28 March, Lansdowne delivered a speech in the Lords designed to build 'mutual confidence' and to make it plain to Russia that Britain had no desire to go to war with her or to use Japan as her catspaw.[71]

At first it seemed as though this mixture of firmness and conciliation might pay dividends. On 5 April, the Russians ended their attempt to force the Chinese into an agreement.[72] On 14

April, Vladimir Lamsdorff, the Russian Foreign Minister, told the British Ambassador, Sir Charles Scott, that there was no problem in Anglo-Russian relations 'that could not be easily reconciled'. Russian troops would remain in China only until a 'normal state of affairs' had been established. Scott was inclined to take Lamsdorff's words at face value and attributed the amelioration in Russian policy to the intervention of Nicholas II.[73] Lansdowne was less convinced that Russia's policy had really changed and suspected that she had backed down under pressure, but he was quite willing to work with the Russians if they showed themselves halfway trustworthy.[74] The Japanese were also of the opinion that it was joint pressure which had produced the change in Russia's policy – and valued the British connection all the more for it.[75]

Whether for this reason, or because of Eckardstein's hints about a triple alliance in the Far East,[76] Hayashi asked Lansdowne on 17 April whether it was possible to have some 'permanent understanding' between the two Governments for the protection of their interests in China.[77] He emphasised that he was speaking in a purely personal capacity, but the fact that Eckardstein had mentioned the same thing to him a few days before showed Lansdowne that the idea came from more than one source. In this sense Eckardstein's lies have misled historians as much as they did his masters in Berlin; in both cases it was supposed that the British wanted a German alliance for its own sake. In so far as Lansdowne considered it, it was because he had been led to believe that the Kaiser wanted it – and because he thought it might be useful in the Far East.

There is a macabre fascination to be had from watching the serpentine movements of Eckardstein as he twisted and turned to escape from his own lies by trying to make them into reality. When he saw Lansdowne in mid April, he 'hummed and ha'd' a great deal before saying that 'what had been done had been done with the knowledge of persons very near the Emperor' – mentioning Holstein by name. Lansdowne still doubted 'whether much would come of the project. In principle the idea is good enough.

But when each side comes, if it ever does, to formulate its terms we shall break down.'[78]

Eckardstein led his masters to believe that the British Cabinet was coming round to the idea of an alliance when, in fact, it was under the impression that Berlin was making the running.[79] In an attempt to get a text of an alliance from someone, Eckardstein tried to get Hayashi to take the initiative with Lansdowne in proposing a new triple alliance of Britain, Japan and Germany; he denied having done so when tasked by Berlin[80] and put the blame on Hayashi.[81] Holstein, seeing no reason to disbelieve Eckardstein, confined himself to warning him to 'be careful' because the 'limited' treaty which the British and the Japanese wanted would be directly 'contrary to *our* interests' because it would 'put an end to the *necessity* for England to link herself by a *general* treaty with Germany, or rather with the Triple Alliance'. It was typical of Holstein to assume that Britain and Japan had no choice other than to be 'content with our neutrality' until 'this linking-up has taken place'.[82] Eckardstein assured Holstein that Lansdowne appreciated this, and that the British had no immediate intention of concluding a deal with the Japanese.[83]

In fact, Lansdowne's attention was focused not on Germany, but on trying to get a deal with the Russians. Salisbury's description of the Russian method of dealing with a proposal they disliked cannot be bettered: 'She will pretend to consider it – will waste time in colourable negotiations, and when she has arranged matters to her own liking will decline any cooperation with us';[84] so it proved on this occasion. On 20 April, the Russians, having assured the British of their desire for better relations, proposed to the Germans the reconstruction of the Far Eastern Triplice: Russia, Germany and France were to guarantee the Chinese a loan equal to the value of the sum which the three Powers would demand from her as compensation.[85] Hatzfeldt was 'tremendously' pleased with this notion, which he felt would 'make people here finally see the light'. This 'Triple Alliance' would be 'absolutely disastrous both for English interests in China and for England's prestige in the whole world. Even Salisbury will hardly be able to close his eyes to this fact.' This would be 'the best and most effective means of pressure on the political decisions of the English Government at our disposal'.[86]

To Hatzfeldt's surprise, Lansdowne did not seem unduly worried by events in the Far East.[87] With Salisbury about to return to London, Hatzfeldt thought it undesirable to make a move which would be interpreted as another example of 'blackmail'. Holstein tried to use rumours of a French advance in southern China to secure further Anglo-German co-operation under the terms of the October agreement. Salisbury should be brought to realise, he told Hatzfeldt, that as a member of a five-Power bloc, 'England can push the Dual Alliance about at will *without* war', but that if he did nothing then he would be at its mercy.[88] Eckardstein's lies strengthened Holstein and Bülow in their serious misreading of British intentions.[89] On 15 May, he reported that Lansdowne wanted to prepare a draft Anglo-German treaty, with the two Powers putting their ideas on paper and discussing them point by point. Unfortunately for Eckardstein, it was at this moment that Hatzfeldt's doctors pronounced him well enough to return to work, so it was he, and not his junior, who went to see Lansdowne on 23 May.

Lansdowne expected a memorandum containing the German terms,[90] and had arranged with Salisbury for it to be discussed by an *ad hoc* committee of the two of them with Balfour, Chamberlain and Hicks Beach;[91] instead, he found himself engaged in a dialogue of the mutually misinformed with Hatzfeldt.[92] When Hatzfeldt confirmed that the 'proposal' was for Britain to join the Triple Alliance, Lansdowne was quick with his caveats: 'it seemed to me to follow . . . that each of the allies would have a right to a voice in guiding and controlling the external policy of the other'; he also stressed the difficulties this would cause with public opinion. For his part, Hatzfeldt emphasised that Britain could not have the advantages of an alliance without some disadvantages; the alternative was 'isolation'. A deal with Russia would cost the British too much, and Germany could always look elsewhere for allies. Hatzfeldt stressed that he was not 'using the language of menace', simply remarking that Germany found it inconvenient to have a bad relationship with Russia and might try to 'square' her. 'Now', said Holstein, 'we will await the English decision without showing impatience.' If the English declined an alliance, it would be the end of the matter.[93]

Lansdowne wrote to Eckardstein on 24 May asking for the text of the German memorandum, but his letter arrived when the Minister was out of town and was opened by Hatzfeldt, who, for the first time, began to get an inkling of what was going on.[94] Hatzfeldt replied that he knew nothing whatsoever about any memorandum, and hoped that the matter would keep until Lansdowne could tell him exactly what it was supposed to be about.[95] Lansdowne replied with details of his talks with Eckardstein and renewed his request for the famous 'memorandum'.[96]

Since Hatzfeldt had known nothing about any memorandum and knew that he had not promised one to Lansdowne, he began to suspect Eckardstein of exceeding his instructions.[97] But Holstein refused to believe this and warned his old colleague against raising the question of personnel since there were those who thought that it was time that the ailing Ambassador himself went. As for the British and the alliance proposals, 'there can be no question of a *written* memorandum for the present, that is not until we are agreed on the *basic principles*'.[98]

By this stage Eckardstein was in a state of blue funk. Fearing discovery, he told Sir Thomas Sanderson that Hatzfeldt was in an awful 'state of excitement . . . [and] was quite misrepresenting the position of his discussions to the Government at Berlin and that he was afraid there would be a regular muddle'. Sanderson, who thought that the German was 'becoming a very horrible and portentous bore', showed how seriously the British were taking the matter by telling him that there was no great hurry and that, in any event, 'unless the German Gov[ernmen]t did something, nothing as far as I could see, could possibly happen'.[99]

It was in response to Eckardstein's initiative that Sanderson drew up the draft of an Anglo-German alliance.[100] It was a modest proposal, which excluded from its scope the American continent, and which would come into force only when either of the two Powers was attacked by two others; it would last for a term of five years.[101] Lansdowne himself, having studied the text of the Triple Alliance, thought there were 'a number of cardinal points which require to be cleared up before we can seriously take up the great proposal'.[102]

But before Lansdowne could set his mind to this task, Salisbury did it incomparably better than anyone else could have done. On 29 May, he drew up a masterly statement of the principles of his own diplomacy to show why an alliance with Germany was unnecessary.[103] For Britain to join the Triple Alliance was, 'even in its most naked aspect', a 'bad' bargain, since the obligation of having to defend Germany's and Austria's frontiers against Russia was far heavier than having to defend the British Isles against France. As for Hatzfeldt's statement (and by implication that of so many of his colleagues) that 'isolation' was a danger, Salisbury had one simple question: '*Have we ever felt that danger practically?*' Britain had, after all, survived both the Napoleonic and Boer Wars. In characteristically mordant fashion, Salisbury observed: 'It would hardly be wise to incur novel and most onerous obligations, in order to guard against *a danger in whose existence we have no historical reason for believing.*' Neither Power could be sure that in a given set of unforeseeable circumstances the parliament and government of the day would honour the obligations of its predecessor; and quite apart from that, an alliance would be unpopular with current public opinion.

It is often assumed that Salisbury scuppered Lansdowne's alliance plans, but that is not so. In the first place, there was nothing new in any of these arguments; indeed, Lansdowne had used a variant of them himself when writing to Lascelles in April.[104] The document had been drawn up in response to Eckardstein's initiative and not as part of some long-planned scheme.

Despite Holstein's warning that sending any letter to Lansdowne would lay Germany open to the charge that 'the formal proposal of the alliance idea has come from us – precisely what we want to avoid',[105] Hatzfeldt managed to persuade him that without some reply the British would be frightened off.[106] Thus it was that on 30 May, Hatzfeldt wrote apologising if Lansdowne had got the impression that he was going to send him a document. What he had meant to say was that if they were in agreement on basic principles, then such a document could form the basis for a detailed discussion of the actual terms of an alliance.[107] Eckardstein suggested that because Hatzfeldt had muddied the waters, 'for the time the discussions should be discontinued'.[108] Lansdowne was quite 'content to mark time for a while', particularly in view of Hatzfeldt's imminent retirement.[109]

But Eckardstein continued to feed his master in Berlin the line that it was Hatzfeldt who had ruined a splendid opportunity for an alliance by pressing the British and claiming that his successor would be less friendly. Eckardstein claimed that Salisbury had 'refused to negotiate at pistol-point', but he added that when he had spoken with Lansdowne on 10 June there had been encouraging signs.[110] Count Paul Metternich, the now German Ambassador in London, and Holstein both drew up long memoranda on the alliance question and clearly expected it to be one of the first issues with which the new Ambassador would have to deal.[111] Eckardstein kept up these hopes by telegraphing in late July that although Lansdowne was discouraged by the failure of the earlier negotiations, and that Salisbury was now less keen, he thought that French ambitions in Morocco might yet force the British to renew negotiations.[112] He made free with the Kaiser's name to both the British Ambassador and to Holstein.

The dangers of monarchical diplomacy loomed only too large in the suspicious mind of Holstein, who particularly feared the effects of the forthcoming meeting between the Kaiser and his uncle. Edward was due to come to Homburg to see his dying sister, the Empress Frederick, and Holstein was anxious that Wilhelm should do nothing which would imply that Germany needed Britain's friendship. This meant that he must give no hint that Germany had any quarrels with Russia and France; indeed, it meant that the Kaiser would have to agree to let those two countries in on his pet project of the Berlin to Baghdad railway.[113] The Kaiser agreed to let the Russians in, and argued strongly that any alliance must be between Britain and the Triplice.[114]

Edward VII was the great *bête noire* of the Kaiser. He 'hated his "wicked uncle", whom he suspected of machiavellian cleverness, and, like most Germans, thought that the King exercised a great deal of power'.[115] Bülow, who once described the relationship between uncle and nephew as 'a fat malicious tom-cat playing with a shrewmouse',[116] made the same mistake about the King's powers as his fellow countrymen. He called Edward VII a man of 'much natural intelligence, of very great tact, [and] of very great manners'.[117] After Edward's visit to Homburg, it was only courtliness which prevented Edward's Ministers from applying to him the opprobrious phrase which the Kaiser had used of them – 'unmitigated noodles'.[118]

Before he left London, Edward had been given a briefing document against the chance that he would engage in political conversations with the Kaiser; at their first meeting the King simply handed the thing over to the Kaiser.[119] To anyone less blinded by Eckardstein's lies the most obvious fact about the document was that it did not mention an alliance with Germany. The subject of the alliance was not mentioned until the two monarchs met on 23 August. Imagining that the arrogant British were getting into desperate straits, Wilhelm sanctimoniously declared that they 'will have to decide which side they are on and will finally have to show their colours', nor should they 'be surprised that we no longer react to general sentiments about friendship and solidarity. We can only negotiate on the basis of absolutely firm treaties.'[120] Lascelles responded by saying that Lansdowne too favoured an alliance, but that it would not be easy to depart from traditional British policy, and that he had understood from Bülow that there was no need for haste.[121]

At this point Lansdowne is supposed to have had a 'change of heart',[122] but if the line argued here is taken further, then all that happened is that he had his existing reservations about the possibility of an alliance confirmed. He told Lascelles on 28

August that 'no one could have striven harder than I have' (Eckardstein might have dissented from this verdict), but that an 'alliance' was 'a big fence' to 'ride at': 'I should not mind having a try if I knew what was on the other side.' It was, he concluded, something for the Cabinet to consider in the autumn.[123] Lansdowne, like Salisbury, was primarily concerned with Russian expansion in the Far East: if he could get no *entente* with Russia herself, and if the Germans wanted too much for their cooperation, there was another option – Japan.

18

Alliances and Understandings

Some historians have seen the alliance with Japan as a first step out of isolation,[1] others have seen it as reinforcing it.[2] Both interpretations have elements of truth in them once the nature of Salisbury's 'isolationism' is appreciated: its traditional Tory distrust of entangling Continental alliances; its reliance on British naval power; its preference for a defence policy which kept taxation low (particularly in view of the cost of the Boer War); all these were compatible with a Japanese alliance. Lansdowne's main objective was to bring about a 'frank understanding' between Russia and Britain 'as to Manchuria, Tibet, Afghanistan, Persia, etc.', and it was only continued Russian obduracy on these issues which led him to look for an alternative solution.[3]

In this sense the Japanese alliance, even if Salisbury disapproved of it, provided a Salisburian rather than a Chamberlainite answer to the problem of how to safeguard British interests in the Far East. As Lansdowne pointed out to Hayashi at the end of July, both of their countries had a common interest in maintaining the 'balance of power' in the Far East against Russia.[4] Salisbury had an instinctive understanding of what the Liberal politician, John Morley, came to see as the first essential for a 'statesman' concerned with 'high politics', namely that 'in the great high latitudes of policy, all is fluid, elastic, mutable; the friend to-day, the foe tomorrow; the ally and confederate against your enemy, suddenly *his* confederate against you: Russia or France or Germany or America, one sort of Power this year, quite another sort and in deeply changed relations to you, the year after'.[5] Chamberlain quite lacked this sense, and none of Salisbury's colleagues or successors possessed it in the same way. In so far as the Japanese alliance sprang from a belief that Britain needed an ally in the Far East, it was a departure from Salisbury's views; in so far as Lansdowne regarded it as a purely local arrangement to secure limited objectives, it was not a Chamberlainite solution to the major problems he believed existed.

The case for the Japanese alliance was ably made by one of the Assistant Under-Secretaries at the Foreign Office, Francis Bertie, one of the rising men in the diplomatic service – if he could keep his temper.[6] He saw that 'if we do nothing to encourage Japan to look on us as a friend and possible ally against Russia and France, we may drive her to a policy of despair, in which she may come to some sort of terms with Russia'.[7] He thought that an Anglo-Japanese alliance would serve Britain's purposes better than one with Germany:[8] Japan would be a 'powerful and *sure* ally for the contingency of an attack on the British Empire by two Powers such as Russia and France combined'; Germany was more interested in fomenting disagreements between Britain and those Powers, and would never really help Britain; nor were British and German interests 'everywhere identical' – indeed, in some parts of the world they were 'irreconcilable'; and a formal alliance with Germany would mean shaping British foreign policy 'in accordance with her views and subordinate our policy to hers as is the case with Austria and Italy'. Germany could hardly stand by and watch Britain defeated by the Franco-Russian Alliance, since the effects on the balance of power would be disastrous. To give up the 'liberty to pursue a British world policy' would, he concluded, be too high a price to pay for a German alliance.[9]

When Hayashi saw Lansdowne on 16 October and proposed an Anglo-Japanese alliance, the British considered it carefully and argued its relative advantages and disadvantages.[10] The arguments highlighted the different assumptions upon which Salisbury and his critics were proceeding. His own son-in-law, Lord Selborne, was one of its foremost proponents, but then, as First Lord of the Admiralty, he saw Britain not simply as an island Empire, but as one 'with all the difficulties and responsibilities of a military power in Asia'; it was easy to be 'a great military power for home defence or European warfare' if you had 'compulsory military service', but it was a 'terrific task to remain the greatest Naval Power when Naval Powers are year by year increasing in numbers and in naval strength, and at the same time to be a Military Power strong enough to meet the greatest Military Power in Asia'.[11] This was literally a world away from the traditional Conservative view of Derby and Salisbury, which saw Britain as primarily an island Empire. What Selborne wanted was an alliance with Japan which would enable Britain to maintain the Two-Power Standard against Russia and France.[12] Lansdowne was simply preoccupied with the possibility of crises arising from the simultaneous demise of the 'sick' men of Turkey and China, and wanted to relieve the pressure on Britain somewhere.[13] Salisbury was well aware of the problems – he had been wrestling with them for two decades – but never having seen Britain as primarily an Asiatic power, he could contemplate with more equanimity the possibility of being unable to maintain that position: as he told his former private secretary, Lord Currie, in June 1900, in those regions 'Other nations can lend money and we cannot.'[14]

This was at the heart of the differences between Salisbury and his critics. Under the impact of Beaconsfieldism, they believed in Britain's destiny as an imperial power; Salisbury suspected that they were being led astray by mirages. He warned the impulsive Curzon in September that: 'In the last generation we did much what we liked in the East by force of threats: by squadrons and tall talk', but those days had passed and 'for some years to come Eastern advance must largely depend upon payment; and I fear in that race England will seldom win.'[15]

Cecil Spring-Rice, the Minister to Persia, had to watch the

Russians greatly increase their hold over the Shah's Government in 1900 with the offer of a loan of £2.4 million, which both he and Curzon thought the British should have made: 'it is simply big battalions and money bags which have done the trick'.[16] Yet, despite the fact that Persia was considered a vital buffer zone against Russia's advance towards the frontiers of India, the Chancellor of the Exchequer would not relax his financial vigilance. Despite Lansdowne's efforts, he could not extract more money from the Treasury, the Bank of England or the India Office.[17] 'The situation', Salisbury declared, 'seems sufficiently hopeless.'[18] Curzon, whose impatience and ambition were never constrained by thoughts of finance, failed to understand why he could not have the 'forward policy' he wanted in the Gulf; but the reasons were familiar enough to Salisbury.

The Boer War meant that £200 million extra a year had to be found to sustain government expenditure, a sum which Salisbury complained would mean one penny on income tax in perpetuity.[19] In strict financial terms, despite the rise in naval expenditure in the 1890s, the total tax burden per head of population had declined since the 1860s, and an increase to meet Britain's naval commitments would certainly have been possible, but that would have meant an increase in taxation. To raise indirect taxes would have affected the cost of living; to raise income tax was even less desirable from Salisbury's point of view. He had always believed that income tax was 'demoralizing, inquisitorial' and 'intolerable'. If applied to the populace at large, it would lead to demands for more democracy; if confined to the wealthy few, it would be fatal to the rights of property to raise it any higher than necessary.[20] Disraeli had once asked whether the British would become an 'imperial people'; Salisbury doubted they would be willing to pay for the privilege.

It is now a commonplace that Germany's *Weltpolitik* was constrained by her financial system, which left the central government short of money since it was unable to raise direct taxation,[21] but Britain's own 'World Policy' was subject to not dissimilar restraints. The British system of government was designed to reinforce fiscal conservatism. All departmental estimates were subject to approval by the Treasury before they could be submitted to Parliament. Once funds had been allocated to the spending departments, the comptroller and auditor-general scrutinised spending habits, thus tightening the grip of the Treasury still further.[22] Treasury orthodoxy rarely allowed the use of funds for foreign loans: there had been one in 1833 to help finance the kingdom of Greece, but that had been the act of a Whig Government which had become notorious for its financial laxity, and it had occurred before the Gladstonian reforms of the 1860s, as had the loan to Turkey in 1855. A loan to a spendthrift oriental despotism like Persia or China would have led to a flood of applications from British businessmen in Latin America and Africa, which was why Hicks Beach had no trouble turning down the request for a Persian loan in 1900.[23] Despite Lansdowne's protests in 1901 that British troops needed to remain in China after the Boxer rebellion as a counterweight to Russian influence, Hicks Beach successfully insisted that they should be removed for financial reasons.[24] Salisbury concurred with this line of policy. His response to the constant calls to action which Curzon made from the Viceregal throne was that 'he always wants me to negotiate with Russia as if I had 500,000 men at my back, and I have not'.[25]

The Boer War simply added to the constraints on expenditure; indeed, 'Joe's war' made 'Joe's diplomacy' impossible, at least in Salisbury's eyes. Chamberlain's South African Beaconsfieldism had cost more than enough. But those who believed in the imperial destiny could not and did not see the world this way. Selborne wanted a Japanese alliance for much the same reason Chamberlain wanted a German one: it was the only way to pursue the policy of prestige which the British electorate expected from Disraeli's successors; in this sense, Disraeli's legacy was Salisbury's Nemesis.

Holstein, who was increasingly frustrated by the failure of the British to propose any agreement, blamed 'the paralyzing, or at least delaying influence of Lord Salisbury' for the failure to secure an Anglo-German agreement.[26] He supported his complaints by letting *The Times*' correspondent, Valentine Chirol, see the reports which Hatzfeldt had made in 1895 on Salisbury's attitude towards the Ottoman Empire. But Sir Thomas Sanderson flatly refuted the notion that Salisbury had been considering dismembering it.[27] In his urgency to get the British to come to heel, Holstein had ignored Hatzfeldt's warning that Chamberlain would swing against Germany; the old diplomat lived just long enough to see his words on this subject vindicated. Speaking in Edinburgh on 25 October, Chamberlain bitterly attacked those who had criticised the conduct of the British army in South Africa and pointed out, *inter alia*, that the Germans had used methods during the Franco-Prussian War which were far more brutal. The speech created an uproar – and a demand from Bülow for an official apology, which Lansdowne declined.[28]

Following his conversations with Hayashi on 16 October, Lansdowne had drawn up the 'sketch' of an agreement with Japan, which, with Salisbury's permission, he placed before the Cabinet on 25 October.[29] It provided for Britain and Japan to offer mutual support if they faced more than one other Power in pursuit of their objective of maintaining the independence and integrity of China.[30] But for all its advantages to both sides, there were those in Britain and Japan who doubted its utility. Lansdowne had still not given up the hope of coming to an agreement with the Russians over the Far East and Persia, and he sent his proposals for such a settlement to the Cabinet on the same day (25 October) that he sent the draft treaty with Japan to Salisbury.[31] It was only the complete failure of the Russians to respond which ensured that the Japanese alliance held the stage alone.[32]

Lansdowne, who failed to appreciate that the Germans were not interested in an agreement confined to Asia, disagreed with Salisbury that Britain would incur more 'onerous obligations' by an alliance with Germany. He accepted Salisbury's argument that 'isolation' had not thus far been dangerous, but thought that 'we may push . . . [it] too far'; the fact that they were talking to the Japanese about an alliance showed that 'we do not wish to continue to stand alone'. Lansdowne acknowledged that the 'difficulties in the way of a full-blown defensive alliance' with Germany were 'at the present moment virtually insuperable', but a limited declaration of common interests in certain areas would meet the charge that Britain had 'inconsiderately or brusquely rejected their overtures'.[33]

Balfour, who still wanted a German alliance, argued that 'the Japanese Treaty, if it ends in war, brings us into collision with the same opponents as a German alliance, but with a much weaker partner'. The interests which would be protected by the alliance were of less importance than those which a connection to the Triple Alliance would guarantee: 'It is a matter of supreme moment to us that Italy should not be crushed, that Austria should not be dismembered and ... that Germany should not be squeezed to death between the hammer of Russia and the anvil of France.' The fact that the Japanese refused to guarantee the Indian frontiers deprived the alliance of what little attraction it might have had for Balfour: 'The weakest spot in the Empire is probably the Indian frontier.... A quarrel with Russia anywhere, about anything, means the invasion of India.'[34]

Balfour's objections were presented as late as 12 December because it took that long for the Japanese to respond to Lansdowne's terms. Part of the delay stemmed from the fact that the former Foreign Minister, Count Ito, was on his way to Russia. Ito belonged to that section of the Japanese elite who favoured an alliance with Russia rather than one with Britain, and the Japanese desire for consensus made it impossible to proceed until the results of his talks with Witte were known.[35] Bertie made it clear to Hayashi that the British would be mightily offended if the Japanese were now to conclude a separate agreement with Russia,[36] and he wondered whether the Germans were playing a part in the delay.[37] The Japanese Prime Minister, Marquis Jutaro Nomura, who was committed to the alliance with Britain, expedited matters at his end by submitting a draft treaty to the Emperor on 3 December.[38] On 12 December, Hayashi gave the text to Lansdowne.[39]

British Ministers disliked both the proposal that they should maintain a fixed naval force in the Far East, and the Japanese refusal to extend the alliance to Siam and India; it was felt that both restrictions deprived the arrangement of some of its attraction. Lansdowne put these caveats to Hayashi on 19 December,[40] explaining the need to satisfy Parliament that this 'entirely new departure' was worth it.[41] He warned Salisbury on 22 December that 'it is just possible' that the Japanese would 'break over the two amendments dealing with the strengths of the fleets and Japan's interest in Corea. The first we cannot accept, and the second will be very difficult to deal with.'[42]

Balfour's preference for a German alliance ensured that option remained on the table. On 4 December, whilst he was waiting to hear from the Japanese, and in response to Salisbury's request for one, Lansdowne submitted a sketch of the sort of 'understanding' which he had in mind: it provided for the maintenance of the territorial *status quo* in areas of common interest and amounted to 'little more than a declaration of common policy and of a desire to maintain close diplomatic relations'. He had no great expectation that it would be the sort of thing the Germans wanted, but it would get Britain off the hook as far as being accused of 'dropping' Germany was concerned, and that was its clear motive. But for Salisbury, even this was too much.[43]

Because of the unsatisfactory nature of the state of negotiations with the Japanese, and the fact that the Cabinet had not yet considered the amendments, Lansdowne decided not to mention the subject when he saw Metternich on 19 December; he was convinced, in any case, that Ito, who was travelling to St Petersburg via Berlin, would have given the game away.[44] Instead, Lansdowne brought up his ideas for a bilateral Anglo-German agreement. He told Metternich that he had been waiting for him to raise the issue, but that as he had not done so, and in order to avoid any 'misconception', he thought that he had better do so. Whilst not regarding the German idea 'with an unfriendly or indifferent eye', he made it plain that a full alliance was too 'stiff a fence to ride at'. Metternich made it clear that the German proposal was for an alliance between the British Empire and the Triple Alliance, which 'would probably have ensured peace for half a century'. He found the British refusal to 'jump at it' quite 'unintelligible'. He warned Lansdowne that 'things never stand still' and rejected his suggestion of an understanding on certain issues: it was 'the whole or none'.[45]

The failure to secure an agreement with the Germans did not make anyone in the Cabinet desperate for an alliance with the Japanese. Hicks Beach did not 'think that we gain enough from the treaty to outweigh the obvious objections', a point of view with which Chamberlain was inclined to concur.[46] The Home Secretary, Charles Ritchie, shared Balfour's preference for a German alliance, whilst neither Selborne nor the Indian Secretary, Lord George Hamilton, liked the Japanese alliance;[47] but the most formidable voice raised against it was that of Salisbury.

Salisbury's letter to Lansdowne on 7 January 1902 was almost his last considerable reflection on foreign affairs. He thought that Japan's reluctance to accept 'a stipulation that she is not to be allowed to take without our permission measures which we might regard as provocative' was 'disquieting' because 'it involves a pledge on our part to defend Japanese action in Corea and in China against France and Russia, no matter what the *casus belli* may be. There is no limit: and no escape. We are pledged to war', whatever the conduct of Japan. He thought that Parliament would not sanction 'such a pledge' and that 'in the interests of the Empire it ought not to be taken'. The treaty surrendered 'without reserve into the hands of another Power the right of deciding whether we shall or shall not stake the resources of the Empire on the issue of a mighty conflict'.[48] Salisbury did not push his objections, and ended on a dying fall by commenting that he could not believe that Japan would 'refuse us some discretion' on the question of the *casus belli*. This may have been 'wishful thinking',[49] but his failure to press his objections was more likely to have been due to the fact that his minute crossed with Lansdowne's of the same date which explained that some of the more objectionable features of the draft treaty had been toned down.[50]

Salisbury once commented that Holstein appeared to believe that 'the mutual conduct of nations can be arranged beforehand like a game of chess', but in his view 'no one can foresee or predict what in any future contingency a democratic parliament may do': 'Tell me what is the *casus belli* and I may be able to give a guess at the conduct England will pursue. But without such information we cannot only not guess what England will do, but we cannot determine beforehand her course by any pledges or any arguments derived from general interests.'[51]

Lansdowne insisted that Britain would only recognise Japan's right to take action in Korea if she was threatened by the 'aggressive action' of another Power. In the end, the British agreed to accept the requirement that the alliance should be confined to the Far East, if only because it seemed to be a *sine qua non* for Tokyo. But they would not commit themselves to a fixed naval force, merely promising to maintain a force as large as that of any third Power.[52] Both sides could interpret the wording of the clauses as giving them what they wanted, and the alliance was signed on 30 January 1902. Defending the alliance in the Lords, Lansdowne asked his colleagues to 'look on the matter strictly on its merits' and not to allow their judgment to 'be swayed by any old formula or old-fashioned superstitions as to the desirability of pursuing a policy of isolation for our country'.[53]

Salisbury had let himself be persuaded by Lansdowne's arguments that the alliance was more in the nature of an insurance policy, but he had been right to fear that it would have unforeseen effects. One of his, and Lansdowne's, priorities had been to get on better terms with Russia and France. As Russia became more 'openly hostile' in the Far East, Lansdowne thought of trying to strengthen the alliance, with a view to bringing about 'a frank understanding' with Russia, rather than to fight her.[54] But the Russians remained unwilling to restrict their ambitions in the Far East. This raised the awkward question which Balfour had referred to back in December 1901 – namely the impact of an alliance with the enemy of France's ally on Anglo-French relations. For so many years a *détente* with France had been Salisbury's objective; it was ironic that just as he retired in June 1902, the French should finally have shown signs of being willing to talk seriously about the problems between the two countries.

French foreign policy was directly affected by the instability of the governments of the Third Republic. Ambassadors, once in post, could build up an almost feudal empire which made transient ministers reluctant to interfere with their semi-independent policies, let alone remove them.[55] Although the length of Delcassé's tenure gave him an influence beyond that of other Foreign Ministers, the formulation of his policy still owed much to his ambassadors – and, in the case of England, Cambon's influence was decisive.

Cambon had a natural empathy with Salisbury.[56] He recognised the central rule of *Realpolitik*, that 'nothing was ever absolute, finished, or straightforward'.[57] Brilliant diplomatic victories were usually nothing of the sort, since they were invariably accompanied by the humiliation of another Power; skilful and patient diplomacy was what was needed.[58] Cambon had a high view of the ambassadorial role, and he took pride in the fact that he had gained a position of authority by expressing his 'ideas in complete freedom' without 'worrying myself about the opinion of Paris or the pretended inclinations of the government'.[59] He was even known to burn his instructions when he disagreed with them.[60]

Delcassé's own objective during the period 1901–2 was to gain for France's Mediterranean empire the missing piece of Morocco. But Morocco was an object of interest to other European Powers. Germany, Britain and America had commercial interests there, and Spain, Italy and Britain had strategic ones, so its acquisition would not be easy. In December 1900, Delcassé came to an agreement with Italy which recognised French preponderance in Morocco in the event of the Sultan's authority being destroyed, and he followed this up in early 1901 with conversations with the Spaniards. He was even prepared, should it prove necessary, to offer the Germans compensation in the Congo for any losses in

Morocco.[61] It was England that he regarded as the greatest obstacle to his policy.[62]

At a banquet at Marlborough House on 8 February 1902, Eckardstein spotted Cambon and Chamberlain withdrawing into the billiards-room, and although he was unable to hear what was being said, he picked up the words 'Morocco' and 'Egypt'.[63] This fitted with a report from Metternich a week earlier which said that negotiations had been proceeding between Chamberlain and Cambon 'for the settlement of all outstanding differences between France and England in colonial questions'.[64] In March, Chamberlain suggested to Lansdowne that an Anglo-French agreement might be constructed around a settlement of the various problems between the two Powers in Newfoundland, West Africa, the New Hebrides and Siam; such an arrangement would also take in an understanding over Morocco. Lansdowne was well aware of the 'value of what we have to sell and its immense importance to the French',[65] and let Cambon know that he had never 'excluded the idea of reasonable "give and take" arrangements in regard to their possessions in different parts of the world'.[66]

Delcassé wanted an agreement with Britain, but he shrank from paying the price of Egypt, and hoped to be able to circumvent British interests in Morocco by deals with other Powers. Cambon pursued his lone hand, seeking to use the British willingness to deal and waiting for a propitious time. In this sense, the *entente* was Cambon's creation. It was not that he had a more Anglophile point of view than Delcassé, or valued Morocco less; he simply could not see how French interests were to be secured without discussion with the British and was therefore anxious to have something to bargain with.[67] It was Cambon who first linked Morocco with Egypt, and Eckardstein had overheard the kernel of the eventual agreement. The British Ambassador in Paris, Sir Edmund Monson, reported in August that Cambon was proceeding with a general exchange of views over Franco-British difficulties in Morocco despite Delcassé's caution: 'He himself has improved upon his instructions by filling in the picture with details of his own.'[68] Nor was he above distorting Lansdowne's exact words to give Delcassé the impression that the British were considering a Newfoundland–Morocco bargain.[69]

When Cambon stretched his instructions in August 1902 to discuss the question of the future of Morocco, Lansdowne thought this was somewhat 'premature',[70] but a rebellion against the Sultan's authority in December made matters look rather more urgent. When he discussed the subject again with Lansdowne on 17 December, Cambon reported him as 'anxious to enter into my views'.[71] Cambon was going further than the facts quite warranted, but was clearly trying to calm Delcassé's suspicions of British intentions.

Cambon was well aware that the British were suspicious that the French would use the trouble in Morocco to precipitate a crisis which would require their intervention. But Delcassé, although he might once have pursued such a policy, knew that he could not do so without agreements with either Britain or Germany, so when Cambon saw Lansdowne on the last day of 1902, the Frenchman took good care to stress that French policy was to retain the *status quo*. He took the line that an Anglo-French agreement was essential if other Powers such as Germany were to be prevented from fishing in troubled waters. He had, in fact, succeeded in calming Lansdowne's fears.[72] Lansdowne and Balfour were, above all, anxious to avoid being dragged into any scramble for Morocco, and any attempt to internationalise the problem was welcome to the latter, who took the view that 'the more intervention in the affairs of these semi-barbarous States (when it becomes inevitable) is made a matter of European concern, the better'.[73]

The improvement in relations with France was welcome for the same reason that it was desirable to avoid complications in Morocco; namely the deteriorating state of Anglo-Russian relations in Persia. As Lord George Hamilton, the Secretary of State for India, told Curzon in August 1902, 'both in this Office and the Foreign Office' Persia 'is the question which more constantly occupies the official mind than any other subject connected with foreign politics'.[74] In November 1902, an interdepartmental conference, the first of its kind, with representatives from the Foreign, India and War Offices, as well as the Admiralty, met to discuss the future of Persia, in particular what to do if the situation deteriorated to the stage where Britain found herself at war with Russia, and how to react if Russia occupied the north of the country under the pretext of quelling disorder.[75] Balfour, now Prime Minister, thought that the 'fundamental principle' which should govern British policy in Persia was 'simple': 'until Russia moves, we remain still; as soon as Russia moves in the north we move in the south'; but 'application of that principle was not so simple'.[76] No troops were available for the occupation of any Persian territory, nor could operations inland be considered. All that could be done was to secure the route to India by operations in the south-eastern corner of Persia. The only note of cheer came from a report from the military which stated that the Russians were in no way prepared for operations in Central Asia; but even that was a stay of execution, pending the completion of the Orenburg–Tashkent railway in two and a half years' time.[77]

Curzon's idea of browbeating the Emir of Afghanistan and asserting British interests in Persia was not one which appealed to the Cabinet, and Lansdowne's preferred policy of looking for an agreement with the Russians easily won the day.[78] But if there was the same British willingness to make concessions which marked the talks with the French, there was no reciprocation from St Petersburg. In April 1903, Lansdowne told Balfour: 'I doubt extremely whether the Russians wish to force the pace anywhere just at present, and I don't despair of finding a reasonable solution of the Russo-Afghan difficulty, and perhaps of other tiresome questions which concern Russia and us.'[79] But on 15 May, Nicholas II inaugurated the new course in Russian foreign policy in the Far East which was to lead to the war with Japan.[80] By December 1903, Balfour's gloomy view was that 'little confidence' should be placed in 'Russian assurances'. Given the obvious signs of Russian expansionism, and Britain's desire to maintain the *status quo*, 'the elements of a bargain' were hardly present; Balfour was 'not hopeful of a thoroughly satisfactory permanent arrangement', although he would take a temporary one if it came along.[81]

Lansdowne was no more successful than Salisbury had been in coming to terms with Russia. He was, however, fortunate in dealing with a French Ambassador and Foreign Minister who saw advantages in coming to terms with Britain. King Edward's visit to Paris in May 1903 helped to create a public atmosphere in both countries where a *rapprochement* would be welcomed, but the key point in enabling a deal to be struck was the identification of possible 'compensation' for Egypt in the form of Morocco. In a letter to Lansdowne on 29 May 1903, the British Agent-General in Egypt, Lord Cromer, suggested that they might use Morocco as a bargaining counter to remove French obstructionism on the *caisse de la dette* which dealt with Egypt's finances; Lansdowne thought that there might be mileage in such an idea.[82] This laid the groundwork for the formal conversations which began on 7 July when Delcassé met Lansdowne.

The talks with the French were, however, only a part of Lansdowne's overall efforts to reduce the pressures on the British Empire; he placed hope in Delcassé's assurances that he would 'exercise a restraining influence upon Russia, if not in fact intimate to Russia that she could not rely upon French support if she picked a quarrel with us'.[83] The Anglo-French negotiations, as well as being a means to a desirable end, were also a possible 'precursor of a better understanding with Russia'.[84]

Lansdowne pursued a Russian settlement simultaneously with the French negotiations and, by January 1904, had actually progressed as far as circulating a draft agreement to the Cabinet.[85] However, the Russo-Japanese tension which had been worsening during the period of the Anglo-French talks finally resulted in the outbreak of war in the Far East, which put an end to the negotiations with Russia. Balfour hoped that Britain would not be 'dragged into hostilities' which would involve more than 'half the world' in a war which 'would benefit nobody but the neutrals and chiefly Germany'.[86] He could, however, see advantages in a Russo-Japanese war for Britain: 'though Russia's resources in men are unlimited, her resources in money are not; and . . . if she chooses to squander both her naval and her financial strength in this extreme corner of the world, she is rendering herself impotent everywhere else'.[87] Lansdowne wondered whether it would not be safer to abandon the alliance with Japan, to avoid being dragged into the war, but the Cabinet quashed that idea.[88]

The failure of the Russians to come to terms did not affect the talks with the French. The course of negotiations did not go with all the smoothness either side would have liked, but that was because they were both trying to get the best terms they could. Balfour was 'sorry, but not surprised' to be told in January 1904 that the negotiations had hit a snag over the question of Newfoundland. It would be, he told Lansdowne, 'an international misfortune if they broke down, and unsatisfactory as any negotiation must be which does not include the vexed question of Newfoundland, I would rather that we settled England, Morocco, and Siam, without Newfoundland than that we settled nothing at all'.[89]

Balfour's anxiety was to be explained by his preoccupation with the momentous events in the Far East. If the Russians won their war with Japan, they would try to acquire the whole of Manchuria; in that event, the British would have to face up to the question which the Japanese alliance had been designed to avoid: how could Russia be stopped? 'Are the Americans', Balfour asked Lansdowne in February 1904, 'prepared to help us by force . . .?' He thought that they 'ought not to be under the illusion that anything *short* of this will be of the slightest use, or that mere diplomacy will snatch from Russia the fruits of the victories, if victories she is destined to obtain'. But it was asking a lot of the Americans to expect them to 'violate their traditions' by making an alliance for preserving the integrity of China; it would 'open a new era in the history of the world'. Balfour did not expect that to happen – which was why he wanted to get on better terms with Russia's ally.[90]

Lansdowne was quite capable of interposing across the imperatives of geopolitics those of the negotiating process. He did not want to leave the Newfoundland fisheries out of the deal, because 'the arrangement would be very incomplete without it, and we shall be less liable to attack if we are able to show that we have succeeded in clearing the French, bag and baggage, out of a British colony',[91] so he continued to negotiate hard over African frontiers and Newfoundland fisheries. Indeed, as late as 2 April, Landsdowne complained to Balfour that with the French getting increasingly querulous over Newfoundland, and the permanency of Britain's occupation of Egypt, 'we ought in my opinion to break off and I have told Cambon that if we cannot come to terms over Nfoundland [sic] the whole arrangement will have to go'.[92] Unnoticed by historians anxious to stress the importance of the *entente*, the fact that Lansdowne was prepared to drop the whole thing only six days before it was signed indicates that it was indeed on the same level as the Anglo-German and even the Anglo-Russian negotiations – a welcome limitation of Britain's liabilities, but by no means a vital or indispensable part of a new course in British foreign policy.

19

The Myth of 'Continuity'

When Hatzfeldt used to complain that he could not work out the 'politique' of the British Government, Sanderson used to reply 'that he ought to know that we had not got a policy and worked from hand to mouth'. Salisbury, who took a wry amusement in the portentous meanings which the German was wont to attach to his *obiter dicta*, once told Sanderson to tell him that 'with a parliamentary régime like ours, it is impossible to pledge the Gov[ernmen]t as to the course it will take in case of some future emergency'.[1] The French *entente* was fully in accord with this 'policy', not a departure from it. The Khedival decree embodying the changes which would give the Egyptian Government control over its own finance needed the approval of other Powers, and Lansdowne immediately set about obtaining it.[2] It was in no wise directed against Germany, nor was it meant by Lansdowne to mark a change in the direction of British policy; quite the opposite. Lansdowne had now fulfilled the task Salisbury had set himself of getting on better terms with the French, which restored to British diplomacy that flexibility it had lost after 1882. Lansdowne hoped that this would help Anglo-Russian relations, although he made it clear to the French that any attempt by the Russians to send their Black Sea fleet through the Straits would cause 'really serious trouble'.[3] The French connection was, indeed, useful in October after the Dogger Bank incident, when Russian warships fired on Hull trawlers; French mediation helped defuse Anglo-Russian tension.[4] But the *entente* was not a departure from the 'hand to mouth' policy dictated by the 'parliamentary nature of our institutions'.

By the spring of 1905, that policy could be seen to have brought Britain into a better diplomatic situation than she had enjoyed at any time in the previous half century. The *entente* meant an end to the assumption that an Anglo-French war was always likely; Japan's defeat of Russia did the same for assumptions of Anglo-Russian conflict. For the first time in half a century Britain had no need to fear Russian expansionism: the Russian navy had all but ceased to exist; her armies were defeated; and her political system was in turmoil. There was no danger now to British interests at any of the points where the tectonic plates of Russian and British imperialism met. In the negotiations to renew the Anglo-Japanese alliance in May 1905, the British were able to extend its terms so that the Japanese accepted an obligation to send troops to India in return for a British promise to support them in Korea.

By the spring of 1905, the British were able to face the international scene with more equanimity than they had been able to muster in a decade. It was true that the Moroccan situation was giving cause for concern as civil disorder grew, but as far as Lansdowne was concerned, 'we may in our secret hearts congratulate ourselves on having left to another Power the responsibility of dealing with so helpless and hopeless a country'.[5] It is some indication of the improvement in Britain's diplomatic position that Balfour's main worry was over the intentions of Austria-Hungary, and whether, with the weakening of Russia, she would pursue a 'deliberate policy of further territorial aggrandizement in the Balkan Peninsula'.[6] Lansdowne's own view was that Austria's policy was 'inexplicable' because it consisted of nothing more than a series of 'hand to mouth' expedients.[7]

There were those, like the Marquis de Soveral, the Portuguese

Ambassador in London, who thought that the British should take advantage of this happy situation to settle scores with the Germans,[8] and others who thought that they should try to break up the Franco-Russian alliance. But Lansdowne did not see himself as the arbiter of Europe. He wanted stability in international affairs, not disorder. He thought that 'the intimate relations which prevail between France and ourselves and between France and Russia may be advantageous, particularly when we come to the critical period' when the terms of peace between Japan and Russia were being discussed.[9]

It was certainly the case that Germany's attempts to exact her pound of flesh (and more) for adherence to the Khedival decree aroused ill-feeling in London,[10] and even the imperturbable Lansdowne regarded their offer to surrender their minor claims for £70,000 as a 'great piece of effrontery'; he was still less impressed by the threat to move closer to Russia.[11] However, to write of a 'new estrangement from Germany'[12] is to exaggerate. No doubt articles in periodicals advocating a *coup* against the growing German navy upset the Germans,[13] and experts at the Admiralty, the Foreign Office and in the army all worried about German naval and military power, and diplomacy, but it can hardly be emphasised sufficiently that under Balfour and Lansdowne these people, however interesting and even prophetic their views may appear in retrospect, did not make policy. It was true that Bülow's language about cleaving to Russia aroused the indignation of the new Chancellor, Austen Chamberlain, who in an outburst worthy of his father protested that Germany had never 'made any attempt to cultivate even the appearance of good relations with England except for the purposes of making a better bargain with some third Power!' Writing in January 1905, he told Lansdowne that despite Bülow's denials, the German navy 'is a standing menace to this country'.[14] But his Germanophobia, although not uncommon, did not determine the tenor or the content of British diplomacy.

Sanderson, who as Permanent Under-Secretary counted for a good deal more than some of those diplomats historians have been fonder of quoting, was more impressed by the weakness of Germany's position than by its strength. As he told Lansdowne on 20 January 1905, Germany was confronted by a Franco-Russian alliance against which she could deploy only Austria, which was, in any case, working in co-operation with Russia in the Balkans; the Italians had made friends with the French, as had the British. In these circumstances, it was inevitable that the Germans should lean towards the Russians: 'I do not see that we can reasonably resent this, and as a matter of fact a certain amount of friendship with Germany would be valuable for us in any bargaining with Russia.'[15] Lansdowne also took a less tragic view than Chamberlain of relations with Germany, having 'perhaps become so much used to the querulous tone of the German Government'. He felt that 'the Germans have no doubt behaved shabbily to us on a good many occasions', but that it was untrue to say that 'they have never made any attempt to cultivate good relations with us'. He was not inclined to take the remarks of Bülow and Holstein *au grand sérieux*.[16] He shared Sanderson's opinion that Germany's diplomatic situation was now rather weak, and he was disinclined to let temporary emotion obstruct diplomatic reality.[17] Given the nature of that reality, this need occasion no surprise.

The gloomy prognostications which had inspired so much of the criticism directed at Salisbury had none of them come to pass: Britain had not missed out on the scramble for China; nor had her interests been ignored in a carve-up of the Ottoman Empire; there had been no Continental League; there would be no war against France and Russia; nor was there, any longer, a need for dependence upon German support. Of course the German naval build-up was a cause for concern, but it was no more than that, and the building programme announced by the First Lord of the Admiralty, Cawdor, in 1905 would ensure that Britain would be able to keep ahead of Germany; moreover, there was no immediate need to worry about the Russian navy. The 'experts' would be gloomy, they always were: there was never a general who did not want more troops, never an admiral who could not find a reason to have more ships; but the horizon was, nonetheless, brighter than it had been for half a century. Then, on 31 March 1905, the Kaiser landed at Tangiers.

Before the *entente* was signed, Cromer had warned Lansdowne that 'one of the main attractions in the whole business to the authorities of the Quai d'Orsay is the hope of leading up to an Anglo-Russian arrangement, and thus isolating Germany'.[18] But neither Lansdowne nor Sanderson had any interest in such a notion. Lansdowne had made it clear to Berlin that the *entente* was 'not directed against Germany'. Bülow told Lascelles that 'we had not thought so', and that Germany welcomed the agreement as a contribution to 'world peace'.[19] But behind this public façade, Holstein made the same mistake which generations of undergraduates have, and regarded the agreement as an 'Anglo-French alliance'.[20]

The Kaiser's landing at Tangiers nearly a year after the signing of the *entente* was as much a product of frustration with the paucity of results from *Weltpolitik* as it was an attempt to disrupt Franco-British harmony. The rumours about an attempted *rapprochement* with Russia were quite correct, and the Kaiser had tried to use the Dogger Bank incident to draw Russia into an alliance.[21] But when the Russians eventually admitted that such an agreement would be conditional on France's consent, the initiative foundered. Bülow feared that such an alliance might actually provoke war with Britain, which would be condemned by most sections of German opinion.[22] With the British taking steps to build up their navy in the North Sea, the wisest course was for Germany to avoid antagonising her.[23] Bülow told Holstein in early 1905 that it was essential to avoid 'creating the impression' that Germany 'wanted to draw England from France's side and to sow enmity between England and Russia'.[24]

But the failure to win concessions from Britain, or to weaken the Dual Alliance, left Germany remarkably bereft of any positive result from nearly a decade of *Weltpolitik*. With French attempts in early 1905 to negotiate a privileged position for themselves in Morocco, the prospect of another defeat for German diplomacy exercised minds in the Wilhelmstraße; they could either have tried to cut a deal with France; or they could have demanded an international conference to revise the 1880 Madrid Convention which dealt with the future of Morocco; but fatally, German policy-makers could not decide whether they were trying to get something for themselves in Morocco, or whether they were trying to humiliate the French, so they tried both approaches.

Bülow assured a nervous Kaiser that his visit to Morocco would 'embarrass M. Delcassé, frustrate his plans, and benefit our economic interests in Morocco'.[25] When Wilhelm proved reluctant to go ashore, Bülow reminded him that Delcassé would claim that he had retreated because of French pressure.[26] Once he had conquered his nerves, Wilhelm went much further in opposing French penetration of Morocco than Bülow had wanted,[27] thus creating an international crisis.

The reaction to the German initiative varied. Delcassé had been warned that he ought to have negotiated with Germany over her position in Morocco, but his fear of her Mediterranean ambitions and his belief that she would demand a second ratification of the Treaty of Frankfurt meant that he did not do so.[28] Now, as the Grand Vizier of Morocco put it, 'Whilst France was raping Morocco, Kaiser William came along and gave it a sharp kick up the backside.'[29] The new French Premier, Maurice Rouvier, an industrialist and banker who wanted better relations with the Germans, was seriously concerned at the crisis which Delcassé's attitude had caused.[30] He was willing to talk about German commercial interests, but Bülow declared in the Reichstag that Germany would negotiate directly with the Sultan on such matters, thus driving up the tension.[31] Despite Rouvier's continued anxiety to reach a bilateral settlement of the Moroccan issue which would have conceded most of Germany's demands,[32] he received no positive response.

The problem with this approach was that it passed up the certain gains on offer from a deal with France for the uncertainty of an international conference. But this was not perceived as a problem by the self-confident and self-deluding Bülow, who saw a conference as offering considerable diplomatic gains: France 'will become yet more isolated through the developments of her policy', with Russia 'occupied with her own affairs' and with England unlikely to support her because of the 'Open Door' policy. Bülow told the Kaiser in April that he could 'await the settlement of the Moroccan position with calm'.[33] Bülow was assured that if France called his bluff and war resulted, Germany would win.[34] He was gambling that the British would not support the French in Morocco, but the very virulence of the German assault on Delcassé's position threatened to push the focus from Germany's legitimate interests in Morocco to her attitude towards the author of the *entente* with Britian.

Lansdowne's first reaction to the German initiative in Morocco was to dismiss it as 'an extraordinary clumsy bit of diplomacy'. He thought that it stemmed from German annoyance at the *entente* and suspected that in future the Kaiser would avail himself of every opportunity to 'put a spoke in our wheels'.[85] Others took the business a good deal more tragically. Bertie, like Landsowne's private secretary, Louis Mallet, saw it as a deliberate German attempt to disrupt the *entente* and reacted accordingly, with the latter stoking up the First Sea Lord, Sir John Fisher, to warn of the dangers which might follow Germany acquiring a Moroccan port.[36] Lansdowne thought that it would be a 'bad thing' if the Germans were able to 'discredit the entente', but he regarded Fisher's bloodthirsty desires to attack the German fleet and seize Kiel as a 'characteristic effusion', and thus as an object of amusement rather than anything serious.

But with Delcassé resigning on 22 April (and rescinding it straight away), and with Germany still pressing the French, Lansdowne was 'not happy at the turn which the Germany and France about Morocco [*sic*] dispute is taking'. The French, he thought, were 'thoroughly frightened and realize that they are in a very bad mess – Russia cannot help them and they are not at all sure that we might do so except in certain eventualities'. He thought that it might be necessary to cede a 'Moorish port' as 'atonement' to Germany.[37] The Admiralty warned him that this would be 'fatal', and Lansdowne wanted to advise the French 'not to concede without giving us [a] full opportunity of conferring with them as to [the] manner in which the demand might be met'.[38] Even as he was collecting these thoughts, Lansdowne was interrupted by the arrival of Balfour at his Bowood estate in Wiltshire. After hasty consultation, the two men drafted a telegram to Bertie in Paris authorising him to tell Delcassé that Britain was prepared to join him in offering 'strong opposition' to any German demand for a port, adding that they wanted the opportunity of consultation with the French if any such demand was made. The telegram finished by calling the German attitude 'unreasonable' and by offering Delcassé 'all the support we can'.[39]

It is clear from the context that Lansdowne's main concern was to prevent a bilateral deal between the French and the Germans which would be unfavourable to British interests. However, the context in which Cambon and Delcassé received the British message was one in which the latter was fighting for his political life, and the former wanted to block those Ministers who would have done a deal with the Germans.[40] Naturally enough both Cambon and Delcassé chose to characterise Lansdowne's telegram of 22 April as something close to an offer of an alliance, when the latter revealed it to his colleagues.[41] But when Cambon asked on 3 May exactly what the British meant by 'support', Lansdowne's answer hardly bore out his optimistic reading. He said that Britain would wait and see what the Germans intended to do, adding that it was enough that it was known that Britain and France were at one on the issue.[42] Delcassé and Cambon once again used their interpretation of Lansdowne's remarks to try to bolster the former's position within the French Cabinet, with the Ambassador providing useful supplementary evidence in the form of his account of a conversation on 17 May, when Lansdowne had said that the 'two Governments should continue to treat each other with the most absolute confidence' and 'discuss any contingencies by which they might in the course of events find themselves confronted'. This, Cambon declared, was a 'most clear' and 'spontaneous' British offer to co-ordinate policies, and Delcassé used it at an important Cabinet meeting on 21 May to show that France had the total support of Britain in the event of a conflict with Germany.[43]

These French reports were, as Lansdowne much later assumed, 'origin of the offensive and defensive alliance'[44] stories which circulated thereafter, and which led to the belief that there was 'continuity between his policy and that of Grey'.[45] By the 1920s, when the Anglo-French alliance was generally held to have been a good thing, old men did not so much forget what they had done in 1905 as embellish it to fit in with the way they were sure things must have happened.[46] At the time Lansdowne moved to clarify his remarks at once, telling Cambon on 25 May that his desire for 'full and confidential discussions' between the two Governments was not so much 'in consequence of some acts of unprovoked aggression on the part of another Power, as in anticipation of some acts of unprovoked aggression during the somewhat anxious period through which we are at present passing'.[47] There was no offer, or authorisation, of military talks, nor was there any commitment to future co-ordination of policy. What Lansdowne was trying to do was to prevent the French from caving in to German demands whilst simultaneously trying to ensure that Britain retained the power to restrain them if they became over-excited; in these objectives he failed. Delcassé was beyond saving, and had Rouvier's willingness to negotiate over Morocco been matched in Berlin, then concessions would indeed have been made.

Lansdowne's comment that Delcassé's resignation 'produced a very painful impression here' was something of an understatement. The *entente* was, he told Bertie on 9 June, 'quoted at a much lower price than it was a fortnight ago'.[48] With Rouvier pinning his hopes on Franco-German co-operation and accepting the idea of a conference, the lines from Paris to London went dead. By July, Lansdowne was complaining that he had heard nothing from the French about what support they wanted. His own view, cautious and conservative as ever, was that they should avoid volunteering a 'statement'. The moment was not, he thought, 'opportune . . . for suggesting either to the Cabinet or to the country an extension of the understanding arrived at'.[49]

Unable to anticipate how ham-fisted the Germans would manage to be, Lansdowne was quite prepared to protect Britain's interests in the western Mediterranean through a deal with the Spanish, although he was also happy to reassure Rouvier that if the French persisted in refusing the German demands for a conference, Britain would support them.[50] In short, whatever Germanophobe and Francophile views may have been expressed by subordinate officials at the Foreign Office, Lansdowne's eyes remained firmly fixed on 'British interests' rather than on Franco-British ones. He authorised no military conversations and gave no assurances that Britain would support France in the event of a war with Germany. Naturally enough, rumours that the French were claiming that they had had the offer of an alliance from the British reached German ears.

Bülow raised the matter with Lascelles on 10 June, saying that he had had it from an unimpeachable source, a line followed by Holstein two days later.[51] Lansdowne told Metternich on 16 June that he could hardly believe that the alliance story was worth contradicting, but that if it would 'serve a useful purpose, I was glad to assure him that no offensive and defensive alliance had ever been offered or discussed on either side'.[52] As far as he was concerned, if German interest in Morocco was confined to economic matters, there was 'no antagonism between the British and the German policy'. Metternich reported on 28 June that Lansdowne had told him that if Germany did attack France, it was unlikely that Britain would just stand by and let her.[53] Lansdowne's own report of this conversation was less specific than Metternich's,[54] and he later suspected that the German had 'made a good deal of my observation that, although there was no alliance, public opinion here might become uncontrollable if Germany were to fasten a quarrel upon France merely because the latter had come to a friendly arrangement with us'.[55] Lansdowne never told the French of his warning to Metternich, and he thought that they had 'played their cards badly in Morocco, and are suffering heavily for it'.[56] He was pleased when on 1 July the Germans agreed to the French conditions for a conference on Morocco, but there was no solidarity with France, neither was there a desire to maintain some 'balance of power'. Lansdowne's policy during the Moroccan crisis was recognisably a continuation of business as usual, not an anticipation of Grey.

It is true that the Committee of Imperial Defence (CID) considered the mechanics and possible implications of a German war, and that topics such as the neutrality of Belgium were raised,[57] but it is only in retrospect that these things loom larger than the fact that Balfour and Lansdowne were more concerned with renewing the Japanese alliance and protecting British interests generally than they were with any German 'antagonism'. They had lived for years with Germany's odd diplomacy, and whilst they took its possible consequences seriously, they did not take a tragic view of Anglo-German relations.

Lansdowne picked up rumours about the discussions which took place at Björkö in late July between the Kaiser and the Tsar. The so-called Björkö Treaty was designed by Bülow to try to preclude the possibility of France presiding over an Anglo-Russian reconciliation,[58] and in securing Nicholas's signature to it, the Kaiser though that he had brought European diplomacy to a 'turning-point'.[59] It did not turn. Wilhelm's version of the alliance confined it to Europe, which made it worthless in terms of Morocco or of putting pressure on the British in the Far East; and the usual Russian condition, that it was dependent upon French assent, gave the latter a lever over German policy.[60] Bülow threatened to resign unless the Kaiser allowed him to try to renegotiate the treaty.[61] The Kaiser, who threatened suicide if Bülow went, abjured him to 'think of my poor wife and children!'[62] But although Bülow graciously consented to remain,[63] his idea that he could secure French consent for a renegotiated alliance by soft-peddling on Morocco[64] led him to agree to Witte's request that as a step towards a Franco-Russian-German union against Britain, Germany should concede France's requests concerning the agenda for the conference at Algeciras.[65]

Salisbury, when confronted with the simulacrum of the Continental League, had always refused to take it seriously, and that was when most of the British army was occupied in a war in South Africa, relations with France were strained, and Russia in the full flower of her expansionist ambitions. Now, with France needing British support in Morocco, the Russians powerless and the British strengthened by the renewal of the Japanese alliance, there was even less to fear. On a long historical perspective, particularly one tinctured by the search for the origins of the war and the knowledge of British decline, it is easy to forget how much better the diplomatic prospects looked for Britain in late 1905. No doubt, as the fourth Marquess of Salisbury commented to Balfour in November, 'circumstances' had 'driven us in respect to France further than we intended', but he was correct to point out that 'originally French policy was wholly different from the Japanese', and that the agreement with France was 'a development of past policy' rather than a new departure. Lansdowne had continued the Salisburian policy of 'adjusting conflicting claims, and . . . bargaining so as to get rid of causes of friction'.[66]

There were those, like Sir Charles Hardinge, Francis Bertie and Austen Chamberlain, who all urged Lansdowne to take advantage of Russia's current weakness to conclude an agreement with her which would, in Chamberlain's words, clip the 'German eagle's claws',[67] but when the Russian Ambassador raised the question officially on 3 October, Lansdowne told him that 'it would be a mistake to attempt a transaction analogous to that which had taken place between France and Great Britain'.[68] He was quite willing to discuss matters such as Persia with the Russians, and when the Russian Ambassador stressed that such talks should not be seen as in any way hostile to Germany, Lansdowne said that 'nothing was further from my thoughts'.[69] This would not be true of his successor.

If Britain's diplomatic position was the strongest it had been for a generation, the same could not be said of the political position of Balfour's administration. Riven by disputes over Chamberlain's schemes for Tariff reform, tired after a decade in office, the Conservatives had entered one of their periodic phases of self-destruction. Balfour proved adroit in finding formulae which would prevent the warring factions within his Party from rending it apart, but, as with later successors, he could not provide leadership to those who were determined not to be led. To Joseph Chamberlain and his supporters the issue surrounding Tariff reform transcended mere Party politics, and the word compromise was foreign to their vocabulary. The only question was whether the Unionists would be able to see out their term of office, which was due to expire in 1907. In November 1905, Balfour answered the question by resigning.

The Liberals had not been famous for their Party unity over the past decade. Following Rosebery's resignation in 1895, the Party had staggered from one stop-gap leader to another, with Rosebery himself forever hovering in the wings threatening to come back. In 1900, the Party had settled on the former War Minister, Sir Henry Campbell-Bannerman. 'C-B', as he was known, had just about managed to hold his own Party together during the furore generated by the Boer War, and the so-called Liberal imperialists had little time for him. Indeed, during September 1905 some of them were in touch with the King about what arrangements might be made in the event of C-B being asked to form a government in the near future;[70] it may well have been these manoeuvrings which convinced Balfour to go when he did. If so, he made a serious tactical mistake.

The three leading Liberal imperialists were Henry Herbert Asquith, Sir Edward Grey and Richard Burdon Haldane. They shared the view, common on their wing of the Party, that the old Gladstonian methods favoured by the likes of Campbell-Bannerman would not rally the 'great progressive force', which needed something more positive than a defence of free trade around which to coalesce.[71] In September 1905, at Grey's fishing lodge at Relugas in north-eastern Scotland, the three men agreed that they would not take office unless Campbell-Bannerman agreed to their terms, which were that he should go to the Lords, leaving Asquith as Leader of the Commons and Chancellor of the Exchequer, whilst Haldane became Lord Chancellor and Grey went to the Foreign Office. The conspirators had presumed that they would be asked to take office following an electoral victory, but thanks to Balfour's resignation Campbell-Bannerman enjoyed the luxury of being able to approach them from a position of strength as Prime Minister.

The ensuing events reflected little credit on Asquith's sense of loyalty, but threw much light on his character; they also revealed Campbell-Bannerman as a shrewd judge of human nature. Asquith was the most important of the three figures – and the most ambitious – so it was to him that the bribe was made. Campbell-Bannerman offered him any office he wanted, and without a mention of his friends he took the Exchequer.[72] Haldane was offered the post of Attorney-General, whilst Grey let it be known that he did not want any post – not that he was being offered one. Haldane did not want the job he had been offered, and he did not want to take office without Grey, whom he tried to persuade to join the administration for the sake of the Liberal imperialist cause.[73] But it proved impossible for Campbell-Bannerman to avoid Grey. Lord Cromer refused to leave Egypt for the uncertainties of office in a minority Liberal administration, whilst the other choice, Lord Elgin, was perceived to be lacking in the political weight required; so on 8 December, Grey agreed to take on the Foreign Office. As for Haldane, Campbell-Bannerman took some pleasure in putting 'Schopenhauer' to the 'kailyard' to grapple with the thorny question of army reform which had seen off two of his two Unionist predecessors.[74]

Grey had already stated that there would be 'continuity' between his policy and that of the Unionists: this was as much a cause for joy amongst Unionists as it was for regret amongst radical Liberals; but the notion can only be maintained if the Salisburian basis of Lansdowne's policy is ignored, and if the Germanophobia present in Grey's thought is attributed to his predecessor. In short, 'continuity' exists only in the eye of the historian – and the contemporary polemicist. On a long view of Conservative foreign policy, its intellectual and emotional bases, what is striking about the period after 1905 is precisely a lack of continuity between it and the policy which followed.

Part Three

Balance of Power

'We have all the obligations of an alliance without its advantages.'

Churchill to Asquith, 22 August 1912

20

Grey and the Balance of Power

Lloyd George's comment that 'Edward Grey is one of the two men primarily responsible for the war',[1] has not prevented him receiving a generally favourable press from historians; the English have always preferred 'character' to intellect. As a youth Grey took no interest in public affairs, or anything beyond 'sport and games'.[2] A gentleman, *sans peur et sans reproche*, with his clean-cut, aquiline aristocratic features, his unworldly, almost diffident manner, his lack of intellectual pretensions, and his love of the gentler country pursuits, Grey was the image of God's Englishman in its Victorian incarnation.[3] The fact that his personal life was twice touched by the tragedy of losing a young and beautiful wife made him 'indeed one whom fortune loved and hated out of the common measure';[4] 'fortune' was not alone.

Grey may have posed as the *preux chevalier* of the Liberal Party, but the distrust felt for him by old Gladstonians like Morley, who went to the India Office, was well-justified.[5] Relugas had failed to remove Campbell-Bannerman, but it had left the foreign and military policy of the Government largely in the hands of Liberal imperialists.[6] The unity of the 'Liberal Leaguers' should not be exaggerated: Asquith took little interest in foreign affairs, and Haldane could hardly be classed as a Germanophobe; there is, nevertheless, a kernel of truth in the comment that 'the Liberal League did not vanish. What happened is simply that in 1905 it absorbed the Liberal Government. And that is why we went to war in 1914.'[7] The Government was not 'absorbed', but foreign policy was.

Trevelyan correctly identified the French *entente* as 'the first and most important aspect' of Grey's policy.[8] In October 1905, Grey had declared that the 'spirit' of the *entente* was more important than its exact terms, adding that 'if anyone is disturbed by the diplomatic trouble which has taken place, I would advise him to ask himself, whether, if there had been no agreement between us and France, it is not possible that there would have been trouble more serious for France and possibly for ourselves'.[9] This was the exact opposite of Lansdowne's position, where the 'exact terms' mattered more than 'the spirit'. Grey made it 'an object to maintain the *entente* with France' and would have found his position 'intolerable' had France not been supported at Morocco.[10] Sir Arthur Nicolson, the British representative at Algeçiras, also regarded it as essential to stay on side with the French. Neither would Grey make any deal with Germany before the conference; he told Lascelles that 'fine words butter no parsnips, and if the parsnips are to be buttered, it must be done at the Conference. If that ends in conclusions not adverse to the Anglo-French Entente, there will be a real clearing of the skies and an assurance of peace.'[11]

This amounted to a level of commitment to France far beyond anything which Lansdowne had offered, but it fitted very nicely with what had been going on behind the scenes during December whilst British politicians had been electioneering. The activities of busybodies like Lord Esher and Sir George Clark, and of soldiers and journalists like Major-General Grierson and Colonel Repington, in initiating talks with the French military in early December have been well-chronicled. Any claims that such talks had taken place in Lansdowne's day were either the result of memory lapses in the 1920s, or of an understandable desire to minimise the irregular nature of what had gone on.[12] By themselves, meetings between Grierson, the British Director of Military Intelligence, and the French Military Attaché, Major Huguet, had no significance. Even the initiative of the Chairman of the CID, Sir George Clark, in organising an informal conference of experts on 19 December to discuss joint Anglo-French naval action in the event of a war with Germany had no significance beyond its conclusion that it would be useful if something could be learned about French military plans. The intervention of a professional busybody in the form of the military correspondent of *The Times*, Colonel Repington, reassuring Huguet at the end of December that the new Government would not desert the French over Morocco, meant nothing more than an individual talking loosely. Collectively this burst of activity showed how worried some people were by French fears that the new Government would revert to Gladstonianism;[13] but what gave it significance was Grey's endorsement – and his deliberate and successful attempt to conceal not only from the Cabinet, but from the Prime Minister himself, what had gone on.

Grey professed a desire for better relations with Germany, but something always got in the way. At first it was the Algeçiras conference. He told Metternich on 3 January 1906 of his desire to improve Anglo-German relations, but only after France had been supported at Morocco.[14] The following day he warned Bülow that: 'Here the Morocco question is generally regarded as a test of the Anglo-French Entente, and [y]our Morocco policy as an attempt to smash it up';[15] that was certainly true of Grey.

When Cambon saw Grey for the first time on 20 December, he assured him that he supported the *entente*, but the conversation did not touch upon any extension of it.[16] It was only on his way out that Cambon raised the issue of the 'co-operation' which Lansdowne had offered; but Sanderson, to whom he mentioned it, said that it was limited to the case of Morocco itself.[17] Since Cambon had interpreted Lansdowne's words back in May as having meant more than this, he now expressed his anxiety to Repington about Grey's failure to confirm his predecessor's 'assurance'. Repington reported this to Grey, who responded on 30 December that he had 'not receded from anything that Lord Lansdowne said to the French and have no hesitation in confirming it'.[18] But from whom had Grey gained his impression of what Lansdowne had said? Certainly not from Lansdowne, but Sanderson's comment to Cambon was an accurate representation of what had passed in May. However, from his private secretary, Mallet, and from Bertie in Paris, Grey was likely to have gained the same impression about Lansdowne's position as Cambon had; at any rate, Grey certainly went way beyond it and authorised military conversations with the French.

An informal meeting of the CID on 6 January 1906 came up with a questionnaire which was put to Huguet, who responded on 11 January with a French statement that the best help the British could offer would be to send one or two divisions to France as soon as possible after war broke out. Clark told Grey the gist of what was going on,[19] and so Grey's statement to Campbell-Bannerman on 9 January that on the Moroccan issue matters with the French 'stand as Lord Lansdowne left them' was probably inaccurate when made. Grey was technically correct on 9 January to say that the French had been offered only 'diplomatic support' and had 'asked no inconvenient questions';[20] but by the time the Prime Minister received the letter, this was no longer the case. Grey did tell him that the War Office 'seems . . . to be ready to answer the question, what could they do if we had to take part against Germany, if for instance the neutrality of Belgium was violated', but he did not mention the questionnaire or the French response; selective reporting was, it transpired, a characteristic of Grey's diplomatic style.

When Cambon met Grey on 10 January, he said that it was necessary to 'discuss the eventuality of war'.[21] Grey could have replied that he saw no such need, but he did not. He knew from Repington that Huguet had expressed his anxieties about the likely attitude of the Liberal administration, and it is probable that he knew about the French reply to the CID questionnaire.[22] He stated as his 'personal opinion' that 'public opinion in England would be strongly moved in favour of France'.[23] That did not go beyond what Lansdowne had said, but Sanderson was seriously worried about the fact that Grey assented to Cambon's request for the unofficial conversations between the British and French military to be continued: 'I thought this latter remark looked very much as if the conversations which we know that . . . Repington has had with the French military attaché had been taken by the latter and by the Embassy as being authorized by our General Staff'; he wondered whether Grey really wanted to authorise official talks.[24] Grey went ahead and did just that – without informing the Prime Minister, or his colleagues.[25] He ordered the full text of the conversation to be kept in the department,[26] and sent Campbell-Bannerman an edited version which omitted all reference to military conversations.[27] Grey, and Campbell-Bannerman's official biographer, the Liberal journalist J.A. Spender, both chose to print the account which was sent to Bertie on 10 January as though it was the version which was sent to the Prime Minister, thus creating the misleading impression that Grey had been open and frank with 'C-B' about the military conversations. He was not. Two days after his meeting with Cambon, Grey had a long conversation with Haldane, who had come down from Lothian to Berwick to help in his election campaign, in which the two men agreed that there should be staff conversations with the French which would be 'wholly non-committal'; Haldane promised to consult Campbell-Bannerman.[28]

There was already unease in some Liberal quarters about the extent to which Britain was committed to the French. The Liberal leader in the Lords, the seventy-nine-year-old Lord Ripon, feared that the French would expect more than diplomatic support if the conference at Algeçiras broke down, and thought that 'we ought to decline to go further than diplomacy will reach'. But he could foresee that there might be a cry of *perfide Albion* and a destruction of the present friendship between the two nations. The situation requires great wariness, but we may trust to Grey for that.'[29] Grey's 'wariness' had certainly helped smooth over the problem of the military conversations, since Campbell-Bannerman's response to the edited version of Grey's conversation with Cambon was that: 'We have happily a little more time for reflection, as the French Ambassador cannot expect an answer during the elections.'[30]

Grey authorised the talks on 13 January, two days before Campbell-Bannerman even acknowledged receiving an account of his interview with Cambon.[31] Grey told Bertie that 'a promise in advance committing this country to take part in a Continental war is . . . a very serious one . . . it changes an Entente into an Alliance – and Alliances, especially continental Alliances are not in accord with our traditions'.[32] This was strictly true, and it would remain so, but what it showed was a capacity for ignoring the consequences of events which was awesome. Grey had authorised talks about military co-operation with the French in a situation where, as he acknowledged to the German Ambassador, 'if there was trouble we should be involved in it'.[33] As A.J.P. Taylor put it many years ago: 'However strong the technical justification, the military talks were a political act.'[34]

Reporting another conversation with Cambon at the end of January, Grey commented, 'I do not know that I did well, but I did honestly';[35] it is tempting to reverse that verdict. Grey told Cambon on 31 January that, 'if France is let in for a war with Germany arising out of our agreement . . . about Morocco we cannot stand aside, but must take part with France'. Cambon was not happy about an assurance from Grey alone, and made plain his desire for one from the Cabinet. Grey's response was a masterpiece of 'wariness' – not to say casuistry. He told Cambon that although he had no doubts about the 'good disposition of the Cabinet', he 'did think there would be difficulties in putting such an undertaking in writing'.[36] The nature of those 'difficulties' was made plain by Sanderson to Cambon on 1 February: 'it was not wise to bring before a Cabinet the question of the course to be pursued in hypothetical cases which had not arisen. A discussion . . . invariably gave rise to divergences of opinion on questions of principle, whereas in a concrete case unanimity would very likely be assured.' It was not surprising that Grey was 'glad that this point was so well pointed out'.[37] Translated out of 'diplomatic' language, Sanderson's comment amounted to an admission that large sections of the Cabinet would have refused to give a hypothetical commitment, but they might be prepared to give one if Germany was actually attacking France; at this level matters did not change until early August 1914. Campbell-Bannerman disliked 'the stress laid upon joint preparations', which he thought came 'very close to an honourable undertaking';[38] but he too preferred to keep the matter away from the Cabinet.

Grey's sanctioning of the military talks, like his readiness to stand by the French, was all predicated on his view of German policy; unfortunately, his actions played into the hands of those in Berlin who thought that the British could not be trusted. When the Unionists were still in power, Holstein looked to the Algeçiras conference with some trepidation, suspecting that the British looked forward to 'presenting us with the bill for the Kruger Telegram, the Boer War episode, the naval drive and other items'.[39] He regarded the change of Government as 'an unexpected stroke of luck for us which we should make use of', and wanted to try to convince the British that 'we are not planning a war against them'; he thought that they should 'hurry to improve our relations with England in the next few years while the new Russia is still busy at home'. Bülow's distrust of the English led him to prefer to see whether he could get a deal with the French at Algeçiras.[40] Holstein tried to convince him that this was a 'mistake' and that 'the place where German policy should dig is England and not France . . . without England, even the Dual Alliance will think twice before waging war on us'.[41]

Bülow recognised that the British were 'the key to the Moroccan situation',[42] but he suspected that 'England has, in effect, made an offer of armed support to France' and that Lansdowne had been 'lying' when he had told Metternich that he had not offered to support France.[43] Bülow, like the French, saw a 'continuity' between Lansdowne and Grey that did not exist. Convinced that Britain and France were ready to strike if war broke out, the Kaiser told Bülow on 29 December 1905 that there must be a diplomatic rather than a military solution to the crisis.[44]

Lansdowne and Sanderson were well aware that Germany's international position was weaker than it had been, but Grey insisted on acting as though she was in a position of European hegemony. His views about Germany stemmed from the experiences of the 1890s, when Britain's diplomatic dependency on her had meant that 'we were kept on bad terms with France and Russia . . . and Germany took toll of us when it suited her'.[45] 'Isolation' haunted his imagination in much the way it had Joseph Chamberlain. Grey feared the effects on the balance of power if Britain left France 'in the lurch': there would be 'a general feeling that we had behaved meanly'; America 'would despise us'; Russia 'would not think it worth while to make a friendly arrangement with us about Asia'; Japan would 'prepare to insure herself elsewhere'; in short, Britain would 'be left without a friend and without the power of making a friend and Germany would take some pleasure . . . in exploiting the whole situation to our disadvantage'. Although he shrank from the 'prospect of a European War and of our being involved in it', he thought that an *entente* with Russia to match the one with France would mean that 'If it is necessary to check Germany then it could be done.' Grey himself saw that in the event of a war with Germany, Britain's 'liabilities' would be minimal: 'We should risk little or nothing on land, and at sea we might shut the German fleet up in Kiel and keep it there without losing a ship or a man or even firing a shot.'[46] It was this attitude which tied Grey to France throughout the Algeçiras conference, which finished on 7 April in 'dismal failure' for the Germans, who found themselves supported only by the Austrians.[47]

Grey had told Metternich in January that once the conference was over, he was eager to establish better relations with the Germans, but when the Kaiser raised the subject of an understanding between the two countries in May, the British reaction was that there was no need for one because, in Crowe's words, 'we have no differences whatsoever' with Germany.[48] When the British press advocated such an understanding, Grey dismissed such talk as 'gush'.[49] He thought that the Germans 'do not realize that England has always drifted or deliberately gone into opposition to any Power which establishes a hegemony in Europe'.[50] This statement of belief in the balance of power reads oddly when set against Grey's claim in his memoirs that he had 'never, so far as I recollect, used the phrase "Balance of Power". I have often deliberately avoided the use of it, and I have never consciously set it before me as something to be pursued, attained and preserved. I am not, therefore, qualified to explain or define what it is.'[51] Despite this, he failed to contradict Bertie's comment to the Germans in 1911 that 'the policy of England has always been the maintenance of the Balance of Power'.[52]

Grey told the Dominion Prime Ministers in May 1911 that Britain's 'Foreign Policy is anything but a Machiavellian one; it is most simple and straightforward';[53] so it was, and it was based on the principle that 'the balance of power in Europe was preserved by the present grouping, and I should not think of disturbing it'.[54] This comment, made in 1909 after the Russian *entente*, shows Grey inflexibly wedded to maintaining a temporary diplomatic alignment. When he told the Dominion Prime Ministers that the *entente* with France had inaugurated a new phase in Britain's relations with the Continental Powers, this was his doing, not Lansdowne's. Lansdowne thought that a German attack on France over the Moroccan issue would 'dangerously excite' British public opinion',[55] a view Grey shared; but unlike Lansdowne, he shared it with the Germans. He also authorised staff talks with the French, and pursued the goal of an agreement with Russia to help cement the French connection.

Grey's views on Russia were quite different from those of his predecessors. Where Lansdowne had seen the French *entente* as a settlement of colonial differences which would restore some flexibility to his diplomacy, Grey saw the *entente* with Russia as being 'necessary to check Germany', and thus as a complement to his vision of the Anglo-French *entente*.[56] He also believed that trying to 'head back Russia in every direction' was profoundly 'mistaken', and thought that the best way of preventing the threat to the North-West Frontier of India was to 'come to an agreement with Russia'.[57] But recent arguments to the effect that this was his main concern, as it had been Lansdowne's, and that Grey's evocations of the 'balance of power' were, in fact, a way of concealing this fact, are ingenious rather than convincing.[58] Grey never thought that Russia 'seriously had designs for invading India'.[59] For him, Russia was a vital element in balancing German power in Europe, and he was 'impatient to see Russia re-established as a factor in European politics'.[60] 'Asiatic questions' occupied a secondary place in Grey's scheme of things, and his approach to Russia was dictated by the fact that since she was the ally of France, 'we could not pursue at one and the same time a policy of agreement with France and a policy of counter-alliances with Russia'.[61] Once the connection had been made, it would always steer Grey away from his own proclaimed desire for better relations with Germany, because if France and Russia should ever become convinced that they could not rely on Britain, 'they must abandon her and make friends with the Triple Alliance, the result would be a quintuple Alliance which would leave England isolated'.[62]

Grey's admiring Whig biographer, Trevelyan, described his policy as being to 'preserve the peace of Europe' and 'at the same time to provide that, if war came, England should not be without friends';[63] but his conception of who those 'friends' might be, and the direction from which the threat to the 'peace of Europe' might come, lacked all flexibility. For Grey, Germany was always the danger; France and Russia were always the 'friends'. German motives and actions were always suspect; those of France and Russia were always given the benefit of the doubt. That Grey should have thought that this retained the 'free hand' for Britain is testimony only to the blinkered nature of his diplomatic vision.

Perhaps Grey's opinions would not have been so inflexible had they been challenged, but they were not – at least not very often. It was only senior diplomats of the old school like Sanderson and Lascelles who argued for a more flexible view of Germany, but the former retired in 1906, and although the latter kept going until 1908, his views were little regarded by the younger men at the

Foreign Office, who very largely shared Grey's views, and certainly did not question them.[64] It has been argued that Grey's view of Germany 'remained more flexible that that of Crowe, and that he remained fully aware of the advantages which a limited agreement with Germany, which did not undermine the *entente* with France might produce';[65] but since Crowe's views became increasingly extreme, and Grey appeared to regard any agreement with Germany as having the potential to undermine the *entente*,[66] the practical difference between the two men was negligible. Neither was there much in the way of dissent from the Cabinet, despite, or more probably because of, the fact that Grey's views were not widely shared there. Grey issued few 'Blue Books' on his diplomacy and shied away from Cabinet discussion of his policy; most of the Cabinet only learned about the staff talks with the French in 1911. When Crowe rejected the idea of an understanding with Germany in 1906, he commented that an *entente* 'means nothing more than a frame of mind, a disposition to view the actions and thoughts of another power with friendly sympathy';[67] it was the 'frame of mind' which Grey and men like Crowe brought to the German question which made the French *entente* the cornerstone of Grey's policy.

When Crowe described German policy as being 'to make herself so strong that in all matters in which she considers German interests to be involved, she will have her own way', he also acknowledged that this was 'not deserving of moral censure' because the same ambition 'inspires the policy of every Great Power worthy of the name, to a certain degree'. But his view that 'the uniform experience of history shows that if this ambition is absolutely realized, the unquestioned supremacy of one State reacts disastrously on all the others',[68] permeated the analysis of German policy contained in his famous memorandum of 1 January 1907. However much inter-war historians may have distorted its importance, its significance lies in the fact that it was this view of Germany as potential hegemon which came to dominate British official thinking, rather than the alternative version offered by Crowe himself.

Crowe acknowledged that it was possible that German policy was 'in reality no more than the expression of a vague, confused, and unpractical statesmanship, not fully realizing its own drift';[69] German policy during the first Moroccan crisis certainly suggested such a conclusion, as did other evidence. Sir Edward Goschen, who succeeded Lascelles as Ambassador in Berlin in 1908, found 'more muddle – more confusion – than I have found in any country during my 35 years experience', and characterised German foreign policy as marked by 'chaos'. He thought that the 'admitted failures of German diplomacy in recent years' were 'the result' of the confusion and chaos, rather than of malice aforethought.[70] Sanderson, who had served under Derby, Salisbury and Lansdowne, and had lived through the period which Crowe was theorising about, actually preferred this last explanation: it was 'inevitable that a nation flushed with success which had been obtained at the cost of great sacrifices, should be somewhat arrogant and over-eager'. He thought it was absurd to suppose that a Great Power like Germany would renounce her colonial ambitions, or the naval policy which they entailed. In his view, Germany was 'a helpful, though somewhat exacting friend . . . a tight and tenacious bargainer, and a most disagreeable antagonist. She is oversensitive about being consulted on all the questions on which she can claim a voice, either as a Great Power or on account of special interests, and it is never prudent to neglect her on such occasions.' Sanderson doubted whether the Germans actually wished to quarrel with the British, but warned that 'a great and growing nation cannot be repressed' and that it would be 'a misfortune that she should be led to believe that in whatever direction she seeks to expand she will find the British lion in her path'.[71] Yet it was precisely along that path that fear of German hegemony pushed Grey, who, in following it, helped create the very danger he was trying to avoid.

Grey may have wanted an *entente* with Russia to 'check Germany',[72] but the Russians responded to his overtures because their weakness in the aftermath of their defeat by Japan made them anxious that the British would steal a march on them in

Central Asia.[73] The appointment of Alexander Izvolsky as Foreign Minister in early 1906 marked a reorientation in Russian foreign policy: there was a move from Asia back to Europe; and a move to mend fences with Japan, Austria-Hungary, Germany and Great Britain. Izvolsky thought that a 'Triple *Entente*' of France, Russia and Britain would provide a diplomatic context in which he could restore Russia's prestige; however, he did not see it as an exclusive relationship, but rather as allowing Russia some diplomatic leverage vis-à-vis Germany, and an opportunity to adjust the balance of power in the Balkans.[74] Izvolsky was, and remained, nervous about the German reaction to an Anglo-Russian *rapprochement*; he was careful to keep Berlin informed and to stress that any agreement would not be at Germany's expense.[75] It is difficult to avoid the conclusion that where Grey wanted the agreement for European reasons, Izvolsky wanted it for imperial ones: Grey wanted to 'check' Germany should that become necessary; Izvolsky wanted to prevent the British taking advantage in Persia of Russia's temporary weakness.

Such an interpretation is reinforced by the course of the negotiations and by the settlement itself. The final agreement covered three areas, and it was bitterly condemned by Curzon in the Lords as sacrificing positions which, as Viceroy of India, he had helped establish; but he was looking through Indian eyes at an *entente* concluded for European reasons. Curzon had been concerned to try to establish Tibet as a *glacis* between the Indian and the Russian Empires.[76] Grey neither knew nor cared about the details of Tibet's frontiers, but he was willing to use a relatively unimportant issue as a means of making concessions to convince the Russians of his good intentions, in order to make an agreement over Persia and Afghanistan possible.[77]

Grey was able to succeed in making an agreement with the Russians over Persia where the Unionists had failed because he was willing to make concessions they had declined to make. Cecil Spring-Rice, newly appointed to Tehran, bemoaned the new tendency to 'take for granted that Russia means what she says when she says she does not intend to take up a position in Persia which would facilitate the invasion of India'; this despite 'certain indications, which if generally known would not increase the ardour of the British action in persisting'.[78] Those like Hardinge, who wanted the *entente* for European reasons, dismissed such fears as the result of a propensity to believe in the last rumour from the bazaar.[79] But Sir Arthur Nicolson, Hardinge and Grey were willing to buy the Russians off with concessions in Persia because it suited their wider purpose. Lord Sanderson was probably correct when he told Spring-Rice: 'We could not pursue a really successful policy of antagonism to Russia without efforts and sacrifices which the public and Parliament would not agree to';[80] but Russia was in no position in 1907 to drive the bargain she was accorded. The final agreement conceded her dominance in the north of Persia in return for a British sphere of influence in the south. The long discussions of Persian policy which had marked the Salisbury years were no more; the same was true of the issue of the Straits.

Grey told Izvolsky in March 1907 that he had felt 'all through these negotiations that good relations with Russia meant that our old policy of closing the Straits against her, and throwing our weight against her at any conference of the Powers must be abandoned'.[81] Izvolsky, naturally, expressed his delight that 'the closing of the Straits is no longer a cardinal point of British policy'.[82] Grey used the Straits as a bargaining counter to get concessions on Persia, which were necessary if the agreement as a whole was to be sold to his own Party. He was 'quite satisfied with the way in which our Russian agreement has been received'. Grey himself acknowledged that 'as an isolated bargain' many people regarded it as a 'bad one', and whilst not agreeing with them, he told Nicolson that it was 'most important that public opinion here should be favourably impressed by the attitude of the Russians towards us during the next year or two'. This was because the only real justification for the agreement was that it might lead to 'a generally friendly attitude of Russia towards us'. Grey thought that a 'combination of Britain, Russia, and France', although 'for the present . . . a weak one', could potentially 'dominate Near Eastern policy'.[83]

Grey believed in the potential German hegemony, the utility of the Russian *entente*, the seminal importance of the French connection and the maintenance of the balance of power; ironically his steps to maintain the latter actually helped undermine it still further.

21

Unbalancing Europe

Morley's comment that 'one great spring of mischief in these high politics is to suppose that the situation of to-day will be the situation of tomorrow',[1] described the besetting sin of Grey's diplomacy: his conception of the balance of power was rigidly fixed. Professing always a desire to get on better terms with the Germans, Grey constantly feared that the French would read any such attempts as a sign that 'we intend to leave her in the lurch, and draw towards Germany to see what we can get in that quarter . . . and so we shall run the risk of returning to our position of isolation in Europe, and of losing much of the strong position which our recent policy has won for us'.[2] Grey was never prepared to run that risk.

One of Crowe's reasons for not definitely accepting 'the view that Germany was deliberately pursuing an anti-English policy' was that 'pending the necessary development of the German forces, such a policy must compel Germany to make every effort to win and retain England's friendship temporarily', and she had not done so. So, when the Germans did try to win Britain's friendship in 1908, they found themselves in a diplomatic version of 'Morton's Fork', since Crowe took it as a sign that they had realised that they needed to lull England into a false sense of security, whilst their 'whole energy . . . is directed towards the coming struggle with England'. On Crowe's logic, Germany's unwillingness to cut back her naval-building programme should have been taken as a sign that she had no evil intent towards Britain, but that was not how Grey saw it: 'We cannot be comfortable as long as the German navy is increasing.'[3] Explaining a reluctance to respond to German overtures in terms either of not wanting to upset the French, or of the exigencies of the balance of power, would hardly have gone down well with large sections of the Liberal Party; fear of the German navy was a much better excuse. Yet that fear was not so deeply ingrained that it had prevented the Liberals from cutting Britain's own naval programme.

Conservative defence policies had proceeded upon imperial assumptions, with the army being reorganised for imperial responsibilities, and emphasis in spending being placed mainly upon the navy.[4] Although Grey's foreign policy carried with it, from Algeçiras onwards, the risk of involvement in a Continental war, the Liberals continued with the 'strategy of business as usual'.[5] This assumed that the Royal Navy would help bring about the collapse of the German economy by blockade, whilst Britain's Continental allies would hold the German colossus at bay; at worst, Britain would have to pay her allies to fight for her as she had before in her history. The notion that she might find herself involved in a Continental land campaign of prolonged length and bloody severity was not one which occurred to those who directed British diplomacy to the task of limiting Germany's supposed ambitions.[6]

As early as 1904, Selborne had concluded that 'the great new German navy is being carefully built up from the point of view of a war with us',[7] and the Unionists had responded according to type – not with *ententes* but with the Cawdor programme, which provided for the laying down of four dreadnoughts a year. This was fully in accord with the old Country Party preference for basing British power on the navy, rather than 'the shifting sands of any temporary and unofficial international relationships', as the

Board of Admiralty put it in February 1906.[8] But as the new Chancellor, Asquith, told the First Lord, Lord Tweedmouth, with the Kaiser having increasing difficulty in getting his way in the Reichstag, and with the international position looking favourable, there was no longer any need for it.[9] So the Cawdor programme was cut.

Liberalism has usually placed a higher priority on 'butter' than it has on 'guns', and Grey's willingness to cut the Cawdor programme despite his own views on Germany reflected his faith in Britain's ability to lead the way towards a general reduction of armaments in Europe.[10] In April 1906, the Tsar had issued an invitation to a conference at The Hague to discuss disarmament, which met in early 1907. To those who argued that the timing was 'inopportune', Campbell-Bannerman, in good old Liberal fashion, replied that Britain had already set a 'moral' lead by her own policy, and that her reliance on naval power carried with it 'no menace across the waters of the world'.[11] It was characteristic of Grey to have been disappointed at the Kaiser's refusal to consider measures of disarmament, but also to reject his argument that since the British had a 'Two-Power' naval standard, it was unfair of them to object to the German naval programme.[12] Ignoring the weakness of Germany's diplomatic and strategic position, Grey took the view that if the Kaiser caused the conference to fail and Britain had to increase her naval programme: 'I want people here and in Germany . . . to realize that it is he, who has forced our hand in spite of our wish to limit expenditure.'[13] The fact that in German eyes it looked pretty rich for the British, from their position of naval supremacy, to be telling them that they must halt their 'progress to world power', or be branded as 'the one determined disturber of the peace of the world',[14] never seems to have occurred to Grey. Grey himself refused to allow Britain's delegate at the conference to agree to 'any resolution which would diminish the effective means which the Navy has of bringing pressure to bear on the enemy',[15] but he saw that as an act of self-defence, and thus as being in a different category from the German attitude.

The failure of the conference exposed the Government to the criticism that in cutting the Cawdor programme, it had allowed Britain to fall behind Germany in the naval race. The Russian *entente* helped to deflect some of this criticism, though Grey can hardly have welcomed the commendation he received from the Chamberlainite journalist, J.L. Garvin, that it was 'a necessary response to Germany's challenge to our naval supremacy which is the life of our race'.[16] But many Conservatives and imperialists wanted a stepping up of the direct naval challenge, which led to the great 'naval scare' of 1908, with the slogan 'we want eight and we won't wait'. Had the Government continued with the Cawdor programme, there would have been no 'scare', but as things were, it put an end to any hopes of better relations with Germany. As Bülow told Holstein in December 1908, 'the growing agitation in England is entirely the result of our ship-building'.[17] Holstein was equally correct that 'all efforts to bring about better relations with England would be fruitless as long as we continued our naval policy'.[18]

When the Kaiser asked why, since England 'had the right to build as many ships as she considered necessary', the 'blame' was placed 'exclusively on Germany' when other nations were 'increasing their naval armaments';[19] the real answer was that Grey considered the Germans a unique danger. He and his diplomats were convinced that the Germans were carefully preparing 'the future invasion of England',[20] and although they all stoutly denied being 'peculiarly anti-German',[21] their version of the balance of power meant that only German hostility needed to be guarded against. When Winston Churchill 'greatly deprecated that persons should try to spread the belief . . . that war between Great Britain and Germany is inevitable',[22] and tried, along with Lloyd George, to resist the clamour for an increase in British spending on the navy to keep in line with that of Germany, the Liberal Cabinet found itself convulsed.

Asquith had become Prime Minister in 1908 and was widely expected to provide new initiatives in social policy. His Chancellor, Lloyd George, warned him in February 1909 that there were 'millions of earnest Liberals in the country who are beginning rather to lose confidence in the Government',[23] The argumetnover 'guns versus butter' was one which tested all Asquith's considerable political skills, but he managed to find a compromise which kept Lloyd George and Churchill in the same Government as Grey.

But the greatest threat to the balance of power came neither from German ambitions nor yet from the naval race, but rather from a direction Salisbury would have been familiar with – the Near East. When Salisbury had talked about the importance of Austria to British policy in 1886, he had been recognising that two conservative Empires had a common interest in acting as a bulwark against Russian expansionism in the Balkans; he was aware that without British help, Austria would have only the alternatives of trying to cut a deal with the Russians, or of falling back on German support.[24] Grey's policy left Austria with such a choice. The brief period of Anglo-Austrian *rapprochement* which had followed his arrival at the Foreign Office gave way to recriminations and ill-will in the aftermath of the *entente* with Russia, which in Vienna was seen as an abandonment of Britain's old policy.[25] The loss of the British connection left the Austrians to face the dangers of Pan-Slavism without support from anyone save the Germans. If those forces proved too strong for the Habsburg Empire, then there would be no balance of power – because the war of the Austrian succession would bring the old Eastern Question right into the heart of Europe.[26] In an era of triumphant nationalism, it was easy for liberals to assume that the Habsburg Empire was the next 'sick man' of Europe. But of the three destabilising forces by which it was beset, Irredentism, Pan-Germanism and Pan-Slavism,[27] only the last posed a deadly threat: Italian claims against the Empire could be contained by the Triple Alliance; Pan-Germanism was defused by the German alliance; but Pan-Slavism was a real danger, not because of the anti-Austrian policy which the Serbs had pursued since 1903, but because the Serbs could look to Russia for support.[28]

When Count Lexa von Aehrenthal had succeeded Count

Agenor Goluchowski in October 1906 as Habsburg Foreign Minister, his aim had been to seek a renewed *Dreikaiserbund*,[29] but the agreement between England and Russia cut the ground from under him in two ways: it seemed to rule out any need for the Russians to seek Austrian co-operation; and it seemed to herald a Russo-British partnership in the Balkans.[30] What was left of the Russo-Austrian *entente* depended on the ability of the two Powers to co-operate in sponsoring reform in the troubled Ottoman province of Macedonia. The activities of Greek bandits there, which were unchecked because of the refusal of the Great Powers to allow the usual repressive methods favoured by the Porte, were making the area ungovernable. In 1903, the two Powers had come up with a scheme of reform, the *Mürzsteg Punctation*, which they endeavoured to persuade the Sultan to adopt.[31] Lansdowne had welcomed the agreement, recognised the 'special interest' of Austria and Russia in the area, and steered Britain away from any involvement.[32] But after the 1907 *entente*, it seemed as though Grey was bent upon securing an Anglo-Russian solution to the Macedonian problem.[33] In German eyes this looked like a British attempt to break the Austro-Russian understanding.[34] Aehrenthal, who feared that Austria-Hungary would become the main victim of an Anglo-Russian partnership,[35] therefore responded enthusiastically to overtures from Izvolsky in July 1908 which seemed to offer an opportunity of averting such a development.[36] If the British would no longer work with Austria to preserve the *status quo*, then Aehrenthal was willing to seek an agreement *à deux* with the Russians to alter it in a way which suited him.[37]

At Buchlau in September, the two men agreed that 'if Austria-Hungary were forced to proceed to annexation of Bosnia-Herzegovina, Russia would assume a friendly and benevolent attitude'; in return, Izvolsky expected reciprocation from Aehrenthal over the Straits.[38] Izvolsky thought that the changes would be simultaneously announced; but, confident that he could rely on German help, Aehrenthal acted at once. In Aehrenthal's opinion, the Germans were 'now absolutely dependent upon Austria-

Hungary'.[39] He got the Italians on side,[40] and, anticipating no trouble from the British, he announced on 6 October 1908 that Austria was annexing Bosnia-Herzegovina.[41] This left Izvolsky high and dry. He claimed that there had been no agreement with Aehrenthal, merely an 'academic' discussion; but that did not save him from the criticism that he had been tricked by Aehrenthal and that he had betrayed Pan-Slavism.[42]

It was the decision to occupy Bosnia and Herzegovina in 1908 which, far more than any Anglo-German antagonism, led the way to the conflagration of 1914. It marked a new willingness by the Austrians to use force to deny territory to the Pan-Serbian agitators in Belgrade,[43] which showed the increasing influence of the Austrian Chief of the General Staff, Field-Marshal Franz Conrad Von Hötzendorff, who advocated a forceful solution to the problems which beset the Dual Monarchy.[44] It marked also a new, almost reckless style of diplomacy, the success of which inculcated lessons which would be remembered in 1914. The Bosnian crisis brought Europe to the verge of war for the first time since the 1870s.[45] Aehrenthal ruthlessly overplayed his hand, but felt that he had no alternative if Austria was to be saved.[46] The crisis opened up a new and fatal stage of the Eastern Question; it also revealed how far Grey might have to go to keep his balance of power.

Failing to see that it was his own backing for reforms in Macedonia which had helped to create the crisis, Grey thought that the Austrians had struck a 'cruel blow' at the Young Turk reformers;[47] he also objected to their unilateral abrogation of an international treaty. Feeling 'justly aggrieved' at being treated with such 'bad faith' by Aehrenthal, Grey authorised Goschen to tell him as much.[48] German protestations of innocence were not believed, and for a moment even Izvolsky and the Russians came under private censure as having shown that they had their 'price'.[49] British suspicions of the immortality of Continental diplomacy lay very near the surface. For a brief moment German hopes were raised that the crisis might scupper the Anglo-Russian *entente*.[50] Aehrenthal was unimpressed by Grey's 'sickening' hypocrisy, noting that he had sanctioned changes in the 1880 Madrid Convention over the future of Morocco readily enough when it had suited him.[51] His refusal to agree to submit the Austrian action to that 'Concert' of Europe which had so studiously ignored Vienna's interest forced Grey to consider his relations with Russia.

Just before the crisis broke, Nicolson had warned Grey that: 'The understanding with Russia is in its early infancy and will require . . . careful nurture and treatment. Any serious check . . . may kill it.'[52] Grey accordingly decided to back Izvolsky in calling for a conference to discuss the 1878 Berlin settlement.[53] But the Serbs, who regarded the annexation as a 'great national catastrophe',[54] proceeded to mobilise their forces.[55] Izvolsky, in a bid to shore up his position, promised to support their claims for compensation.[56] Aehrenthal warned Grey against supporting the Russians,[57] but it was a sign of how seriously Grey took the new *entente* that he told the Serbs that he would support Izvolsky's demands.[58] Despite Grey's claims that his policy was motivated solely by 'disinterested motives',[59] it was entirely pro-Russian in orientation. Grey was persuaded by Izvolsky's portrayal of himself as a sort of Russian Delcassé, whose disappearance would be a blow to the *entente*; and Sir Charles Hardinge wrote that it was 'evident that we must do our best to support him, such as he is'.[60] Britain had hitherto always sought to mediate between Russia and Austria; now she was firmly aligned with the Russians.

Grey's habit of treating the Austro-German alliance as a monolithic bloc was never more wrong-headed than at this juncture. The Germans had known nothing of Aehrenthal's plans, and were both surprised and dismayed by the crisis over Bosnia.[61] Their subsequent support for Austria was a sign not of German aggression, but of her weakness. Bülow took the view that whatever the rights or wrongs of the business, Germany had no alternative but to stand by her ally: the slogan must be '*la loyauté sans phrases*'.[62] Thus, when Izvolsky went to Berlin with British backing to secure support for the agenda of the proposed conference, he met a German *non possumus*; Germany, he was told bluntly, would stand by her ally.[63] Aehrenthal warned the British that they were 'incurring a great responsibility', and that 'if Russia wants war she shall have it'.[64]

Grey heard German complaints that they were being 'ringed in', but dismissed them as incompatible with his view of Germany as potential hegemon. As he told the Russian Ambassador, Count Benckendorff, there was no reason why Germany should be worried when she had 'two allies in Europe', whilst 'France and Russia had one each': Germany stood in the 'middle of Europe, with two allies and the strongest army in the world, and no one dreamt of attacking her'.[65] This displayed a level of complacency staggering even in an insular English politician: of Germany's 'two allies', Italy was militarily of small value and had already drawn closer to France, whilst Austria was fast becoming a worm-eaten galleon; being 'in the middle of Europe' meant that Germany was vulnerable from both Russia and France, and it would have been the height of folly for the Germans to have assumed that neither of those Powers 'dreamt of attacking her'.

Indeed, it was the very consciousness of the weakness of their position which led the Austrian and German military to concert, for the first time, plans for action in the event of a war with the Dual Alliance.[66] Bülow's policy of *'Festigkeit'* (firmness) was founded on the assumption that if Germany did not stand by her ally, she would be left isolated. Germany had to back her only reliable ally, and a show of firmness might even weaken the *'Einkreisungring'* (encircling ring) around her, at the same time.[67] Had Bülow been determined on war, then 1909 would have been, as Wilhelm II realised, 'the best moment to settle accounts with the Russians'.[68] Baron Franz Conrad Von Hötzendorff, the Chief of the Austrian army, calculating that the balance of forces gave Austria an overwhelming advantage over the Balkan states, wanted to take the opportunity to crush Serbia and Montenegro, but Aehrenthal's view was that 'today one does not fight preventive wars';[69] he relied upon Belgrade backing down.[70]

Aehrenthal thought that Grey's backing for Izvolsky had encouraged both the Russians and the Serbs to hold out for territorial compensation.[71] He told Albert Mensdorff, the Austrian Ambassor in England, in late December that he suspected that British policy was inspired by a desire to strike at the Germans indirectly. He simply did not believe Grey's assurances that he had never sought to sow discord between members of the Triple Alliance, and he thought that his ultimate aim was a formal alliance with France and Russia.[72]

The British totally failed to understand the depth of Austrian resentment against them. Edward VII, like Grey and the rest of those in England who had any interest in the subject, thought that Aehrenthal's attitude was uncalled for.[73] Grey 'had carefully abstained from any attempt on any occasion to make mischief between Austria and Germany', and since 'the balance of power in Europe was preserved by the present grouping', he would not 'think of wishing to disturb it'.[74] But as Hardinge acknowledged to the new British Ambassador in Vienna, Sir Fairfax Cartwright, the Triple Alliance was already so weak 'that there would be danger of its falling through altogether if it grew weaker';[75] Grey's 'Triple *Entente*' had just that effect.

The Austrians warned that they would take firm action against 'provocation' from Belgrade.[76] Hardinge thought that it was 'high time' that the Russians told the Serbs that they were not going to get any compensation,[77] but when the Germans suggested that step in late February, Grey declined to act without Russian consent.[78] This was a perfect example of the loss of flexibility which was Grey's outstanding contribution to British diplomacy. Having promised his support to Izvolsky for the Russian position on Serbia 'whatever that might be',[79] Grey now found himself facing the prospect of redeeming his word at a high cost. Nicolson warned him on 24 February 1909 that in the event of a war between Austria and Serbia, 'Russia would actively intervene'.[80] Grey's private secretary, Louis Mallet, thought that there would be 'few who would think that Britain would not fight alongside France and Russia in a war over Serbia',[81] and by the end of February Hardinge did not 'see how war is to be avoided'.[82]

The resemblance to the crisis of 1914 is obvious, and had the parties involved behaved as they did then, Hardinge's gloomy prediction would have been borne out. Grey's policy amounted to writing out blank cheques to Russia and France and hoping they would not be cashed. The only reason they were not on this occasion is that Aehrenthal had guessed correctly about how far the Russians could be pushed. At the end of February, Izvolsky advised the Serbs to drop the demand for territorial compensation;[83] but Grey still agreed to back his secondary demand for a conference at which the Serbs should be given some economic compensation.[84] He spoke patronisingly to Mensdorff about Austria manifesting the same 'conciliatory spirit' as the Russians, saying that he would 'despair' about European politics if the Austrians insisted on a bilateral solution of the problem.[85] It never occurred to Grey that 'these Near East questions' were a matter of life and death to Austria. Once the Turks had been paid to agree to the annexation, for Serbia to refuse to do so was, in Aehrenthal's eyes, another sign of her irredentist ambitions,[86] and he had as little intention of compromising as Grey had of doing so in the naval race.

Aehrenthal was not planning to attack Serbia unless the Serbs provoked him. His ambition was not to annex Serbia, but to reassert the sort of economic and military hegemony which Austria had enjoyed in Belgrade before 1903. Even after a successful war, it would still be in Austria's interests to maintain an independent Serbia, and so he endeavoured to solve the crisis by offering the Serbs economic concessions.[87] But it was essential that the negotiations should be between Austria and Serbia alone, and he was determined to 'never admit' the 'mad claim' of Russia to act as the protector of Serbia.[88] Yet it was precisely that claim which Grey was supporting by insisting that 'the Powers' should frame the Serbian reply to Austria's demands for assurances about their intentions.[89] The Serbs duly played up to the policy of their patrons by returning a response which the Austrians were bound to find inadequate, not least because it left Serbia's 'cause' in the 'hands' of the other Powers.[90] Even Mallet had to agree that the tone of the Serb reply had put her *'and the Powers* in the wrong'.[91]

The Germans were correct to observe that if the British really wanted to see the crisis resolved, the best thing they could do was to leave the Serbs and the Austrians to sort it out between themselves;[92] but that was exactly what Grey would not do. Britain's attitude, as Hardinge acknowledged, depended 'entirely upon that of M.Izvolsky'.[93] Even so, Nicolson reported from St Petersburg that Russian opinion was contrasting Britain's want of enthusiasm for the Russian cause with the firm support which the Austrians were getting from Germany.[94]

The reason for Germany's support for Aehrenthal was not far to seek. Despite British delusions that Germany was threatening the balance of power in Europe, the men in Berlin were only too well aware that it was the balance of power which was threatening them; the fact that their own miscalculations had contributed to this situation would not, had it occurred to them, have made them feel any better. The maintenance of the integrity of the Habsburg Empire was 'a necessity for the safety of the German Empire', and if Austria-Hungary found herself involved in a war with Russia which looked like seriously damaging her, 'Germany would draw her sword'.[95] For that reason Germany was, as the British Ambassador in Berlin noted, 'more Austrian than the Austrians'.[96] On 21 March, the Germans presented Izvolsky with an ultimatum: either accept the annexation of Bosnia, or 'we shall draw back and let events take their course'.[97]

Grey, who was deep into fruitless negotiations with Aehrenthal about the text of a more acceptable Serbian reply, was left high and dry by Izvolsky's climb-down.[98] Russia was not prepared to go to war, not least because of the possible consequences on the domestic front; faced with a resolute front by the Dual Alliance, and without any real support from France, Izvolsky had no alternative but to back down.[99] The crisis certainly invoked in Serbia and Russia a desire for revenge;[100] but the Germans and Austrians had given notice that they could not compromise on an issue so closely associated with the survival of the Habsburg Empire.

It was only natural that Izvolsky should have felt that his defeat in the Bosnian crisis marked the establishment of 'German hegemony' over Europe;[101] but it is revealing that there were those on the British side who also saw it as a defeat for the 'Triple *Entente*'. In St Petersburg the architect of the *entente*, Nicolson, saw in it a premeditated campaign of 'revenge' for Algeçiras: the fact that the French were in the process of signing an agreement with Germany over Morocco, and that Germany was redoubling her naval programme, showed that with the Anglo-Russian *entente* 'not sufficiently strong or sufficiently deep-rooted to have any appreciable influence', the 'hegemony of the Central Powers will be established in Europe'. His own solution to this problem was to 'extend and strengthen' the *entente* 'by bringing it nearer to the nature of an alliance'. Without that, he feared, both France and Russia might gravitate into the German orbit and 'England will be isolated'.[102] Mallet disagreed with the diagnosis that the 'Triple Entente was too weak to resist the Central Powers'; it was simply that 'it was not worth their while to do so'. Grey too did not think that he had let Russia down: 'Izvolsky did not give either us or France the chance of saying whether we should help him to make better terms.'[103] Hardinge doubted whether the pessimistic view of Nicolson about a reorientation of Russian policy was justified: 'My own belief is that the anti-German feeling in Russia is too strong at present.'[104] He wondered whether Nicholas II would 'ever get over the brutality of German methods and the humiliation which has been inflicted upon him'.[105]

Aehrenthal was quite right in thinking that the British had 'Germany on the brain'. They insisted on seeing the hand of Germany behind the Bosnian crisis, and, as Hardinge wrote during its final stages, 'Germany may be regarded as our only potential enemy in Europe.'[106] This preoccupation blinded Grey and his diplomats to the fact that in their desire to maintain the balance of power in Europe, they had aligned themselves with two Powers which had good reason to wish to revise that balance, and they had spurned Austria, which had the greatest interest in maintaining it.

Aehrenthal's actions during the Bosnian crisis had been designed to maintain Austria as a Great Power; Germany's actions, however the motive behind them was interpreted, had hardly produced the situation Bülow wanted. *Weltpolitik* had destroyed the international position which Germany had occupied under Bismarck. Indeed, by the summer the Chancellor's own position had become untenable and he was succeeded by Theodore von Bethmann-Hollweg, who came into office determined to effect an improvement in relations with London.[107]

But, of course, Bethmann-Hollweg's hopes were to founder on 'Crowe's fork'. When the Reichstag debates of early 1909 on the Naval Estimates failed to produce any anti-English outbursts, Crowe put it down to manipulation of the German press, whilst Hardinge thought that if the German fleet had actually been ready, 'the tone of the . . . press would probably be very different'.[108] The very notion of an *entente* was dismissed, yet again, as nothing more than an attempt to lull Britain into a false sense of security until Germany was ready to strike.[109] Only time, Grey told the Germans in March 1909, could tell whether the assurances they were offering about their naval programme and its purposes were true. Despite his recognition of the fact that 'German isolation' might lead to a war,[110] Grey never realised that the effect of his diplomacy was to create and intensify just that feeling in Berlin, even though Metternich warned him in June 1909 that Germany felt threatened by the new 'grouping of the Powers' since 1904.[111]

Although undoubtedly a matter of genuine concern, the German naval programme also provided Grey with a good excuse not to pursue any understanding with the Germans. The German attempt to secure an *entente* in early 1909 foundered on British objections to the fact that, under the suggested terms, Germany would have been able to 'increase her fleet to any size desired' and 'fall upon France or Russia without fear of English interference', as well as being able to 'impose her hegemony on any of the less powerful States'. It was true that 'analogous advantages could simultaneously be secured' to Britain, but, as Crowe noted, since 'we have no desire whatever of carrying on a policy of aggression, those paper advantages are in fact null for us. The whole proposal does not merit serious consideration.'[112] Grey also thought that the sort of *entente* the Germans wanted would 'serve to establish German hegemony of Europe'.[113] Not even the fact that Britain proved more than capable of maintaining her naval supremacy over Germany would do anything to diminish Grey's sense that Britain needed France and Russia to maintain the balance of power against the Germans.[114]

22

Responsibility without Power

Grey consistently denied that his diplomacy had created something called 'the Triple *Entente*'.[1] Indeed, in April 1908 Hardinge warned Nicolson to desist from using the phrase;[2] but the fact that it had occurred often enough in his correspondence to alarm some Ministers was, in itself, revealing. If, as Crowe noted in February 1911, an *entente* was 'nothing more than a frame of mind . . . which may be, or become, so vague as to lose all content',[3] then Grey's 'frame of mind' ensured that the *entente* acquired rather than lost content.

The fear of losing Russia and France and once more becoming isolated may not have pushed Grey quite as far as Nicolson wanted him to go during the Bosnian crisis, but it stood firmly in the way of Bethmann-Hollweg's attempts later in 1909 to improve Anglo-German relations, which were seen by Crowe as 'directed to the dissolution of the understanding between England, France, and Russia'.[4] It was 'difficult to think of any formula for an understanding with Germany which will not fetter our freedom of action and disturb the minds of France and Russia';[5] which makes it difficult to see how Grey's desire for a 'good understanding with Germany' which would not 'imperil' the two *ententes* could ever have been realised.[6] Under Grey,

Britain followed a policy of the *ententes*, and the phrase 'Triple Entente' appeared in all the glories of capitals and italics' regularly in diplomatic correspondence despite the 1908 ban on it; yet, as the Colonial Secretary, Lewis Harcourt, sharply reminded him in January 1914, 'no such thing has ever been considered or approved by the Cabinet'.[7]

Germany's bad faith was taken for granted in the same way as her presumed desire for European hegemony. It has been argued that this 'invention of Germany' as a threat to Britain's position 'served to conceal British weakness', and that by playing up the danger to be apprehended from Germany, the diplomats were flattering themselves that Britain still had a role to play in the world.[8] But this assumes that Edwardian diplomats shared the perception of 'decline' which has preoccupied later-twentieth-century historians and commentators; they did not, and both Grey and the Kaiser acted on the assumption that Britain's diplomatic alignment had a crucial effect on the balance of power.

Sir Edward Goschen once remarked that the 'balance of Power theory does not appeal to the German mind';[9] there was every reason for this, given the actual balance in 1909. Bethmann-Hollweg noted that, 'the maintenance of the alleged balance of power policy . . . actually results in a limitation of German power', but he feared that it was 'such a firmly founded principle of British foreign policy that even the most far-reaching concessions regarding our naval armaments are unlikely to be sufficient to make them abandon it'.[10] The Germans certainly failed to realise how vulnerable their *Flottenpolitik* made the British feel, but the British failure of imagination was not to realise that Grey's balance-of-power politics had the same effect in Berlin.[11] Germany 'took no steps to convert her undoubted ascendancy into unwanted supremacy' at times such as 1906 and 1909, when she would have had a good chance of being able to do so with little resistance.[12] To read either the period from the Great Eastern Crisis, or the period after 1898, as the incubation period for a series of crises which culminated in the war, is tempting, but dubious.[13] Despite the increasing sophistication and complexity of the debate over the origins of the First World War, it has never really moved very far from the 'War Guilt' clause of the Treaty of Versailles: if German *Weltpolitik* was aggressive, whether because of the primacy of *Innenpolitik* or *Aussenpolitik* the assumption remains that Germany is at the centre of what needs to be explained, and we are still left with a variant of the old theme of '*[la] militarisme allemand se jetant un beau jour sur la France pacifique* [German militarism attacks pacific France out of the blue]'.[14] But Grey's attitude towards his *entente* partners allowed them to disturb the existing balance in Europe far more successfully than Germany ever managed to do.

The concern for the sanctity of treaties which Grey had manifested when it came to Austria-Hungary and Bosnia was absent when it came to French actions in Morocco.[15] The French and the Germans had reached an agreement in 1909 to supplement the Algeçiras convention, but it did not retard French attempts to consolidate control over Morocco. The Germans were well within their rights to protest at further French attempts to tighten their hold on Morocco without offering compensation, but as usual they managed to put themselves in the wrong. Sending the gunboat *Panther* to Agadir on 1 July 1911 precipitated another crisis, which revealed the extent to which Grey felt he was bound to the French. He insisted on regarding the German protest as an assault on his beloved *entente*, and acted like a mother hen protecting her young, which allowed the French to play on his fears in order to secure British support against the Germans.[16]

Although Grey had 'always felt that if Germany fastened war upon France in connection with Morocco' Britain would have to help her, otherwise 'the world would say that France was being attacked because she had made friends with us, and for us to fold our hands and look on would not be a very respectable part',[17] initially he followed the moderate line favoured by his colleagues, which involved getting the French to negotiate with the Germans. This 'weakness' irritated the French and produced a litany of complaints from his own officials.[18] His new private secretary, William Tyrrell, was 'depressed' that 'after six years' experience of Germany the inclination here is still to believe she can be placated by small concessions. . . . What she wants is the hegemony of Europe.' Despite the fact that French actions in Morocco were 'stupid and dishonest', he thought that it was 'a vital interest to support her on this occasion'.[19] Bertie's line was that 'if the French get to think that we are ready to give way to Germany we shall help throw them into the Teutonic embrace'.[20] Crowe harped on the theme that unless supported by Britain, France might 'barter away' British economic interests in Morocco.[21] When the Germans finally presented their demands to the French on 15 July, Crowe thought that they were 'playing for the highest stakes', and that if their demands were conceded it would mean 'the subjection of France . . . this is a trial of strength'.[22] Nicolson commented that unless Britain ranged herself 'alongside France' as she had in 1905 and 1906, 'German hegemony would become solidly established, with all its consequences, immediate and prospective'.[23] Since this analysis fitted so well into Grey's own preconceptions, it is not surprising that he adopted it. At Cabinet on 19 July, he advocated telling the Germans that unless they agreed to a conference on Morocco, 'we should take steps to assert and protect British interests'.[24]

But now the more radical members of the Government finally received the opportunity to make some comments on Grey's foreign policy.[25] The Lord Chancellor, Loreburn, who possessed 'all the radical's distrust of France and her politicians',[26] resisted Grey's proposal, arguing that British interests in Morocco were negligible and certainly not worth running the risk of war with Germany.[27] This meant that the French were not given the sort of message which Crowe had wanted, leaving him to lament that 'the Cabinet are all on the run'.[28] Grey told Asquith that he feared that if Britain remained silent, the Germans would assume that they would not intervene and would increase their own demands.[29]

On 21 July, the Cabinet met again and decided that Grey should tell the Germans that Britain would recognise no settlement in which 'we had not a voice'.[30] Grey did indeed convey this to Metternich, but far more dramatic was Lloyd George's speech at the Mansion House the same evening. There the great radical opponent of increased naval spending in 1908 announced that Britain would not be treated as of 'no account in the Cabinet of nations' where her interests were 'vitally affected'.[31] The speech, which had been cleared with Grey and Asquith first,[32] had, as Grey put it, much greater effect 'than any words of mine'.[33] Morley and Loreburn both protested about the 'provocative' tone of Lloyd George's speech, as did the Germans,[34] and there is no doubt that its consequence was to ratchet up the crisis to the stage that what had begun as a Franco-German dispute over Morocco, risked becoming an Anglo-German war. Once again, as over Bosnia, Grey's concern to maintain the solidity of the *entente* triumphed over any desire to resolve a crisis. Grey denied that the speech had been provocative, and told the editor of the *Manchester Guardian*, C.P. Scott, that his policy was designed to stop France from falling under German influence, which would lead to the collapse of the Triple *Entente* and German hegemony in Europe.[35] He wrote to the First Lord of the Admiralty, Reginald McKenna, on 24 July warning him that relations with Germany might 'at any moment become strained', adding that 'we are dealing with people who recognize no law except that of force between nations'.[36]

McKenna and other members of the Cabinet were still unaware of the military conversations which had taken place between Britain and France. The lengths to which Grey and Asquith went to keep them secret can be seen from the fact that when a special meeting of the CID was called on 23 August, the Cabinet was not informed, and with the exception of McKenna (who as First Lord could not be kept away), all those Ministers invited were in favour of the policy of the *entente*.[37] This may have been accidental, but Asquith's' comment on learning that Morley had been informed of the meeting: 'I wonder by whom?',[38] suggests otherwise.

Churchill and Lloyd George were 'the readiest to go to the utmost extremities'.[39] Indeed Churchill, with his customary impetuosity, decided that 'perhaps the time is coming when decisive action will be necessary', and pressed Grey to consider the advantages of a 'triple alliance' with France and Russia.[40] He circulated a typically long paper on this theme in advance of the CID meeting.[41] At the meeting Asquith, whilst stressing that it was for the Cabinet to take the final decision, proceeded to recommend acceptance of the army's plan, which was that in the event of a Franco-German war, a British Expeditionary Force should be despatched to France. But this was not at all what the Admiralty had in mind. McKenna's plans were still based on the old, pre-1906 assumption that the navy's role would be to protect the sea-lanes and harass German shipping. Given the divergence between the army's and the navy's plans, it rather looked as though the Expeditionary Force had better book itself on a day-steamer to Calais, since the navy would not be available to transport it.

The meeting did not long remain secret. The President of the Board of Education, Walter Runciman, wrote in alarm to Lewis Harcourt telling him that the 'stability or balance of opinion of the Cabinet cannot now be relied on by us', and that 'in the most unexpected quarters I find something more than a merely negative attitude, *a positive desire for conflict*'.[42] Harcourt responded with news of the CID meeting, which he called criminal folly, and accused Churchill of 'going out of his mind with military mania'.[43] Loreburn told Grey that if he tried to give military and naval support in what was a 'purely French quarrel', he would only be able to get it through the Commons 'by a majority very largely composed of Conservatives and with a very large number of the Ministerial side against you. And this would mean that the present Government could not carry on.'[44] Loreburn warned Grey of the 'ruinous consequences on our future history' of a war with Germany, and argued against giving the impression that Britain was implacably opposed to Germany's expansion.[45] But Grey resisted any suggestion that he should give assurances to Berlin about British neutrality in the event of a Franco-German war.[46] Asquith had no intention of breaking up his Government, and by removing McKenna, who had opposed the idea of an Expeditionary Force as tying Britain too closely to France, and replacing him with Churchill, he deftly switched the balance in the crucial Cabinet positions in Grey's favour.[47]

As the crisis dragged on, even Asquith became rather alarmed at the extent to which the French might be encouraged to assume that they could rely on British military assistance, and he wrote to Grey on 5 September to express his anxieties.[48] Grey's response, which was to point out that he was counselling caution to the French, and that it would only upset them to stop the military conversations, hardly addressed Asquith's concerns.[49] In fact, Grey felt himself to have little leverage in Paris, confessing to Goschen that he 'dare not press the French more about the Congo. If I do we may eventually get the odium in France for an unpopular concession and the whole entente may go.'[50]

Grey was also paralysed by his fear that if France and Russia became convinced that 'England was no use', they would 'abandon her and make friends with the Triple Alliance', which would produce a 'Quintuple Alliance which would leave England isolated'.[51] This was an absurdly mechanistic way of looking at international affairs, regarding them as little more than a chess game in which pieces could be moved at will, and in which all players had complete freedom of movement. The notion that as the result of advocating moderation to the French in 1911 they might simply conclude an alliance with Germany, not only flew in the face of common sense, but flew counter to everything which had happened since 1871, as well as ignoring the obvious reflection that if French policy was that fickle, then what was the point of cultivating such close relations.

In fact, the Franco-German negotiations did produce a satisfactory solution to the crisis and an agreement was signed in Berlin on 4 November. But the crisis had shown the implications of Grey's policy. Morley raised the whole question of the Anglo-French staff talks in Cabinet on 1 November, arguing that there was a serious risk that Britain might be dragged into war with Germany for French interests. He found a good deal of support, but the radicals could not push their dissent too far. Haldane, Churchill and Lloyd George all supported the policy, and the former made plain his determination to resign if it were overruled.[52] When the matter was discussed a fortnight later, Loreburn, Morley and Harcourt all seemed on the verge of resigning, but eventually Asquith held his Cabinet together. Grey promised that no decision had been taken that would compromise 'our freedom of decision' in the event of a Franco-German war, and gave an assurance that in future no military talks should take place that would commit Britain to military or naval intervention without Cabinet approval. Grey thought this last decision 'a little tight', but he abided by it for the sake of the Government.[53]

It is easy to see from this, and from British policy during the Bosnian crisis, why the Kaiser complained that 'the balance of power was upset in Europe when you ranged yourselves on the side of Russia and France. . . . If England had stayed out of it, the balance of power would have been preserved.'[54] Yet when the German Ambassador, Count Metternich, told Nicolson at the height of the Agadir crisis that British policy had changed since 1900, and that she had 'ranged' herself with France and Russia, he was told that 'no change in our policy had taken place', and that 'Germany could have no complaints against England, for our attitude had been quite natural and logical'.[55] It was equally 'logical and natural' for the Germans to feel worried about a Triple *Entente* which seemed to give the French and the Russians *carte blanche* to pursue objectives which were detrimental to Germany's interests.

Following the Bosnian crisis, Russia and her Slav protégés were very active in attempting to ensure that Austria-Hungary was not able to consolidate her position in the Balkans.[56] Izvolsky's immediate response to his defeat in the Bosnian crisis had been to take steps to stimulate the creation of a Balkan League by appointing Nicholas Hartwig to Belgrade; he was, in the words of the Russian Ambassador in Vienna, an 'incurable Austrophobe', who soon gained great influence over Serbian policy.[57] During the winter of 1911–12, Hartwig and the Russian Minister in Sofia, Count A.V. Nekliudov, promoted discussions for a Serb-Bulgarian alliance, which would, in the words of the Russian Foreign

Minister Sergei Sazonov, 'bar the road forever to German penetration [and] Austrian invasion'.[58] The British Minister in Sofia, Sir Henry Bax-Ironside, reported in October 1911 that Russo-Bulgarian discussions were taking place: 'When Russian policy is evolved, it will presumably be made known to other members of the Triple Entente from headquarters.'[59] Sir Henry had evidently forgotten that there was no such thing as the 'Triple *Entente*'.

If the Russians were active in the Balkans preparing a counter-coup to Aehrenthal's Bosnian success, they were equally so in Paris, where Izvolsky, as Ambassador after December 1910, was assiduous in his attempts to fund those sections of the French press which warned against any *entente* with Germany.[60] He also strongly encouraged those like Delcassé and the author of the Dual Alliance, Alexandre Ribot, who argued for a strengthening of the 'Triple *Entente*'.[61] This reinforced the position of those at the Quai d'Orsay who argued that any *détente* between Germany and France would damage the position of the latter vis-à-vis her allies; not that this was a view that was in much danger of being overturned. Of the influential French ambassadors, only Jules Cambon consistently argued for a better Franco-German understanding.[62]

Cambon's view, based on extensive contacts with Bülow, the Kaiser and other German policy-makers, tended towards the 'Sanderson' position of German diplomacy. Obviously the Germans wished to pursue their own national interests and regarded the French and the Russians as obstacles to this, but that did not mean that they were bent on unleashing a European conflagration; indeed, from his experience of them, Cambon thought it most unlikely that either Bülow or the Kaiser would go down such a road. The growth of German power, in Europe and abroad, was simply a natural phenomenon. Prime Minister Georges Clemençeau summarised Cambon's position as wanting to go 'neither to Ems nor Fashoda';[63] but for Cambon, French policy in Morocco entailed the risk of 'going to Fashoda by way of Ems, which is more stupid than anything'.[64] A policy of constantly stimulating German fears was not, he thought, the best way to preserve peace in Europe. But to the 'bureaux' at the Quai, the British alignment had enabled them to get away with their Moroccan policy, and they saw no need for an understanding with Germany.

It was not the Austrians or the Germans who were destabilising the balance of power in Europe, but Russia and France, encouraged by the knowledge that the British would support them. France's success in Morocco sparked off what was, in effect, the war of the Ottoman succession. First the Italians, and then the Balkan Powers, scrambled to grab as much of the Turkish Empire as they could. The British did nothing to discourage this process and, out of fear of losing Russian support, found themselves in effect underwriting Slav ambitions in the Balkans.

The Italians, who had long had an agreement with the French that they should receive compensation for Morocco, decided that the time was ripe to seize the Turkish territory of Tripolitania.[65] Once more Grey proved less concerned about the sanctity of the international order when it was being disturbed by someone other than the Germans. Consulted by the Italians in July, Grey told the Italian Ambassador that if Italy's 'hand was forced', Britain would not help the Turks.[66] San Guiliano, the Italian Foreign Minister, 'read these words as a green light'.[67] Italy's allies, Germany and Austria-Hungary, were not informed in advance of her intentions,[68] and Aehrenthal was furious when he learned of Italy's invasion of Tripoli. He knew that it was bound to encourage Turkey's Balkan enemies,[69] and feared that the disruption caused by the war would lead to unrest in the Balkans which might lead to war with Russia.[70] Neither was Berlin any more pleased, with the Kaiser finding it 'strange that Italy hid her plans from her allies, whilst she arranged a step with the opponents of the Triple Alliance, frankly with the object of embroiling us with Turkey'.[71] But the fear of driving Italy from her tenuous place in the Triple Alliance prevented Berlin or Vienna from withholding their approval.

It was a sign of the persistence of old habits that Aehrenthal should have hoped that the British might be able to use their influence with the Italians to dissuade them from resorting to arms, or at least to localise the war.[72] But Grey's policy was summed up in Mallet's words that 'it would be best to consult Petersburg and Paris before moving'.[73] Had the Turks quickly capitulated, as the Italians expected, then perhaps the conflict could have been localised, but the splendid resistance put up by Turkish forces meant that the war dragged on into 1912, and the absence of Turkish troops from the Balkans gave encouragement to the forces of the Balkan League to strike whilst their iron was hot.

The Russians, who were encouraging the League, also seemed set to raise the question of the Straits.[74] Grey told the Germans, who were clearly alarmed, that Britain 'no longer contended that the Straits should be closed', but that 'the actual conditions on which they might be opened' was a matter for discussion with the Powers.[75] But Izvolsky did not see matters in quite that light. He sought French help to ensure that Russia got her way. The new French Foreign Minister, Justin de Selves, professed his complete ignorance of the history of the matter, but was profuse in his assurance that Russia could rely upon France totally.[76] The Turks, still operating on the assumption that Salisbury, if not Palmerston himself, was directing British policy, approached Grey about the possibility of an Anglo-Turkish alliance to guarantee the Straits;[77] but the British would no longer cross Russia for the sake of Turkey. In future, the Turks would look towards Berlin for support.[78]

A war between Austria and Russia would be 'very inconvenient' for Grey, because it was most unlikely that Britain could take part in it on Russia's side.[79] Aware of the development of the Balkan League, but not of the detail of Russia's involvement, the British would have preferred it to have been directed at the maintenance of the *status quo* in the region, but realised that it was directed at the exclusion of Austria.[80] Nicolson's sanguine view that neither Sazonov nor his colleagues wished to 'provoke conflicts' was well wide of the mark, but characteristic of the British reluctance to attribute malign motives to anyone save the Germans.[81]

Whilst the tension in the Balkans mounted, an opportunity arose to undo some of the harm inflicted on Anglo-German relations by the Agadir crisis; but the sort of assumptions made about Russian policy in the Balkans were quite lacking when it came to Germany. It was somehow typical that yet again an attempt to improve Anglo-German relations should begin with an amateur, unofficial initiative and end up stymied by the naval race. Churchill heard from the great financier, Sir Ernest Cassell, that the Kaiser would be willing to invite Grey to Berlin to discuss matters;[82] taking the view that 'this would never do', Grey sent Haldane instead.[83] Haldane was a notable admirer of German culture and spoke the language well, so he was the ideal person to undertake a task which it was hoped would improve Anglo-German relations.[84] The French, who were naturally uneasy at the notion of an Anglo-German *rapproachement*, were reassured that *'le maintien des relations existant entre l'Angleterre, la France et la Russie doit être la condition de tout essai de conversation entre les cabinets de Londres et de Berlin* [the maintenance of the existing relations between Britain, France and Russia ought to be a condition preceding any talks between London and Berlin]'.[85] This condition alone made it unlikely that anything would come of the talks; the fact that neither side was actually willing to pay any price made it certain. The British continued to insist that the Germans should reduce their naval programme; the Germans continued to insist that they would not do so unless the British concluded a non-aggression pact.[86] Haldane hinted that the British might be willing to do this if the Germans first reduced their naval estimates, and on 12 March the Germans offered to withdraw their next Novelle (or Naval Law) if the British would agree to serious political discussions.[87]

On 14 March, Haldane and Grey reported to the Cabinet that it seemed as though Bethmann-Hollweg had, for the moment, got the upper hand over Admiral Tirpitz. Harcourt and Haldane pressed Grey to agree to the German request that the British should include a promise of neutrality in any non-aggression pact, but Grey refused, saying that it would 'tie Britain's hands in the event of a war'.[88] Here Grey was being guided by the view that the Germans were still just trying to lull the British into a false sense of security – and woo them away from the French; 'Crowe's fork' caught the Germans out once more.[89] The failure to come to any agreement with Germany meant, as Crowe had realised, that Britain had 'to keep up our own strength and to consolidate our international friendships'.[90]

The French, who had been worried by the Haldane mission, were anxious to 'strengthen and extend' their understanding with the British, and Cambon, claiming that Lansdowne had always meant to expand the area of the military conversations to include the navy, approached Grey in mid-April, just after the failure of the Haldane talks. He said that the French President, Raymond Poincaré, was always being asked 'how far France could rely upon British support in the event of difficulties with Germany'. But Nicolson had deprecated trying to strengthen the *entente* then, mainly because it would have looked rather pointed to have done so just after the failure of talks with Germany.[91] Nicolson had given this advice 'very much against the grain' and so welcomed an initiative from Cambon in May for closer naval co-operation between the two countries.[92]

The failure of the Haldane mission meant that the British would have to build their way to victory in the naval race, but committed as the Government was to an ambitious programme of domestic reform, the finance was not there. Churchill, now First Lord of the Admiralty, and always inclined to take a departmental view, argued that Britain should cut her coat according to her cloth and abandon the Mediterranean in order to concentrate her forces in the North Sea and the Channel. But that was going too far for Grey, who feared the effect which this would have on Britain's relations with her partners in the Triplice.[93] However, the French were willing to enter a naval agreement by which they would cover the Mediterranean in return for the British covering the North Sea area, which would meet Churchill's requirements in a way which would most definitely not damage Anglo-French relations.[94] But Harcourt,

Morley and others objected that starting naval conversations with France meant 'an alliance . . . under cover of "conversations" '.[95] McKenna argued powerfully in this vein in a paper to the CID in July, and wondered what price the French would demand 'for protecting us in the Mediterranean'.[96] An answer was not long in coming: the French would not transfer their fleet without a British pledge to intervene in a Continental war.[97] But having decided not to abandon the Mediterranean, it was, as Churchill reminded the CID, impossible to turn the French down flat.

When the Cabinet discussed the matter on 15 and 16 July, tempers became heated, with Churchill abusing and insulting McKenna for refusing to accept the logic of his case. It was agreed that there would be conversations with the French, but that the critics would be satisfied by being given assurances that they would not prejudice Britain's actions in the event of a war.[98] This was duly acknowledged in the draft agreement given to the French on 23 July.[99] But Churchill's view, that as the French had already decided to deploy their fleet in the Mediterranean they could hardly expect to be rewarded for it by the British, was too naïve by half.[100]

Grey, Asquith and Churchill wanted to be able to claim that they still had a 'free hand', but that they could also rely on the French fleet in the event of a war with Germany. Knowing the problems which the discussion was creating for Grey inside the Cabinet, Bertie advised Poincaré not to 'press his views', assuring him that as long as Grey remained, 'he might be sure that there would be no abandonment of the spirit of the entente'. But Poincaré replied that to begin a military and naval convention by pointing out that 'it means nothing so far as the Governments are concerned is superfluous and quite out of place'.[101] Grey risked losing the French if he made no commitment, but he risked a Cabinet crisis if he made the one the French wanted. Fortunately, the resources of diplomacy were equal to the job. A naval agreement which stated how the two Powers would co-operate *should* they become allies in the event of a war would not, technically, tie Britain's hands, and this ingenious suggestion of Bertie's provided the way out of Grey's dilemma.[102]

Churchill complained to Asquith on 22 August that to anyone who 'knows the facts', it would look as though 'we have all the obligations of an alliance without its advantages and above all without its precise definitions';[103] it is impossible to define the flaw in Grey's diplomacy better than this. Because he could not get precise commitments to the French past the Cabinet, Grey acquiesced in a series of diplomatic nudges and winks which meant whatever the French wanted. The three 'Grey–Cambon notes' which were eventually exchanged in November recognised that conversations between experts had taken place; that they were not binding on their Governments; and that in the event of a threatening situation arising, the two Governments would consult with each other.[104]

Grey knew that 'public opinion would not support an aggressive war for *revanche* or to hem Germany in', but he was convinced that if she 'was led by her great, I might say unprecedented strength, to attempt to crush France, I did not think we should stand by and look on, but should do all we could to prevent France from being crushed'.[105] But Grey's assumptions about public opinion would not, as he realised, apply in the event of a war in the Balkans between Russia and Austria – 'yet our abstention would prove a danger to the present grouping of the European Powers'.[106] Grey's policy would only work if the Germans actually attacked the French, and even then, as Salisbury had always said it would, much depended upon circumstances.

23

'Measurable distance of Armageddon'

Grey's fixed version of the 'balance of power' prevented him from appreciating what was becoming only too apparent to the Germans, which was that changes in it since 1906 had been uniformly unfavourable to Germany. The Agadir crisis had forced the Germans to contemplate a war against the Dual Alliance, and the prospect had not been a reassuring one. Against France, as in the first Moroccan crisis, the Germans would have a chance since they had nearly 613,000 men available compared with France's 593,000 and a superiority in armament;[1] but as Count Helmuth von Moltke, the Chief of the German General Staff, warned Bethmann-Hollweg on 2 December 1911: 'The political grouping of Europe today will make an isolated war between France and Germany as far as can be foreseen impossible . . . the remaining Great Powers will be drawn in in such a way as to force active intervention upon them.'[2] If the Russian army of 1,345,000 was added to the equation, along with the British army of 130,000–150,000 men, then the German Empire was in trouble, which would be made worse by the fact that Austria's army would have to be divided to take account of the danger from Serbia on her southern borders.

In this ominous situation it had been decided to embark upon a massive expansion of the army. For Bethmann-Hollweg this had the additional benefit of restricting Tirpitz's demands for more money for his navy, which ought to have helped him improve relations with Britain. Germany's programme may have looked threatening, but it was inspired by the feeling of being threatened. For a decade and more money had been poured into battleships, but the British were winning the naval race, Anglo-German relations had been damaged and the real source of German power, her army, had been neglected.[3] Germany's position deteriorated still further in the aftermath of the Balkan wars of 1912 and 1913, which eliminated Turkey as any sort of military factor and provided a League of Balkan States viscerally hostile to Austria.

Developments in the west seemed almost equally threatening to Germany. In the aftermath of Agadir, a great revival of French nationalism had brought the combative Lorrainer, Poincaré, to power, and he had responded to the German military law with measures of his own, designed to increase the size of the French army. In July 1912, the Russians increased the annual call-up by 20,000 men to 450,000 a year, which meant that by 1913 they had 1,300,000 men ready, whilst the French had about 700,000. Germany, by comparison, had only 782,000 troops available, and the Austrians could only provide 400,000 men. But Vienna would have to face a challenge from Serbia and Montenegro, who might be able to muster nearly the same number of men – and they only had to fight on one front.[4] With French finance, the Russians were improving their railway system, and would soon be able to mobilise more swiftly and move troops towards East Prussia more speedily than the Schlieffen plan allowed for.[5] The development of the Balkan League provided Russia with a proxy alliance on Austria's southern flank, and as consultations with the French in September 1912 showed, if a general war did break out over the spoils of the Ottoman Empire, France would stand by her alliance.

By September 1912, the Balkan League was in place and ready to attack the Turks.[6] Poincaré was right to see it as 'an agreement for war' against Austria as well, but he did nothing to dissuade the

Russians from launching their unguided missile into the Balkan powder-keg.[7] The French were confident that a war in the Balkans would work to their advantage. The General Staff doubted whether Berlin would let the Austrians become involved in any Balkan adventure, but if they did, and a general war resulted, then they reckoned that the 'Triple Entente would have the best chances of success and might gain a victory which would enable the map of Europe to be redrawn'. The Austrians would have to keep at least seven of their sixteen army corps in the Balkans, which would so weaken their ability to attack Russia in Galicia that the Russians would be able to launch an all-out offensive on the weak German forces stationed in East Prussia. If the Germans countered by strengthening those forces, then with British help, the French would enjoy a numerical superiority in an attack on Lorraine.[8]

When Poincaré saw Izvolsky after returning from St Petersburg, he reaffirmed his view that the Balkan League was *'un instrument de guerre'*. He expected a Serbian attack on Turkey to produce an Austrian declaration of war on Serbia, in which case Russia would not remain indifferent – and there would probably be *'la guerre générale'*. It was hardly likely that the 'Concert' could put pressure on Turkey to yield territory without a war, and it was equally unlikely that the Balkan states would listen to counsels of moderation; all that could be done was to try to intervene quickly with proposals of mediation if war did break out. But a Bulgarian defeat, or an attack by Austria on Serbia, must bring Russia into military action against either Turkey or Austria. Poincaré confirmed that France would abide by her alliance and offer all possible diplomatic support, but military action would depend upon the state of parliamentary and public opinion. However, if Germany entered the fray, then the Dual Alliance would come into play and France would recognise the *casus fœderis* and would fulfil her obligations. France was undoubtedly *'pacifiquement'*, but German intervention would *'modifierait immédiatement cette état d'esprit'*. He told Izvolsky about the optimistic views of the French General Staff; the fact that Italy would be unable to intervene on the side of the Triple Alliance because of her involvement in

Tripoli was, of course, an uncovenanted bonus for the Dual Alliance.[9]

When Grey was canvassed on the question of what Britain would do in the event of a Russo-German war, he told Sazonov on 24 September that although it would depend on the circumstances of such a war, if it involved the danger of France being crushed then it was unlikely Britain could stand aside. Britain would not guarantee Berlin that she would stay out of a war: 'If Germany dominated the policy of the Continent it would be disagreeable to us as well as to others, for we would be isolated.'[10]

The Balkan League's assault on Turkey, which began in early October, had, by November, ejected the Grand Turk from most of his European provinces; outside the great imperial capital only the fortresses of Adrianople, Janina and Scutari remained, along with the heavily defended Gallipoli Peninsula. Slavdom was triumphant. The victory of the Balkan League was, in A.J.P. Taylor's plangent phrase, 'a disaster beyond remedy for the Habsburg Monarchy'.[11] Russia was obviously bound to support the territorial demands of her Balkan allies, and Austria was equally bound to oppose any demands which worsened her strategic situation. Sir George Buchanan, the new British Ambassador in Russia, reported that the expectation there was that Britain, 'as a member of the Triple Entente', would 'support Russia in advocating the cause of the Balkan States'. This meant that the 'ultimate fate' of the *entente* was 'now in England's hands', and if she failed 'the first time she was appealed to', it would 'lose its value' in Russian eyes. Grey, who doubted that the Russians would support an annexationist peace, thought that 'we should . . . try to steer a moderate course as long as we can'.[12]

As it transpired, it was only the fact that the Germans, too, wished to steer their ally into a moderate course, that prevented a general war from breaking out in 1913. Bethmann-Hollweg shared Grey's view that the Powers should stay out of the war and try to mediate when the occasion arose.[13] In late October, he told Goschen that although the moment was not yet right for mediation, he hoped the Powers would keep in touch so that when it was 'they could act without hesitation or delay'. He also laid 'stress upon the good effect which common action between England and Germany would have on Anglo-German relations' by drawing public attention away from areas of conflict to ones where they had similar interests; that would conduce to the creation of an atmosphere in which other matters might be discussed.[14] The German Chargé, Richard von Kühlmann, reported that Tyrrell, Grey's private secretary, had said that the Foreign Secretary wanted to use the discussions to move towards some sort of 'confidential political relationship' with Germany.[15]

Sir Lewis Namier argued that this report was, in effect, a replay of Eckardstein's clumsy manoeuvres, and that whatever the faults of Grey's new private secretary, he was not a 'pro-German'; but that is testimony more to Namier's feelings about Germany than to the accuracy of Kühlmann's account.[16] Bethmann-Hollweg was cautious about the indirect method of approach which Grey had chosen, but he was quite happy to propose that the two Powers should co-operate on Balkan matters.[17] Grey agreed that they should stay in touch and let Austria and Russia take the leading part on behalf of the 'Concert of Europe'.[18]

The Austrians were prepared to acquiesce in what could not be remedied and to acknowledge the territorial acquisitions of the Balkan League, but when the Serbs and Montenegrins showed every sign of wanting to take over most of Albania and to acquire access to the Adriatic, that was more than they were willing to accept. The Italians, who had as little desire as the Austrians to see competitors in the Adriatic, joined in their protests.[19] The fact that the Russians seemed prepared to back the Balkan states raised the spectre of a general war.[20]

In early November, the Russians ordered a highly provocative 'trial mobilisation' in Poland and retained nearly half a million conscripts who were due for release. The Russian War Minister, General Sukhomilinov, decided to mobilise the entire Kiev district and part of the Warsaw district, and was even prepared to order a partial mobilisation of the whole army, which under the terms of the Dual Alliance would have brought Germany to

Austria's side.[21] At a meeting at Tsarskoe Selo on 23 November, Vladimir Kokovtsov, the Russian Minister of Finance, was able to combine with Sazonov and other politicians to warn the Tsar that the result of this policy would be a war against the Dual Alliance Powers;[22] reluctantly Nicholas agreed not to go ahead with the mobilisation orders.

Similar scenes were enacted in Vienna. The ever-bellicose Conrad, now returned to office, demanded action in the face of Russian provocation.[23] Franz Ferdinand, in contrast to his attitude during the Bosnian crisis, also favoured stern measures and argued strongly in early December that the decisive moment had come.[24] Again, it was the combination of Finance Ministers and the Foreign Minister, Leopold Berchtold, which prevailed when Franz Joseph met with his counsellors on 11 December at the Schönbrunn Palace. Conrad still pressed for war, but with Franz Joseph against 'military adventure', Berchtold's arguments against it prevailed. It is in this context, rather than as a prelude to World War I, that the famous 'War Council' of the Kaiser's on 8 December should be considered.

A good deal of the thesis propounded by the eminent German historian, Fritz Fischer, which posits aggressive German designs for European hegemony, rests upon the so-called 'War Council' of 8 December 1912.[25] According to this line of argument, the Kaiser and his advisers took the decision to go to war at this meeting, but decided that it must be postponed until 1914 when Germany would be ready for the conflict. But Fischer's critics have cited four main arguments against this interpretation: in the first place, the meeting was not a properly constituted 'War Council', since Bethmann-Hollweg and other Ministers were absent; in the second place, Poincaré's promise to Izvolsky in September essentially transformed the nature of the Dual Alliance from a defensive to an offensive arrangement; thirdly, the first Balkan war was, in effect, a Russian war of aggression by proxy; and finally, the so-called 'decisions' were all soon cancelled by Bethmann-Hollweg as soon as he learned of them.[26] The 'Council', like the meetings in St Petersburg and Vienna, showed that the military were quite prepared to go to war – but that the politicians remained firmly against it, and that they were in control.

In an attempt to ensure that the Great Powers retained some control over the situation, Bethmann-Hollweg and Grey agreed to sponsor the idea of a conference of ambassadors;[27] but neither the Germans nor the Austrians were keen on Paris as the venue for this, since it would allow Izvolsky too much latitude for interference.[28] The conference, which started meeting just before Christmas, took until May to reach a conclusion satisfactory to the Great Powers, but its achievements should not be oversold: it did not witness any loosening of the tie which bound the two rival camps, and the final settlement owed as much to unilateral action as to co-operation.

The Germans did not abandon the Austrians. They made it perfectly plain from an early stage that Germany would stand by her ally in resisting Russian support for Serb claims to an Adriatic port.[29] Bethmann-Hollweg's oration in the Reichstag on 3 December declaring support for Austria surprised the British, but the Germans maintained that the speech had been designed to calm down the hotheads in Vienna by assuring them that they needed to take no impulsive actions.[30] The sudden and unexpected death of Alfred von Kiderlen-Wachter brought a new German Foreign Minister, Gottlieb von Jagow, to office, but he assured Grey of his eagerness to continue the co-operation begun under his predecessor. He was willing to admit that German diplomacy had given rise to much anxiety in Britain and elsewhere, but he protested his desire to work for better Anglo-German relations, and to begin in the Balkans, where neither side wished to see a Russo-Austrian war. He candidly admitted that the consequences of the dissolution of the Habsburg Empire would be disastrous for Germany.[31] Wilhelm himself, for all his bellicose talk, was anxious lest the refusal of the Turks to conclude an armistice would lead Russia to intervene, and he was keen that Britain and Germany, as the two Powers 'least interested in the Balkans', should mediate.[32] Nearly a quarter of a century after dismissing Bismarck, Wilhelm had finally turned to his old policy of Anglo-German co-operation as a way of preventing the Balkans from causing an Austro-Russian war from which Germany would be the loser.

But in 1877, 1887 and even a decade later, Britain had been a genuine counter-weight to Russian ambitions; now Grey was simply anxious lest his support for Russia should drag him into a war he did not want. Thus, whilst he would co-operate with Germany, there were limits to how far he would go. He approved of George V's statement to the Kaiser's son, Prince Henry, that 'under certain circumstances' Britain would 'come to the assistance' of France and Russia.[33] Grey doubted whether public opinion would favour a war over Serbia, but he thought that if Austria attacked her and Russia came to her assistance, 'and France were then involved, it might become necessary for England to fight . . . for the defence of her position in Europe and for the protection of her own future and security'.[34]

Similarly Germany was now bound to Austria-Hungary in a way which had not been the case three decades earlier, as her position now seemed to be critical; the dissolution of the Habsburg Empire would have incalculable consequences for Germany.[35] The real common ground between Grey and Jagow was a desire to restrain their partners. The London conference proved fruitful in getting acceptance of the idea of Albanian independence, but the resumption of the war by the Turks in February, and the refusal of the Montenegrins and the Serbs to surrender access to the Adriatic put strains upon this renewal of the Concert of Europe.[36] Throughout the crisis Grey had been concerned not to divide Europe along the lines of the Triple *Entente* and the Triple Alliance,[37] despite Nicolson's fear that the Russians and the French would misinterpret this as a move towards Germany.[38] In fact, Izvolsky reassured Sazonov on this score, citing the Anglo-French naval conversations as evidence. Izvolsky knew all about Britain's famous 'free hand', but his view that the *'cours irrésistible des événements'* would bring her to *'une intervention armée contre l'Allemagne* [the irresistible course of events would bring her to an armed intervention against Germany]' was given powerful support by Grey's actions in the crisis which developed over the question of whether or not the Albanians had Scutari.[39]

Nicolson thought that irrespective of the merits of the Austrian case, the fact that the Russians were under the impression that the 'Triple *Entente*' had not brought them any gains obliged Britain to support them regardless of the merits of the case.[40] Grey made it plain that he could give no more than 'diplomatic support as it would be considered here that these questions are not, if taken by themselves sufficient cause for a European war'.[41] But this caveat remained verbal and was never presented to Sazonov in writing;[42] it was also subject to Grey's comment to the King that an attack by Austria on Serbia might well bring England into a war.[43]

During January 1913, it gradually dawned upon Grey that the issue of the future of Scutari could actually lead to war; fortunately, Bethmann-Hollweg had had the same epiphany. Berchtold had sent a special envoy to Berlin in mid-January, but he reported that there would be no support at all for a war against Russia.[44] The Kaiser wrote to Franz Ferdinand on 13 February telling him bluntly that it was Austria and Russia and their mobilisation of troops which prevented a calming down, and he asked whether Scutari was really that important.[45] Under this pressure the Austrians decided to compromise on the question of Albania's frontiers. But on 23 April, Scutari fell to the Montenegrins, who refused Austrian demands to leave;[46] the ambassadors' conference agreed that King Nikita should be informed that he was expected to evacuate the port.[47] The Austrians had reached the limit of their patience. Berchtold had made concession after concession to keep the 'Concert' together, and from Vienna the British Ambassador, Sir Fairfax Cartwright, reported that the general view was that she could concede no more without a fatal blow being struck to her prestige.[48] Conrad, taking the position that he had been right all along and that force should have been used, redoubled his attempts to go down that route; but Berchtold held out for a diplomatic solution.[49]

The Germans continued to support Berchtold's line, but were

anxious not to push the Austrians too far. Prince Karl Max Lichnowsky, the German Ambassador at the conference, proposed that the Powers should agree either to collective action against the Montenegrins, or, if that failed, to allow Austria to act either alone or with Italian help.[50] The Kaiser, who criticised Grey for 'flabbiness', was correct in his instinct that he did not want to offend the Russians.[51] Grey had discussed the line to be taken over Austria's demands with France and Russia on 28 April,[52] and he was unwilling to participate in anything which had the 'appearance of acting against the wishes of Russia and separating ourselves from France', particularly at a moment when 'it seems most necessary that we should keep in touch with her and with Russia'.[53]

In the face of inaction from London, even Berchtold now began to look towards a military solution. At a tense Crown Council meeting on 2 May, he agreed that the Empire could not afford to be defied by Montenegro, and that they could not let Serbia have an outlet to the Adriatic, even if the attempt to prevent these things led to war. It was agreed to deploy 50,000 troops against Montenegro, and steps were to be taken to get the army ready for war.[54] The 'Concert' had now broken down. Had the Montenegrins persisted in their obduracy, then it is difficult to see how war could have been avoided.[55] The Austrians were determined to act; the Germans were committed to helping them if Russia intervened; Russia was committed to her Slav protégés; and although France did not want to go to war, as recently as November Poincaré had told Izvolsky that *'si la Russie fait la guerre, La France la fera aussi'*.[56] Britain's 'free hand' amounted to little in these circumstances, as Grey's comments to George V had revealed. Yet war over Scutari was hardly something which could have been sold very easily to the British public, or his colleagues in the Liberal Party; there was even a sizeable segment of the Cabinet which would have jibbed at the notion.[57] From these snares of his own devising Grey was spared by King Nikita of Montenegro. On the evening of 4 May, the conference in London received the news that the Montenegrins had agreed to the demands of the Powers and were going to evacuate Scutari.

Grey 'had felt throughout this crisis, that if Russia and Austria went to war, there was not one of us . . . that might not be drawn into it'.[58] If that had happened, then the Germans could no longer be in any doubt about the likely British attitude. On 25 November, Goschen had asked Nicolson what Britain would do in the event of a war,[59] and whilst Nicolson skirted giving a straight answer,[60] he warned him not to assume that Britain would only go to war if she were to be attacked.[61] On 3 December, Lichnowsky reported Haldane's comment that British policy was to maintain the existing balance of forces, and that she could never allow France to be overthrown, or allow Germany to secure hegemony in Europe.[62] When this catalogue is set alongside George V's comments to Prince Henry of Prussia, it was not surprising that the Germans might have concluded by December 1912 that war might be inevitable.

Cartwright had thought that Europe would be lucky to escape without a major war from the crisis; his fear that 'next time a Serbian crisis arises' Austria 'will refuse to admit of any Russian interference in the dispute', and 'proceed to settle her difference' whatever the cost,[63] turned out to be only too accurate. He thought that even if there was not another crisis immediately, the Austrians would be provoked by the new Serb self-confidence into taking action against the Piedmont of the South Slavs. Such action, he predicted, would lead to 'a war with Russia, and probably to a general conflict in Europe'.[64] But, as Grey's attitude throughout the 1913 crisis had revealed, it would be far from easy to secure parliamentary and public approval for a war originating in the Balkans; and so it proved the following year.

The assassination of Franz Ferdinand on 28 June 1914 seemed, at first, to presage simply another tiresome crisis over the Balkans. Most Liberal Ministers thought little of it, and even fewer would have been willing to go to war over a far-away country about which most of them knew nothing.[65] In so far as the thought of war entered the minds of most Ministers in July 1914, it was in the context of a possible civil war breaking out over Unionist resistance to their Home Rule plans for Ireland. The Prime Minister himself gave little or no attention to the incipient European crisis before 24 July – nearly a month after the assassination.[66] Speaking at the Mansion House on 17 July, Lloyd George declared that while there was never a 'perfect blue sky in foreign affairs', he expected to get over the current difficulties well enough. On 23 July, he told the Commons that relations with Germany were 'very much better' than they had been a 'few years before'. That same day the Austrians delivered an ultimatum to the Serbs which required them, in effect, to submit to Austrian domination or fight.[67] Grey told his colleagues on 24 July that Serbia would fight, which would mean that Russia would declare war on Austria, which, in turn, would make it 'difficult both for Germany and France to refrain from lending a helping hand to one side or the other'. As Asquith put it to his confidante, Venetia Stanley, 'we are within measurable, or unimaginable, distance of a real Armageddon'.[68] On 28 July, that distance was reduced considerably with the issuing of the Austrian declaration of war against Serbia.

This did not produce some great outburst in favour of going to war for Serbia. The Conservative leader, Andrew Bonar Law, told Grey on 29 July that he doubted whether his Party 'would be unanimous or overwhelmingly in favour of war, unless Belgian neutrality were invaded; in that event, he said, it would be unanimous'.[69] The problem for Grey was that Britain's 'Triple *Entente*' partners now presented their cheques for encashment. On 27 July, the Russians made it plain that they expected Britain to declare solidarity with them.[70] On 30 July, Cambon called at the Foreign Office to remind Grey of the letters which they had exchanged in 1912 in which it had been agreed that if the peace of Europe were ever seriously threatened, the two Governments would consult about what action to take. Grey took note of his remarks and promised to see him after the following morning's Cabinet.[71] When Cambon turned up on 31 July, it was to hear the news that no pledge could be given. As Grey told Bertie, 'Feeling is quite different from what it was in the Morocco question.'[72] It had been agreed in Cabinet that 'British public opinion would not now enable us to support France'; that doughty opponent of the 'Triple *Entente*', Harcourt, noted with satisfaction that, 'It is now clear that *this* Cabinet will not join in the war.'[73]

The news was no more cheerful from the French point of view on 1 August. After the Cabinet had met, Grey told Cambon that 'France must take her own decision at this moment without reckoning on an assistance which we were not now in a position to promise.' Cambon refused to transmit such a message to his Government. 'White and speechless', he staggered into Sir Arthur Nicolson's room; when he could pluck up speech, it was to mutter '*Ils vont nous lâcher*' – 'They are going to abandon us.' Nicolson told Grey angrily that 'You will render us a by-word among nations.' After consultation with Cambon, Nicolson reminded Grey that, in accordance with the 1912 naval agreements, the French had deprived their northern coasts of all naval defence. It was little wonder that when he saw the foreign editor of *The Times*, Henry Wickham-Steed, Cambon should have declared: '*J'attends de savoir si le mot honneur doit être rayé du vocabularie anglais* [I am waiting to see whether the word honour ought to be erased from the English language].'

The Cabinet had been informed of Bethmann-Hollweg's assurance to Grey on 30 July that provided Britain remained neutral, Germany would exact no territorial penalties from Metropolitan France, neither would she attack Holland, nor yet Belgium, provided the latter did not take sides against Germany. Grey had refused to guarantee British neutrality on such terms,[74] but he was unable to deliver a British declaration of war on them either. The crisis had come over the wrong issue. No British Foreign Secretary could make commitments involving a *casus belli* in advance; everything depended on the circumstances, and the circumstances on 1 August 1914 failed to command the assent of the Liberal Party to a declaration of support for France and Russia.

Campbell-Bannerman's former private secretary and successor as Liberal MP for Stirling Burghs, the radical Arthur Ponsonby, wrote to Churchill on 31 July saying that although MPs had 'held back so far' because they did not want to embarrass Grey, 'the most emphatic opinion has been expressed that we should on no account be drawn into war when our interests are not immediately affected and no treaty obligations bind us'. Churchill agreed that so long as that situation obtained, 'we sh[oul]d remain neutral. Balkan quarrels are no vital concern of ours'; but he warned that a 'German attack upon France or Belgium w[oul]d raise other issues'.[75] Churchill's answer was politically astute. Whatever his own feelings, and whatever moral obligations Grey supposed that Britain was under, there was no reason which public opinion would have accepted as being a sufficient excuse for Britain to participate in a European war.

Before news of Germany's declaration of war on Russia reached London on 1 August, the Cabinet had had a stormy session. Churchill wanted to mobilise the Royal Navy completely, but he could not secure the approval of the Cabinet. Lord Morley was completely against any intervention, as was Edwin Montagu; but the crucial man was Lloyd George. As Chancellor, and the leading radical figure in the Government, he commanded a powerful position; as the author of the Mansion House speech in 1911, he could no longer be accused of pacifism, and he was firmly against going to war in the present circumstances. But he was also firmly against declaring in favour of neutrality. If Lloyd George was a definite 'maybe', Grey was, of course, decidedly in favour of helping the French – provided the circumstances were right.[76] Here the key question was the position if Belgium was attacked by Germany. Churchill tried to persuade Lloyd George to declare himself in favour of war in that event, but he would not, despite Churchill's urgings that the naval war 'will be cheap – not more than 25 millions a year'.[77] When the news of Germany's declaration of war reached London, Asquith approved the mobilisation of the fleet. On the morning of 2 August, news came through that the Germans were rumoured to have violated French territory.

Two phenomena now began to shift the balance towards war: the first, of course, was the possibility that the Germans were going to attack the French; the second was the nature of the war which many politicians thought they were getting themselves into. Grey assured Cambon on the morning of 2 August that the British 'fleet would not allow the Germans to make the Channel the basis of hostile operations';[78] this was a statement which commanded almost universal support in the Cabinet. With the exception of the pacifist John Burns, even the non-interventionists could agree with it; after all, it did not mean a declaration of war – unless the Germans mounted naval operations in the Channel; and even then, it only meant Churchill's 'cheap' naval war.

The Cabinet which decided to issue the assurance to Cambon on 2 August had also revealed that the Government was 'on the brink of a split'. Lloyd George, Morley, Harcourt and some less senior figures all stood out against intervention. Had the Cabinet actually split, Asquith knew that the Unionist leadership was promising him support, but he thought that three-quarters of his own Party were 'for absolute non-interference at any price', and doubted whether an alternative Government could be formed.[79] Grey was willing to break up the Government: 'I believe war will come and it is due to France they shall have our support'. He told his colleagues that 'We have led France to rely upon us, and unless we support her in her agony, I cannot continue at the Foreign Office.'[80] At dinner that evening Lloyd George said he would be willing to fight if Belgium was attacked, but 'strongly insisted upon the danger of aggrandizing Russia'. Sir John Simon went even further and argued that, 'We have always been wrong when we have intervened. Look at the Crimea. The Triple Entente was a terrible mistake. Why should we support a country like Russia?' Lloyd George doubted whether the Cabinet would actually hold together.[81]

By the morning of 3 August, Asquith had written out the mobilisation orders for the army; he had also had letters of resignation from the three Johns – Burns, Morley and Simon – and from Lord Beauchamp. Only the news of the German ultimatum to Belgium offered Asquith, in a perverse sort of way, any political hope.[82] It was in this highly charged atmosphere that Grey rose to address the House that afternoon on the theme of why 'British interests . . . honour and . . . obligations' all justified entry into the war.[83]

Grey denied that Britain had any 'obligations' deriving from the 'Triple *Entente*' which forced her into war; although literally true, it hardly tallied with his statement to the Cabinet that 'We have led France to rely on us.' It was true only in that literal way in which politicians use the truth when they want to gloss over inconvenient facts, as Grey implicitly acknowledged when he asked 'every man' to 'look into his own heart' to decide 'how far' the Anglo-French 'friendship' entailed 'obligation'. But he knew he could not carry the House on a point which had failed to deliver full Cabinet support, and by switching to the subject of Britain's obligations to Belgium, Grey was on safer ground; even Harcourt had agreed that that constituted a *casus belli*. It was a sign of the skill with which the speech had been drafted that having won over his audience, Grey then moved to the theme which had been so much a part of his thinking over the past eight years – the danger of German hegemony, which, he argued, it was in England's interests to prevent. He did not believe that 'at the end of this war, even if we stood aside and remained aside', Britain would be able to 'undo what had happened in the course of the war'. Britain would have to go to war.

When the Cabinet met again at six o'clock to consider what response to make to Germany's ultimatum to Belgium, it was announced that Sir John Simon and Lord Beauchamp had withdrawn their resignations. Although the Belgian issue was the occasion for Simon's action, it was hardly the only cause, as he told a fellow Liberal MP, Christopher Addison: 'an important consideration with him was that . . . if a block were to leave the Government at this juncture, their action would necessitate a Coalition Government which would assuredly be the grave of Liberalism'.[84]

At 11 p.m. on 4 August, Britain's ultimatum to Germany requiring her to withdraw from Belgium expired, and from that point a state of war existed between the two countries. In 1912, Churchill had pointed out the danger that the naval agreement

SPLENDID ISOLATION?

with France would oblige Britain to go to her rescue; now it had; or rather, Grey's insistence that he would break up the Government rather than leave France in the lurch had done so. In 1906, he had thought that deserting France would lead Britain into dangerous isolation, and he had learnt and forgotten nothing since then. The decision for war was eased by the fact that most Ministers expected Britain's commitment to be mainly naval in character, and no one could anticipate that in escaping from the 'isolation' Grey so feared, Britain had taken a leap into the dark.

Conclusion

In 1872, Disraeli had told his audience at the Crystal Palace that they faced a choice: 'whether you will be content to be a comfortable England, modelled and moulded upon Continental principles . . . or whether you will be a great country, an Imperial country'.[1] Disraeli's vision of England's role in the world was of a cosmopolitan military Empire with a group of English-speaking colonies who might be forged into an Imperial Federation; it was a vision he bequeathed to the Conservative Party, and which provided the real connection between it and Joseph Chamberlain. This Disraelian vision could attract the new democracy to the old order, and its assertion that England's freedom should not be trammelled by any considerations save that of her self-interest, played well to the gallery of popular opinion.

But, as Disraeli had acknowledged, there were other versions of England's role in the world. The Liberal vision saw England as part of the Concert of Europe, owing and owning a moral duty towards other States, and was suitably outraged at the amorality, if not downright immorality, of Beaconsfieldism. Gladstone explicitly subscribed to the notion of a community of nations, and implicitly acknowledged that there were laws by which it should be governed. His ideals were noble ones, but ill-suited to the Bismarckian era. With the ruin of Prussian militarism in 1918, they would re-emerge with an American accent to inspire the League of Nations. But as one of the architects of the military talks with France, Sir Henry Wilson, commented to the liberal historian Harold Temperley even before the League was functioning: 'You're trying to run a League of Nations – on a basis of what – not of force – You can't';[2] nor, in the era of Hitler and Stalin could they. But that did not stop Roosevelt from trying it again in 1945, although his conception of the United Nations gave more of a role to the Great Powers, who would, he hoped, have the same interest in maintaining order. But since Russia and the United States could not agree on the nature of that order, the neo-Gladstonism of the United Nations was not noticeably more successful than its predecessors. The end of the Cold War would bring with it hopes of a 'new International Order', but what would be most noticeable would be the reassertion of the old international disorder, which would even give rise to lamentations for the certainties of the Cold War era.

There was also a third version of England's role in the world on offer, which Disraeli did not mention because it was the one he was reacting to in calling his Party to a new vision, and that was the old Conservative 'school of Economy, Peace [and] Sound and strict Finance'.[3] Derby's response to the expansion of military power on the Continent in 1875 was to wonder 'how long these enormous armaments will be endured by the masses who are compelled to serve'. As a pragmatic English politician he had no wish to argue against all further expenditure on 'abstract and general grounds', but sought instead to ask what 'is justifiable'. Beyond that 'we cannot go', he warned Disraeli in June 1875.[4] But it was the nature of Disraeli's Conservatism to go beyond what Derby would think was reasonable, and in so doing he could, and did, use the argument that this was what would appeal to the new democracy. Derby's position was strong enough to make Disraeli cautious, but the way he played his political cards allowed Disraeli to win the trick.

But that should not lead to the conclusion that he won the

argument totally. Under Salisbury the Party's image may have been imperial and Disraelian, but its diplomatic practice differed little from the old Country Party line favoured by Derby. Gladstone had complained in 1885 that Conservatism so-called, in its daily practice, now depends largely on inflaming public passion, and thereby has lost the main element which made it really Conservative, and qualified it to resist 'excessive and dangerous innovation';[5] but the outstanding feature of Salisbury's diplomacy was that that was just what did not happen under it. Indeed, inflamed public passion was as much a Salisburian aversion as it was a Gladstonian one, and like the Philistine of old, he was assaulted by the jaw bones of many asses. Salisbury eschewed any general policy and 'worked from hand to mouth', but he thought that a 'European war . . . was . . . a calamity which we should do our utmost to prevent'.[6] The fears about 'isolation' were secondary to the greater fear of the catastrophe of a European war, and Salisbury never moved from the position that a Continental commitment would cost Britain more than it would benefit her.

It was left to Grey to take the view that 'isolation' was the greatest danger, as it would leave Britain facing German hegemony. As early as 1905, it had been apparent to Lansdowne and Sanderson that whatever else was true of Germany, her international position was deteriorating. The assumptions upon which *Weltpolitik* was based were already proving to be incorrect: the 'inevitable' war between Britain and one or both members of the Franco-Russian alliance had not occurred; Britain had not responded to the dangers of isolation by joining the Triple Alliance; and Tirpitz's fleet had, far from intimidating the British, antagonised them. A few more years of Bülow's diplomacy completed the ruin of the diplomatic position which Wilhelm had inherited from Bismarck. This all passed Grey by, as his assumptions remained fixed in the 1890s.

Inherent in the old Country Party view was the belief that provided the Royal Navy was kept up, isolation was not dangerous. Britain had not been threatened by Bismarck's triumphs, and on the eve of war Lloyd George was able to respond to the question: 'How shall we feel if we see France overrun and annihilated by Germany?', with the comment: 'How will you feel if you see Germany overrun and annihilated by Russia?'[7] The war itself spawned arguments which validated, retrospectively, the view that Germany had been bent on mastery in Europe, which allowed the assumptions of Crowe, Grey and company to go unquestioned. The 'traditional British foreign policy' became that encapsulated in Crowe's famous memorandum of 1 January 1907. Yet to Henry Wilson in 1919, before the legends had set in, what was noticeable about what had just happened was that 'for the first time in our history we made war – i.e. really went into the scrum – i.e. reversed our historic role'.[8] The Great War established a different version of Britain's 'historic role', one more in tune with the Disraelian vision of Britain as a Great Power.

But, in reality, Britain had established her position as a Great Power by staying out of the 'scrum' whenever possible. She had grown great by the use of sea power and money, allowing her Continental rivals to exhaust themselves in costly European wars whilst she picked off their colonial possessions. It was true that after 1808 she had finally made a Continental commitment against Napoleon, but that was in Spain, developed by accident, and it could be afforded. However, after 1914 it came to be seen not as the exception to the rule, but as the rule itself. Thus by 1938 Neville Chamberlain came under heavy criticism from those like Churchill who spoke sonorously of his falling below the level of events and acting in a way which was not in accord with the traditions of British foreign policy. Rab Butler, the Foreign Office spokesman in the Commons under Lord Halifax, doubted whether a worldwide Empire had ever had a 'simple traditional policy' because 'British interests and the world itself are too complicated to enable us to follow any one high road'.[9] He was right, but he was right at the wrong time. Butler's attitudes placed him firmly in the Country Party tradition, and he could see a good case for staying out of the affairs of Central Europe and letting the Nazi and Communist dictatorships get on with attacking each other. This was not an easy, or even a practical, line in the aftermath of Munich, when the conviction grew that Hitler, like the Kaiser before him, had in mind European hegemony, and the popular instinct was to go with the Disraelian line of intervention.

The old Country Party Toryism asked whether intervention could be afforded and where it would lead; Winston Churchill's neo-Disraelianism disdained such questions and indulged in heady rhetoric about England's 'destiny'. It was little wonder that Butler should have indulged in spasms of disgust similar to those Derby experienced when he thought about Disraeli's obsession with 'prestige', and have commented that with Churchill's appointment, 'the good clean tradition of English politics, that of Pitt as opposed to Fox, had been sold to the greatest adventurer of modern political history'.[10] From his point of view he was right to see in the passing of Neville Chamberlain the passing of a traditional policy 'which had been responsible for so much of England's greatness'.[11]

Henceforth Britain's commitment would be to an Atlantic alliance that would allow her to play the Disraelian role which would bring its advocates rewards similar to those it had to Disraeli himself. The irony of it would be that it would end not with the 'imperial England' Disraeli – and Churchill – hankered after, but with one which would be 'modelled and moulded upon Continental principles'. But then, as Churchill had warned Grey in another age, the consequences of responsibilities without power cannot be foreseen.

Notes

Introduction

1. P. Smith, *Disraeli: A Brief Life* (Cambridge, 1996), p.217.
2. D.E. Lee, *Great Britain and the Cyprus Convention* (Cambridge, Mass., 1934), p.5.
3. Blake, *Disraeli* (1966), p.570. Other unfavourable analyses are to be found in A.J.P. Taylor, *The Struggle for Mastery in Europe 1848–1918* (1954), Richard Millman, *Britain and the Eastern Question 1875–1878* (Oxford, 1979) and R.W. Seton-Watson, *Disraeli, Gladstone and the Eastern Question* (1935).
4. Sir H. Maxwell, *Life and Letters of the Fourth Earl of Clarendon, vol. II* (1913), p.343.
5. G.E. Buckle, *The Life of Benjamin Disraeli, Earl of Beaconsfield, vol. V* (1920), pp.133–4.
6. *Hansard*, House of Commons, 3rd series, vol. XVI, 12 December 1826, cols 395–6.
7. *Hansard*, House of Commons, 3rd series, vol. CXXXII, 27 March 1854, col. 213.
8. *Hansard*, House of Commons, 3rd series, vol. CXXXII, 27 March 1854, cols 243–67.
9. *Hansard*, House of Commons, 3rd series, vol. CXXXII, 27 March 1854, cols 279–80.

10. J.E. Thorold Rogers (ed.), *Speeches on Questions of Public Policy by John Bright* (1869), pp.331–2.
11. *Hansard*, House of Commons, 3rd series, vol. CLXXXIV, 20 July 1866, col. 1256.
12. Bodleian Library, Oxford, Beaconsfield Papers, Dep. Hughenden 112/1 [henceforth Dep. Hughenden, followed by reference number], Derby to Disraeli, 22 January 1871, fos 185–6.
13. Dudley W.R. Bahlman (ed.), *The Diary of Sir Edward Walter Hamilton 1885–1906* (Hull, 1993), 17 October 1888, p.82.
14. *Hansard*, House of Lords, 3rd series, vol. CLXXXIV, 9 July 1866, cols 736–7.
15. Karl Marx, *The Eighteenth Brumaire of Louis Bonaparte* (Moscow, 1972 edn), p.10.
16. Dep. Hughenden 112/1, note by Mr Currie, 15 May 1876, fos 58–9.
17. Royal Archives, Windsor, R.A. H. 18.52, 57, 68, letters from Dean of Windsor to Queen Victoria, 27, 29 December 1877, 1 January 1878.
18. C. Barnett, *The Collapse of British Power* (1972); P.M. Kennedy, *The Realities Behind Diplomacy* (1980); B. Porter, *The Lion's Share* (1975); D. Reynolds, *Britannia Overruled* (1992); J. Young, *Britain and the World* (1996).

Chapter 1

1. Lee, pp.6–7; see Millman, pp. 4–6, for a survey of the evidence, and also, M. Swartz, *The Politics of British Foreign Policy in the Era of Disraeli and Gladstone* (1985), pp.33–8.
2. Lord Macaulay, *Critical and Historical Essays* (1874 edn), 'Chatham', p.294.
3. A.C. Benson and Viscount Esher (eds), *The Letters of Queen Victoria, 1st series, vol. II, 1844–1853* (1907), Victoria to the King of the Belgians, 23 March 1852, p.467.
4. Quoted in D. Harris, *A Diplomatic History of the Balkan Crisis of 1875–1878: The First Year* (Stanford, CA, 1969 edn), pp.21–2.
5. Dep. Hughenden 111/2, Stanley to Disraeli, 1 November 1855, fo. 41.

6. Dep. Hughenden 111/1, Stanley to Disraeli, 19 July 1852, fo. 93.
7. Dep. Hughenden 111/1, Stanley to Disraeli, 20 July 1853, fos 205–6.
8. J.R. Vincent (ed.), *Disraeli, Derby and the Conservative Party: The Political Journals of Lord Stanley 1849–69* (1978), 18 September 1865, p.236.
9. Dep. Hughenden 111/2, Stanley to Disraeli, 24 October 1852, fo. 18.
10. Lady Bughclere, *A Great Lady's Friendships* (1933), pp.3–5.
11. I owe these suggestions to Professor John Vincent of Bristol, to whom I am most grateful for guidance on this and other matters.
12. S.W. Jackman and H. Haasse (eds), *A Stranger in The Hague: The Letters of Queen Sophie of the Netherlands to Lady Malet, 1842–1877* (Durham, N.C., 1989), p.110.
13. Hatfield House, Papers of the 3rd Marquess of Salisbury [henceforth SP], SP/E/Derby Corr., draft letter, Salisbury to Derby, 1 December 1874.
14. SP/D/71–5, Salisbury to Lady Derby, 11 February 1874.
15. SP/E/Carnarvon Corr., Carnarvon to Salisbury, 7 February 1874.
16. Sir Arthur Hardinge, *The Life of Henry Howard Molyneux Herbert, Fourth Earl of Carnarvon, vol. II* (Oxford, 1925) [henceforth *Carnarvon II*], pp.58–63.
17. Dep. Hughenden 113/4, Lady Derby to Disraeli, 7 August 1874, fo. 66.
18. Blake, p.570.
19. G.E. Buckle (following W.F. Moneypenny), *The Life of Benjamin Disraeli, Earl of Beaconsfield, vol. VI* (1920) [henceforth Buckle VI] pp.546–7.
20. Sir H. Maxwell, *The Life and Letters of the Fourth Earl of Clarendon, vol II* (1913) p. 343.
21. *Hansard*, House of Commons, 3rd series, vol. CLXXVI, 4 July 1864, cols 744–6.
22. G.E. Buckle, *The Life of Benjamin Disraeli, Earl of Beaconsfield, vol. IV* (1916) [henceforth Buckle IV], p.467.
23. C.C. Eldridge, *British Imperialism in the Nineteenth Century* (1987), p. 125.
24. Buckle IV, speech at Aylesbury, April 1859, p. 231.
25. Buckle IV, speech in the Commons, 1866, p.467.

26. Buckle V, pp. 191–2.
27. A.P. Thornton, *The Imperial Idea and its Enemies* (1985 edn), p. xxxiii.
28. J. R. Vincent (ed), *A Selection from the Diaries of Edward Henry Stanley, 15th Earl of Derby 1868–1878* (Cambridge, 1994) [henceforth *Derby Diaries*], 29 November 1875, p.257.
29. Lord Zetland (ed.), *The Letters of Disraeli to Lady Bradford and Lady Chesterfield, vol. I: 1873 to 1875* (1929), Disraeli to Lady Bradford, 3 November 1875, p.298.
30. There is a considerable literature on this subject. In addition to H. Temperley, and L. Penson, *Foundations of British Foreign Policy from Pitt to Salisbury* (Cambridge, 1938) [henceforth *Foundations*] see also, M.S. Anderson, *The Eastern Question* (1966); J.A.R. Marriott, *The Eastern Question* (1917); Edward Ingram, *The Beginning of the Great Game in Asia 1828–1834* (Oxford, 1978).
31. *Foundations*, p.59.
32. F.S. Rodkey, 'Lord Palmerston's Policy for the Rejuvenation of Turkey, 1839–1841', in *Transactions of the Royal Historical Society*, 1929, pp.163–92; Sir Charles Webster, *The Foreign Policy of Palmerston, vol.II* (1951); K. Bourne, *Palmerston: The Early Years 1784–1841* (1982).
33. B.H. Sumner, *Russia and the Balkans 1870–1880* (Oxford, 1937) pp.35–56, for details.
34. J.B. Kelly, *Britain and the Persian Gulf 1785–1880* (Oxford, 1991 edn), p.260.
35. On all this see the brilliant trilogy by Edward Ingram, *The Beginning of the Great Game in Asia 1828–1834* (Oxford, 1979); *Commitment to Empire: Prophecies of the Great Game in Asia 1797–1800* (Oxford, 1981); *Britain's Persian Connection 1798–1828* (Oxford, 1992).
36. SP/D/71–5/29, Salisbury to Derby, 1 August 1874.
37. See Ingram, *Commitment to Empire*, pp. 61–4.
38. SP/E/Disraeli Corr., Disraeli to Salisbury, 28 October 1875.
39. Sir T.H. Sanderson and E.S. Roscoe (eds), *Speeches and Addresses of Edward Henry XVth Earl of Derby, vol. I* (1894) [henceforth *Derby Speeches I*], Edinburgh, 19 December 1875, p.277.
40. William L. Langer, *European Alliances and Alignments* (NY, 1956 revised edn), pp.23–4; Taylor, *The Struggle for Mastery*, pp.219–21.

41. *Derby Diaries*, 5 April 1875, 205.
42. Lothar Gall, *Bismarck: The White Revolutionary, vol. 2:1871–1898*, (1986),pp.45–8.
43. *Derby Diaries*, 20 May 1875, pp.217–18.
44. D. Harris, 'Bismarck's Advance to England, January 1876', in *Journal of Modern History*, vol. III, no. 4, December 1931, Lord Odo Russell to Derby, 3 January 1876, p.447.
45. SP/E/Disraeli Corr., Disraeli to Salisbury, 29 November 1876, fo. 183.
46. Bruce Waller, *Bismarck at the Crossroads* (1974), p.67.
47. E.T.S. Dugdale (ed.), *German Diplomatic Documents, 1871–1914, vol.I* (1928) [henceforth *GD*, followed by volume number] Kissingen memo., 15 June 1877, p. 54.
48. J.Y. Simpson, *The Saburov Memoirs* (Cambridge, 1929), p. 111.
49. G.H. Rupp, *A Wavering Friendship: Russia and Austria 1876–1878* (Cambridge, Mass., 1941) pp.17–44.
50. Barbara Jelavich, *Russia's Balkan Entanglements 1806–1914* (Cambridge, 1991), pp.1–27.
51. Langer, pp. 60–4.
52. Rupp, pp.3–11.
53. *GD I*, p.20; also Taylor, *The Struggle for Mastery*, p.233.
54. Rupp, pp.87–8.
55. Dep. Hughenden 112/4, Derby to Disraeli, 7 January 1876, fos 60–3.
56. *Derby Diaries*, 22 November 1875, p. 255.
57. *Derby Diaries*, 7 January 1876, p. 265.
58. Buckle VI, Disraeli to Derby, 9 January 1876, pp. 18–19.
59. SP/E/Derby Corr., Derby to Salisbury, 9 January 1876; *Derby Diaries*, 5, 7 January 1876, pp.265–6.
60. Harris, 'Bismarck's Advance to England . . .' pp.441–56.
61. *GD I*, II/29, Bülow to Münster, 4 January 1876, pp. 21–2.
62. *GD I*, II/29, Bülow to Münster, 4 January 1876, pp.21–2. The British version is at P[ublic] R[ecord] O[ffice], F[oreign] O[ffice] 64/850, no. 8, Lord Odo Russell to Derby, 2 January 1876.
63. SP/E/Currie Corr., Currie to Salisbury, 31 January 1880.
64. Quoted in Harris, p.22.
65. Borthwick Institute, York, Papers of the 1st Viscount Halifax, A 4/87a, Pt I, Lady Derby to Lord Halifax, 20 November 1878.

66. SP/E/Derby Corr., Derby to Salisbury, 2 December 1874.
67. British Library, Papers of the Ist Earl of Iddesleigh, Add. Mss. 50022, Derby to Northcote, 26 February 1877.
68. *Derby Speeches I*, Edinburgh, 19 December 1875, p.276.
69. Dep. Hughenden 112/2, Derby to Disraeli, June 1875, fo.202.
70. Halifax Mss., A 4/87a, Pt I, Lady Derby to Halifax, 24 November 1877.
71. G.E. Buckle (ed.), *The Letters of Queen Victoria, Second Series, vol. II* (1926) [henceforth *LQV II*], Queen Victoria to Crown Prince of Germany, 8 June 1875, p. 405.
72. *LQV II*, Queen Victoria to Derby, 9 February 1876, p.448.
73. SP/E/Derby Corr., Derby to Salisbury, 22 November 1876; *Derby Diaries*, 9 February 1876, p. 276.
74. Buckle VI, Derby to the Queen, 10 February 1876, pp.20–1.
75. FO 64/850, no. 9, Lord Odo Russell to Derby, 3 January 1876.
76. *Derby Diaries*, 11 January 1875, p.267.
77. Dep. Hughenden 112/4, Derby to Disraeli, 15 February 1876.
78. Buckle VI, Disraeli to Derby, 15 February 1876, p.21.
79. Dep. Hughenden 112/3, Derby to Disraeli, 27 April 1876, fo. 44.
80. Buckle VI, pp. 23–4.
81. Buckle VI, Disraeli to Derby, 15 May 1876, p.24.
82. Dep. Hughenden, Currie to Tenterden, 15 May 1876, fos 58–9.
83. Buckle VI pp. 24–5.
84. *Derby Diaries*, 16 May 1876, p. 297.
85. Dep. Hughenden 79/3, Ponsonby to Disraeli, 16 May 1876, fos 32–3.
86. Seton-Watson, p.35.
87. Seton-Watson, p.35.
88. Dep. Hughenden 107/1, Northcote to Disraeli, 4 January 1878, fos 139–40; 100/1, Carnarvon to Disraeli, 6 September 1876, fos 176–80.
89. Buckle VI, Disraeli to Derby, 25 May 1876, p.29.
90. Sumner, pp.56–80.
91. Sumner, p.31.
92. Sumner, pp.75–6.
93. Rupp, pp. 8–11.
94. Sumner, p.125.

95. Sumner, pp.131–4.
96. *Derby Diaries*, 9 June 1876, p.301; Dep. Hughenden 112/4, Derby to Disraeli, 4 June 1876, fo. 97.

Chapter 2

1. Buckle VI, Disraeli to Lady Bradford, 7 June 1876, p. 31.
2. Lord Zetland (ed.), *The Letters of Disraeli to Lady Bradford and Lady Chesterfield, vol. II: 1876–1881* (1929) [henceforth Zetland II] Disraeli to Lady Bradford, 13 June 1876, p.54.
3. Lee, pp.6–7, for the critics.
4. Charles and Barbara Jelavich, *Russia in the East 1876–1880* (Leiden, 1959), Jomini to Giers, 30 May/11 June 1876, p.13.
5. Seton-Watson, p. 103.
6. R.T. Shannon, *The Age of Disraeli 1868–1881* (1992), p.270.
7. Lady G. Cecil, *Life of Robert, Marquis of Salisbury, vol.II* (1921) [henceforth *Salisbury II*] Salisbury to Disraeli, 23 September 1876, p. 85.
8. Shannon, p. 271.
9. *Derby Diaries*, 9 June 1876, pp.300–1.
10. *Salisbury II*, p.136.
11. Dep. Hughenden 79/3, Lord John Manners to Disraeli, 1 June 1876, fos 74–5; *LOV II*, General Ponsonby to Derby, 18 June 1876, pp. 464–5; FO 64/852, Lord Odo Russell to Derby, 16 May 1876.
12. Dep. Hughenden 112/4, Russell to Derby, 3 June 1876, fos 103–4.
13. *LOV II*, Disraeli to the Queen, 7 June 1876, p.457.
14. Buckle VI, Disraeli to Manners, 7 June 1876, p.31.
15. Alan Cassels, *Ideology & International Relations in the Modern World* (1996), pp.85–6.
16. David F. Krein, *The Last Palmerston Government* (Iowa, 1978), p.170.
17. Dep. Hughenden 112/4, Russell to Derby, 3 June 1876, fos 103–4.
18. Dep. Hughenden 112/4, Russell to Derby, 10 June 1876, fos 109–10.
19. Buckle VI, Disraeli to the Queen, 18 June 1876; Derby to Ponsonby, 20 June 1876, pp. 33–4.

20. Dep. Hughenden 112/4, Russell to Derby, 10 June 1876, fo. 111.
21. Buckle VI, Disraeli to Lady Bradford, 13 June 1876 p.32; *Derby Diaries*, 26 July 1876, p.313.
22. R.W. Seton-Watson, 'Russo-British relations during the Eastern Crisis', *Slavonic and East European Review*, vol. III, 1934, Shuvalov to Gorchakov, 11 June 1876, pp. 672–5; Sumner, pp. 166–7.
23. Buckle VI, pp. 34–6.
24. Jelavich, Jomini to Giers, 30 May/11 June 1876, p. 12; Seton-Watson, 'Russo-British relations . . .', Gorchakov to Shuvalov, 14 June 1876.
25. Zetland II, Disraeli to Lady Chesterfield and Lady Bradford, 9 and 13 July 1876, pp. 57–8.
26. Buckle VI, Derby to General Ponsonby, 20 June 1876, pp.33–4.
27. Rupp, pp.126–7; Sumner, pp. 18–35; Hugh Seton-Watson, *The Russian Empire 1801–1917* (Oxford, 1967), pp. 449–51.
28. Jelavich, pp.5–6; Rupp, pp. 53–8.
29. Sumner, p. 19; Barbara Jelavich, *Russia's Balkan Entanglements*, pp. 143–4.
30. Jelavich, Jomini to Giers, 30 May/11 June 1876, p. 14.
31. A. Hawkins and J. Powell (eds), *The Journal of John Wodehouse, First Earl of Kimberley for 1862–1902* (1997), p.54.
32. Jelavich, Jomini to Giers, 3/15 June 1876, p.16.
33. Lord Edmond Fitzmaurice, *Life of the Second Earl Granville, vol. I* (1905), Granville to Canning, 8 August 1856, p. 187.
34. Sumner, p.22.
35. Waller, p. 67.
36. Rupp, pp.18–19, 25, 72–3.
37. Rupp, pp.72–3.
38. Alan Sked, *The Decline and Fall of the Habsburg Empire 1814–1918* (1989), pp. 189–94.
39. Sked, p.190.
40. Rupp, p.75; see also pp. 34–5, 63–6.
41. Quoted in Rupp, p.539.
42. Dep. Hughenden 70/1, Sir Henry Elliot to Disraeli, 21 March 1878, fo. 212.
43. Rupp, p. 41, for the quotation; see also pp. 26–9, 74–5.
44. István Diószegi, *Hungarians in the Ballhausplatz: Studies in the Austro-Hungarian Common Foreign Policy* (Budapest, 1983), p. 147.

45. Rupp, p.35.
46. Rupp, pp.39–41, 67.
47. Rupp, Chapter 3, for the details.
48. Seton-Watson, *Eastern Question*, pp.46–8; Sumner, pp.173–5; Langer, pp. 92–3; Rupp, pp. 137–46.
49. Rupp, pp. 55, 143–4, quoting Shuvalov's memoirs.
50. Sumner, p. 175.
51. Rupp, p.149.
52. Sumner, pp. 170–2, for the details.
53. Sumner, p. 206.
54. Buckle VI, p. 46.
55. Buckle VI p.44.
56. Buckle VI, pp.43–5.
57. Dep. Hughenden 112/4, memo. by Tenterden, 14 July 1876, fos 129–34.
58. SP/D/20/104, Salisbury to Disraeli, 29 August 1876.
59. R.T. Shannon, *Gladstone and the Bulgarian Agitation* (1963), p. 13.
60. Shannon, *Gladstone*, pp. 23–41.
61. Shannon, *Gladstone*, p.14.
62. Jeremy Salt, *Imperialism, Evangelism and the Ottoman Armenians 1878–1896* (1993), p.11.
63. Dep. Hughenden 79/4, Derby to Disraeli, 13 July 1876, fo. 12.
64. Parliamentary Papers, *Accounts and Papers, State Papers, Turkey*, XC (1877), Elliot to Derby, 4 September 1876.
65. Buckle VI p. 48.
66. Dep. Hughenden 99/3, Malmesbury to Disraeli, 8 June 1876, fo. 106.
67. Dep. Hughenden 112/2, Derby to Disraeli, 'J24' 1876, fo. 138. Here Derby's example of always calling him 'Disraeli' will be followed.
68. Buckle VI, Disraeli to Salisbury, 3 September 1876, pp. 51–2.
69. *Carnarvon II*, Northcote to Carnarvon, 4 September 1876, p. 335.
70. *Derby Diaries*, 26 August 1876, p. 321.
71. Buckle VI, Disraeli to Northcote, 2 September 1876, p.51; FO 424/42, no. 381, Derby to Elliot, 29 August 1876.
72. *Derby Diaries*, 2 September 1876, p. 323.
73. *Derby Diaries*, 10 October 1876, p. 332.
74. Buckle VI, Disraeli to Northcote, 11 September 1876, pp. 61–2.

75. Buckle VI, Disraeli to Salisbury, 26 September 1876, pp. 71–2.
76. Buckle VI, pp. 51–5; Millman, pp. 169–71.
77. Dep. Hughenden 91/3, Cairns to Disraeli, 31 August 1876, fos 62–3.
78. *Carnarvon II*, Carnarvon to Northcote, 9 September 1876, p.334.
79. SP/E/Carnarvon Corr., Carnarvon to Salisbury, 9 September 1876.
80. Dep. Hughenden 100/1, Carnarvon to Disraeli, 6 September 1876, fos 176–80.
81. Dep. Hughenden 107/1, Northcote to Disraeli, 30 August 1876, fos 32–3.
82. Buckle VI, Disraeli to Derby, 6 September 1876, p. 53.
83. Dep. Hughenden 112/4, Derby to Disraeli, 5 September 1876, fos 159–60.
84. Buckle VI, Disraeli to Salisbury, 26 September 1876, p. 72.
85. Shannon, *Gladstone*, p.92.
86. A. Ramm (ed.), *The Political Correspondence of Mr Gladstone and Lord Granville, vol. I: 1876–1882* (Oxford, 1962) [henceforth *Gladstone Corr. I*] pp. 1–5.
87. Seton-Watson, *Eastern Question*, p. 78.
88. *Gladstone Corr. I*, Gladstone to Granville, 20 August 1876, p. 1.
89. J. Brooke and M. Sorensen (eds), *W.E. Gladstone IV: Autobiographical Memoranda, 1868–1894*, (1981), memo., 28 February, 1885, p. 103; Seton-Watson, *Eastern Question*, p.78.
90. John Morley, *The Life of William Ewart Gladstone, vol. II* (1903), p. 552.
91. Seton-Watson, *Eastern Question*, p. 113.
92. Millman, pp. 180–1.
93. *Gladstone Corr. I* Gladstone to Granville, 3, 7 October 1876, pp. 10–11, 13–14.
94. Buckle VI, Disraeli to Derby, 8 September 1876, p. 60.
95. Hatfield House, Papers of Mary, Countess of Derby, MCD/80/31, Cross to Lady Derby, September 1876.
96. Dep. Hughenden 67/2/53, Lord Derby's Reply to a Deputation of Working Men, 11 September 1876.
97. Dep. Hughenden 91/3, Cairns to Disraeli, 16 September 1876, fo. 68.

SPLENDID ISOLATION?

Chapter 3

1. Iddesleigh Papers, Add. Mss. 50022, Northcote to Carnarvon, 27 October 1876.
2. Dep. Hughenden 81/3, Cairns to Disraeli, 16 September 1876, fos 69–70.
3. Buckle VI, Disraeli to Derby, 4 September 1876, pp. 52–3.
4. *GD I*, II/31, Bismarck to Bülow, 14 August 1876, pp. 23–4.
5. *GD I*, II/34, memo. 30 August 1876, pp. 25–7.
6. Lamar Cecil, *The German Diplomatic Service 1871–1914* (Princeton, 1976), pp. 110–11.
7. Cecil, p. 121.
8. Cecil, pp. 122–3.
9. *LQV II*, memo. by Wilhelm I, 8 October 1876, pp. 484–6.
10. Sumner, pp. 202–3, for this.
11. Buckle VI, Disraeli to Derby, 4 September 1876, pp. 52–3.
12. Buckle VI, Disraeli to Derby, 6 September 1876, pp. 53–4.
13. FO 424/43, no. 426, Buchanan to Derby, 2 September 1876.
14. Seton-Watson, 'Russo-British relations . . .', Slavonic and East European Review vol. IV [henceforth *RBD*, followed by volume number], Shuvalov to Gorchakov, 3 September 1876, p. 183.
15. Jelavich, *Russia in the East*, Jomini to Giers, 13 September 1876, p. 24.
16. Rupp, p.168.
17. FO 424/43, nos 584, 623, from Buchanan, 12 September, Derby's reply, 15 September.
18. *Salisbury II*, Salisbury to Disraeli 23 September 1876, pp. 85–6.
19. *Salisbury II*, Salisbury to Sir Louis Mallet, 23 September 1876, pp. 86–7.
20. Dep. Hughenden 112/4, Derby to Disraeli, 26 September 1876, fo. 185.
21. Buckle VI, Disraeli to Salisbury, 26 September 1876, pp. 71–2.
22. Sumner, p. 206.
23. Buckle VI, Derby to the Queen, 29 September 1876, p. 75.
24. *Derby Diaries*, 26 September 1876, p. 329.
25. Johnson Nancy E. (ed.), *The Diary of Gathorne-Hardy 1866–1892* (Oxford, 1981) [henceforth *Gathorne-Hardy Diary*], 1 October 1876, p. 292.

413

26. Buckle VI, Disraeli to Northcote, 11 September 1876, pp. 51–62.
27. Dep. Hughenden 107/1, Northcote to Disraeli, 28 September 1876, fo. 46.
28. Rupp, pp. 174–6.
29. Otto Pflanze, *Bismarck and the Development of Germany, vol. II* (Princeton, 1990), p. 355.
30. A. Mendelsohn-Bartholdy *et al* (eds) *Die Große Politik der Europäischen Kabinette, 1871–1914*, 40 vols (Berlin, 1922–6) [henceforth *GP*, followed by volume number], *2. Band: Der Berliner Kongreß und seine Vorgeschichte* (Berlin, 1922), nr. 241, Diktat des . . . Bismarck, 2 October 1876.
31. Otto von Bismarck, *Bismarck's Autobiography, vol. II* (NY, 1899) [henceforth *Bismarck's Autobiography II*], p.232.
32. Rupp, p. 211.
33. *GP II*, nr. 229, Diktat . . . des Bismarck, 30 August 1876.
34. *Bismarck's Autobiography II*, p. 234.
35. *GP II*, nrs 243–5, 7–10 October 1876, pp. 61–4.
36. *GP II*, nr. 251, Bülow an Schweinitz, 23 October 1876, p. 76; Taylor, p. 239; Pflanze, p.424, quoting *Gedanken und Erinnerungen II*, p. 214.
37. Rupp, pp. 194–7.
38. Felix Rachfahl, *Deutschland und die Weltpolitik, 1871–1914* (Stuttgart, 1923), pp. 119–21, goes so far as to see the origins of the Great War in this act – which is going a little too far.
39. Buckle VI, pp. 65–8.
40. Buckle VI, Disraeli to Lady Bradford, 5 October 1876, p. 79.
41. *Derby Diaries*, 4 October 1876, pp. 331–2; *Gathorne-Hardy Diary*, 5 October 1876, p. 293.
42. Buckle VI, Disraeli to Lady Bradford, 12 October 1876, p. 80: *Gathorne-Hardy, Diary*, 12 October 1876, p. 294.
43. Buckle VI, Disraeli to Derby, 17 October 1876, p.81.
44. *LQV II*, Queen Victoria to Beaconsfield, 18 October 1876, p.489.
45. Dep. Hughenden 112/4, Derby to Disraeli, 10 October 1876, fo. 211.
46. *LQV II*, Derby to the Queen, 25 October 1876, pp. 490–1; *Derby Diaries*, 4–19 October 1876, pp. 331–6.
47. Dep. Hughenden 112/4, Derby to Disraeli, 16 October 1876, fo. 291.

48. Dep. Hughenden 112/4, Derby to Disraeli, 17 October 1876, fo. 222.
49. SP/Disraeli I/D/20/111, Salisbury to Disraeli, 18 October 1876.
50. *GD I*, II/69, Bismarck memo. 20 October 1876, pp. 31–3; also at *GP II*, nr. 250.
51. *GD I*, Bismarck memo. 20 October 1876, p. 32.
52. Langer, pp. 101–2.
53. Buckle VI, memo. by Lord Barrington, 23 October 1876, p.84.
54. Lee, p. 32; *Derby Diaries*, 19 October 1876, p. 336.
55. Dep. Hughenden 112/4, Derby to Disraeli, 22 October 1876, fo. 226.
56. *Derby Diaries*, 22, 23 October 1876, pp. 336–7.
57. Dep. Hughenden 112/4, Derby to Hunt, 24 October 1876, fo. 228.
58. Dep. Hughenden 112/4, Derby to Disraeli, 25 October 1876, fo. 232.
59. Millman, pp. 192–3.
60. SP/Derby/38, Salisbury to Derby, 5 October 1876.
61. Millman. p.193.
62. Brooke and Sorensen (eds), undated memo., p.104.
63. *Derby Diaries*, 24 October 1876, p.337.
64. Sumner, pp.216–220; Rupp, pp.237–42.
65. *RBD IV*, 11, December 1925, Gorchakov to Shuvalov, 5 November 1876, pp.433–4.
66. Dep. Hughenden 113/1, Derby to Disraeli, 7 November 1876, fo. 9.
67. Dep. Hughenden 113/1, Derby to Disraeli, 10 November 1876, fo. 11; *RBD IV*, Gorchakov to Shuvalov, 9 November 1876, p.434.
68. *RBD IV*, Gorchakov to Shuvalov, 29 November 1876, p.443.
69. *RBD IV*, Gorchakov to Shuvalov, 19 November 1876, pp.435–8; Rupp, pp.240, 245–7.
70. Dep. Hughenden 92/4, undated note from Disraeli, fo. 130.
71. Lady Derby Mss, MCD 65/9, Salisbury to Lady Derby, 5 November 1876.
72. Dep. Hughenden 92/4, undated note from Salisbury, fo. 130.
73. Seton-Watson, *Eastern Question*, quoting Gladstone to Mme, Novikov, p.102.
74. *Salisbury II*, Derby to Salisbury, 3 November 1876, p.90.
75. For Salisbury's background see: Lady Gwendolen Cecil, *Life of Robert, Marquis of Salisbury*. 4 vols (1921–32); R. Blake and Hugh

Cecil (eds), *Salisbury: The Man and his Policies* (1987); Paul Smith (ed.), *Lord Salisbury on Politics* (Cambridge, 1982).

76. Lady Derby papers, MCD 264/7, Shouvaloff to Lady Derby, October 1876.
77. Lady Derby papers, MCD 65/11, Salisbury to Lady Derby, 14 November 1876.
78. Dep. Hughenden 92/4, note by Salisbury, 17 November 1876, fos 126–8.
79. *Derby Diaries*, 30 October 1876, p.339; *Salisbury II*, pp.90–3; Buckle VI, p.87–90; Shannon, *Age of Disraeli*, pp.290–1.
80. *Salisbury II*, p.91.
81. *Salisbury II*, Salisbury to Derby, 3 November 1876, p.90; Lady Derby papers, MCD 65/10, Salisbury to Lady Derby, 10 November 1876.
82. SP/Disraeli I, Disraeli to Salisbury, 10 November 1876, fos 172–3.
83. *Derby Diaries*, 18 December 1876, p.353.
84. *GD I*, Bülow to Münster, 27 November 1876, pp.40–1; original in *GP II*, nr. 263, p.105.
85. *Salisbury II*, Salisbury to Derby. 23 November 1876, pp.96–7; Dep. Hughenden 92/3, Salisbury to Disraeli, 24 November 1876, fo. 38.
86. SP/E/Derby/52, Derby to Salisbury, 28 November 1876.
87. *Salisbury II*, Salisbury to Derby, 25 November 1876, p.99.
88. Langer, pp.76–8; Bruce Waller, 'Bismarck and Gorchakov in 1879: "The Two Chancellors' War" ', in K. Bourne and D.C. Watt (eds), *Studies in International History* (1967).
89. Rupp, p.220; Pflanze, pp.422–4.
90. P.M. Kennedy, *The Rise of the Anglo-German Antagonism* (1981), p.33 and references given there.
91. Rupp, pp.212–15; Lothar Gall, *Bismarck: The White Revolutionary, Vol. II: 1871–1898* (1986), pp.52–2.
92. Rupp, p.212.
93. *Salisbury II*, Salisbury to Derby, 26 November 1876, pp.100–3.
94. *Salisbury II*, pp.107–8.
95. Buckle VI, Disraeli to Salisbury, 29 November 1876, p.104.
96. *Derby Diaries*, 28 November, 5,7 December 1876, pp.348–49.
97. Buckle VI, Disraeli to Derby, 28 December 1876, p.111.

Chapter 4

1. Lady Derby Papers, MCD 313/329, Cowley to Lady Derby, 28 November 1876.
2. Dep. Hughenden 69/2, Tenterden note, 20 November 1876, fo. 61.
3. Dep. Hughenden 113/4, Lady Derby to Disraeli, n.d., fo. 122.
4. Dep. Hughenden 69/1, Disraeli to Corry, 15 November 1896, fo.7.
5. Lady Derby Papers, MCD 65/13, Salisbury to Lady 'Salisbury' [*sic* Derby], 22 December 1876.
6. Millman, p.211; *RBD IV*, December 1925, lgnatyev to Gorchakov, 22 January 1877, p.460.
7. *Derby Diaries*, 12,14 December 1876, pp.351–2.
8. Sumner, pp.30–3; Rupp, pp.49–52; there is a fuller account by Sumner, 'lgnatyev at Constantinople 1864–1874', in *Slavonic and East European Review*, vol. XI, pp.341–54, 556–71.
9. *Salisbury II*, p.110.
10. Shannon, *Age of Disraeli*, p.271.
11. Lady Derby Papers, MCD 62/2, Lady Salisbury to Lady Derby, 30 December 1876.
12. Dep. Hughenden 107/1, Northcote to Disraeli, 15 December 1876, fos 54–6.
13. Lady Derby Papers, MCD 82/42, Cross to Lady Derby, December 1876.
14. *Derby Diaries*, 15 December 1876, p.352.
15. *Derby Diaries*, 18 December 1876, p.353.
16. *Derby Diaries*, 22 December 1876, p.354–5.
17. *Carnarvon II* pp.347–8; also at SP/D/31/134, fo. pp.270 foll.
18. *Derby Diaries*, 13 December 1876, p.351.
19. *Derby Diaries*, 21 January 1877, pp.368–9.
20. *Derby Diaries*, 26 December 1876, p.357.
21. Lord Salisbury, *Biographical Essays* (1903), 'Lord Castlereagh', January 1862, p.62.
22. Lady G. Cecil, *Life of Robert, Marquis of Salisbury, vol. I* (1921), pp.314–16.
23. SP/D/31/Herbert VII, Salisbury to Carnarvon, 14 December 1876, fo. 51.
24. *Salisbury II*, to Sir Louis Mallet, 11 January 1877, p.123.
25. *Salisbury II*, to Carnarvon, 11 January 1877, p.122.

26. Millman, p.537, fn. 48.
27. Dep. Hughenden 92/3, Salisbury to Disraeli, 28 December 1876, fos 48–9.
28. Lady Derby Papers, MCD 62/2, Lady Salisbury to Lady Derby, 30 December 1876.
29. *Salisbury II*, pp.114–16; *Slavonic Review*, vol. IV, December 1925, Ignatyev to Gorchakov 22 January 1877, pp.460–1.
30. Lady Derby Papers, MCD 62/2, Lady Salisbury to Lady Derby, 30 December 1876.
31. Dep. Hughenden 92/3, Disraeli to Salisbury, 1 January 1877.
32. *RBD V* March 1926, Shuvalov to Gorchakov, 7 February 1877, p.740.
33. Millman, pp.210–15 for the details.
34. *RBD V*, Shuvalov to Gorchakov, 21 February 1877, p.748.
35. Buckle VI, Disraeli to Derby, 30 December 1876, p.111.
36. Dep. Hughenden 69/2, Mr Scudamore to Corry, 11 January 1877, fo.73.
37. *Derby Diaries*, 7 January 1877, p.365.
38. Seton-Watson, *Eastern Question*, pp.146–8; Millman, pp.226–9.
39. Allan Cunningham, *Eastern Questions in the Nineteenth Century*, vol. 2 (1993), *passim*.
40. Sumner, p.244.
41. Dep. Hughenden 92/3, Salisbury to Disraeli, 31 December 1876, fo. 63; *RBD IV*, Ignatyev to Shuvalov, 29, 31 December 1876, pp.456–7.
42. *Salisbury II*, p.124.
43. Seton-Watson, *Eastern Question*, p.120.
44. Seton-Watson, *Eastern Question*, p.121.
45. *GD I*, Bismarck to Schweinitz, 24 January 1877, pp.47–8.
46. FO 64/876, tel. 36, Russell to Derby, 16 January 1877; SP/D/61, Salisbury to Derby, January 1877; Dep. Hughenden 80/1, Derby to Disraeli, 20 January 1877, fo. 33.
47. *RBD V*, Shuvalov to Gorchakov, 4 February 1877, p.739.
48. *Derby Diaries*, 30 January 1877, pp.372–3; *RBD IV* March 1926, Shuvalov to Gorchakov, 30 January 1877, pp.737–8.
49. Diószegi, pp.47–57; M.D. Stojanovic, *The Great Powers and the Balkans 1875–1878* (Cambridge, 1939), pp.135–9.
50. *RBD V*, Shuvalov to Gorchakov, 20 February 1877, p.747; Stojanovic, pp.138–9.

51. *RBD V*, Shuvalov to Gorchakov, January 1877, p.738.
52. Rupp, pp.270–4.
53. Millman, pp.232–3.
54. Lord Newton, *Lord Lyons, vol. II* (1913) [henceforth *Lyons II*], Derby to Lord Odo Russell, 24 January 1877, p.107.
55. *Gathorne-Hardy Diary*, 10 February 1877, pp.306.
56. SP/E/Derby/76, Derby to Salisbury, 8 January 1877.
57. Buckle VI, p.113.
58. *Derby Diaries*, 30 January 1877, p.373; Buckle VI, Queen Victoria to Disraeli, 22 February 1877, p.123; *Carnarvon II* pp.350–1.
59. Millman, pp. 251–2; *Salisbury II*, pp.129–30; Buckle VI, pp.126–7.
60. *Derby Diaries*, 11 February 1877, p.377.
61. *Salisbury II*, p.127.
62. Iddesleigh Papers, Add. Mss. 50022, Northcote to Derby, 4 February 1877, fo. 128.
63. *Lyons II*, p.107.
64. SP/E/Iddesleigh, Northcote to Salisbury, 22 January 1877.
65. Lady Derby Papers, MCD 80/46, Cross to Lady Derby, 5 February 1877.
66. Lady Derby Papers, MCD 80/47, Cross to Lady Derby, 6 February 1877.
67. *Hansard*, House of Lords, vol. CCXXXII, 8 February 1877, col. 42.
68. Buckle VI, p.122.
69. *Gathorne-Hardy Diary*, 25 February 1877, p.308; *Derby Diaries*, 28 February 1877, p.380; Buckle VI, pp.128–9.
70. Zetland II, Disraeli letter, 26 February 1877, p.106.
71. Buckle VI, Disraeli to Derby, 9 February 1877, pp.126–7.
72. *RBD V*, Shuvalov to Gorchakov, 21 February 1877, pp.747–9.
73. Seton-Watson, *Eastern Question*, pp.126–33.
74. *RBD IV*, Ignatyev to Gorchakov, 26 November 1876, p.451.
75. Sumner, p.229.
76. Sumner, pp.230–1.
77. *RBD V*, Shuvalov to Gorchakov, January 1877, p.745.
78. Jelavich, *Balkan Entanglements*, p.172.
79. *Carnarvon II*, p.351, letter, 13 March 1877.
80. *Salisbury II*, p.134.
81. Lady Derby Papers, MCD 65/15, Salisbury to Lady Derby '11.45' (n.d., but c. late February 1877).

82. *RDB V*, Shuvalov to Gorchakov, 1, 11 March 1877, pp.753–4.
83. PRO, Cab/41/8/5, Disraeli to the Queen, 13 March 1877.
84. *Salisbury II*, Salisbury to Disraeli, 12 March 1877, p.132.
85. *Derby Diaries*, 9 February, 1 march 1877, pp.376, 380.
86. *Derby Diaries*, 13 March 1877, p.382; *Gathorne-Hardy Diary*, 14 March 1877, p.310.
87. Buckle VI, Disraeli to the Queen, 24 March 1877, p.129.
88. *LQV II*, Disraeli to the Queen, 23 March 1877, p.525.
89. *Gathorne-Hardy Diary*, 24 March 1877 p.314.
90. SP/E/Carnarvon, Carnarvon to Salisbury, 25 March 1877.
91. Buckle VI, Disraeli to the Queen, 24 March 1877, p.129.
92. SP/E/Carnarvon, Carnarvon to Salisbury, 25 March 1877.
93. *Salisbury II*, Salisbury to Carnarvon, 26 March 1877, pp.138–9.
94. *Salisbury II*, Salisbury to Lytton, 9 March 1877, p.130. Contrary to the assumption of some who quote this, Salisbury did not mean it as a mark of approval.
95. Sumner, p.267.
96. Sumner, p.270.
97. Swartz, pp.62–5.
98. Buckle VI, p.139.
99. Iddesleigh papers, Add. Mss. 50018, Northcote to Disraeli, 21 April 1877.
100. Dep. Hughenden 107/1, Northcote to Derby, 29 April 1877, fo. 77.
101. Lady Derby Papers, MCD 80/50, Cross to Lady Derby, 30 April 1877.
102. Dep. Hughenden 107/1, Northcote to Derby, 29 April 1877, fo. 77.
103. Buckle VI, Disraeli to the Queen, 5 May 1877, p.135.
104. Dep. Hughenden 91/3, Cairns to Disraeli, 24 May 1877, fos 138–9.
105. Buckle VI, Queen Victoria to Disraeli, 25 April 1877, p.133.
106. Dep. Hughenden 113/1, Derby to Disraeli, 8 May 1877, fo. 120.
107. Dep. Hughenden 113/1, Derby to Disraeli, 17 May 1877, fo. 125.
108. Buckle VI, pp.138–40.

Chapter 5

1. Once again I must express my gratitude to Professor John Vincent for his guidance here.

2. Lady Derby Papers, MCD 65/13, Salisbury to 'Lady Salisbury', 22 December 1876.
3. Letter to the author from Professor Vincent, 30 July 1998.
4. Professor Vincent's information; the author's speculation!
5. *Derby Diaries*, 14 July 1877, p.420.
6. *Salisbury II*, to Lytton, 25 May 1877, p.145.
7. *Salisbury II*, to Lytton, 27 April 1877, p.142.
8. *Salisbury II*, speech in the Lords, 11 June 1877, p.156.
9. *Salisbury II*, to Lytton, 27 May 1877, p.141.
10. *Salisbury II*, to Lytton, 15 June 1877, p.146.
11. *Derby Diaries*, 23 May, 12 July 1877, p.402, 418; Buckle VI, Disraeli to Derby, 22 May 1877, p.140.
12. British Library, papers of the 1st Earl Balfour, Add. Mss. 49688, Balfour's memo., 8 May 1880, informed the views in Buckle VI, pp.139–46, 184–96, 247–50, 217–18, and in *Salisbury II*, pp.114, 184, 208, 219–24. Those in Blake, pp.623–7; Millman, pp.7–11, 359–60, 575; Swartz, pp.262–3; Shannon, *Age of Disraeli*, pp. 295–7, and S. Weintraub, *Disraeli* (1993), follow this line.
13. *Derby Diaries*, 2 August 1877, p.427.
14. *Derby Diaries*, 25 April 1877, p.394.
15. Buckle VI, pp.140–1; Dep. Hughenden 113/1, Derby to Disraeli, 24 May 1877, fo. 133.
16. *Derby Diaries*, 21 April 1877, p.392.
17. Dep. Hughenden 113/1, Derby to Disraeli, 28 May 1877, fo. 135.
18. Buckle VI, Disraeli to Layard, 6 June 1877, pp.142–3.
19. Buckle VI, Queen Victoria to Disraeli, 7 June 1877, pp.143–4.
20. *LOV II*, Queen Victoria to Derby, 8 June 1877, p.540.
21. *LOV II*, Derby to the Queen, 11 June 1877, p.542.
22. Buckle VI, Disraeli to Salisbury, 14 June 1877, pp.144–5.
23. *Derby Diaries*, 8 June 1877, p.407.
24. *Derby Diaries*, 16 June 1877, pp.409–10.
25. Buckle VI, Disraeli to Derby, 17 June 1877, pp.145–6.
26. Buckle VI, Derby to Disraeli, 17 June 1877, p.146.
27. *Derby Diaries*, 17 June 1877, p.410.
28. *Derby Diaries*, 20 June 1877, p.411.
29. *Derby Diaries*, 22 June 1877, p.412.
30. Buckle VI, Queen Victoria to Disraeli, 25 June 1877, pp.147–8.
31. Buckle VI, Disraeli to the Queen, 26 June 1877, p.148.

32. Buckle VI, Queen Victoria to Disraeli, 27 June 1877, pp.148–9.
33. Buckle VI, Disraeli to the Queen, 28 June 1877, p.149.
34. *Derby Diaries*, 29 June 1877, p.413.
35. *Derby Diaries*, 28 June 1877, pp.412–13.
36. *Derby Diaries*, 30 June 1877, p.413.
37. *Derby Diaries*, 1 July 1877, p.414.
38. *Derby Diaries*, 30 June 1877, pp.413–14.
39. *Derby Diaries*, 11 July 1877, p.417.
40. *Derby Diaries*, 12 July 1877, p.418.
41. Halifax Mss., A4/87a, Pt I, Lady Derby to Halifax, 12 August 1877.
42. *LOV II*, Queen Victoria to Disraeli, 15 July 1877, p.548.
43. Buckle VI, Disraeli to the Queen, 12 July 1877, pp.150–2.
44. Dep. Hughenden 113/1, Derby to Disraeli, 14 July 1877, fo. 169.
45. *Derby Diaries*, 17 July 1877, p.421.
46. Buckle VI, Queen Victoria to Disraeli, 20 July 1877, p.153.
47. *Derby Diaries*, 21 July 1877, p.422; Buckle VI, Disraeli to the Queen, 22 July 1877, pp.153–4.
48. Buckle VI, Disraeli to the Queen, 21 July 1877, p.154.
49. Buckle VI, Disraeli to the Queen, 22 July 1877, pp.153–4.
50. *Carnarvon II*, p.359.
51. *Derby Diaries*, 28 July 1877, pp.423–4.
52. *Derby Diaries*, 30 July 1877, p.425.
53. *Carnarvon II*, p.360.
54. *Salisbury II*, p.156.
55. *Carnarvon II*, p.360.
56. Buckle VI, Derby to the Queen, 28 July 1877, pp.157–8.
57. *Derby Diaries*, 28 July 1877, p.424.
58. *Derby Diaries*, 30 July 1877, p.425.
59. *Gathorne-Hardy Diary*, 31 July 1877, p.333.
60. *Derby Diaries*, 31 July 1877, p.426.
61. Lady Bughclere, *A Great Lady's Friendships*, (1933), pp.4–6
62. Col. the Hon. Frederick Wellesley, *Recollections of a Soldier-Diplomat* (n.d., c. 1946), chapter VII, for some evidence here!
63. Lady Derby Papers, MCD 313/304, 307, Cowley to Lady Derby, 6, 10 January 1876.

64. Lady Derby Papers, MCD 313/314, 384, Cowley to Lady Derby, 1 August 1876, 17 January 1877.
65. Wellesley, p.138.
66. Dep. Hughenden 80/3, Queen Victoria to Disraeli, 5 August 1877, fo.18.
67. Dep. Hughenden 80/3, Queen Victoria to Disraeli, 15 August 1877, fo. 22.
68. Dep. Hughenden 80/3, Disraeli to the Queen, 15 August 1877, fo. 55.
69. Wellesley, p.145.
70. Buckle VI, pp.174–6; also at Dep. Hughenden 80/3, Wellesley to Corry, 17 August 1877, fos 59–64; Wellesley, pp.143–5.
71. Buckle VI, p.176.
72. *Derby Diaries*, 14 August 1877, pp.431–2.
73. Halifax Mss. A4/87a, Pt I, Lady Derby to Halifax, 24 November 1877.
74. Buckle VI, Disraeli to Derby, I September 1877, pp.177–8.
75. Dep. Hughenden 80/4, Disraeli to the Queen, 8 October 1877, fo. 21.
76. Dep. Hughenden 80/3, Disraeli to the Queen, 11 September 1877, fo. 134.
77. *Derby Diaries*, 20 September 1877, p.439.
78. Lady Derby Papers, MCD 141/68, Carnarvon to Lady Derby, 5 September 1877.
79. *Derby Diaries*, 23 September 1877, p.439.
80. Buckle VI, Queen Victoria to Disraeli, 26 September 1877, p.181.
81. Dep. Hughenden, Disraeli to Salisbury, 3 October 1877, fos 88–91.
82. Buckle VI, Disraeli to Derby, 28 September 1877, p.182; *Derby Diaries*, 5 October 1877, p.442.
83. *Derby Diaries*, 29 September 1877, p.440.
84. Buckle VI, Derby to Disraeli, 29 September 1877, p.183.
85. *Derby Diaries*, 2 October 1877, p.441.
86. Dep. Hughenden 107/1, Northcote to Disraeli, 1 October 1877, fo. 125.
87. Buckle VI, Disraeli to the Queen, 5 October 1877, p.183.
88. *Gathorne-Hardy Diary*, 9 October 1877, p.340.

89. Buckle VI, Disraeli to the Queen, 6 October 1877, p.183.
90. *Carnarvon II* p.363, Lady Derby to Carnarvon, 8 October 1877.
91. Lady Derby Papers, MCD 141/71, Carnarvon to Lady Derby, 15 October 1877.

Chapter 6

1. *Derby Diaries*, 21 October 1877, p.446.
2. Bucke VI, Disraeli to the Queen, I November 1877, p.193.
3. British Library, Papers of The 4th Earl of Carnarvon, Add. Mss. 60765, Lady Derby to Carnarvon, 26 October 1877, fo. 137.
4. *Derby Diaries*, 11 October 1877, p.444.
5. Buckle VI, Disraeli to the Queen, 10 October 1877, pp.185–6.
6. Dep. Hughenden 69/1, Disraeli to Corry, 20 October 1877, fo. 18.
7. Buckle VI, Disraeli to the Queen, 18 October 1877, p.189.
8. Dep. Hughenden 69/1, Corry to Disraeli, 31 October 1877, fos 177–8.
9. *Derby Diaries*, 31 October 1877, p.499.
10. Buckle VI, Disraeli to the Queen, 1 November 1877, p.193.
11. *Derby Diaries*, 31 October 1877, p.499.
12. Dep. Hughenden 80/4, Derby to Disraeli, 1 November 1877, fos 89–90.
13. Buckle VI, Disraeli to the Queen, 5 November 1877, p.195.
14. Buckle VI, p.196.
15. *LOV II*, Queen Victoria to Disraeli, 13 November 1877, pp.573–4.
16. Dep. Hughenden 113/1, Derby to Disraeli, 19 November 1877, fo.223.
17. Dep. Hughenden 80/4, Derby to Disraeli, 24 November 1877, fos 157–9.
18. *Derby Diaries*, 24 November 1877, p.456.
19. Dep. Hughenden 80/4, Disraeli to Derby, 24 November 1877, fos 161–2.
20. Halifax Mss. A4/87a, Pt I, Lady Derby to Halifax, 24 November 1877
21. *Derby Diaries*, 4 December 1877, p.450.
22. *Derby Diaries*, 4 December 1877, p.450; Buckle VI, Manners to

the Queen, 4 December 1877, p.198; *Gathorne-Hardy Diary*, 5 December 1877, p.343.
23. Buckle VI, Disraeli to Derby, 5 December 1877, p.199.
24. Dep. Hughenden 80/4, Disraeli to the Queen, 4 December 1877, fo.174.
25. *Derby Diaries*, 26 November 1877, p.457.
26. *Salisbury II*, Salisbury to Carnarvon, 14 October 1877, p.162.
27. Dep. Hughenden 80/4, Derby to Ponsonby, 20 November 1877, fos 150–1.
28. *Derby Diaries*, 6 December 1877, p.461.
29. Dep. Hughenden, Queen Victoria to Disraeli, 7 December 1877.
30. Millman, p.302, takes it for granted that Lady Derby's honour was compromised; Blake, p. 623, does not concur on this point; Rupp, p.372, offers sources upon which Millman relies; there is no sign of this in Derby's diary. Swartz pp.69–71, 187, accepts the stories.
31. Dep. Hughenden 80/4, Disraeli to Salisbury, 7 December 1877.
32. Dep. Hughenden 80/4, Disraeli to the Queen, 8 December 1877.
33. *Derby Diaries*, 12, 14 December 1877, pp.462–3.
34. *LOV II*, Queen Victoria to Disraeli, 13 December 1877, p.576.
35. *Derby Diaries*, 14 December 1877, p.463. Other accounts substantially agreed, see: Buckle VI, Disraeli to the Queen, 14 December 1877, p. 344.
36. Buckle VI, Disraeli to the Queen, 14 December 1877, p.202.
37. *Derby Diaries*, 14 December 1877, p.463.
38. *Carnarvon II* p.365; full text Carnarvon Papers, Add. Mss. 60765, fos 143–4.
39. Iddesleigh, Corr./D/XIV133, Northcote to Salisbury, 15 December 1877.
40. *Salisbury II*, Salisbury to Northcote, 15 December 1877, pp.163–6; also at Iddesleigh Papers, Add. Mss. 50019, fos 53–9.
41. Blake, p.637
42. *Derby Diaries*, 17 December 1877, pp.464–5; Buckle VI, Disraeli to the Queen, 17 December 1877, p.204.
43. Buckle VI, Disraeli to the Queen, 17 December 1877, p.205.
44. Dep. Hughenden 107/1, Northcote to Disraeli, 17 December 1877, fo. 135.
45. Buckle VI, Disraeli to the Queen, 17 December 1877, p.204.
46. Buckle VI, Derby to Disraeli, 17 [? 18] December 1877, p.205.

47. *Derby Diaries*, 18 December 1877, pp.465–6.
48. *Derby Diaries*, 18 December 1877, p.466; Buckle VI, Disraeli to the Queen, 18 December 1877, pp.206–7.
49. *Salisbury II*, Derby to Salisbury, 23 December 1877, p.171.
50. Salisbury II, Disraeli to Salisbury, 24 December 1877, p.169.
51. Buckle VI, Salisbury to Disraeli, 26 December 1877, p.211.
52. Buckle VI, p.205.
53. Carnarvon Papers, Add. Mss. 60817, Carnarvon's memo. on his resignation, fos 40–1.
54. *Salisbury II*, pp.172–3.
55. Iddesleigh Mss. 50019, Salisbury to Northcote, 18 December 1878, fo. 61.
56. Halifax Mss. A4/87a, Pt I, Lady Derby to Halifax, 12 August 1877.
57. *Derby Diaries*, Professor Vincent's introduction, p.29.
58. R.A., H. 18.52, Dean of Windsor to the Queen, 27 December 1877.
59. *Derby Diaries*, Professor Vincent's note, p.473.
60. Lady Derby Papers, MCD 264/59, 'Dec. 1877', manuscript notes on Knowsley writing-paper. The hand is not Shuvalov's nor, as Robin Harcourt-Williams, the archivist at Hatfield confirms, is it Mary Derby's; there appears to be more than one hand at work.
61. R.A., H. 18.69, Lady Derby to the Dean of Windsor, 29 December 1877.
62. Professor Vincent to the author.
63. *Derby Diaries*, p.471, n.92.
64. Swartz, pp.69–70.
65. Sumner, *Russia and the Balkans*, pp.320–2.
66. *Derby Diaries*, pp.471–2, Professor Vincent's comments.
67. Iddesleigh Papers, Add. Mss. 50022, Derby to Northcote, 28 February 1878, fo. 166.
68. Weintraub, p.584.
69. Add. MSS. 60765, Lady Derby to Carnarvon, 15 December 1877, fo. 144.
70. PRO, Cab. 41/10/2, Disraeli to the Queen, 3 January 1878.
71. *Derby Diaries*, 3 January 1878, p.477.
72. Carnarvon Papers, Add. Mss. 60759, Carnarvon to Salisbury, 3 January 1878, fo. 44.
73. SP/E/Iddesleigh/1/51, Northcote to Salisbury, 4 January 1878, fo. 131.

SPLENDID ISOLATION?

74. *Salisbury II*, Salisbury to Carnarvon, 8 January 1878, p.175.
75. Millman, p.355.
76. Dep. Hughenden 100/1, Carnarvon to Disraeli, 8 January 1878, fos 220–4.
77. Carnarvon Papers, Add. Mss. 60817, Carnarvon's memo. on his resignation, fos 34–40. This was written in September 1879 and is omitted from Hardinge's account.
78. *Derby Diaries*, 4 January 1878, p.479.
79. *Derby Diaries*, 1 January 1878, p.475.
80. PRO. Cab. 41/4, Disraeli to the Queen, 9 January 1878; *Derby Diaries*, 9 January 1877, pp.481–2; *Carnarvon II*, p.371; *Gathorne-Hardy Diary*, 10 January 1878, p.347.
81. F. Dwyer, 'R.A. Cross and the Eastern Crisis of 1875–8', In *Slavonic Review*, vol. XXXIX June 1961, p.451.
82. Dep. Hughenden 81/1, Disraeli to the Queen, 9 January 1878, fo. 44.
83. Buckle VI, Disraeli to the Queen, 9 January 1878, pp.216–17; *Derby Diaries*, 9 January 1878, p.482.
84. *Derby Diaries*, 9 January 1878, p.482.
85. *Carnarvon II*, p.371.
86. Buckle VI, Queen Victoria to Disraeli, 10 January 1878, p.217.

Chapter 7

1. Dep. Hughenden 81/1, Queen Victoria to Disraeli, 8 p.m., 11 January 1877, fo. 95.
2. Dep. Hughenden 81/1, Queen Victoria to Disraeli, 11.55 a.m., 12 January 1877, fo. 101.
3. Buckle VI, memo. by the Queen, 11 January 1878, pp.218–19.
4. Seton-Watson, *Eastern Question*, pp.304–5.
5. PRO, Cab. 41/5 Disraeli to the Queen, 12 January 1878.
6. PRO, Cab. 41/5 Disraeli to the Queen, 12 January 1878.
7. *Carnarvon II*, p.372.
8. *Derby Diaries*, 12 January 1878, p.483.
9. *Gathorne-Hardy Diary*, 13 January 1878, pp.347–8.
10. PRO, Cab. 41/5, Disraeli to the Queen, 12 January 1878.
11. *Derby Diaries*, 12 January 1878, p.483; Buckle VI, p.219, for Disraeli's fury.

12. *Derby Diaries*, 10 January 1878, p.482.
13. *Derby Diaries*, 14 January 1878, p.483.
14. *Carnarvon II*, p.373; Millman, p.575, fn. 40, for more details.
15. Dep. Hughenden 113/2, Derby to Disraeli, 15 January 1878, fos 5–6.
16. *Derby Diaries*, 9–18 January 1878, pp.482–5.
17. Dep. Hughenden 81/1, Queen Victoria to Disraeli, 14 January 1878, fo. 70.
18. Buckle VI, Tsar Alexander to Queen Victoria, 15 January 1878, p.220.
19. Dep. Hughenden 81/1, Queen Victoria to Disraeli, 15 January 1878, fo. 112.
20. Dep. Hughenden 81/1/ Queen Victoria to Disraeli, 14 January 1878, fo. 114.
21. *Gathorne-Hardy Diary*, 15 January 1878, p.348.
22. Dep. Hughenden 113/2, Derby to Disraeli, 15 January 1878, fo. 5.
23. *Gathorne-Hardy Diary*, 15 January 1878, p.348; Millman, p.360 and sources cited there.
24. *Carnarvon II*, p.374.
25. *Gathorne-Hardy Diary*, 15 January 1878, p.349.
26. *Derby Diaries*, 15 January 1878, p.483–4.
27. Dep. Hughenden 100/1, Carnarvon to Disraeli, 15 January 1878, fos 226–8.
28. Dep. Hughenden 113/4, Sanderson to Disraeli, 16 January 1878, fo. 7.
29. Dep. Hughenden 113/2, Derby to Disraeli, 16 January 1878, fos 9–11.
30. *Derby Diaries*, 15 January 1878, p.484.
31. E.A. Chilston, *W.H. Smith* (1967) p. 102, quoting Smith to Northcote, 15 January 1878.
32. *Gathorne-Hardy Diary*, 16 January 1878, p.349.
33. *Derby Diaries*, 17 January 1878, p.485.
34. Buckle VI, Carnarvon to Disraeli, 18 January 1878, pp.220–2.
35. Dep. Hughenden 100/1, Carnarvon to Disraeli, 18 January 1878, fos 230–4.
36. *LOV II*, Disraeli to the Queen, 4 January 1878, pp.587–8.
37. Buckle VI, Disraeli to Carnarvon, 18 January 1878, p.223.
38. *Salisbury II*, Salisbury's speech, 17 January 1878, p.189.

39. Seton-Watson, *Eastern Question*, p. 290.
40. Buckle VI, Disraeli to the Queen, 18 January 1878, p.225.
41. *LOV II*, Queen Victoria to Disraeli, 20 January 1878, pp.597–8; Buckle VI, p.226, for his reply.
42. Dep. Hughenden 81/1, Leopold to Corry, 20 July 1878, fos 154–7.
43. *Derby Diaries*, 19 January 1878, p.486.
44. Buckle VI, Disraeli to the Queen, 21 January 1878, p.227.
45. *Gathorne-Hardy Diary*, 22 January 1877, p.350.
46. *Derby Diaries*, 21 January 1978, p.488.
47. Dep Hughenden 113/2, Salisbury's ms. note, 21 January 1878, fo. 29.
48. Cab. 41/10/10, Disraeli to the Queen, 22 January 1878.
49. Millman, p.366.
50. Cab. 41/10/11, Disraeli to the Queen, 23 January 1878.
51. *Derby Diaries*, 23 January 1878, p.490.
52. Dep. Hughenden 113/2, Hart-Dyke to Disraeli, 23 January 1878; also printed in Swartz, Appendix B, pp.157–8, and quoted in Shannon, *Age of Disraeli*, p.300.
53. *Derby Diaries*, 23 January 1878, p.490; *Carnarvon II*, p.376; *Gathorne-Hardy Diary*, 24 January 1878, p.351.
54. Dep. Hughenden 113/2, fo. 37. clearly notes the resignation as taking place on 23 January.
55. Buckle VI, Derby to Disraeli, 23 January 1878, p.228.
56. *Derby Diaries*, 24 January 1878, p.491.
57. Dep. Hughenden 113/2, Derby to Disraeli, 24 January 1878, fo. 42.
58. Buckle VI, Queen Victoria to Disraeli, 24 January 1878, pp.229–30.
59. Dep. Hughenden 113/2, Derby to Disraeli, 25 January 1878, fo. 44.
60. Seton-Watson, *Eastern Question*, p.298, citing Shuvalov, who does not name his source; Millman, p.367, bases himself on this, but also cites a despatch from the Belgian Minister dated 2 February.
61. Buckle VI, pp.230–1.
62. Seton-Watson, *Eastern Question*, p.299.
63. Millman, pp.368–9.
64. Sumner, pp.355, 356, quoting Layard's letter to Admiral Hornby, 25 January 1878.
65. *Derby Diaries*, 24 January 1878, p.491.

66. Dep. Hughenden 113/2, Derby to Disraeli, 24 January 1878, fo. 42.
67. *Derby Diaries*, 24 January 1878, p.491; Buckle VI, pp.230–1.
68. Dep. Hughenden 113/2, Derby to Disraeli, 25 January 1878, fo. 44.
69. Dep. Hughenden 107/1, Northcote to Disraeli, 25 January 1878, fos 179–80.
70. *Derby Diaries*, 25 January 1878, p.492.
71. Dep. Hughenden 113/2 Hart-Dyke to Disraeli, 25 January 1878, fo. 50.
72. *Derby Diaries*, 25 January 1878, p.491; Buckle VI, pp.232–3.
73. *Derby Diaries*, 26 January 1878, p.493.
74. Dep. Hughenden 107/1 Northcote to Disraeli, 26 January 1878, fo. 181.
75. *LQV II*, Northcote to the Queen, 26 January 1878, pp.598–9.
76. Carnarvon Papers, Add. Mss. 60765, Lady Derby to Carnarvon, 7.30 p.m., 26 January 1878.
77. Iddesleigh Papers, Add. Mss. 50023, Derby to Northcote, 25 January 1878, fo. 160.
78. Carnarvon Papers, Add. Mss. 60765, Lady Derby to Carnarvon, 26 January 1878.
79. Buckle VI, Disraeli to the Queen, 26 January 1878, pp.232–4.
80. Dep. Hughenden 92/4, Salisbury to Disraeli, 27 January 1878, fos 47–8.
81. Cab. 41/10/13, Disraeli to the Queen, 25 January 1878.
82. Blake, p.638; Weintraub, pp.586–7.
83. Buckle VI, p.247.
84. *Salisbury II*, p.209.
85. Balfour Papers, Add. Mss. 49688, Balfour memo., 8 May 1880, fo. 26.
86. Dep. Hughenden 113/2, Derby to Disraeli, 28 January 1878, fos 59–60.

Chapter 8

1. *Derby Diaries*, 24 January 1878, p.491.
2. *Derby Diaries*, 29 January 1878, p.495.

SPLENDID ISOLATION?

3. Seton-Watson, *Eastern Question*, pp.303–6, for the best bits.
4. Seton-Watson, *Eastern Question*, p.304; *Gathorne-Hardy Diary*, p.354.
5. Seton-Watson *Eastern Question*, p.305.
6. Buckle VI, Disraeli to Lady Bradford, 1 February 1878, p.239.
7. *Derby Diaries*, 31 January 1878, p.497.
8. *RBD VI*, April 1947, Shuvalov to Gorchakov, 31 January 1878.
9. PRO. FO 65/1023, 'Observations by Lord Tenterden on Russian conditions of peace', 29 January 1878, printed for the Cabinet on 30 January.
10. Sumner, Appendix VI, pp.625–6.
11. Sumner, p.359.
12. *Derby Diaries*, 1 February 1878, p.497.
13. Milliman, p.580, fn. 7, for these.
14. Dep. Hughenden 81/2, Queen Victoria to Disraeli, 1 February 1878, 2.45 p.m., fo. 1.
15. Dep. Hughenden 81/2, Queen Victoria to Disraeli, 1 February 1878 7.40 p.m., fo. 2.
16. Dep. Hughenden 81/2, Queen Victoria to Disraeli, 1 February 1878, 11.22 p.m., fo. 3.
17. Millman pp.372–3.
18. FO 64/902, Russell to Derby, 1 February 1878.
19. FO 424/67, Elliot to Derby, 31 January 1878.
20. FO 424/67, Paget to Derby, 1 February 1878.
21. *Derby Diaries*, 2 February 1878, p.498.
22. *Derby Diaries*, 4 February 1878, pp.499–500.
23. Dep. Hughenden 81/2, Queen Victoria to Disraeli, 4 February 1878, fo. 25.
24. Deo. Hughenden 81/2, Derby to Disraeli, 5 February 1878, fo. 20.
25. *LQV II*, Northcote to the Queen, 7 February 1878, pp.601–2.
26. Dep. Hughenden 92/4, Salisbury to Disraeli, 6 February 1878, fo. 51.
27. Dep. Hughenden 113/2, Disraeli to Derby, 6 February 1878.
28. *Derby Diaries*, 7 February 1878, pp.502–3.
29. Iddesleigh Papers, Add. Mss. 50019, Salisbury to Northcote, 7 February 1878, fo. 64.
30. *Derby Diaries*, 7 February 1878, p.502.
31. *Derby Diaries*, 7 February 1878, p.502.

32. Millman, p.381.
33. Buckle VI, Queen Victoria to Disraeli, 7 February 1878, p.243.
34. SP/E/Iddesleigh, Northcote to Salisbury, 8 February 1878.
35. *Derby Diaries*, 8 February 1878, p.503.
36. R.A., H.20, Derby to Queen Victoria, 8 February 1878.
37. Buckle VI. Disraeli to the Queen, 6 February 1878, p.244.
38. Dep. Hughenden 81/2 Queen Victoria to Disraeli, 9 February 1878, fos 59–66; the adjective 'cowardly' was tactfully omitted by Buckle, p.245.
39. Buckle VI, Disraeli to the Queen, 10 February 1878, pp.245–6.
40. *Derby Diaries*, 10 February 1878, pp.504–5.
41. Millman, p.404.
42. Millman, pp.386–7, 404–5.
43. Seton-Watson, *Eastern Question*, Shuvalov to Gorchakov, 14 February 1878, p.318.
44. *Salisbury II*, Salisbury to Disraeli, 10 February 1878, p.198.
45. *Derby Diaries*, 11 February 1878, p.505.
46. Dep. Hughenden 113/2, Derby to Disraeli, 10 February 1878, fo. 79.
47. Dep. Hughenden 113/2, Derby to Disraeli, 10 February 1878, fos 81–3.
48. *Derby Diaries*, 11 February 1878, p.505.
49. *Gathorne-Hardy Diary*, 12 February 1878, p.355.
50. FO 424/67, Derby to Musurus Pasha, 12 February 1878.
51. *Derby Diaries*, 11 February 1878, p.506.
52. *Derby Diaries*, 12 February 1878, p.506.
53. *Derby Diaries*, 13 February 1878, pp.506–7: FO 424/67, Derby to Loftus, 13 February 1878.
54. *Derby Diaries*, 13 February 1878, p.507.
55. *RBD VI*, Shuvalov to Gorchakov, 14 February 1878, pp.545–8.
56. Buckle VI, Disraeli to Layard, 22 November 1877, pp.251–2.
57. *Derby Diaries*, 14 February 1878, pp.507–8.
58. Millman, p.591.
59. Sumner, pp.374–8, for this.
60. *Derby Diaries*, 15 February 1878, pp.508–9.
61. *RBD VI*, Shuvalov to Gorchakov, 16 February 1878, pp.548–52.
62. Millman, p.586, fn. 40. I do wish Millman, whose book is in so many ways splendid, had not insisted on carrying on a second volume hidden in his footnotes!

63. *Derby Diaries*, 16 February 1878, p.510.
64. Seton-Watson, *Eastern Question*, p.320.
65. Sumner, pp.382–3, for the damage to Shuvalov.
66. Seton-Watson, *Eastern Question*, pp.321–2; Sumner, pp.379–81, quoting Shuvalov to Gorchakov, 14 February 1878.
67. FO 424/67, Derby to all ambassadors, 16 February 1878.
68. Buckle VI, p.251.
69. *Derby Diaries*, 18 February 1878, p.511; *Gathorne Hardy Diary*, 19 February 1878, p.357, gives the timing for the day before.
70. *Derby Diaries*, 18 February 1878, p.511.
71. *GD II*, memo. by Bismarck, 2 February 1878, pp.62–3.
72. Dep. Hughenden 81/2, Princess Victoria to Queen Victoria, 23 February 1878, fo. 129.
73. *GD II*, Bismarck to Bülow, 6 February 1878, pp.63–4.
74. Seton-Watson, *Eastern Question*, p.328; Gall, *Bismarck II*, p.54.
75. *Derby Diaries*, 20 February 1878, p.512; Seton-Watson, *Eastern Question*, p.338.
76. *Derby Diaries*, 19 February 1878, p.512.
77. *Derby Diaries*, 20 February 1878, p.513.
78. *Derby Diaries*, 21 February 1878, pp.513–14.
79. Millman, p.398.
80. PRO, Cab. 41/10/21, Disraeli to Queen Victoria, 23 February 1878.
81. *Derby Diaries*, 23 February 1878, pp.514–15.
82. *Derby Diaries*, 24 February 1878, p.516.
83. *Derby Diaries*, 27 February 1878, p.518.

Chapter 9

1. E.J. Feuchtwanger, *Disraeli, Democracy and The Tory Party* (Oxford, 1968), p.217, Edward Whitley to Sandon, 1 January 1878; see also Shannon, *Gladstone*, p.152.
2. *Hansard*, Lords Debates, CCXXXVIII, 25 February 1878, col. 289.
3. Arthur Forwood to Lord Sandon, 30 January 1878, quoted in Feuchtwanger, p.217.
4. *Derby Diaries*, 27 February 1878, p.517.

5. Dep. Hughenden 107/1, Northcote to Disraeli, 27 February 1878, fos 197–8.
6. Iddesleigh Papers, Add. Mss. 50022, Derby to Northcote, 28 February 1878, fos 166–7.
7. British Library, Papers of Sir Henry Layard, Add. Mss. 39018, Currie to Layard, 28 February 1878.
8. Dep. Hughenden 91/3, Cairns to Disraeli, 28 February 1878, fos 178–9.
9. Buckle VI, Disraeli to Derby, 28 February 1878, p.249.
10. Dep. Hughenden 113/2 Derby to Disraeli, 28 February 1878.
11. *Derby Diaries*, 2 March 1876, pp.518–19.
12. Buckle VI, Northcote to the Queen, 2 March 1878, p.253.
13. D.E. Lee, 'The Proposed Mediterranean League of 1878', in *Journal of Modern History*, 1931, pp.39–42, for Italy.
14. PRO, Cab. 41/10/23, Disraeli to the Queen, 6 March 1878.
15. *Derby Diaries*, 6 March 1878, p.522.
16. PRO, Cab. 41/10/22, Disraeli to the Queen, 2 March 1878.
17. *GD I*, memo. by Bülow, 23 February 1878, pp.66–7.
18. *Derby Diaries*, 4 March 1878, pp.519–20.
19. *Derby Diaries*, 7 March 1878, p.522.
20. Buckle VI, Disraeli to the Queen, 8 March 1878, p.255.
21. *Derby Diaries*, 8 March 1878, p.523.
22. Buckle VI, Disraeli to the Queen, 8 March 1878, pp.255–6.
23. *Derby Diaries*, 8 March 1878, p.523.
24. *Hansard*, House of Lords, vol. CCXXXVIII, 8 March 1878, cols 866–9.
25. Seton-Watson, *Eastern Question*, p.339, quoting Shuvalov to Gorchakov, 20 March 1878.
26. *Derby Diaries*, 20 March 1878, p.528.
27. PRO, Cab. 41/11/4, Disraeli to the Queen, 18 March 1878.
28. *Derby Diaries*, 18, 19 March 1878, pp.527–8.
29. Dep. Hughenden 113/2, Derby to Disraeli, 19 March 1878, fos 114–16.
30. Dep. Hughenden 113/2, Salisbury to Disraeli, 19 March 1878, fo. 118.
31. Seton-Watson, *Eastern Question*, p.342, quoting Gorchakov to Shuvalov, 17 March 1878.
32. Seton-Watson, *Eastern Question*, pp.342–4.

33. Buckle VI, Disraeli to Lady Bradford, 24 March 1876, p.260.
34. Buckle VI, Disraeli to the Queen, 26 March 1878, p.262.
35. Buckle VI, pp.261–2; see also *GD I* 249, Münster to Bismarck, 29 March 1978, pp.88–90, for a well-informed view of the damage to Derby's reputation.
36. *Derby Diaries*, 27 March 1878, p.532; Buckle VI, pp.264–6.
37. *Derby Diaries*, 27 March 1878, p.533.
38. Seton-Watson, *Eastern Question*, p.365, quoting Shuvalov to Gorchakov, 28 March 1878.
39. Millman, p.414.
40. Dep. Hughenden 81/3, Derby to the Queen, 1 April 1878, fos 1–2.
41. Lady Derby Papers, MCD 311/58, Dean Wellesley to Lady Derby, 28 March 1878.
42. *Derby Diaries*, 15 March 1878, p.527.
43. Buckle VI, pp.269–70, for the correspondence between Derby and Disraeli.
44. Iddesleigh 50022, Derby to Northcote, 28 March 1878, fos 170–1.
45. *Derby Diaries*, 24 February 1878, p.515.
46. *Derby Diaries*, 7 March 1878, p.522.
47. *Derby Diaries*, 24 March 1878, p.531.
48. E.D. Steele, *Palmerston and Liberalism 1855–1865* (Cambridge, 1991), p.275.
49. Balfour Papers, Add. Mss. 49688, Balfour's notes of Salisbury's account of Disraeli's part in 'the secret history of their foreign policy', 8 May 1880.
50. K. Bourne, *The Foreign Policy of Victorian England* (1970), p.133.
51. Millman, p.416.
52. Cab. 41/11/10, Disraeli to the Queen, 12 April 1878.
53. Lee, 'The Proposed Mediterranean League', pp.43–4.
54. *Foundations*, Doc. 144, Salisbury's Circular, 1 April 1878, pp.372–80.
55. Rupp, pp.459–93; Seton-Watson, *Eastern Question*, pp.368–71.
56. *LQV II*, Salisbury to Russell and his responses, 6, 7, 9 April 1878, pp.612–14.
57. Seton-Watson, *Eastern Question*, p.414; Sumner, pp.487–8.
58. Dep. Hughenden 92/4, Salisbury's note, 25 April 1878, fos 67–8.
59. *LQV II*, Queen Victoria to Disraeli, 23, 31 May 1878, pp.622, 625–6, C.H.D. Howard and P. Gordon (eds), *The Cabinet Journal*

of Dudley Ryder, Viscount Sandon, 11 May–10 August 1878 (1974) [henceforth *Sandon Journal*], 24 May 1878, pp.7–10.
60. Sumner, Cabinet memo., 3 May 1878, pp.638–40.
61. Sumner, Shuvalov's memos, 23 May 1878, pp.640–2.
62. *Salisbury II*, Salisbury to Disraeli, 21 March 1878, p.213; *GD I*, 257, Münster to Bülow, 2 April 1878, pp.90–1.
63. *Sandon Journal*, 25, 26, 30 May 1878, pp.11–14; *Gathorne-Hardy Diary*, 30 May 1878, p.374.
64. Buckle VI, Disraeli to the Queen, 5 May 1878, p.291.
65. A.J.P. Taylor, *Bismarck* (1955), p.147.
66. Lee, *Great Britain and the Cyprus Convention*, p.75, quoting Salisbury to Layard, 18 April 1878.
67. Gall, *Bismarck II*, p.57.
68. Prince von Bülow, *Memoirs 1849–1897* (1932), pp.442–3; Taylor, *Bismarck*, pp.171–6; W.N. Medlicott, *The Congress of Berlin* (1965 edn), pp.37–8; Gall, *Bismarck II*, pp.55–7.
69. Zetland II, Disraeli to Lady Bradford, 15 June 1878, p.170.
70. Dep. Hughenden 73/1, fos 28–30, 38–40, for these threats.
71. Buckle VI, Disraeli to the Queen, 31 May 1878, pp.306–7.
72. Zetland II, Disraeli to Lady Bradford, 1 November 1877, p.144.
73. Bülow, p.453.
74. 'I don't want to go out like a spluttering lamp, but rather like a falling star': quoted in Bülow, p.443.
75. Sumner, p.501.
76. *Salisbury II*, pp.280–1.
77. Bülow, p.445.
78. Buckle VI, p.312.
79. Medlicott, p.49.
80. Sumner, pp.516–17.
81. Buckle VI, pp.322–3; *Salisbury II*, p.282; Medlicott, pp.53–5; Sumner, pp.519–20.
82. Buckle VI, p.325.
83. Medlicott, p.62.
84. Buckle VI, p.325; Sumner, pp.522–8, for the detail.
85. Buckle VI, p.324; *Salisbury II*, p.286.
86. *Salisbury II*., Salisbury to Lady Salisbury, 23 June 1878, p.287.
87. Sumner, pp.506–7, and Seton-Watson, Eastern Question, p.439, for the views of Salisbury.

88. *Salisbury II*, p.288.
89. Buckle VI, Disraeli to the Queen, 13 June 1878, p.317.
90. Buckle VI, Disraeli to the Queen, 14 June 1878, p.319.
91. Buckle VI, p.324.
92. *Sandon Journal*, 19 June 1878, p.27.
93. *Sandon Journal*, 10 July 1878, p.39.
94. *Salisbury II*, Salisbury to Lady Salisbury, 22 June 1878, p.287.
95. Sumner, pp.540–1.
96. Dep. Hughenden 92/4, Salisbury to Disraeli, 2 July 1878, fos 84–5.
97. Sumner, p.543.
98. Dep. Hughenden 82/1, Princess Victoria to Queen Victoria, 16 July 1878, fos 45–6
99. A.F. Pribram, *England and the International Policy of the European Great Powers 1871–1914* (Oxford, 1931), p.13.
100. Buckle VI, p.346.
101. Langer, p.162.
102. Seton-Watson, *Eastern Question*, p.503.
103. Seton-Watson, *Eastern Question*, pp.497–8.
104. *Hansard*, House of Lords VI, cols 789–801.
105. Buckle VI, pp.273–7, for the details.
106. G.C. Thompson, *Public Opinion and Lord Beaconsfield, vol. I* (1886), p.70, quoting the *PMG*, 13 April 1878.
107. Thompson p.61.
108. Thompson p.62.
109. *Derby Speeches I*, p.xvi.
110. British Library, Papers of the Ist Earl Cross, Add. Mss. 51266, Derby to Cross, 29 March 1878.
111. Lady Derby Papers, MCD 329/96, Halifax to Lady Derby, 5 April 1880.

Chapter 10

1. Thompson I, p.79, quoting the *PMG*, 13 April 1878.
2. SP/A/Disraeli II, Disraeli to Salisbury, 1 October 1879, fos 480–1.
3. SP/A/Disraeli II, Disraeli to Salisbury, 17 September 1878, fos 311–13.

4. SP/A/Disraeli II, Disraeli to Salisbury, 17 September 1878, fo. 311.
5. M. Cowling, 'Lytton, the Cabinet, and the Russians, August to November 1878', in *English Historical Review*, 1961, pp.59–79.
6. SP/A/Disraeli II, Disraeli to Salisbury, 17 September 1878, fo. 311.
7. SP/A/Disraeli II/D/20/253, Salisbury to Disraeli, 10 October 1878.
8. SP/A/Disraeli I/D/20/120, Salisbury to Disraeli, 31 October 1876.
9. SP/Stanley/D/72, Salisbury to Derby, 21 June 1877.
10. SP/A/Disraeli I/D/20/168, Salisbury to Disraeli, 11 June 1877.
11. Dep. Hughenden 113/3 Derby to Disraeli, 9 October 1877, fo. 14.
12. Dep. Hughenden 113/3 Derby to Disraeli, 11 October 1877, fo. 16.
13. Cowling, p.63.
14. SP/A/Disraeli II/D20/247, Salisbury to Disraeli, 24 September 1878.
15. Buckle VI, Disraeli to the Queen, 26 October 1878, p.387.
16. *Gathorne-Hardy Diary*, 26 October 1878, p.389.
17. Cowling p.70, quoting Lytton to Cranbrook, 27 May 1878.
18. Cowling, p.70, quoting Lytton to F.J. Stephen, 28 January 1878.
19. G.C.Thompson, *Public Opinion and Lord Beaconsfield, vol. II* (1886), p.501.
20. Buckle VI, pp.390–1.
21. Buckle VI, p.401.
22. Thompson II, p.501.
23. Buckle VI, pp.418–24.
24. Buckle VI, Disraeli to the Queen, 24 July 1879, p.447.
25. Thompson II, p.505, quoting Gladstone in November 1879.
26. Buckle VI, Disraeli to Salisbury, 9 September 1879, p.479.
27. Halifax Mss., A4/87a, Pt I, draft letter to Lady Derby, November 1878.
28. Thompson I, p.62.
29. Thompson II, p.280, quoting Chamberlain at Birmingham, 12 January 1878.
30. SP/E/Disraeli II, memo. by Disraeli, 27 September 1879, fos 472–8, for the British account, which is also published in Buckle VI, pp.486–8; *GD I*, Münster to Bismarck, 27 September 1878, pp.146–8, for the German account.
31. *GD I*, p.147.

32. Medlicott, pp.385–8, surveys the arguments.
33. SP/E/Disraeli II, Disraeli to Salisbury, 1 October 1879, fos 480–2.
34. *Salisbury II*, Salisbury to Disraeli, 29 September 1879, pp.365–6.
35. SP/E/Disraeli II, Salisbury to Disraeli, 13 October 1879, fo. 518.
36. SP/E/Disraeli II, Disraeli to Salisbury, 14 October 1879, fos 487–8.
37. Waller, chapter 1; Gall, *Bismarck II*, chapter 12.
38. Langer, pp.174–6.
39. Taylor, *The Struggle for Mastery in Europe*, pp.265–6.
40. *Bismarck's Autobiography II*, pp.255–60.
41. Langer, p.195.
42. SP/E/Disraeli II, Disraeli to Salisbury, 14 October 1879, fos 488–90.
43. Buckle VI, Salisbury to Disraeli, 15 October 1879, p.491.
44. SP/E/Disraeli II, Disraeli to Salisbury, 19 October 1879, fo. 493.
45. *GD I*, p.147.
46. Thompson I, p.56.
47. Thompson II, p.327, quoting Gladstone's speech in Oxford, 30 January 1878.
48. J. Joll (ed.), *Britain and Europe 1793–1940* (1961), pp.184–8.
49. A.E. Houseman, 'A Shropshire Lad'.
50. *Gladstone-Granville Corr. I*, Gladstone to Granville, 21 December 1879, p.105.
51. Thompson II, p.523, quoting the *Daily News*, 15 March 1880.
52. Lady Derby Papers, MCD 329/96, Halifax to Lady Derby, 5 April 1880.
53. Balfour Mss. 49688, Salisbury to Balfour, 15 June 1881, fo. 37.
54. Fitsmaurice II, pp.209–13; *Gladstone-Granville Corr. I*, pp.123–6; W.N. Medlicott, *Bismarck, Gladstone and the Concert of Europe* (1956), pp.79–83.
55. *LQV III*, Granville to the Queen, 27 July 1880, pp.122–3.
56. Paul Knaplund (ed.), *Letters from the Berlin Embassy* (Washington, 1944), [henceforth *Letters from Berlin*]., Lord Odo Russell to Granville, 10 July 1880, p.153.
57. Kennedy, p.158.
58. J.Y. Simpson (ed.), *The Saburov Memoirs*, (Cambridge, 1929), pp.72–3.
59. *Bismarck's Autobiography II*, pp.255–6.
60. Simpson, Saburov to Jomini, 12 May 1880, pp.137.

61. Simpson, Saburov to Jomini, 12 May 1880, p.137.
62. *Letters from Berlin*, Russell to Granville, 19 June 1880, p.148.
63. *Letters from Berlin*, Russell to Granville, 29 May 1880, p.145.
64. *Bismarck's Autobiography II*, p.277.
65. *Letters from Berlin*, Russell to Granville, 8 May 1880, p.141.
66. *Letters from Berlin*, Russell to Granville, 19 June 1880, p.148.
67. *GD I* 'Draft of a General Instruction . . . in Eastern Affairs', 7 November 1880, pp.153–4.
68. Medlicott, *Bismarck, Gladstone . . .*, p.163.
69. Simpson, p.111.
70. Simpson, 'Instructions given at Livadia', 8 September 1879, pp.66–7.
71. Simpson, p.124.
72. A.J.P. Taylor, *The Trouble Makers* (1956) p.72.
73. *Gladstone-Granville Corr. I*, Granville to Gladstone, 29 June 1880, p.140.
74. *Foundations*, Gladstone to Lord Reay, 16 September 1880, pp.407–8.
75. *Foundations*, Gladstone to Mrs Gladstone, 10, 11 October 1880, p.410.
76. Simpson, Saburov to Jomini, 12 May 1880, p.138.
77. Simpson, Saburov's memo. to Giers, 5 August 1879, pp.57–63.
78. Diósegi, pp.65–6; F.R. Bridge, *From Sadowa to Sarajevo* (1972), pp.108–9.
79. Bridge, pp.114–15; Medlicott, *Bismarck, Gladstone . . .* pp.172–89.
80. *Letters from Berlin*, Russell to Granville, 18 October 1880, p.168.
81. *Foundations*, pp.406–7.
82. C.J. Lowe, *The Reluctant Imperialists: British Foreign Policy 1878-1902*, vol.11 (1967) [henceforth *Reluctant Imperialists*, followed by volume numbers], pp. 35–6.
83. *Letters from Berlin*, Russell to Granville, 18 October 1880, p.169.
84. Simpson, Saburov to Jomini, 12 May 1889, p.137.
85. Simpson, p.75.
86. Simpson, p.79.
87. Waller, *Bismarck at the Crossroads*, p.1; whose views are supported by Kennedy, pp.49–54, 66–80, 146–53.
88. Lady Derby Papers, MCD 262/73, Lord Odo Russell to Lady Derby, 13 October 1879.

89. D.W.R. Bahlman, *The Diary of Sir Edward Walter Hamilton, vol. I* (Oxford, 1972) [henceforth *Hamilton Diary*], 11 May 1880, p.12.
90. Thompson II, p.508, quoting Gladstone, 20 July 1878.

Chapter 11

1. Morley, p.615.
2. John Morley, *The Life of William Ewart Gladstone, vol.III* (1903), pp.27–8.
3. Paul Knaplund, *Gladstone's Foreign Policy* (1970 edn), pp.87–90.
4. *Lyons II*, Granville to Lyons, 5 April 1881, p.241; on the background see A. Marsden, *British Diplomacy and Tunis 1875–1902* (Edinburgh, 1971), pp.66–76.
5. *Lyons II*, p.241.
6. *Lyons II*, Granville to Lyons, 22 April 1881, p.242.
7. Marsden, p.74.
8. *Lyons II*, Lyons to Granville, 13 May 1881, pp.243–4.
9. *Gladstone-Granville Corr. I*, Gladstone to Granville, 30 August 1881, p.288.
10. *Gladstone-Granville Corr. I*, Gladstone to Granville, 12 September 1881, p.290.
11. *Lyons II*, Lyons to Granville, 30 September 1881, pp.258–9.
12. *Letters from Berlin*, Granville to Ampthill, 21 September 1881, p.224.
13. *Letters from Berlin*, Ampthill to Granville, 24 September 1881, p.225.
14. *Gladstone-Granville Corr. I*, Gladstone to Granville, 4 January 1882, p.327.
15. *Gladstone-Granville Corr. I*, Granville to Gladstone, 30 December 1881, p.325.
16. H.G.C. Matthew, *Gladstone*, vol. II (1995), pp.135–7.
17. *Gladstone-Granville Corr. I*, Granville to Gladstone, 15 December 1881, p.320; 12 January 1882, p.328.
18. *Letters from Berlin*, Ampthill to Granville, 19 February 1881, p.197.
19. *Letters from Berlin*, Ampthill to Granville, 19 November 1881, p.234.

20. *Gladstone-Granville Corr. I*, Gladstone to Granville, 9 October 1881, p.302.
21. Knaplund, p.173.
22. *Gladstone-Granville Corr. I*, Gladstone to Granville, 22 January 1882, p.335.
23. *Lyons II*, Lyons to Granville, 19 January 1882, pp.271–4.
24. *Lyons II*, Granville to Lyons, 21 January 1882, p.274.
25. *Lyons II*, p.285.
26. *Hamilton Diary*, 25 June 1882, p.293.
27. Lord. E. Fitzmaurice, *Life of the Second Earl Granville, vol. II*, (1913) [henceforth *Granville II*], Granville to Spencer, 22 June 1882, p. 265.
28. *Letters from Berlin*, Ampthill to Granville, 15 July 1882, p.271.
29. *Gladstone-Granville Corr. I*, Gladstone memo., 21 June 1882, p.381.
30. H.C.G. Matthew (ed.), *The Gladstone Diaries, vol. X* (Oxford, 1990) [henceforth *Gladstone Diaries X*], Gladstone memo., 21 June 1882, p.284.
31. *Gladstone-Granville Corr. I, p.381,* fn. 4; *Hamilton Diary*, 26 June 1882, p.296.
32. *Gladstone-Granville Corr. I*, Gladstone to Granville, 25 June 1882, p.382.
33. *Gladstone-Granville Corr. I*, Gladstone to Granville, 1 July 1882, p.383.
34. *Gladstone Diaries X*, Gladstone minute, 3 July 1882, p.291.
35. *Gladstone-Granville Corr. I*, Gladstone to Granville, 5 July 1882, p.386.
36. *Granville II*, p.266.
37. *Hamilton Diary*, 14 July 1882, p.306.
38. *Gladstone Diaries X*, Gladstone to John Bright, 12 July 1882, p.296.
39. *Gladstone Diaries X*, Gladstone to Bright, 14 July 1882, p.298.
40. *Letters from Berlin*, Ampthill to Granville, 15 July 1882, p.271.
41. *LQV III*, Queen Victoria to Gladstone and his response, 1 August 1882, pp.317–18.
42. *Gladstone-Granville Corr. I*, Gladstone to Granville, 16, 21 July 1882, pp.397–8, 400; *Gladstone Diaries X*, Cabinet minute, 24 July 1882, p.304.

43. *Gladstone-Granville Corr. I*, Granville to Gladstone, 21 July 1882, p.401.
44. *Gladstone-Granville Corr. I*, Gladstone to Granville, 22 July 1882, p.401.
45. *Granville II*, p.272.
46. *Gladstone Diaries X*, Cabinet minute, 31 July 1882, p.306.
47. *Gladstone-Granville Corr. I*, Gladstone to Granville, 11 August 1882, p.409.
48. *Gladstone-Granville Corr. I*, Gladstone to Granville, 14 August 1882, p.410; the statement came on 11 August.
49. *Gladstone Diaries X*, Gladstone to Northbrook, 6 September 1882, p.327.
50. *Gladstone-Granville Corr. I*, Gladstone to Granville, 9 September 1882, p.419.
51. *Gladstone Diaries X*, Gladstone to Childers, 16 September 1882, p.335.
52. *Gladstone Diaries X*, Gladstone to Mme Novikov, 15 September 1882, p.334.
53. Knaplund, Appendix II, Gladstone memo., 15 September 1882, p.281.
54. *Gladstone Diaries X*, Gladstone to Northbrook, p.327.
55. *Gladstone-Granville Corr. I*, Gladstone to Granville, 16 September 1882, p.422.
56. *LQV III*, Queen Victoria to Granville, 17 September 1882, p.334. The 'Convention' referred to was the attempt by the Government to come to a military agreement with the Porte.
57. *Letters from Berlin*, Ampthill to Granville, 9 September 1882, p.273.
58. *LQV III*, Granville to the Queen, 10 September 1882, p.322.
59. *Reluctant Imperialists II*, Granville circular, 14 December 1882, p.19.
60. P. M. Hayes, *Late Victorian Foreign Policy* (1977), p.14.
61. The literature here is immense. I have relied upon: Kennedy, *Anglo-German Antagonism*, chapter 10; H. Pogge von Strandman, 'Domestic origins of Germany's colonial expansion under Bismarck', in *Past and Present*, 1969, pp.140–59; A.J.P. Taylor, *Germany's First Bid for Colonies 1884–1885* (1938); H.A. Turner, 'Bismarck's imperialist venture: anti-British in origin?', In P.

Gifford and W.R. Louis (eds), *Britain and Germany in Africa* (New Haven, 1967); Pflanze, *Bismarck III* pp.119–42.
62. Pflanze, *Bismarck III*, p.122.
63. Lady G. Cecil, *Life of Robert, Marquis of Salisbury, vol. IV* (1932), p.41.
64. N. Rich and M.H. Fisher (eds), *The Holstein Papers, vol. III: Correspondence 1861–1896* (Cambridge, 1962) [henceforth *Holstein Papers*, followed by volume numbers], p. 131.
65. *Foundations*, Granville to Goschen, 14 March 1881, p.412.
66. *Letters from Berlin*, Ampthill to Granville, 7 October 1884, p.275.
67. *Foundations*, Granville to Ampthill, 14 June 1884, p.425.
68. H.C.G. Matthew (ed.), *The Gladstone Diaries, vol. XI* (Oxford 1990), p.160.
69. *Letters from Berlin*, Ampthill to Granville, 9 May 1883, p.298.
70. *Letters from Berlin*, Ampthill to Granville, 16 March 1884, p.317.
71. *GD I*, pp.169–74.
72. *Granville II* pp.346–7.
73. *Granville II*, Granville to Ampthill, 21 November 1883, p.349.
74. *GD I*, pp.169–71.
75. *Granville II*, Granville memo., 17 May 1884, pp.351.
76. *GD I*, Bismarck to Münster, 5 May 1884, pp.170–1.
77. *GD I*, Bismarck to Münster, 1 June 1884, pp.175–7.
78. *Letters from Berlin*, Ampthill to Granville, 26 June 1884, p.336.
79. *GD I*, p.135.
80. A. Raman (ed), *The Political Correspondence of Mr Gladstone and Lord Granville vol. II: 1883–1886* (Oxford, 1962) [henceforth *Gladstone-Granville Corr. II*], Gladstone to Granville, 5 September 1884, p.246.
81. *Letters from Berlin*, Ampthill to Granville, 2 August 1884, p.339.
82. *Gladstone-Granville Corr. II*, Gladstone to Granville, 7 December 1884, p.290.
83. *Gladstone-Granville Corr. II*, Granville to Gladstone, 9 December 1884, p.292.
84. *Gladstone-Granville Corr. II*, Gladstone to Granville, 2 December 1884, pp.294–5.
85. *Gladstone-Granville Corr. II*, Gladstone to Granville, 31 December 1884, p.309.
86. *Granville II*, Granville to Gladstone, 25 December 1884, p.371.

SPLENDID ISOLATION?

87. *Gladstone Diaries X*, Gladstone to the Rev. E.A. Abbot, 17 September 1882, p.336.
88. *Lyons II*, Granville to Lyons, 10 April 1885, p.349.
89. *GD I* Prince Reuss to Bismarck, 15 April 1885, pp.199–200.
90. *GD I*, Reuss to Bismarck, 6 May 1885, pp.202–3.
91. *Hamilton Diary*, 25 June 1882, p.294.
92. Thompson I, p.60.

Chapter 12

1. Lady G. Cecil, *Life of Robert, Marquis of Salisbury, vol. III* (1931) [henceforth *Salisbury III*], p. 136.
2. *LQV III*, Queen's Journal, 13 June 1885, pp.666–7.
3. It has only happened once since, in 1924 with Ramsay MacDonald.
4. *LQV III*, Queen's Journal, 12 June 1885, p.663.
5. *Salisbury III*, p.141.
6. *Gathorne-Hardy Diary*, 13 June 1885, p.560.
7. *Salisbury III*, p.138.
8. *Gathorne-Hardy Diary*, 16 June 1885, p.561; A.B. Cooke and J.R.Vincent, *The Governing Passion* (1974), pp.70, 262–9, for a detailed account.
9. *Salisbury III*, pp.138–40; Cooke and Vincent, pp.264–6, for the details.
10. Balfour Papers, Add. Mss. 49688, Balfour's note, 8 May 1880, fo. 24.
11. *Salisbury III*, pp.169–70.
12. Thompson I, pp.69–70, quoting Salisbury, 12 May 1885.
13. *Letters from Berlin*, Ampthill to Granville, 15 July 1882, pp.271–2.
14. C.H.D. Howard, *Splendid Isolation* (1967), pp.76–83, for what follows.
15. F.H., Hinsley, 'Bismarck, Salisbury and the Mediterranean Agreements of 1887', in *Historical Journal*, 1958, p.76.
16. *GD I*, Münster to Bismarck, 26 June 1885, p.207.
17. *GD I*, Salisbury to Bismarck, 2 July 1885, p.208.
18. *Lyons II*, p.354; see also *GD I*, Herbert Bismarck to Bismarck, 1 October 1884, p.185.
19. *GD I*, Herbert Bismarck to Bismarck, 1 October, p.185; Bismarck to Münster, 5 December 1884, p.188.

20. SP/E/Currie 1/96, Currie to Salibsury, 28 September 1885, fo. 203.
21. *Reluctant Imperialists I*, p.63.
22. Langer, p.189.
23. *Salisbury III*, p.167.
24. *Salisbury III*, Salisbury to Sir E. Thornton, 21 July 1885, p.226.
25. SP/E/Currie 1/60, Currie to Salisbury, 4 August 1885, of. 128.
26. SP/E/Currie 1/60, 'Paper shown to Ct. Herbert Bismarck . . .', 3 August 1885, fos 122–7.
27. SP/E/Currie 1/62, Currie to Salisbury, 7 August 1885, fo. 128.
28. SP/E /Currie 1/64, Currie to Salisbury, 10 August 1885, fos 134–6.
29. *LQV III*, Salisbury to the Queen, 4 July 1885, p.684.
30. *GD I*, Bismarck to Wilhelm I, 27 May 1885, pp.204–6.
31. A. Ramm, *Sir Robert Morier* (Oxford, 1973), p.217.
32. SP/D/Morier, Salisbury to Sir Robert Morier, 15 September 1885.
33. *Reluctant Imperialists, I* pp.90–2, for Russian policy.
34. Ramm, *Morier*, p.208, quoting Salisbury to Morier, 16 September 1885.
35. Colin L. Smith, *The Embassy of Sir William White at Constantinople 1886–1891* (Oxford, 1957), p.162.
36. *Salisbury III*, Salisbury to Lyons, 16 October 1885, p.245.
37. W.N. Medlicott, 'The Powers and the Unification of the Two Bulgarias, 1885', in *English Historical Review*, 1939, p.276.
38. *Salisbury III*, pp.242–5.
39. *GD I*, Hatzfeldt to Herbert Bismarck, 5 December 1885, pp.212–13, for Churchill.
40. *Salisbury III*, Salisbury to Sir Robert Morier, 2 December 1885, p.251.
41. *Salisbury III*, Salisbury to the Queen, 20 November 1885 p.251.
42. Langer, pp.356–7.
43. *LQV III*, Queen Victoria to Salisbury, 29 January 1886, p.31.
44. *Foundations*, p.431.
45. *Salisbury III*, p.224–5.
46. G. Martel, *Imperial Diplomacy: Rosebery and the Failure of Foreign Policy* (1986), p.15.
47. Martel, p.17.
48. Martel, p.30.
49. SP/E/ lddesleigh/322, Salisbury to Northcote, 16 January 1885, fo. 790.

50. R. Shannon, *The Age of Salisbury 1881–1902* (1995), pp.209–15, for a perceptive account of the political scene.
51. *Salisbury III*, p.311; *Gathorne-Hardy Diary*, 28 July 1886, pp. 614–15.
52. *Salisbury III*, pp.309–11, for details.
53. J.R. Vincent (ed.), *The Later Derby Diaries* (Bristol, 1981) [henceforth *Later Derby Diaries*], 23 July 1886, p.72.
54. *Lyons II*, Salisbury to Lyons, 26 July 1886, p.371.
55. *Gathorne-Hardy Diary*, 28 July 1886, p.616.
56. *LQV III*, Queen's Journal, 24 July 1886, pp.165–6.
57. *Reluctant Imperialists I* p.104.
58. *Salisbury III*, Salisbury to the Queen, 7 September 1886, p.319.
59. Winston S. Churchill, *Lord Randolph Churchill* (1974 edn), pp.516–18.
60. Churchill, Salisbury to Churchill, 28 September 1886, p.519.
61. Churchill, Salisbury to Churchill, 1 October 1886, p.520.
62. Churchill, Churchill to Salisbury, 30 September 1886, pp.519–20.
63. *Salisbury III*, pp.322–3.
64. Hinsley, 'Bismarck, Salisbury and the Mediterranean Agreements . . .', p.77.
65. *Salisbury III*, Cranbrook to Salisbury, 23 November 1886, p.326; *Gathorne-Hardy Diary*, 23 November 1886, p.636.
66. *Salisbury III*, Salisbury to Cranbrook, 25 November 1886, pp.326–7.
67. *LQV III*, Salisbury to the Queen, 29 July 1886, p.168.
68. *GDI*, Hatzfeldt to Herbert Bismarck, 26 October 1886, pp.259–62.
69. Ramm, *Morier*, Morier to Salisbury, 14 September 1886, p.232.

Chapter 13

1. Lady G. Cecil, *Life of Robert, Marquis of Salisbury, vol. IV* (1932) [henceforth *Salisbury IV*], Salisbury to the Queen, 29 August 1886, p.3.
2. *Salisbury IV*, Salisbury to the Queen, 24 January 1887, p.15.
3. SP/E/lddesleigh IV/432, Iddesleigh to Salisbury, 18 September 1886, fo. 1041.
4. SP/E/Currie 1/96, 'Notes of conversation with Prince Bismarck . . . 28 September 1885', fo. 206 foll.

5. SP/E Iddesleigh IV/432, Iddesleigh to Salisbury, 18 September 1886, fo. 1042.
6. Ramm, *Morier*, Salisbury to Morier, 2 October 1886, pp.235–8.
7. SP/E/Currie 1/96, 'Notes of Conversation with Prince Bismarck . . . 28 September 1885', fo. 206 foll.
8. *Foundations*, memo. communicated to Austria-Hungary on 2 October 1886, pp.442–5.
9. *GD I*, note, pp.270–1.
10. C.J. Lowe, *Salisbury and the Mediterranean 1886–1896* (1965), p.7, quoting Bismarck, 29 September 1886.
11. *Salisbury IV*, Salisbury to Wolff, 23 February 1887, p.42.
12. *Salisbury IV*, Salisbury to Baring, 6 May 1887, p.45.
13. *Salisbury IV*, Salisbury to Malet, 23 February 1887, pp.40–1.
14. *Salisbury IV*, Salisbury to Wolff, 23 February 1887, p.41.
15. *Lyons II*, Lyons to Iddesleigh, 23 November 1886, pp.377–8.
16. Hinsely, 'Bismarck, Salisbury and the Mediterranean Agreements . . .', p.79.
17. *Lyons II*, Lyons to Iddesleigh, 21 December 1886, pp.381–2.
18. *Salisbury IV*, Salisbury to Malet, 23 February 1887, pp.40–1.
19. *Salisbury IV*, p.247.
20. G.P. Gooch & H. Temperley (eds), *British Documents on the Origins of the War, 1898–1914, vol. VIII: Arbitration and Neutrality* (1932) [henceforth *BD*, followed by volume number], pp.1–6.
21. Lowe, *Salisbury and the Mediterranean*, pp.12–14.
22. *Salisbury IV*, Salisbury to Sir Augustus Paget, 9 February 1887, p.23.
23. *Gathorne-Hardy Diary*, 2 February 1887, p.649.
24. *LQV III*, Salisbury to the Queen, 2 February 1887, pp.277–9.
25. *Gathorne-Hardy Diary*, 6 February 1887, p.650.
26. *Parliamentary Papers*, vol. CIX (1888), C.5256, *France No. 1* (1888).
27. *Gathorne-Hardy Diary*, 2 February 1887, p.649.
28. *Salisbury IV*, Salisbury to Lyons, 5 February 1887, pp.29–30.
29. *Gathorne-Hardy Diary*, 6 February 1887, p.650.
30. *LQV III*, Salisbury to the Queen, 10 February 1887, p.272.
31. *BD VIII*, exchange of notes, 12 February 1887, pp.1–3.
32. *LQV III* Salisbury to the Queen, 10 February 1887, p.272.
33. *Salisbury IV*, Salisbury to Goschen, 5 February 1887, p.22.

SPLENDID ISOLATION?

34. Lowe, *Salisbury and the Mediterranean*, pp.17–18.
35. Ramm, *Morier*, Salisbury to Morier, 19 January 1887, p.245.
36. *Salisbury IV*, Salisbury to Sir Edward Malet, 23 February 1887, pp.40–1.
37. *Salisbury IV*, Salisbury to Mr Scott (Berlin), 4 May 1887, p.43.
38. *Lyons II., Salisbury to Lyons, 20 July 1887, p.409.*
39. *Lyons II., Salisbury to Lyons, 20 July 1887, p.409.*
40. *Salisbury IV*, Sailsbury to Sir William White, 10 August 1887, pp.50–1.
41. *Salisbury IV*, p.53.
42. *Salisbury IV*, Salisbury to Alfred Austin, 27 October 1887 p.54.
43. Ramm, *Morier*, pp.232–41, for the details.
44. *Salisbury IV*, Salisbury to Sir William White, 10 August 1887, p.51.
45. *GD I*, Hatzfeldt to Bismarck, 3 August 1887, pp.308–10.
46. *GD I*, Bismarck to Hatzfeldt, 8 August 1887, pp.310–12.
47. *GD I*, Bismarck minute, August 1887, p.315.
48. *GD I*, Bismarck's minutes on Hatzfeldt's despatch of 10 August 1887, p.315.
49. *GD I*, memo. by Herbert Bismarck, 24 August 1887, pp.316–20.
50. Lowe, *Salisbury and the Mediterranean Agreements*, pp.20–1, for the background.
51. *Salisbury IV* p.69.
52. *Salisbury IV*, Salisbury to the Queen, 28 October 1887, p.69.
53. *Salisbiury IV*, Salisbury to Sir William White, 2 November 1887, p.70.
54. Hinsley, 'Bismarck, Salisbury and the Mediterranean Agreements . . .', pp.80–1.
55. *Salisbury IV*, Salisbury to Malet, 16 November 1887, p.72; *GDI*, Hatzfeldt to Bismarck, 12 November 1887, pp. 337–42.
56. *GD I*, Bismarck to Salisbury, 22 November 1887, pp.345–8. The translations are mine. The German text is in *GD IV*, pp.376–80.
57. *Salisbury IV*, Salisbury to Bismarck, 30 November 1998, pp.75–7.
58. *BD VIII*, Salisbury's reply to the Austrian and Italian Ambassadors, 12 December 1887, pp.12–13.
59. *Salisbury IV*, p.80.
60. *GD I*, Bismarck to Hatzfeldt, 11 January 1889, pp.369–72.
61. *GD I*, Herbert Bismarck to Bismarck, 22 March 1889, pp.373–5.
62. *Later Derby Diaries*, 14 January 1887, pp.76–7.

63. *GD I*, Hatzfeldt to Bismarck, 13 August 1887, p.249.
64. A.N. Porter, 'Lord Salisbury, Foreign Policy and Domestic Finance, 1860–1900', in R. and H. Cecil (eds), *Salisbury: the Man and his Policies* (1987), Chapter 7.
65. A.J. Marder, *The Anatomy of British Sea Power, 1880–1905* (NY, 1940), pp.45–6.
66. Marder, pp.132–6; Jon Tetsuro Sumida, *In Defence of Naval Supremacy: Finance, Technology and British Naval Policy 1889–1914* (1989), pp.11–13; C.J. Bartlett, *Defence and Diplomacy: Britain and the Great Powers 1815–1914* (Manchester, 1993), pp.86–8.
67. In addition to Marder, Sumida and Bartlett, see also Lowe, *Salisbury and the Mediterranean Agreements*, pp.41–53.
68. Sumida, p.13.
69. R. Oliver and T. Matthew, *History of East Africa, Vol. I* (Oxford, 1963), pp.355-72.
70. *GD I*, Herbert Bismarck to Bismarck, 27 March 1889, p.375.
71. *Salisbury IV* pp.247–8.
72. *Reluctant Imperialists I*, p.129.
73. D.R. Gillard, 'Salisbury's African policy and the Heligoland Offer of 1890' in *English Historical Review*, 1960; Kennedy, pp.205–10.
74. *Reluctant Imperialists I*, p.136.
75. *LQV III*, Salisbury to the Queen, 10 June 1890, p.614

Chapter 14

1. *Salisbury IV*, Salisbury to Currie, 18 August 1892, pp.404–5.
2. G. N. Sanderson, *England, Europe and the Upper Nile 1882–1899* (Edinburgh, 1965), pp.102–9.
3. Sanderson, pp.113–15.
4. *Salisbury IV*, Salisbury to Lytton, 16 June 1891, p.381.
5. *Holstein Papers I*, 126–8; N. Rich, *Friedrich von Holstein 2vols* (Cambridge 1965) [henceforth *Holstein*, followed by volume number], pp.307–17, for the full story.
6. J.C.G. Röhl, *Germany without Bismarck* (1967), pp.63–75; *Holstein I*, pp.287–99; I. Geiss, *German Foreign Policy 1871–1914* (1970), pp.62–4.
7. Prince von Bülow, *Memoirs 1897–1903* (1931), p.38.

8. Marder, p.241.
9. Martel, pp.125–36; Langer, pp.43–6.
10. Martel, pp.202–15; A.J.P. Taylor, *Essays in English History* (1976), 'Prelude to Fashoda', pp.129–69.
11. Martel, p.123.
12. Martel, p.255, quoting Rosebery to Cromer, 22 April 1895.
13. Martel, p.249.
14. *Holstein II*, pp.464–5.
15. *Holstein II*, p.438.
16. PRO, Malet Papers, FO 343/3, Rosebery to Malet, 3 January 1894.
17. Martel, p.174.
18. Martel pp.179–84.
19. Shannon, *Age of Salisbury*, pp.407–9.
20. Shannon, *Age of Salisbury*, pp.413–16.
21. Smith, *Lord Salisbury on Politics*, p.34.
22. Smith, p.100.
23. Smith, p.42.
24. J.A.S. Grenville, *Lord Salisbury and Foreign Policy: The Close of the Nineteenth Century* (1964), p.17.
25. *BD I*, Salisbury to Currie, 12 October 1900, p.350.
26. *Salisbury IV*, p.162.
27. Shannon, *Age of Salisbury*, p.485.
28. Neilson, chapter 1.
29. Henry Kissinger, *Diplomacy* (1993), p.187.
30. L.M. Penson, 'The new course in British Foreign Policy, 1892–1902', in *Transactions of the Royal Historical Society*, 1943; J.D. Hargreaves, '*Entente Manqée;* Anglo-French Relations '1895–1896', *Cambridge Historical Journal*, 1953, pp.69–70.
31. Hargreaves, pp.70–1.
32. *Documents Diplomatiques Français 1ère série, tome XII* [henceforth *DDF*, followed by volume number] nos 69, 75, 144, Councel to Hanotaux, 17, 27 June, 29 August 1895.
33. Salt, pp.71–81, for an account which lacks the usual anti-Ottoman bias.
34. British Library Papers of the 5th Marquis of Lansdowne (not yet numbered), Private Letters [henceforth Lansdowne Pte Letters] Corr. after 1900, S, memo. By Sir Thomas Sanderson, 11 November 1901. This material has only just become available.

35. Grenville, pp.109–10, thinks there was a change of policy; Neilson, pp.113–14, 167–9, generally follows him; K. Wilson, 'Constantinople or Cairo: Lord Salisbury and the Partition of the Ottoman Empire 1886–97', in K. Wilson (ed.), *Empire* and *Continent* (1987), offers ingenious arguments the other way.
36. Grenville, pp.30–7, for detailed references.
37. M.M. Jefferson, 'Lord Salisbury's Conversations with the Tsar at Balmoral, 27 and 29 September 1896', in *Slavonic and East European Review*, December 1960, pp.216–22.
38. Salt, p.52, quoting FO 800/32, Vambéry to Currie, June 1890.
39. Marder, pp.158–60.
40. *Hansard*, Lords debates, 4th Series, vol. XLVII, 19 March 1897, cols 1011–12.
41. Lowe, *Salisbury and the Mediterranean*, pp.100–1, quoting SP, Salisbury to Currie, 27 August, 17 December 1895.
42. Marder, pp.244–7.
43. *Reluctant Imperialists II*, pp.45–7, 85–91; Neilson, p.113.
44. Lowe, *Salisbury and the Mediterranean*, pp.101, 105.
45. Lansdowne Pte Letters, Corr. after 1900, S, memo. by Sir Thomas Sanderson, 11 November 1901.
46. *GD II*, Rothenham to Hatzfeldt, 1 August 1895, p.331.
47. *GD II*, Hatzfeldt to Holstein, 3 August 1895, pp.332–4.
48. *Holstein II*, p.452.
49. Grenville, p.39, claims this, but the material in the Lansdowne Mss., Corr. After 1900, S, in particular Chirol to Lansdowne, 7 November 1901, shows that it still rankled with the Kaiser.
50. *GD II* editorial note, pp.339–40.
51. Lansdowne Mss., Corr. after 1900, S, Chirol to Lansdowne, 7 November 1901.
52. Lansdowne Mss., Corr. after 1900, S, Sanderson's memo. 11 November 1901.
53. Grenville, pp.40–3, for the detail.
54. *GP XI*, Wilhelm II to Marschall, 25 October 1895, pp.8–11.
55. Grenville, pp.65–6.
56. G.J. Renier, *Great Britain and the Netherlands 1813–1815* (1930), pp.321–4.
57. A.E.Campbell, 'Great Britain and the United States in the Far

East, 1895-1903', in *Historical Journal*, 1958, pp.12–13; Grenville pp.57–8; Walter LeFeber, *The Cambridge History of American Foreign Relations, vol II: The American Search for Opportunity 1865–1913 (1993)*, pp.124–5.
58. LeFeber p.124.
59. S. Gwynne (ed.), *The Letters and Friendships of Sir Cecil Spring-Rice: A Record, vol. I* (1929) [henceforth *Spring-Rice I*] Spring-Rice to Villiers, 12 April 1895, p.175.
60. Grenville, pp.60–3.
61. Allan Nevins, *Henry White; Thirty Years of American Diplomacy* (NY, 1930), White to William H. Buckler, 21 February 1896, p.110.
62. *Holstein II*, pp.450–1.
63. *GD II*, Wilhelm II to Marschall, 25 October 1895, p.368.
64. *GD II*, Wilhelm's marginal notes, 25 October 1895, p.369.
65. *GD II*, Holstein's memo., 30 December 1895, p.373–4.
66. *Holstein II* p.465.
67. *GP XI*, Marschall to Hatzfeldt, 31 December 1895, pp.18–19.
68. *Spring-Rice I*, Spring-Rice to Villiers, 11 January 1896, p.188.
69. Langer, p.235, quoting from the extracts quoted in F. Thimme, 'Die Krüger-Depesche', in *Europäische Gespräche*, Jahrgang 2, 1924, p.212; *Holstein II* pp.469–70.
70. *GP XI*, no. 2610, pp.31–2.
71. *The Times*, 6 January 1896.
72. Langer, pp.241–2.
73. *GP XI*, no.2636.
74. *Holstein II*, p.469.
75. Lowe, *Salisbury and the Mediterranean*, p.107, quoting Hohenloe to Munster, early 1896.
76. J.L. Garvin, *The Life of Joseph Chamberlain vol. III* (1934) [henceforth *Chamberlain III*], Chamberlain diary, 11 January 1896, p.161.
77. *Chamberlain III*, Chamberlain to Salisbury, 4 January 1896, p.95.
78. *LQV III*, p.22.
79. Lansdowne Mss. Corr. after 1900, S, Salisbury to Lansdowne, 30 September 1901.
80. A. Porter, *Origins of the South African War* (1975), pp.36–8.
81. Balfour Papers, Add. Mss. 49778, Hamilton to Balfour, 12 January 1898.

82. Marder, p.264.
83. Howard, pp.12–13.
84. *BD VI*, Appendix IV, Salisbury to Mr E.B. Iwan-Muller, 31 August 1896, p.780.
85. Lowe, *Salisbury and the Mediterranean*, p.112.
86. Lowe, *Salisbury and the Mediterranean*, pp.110–11.
87. *BD VIII*, nos 1 (f) and (g), Salisbury to Monson, 4, 26 February 1896, pp.4–5; for the Austrian report, see *Reluctant Imperialists II*, Deym to Goluchowski, 6 February 1896, pp.108–9.
88. Jefferson, Salisbury to the Tsar, 27 September 1896, p.219.
89. *Reluctant Imperialists II*, Salisbury to the Queen, 19 February 1896, pp.109–10.
90. *Reluctant Imperialists II*, Salisbury to Lascelles, 10 March 1896, pp.110–11
91. *BD VIII*. Annexe 1, 6, for the agreement of March 1887, and 2(f), 13, for the December agreement.
92. *BD VI*, Appendix IV.
93. Lords debates, *Hansard*, 4th series vol. XLVII, 19 March 1897, cols 1008–18.
94. Lords debates, *Hansard*, 4th series vol. XXXVI, 15 August 1895, col. 49.
95. K. Wilson, 'Constantinople or Cairo . . .', p.18.
96. PRO, Cab. 37/42, no. 35, Salisbury's report, 27, 29 September 1896.

Chapter 15

1. Thompson I, p.57.
2. J.L. Garvin, *The Life of Joseph Chamberlain, vol. II* (1934), p.641.
3. Porter, pp.32, 51.
4. *Chamberlain III*, p.27.
5. Randolph Churchill, *Winston S. Churchill. Companion vol. 1. part 2 1896–1900* (1967), Churchill to Lady Randolph Churchill, 25 February 1897, p.734.
6. *Holstein Papers III*, Hatzfeldt to Holstein, 28 April 1896; p.607.
7. *BD VI*, Appendix IV, Salisbury to Iwan-Muller, 31 August 1896, p.780.

8. *The Times*, 10 November 1896.
9. Lords debates, *Hansard*, 4th series, vol. XLV, 19 January 1897, cols 28–9.
10. Langer, pp.347–55.
11. The Earl of Ronaldshay, *The Life of Lord Curzon, vol. I* (1928) [henceforth *Curzon I*], Curzon to Mary Curzon, 9 November 1896, p.264.
12. Grenville, pp.109–10.
13. *Chamberlain III*, p.203.
14. *Chamberlain III*, Chamberlain to Salisbury, 6 June 1897, p.204.
15. *Chamberlain III*, Chamberlain to Selborne, 12 September 1897, p.204.
16. *Chamberlain III*, Chamberlain to Selborne, 29 September 1897, p.211.
17. *LQV III*, Queen's Journal, 14 November 1897, p.209.
18. *DDF XIV*, Courcel to Hanotaux, 12 March 1898, p.135.
19. Grenville, pp.111–13.
20. *Holstein Papers IV*, Hatzfeldt to Holstein, 23 April 1897, p.31.
21. *Holstein Papers III*, Hatzfeldt to Holstein, 15 March 1896, p.598.
22. G.N. Sanderson, *England, Europe and the Upper Nile 1882–1889* (Edinburgh, 1965), pp.243–6.
23. Lord Zetland, *Lord Cromer* (1932), Salisbury to Cromer, 13 March 1897, p.223.
24. Lansdowne Mss., Corr. after 1900, S, Sanderson memo., 11 November 1901.
25. *Holstein Papers III*, Holstein to Radolin, 22 March 1896, p.601.
26. Geiss, p.78.
27. Röhl, *Germany without Bismarck*, pp.162–3.
28. Taylor, *The Struggle for Mastery*, p.586.
29. K.A. Lerman, *The Chancellor as Courtier* (Cambridge, 1990), p.2.
30. F. Whyte (ed.), *Letters of Prince Bülow* (n.d.).
31. *BD VI*, p.198.
32. Peter Winzen, *Bülows Weltmachtkonzept: Untersuchungen zur Führphase seiner Aussenpolitik 1897–1901* (Boppard-am-Rhein, 1997).
33. See Lerman pp.3–9, for a review of the arguments.
34. Ian F.D. Morrow, 'The Foreign Policy of Prince von Bülow', in *Cambridge Historical Journal*, 1932, pp.63–93 was the last English-language attempt to do this!

35. F. Fischer, *Germany's Aims in the First World War* (1967) and his *War of Illusions* (1975) are the classic statements of this view which he has restated more recently in G. Shöllegen (ed.) *Escape into War* (Oxford, 1990), pp.19–40.
36. *BD III*, Appendix A, memo. by Mr Eyre Crowe on the Present State of British Relations with France and Germany, 1 January 1907, p.414.
37. *BD III*, Crowe memo., 1 January 1907, p.415.
38. *BD VI*, Crowe memo. 14 May 1911, pp.627–8.
39. James Ratallack, *Germany in the Age of Kaiser Wilhelm II* (1996), p.74, for some suitably trenchant views on this.
40. Ratallack p.73.
41. Bülow, Memoirs 1897–1903 pp.86–7.
42. *Spring-Rice I*, letter 24 July 1897, p.226.
43. J.A. White *Transition to Global Rivalry* (Cambridge, 1995), pp.63–4.
44. Langer, p.451.
45. E. Johann (ed.) *Reden des Kaisers: Ansprachen, Predigten und Trinksprüche Wilhelms II* (Munich, 1966), pp.86–8, for the authoritative texts.
46. *BD I*, Salisbury to Lascelles, 12 January 1898, p.4.
47. *Holstein Papers IV*, Hatzfeldt to Holstein, 12 May 1897, p.36.
48. *Chamberlain III*. p.251.
49. *Spring-Rice I*. letter 1 January 1898, p.245.
50. Blanche E.C. Dugdale, *Arthur James Balfour; Years 1848–1906* (1939) [henceforth *Balfour*], Chamberlain to Balfour, 3 February 1898, p.191–2.
51. *Chamberlain III*, Salisbury to Chamberlain, 30 December 1897, p.249.
52. *BD I*, Salisbury to O'Conor, 25 January, O'Conor to Salisbury, 2,3,7 February 1898, pp.8–10.
53. *BD I*, memo. by J.A.C. Tilley, 14 January 1904, pp.1–3; Grenville, pp.140–1.
54. *BD I*, Salisbury to O'Conor, 8 February 1898, p.11
55. *BD I*, note to doc. 14, p.11.
56. *BD I*, Salisbury to Sir C. MacDonald, 11 February 1898, p.11.
57. *BD I*, Tilley memo. 14 January 1904, p.2.
58. *Balfour*, Chamberlain to Balfour, 3 February 1898, pp.191–2.

59. Nevins, White to Hay, 6 March 1898, pp.162–4; *Chamberlain III*, p.252; *Balfour I*, pp.192–3.
60. *BD I*, O'Conor to Salisbury, 19 February 1898, p.14.
61. *BD I*, O'Conor to Salisbury, 3, 13 March 1898, pp.16–17.
62. *BD I*, O'Conor to Salisbury, 3, 13 March 1898, pp.16–17.
63. *BD I*, Salisbury minute, 22 March 1898, pp.22–3.
64. *BD I*, Sir E. Monson to Salisbury, 20 January 1898, pp.136–8.
65. *BD I*, Monson to Salisbury, 26 February 1898, p.146.
66. PRO, Private Papers of British Diplomats, FO 800 series, papers of Sir Frank Lascelles, FO 800/16 O'Conor to Lascelles, 7 April 1898; *Holstein Papers IV*, Hatzfeldt to Holstein, 28 March 1898, p.67.
67. *Curzon I*, pp.280–1, for quotations; see also *The Times*, the *Morning Post* and the *Saturday Review* throughout March and April.
68. *Curzon I*, pp.284–5; *Balfour I*, Balfour to the Queen, 26 March 1898, p.193.
69. India Office Library, Curzon Papers, Mss. Eur F/112b, Salisbury to Curzon, 9 April 1898.
70. Lansdowne Mss. Pte letters, vol. 5, Prime Minister, Balfour to Lansdowne, 11 October 1905.
71. A.E. Campbell, 'Great Britain and the United States . . .', p.161.
72. *GP XIV/I* nr. 3782, Hatzfeldt to Bülow, 29 March 1898, pp.196–9. *Chamberlain III*, pp.259–61, for the text; Grenville, *Salisbury* pp.153–68; J.M. Goudswaard, *Some Aspects of the End of Britain's 'Splendid Isolation' 1898–1904* (Rotterdam, 1952), pp.14–22.
73. Lerman, p.12.
74. *Holstein Papers IV*, Holstein to Brandt, 23 December 1905, p.377.
75. *DDF XIV*, no. 1, Billot to Hanotaux, 4 January 1898, pp.1–2.
76. Kennedy, p.226, quoting Bülow in 1886 and 1895.
77. Kennedy, p.226.
78. Winzen *passim*; Kenndey, pp.226–7.
79. *GP XIV/I* nr. 3784, Bülow to Hatzfeldt, 30 March 1898, pp.199–202.
80. *Chamberlain III*, Chamberlain's second memo. 1 April 1898, pp.263–6.
81. *Holstein Papers IV,* Holstein to Hatzfeldt, 3 April 1898, pp.68–70
82. *Holstein Papers IV,* Hatzfeldt to Holstein, 17 May 1898, pp.77–9.
83. *GP XIV/I* nr. 3785, Bülow to Hatzfeldt, pp.204–7.

84. *GP XIV/I* nr. 3788, Hatzfeldt to Höhenloe, 7 April 1898, pp.211–16.
85. *Balfour I*, Salisbury to Balfour, 9 April 1898, p.195.
86. *Balfour I*, Balfour to Salisbury, 14 April 1898, p.196–8.
87. *Holstein Papers IV*, Hatzfeldt to Bülow, 20 April 1898, pp.70–4.
88. *GP XIV/I*, nr. 3789, Kaiser's notes, p.216.
89. *GP XIV/I*, nr. 3769, Bülow to Wilhelm II, 9 April 1898, pp.169–70.
90. *Balfour I*, Balfour to Salisbury, 14 April 1898, p.198.
91. *Holstein II*, p.575.
92. *GP XIV/I*, nr. 3790, Wilhelm II to Bülow, 10 April, and Bülow's notes, pp.217–18.
93. *GP XIV/I*, nr. 3791 Hatzfeldt to Bülow, 23 April 1898, p.218.
94. *Chamberlain III*, Chamberlain's third memo. 22 April 1898, pp.271–2.
95. *GP XIV/I*, nr. 3791, Hatzfeldt to Bülow 23 April 1898, p.218.
96. *GP XIV/I*, nr. 3792, Bülow to Hatzfeldt, 24 April 1898, pp.218–21.
97. *GP XIV/I*, nr. 3793, Hatzfeldt to Bülow, 26 April 1898, pp.221–6, for Hatzfeldt's much fuller account; *Chamberlain III*, pp.273–4, for the British side.
98. *GP XIV/I*, nr. 3793, Hatzfeldt to Bülow, 26 April 1898, Kaiser's notes. p.226.
99. *Chamberlain III*, pp.276–7.
100. *Chamberlain III*, Chamberlain to Salisbury, 29 April 1898, pp.278–9.
101. *Chamberlain III*, Salisbury to Chamberlain, 2 May 1898, p.279.
102. *Chamberlain III*, p.281.
103. *DDF XIV*, no. 181, Geoffray to Hanotaux, 7 May 1898, pp.265–7.
104. *GP XIV/I*, n. to nr. 3796, p.230; *Holstein Papers IV*, Hatzfeldt to Holstein, 17 June 1898, p.88.
105. *GP XIV/I*, nr. 3798, Hatzfeldt to Hohenloe, 20 May 1898, pp.235–7.
106. Grenville pp.166–8.

Chapter 16

1. *DDF XIV*, no. 193, Geoffray to Hanotaux, 17 May 1898, pp.288–9; Goudswaard, pp.25–6.
2. *Chamberlain III*, p.283.

3. *Chamberlain III*, pp.282.
4. *Chamberlain III*, pp.301–2.
5. *DDF XIV*, no. 193, Geoffray to Hanotaux, 17 May 1898, pp.290–2, for this.
6. Baron A. Meyendorff (ed.), *Correspondence Diplomatique de M. De Staal. Tome II 1889–1900* (Paris, 1929), Staal to Muraviev, 13/25 May 1898, pp.384–6.
7. *Holstein Papers IV*, Hatzfeldt to Holstein, 17 May 1898, p.78.
8. *DDF XIV*, no. 193, Geoffray to Hanotaux, 17 May 1898, pp.288–9; Meyendorff (ed.), Staal to Muraviev, 13/25 May 1898, pp.384–6; *GP XIV I*, nr. 3797, Hatzfeldt to Foreign Office, 15 May 1898, pp.233–5.
9. Grenville p.171; *DDF XIV*, no. 198, note by Hanotaux, 18 May 1898, pp.294–5.
10. Hawkins and Powell, *Kimberley's Journal*, 19 May 1898, p.460.
11. *GP XIV/I, nr. 3795, Hatzfeldt to the Foreign Office, 13 May 1898, p.229.*
12. *BD I*, Lascelles to Salisbury, 26 May 1898, pp.34–5.
13. *Holstein Papers IV*, p.79.
14. *GP XIV/I*, nr. 3799, the Kaiser's secret memo., n.d., pp.239–40.
15. *Holstein II*, p.582.
16. *Holstein Papers IV*, Hatzfeldt to Holstein, 2 June 1989, p.583.
17. *GP XIV/I*, nr. 3803, Nicholas II to Wilhelm II, 22 May/3 June 1898, pp.250–1.
18. *GP XIV/I)*, nr. 3800, Hatzfeldt to Foreign Office, 2 June 1898, pp.240–1.
19. *BD I*, memo. by Mr Bertie, 1 May 1898, pp.44–8; *Holstein Papers IV*, Hatzfeldt to Holstein, 28 April 1899, pp.110–11.
20. *GP XIV/I*, nr. 3806 Bülow to Hatzfeldt, 8 June 1898, pp.259–61; nr. 3817, Hatzfeldt to Foreign Office, 21 June 1898, p.270–1; nr. 3818, Bülow to Hatzfeldt, 22 June 1898, pp.272–6.
21. *BD I*, Salisbury to Viscount Gough, 21 June 1898, p.49.
22. *BD I*, Salisbury to MacDonell, 23 June 1898 plus enclosures, pp.51–2.
23. *BD I*, Salisbury's despatches, 21, 22, 23, 29 June, pp.44–53.
24. *GP XIV/I* nr. 3807, Hatzfeldt to Foreign Office, 14 June 1898, pp.261–3.
25. *BD I*, Salisbury to Gough, 23 June 1898, pp.52–3.

26. *Chamberlain III*, Milner to Chamberlain, 5 July 1898, pp.311.
27. *GP XIV/I*, nr. 3831, 3833, 3834–9, Bülow-Hatzfeldt correspondence, 13–24 July 1898, pp.293–303.
28. *Chamberlain III*, p.314.
29. *Chamberlain III*, Chamberlain to Balfour, 19 August 1898, p.315.
30. D.G. Boyce (ed.), *The Crisis of British Power: The Imperial and Naval Papers of the Second Earl of Selborne, 1895–1910* (1990) [henceforth *Crisis of British Power*], Selborne to Balfour, 7 July 1898, p.65.
31. *Chamberlain III*, p.315–16.
32. *GP. XIV/I* nr. 3805, Bülow memo. 11 June 1898, pp.253–5.
33. *Chamberlain III*, p.290.
34. *LQV III*, Empress Frederick to the Queen, 15 July 1898, pp.258–9.
35. *LQV III*, Salisbury to the Queen, 4 August 1898, pp.262–3.
36. *Balfour*, Chamberlain to Balfour, 17 August 1898, pp.204–6.
37. *GP XIV*, nr. 3850, 3854, Richthofen to Hatzfeldt, 12, 19 August 1898, pp.317–18, 321–2.
38. *BD I* Lascelles to Balfour, 23 August 1898, pp.100–1.
39. *GP XIV/I*, nr. 3865, Wilhelm's memo. 22 August 1898, pp.333–8.
40. *BD I*, Balfour to Lascelles, 31 August 1898, pp.71–5.
41. Granville, quoting Balfour to Salisbury, 1 September 1898, p.197.
42. *BD I*, Salisbury's minute to Balfour and Lascelles, 1 September 1898, p.76.
43. *GP XIV/I*, nr. 3867, Bülow to the Kaiser, 24 August 1898, pp.339–42.
44. *GP XIV/I*, nr. 3795, Holstein to Hatzfeldt, 15 May 1898, p.229.
45. *Curzon I*, Curzon to Selborne, 9 April 1898, p.254.
46. *Holstein Papers IV*, Hatzfeldt to Holstein, 17 May 1898, p.78.
47. Campbell, 'Great Britain and the US . . .', pp.162–3.
48. Eric Stokes, 'Milnerism', *Historical Journal*, 1962, p.51.
49. Sanderson, *England, Europe and the Upper Nile*, pp.269–89, 314–29; D. Levering Lewis, *The Race to Fashoda*, (1988), pp.175–205, for the background.
50. *DDF XIV*, no. 283. Geoffray to Delcassé, 9 August 1898, pp.440–3.
51. Meyendorff (ed.), Staal to Lamsdorff, 11/23 October 1898, pp.393–4.

52. *GP XIV/I* nr. 3812, 3818, Bülow to Hatzfeldt, 17, 22, June 1898, pp.266, 272–6.
53. *BD I*, Salisbury to Cromer, 2 August 1898, pp.150–60.
54. *BD I*, Monson to Salisbury, 27 September 1898, pp.169–70; DDF XIV, nos 384, Delcassé's note, 27 September 1898, p.386, Delcassé to Geoffray, 28 September 1898, pp.593, 594.
55. *BD I*, Monson to Salisbury, 28, 30 September, 7, 11 October, 1898, pp.171, 172, 175–6, 178; *DDF XIV*, nos 400, Delcassé's note, 30 September 1898, pp.612–13.
56. *BD I*, Salisbury to Monson, 9 September 1898, p.164.
57. *BD I*, Monson to Salisbury, 27 October 1898, p.183.
58. *BD I*, Salisbury to Monson, 27 October 1898, p.183.
59. C. Andrew, *Théophile Delcassé and the Making of the Anglo-French Entente* (1968), p.98.
60. *DDF XIV*, no., 412, Delcassé to Courcel, 4 October 1898, pp.629–31.
61. *BD I*, Monson to Salisbury, 11 October 1898, pp.178–9.
62. *DDF XIV*, no. 433, Courcel to Delcassé, 13 October 1898, pp.663–6.
63. *BD I*, Courcel to Salisbury, 12 October, Salisbury to Courcel, 13 October 1898, p.180.
64. *DDF XIV*, no. 443, Geoffray to Delcassé, 20 October 1898, pp.678–81.
65. Meyendorff II (ed.), Staal to Lamsdorff, 11/23 October 1898, pp.393.
66. *DDF XIV*, nos 478, 480, Delcassé's telegrams, 2, 3 November 1898, pp.750, 751.
67. Andrew, pp.103–4.
68. Andrew, pp.111–12.
69. *DDF XIV*, no. 477, Cambon to Delcassé, 22 December 1898, pp.881–2; *BD I*, Monson to Salisbury, 9 December 1898, pp.196–7.
70. *The Times*, 10 November 1898.
71. P.M. Kennedy, *The Samoan Tangle: A study in Anglo-German Relations 1878–1900* (Dublin, 1974), pp.155–88 in particular.
72. *Chamberlain III*, p.331.
73. *LQV III*, Queen's Journal, 17 February 1898, pp.340–1.
74. *GP XIV/II*, nr. 4044, Hatzfeldt to Foreign Office, 23 February 1899, pp.579–80.

75. *GP XIV\II*, nr. 4045, Holstein to Hatzfeldt, 24 February 1899, p.580.
76. Kennedy, *Samoan Tangle*; pp.145–55.
77. *BD I*, Lascelles to Salisbury, 24 March 1899, p.111.
78. Kennedy, *Samoan Tangle*, pp.164–5, for the pressures.
79. *GP XIV/II*, nr. 4052, Richtofen to Hatzfeldt, 30 March 1899, pp.589–90.
80. *GP XIV/II*, nr. 4053, Bülow to the Kaiser, 1 April 1899, pp.590–2.
81. *BD I*, Lascelles to Salisbury, 31 March, 2, 6 April 1899, pp.112–14.
82. *BD I*, Salisbury to Lascelles, 4 April 1899, pp.114–15.
83. *GP XIV/II* nr. 4064, Bülow to Hatzfeldt, 12 April 1899, pp.603–4.
84. Kennedy, *Samoan Tangle* p.167.
85. *LQV III* the Kaiser to Queen Victoria, 27 May 1899, pp.375–9.
86. PRO, Lascelles Papers, FO 800/9, Sir Thomas Sanderson to Lascelles, 12 April 1899.
87. *LQV III*, Salisbury to the Queen, 3 June 1899, pp.379–81; *BD I*, Salisbury to Monson, 15 March 1899, p.202.
88. Kennedy, *Samoan Tangle*, pp.178–240.
89. S P, Section A 134/104, Salisbury to Wolff, 17 July 1898.
90. *GP XIV/II*, nr. 4072, Bülow to Hatzfeldt, 6 May 1898, pp.613–14.
91. *Holstein Papers IV*, Hatzfeldt to Holstein, 4 May 1899, pp.113–18, Bülow's comments are in fn.3, p.118.
92. *Holstein Papers IV*, Hatzfeldt to Holstein, 13 June 1899, pp.120–2.
93. Lansdowne Mss., Corr. after 1900, S, Salisbury to Lansdowne, 12 May 1901.
94. Porter, *Origins of the South African War*, pp.258–61.
95. Balfour Papers, Add. Mss. 49778, Lord George Hamilton to Balfour, 2 December 1899.
96. Meyendorff, II, (ed.), Staal to Lamsdorff, 27 October/8 November 1899, pp.424–6.
97. *BD I*, Monson to Salisbury, 27 October 1899, pp.234–6.
98. Neilson, p.206.
99. Andrew, pp.136–7, 151–4, 162–9; Neilson, pp.206–7.
100. *DDF XV*, no. 283, Noailles to Delcassé, 19 October 1899.
101. *DDF XV*, no. 287, Noailles to Delcassé, 28 October 1899.
102. *Holstein Papers IV*, Holstein memo. 17 November 1899, pp.166–7; Bülow, *Memoirs 1897–1903*, pp. 289–91.

103. Bülow, *Memoirs 1897–1903*, pp.313–14; cf. the account in *GP XV*, nr. 413–20.
104. Bülow, *Memoirs 1897–1903*, pp.314–15.
105. *Chamberlain III*, pp.505–6.
106. *Chamberlain III*, pp.507–8.
107. *Holstein Papers IV*, Eckardstein to Holstein, 2 December 1899, p.169. fn. 1.
108. Bülow *Memoirs 1897–1903*, pp.322–5.
109. Meyendorff II, (ed.), Staal to Muraviev, 24 November/6 December 1899, pp.433–4.
110. *Holstein Papers IV*, Bülow to Hatzfeldt, 28 November 1899, pp.167–8.
111. *Holstein II*, p.615.
112. *Holstein Papers IV*, Bülow to Holstein, 28 November 1899, p.168.
113. *Holstein I*, p.182, fn.2.
114. *GP XV*, Hatzfeldt to Bülow, 20 December, 1899, pp.426–7.
115. *Chamberlain III*, p.510.
116. *Chamberlain III*, Chamberlain to Lascelles, 12 December 1899, p.512.
117. *Chamberlain III*, Chamberlain to Eckardstein, 28 December 1899, p.513.
118. Goudswaard, p.36.
119. *GP XV*, Metternich to Bülow, 19 March 1900, pp.484–91.
120. Sir Sidney Lee, *King Edward VII vol. I* (1925), p.769.
121. *LQV III*, Salisbury to the Queen, 10 April 1900, pp.526–7.
122. Andrew, p.172.

Chapter 17

1. J.D. Hargreaves, 'Lord Salisbury, British Isolation and the Yangtze Valley, June–September 1900; in *Bulletin of the Institute of Historical Research*, 1957, p.63.
2. *Curzon I*, Curzon to St John Brodrick, 18 June 1900, p.282.
3. *Curzon I*, Curzon to Brodrick, 19 July 1900, pp.282–3.
4. *BD II*, Lascelles to Salisbury, 15 June 1900, p.3; 24 August 1900, pp.7–9.
5. *BD II*, Lascelles to Salisbury, 30 August 1900, p.10.

6. *BD II*, Salisbury to Lascelles, 31 August 1900, p.10.
7. Julian Amery, *The Life of Joseph Chamberlain, vol. IV, 1901–1903* (1951) [henceforth *Chamberlain IV*] Goschen to Chamberlain, 1 September 1900, p.139.
8. *Holstein Papers IV*, Holstein to Hatzfeldt, 23 August 1900, p.195; *GP XVI*, Bülow to Hatzfeldt, 1 September 1900, pp.214–15.
9. *BD II*, Lascelles to Salisbury, 24 August 1900, pp.7–9; Grenville, pp.312–14; J. Nish, *The Anglo-Japanese Alliance* (1967), p.1
10. *Chamberlain IV*, p.140; G.A.Monger, *The End of Isolation* (1965), pp.15–16; Grenville, pp.314–16.
11. Monger, p.17, quoting Salisbury to Curzon, 17 October 1900.
12. *BD II*, memo. by Francis Bertie, 13 September 1900, p.11.
13. *GP XVI*, nr. 4716, Hatzfeldt to Bülow, 1 September 1900, pp.216–17.
14. *BD II*, Salisbury to Lascelles, 15 October 1900, pp.15–16.
15. Monger, p.20.
16. *BD II*, enclosure 6 in no. 38, Salisbury to Hatzfeldt, 6 October 1900, p.21.
17. Goudswaard, 49–50, quoting Akers-Douglas to Balfour, 18 October 1900.
18. Hargreaves, 'Lord Salisbury – and the Yangtze Valley', pp.74–5.
19. Shannon, *Age of Salisbury*, p.524.
20. Chateaubriand, *Chateaubriand's Memoirs, vol. IV*, (London, 1882), p.26.
21. Apart from the official biography published in 1929 by Lord Newton, there is no biographical study. Monger's *The End of Isolation* was published in 1965.
22. Jürgen Theiner, *The Foreign Policy of the 5th Marquis of Lansdowne*, unpublished M.A. dissertation (awarded a distinction), University of East Anglia, 1990, pp.1–4.
23. J.A.S. Grenville, 'Lansdowne's abortive project of 12 March 1901 for a secret agreement with Germany', in *Bulletin of the Institute of Historical Research*, 1954, pp.202–3.
24. Lansdowne Papers, FO 800/128, Lansdowne to Lascelles, 11 November 1900.
25. P.J.V. Rolo, 'Lansdowne', in K. Wilson (ed) *British Foreign Secretaries and Foreign Policy* (1987), pp.159–61, reiterates this common view.

26. Lansdowne Mss., Corr. after 1900, S, contains the file of his correspondence with Salisbury which has many such examples; Pte Letters, vol. 5, Prime Ministers, also shows how close the two men were – and who was in charge.
27. FO 800/128, Lascelles to Lansdowne, 17 November 1900.
28. *Holstein Papers IV*, Holstein to Hatzfeldt, 3 December 1900, p.214.
29. *Holstein Papers IV*, Hatzfeldt to Holstein, 5 December 1900, pp.214–15.
30. Lansdowne Mss., Corr. after 1900, S, Salisbury to Lansdowne, 13 December 1900.
31. *Holstein II*, pp.627–8; *GP XVII*, pp.14–16.
32. *GP XVII*, nr. 4982, the Kaiser to Bülow, 20 January 1901, p.19.
33. *GP XVII*, nr. 4983, Bülow to the Kaiser, 21 January 1901, pp.20-1.
34. *GP XVII*, nr. 4983, Holstein to Metternich, 21 January 1901, pp. 20-3.
35. *Holstein IV*, Metternich to Holstein, 22 January 1901, pp. 217-18.
36. FO 46/538 Lansdowne to MacDonald, 12, 15 January 1901.
37. FO 17/1499, Lansdowne to Salisbury and the reply, 15, 17 January 1901.
38. *BD II*, Lansdowne to Lascelles, 22 January 1901, p. 23.
39. *GP XVII*, Eckardstein to Holstein, 2 February 1901, pp. 289-92.
40. *GP XVI*, nrs 4811, 4812, Bülow to Hatzfeldt, 9, 11 February 1901, pp.316-19.
41. *GP XVI*, nr 4989, Holstein to Bülow, 11 February 1901, pp 33-7.
42. *Holstein Papers IV*, Holstein to Hatzfeldt, 13 February 1901, pp.218-19.
43. *Holstein Papers IV*, Holstein to Eckardstein, 2 March 1901, p. 219.
44. Goudswaard, p. 59.
45. *GP XVII*, nr. 4982, Wilhelm II to Bülow, 30 January 1901, p.19.
46. FO 65/1624, Lansdowne's memo., 1 March 1901.
47. *BD II*, Lansdowne to Sir Charles Scott, 4 March 1901, pp.36-7.
48. FO 64/1525, Lascelles to Lansdowne, 7 March 1901.
49. *BD II*, Hayashi to Lansdowne, 9 March 1901, pp.41-2.
50. Grenville, 'Lansdowne's abortive project. , pp.208–9.
51. Goudswaard, p.72-3.
52. Grenville, 'Lansdowne's abortive project, pp.210-11, for the text.

53. *BD II*, no. 32, p.26.
54. FO 800/128, Lascelles to Lansdowne, 16 March 1901.
55. FO 800/128, Lansdowne to Lascelles, 18 March 1901.
56. FO 800/128, Lascelles to Lansdowne, 22 March 1901.
57. *BD II*, Lascelles to Lansdowne, 23 March 1901, pp.61-2.
58. FO 800/128, Lansdowne to Lascelles, 19 March 1901 (fos, 86-7); this letter seems rather too important to have suffered the neglect which it has been accorded by the standard accounts.
59. J.A.S.Grenville, *Lord Salisbury and Foreign Policy: The Close of the Nineteenth Century* (1964),p. 341; Taylor, *The Struggle for Mastery*, pp.396-7.
60. *GP XVII*, nr. 4997, Hatzfeldt to Bülow, 23 March 1901, pp.46-9.
61. FO 800/128, Lansdowne to Lascelles, 1 April 1901.
62. *GP XVII*, nr. 4994, Eckardstein to Foreign Office, 19 March 1901, pp.46-9.
63. *BD II*, Lansdowne to Lascelles, 1 April 1901.
64. *Holstein II*, pp.638-9.
65. *GP XVII*, nr. 4996, Bülow to Hatzfeldt, 20 March 1901, pp.44-5.
66. *GP XVII*, nr. 4998, Bülow to Hatzfeldt, 24 March 1901, pp.48-51.
67. *BD II* Lansdowne to Lascelles, 29 March 1901, p.62.
68. *Holstein Papers IV*, Eckardstein to Holstein, 31 March 1901, pp.219-20.
69. Neilson, p.217, citing Hamilton to Curzon, 15 March 1901.
70. FO 800/140, Lansdowne to Scott, 23 March 1901.
71. FO 800/128, Lansdowne to Lascelles, 4 April 1901.
72. FO 800/125, Monson to Lansdowne, 17 May 1901, for the reasoning.
73. FO 800/140, Scott to Lansdowne, 18 April 1901.
74. FO 800/140, Lansdowne to Scott, 23 April 1901.
75. Nish, pp.118-19.
76. Nish, pp.128-9.
77. *BD II*, Lansdowne to MacDonald, 17 April 1901, p.69.
78. *BD II*, Lansdowne to Lascelles, 13 April 1901, pp.63-4.
79. *GP XVII*, nr. 5001, p.53, fn.
80. *GP XVII*, nrs 5036-8, telegrams from Tokyo, 15 April, and Eckardstein's replies, 16, 17 April 1901, pp.135-8.
81. *Holstein II*, pp.646-7, where Professor Rich accepts that Eckardstein was to blame.

82. *Holstein II*, p.647; Goudswaard, p.75, both quoting Holstein to Eckardstein, 18 April 1901.
83. *Holstein II*, pp.647-8.
84. Lansdowne Mss., Pte letters, vol. 5, Prime Minister, Salisbury to Lansdowne, 18 October 1901.
85. *GP XVI*, nr. 4899, Bülow to Hatzfeldt, 20 April 1901, pp.408-9.
86. *Holstein Papers IV*, Hatzfeldt to Holstein, 20 April 1901, pp.221-2.
87. *Holstein Papers IV*, Hatzfeldt to Holstein, 4 May 1901, pp.223-4.
88. *GP XVI*, nr. 5003, Bülow to Hatzfeldt, 11 May 1901, pp.54-6.
89. *GP XVI*, nr. 5005, 5006, Hatzfeldt to Bülow, 16, 17 May 1901, pp.57-60; Rich in *Holstein II*, pp.649-50, says there is no doubt these came from Eckardstein.
90. *BD II*, Lansdowne to Eckardstein, 24 May 1901, p.66.
91. *BD II*, Lansdowne to Salisbury, 24 May 1901, p.64.
92. *BD II*, memo. by Lansdowne, 24 May 1901, pp.64-5, for the British account which does not differ substantially (for once) from the German in *GP XVI* nr. 5010, Hatzfeldt to Foreign Office, 23 May 1901, pp.65-6.
93. *Holstein II*, p.653.
94. *Holstein II p.654*.
95. *BD II*, Hatzfeldt to Lansdowne, 25 May 1901, p.70.
96. *BD II* Lansdowne to Hatzfeldt, 26 May 1901, pp.70-1.
97. *Holstein Papers IV* Hatzfeldt to Holstein, 26 May 1901, pp.225-7.
98. *Holstein Papers IV*, Holstein to Hatzfeldt, 27 May 1901, pp. 227-8.
99. FO 800/115, Sanderson to Lansdowne, 28 May 1901.
100. FO 800/115, undated minute from Lansdowne to Sanderson, c. 30 May 1901.
101. *BD II*, Sanderson memo., 27 May 1901, pp.66-8.
102. FO800/115, undated minute from Lansdowne to Sanderson, c. 30 May 1901.
103. *BD II*, Salisbury memo., 29 May 1901, pp.68-9.
104. FO 800/128, Lansdowne to Lascelles, 1 April 1901.
105. *GP XVI*, nrs 5014, 5015, Holstein to Hatzfeldt, 28, 29 May 1901, pp.70-1.
106. *GP XVI*, nr. 5016, Hatzfeldt to Holstein, 29 May 1901,p. 72.
107. *BD II* Hatzfeldt to Lansdowne, 30 May 1901, p.71.
108. FO 800/115, Sanderson note, 2 January 1902.

109. *BD II*, Lansdowne to Lascelles, 9 June 1901, pp.71-2.
110. *Holstein Papers IV*, Eckardstein to Holstein, 8 June 1901, pp.231-2.
111. *GP XVI* nr. 5018, 5019, Metternich memo. for Bülow, 1 June 1901, pp.74-83, Holstein's memo., 14 June 1901, pp.83-8.
112. *GP XVI* nr.5021, Eckardstein to Holstein, 29 July 1901, pp.90-2.
113. *GP XVI*, nr.5022, Mühlberg's memo., 2 August 1901, pp.92-3.
114. *Holstein Papers IV*, Bülow to Holstein, 5 August 1901, pp.235-6.
115. Bülow, *Memoirs 1897–1903*, pp.336-9.
116. Bülow, *Memoirs 1897–1903* p.339.
117. Bülow, *Memoirs 1897–1903*, p.336.
118. *BD II* addition to p.53, Lascelles to Lansdowne, 10 April 1901, pp.121–5.
119. *GP XVI* nr. 5033, Lansdowne's memo., 10 August 1901, pp.121–5.
120. *GP XVI* nr. 5023, Wilhelm's notes, 23 August 1901, pp.94–8.
121. *BD II* Lascelles to Lansdowne, 25 August 1901, p.73.
122. Grenville, *Lord Salisbury*, p.358
123. FO 800/128, Lansdowne to Lascelles, 28 August 1901.

Chapter 18

1. Monger, p.62
2. Taylor *The Struggle for Mastery* p.403; C.H.D. Howard, *Britain and the Casus Belli 1822–1902* (1974), p.2.
3. Lansdowne Mss., Pte, letters, vol. 5, Prime Minister, Lansdowne to Balfour, 21 October 1903.
4. *BD II*, Lansdowne to Whitehead, 31 July 1901, pp.90–1.
5. Viscount Morley, *Recollections II* (1918), p.205.
6. Lansdowne Mss., Pte letters, vol. 5, Lansdowne to Balfour, 22 December 1902.
7. *BD II* memo. by Bertie, 11 March 1901, p.43.
8. Grenville, *Lord Salisbury*, Bertie memo., 22 September 1901, p.400.
9. *BD II* memo. by Bertie, 9 November 1901, pp.73–6.
10. *BD II* Lansdowne to Whitehead, 16 October 1901, pp.96–8.
11. *Crisis of British Power*, Selborne to Curzon, 4 January 1903, p.155.

12. *Crisis of British Power*, Selborne's memo., 4 September 1901, pp.123–6.
13. Lansdowne Mss., Corr. after 1900, S, correspondence with Salisbury 1901, *passim*.
14. Theiner, *The Foreign Policy of the 5th Marquis of Lansdowne* (M.A. thesis), p.13.
15. Monger, p.5, quoting Salisbury to Curzon, 23 September 1901.
16. David MacLean, *Britain and Her Buffer State* (1979), p.19.
17. Lansdowne Mss., Pte letters, vol. 5, Correspondence with Salisbury and Hicks Beach, Septemeber to October 1901, for the details.
18. Lansdowne Mss., Pte letters, vol, 5, Salisbury to Lansdowne, 18 October 1901.
19. MacLean, p.45.
20. Porter, 'Lord Salisbury, Foreign Policy and Domestic Finance', p.156.
21. Schöllgen (ed.), Schöllgen's introduction, pp.1–19, and his essay on 'Germany's Foreign Policy', pp.105–20; see also the important article by Niall Ferguson, 'Public Finance and National Security: The Domestic Origins of the First World War Revisited', in *Past & Presnet*, February 1994, pp.141–68.
22. H.Roseveare, *The Treasury: The Evolution of a British Institution* (1969), *passim*; R.V.Kubicek, *The Administration of Imperialism: Joseph chamberlain at the Colonial Office* (Durham, NC, 1969), p.70; Porter, 'Lord Salisbury, Foreign Policy and Domestic Finance', pp.158–60.
23. MacLean, p.35
24. Theiner. p.15.
25. The Earl of Ronaldshay, *The Life of Lord Curzon, vol.II* (1928), p.206.
26. *GP XVII*, nr. 101–9.
27. Lansdowne Mss., Corr. after 1900, S, Chirol to Lansdowne, 7 November 1901, with enclosures. See above, chapter 15.
28. *Chamberlain VI* p.168–9.
29. *BD II*, Lansdowne to MacDonald, 1 November 1901, p.99; Nish, pp.178-9.
30. *BD II*, Lansdowne to MacDonald, 6 November 1901,pp. 99-100.
31. PRO, Cab. 37/58/105, Lansdowne memo., 25 October 1901.

32. Neilson, pp.220-1; Monger, pp.54-6.
33. *BD II*, Lansdowne's memo., 11 November 1901, pp.76-9.
34. Balfour Papers, Add. Mss. 49727, Balfour to Lansdowne, 12 December 1901.
35. Nish, pp.185-6; Goudswaard, pp.81-3.
36. Nish, p.187.
37. K.Hamilton, *Bertie of Thame: Edwardian Ambassador* (Suffolk, 1990). p. 26.
38. Goudswaard, p.83.
39. *BD II*, Lansdowne to MacDonald, 12 December 1901, pp.102-3.
40. *BD II*, Lansdowne to MacDonald, 19 December 1901, pp.103-4.
41. *BD II*, Lansdowne to MacDonald, 7 January 1902, pp.106-11.
42. Lansdowne Mss., Pte letters, vol. 5, Prime Ministers, Lansdowne to Salisbury, 22 December 1901.
43. *BD II*, Lansdowne to Lascelles, 12 December 1901, p.79.
44. Lansdowne Mss., Pte letters, vol. 5. Prime Ministers, Lansdowne to Salisbury, 21 November, 10 December 1901.
45. *BD II*, Lansdowne to Lascelles, 19 December 1901, pp.80-2.
46. Nish, p.209.
47. Monger, pp.59-60, for the details.
48. Bourne, Salibury's memo., 7 January 1902, pp.476-8.
49. Grenville, p.414.
50. Lansdowne Mss., Pte letters, vol.5, Prime Ministers, Lansdowne to Salisbury, 8 January 1901.
51. Grenville, p.364, quoting Salisbury to Sanderson, 15 January 1902.
52. *BD II*, Anglo-Japanese Agreement, 30 January 1902, pp.114-21.
53. *Hansard*, Lords debates, 13 February 1902.
54. Lansdowne Mss., Pte. letters, vol. 5, Prime Ministers, Lansdowne to Balfour, 23 October 1903.
55. J.F.V. Keiger, *France and the Origins of the First World War* (1985), pp.25-43; M.B. Hayne, *The French Foreign Office and the Origins of the First World War* (Oxford, 1993), pp.9-28.
56. Paul Cambon (ed.), *Correspondance, tome II* (Paris, 1940 [henceforth *correspondance II*], Paul to Jules Cambon, 19, 21 January 1899*, pp.17-18.
57. Hayne, p.81.

58. *Correspondance II*, letters to: Delcassé, 1 February 1899, pp.23-4; Jules Cambon, 14 February 1901, pp.53–5; Henri Cambon, 7 February 1909, p.272, for some examples of this.
59. Paul Cambon *Correspondance, tome I* (Paris, 1940), to Mme Cambon, 27 January 1896, pp.400-1; see also K. Eubank (1960), , *Paul Cambon* pp.201-3.
60. Hayne, p.81.
61. *DDF, 2ième série, tome I*, pp.20-3; Andrew, pp.148-51.
62. Andrew, pp.151-2.
63. Goudswaard, p.94.
64. *GP XVII* nr. 5186, Metternich to Foreign Office, 30 January 1902, pp.342-3.
65. *Chamberlain IV* p.181.
66. P.J.V. Rolo, *Entente Cordiale* (1969), p.135.
67. Hayne, pp.102-4.
68. FO 800/124, Monson to Lansdowne, 23 August 1902.
69. Hayne, p.105.
70. *BD II*, Lansdowne to Monson, 6 August 1902, p.266.
71. *DDF 2/II*, Cambon to Delcassé, 17 December 1902, pp.660-2.
72. *BD II* Lansdowne to Monson, 31 December 1902, pp.275-6.
73. Balfour Papers, Add. Mss. 49728, Balfour to Lansdowne, 2 January 1902.
74. Monger, p.87.
75. Monger, pp.90-2; MacLean, pp.47-9; both relying on PRO, FO 60/657.
76. Lansdowne Mss., Pte letters, vol. 5, Prime Ministers, Balfour to Lansdowne, 6 September 1902.
77. FO 65/1643, Colonel Beresford to Hardinge, 20 November 1902, in Hardinge to Lansdowne, 24 November 1902.
78. Monger, pp. 91-2; Neilson, pp.226-7.
79. Balfour Papers, Add. Mss. 49728, Lansdowne to Balfour, 12 April 1903.
80. Neilson, pp.229-30.
81. Balfour Papers, Add. Mss. 49728, Balfour to Lansdowne, 21 December 1903.
82. FO 800/124, Cromer to Lansdowne, 29 May 1903, Lansdowne to Cromer, 8 June 1903.
83. Monger, p.129, quoting Hamilton to Curzon, 9 July 1903.

84. Monger, p.133.
85. Theiner, p.25.
86. Balfour Papers, Add. Mss. 49747, Balfour to Spencer-Wilkinson, 3 January 1904.
87. *Crisis of British Power*, Balfour to Selborne, 29 December 1903, p.165.
88. Balfour Papers, Add. Mss. 49728, Lansdowne to Balfour, 24 December 1903.
89. Lansdowne Mss., Pte letters, vol. 5, Prime Minister, Balfour to Lansdowne, 15 January 1904.
90. Lansdowne Mss., Pte letters, vol. 5, Prime Minister, Balfour to Lansdowne, 11 February 1904.
91. Lansdowne Mss., Pte letters, vol. 5, Prime Minister, Lansdowne to Balfour, 18 January 1904.
92. Balfour Papers, Add. Mss. 49728, Lansdowne to Balfour, 2 April 1904.

Chapter 19

1. *BD II*, draft reply to Chirol by Sanderson, 21 January 1902, p.88.
2. *BD II*, Lansdowne to Monson, 8 April 1904, pp.367-8; *BD III* Lansdowne to Lascelles, 24 May 1904, pp.18-19.
3. *BD II*, Lansdowne to Monson, 29 April 1904, p.401.
4. White, pp.102-10, for this.
5. Lansdowne Papers, FO 800/126, Lansdowne to Monson, 26 December 1904.
6. Lansdowne Mss., Pte letters, vol. 5, Balfour to Lansdowne, 6 January 1905.
7. Balfour Papers, Add. Mss. 49729, Lansdowne to Balfour, 9 January 1905.
8. Lansdowne Mss., Pte letters, vol. 6, Salisbury to Lansdowne, 15 June 1904.
9. Lansdowne Mss., letters, vol. 5, Lansdowne to Balfour, 12 December 1904.
10. *Holstein II*, Bülow to Richthofen, 19 April 1904, p.682; *BD III*, Lascelles to Lansdowne, 18 May 1904. p.1.
11. Lord Newton, *Lord Lansdowne* (1929), pp.329-30.

12. Monger, p.164.
13. *BD III*, Lascelles to Lansdowne, 28 December 1904, pp.56-8.
14. Monger, p.177, quoting Chamberlain memo., 14 January 1905.
15. *BD III*, Sanderson to Lansdowne, 20 January 1905, p.429.
16. Balfour Papers, Add. Mss. 49729, Lansdowne to Balfour, 18 January 1905.
17. Zara Steiner, *The Foreign Office and Foreign Policy 1898–1914* (Cambridge, 1969), p.68.
18. Monger, p.145, quoting Cromer to Lansdowne, 12 December 1903.
19. Whyte (ed.), Bülow to Wilhelm II, 6 April 1904, pp.50–1.
20. *Hostein II*, p.682.
21. *GP XIX I*, nr. 6118–19, for the correspondence between the Kaiser and the Tsar in October 1904, pp.303–8.
22. *Holstein Papers IV*, Bülow to Holstein, 13 December 1904, p.316.
23. *GP XIX II*, nr. 6157, Bülow to the Kaiser, 26 December 1904, pp.372–3.
24. *Holstein Papers IV*, Bülow to Holstein, 15 January 1905, p.323.
25. *Holstein II*, p.694; *GP XXI*, pp.248, 254–5.
26. L. Cecil, *Wilhelm II, vol. II*, (North Carolina, 1996), pp.94–5.
27. *Holstein II.*, pp.694–5; E.N. Anderson, *The First Moroccan Crisis, 1904–1906* (Chicago 1930), for a detailed account.
28. Andrew, pp.269–73.
29. Comte de Saint-Aulaire, *Confession d'un vieux diplomate* (Paris, 1953), p.139: 'Pendant la France était en train de violer le Maroc, l'empereur Guillaume lui a donné un formidable coup de pied au derrière.'
30. Hayne, pp.130-1.
31. Saint-Aulaire, pp.139–40; Andrew, pp.274–5.
32. *GP XX II*, nr. 6635, Radolin to Bülow, 27 April 1905, pp.344–5; see also nr. 6647, Radolin to Bülow, 30 April 1905, see also *Holstein Papers IV*, Holstein to Radolin, 1 May 1905, p.338–9.
33. Whyte (ed.), Bülow to Wilhelm II, 4 April 1905, p.122
34. D.G. Herrmann, *The Arming of Europe and the Making of the First World War* (1996), pp.51–3.
35. Lansdowne Papers, FO 800/119, Lansdowne to Lascelles, 9 April 1905.
36. Monger, p.189, quoting Mallet to Bertie, 24 April 1905.

37. Balfour Papers, Add. Mss. 49729, Lansdowne to Balfour, 23 April 1905.
38. Lansdowne Mss. Pte letters, vol. 5, Lansdowne to Balfour, 23 April 1905.
39. *BD III*, Lansdowne to Bertie, 22 April 1905, pp.72–3.
40. Andrew, pp.281–2, rehearses the evidence; see also Hayne, pp.128–30.
41. Andrew, pp.281–2; Hayne, pp.127–30.
42. *DDF 2 VI*, no. 390, Cambon to Delcassé, 3 May 1905.
43. *DDF VI*, no. 443, Cambon to Delcassé, 18 May 1905; *Correspondance II*, Cambon to Delcassé, 18 May 1905, pp.195–6; Andrew, pp.227–8; S, R.Williamson, *The Politics of Grand Strategy* (Harvard, 1967), pp.36–7.
44. *BD III*, Lansdowne minute, undated, on Lansdowne to Bertie, 17 May 1905, p.76.
45. FO 800/130, Robert Dell to Mr Hirst, 9 September 1929, for an early example of the attempt to clarify matters. Williamson, pp.34–8, and Monger pp.188–92, for some of the comments. Andrew, pp.281–3, gives these accounts too much credence, as he does with Lansdowne's comment to Harold Temperley in 'British Secret Diplomacy from Canning to Grey', in *Cambridge Historical Journal*, 1938, p.26.
46. J.D. Hargreaves, 'The Origin of the Anglo-French military conversations in 1905', in *History*, 1951; Monger, p.199, fn. 2, has it right in my opinion.
47. *BD III*, Lansdowne to Cambon, 25 May 1905, pp.77–8.
48. FO 800/127, Lansdowne to Bertie, 12 June 1905.
49. FO 800/127, Lansdowne to Sir Reginald Lister, 10 July 1905.
50. Monger, p.203.
51. *BD III*, Lascelles to Lansdowne, 12 June 1905, pp.79–81.
52. *BD III*, Lansdowne to Lascelles, 16 June 1905, pp.82–3.
53. *GP XX II*, Metternich to Bülow, 28 June 1905, pp.635–7.
54. *BD III*, Lansdowne to Whithead, 28 June 1905, p.103.
55. FO 800/130, Lansdowne to Lascelles, 5 August 1905; the files here were only discovered in 1942, too late for Gooch and Temperley to use.
56. FO 800/130, Lansdowne to Lascelles, 5 August 1905.
57. Monger, pp.209–12.

58. *GP XIX II*, nr. 6202, Bülow to Holstein, 20 July 1905, pp.435–6.
59. Whyte (ed.), Wilhelm II to Bülow, 25 July 1905, pp.115–6.
60. *GP XIX II*, nr. 6228, 6229, Bülow to the Kaiser, 28, 30 July 1906, pp.476–81.
61. *GP XIX II*, nr. 6230, Bülow to the Kaiser, 2 August 1906, p.481.
62. *GP XIX II*, nr. 6237, Wilhelm II to Bülow, 11 August 1906, pp.496–8.
63. Lerman, p.131–3, and the references she gives.
64. *GP XX II*, Bülow to the Foreign Ministry, 31 July 1905, pp.531–2.
65. *GP XIX II*, nr. 6241, Radolin (Paris) to Bülow, 23 September 1905, pp.503–4; nr. 6243, Bülow to Wilhelm II, 25 September 1905, pp.505–7; nr. 6246, Wilhelm II to Bülow, 27 September, pp.508–11.
66. Balfour Papers, Add. Mss. 48758, Salisbury to Balfour, 9 November 1905.
67. Chamberlain to Lansdowne, 29 October 1905, quoted in Monger, p.218.
68. *BD IV*, Lansdowne to Hardinge, 3 October 1905, p.205.
69. *BD IV*, Lansdowne to Hardinge, 5 October 1905, p.208.
70. R.B. Haldane, *An Autobiography* (1929), pp.158–60, for the details.
71. Haldane, p.158.
72. A. Gollin, 'Asquith: a new view', in M. Gilbert (ed.), *A Century of Conflict, 1850–1950: Essays for A.J.P. Taylor* (1966), pp.109–12.
73. Haldane, pp.170–2.
74. R. Williams, *Defending the Empire* (1991), p.80.

Chapter 20

1. T.Wilson (ed.), *The Political Diaries of C.P. Scott 1911–1928* (1970). p.328.
2. Viscount Grey of Falloden, *Twenty-Five Years, vol. I* (1925) [henceforth *Twenty-Five Years I*], pp.xxiv-xxv.
3. Steiner, pp.83–5, has some useful comments.
4. G.M. Trevelyan, *Grey of Falloden* (1937), p.vi.
5. Haldane, p.171.
6. Wilson, *The Policy of the Entente*, pp.19–22.

7. Monger, p.259, quoting Halévy.
8. Trevelyan, p.108; see also Williamson, pp.60–1.
9. Trevelyan, p.91.
10. *BD III*, Grey memo., 20 February 1906, p.267.
11. PRO, Papers of Sir Edward Grey, FO 800/60, Grey to Lascelles, I January 1906.
12. Monger, pp.236–8.
13. Williamson, pp.59–61.
14. *GD III*, Metternich to Bülow, 3 January 1906, pp.235–7; Trevelyan, p.127.
15. *GD III*, Metternich to Bülow, 4 January 1906, p.237.
16. *BD III*, Grey to Bertie, 20 December 1905, p.160.
17. *DDF 2/VIII*, no. 262, Cambon to Rouvier, 21 December 1905.
18. J.A. Spender, *The Life of the Rt Hon. Sir Henry Campbell-Bannerman.*, vol. II (n.d.), pp.248–9.
19. Monger, p.248, for the evidence.
20. Spender, Grey to C-B, 9 January 1906, p.249.
21. *BD III*, Grey to Bertie, 10 January 1906, pp.170–1.
22. *BD III*, Editorial note, p.169.
23. *BD III*, Grey to Bertie, 10 January 1906, pp.170–1.
24. *BD III*, Sanderson minute, 11 January 1906, pp.171–2.
25. K.A. Hamilton, 'Great Britain and France', in F.H. Hinsley (ed.), *British Foreign Policy under Sir Edward Grey* (Cambridge, 1977), p.114.
26. *BD III*, no. 212, pp.173–4.
27. Spender II, publishes the full version as though it was sent to C-B, the version in C-B's papers, Add. MSS. 41218 is that is Trevelyan, 129 and omits thence to the conversations.
28. Haldane, *Autobiography*, 189–190.
29. L. Wolf, *Life of the First Marquess of Ripon, vol.II* (1921), Ripon to Fitzmaurice, 11 January 1906, pp.292–3.
30. Spender II, C-B to Grey, 14 January 1906, p.252.
31. Williamson, pp.76–7, gives the likeliest explanation.
32. PRO, Bertie Papers, FO 800/162, Grey to Bertie, 15 January 1906.
33. *BD II*, Lansdowne to Lascelles, 9 January 1906, pp.209–10.
34. Taylor, *The Struggle for Mastery*, p.438.
35. Trevelyan, p.103.
36. *BD III*, Grey to Bertie, 31 January 1906, pp.180–2.

37. *BD III*, memo. by Lord Sanderson, 2 February 1906, pp.184–5.
38. Spender II, C-B to Ripon, 2 February 1906, pp.257–9.
39. *Holstein Papers IV*, Holstein memo., 31 July 1905, p.356.
40. *Holstein Papers IV*, Holstein to von Brandt, 23 December 1906, p.377.
41. *Holstein Papers IV*, Holstein to Bülow, January 1906, pp.379–83, unsent.
42. White, p.192.
43. Bülow, *Memoirs 1903–1909*, p.189.
44. *GP XX 2*, nr. 6887, Kaiser to Bülow, 29 December 1905, pp.690–6.
45. *BD VI*, Grey minute, c. 20 April 1909, p.266; see also Grey to Goschen, 9 June 1909, p.275.
46. *BD III* memo. by Grey, 20 February 1906, p.267
47. S.L. Mayer, 'Anglo-German Rivalry at the Algeçiras conference', in P.Gifford and W.R Louis (eds), *Britain and Germany in Africa* (New Haven, 1967), p.241.
48. *BD III*, Crowe minute, 28 May 1906, p.358.
49. *BD III*, Grey minute, c. 26 June 1906, p.360.
50. *BD III*, Grey minute, c. 6 June 1906, p.359.
51. *Twenty-five Years I*, p.5.
52. *BD X(II)*, Bertie to Grey, 21 December 1911, p.423.
53. *BD VI*, Appendix V, p.781.
54. *BD V*, Grey to Cartwright, 6 January 1909, p.557.
55. FO 800/144, Grey to Durrand, 28 June 1905; see also FO 800/130, Grey to Lascelles, 5 August 1905.
56. *BD III*, Grey memo., 20 February 1906, pp.266–7.
57. *BD X(I)*, Grey to Dr T. Hodgkin, 23 January 1912, p.899.
58. Wilson, *Policy of the Entente*, pp.59–89, 100–20, for these ingenious suggestions.
59. *BD VI*, Appendix V, pp.782–3; Trevelyan, pp.115–16.
60. S. Gwynne (ed.), *The Letters and Friendships of Sir Cecil Spring-Rice vol. II* (1929) [henceforth Spring-Rice II], Grey to Spring-Rice, February 1906, p.65.
61. *Twenty-five Years I*, p.152.
62. *BD VI*, Grey to Sir Edward Goschen, 9 June 1909, pp.275–6.
63. Trevelyan, p.108.
64. Steiner, pp.60–1, 67–82; also, Zara Steiner, 'The Foreign Office under Sir Edward Grey', pp.22–69.

65. G. Sweet, 'Great Britain and Germany, 1905–1911', p.219.
66. *BD III*, Grey to Lascelles, 31 July 1906, pp.363–4.
67. C.J. Lowe and M.L. Dockrill, *The Mirage of Power, vol. 3* (1972), Crowe minute, 18 August 1908, p.430.
68. *BD VI*, Eyre Crowe minute, 14 May 1911, pp.627–8.
69. *BD III*, Appendix A, Crowe memo. 1 January 1907, p.415.
70. C.H.D. Howard (ed.), *The Diary of Edward Goschen 1900–1914 (1980)*, Goschen to Hardinge, 26 February 1909, p.28.
71. *BD III*, Appendix B, Sanderson memo., 21 February 1907, p.430.
72. *BD III*, memo. by Grey, 20 February 1906, p.267.
73. Neilson, pp.267–75; A.V. Ignat'ev, 'Foreign Policy of Russia in the Far East', and D.M. McDonald, 'A Lever without a fulcrum: domestic factors and Russian Foreign Policy, 1905–1914', in H. Ragsdale (ed.), *Imperial Russian Foreign Policy* (Cambridge, 1933), pp.264–6, 280–6.
74. White, pp.208–11; Neilson, pp.268–9, 276–85.
75. B. Williams, 'Great Britain and Russia, 1905–1907', in Hinsley (ed.), pp.137–8; White, pp.242–3.
76. A. Lamb, *Britain and Chinese Central Asia: The Road to Lhasa 1767–1905* (1960), pp.239–42.
77. *BD VI*, Draft instructions to Nicolson, 23 May 1906, p.331; Memorandum on correspondence relating to . . . Thibet', 18 April 1907, pp.336–49.
78. *Spring-Rice II*, Spring-Rice to Chirol, 11 October 1906, p.82.
79. PRO, Papers of the 1st Baron Carnock (Sir Arthur Nicolson), FO 800/339, Hardinge to Nicolson, 8 January 1907.
80. PRO, Papers of Sir Cecil Spring-Rice, FO 800/241, Sanderson to Spring-Rice, 6 August 1907.
81. *BD IV*, Grey's memo., 15 March 1907, p.280.
82. *BD IV*, Nicolson to Grey, 14 April 1907, p.286.
83. *BD IV*, Grey to Nicolson, 24 February 1908, pp.616–17.

Chapter 21

1. J. Morley, *Recollections, vol. II* (1923), Morley to Minto, 28 February, 1907, p.205.
2. *BD VI*, Grey to Lascelles, 18 September 1907, p.81.

3. *BD IV*, Crowe minute, 14 January 1908, Grey's undated minute, p.108.
4. N. d'Ombrain, *War Machinery and High Policy*. (Oxford, 1973) pp.ix, 1–3; Herrmann, p.43.
5. D. French, *British Economic and Strategic Planning 1905–1915* (1928), p.1.
6. d'Ombrain, pp.11–13; J. McDermott, 'The Revolution in British Military Thinking from the Boer War to the Moroccan Crisis', in P.Kennedy (ed.), *The War Plans of the Great Powers 1880–1914* (1985), pp.99–100.
7. *Selborne Papers*, memo., 24 February 1904, pp.170–1.
8. Monger, p.310.
9. Spender and Asquith, *Life of Asquith, vol. I*, Asquith to Tweedmouth, 10 July 1906, p.188.
10. *Hansard*, House of Commons, 4th series, vol. 156. 9 May 1906, cols 1412–15.
11. Spender II, pp.328–30.
12. *BD VIII*, Grey minute, c. 16 August 1906, p.193.
13. *BD VIII*, Grey to Knollys, 12 November 1906, p.198.
14. *BD VI*, Captain Dumas to Lascelles, 12 February 1908, p.118.
15. *BD VIII*, Grey to Sir E. Fry, 12 June 1907, p.243.
16. A.J.A. Morris, *The Scaremongers* (1984), p.85.
17. *Holstein IV*, Bülow to Holstein, 4 December 1908, p.600.
18. *Holstein IV*, Holstein memo., 15 August 1908, p.550.
19. *BD VI*, Lascelles to Grey, 30 January 1908, p.111.
20. *BD VI*, minutes on Lascelles to Grey, 4 February 1908, p.117.
21. *BD VI*, minutes on Lascelles to Grey, 27 February 1908, p.139.
22. Randolph S. Churchill, *Winston S. Churchill, vol. II* (1967), 14 August 1908, p.282.
23. John Charmley, *Churchill: The End of Glory* (1993), p.59.
24. Richard B. Elrod, 'The Concert of Europe', in *World Politics*, vol.XXVIII, 1976, p.171.
25. F.R. Bridge, *Great Britain and Austria-Hungary 1906–1914: A Diplomatic History* (1972), pp.41–76.
26. P.W. Schroeder, 'World War One as Galloping Gertie', in H.W. Koch (ed.), *The Origins of the First World War* (1984 edn), pp.116–17.

27. E. Walters, 'Franco-Russian Discussions on the partition of Austria-Hungary, 1899', in *Slavonic and East European Review*, vol. XXVIII, no. 70, December 1949, p.185.
28. S. Wank, 'Foreign Policy and the Nationality Problem in Austria-Hungary, 1867–1914', in *Austrian History Yearbook*, 1967, p.54.
29. Diószegi, pp.202–3; Bridge, pp.20–1, 43–4, 51–2.
30. L. Bittner, A.F. Pribram *et al* (eds), *Österreich-Ungarns Aussenpolitik von der bosnichen Krise 1908 bis zum Kriegsaubruch*, vol. II (1930) [henceforth Ö-U Auss. followed by volume number], doc. 85, 10 September 1908.
31. F.R. Bridge (ed.), *Austro-Hungarian Documents relating to the Macedonian Struggle, 1896–1912* (Thessaloniki, 1976), esp. docs, 68, 77, 79, 80–8, 90, 99, pp.12–15; *BDV* pp.49–56.
32. *BDV* Lansdowne to Plunkett, 6 January 1903, p.50.
33. E. Walters, 'Aehrenthal's attempt in 1907 to Re-Group the European Powers', in *Slavonic and Eastern European Review*, vol. XXX, no. 74, December 1951, Aehrenthal to Berchtold, 14 May 1907, p. 219; see also the references in Ralph R. Menning, 'Origins of a Political Friendship', in *Austrian History Yearbook*, 1993, pp.181–2, esp. fn. 8. S. R. Williamson, *Austria-Hungary and the Origins of the First World War* (1991), pp.66–7.
34. *BD VI*, Cartwright to Grey, 28 March 1908, p.142.
35. Walters 'Aehrenthal's attempt . . .', Aehrenthal to Berchtold, 14 May 1907, p.219.
36. F.R. Bridge, 'Izvolski, Aehrenthal, and the End of the Austro-Russian Entente, 1906–1908', in *Mitteilungen des österreichischen Staatsarchivs*, vol. 29, 1976, pp.315–62.
37. Walters, 'Aehrenthal's attempt . . .', pp.213–18.
38. A.F. Pribram, *Austria-Hungary and Great Britain 1908–1914* (Oxford, 1951) [henceforth Pribram, *A-H*], pp.95–6; *Ö-U Auss. I*, no. 79, for Aehrenthal's account; *GP XXVI/1*, p.190 foll.
39. *Ö-U Auss. I*, doc. 40; Bridge, *Great Britain and Austria-Hungary*, p.97.
40. *Ö-U Auss. III*, no. 67.
41. Diózsegi, p.208.
42. *BD V*, Nicolson despatch, 8 February 1909, pp.367–8.
43. *Ö-U Auss. II* doc. 40, 19 August 1908; Pribram, *England and the International Policy of the European Great Powers*, pp.126–7.

44. L.B. Namier, *In the Margin of History* (1939), pp.227–8.
45. Bernadotte E. Schmitt, *The Annexation of Bosnia* (Cambridge, 1937), is the classic study.
46. O.H. Wedel, 'Austro-Hungarian Diplomatic Documents 1908–1914', in *Journal of Modern History*, vol. 3, no. 1, March 1931, pp.86–9.
47. *Twenty-Five Years I*, p.175.
48. *BD V*, Grey to Goschen, 5 October 1908, p.389.
49. Bridge, *Great Britain and Austria-Hungary*, p.112, for the details; H. Nicolson, *Lord Carnock: A Study in the Old Diplomacy* (1930) [henceforth *Carnock*] pp.278–9, for other examples.
50. *Holstein Papers IV*, Holstein to Bülow, 8, 10 October 1908, pp.577–80.
51. *Ö-U Auss. III*, no. ;681, Aehrenthal to Mensdorff, 30 November 1908.
52. *Carnock*, Nicolson to Grey, 19 July 1908, p.262.
53. *BD V*, Grey to Nicolson, 12 October 1908, pp.429–30.
54. *BD V*, Grey to Whitehead, 5 October 1908, p.394.
55. *BD V*, Whitehead to Grey, 6 October 1908, p.397.
56. *BD V*, Bertie to Grey, 8 October 1908, p.416; Bridge, *Great Britain and Austria-Hungary*, p.117.
57. *BD V*, Goschen to Grey, 19 October 1908, pp.455–6.
58. *BD V*, Grey to Nicolson, 29 October 1908, p.473.
59. *Twenty-Five Years I*, p.173.
60. *Carnock*, Hardinge to Nicolson, 26 October 1908, p.283.
61. *GP XXVI*, nr. 8992; *BD V* Lascelles to Grey, 6 October 1908, p.397; Hardinge memo., 11 February 1909, pp.608–9.
62. *GP XXVI/I*, nr. 8939, Bülow to Wilhelm II, 5 October 1908, pp.50–1.
63. *Carnock* pp.284–5.
64. *BD V*, Goschen to Grey, 5 November 1908, p.485.
65. *BD V*, Grey to Nicolson, 10 November 1908, pp.494–5; *Carnock*, pp.284–5.
66. N. Stone, 'Moltke and Conrad Plan their War', in P. Kennedy (ed.), *The War Plans of the Great Powers 1880–1914* (1985 edn), pp.224–5.
67. *GP XXVI/2*, nr. 9197, Bülow to Wilhelm II, 29 January 1909, pp.409–10; see also nr. 9388, Bülow to Wilhelm II, 22 February 1909, pp.618–20.

68. Herrmann, p.123.
69. Herrmann, p.125.
70. *GP XVI/1*, Aehrenthal to Bülow, 8 December 1908, pp.312–13; *BD V*, Cartwright to Grey, 11 December 1908, pp.526–7.
71. *BD V*, Cartwright to Grey, 11 December 1908, pp.527–30.
72. *Ö-U Auss.I*, no.695, Aehrenthal to Mensdorff, 17 December 1908.
73. *BD V*, Edward VII's minutes on Cartwright to Grey, 11, 24 December 1908, pp.530, 538; Grey to Cartwright, 14, 16 December 1908, pp.530, 531–2.
74. K. Wilson, 'Isolating the Isolater: Cartwright, Grey and the Seduction of Austria-Hungary 1908–1912', in Wilson (ed.), *Empire and Continent* p.78, quoting Grey to Cartwright, 6 January 1909.
75. Wilson, 'Isolating the Isolater', p.79, quoting Hardinge to Cartwright, 8 February 1909.
76. *BD V*, Grey to Cartwright, 19 February 1909, pp.610–11.
77. Bridge, *Great Britain and Austria-Hungary*, p.129.
78. *BD V*, Grey to Nicolson, 25 February 1909, pp.627.
79. Bridge, *Great Britain and Austria-Hungary*, p.127, quoting Nicolson to Grey, 9 December 1908.
80. *BD V*, Nicolson to Grey, 24 February 1909, pp.622–3.
81. Bridge, *Great Britain and Austria-Hungary*, p.280.
82. Bridge, *Great Britian and Austria-Hungary*, p.129, quoting Hardinge to Bryce, 26 February 1909.
83. *BD V*, Nicolson to Grey, 27 February 1909, pp.636–7.
84. *BD V*, Grey to Nicolson, 1 March 1909, pp.642.
85. *BD V*, Cartwright to Grey, 6 March 1909, pp.650–1.
86. *Ö-U Auss. I*, no. 1053, Aehrenthal to Mensdorff, 25 February 1909.
87. Bridge, *Great Britain and Austria-Hungary*, p.130.
88. *BD V*, Cartwright to Grey, 2 March 1909, p.661.
89. *BD V* Grey to Cartwright, 8 March 1909, pp.663–4.
90. Pribram, *Austria Hungary and Gt. Britain*, p.128, for the text of the 10 March note; the text, in French, is also at *BD V*, p.666.
91. *BD V*, Whitehead to Grey, 15 March 1909, Mallet minute, p.680.
92. *BD V*, Cartwright to Grey, 15 March 1909, pp.682–5.
93. *BD V*, Hardinge minute on Cartwright to Grey, 17 March 1909, p.694.

94. *BD V*, Nicolson to Grey, 17 March 1909, p.695.
95. *BD V*, Cartwright to Grey, 15 March 1909, p.684.
96. *BD V*, Goschen to Grey, 16 March 1909, p.692.
97. *GP XXVI/2*, no. 9460, Bülow to Pourtalès. 21 March 1909, p.694.
98. Bridge, *Great Britain and Austria-Hungary*, pp.131–2; Pribram, pp.138–40.
99. *BD V*, Nicolson to Grey, 10, 23 March 1909, *A-H*, pp.667, 726–7; *Carnock*, pp.301–3.
100. *Carnock*, pp.303–4; ;Taylor, *The Struggle for Mastery*, pp.455–6; Trevelyan, p.225.
101. *BD V*, Nicolson to Grey, 23 March ;1909, p.729.
102. *BD V*, Nicolson to Grey, 24 March 1909, p.736–7.
103. *BD V*, minutes on Nicolson to Grey, 29 March 1909, p.758.
104. *BD V*, minutes to Nicolson, 30 March 1909, p.764.
105. *BD V*, Hardinge to Nicolson, 12 April 1909, p.781.
106. *BD V*, Appendix III, Hardinge memo., c. April 1909, p.824.
107. K.H. Jarausch, *The Enigmatic Chancellor: Bethmann-Hollweg and the Hubris of Imperial Germany* (Princeton, 1972), pp.112–14.
108. *BD VI*, Crowe minute, 22 March 1909, p.247.
109. *BD VI*, Crowe minute, 25 March 1909, p.248.
110. *BD VI*, Grey to Goschen, 31 March 1909, p.257–8.
111. *BD VI*, Grey to Goschen, 9 June 1909, p.275.
112. *BD VI*, Crowe minute, 19 April 1909, p.268.
113. *BD VI*, Grey minute, p.266.
114. *BD VI*, Grey's account of his conversation with Metternich, 9 June 1909, p.275 foll.; see also Grey's comments at: *BD IX(I)*, minute 24 September 1912, p.761; *BD X(I)*, letter to Dr T. Hodgkin, 23 January 1912, p.899.

Chapter 22

1. Wilson, *Policy of the Entente*, pp.85–99.
2. *BD IX(I)*, Hardinge to Nicolson, 30 April 1909, p.6
3. Hamilton, Crowe minute, February 1911, p.215.
4. Lowe and Dockrill, Crowe minute, 13 April 1909, p. 430.
5. *BD VII*, minute by Mr Langley, August 1909, p.284.
6. *BD VII*, Grey to Goschen, 1 September 1909, p.239.

7. PRO, Grey papers, FO 800/91, Harcourt to Grey, 14 January 1914.
8. Wilson, *Policy of the Entente*, p.115.
9. *BD VII*, Goschen to Nicolson, 18 August 1911, p.456.
10. Jarausch, p.115.
11. N. Fergusson, 'Germany and the Origins of the First World War: New Perspectives', in *Historical Journal*, 1992, p.725–52, for the most succinct account.
12. Wilson, *Policy of the Entente*, p.105.
13. Geiss, *Die lange Weg in die Katastrophe*, is the best recent example of the tendency to go back to 1875; Gooch and Temperley's whole selection was based on the view that 1898 was the crucial date.
14. *Un Livre Noir: Diplomatie d'avant-guerre d'après les documents des archives Russe, tome 1 ére, November 1910–Juillet 1914* (Paris, 1992) [henceforth *D R*, followed by volume number] p.x.
15. PRO, Cab. 37/107/89, Grey's memo., 2 August 1911.
16. M. L. Dockrill, 'British policy during the Agadir Crisis of 1911' in Hinsley (ed.), p.272.
17. *BD V*, Grey to Nicolson, 10 November 1908, p.495.
18. Dockrill, 'British policy . . .', pp.274–6.
19. Lowe and Dockrill, Tyrrell to Hardinge, 21 July 1911, p.434.
20. *BD VII*, Bertie to Nicolson, 12 July 1911, p.359.
21. *BD VII*, Crowe minute, 15 July 1911, p.363–4.
22. *BD VII*, Crowe minute, 18 July 1911, p.372.
23. *BD VII*, Nicolson minute, n.d. but 18 July 1911, p.373.
24. *BD VII*, Grey to Bertie, 19 July, Grey to Asquith, 19 July 1911, pp.376, 377–8.
25. K. Robbins, 'Foreign Secretaries, Cabinet, Parliament and Parties', in Robbins (ed.), *Politicians, Diplomacy and War in Modern British History* (1994), pp.113–14.
26. R.F.V. Heuston, *Lives of the Lord Chancellors 1885–1940* (Oxford, 1963), pp.173–4.
27. PRO, Cab. 41/33/22, Asquith to the King, 19 July 1911.
28. PRO, Bertie papers FO 800/160, Crowe to Bertie, 20 July 1911.
29. *BD VII*, Grey to Asquith, 19 July 1911, pp.377–8.
30. PRO, Cab. 41/2/3, Asquith to the King, 22 July 1911.
31. M. Dockrill, 'David Lloyd George and Foreign Policy', in A.J.P. Taylor (ed.), *Lloyd George: Twelve Essays* (1971), p.15.
32. John M. McEwen (ed.), *The Riddell Diaries* (1986), pp.25–6.

33. *Twenty-Five Years I*, p.225.
34. Dockrill, 'David Lloyd George . . .', p.17.
35. Dockrill, 'British policy . . .', p.279.
36. BD VII, Grey to McKenna, 24 July 1911, p.625.
37. Robbins p.115.
38. Wilson, *Policy of the Entente*, p.154.
39. Lowe and Dockrill, Nicolson to Hardinge, 17 August, 1911, p.436.
40. W.S. Churchill, *The World Crisis, vol. I* (1974 centenary edn), WSC to Grey, 30 August 1911, pp.65–6.
41. Churchill, *World Crisis I*, pp.60–4.
42. Robbins, p.115, quoting Runciman to Harcourt, 24 August 1911.
43. Robbins, p.115, quoting Harcourt's reply, 26 August 1911.
44. Grey Papers, FO 800/99, Loreburn to Grey, 25 August 1911.
45. Grey Papers FO 800/99, Loreburn to Grey, 26 August 1911.
46. Grey Papers FO 800/99, Grey to Loreburn, 30 August 1911.
47. Charmley, pp.70–1; Wilson, *Policy of the Entente*, pp.27–8; Robbins pp.115–16.
48. Grey Papers FO 800/100, Asquith to Grey, 5 September 1911.
49. Grey Papers FO 800/100, Grey to Asquith, 8 September 1911.
50. BD VII, Grey to Goschen, 27 September 1911, p.545.
51. BD VI, Grey to Goschen, 9 June 1909, p.275.
52. Lowe and Dockrill, p.46, for the best account of this.
53. K. Robbins, *Sir Edward Grey* (1971) pp.246–7.
54. BD X(II), Captain Watson to Goschen, 12 May 1913, p.701.
55. BD VII, Grey to Goschen, 18 August 1911, p.456.
56. BD IX(I), Bax-Ironside (Sofia) to Grey, 12 October 1911, p.531.
57. L.C.F. Turner, *Origins of the First World War* (1970), p.33.
58. Quoted in Turner, p.33.
59. BD IX(I), Bax-Ironside (Sofia) to Grey, 12 October 1911, p.531.
60. DR I, Izvolsky to Sazonov, 2/15 February 1911, pp.35–6.
61. DR I, Izvolsky to Sazonov, 1/14 March 1911, pp.46–9.
62. Hayne, pp.189–95; Keiger, pp.37–43, 68–74, for Cambon, upon which this paragraph is based.
63. Keiger, p.37.
64. Keiger, p.41.
65. R.J.B. Bosworth, *Italy, the Least of the Great Powers* (Cambridge, 1990), pp.135–56.
66. BD IX(I), Grey to Sir R. Rodd, 28 July 1911; GD IV, p.264.

67. Bosworth, p.153.
68. Bosworth, p.157.
69. *GD IV*, Oberndorff (Vienna) to FO, 28 September 1911, p.59; see also *Ö-U Auss. III*, nr. 2673, Aehrenthal's circular, 29 September 1911, p.372.
70. *BD IX(I)*, Nicolson to Cartwright, 2 October 1911, p.297.
71. *GD IV*, Jenisch to FO, 4 October 1911, p.60.
72. *BD IX(I)*, Cartwright to Grey, 28 September 1911, p.281.
73. *BD IX(I)*, Mallet minute on Cartwright to Grey, 23 October 1911, p.313; see also Grey to Lowther, 5 October 1911, pp.300–1.
74. *BD IX(I)*, Lowther to Grey, 16 October 1911, p.308; also editorial note on Bax-Ironside to Grey, 17 October 1911, p.311; also pp.320–50.
75. *BD IX(I)*, Grey to Goschen, 6 November 1911, pp.321.
76. *DR I*, Izvolsky to Nératof, 26 October/8 November 1911, including letter to de Selves, pp.155–9.
77. *BD IX(I)*, Lowther to Grey, 16 October 1911, p.308.
78. *Carnock*, p.360.
79. *BD IX(I)*, Grey to Bertie, 9 January 1912, p.527.
80. *BD IX(I)*, Bax-Ironside to Nicolson, 8 April 1912, pp.564–5.
81. *BD IX(I)*, Nicolson to O'Beirne, 21 May 1912, p.568.
82. *BD VI*, Goschen to Nicolson, 9 February 1912, pp.672–3.
83. *BD VI*, Grey to Bertie, 7 February 1912, p.670.
84. Haldane, pp.239–40.
85. *BD VI*, Cambon to Poincaré, 9 February 1912, p.675.
86. *BD VI*, Haldane's diary, 10 February 1912, pp.676–85.
87. *BD VI*, memo. by Haldane, 12 March 1912, pp.710–11.
88. Robbins, p.119, quoting Harcourt papers.
89. *BD VI*, Crowe minute, 3 March 1912, p.703.
90. *BD VI*, Crowe minute, 3 March 1912, p.703.
91. *BD VI*, Nicolson minute, 15 April 1912, pp.747–8.
92. *BD IX(II)*, Nicolson to Bertie, 6 May 1912, pp.583–4.
93. *BD IX(II)*, FO memo., 8 May 1912, pp.585–9.
94. *BD IX(II)*, Nicolson to Grey, 4 May 1912, pp.582–3.
95. M.V. Brett (ed.), *Journals and Letters of Reginald, Viscount Esher, vol. III: 1910–1915* (1938), Esher to M.V. Brett, 2 July 1912, p.99.
96. Cab. 37/111/86, McKenna memo., 3 July 1912.
97. *BD IX(II)*, Grey to Carnegie, 26 July 1912, pp.604–5.

98. E. David (ed.), *Inside Asquith's Cabinet: The Diary of Charles Hobhouse* (1977), 17 July 1912, p.118.
99. *BD IX(II)*, Grey to Carnegie, 22 July 1912, p.601.
100. *BD IX(II)*, Churchill's note, 29 July 1912, p.605.
101. *BD IX(II)*, Bertie to Grey, 30 July 1912, pp.606–7.
102. *BD IX(II)*, Bertie to Grey, 13 August 1912, pp.609–10.
103. Randolph S. Churchill, *Winston S. Churchill. Companion Volume II, part 3* (1969) [henceforth Churchill II, cv.3], Churchill to Asquith, 22 August 1912, pp.1638–9.
104. *BD X(II)*, nos 413, 416 and 417.
105. *BD IX(I)*, Grey memo. 24 September 1912, p.761.
106. *BD IX(I)*, Grey to Bertie, 9 January, 1912, p.527.

Chapter 23

1. Herrmann, p.234.
2. Herrmann, p.169.
3. Herrmann, pp.161–9.
4. Herrmann, p.178.
5. *BD IX(II)*, Buchanan to Grey, 15 May 1913, pp.792–3.
6. Turner, p.34.
7. Turner, pp.35–6; Keiger, pp.97–9.
8. *DDF 3ème série, tome III*, no. 359.
9. *DR I*, Izvolsky to Sazanov, 30 August/12 September, 1912, pp.323–7.
10. *BD IX(I)*, Grey's memo., 24 September 1912, p.761.
11. Taylor, *The Struggle for Mastery*, p.491.
12. *BD IX(II)*, Buchanan to Grey, 16 October 1912, pp.26–9.
13. *BD IX(II)*, Granville to Nicolson, 18 October 1912, pp.36–8.
14. *BD IX(II)*, Goschen to Grey, 25 October 1912, pp.48–9.
15. *GD IV*, Kühlmann to Bethmann-Hollweg, 15 October 1912, pp.115–17.
16. Namier, p.107.
17. *GD IV*, Kiderlen to Kühlmann, 20 October 1912, pp.117–18.
18. *BD IX(II)*, Grey to Goschen, 25, 28 October 1912, pp.49–51, 55–6.
19. *BD IX(II)*, Rodd (Rome) to Grey, 9 November 1912, pp.124–5; Bosworth, pp. 222–3.

20. *BD IX(II)*, Goschen to Grey, 7, 8, 9 November 1912, pp.114, 118, 126; Cartwright to Grey, 8 November, 1912, pp.122–4.
21. Turner, pp.44–5.
22. Turner, pp.46–7.
23. Williamson, *Politics of Grand Strategy*, p.130; Sir Lewis Namier, *Vanished Supremacies* (1958), 84.
24. S. Williamson, 'Influence, Power and the Policy Process; The Case of Franz Ferdinand', in *Historical Journal*, 1974, pp.428–9.
25. Fischer, *War of Illusions*, esp. pp.161–4.
26. H. W. Koch (ed.), *The Origins of the First World War* (1984 edn), pp.12–14.
27. *BD IX(II)*, Goschen to Grey, 22 November 1912, p.187; Grey to Goschen, 28 November 1912, p.224.
28. *BD IX(II)*, Buchanan to Grey, 4 December 1912, pp.241–2.
29. *BD IX(II)*, Goschen to Grey, 7 November 1912, pp.113–14.
30. *BD IX(II)*, Goschen to Grey, 7 December 1912, pp.261–2.
31. *BD X(II)*, Rodd to Grey, 6 January 1913, pp.659–63.
32. R.J. Crampton, *The Hollow Detente* (1979), p.79.
33. *BD X(II)*, George V to Grey, 8 December 1912, p.658.
34. *BD X(II)*, Grey to George V, 9 December 1912, pp.658–9.
35. *BD X(II)*, Rodd to Grey, 6 January 1913, pp.659–62.
36. *BD IX(II)*, Nicolson to Buchanan, 31 December 1912, pp.325–6.
37. *BD IX(II)*, Nicolson minute on Paget to Grey, 21 November 1912, p.183.
38. *BD IX(II)*, Nicolson to Goschen, 7 January 1913, p.373.
39. *RD I*, Izvolsky to Sazonov, 22 November/5 December 1912, p.368.
40. *BD IX(II)*, Nicolson to Buchanan, 31 December 1912, p.325.
41. *BD IX(II)*, Grey to Buchanan, 1 January 1913, p.326.
42. *BD IX(II)*, editorial note on no. 449, p.353.
43. *BD X(II)* Grey to George V, 9 December 1912, pp.658-9.
44. Willamson, *Politics of Grand Strategy*, p.133.
45. R.A. Kann, 'Wilhelm II and Francis Ferdinand', In *American Historical Review*, 1952, letter dated 13 February 1913, p.346.
46. Crampton, pp.89-91, for the details.
47. *BD IX(II)*, no. 889 record of the meeting, 25 April 1913, pp.720-1.
48. *BD IX(II)*, Cartwright to Grey, 25 April 1913, pp.721-3.

49. *GD IV*, reports from Vienna, 28 and 30 April 1913, pp.172-4.
50. *GD IV*, Jagow to Wilhelm II, 24 April 1913, p.169.
51. *GD IV*, minutes on Tschirschky to FO, 28 April 1913, p.170-1.
52. *BD IX(II)*, Grey to Buchanan, 28 April 1913, p.725.
53. *BD IX(II)*, Grey to Buchanan, 1 May 1913, pp.745-6, except for the last clause which was excised but is quoted in Crampton, p.93.
54. *Ö-U Auss. VI*, no. 6870, record of the meeting of the Crown Council, 2 May 1913.
55. *BD IX(II)*, Buchanan to Nicolson, 1 May 1913, pp.751-2.
56. *DR I*, Izvolsky telegram 1/17 November 1912, p.346.
57. *BD IX(II)*, Grey to Cartwright, 24 April 1913, pp.718-19.
58. *BD IX(II)*, Grey to Mr E. Howard, 6 December 1912, p.257.
59. Carnock Papers, FO 800/360, Goschen to Nicolson, 25 November 1912.
60. FO 800/360, Nicolson to Goschen, 26 November 1912.
61. FO 800/360, Nicolson to Goschen, 27 November 1912.
62. *GP XXXIX*, nr. 15612, Lichnowsky to Bethmann, 3 December 1912.
63. Nicolson, p.390, quoting Cartwright to Nicolson, 31 January 1913.
64. Nicolson, p.390, quoting Cartwright to Nicolson, 23 May 1913; also at *BD IX(II)*, pp.810-11.
65. Wilson *Policy of the Entente*, pp.135-6.
66. M. and E. Brock (eds), *H.H. Asquith: Letters to Venetia Stanley* (Oxford, 1982), p.92.
67. Brock, pp.92-3
68. Brock, 24 July 1914, p.123.
69. *Twenty-Five Years II*, p.331.
70. *BD XI* Buchanan to Grey, 27 July 1914, p.120.
71. *BD XI,*, Grey to Bertie, 30 July 1914, p.201.
72. *BD XI*, Grey to Bertie, 31 July 1914, p.220.
73. Wilson, *Policy of the Entente*, p.136, quoting Pease diary, 31 July 1914.
74. *BD XI*, Goschen to Grey, 29 July 1914; Grey to Goschen, 31 July 1914, pp.185-6, 193-4.
75. *Churchill II, cv. 3*, Ponsonby to Churchill, Churchill's reply, 31 July 1914, pp.1190-1.
76. Brock, 1 August 1914, p.140.
77. *Churchill II, cv. 3*, Cabinet notes, 1 August 1914, pp.1996-7

78. *BD XI*, Grey to Bertie, 2 August 1914, pp.274–5.
79. Brock, 2 August 1914, p.146.
80. Wilson, *Policy of the Entente*, p.138, quoting Pease diary, 2 August 1914.
81. McEwen (ed.), 2 August 1914, p.87.
82. Brock, 3 August 1914, pp.147–8.
83. *Hansfard*, House of Commons, 5th series, vol. LXV, 3 August 1914, cols 1810–27.
84. Wilson, *Policy of the Entente*, p.141.

Conclusion

1. Buckle V, p.186.
2. John D. Fair, *Harold Temperley* (Newark, 1992), p.133.
3. Brooke and Sorenson, undated memo. by Gladstone, p.104.
4. Dep. Hughenden 112/2, Derby to Disraeli, June 1875, fo. 202.
5. Brooke and Sorensen, memo., 28 February 1885, p.103.
6. *BD II*, Sanderson draft response to Chirol, 21 January 1902, p.88.
7. McKewen (ed.), 2 August 1914, p.87.
8. Fair, p.133.
9. Trinity College, Cambridge, R.A. Butler Papers, RAB G.9/13, Butler to Ian Black, 21 April 1938.
10. J. Colville, *The Fringes of Power* (1985), 10 May 1940, p.123.
11. Butler Papers, RAB C.11/180, Butler to Annie Chamberlain, 22 December 1940.

Bibliography

A. MANUSCRIPTS

Bodleian Library, Oxford
Papers of the 1st Earl of Beaconsfield
Microfilm of Correspondance from the Royal Archives on the Oriental Question

Borthwick Institute, York
Paper of the 1st Viscount Halifax

British Library, London
Papers of the 1st Earl Balfour
Papers of the 1st Baron Bertie of Thame
Papers of the 4th Earl of Carnarvon
Papers of the 1st Earl Cross
Papers of the 1st Earl of Iddesleigh (Sir Stafford Northcote)
Papers of Sir Henry Austen Layard
Papers of the 5th Marquis of Lansdowne

University of East Anglia Library
Microfilm of Prime Minister's Correspondence with the Monarch, 1864–1914

Hatfield House, Herts.
Papers of the 3rd Marquess of Salisbury
Papers of the 15th Countess of Derby

Liverpool Record Office
Papers of the 15th Earl of Derby

Public Record Office, London
Foreign Office, Correspondence with Germany
Papers of the 1st Earl Cairns
Papers of the 1st Baron Carnock (Sir Arthur Nicolson)
Papers of Sir Edward Grey
Papers of the 5th Marquis of Lansdowne
Papers of Sir Frank Lascelles
Papers of Sir Cecil Spring-Rice

B. PRINTED DOCUMENTARY SOURCES
(Place of publication is London
unless otherwise stated)

1. OFFICIAL PAPERS

Austro-Hungarian Documents
L.Bittner, A.F. Pribram *et al* (eds), *Österreich-Ungarns Aussenpolitik von der bosnichen Krise 1908 bis zum kriegsausbruch*, 8 vols (Vienna, 1930) (*Ö-U Auss* in notes)
F.R. Bridge (ed.), Austro-Hungarian Documents relating to the Macedonian Struggle, 1896–1912 (Thessaloniki, 1976)

British Documents
G.P. Gooch and H.Temperley (eds), *British Documents on the Origins of the War, 1898–1914*, 11 vols in 13 (1926–38) (*BD* in notes)

Hansard, Parliamentary Debates, House of Commons, House of Lords
  Parliamentary Papers

French Documents
Documents Diplomatiques Français (1930–53) (*DDF* in notes)
Première série, tomes I-XV, 1871–97
Deuxième série, tomes I-XIV, 1898–1911
Troisième série, tomes I-XI, 1911–14

German Documents
A. Mendelsohn-Bartholdy *et al* (eds), *Die Große Politik der Europäischen Kabinette, 1871–1914*, 40 vols (Berlin, 1922–6) (*GP* in notes)
Otto von Bismarck, *Die Gesammelten Werke*, X (Berlin, 1930)
E.T.S. Dugdale (ed) *German Diplomatic Documents, 1871–1914*, 4 vols (1928) (*GD* in notes)
N. Rich and M.H. Fisher (eds) *The Holstein Papers, vol I* (Cambridge, 1955)
N. Rich and M.H. Fisher (eds) *The Holstein Papers, vol III*: Correspondence 1861–1896 (Cambridge, 1962)
N. Rich and M.H. Fisher (eds) *The Holstein Papers, vol IV: Correspondence 1897–1909* (Cambridge, 1963)

Russian Documents
R.W. Seton-Watson, 'Russo-British relations during the Eastern Crisis', *Slavonic and East European Review*, 11 parts (1924–47) (*RBD* in notes)
J.Y. Simpson (ed.), *The Saburov Memoirs* (Cambridge, 1929)
Baron A. Meyendorff (ed.), *Correspondance Diplomatique de M. De Staal, tome II, 1889–1900* (Paris, 1929) *Un Livre Noir: Diplomatie d'avant-guerre d'après les documents des archives Russe, tome 1ère, Novembre 1910–Juillet 1914*, 3 vols (Paris, 1922) (*DR* in notes)

2. PRINTED COLLECTIONS

D.W.R. Bahlman (ed.) *The Diary of Sir Edward Walter Hamilton, vol. I* (Oxford, 1972)
D.W.R. Bahlman (ed.) *The Diary of Sir Edward Walter Hamilton, 1885–1906* (Hull, 1993)

A.C. Benson and Viscount Esher (eds), *The Letters of Queen Victoria, 1st series, vol. II 1844–1853* (1907)

D.G. Boyce (ed.), *The Crisis of British Power: The Imperial and Naval Papers of the Second Earl of Selborne, 1895–1910* (1990)

M.V. Brett (ed.), *Journals and Letters of Reginald, Viscount Esher, vol. III 1910–1915* (1938)

M. and E. Brock (eds) *H.H. Asquith: letters to Venetia Stanley* (Oxford, 1982)

J. Brooke and M. Sorensen (eds) W.E. Gladstone IV: Autobiographical Memoranda, 1868–1894 (1981)

G.E. Buckle (ed.), *The Letters of Queen Victoria, Second Series, vol. II* (1926)

G.E. Buckle (ed.), *The Letters of Queen Victoria, Second Series, vol. III* (1928)

Paul Cambon *Correspondance, tome II* (Paris, 1940)

Randolph Churchill (ed.), *Winston S. Churchill. Companion volume 1., part 2 1896–1900* (1967)

E. David (ed.), *Inside Asquith's Cabinet The Diary of Charles Hobhouse* (1977)

P. Gordon (ed.), *The Red Earl: The Papers of the Fifth Earl Spencer 1835–1910, vol. I* (Northampton, 1981)

S. Gwynne (ed.), *The Letters and Friendships of Sir Cecil Spring-Rice: A Record, 2 vols* (1929)

A. Hawkins and J. Powell (eds), *The Journal of John Wodehouse, First Earl of Kimberley for 1862–1902* (1997)

C.H.D. Howard and P. Gordon (eds), *The Cabinet Journal of Dudley Ryder, Viscout Sandon, 11 May–10 August 1878* (1974)

C.H.D. Howard (ed.), *The Diary of Edward Goschen 1900–1914* (1980)

S.W. Jackman and H. Haasse (eds), *A Stranger in The Hague: The Letters of Queen Sophie of the Netherlands to Lady Malet, 1842–1877* (Durham, N.C., 1989)

M.M Jefferson, 'Lord Salisbury's Conversations with the Tsar at Balmoral, 27 and 29 September 1896', in *Slavonic and East European Review*, XXXIX, vol. 92, December 1960

Paul Knaplund (ed.), *Letters from the Berlin Embassy* (Washington, 1944)

C.J. Lowe, *The Reluctant Imperialists: British Foreign Policy 1878–1902*, 2 vols (1967)

C.J. Lowe and M.L. Dockrill, *The Mirage of Power, vol. 3* (1972)
H.C.G. Matthew (ed.), *The Gladstone Diaries, vol. X* (Oxford, 1990)
H.C.G. Matthew (ed.), *The Gladstone Diaries, vol. XI* (Oxford, 1990)
Nancy E. Johnson (ed.), *The Diary of Gathorne-Hardy 1866–1892* (Oxford, 1981)
John M. McEwen (ed.), *The Riddell Diaries* (1986)
A. Ramm (ed.), *The Political Correspondence of Mr Gladstone and Lord Granville, vol. I: 1876-1882* (Oxford, 1952)
A. Ramm (ed.), *The Political Correspondence of Mr Gladstone and Lord Granville, vol II: 1883-1886* (Oxford, 1962)
N. Rich, *Friedrich von Holstein*, 2 vols (Cambridge, 1965)
Sir T.H. Sanderson and E.S. Roscoe (eds), *Speeches and Addresses of Edward Henry XVth Earl of Derby, vol. I* (1894)
H. Temperley and L. Penson (eds), *Foundations of British Foreign Policy from Pitt to Salisbury* (Cambridge, 1938)
J.R. Vincent (ed.), *Disraeli, Derby and the Conservative Party: The Politicals Journals of Lord Stanley 1849–69* (1978)
J.R. Vincent (ed.), *The Later Derby Diaries* (Bristol, 1981)
J.R. Vincent (ed.), *A Selection from the Diaries of Edward Henry Stanley, 15th Earl of Derby 1868–1878* (Cambridge, 1994)
T. Wilson (ed.), *The Political Diaries of C.P. Scott 1911–1928* (1970)
Lord Zetland (ed.), *The Letters of Disraeli to Lady Bradford and Lady Chesterfield*, 2 vols (1929)

3. AUTOBIOGRAPHIES/BIOGRAPHIES

Julian Amery, *The Life of Joseph Chamberlain, vol. IV: 1901–1903* (1951)
C. Andrew, *Théophile Delcassé and the Making of the Anglo-French Entente* (1968)
Otto von Bismarck, *Bismarck's Autobiography, vol. II*, (NY, 1899)
R. Blake, *Disraeli* (1966)
G.E. Buckle, *The Life of Benjamin Disraeli, Earl of Beaconsfield, vol. IV* (1916)
G.E. Buckle, *The Life of Benjamin Disraeli, Earl of Beaconsfield, vol. V* (1920)
G.E. Buckle, *The Life of Benjamin Disraeli, Earl of Beaconsfield, vol. VI* (1920)

Lady Burghcleve, *A Great Lady's Friendships* (1933)
Prince von Bülow, *Memoirs 1849–1897* (1932)
Prince von Bülow, *Memoirs 1897–1903* (1931)
Lady G. Cecil, *Life of Robert, Marquis of Salisbury, vol. I* (1921)
Lady G. Cecil, *Life of Robert, Marquis of Salisbury, vol. II* (1921)
Lady G. Cecil, *Life of Robert, Marquis of Salisbury, vol. III* (1931)
Lady G. Cecil, *Life of Robert, Marquis of Salisbury, vol. IV* (1932)
L. Cecil, *Wilhelm II, vol. II* (North Carolina, 1996)
John Charmley, *Churchill: The End of Glory* (1993)
E.A. Chilston, *W.H. Smith* (1967)
Winston S. Churchill, *Lord Randolph Churchill* (1974 edn)
Blanche E.C. Dugdale, *Arthur James Balfour: Years 1848–1906* (1939)
Lord E. Fitzmaurice, *Life of the Second Earl Granville, vols. I* (1905)
Lord E. Fitzmaurice, *Life of the Second Earl Granville, vol. II* (1913)
Lothar Gall, *Bismarck: The White Revolutionary, vol. 1: 1815–1871* (1986)
Lothar Gall, *Bismarck: The White Revolutionary, vol. 2: 1871–1898* (1986)
J.L. Garvin, *The Life of Joseph Chamberlain, vols II and III* (1934)
Viscount Grey of Falloden, *Twenty-Five Years*, 2 vols (1925)
K. Hamilton, *Bertie of Thame: Edwardian Ambassador* (Suffolk, 1990)
R.B. Haldane, *An Autobiography* (1929)
Sir Arthur Hardinge, *The Life of Henry Howard Molyneux Herbert, Fourth Earl of Carnarvon, vol. II* (Oxford, 1925)
K. Jarausach, *The Enigmatic Chancellor: Bethmann-Hollweg and the Hubris of Imperial Germany* (Princeton, 1972)
Sir Sidney Lee, *King Edward VII, 2 vols* (1925)
H.G.C. Matthew, *Gladstone, vol. II* (1995)
Sir H. Maxwell, *Life and Letters of the Fourth Earl of Clarendon, 2 vols* (1913)
John Morley, *The Life of William Ewart Gladstone, vols II and III* (1903)
John Morley, *Recollections, vol. II* (1923)
Allan Nevins, *Henry White: Thirty Years of American Diplomacy* (NY, 1930)
Lord Newton, *Lord Lyons, vol. II* (1913)
Lord Newton, *Lord Lansdowne* (1929)
H. Nicolson, *Lord Carnock: A Study in the Old Diplomacy* (1930)
H. Pakula, *An Uncommon Woman* (1996)

A. Ramm, *Sir Robert Morier* (Oxford, 1973)
K. Robbins, *Sir Edward Grey* (1971)
The Earl of Ronaldshay, *The Life of Lord Curzon, 2 vols* (1928)
Comte de Saint-Aulaire, *Confession d'un vieux diplomate* (Paris, 1953)
Lord Salisbury, *Biographical Essays* (1903)
P. Smith, *Disraeli: A Brief Life* (Cambridge, 1996)
J.A. Spender, *The Life of the Rt Hon. Sir Henry Campbell-Bannerman, vol. II* (n.d.)
W. Taffs, *Ambassador to Bismarck: Lord Odo Russell* (1938)
A.J.P. Taylor, *Bismarck* (1955)
G.M. Trevelyan, *Grey of Falloden* (1937)
Bruce Waller, *Bismarck* (1985)
S. Weintraub, *Disraeli* (1993)
Frederick Wellesley, *Recollections of a Soldier-Diplomat* (n.d., c. 1946)
F. Whyte, *Letters of Prince Bülow* (n.d.)
L. Wolf, *Life of the First Marquess of Ripon, vol. II* (1921)
Lord Zetland, *Lord Cromer* (1932)

4. MONOGRAPHS

E.N. Anderson, *The First Moroccan Crisis, 1904–1906* (Chicago, 1930)
M.S. Anderson, *The Eastern Question* (1966)
C.J. Bartlett, *Defence and Diplomacy: Britain and the Great Powers 1815–1914* (Manchester, 1993)
Winfried Baumgart, *Imperialism: The Idea and Reality of British and French Colonial Expansion, 1880–1914* (Oxford, 1982)
J.V. Beckett, *The Aristocracy in England 1660–1914* (1986)
V.R. Berghahn, *Germany and the Approach of War in 1914* (NY, 1973)
R. Blake and Hugh Cecil, *Salisbury: The Man and his Policies* (1987)
R.J.B. Bosworth, *Italy, the Least of the Great Powers* (Cambridge, 1990)
K. Bourne, *The Foreign Policy of Victorian England* (1970)
F. R. Bridge, *From Sadowa to Sarayevo* (1972)
F.R. Bridge, *Great Britain and Austria-Hungary 1906–1914: A Diplomatic History* (1972)
P.J. Cain and A.G. Hopkins, *British Imperialism: Innovation and Expansion 1688–1914* (1993)
David Cannadine, *The Rise and Fall of the British Aristocracy* (1990)

Alan Cassels, *Ideology & International Relations in the Modern World* (1996)

L. Cecil, *The German Diplomatic Service 1871–1914* (Princeton, 1976)

L. Cecil, *Wilhelm II, vol. II* (North Carolina, 1996)

Ian Clark, *Reform and Resistance in the International Order* (Cambridge, 1980)

J.C.D. Clark, *English Society, 1688–1832* (1985)

A.B. Cooke and J.R. Vincent, *The Governing Passion* (1974)

R.J. Crampton, *The Hollow Detente* (1979)

Allan Cunningham, *Eastern Questions in the Nineteenth Century, vol. 2* (1993)

István Diószegi, *Hungarians in the Ballhausplatz: Studies in the Austro-Hungarian Common Foreign Policy* (Budapest, 1983)

N. d'Ombrain, *War Machinery and High Policy* (Oxford, 1973)

C.C. Eldridge, *British Imperialism in the Nineteenth Century* (1987)

Richard J. Evans (ed.), *Rethinking German History* (1987)

John D. Fair, *Harold Temperley* (Newark, 1992)

E.J. Feuchtwanger, *Disraeli, Democracy and the Tory Party* (Oxford, 1968)

F. Fischer, *Germany's Aims in the First World War* (1967)

F. Fischer, *War of Illusions* (1975)

D. French, *British Economic and Strategic Planning 1905–1915* (1982)

I. Geiss, *German Foreign Policy 1871–1914* (1970)

I. Geiss, *Die lange Weg in die Katastrophe. Die Vorgeschichte des Ersten Weltkriegs 1815–1914* (Munich/Zurich, 1990)

P. Gifford and W.R. Louis (eds), *Britain and Germany in Africa* (New Haven, 1967)

J.M. Goudswaard, *Some Aspects of the End of Britain's 'Splendid Isolation' 1898–1904* (Rotterdam, 1952)

J.A.S. Grenville, *Lord Salisbury and Foreign Policy: The Close of the Nineteenth Century* (1964)

D. Harris, *A Diplomatic History of the Balkan Crisis of 1875–1878: The First Year* (Stanford, CA, 1969 edn)

M.B. Hayne, *The French Foreign Office and the Origins of the First World War* (Oxford, 1993)

P.M. Hayes, *Late Victorian Foreign Policy* (1977)

D.G. Herrmann, *The Arming of Europe and the Making of the First World War* (1996)

R.F.V. Heuston, *Lives of the Lord Chancellors 1885–1940* (Oxford, 1963)

SPLENDID ISOLATION?

F.H. Hinsley (ed.), *British Foreign Policy under Sir Edward Grey* (Cambridge, 1977)

C.H.D. Howard, *Splendid Isolation* (1967)

C.H.D. Howard, *Britain and the Casus Belli 1822–1902* (1974)

E. Ingram, *The Beginning of the Great Game in Asia 1828–1834* (Oxford, 1979)

E. Ingram, *Commitment to Empire: Prophecies of the Great Game in Asia 1797–1800* (Oxford, 1981)

E. Ingram, *Britain's Persian Connection 1798–1828* (Oxford, 1992)

Charles and Barbara Jelavich, *Russia in the East 1876–1880* (Leiden, 1959)

Barbara Jelavich, *Russia's Balkan Entanglements 1806–1914* (Cambridge, 1991)

J. Joll (ed.), *Britain and Europe 1793–1940* (1961)

E. Kehr, *Der Primat der Innenpolitik* (Berlin, 1965)

J.F.V. Keiger, *France and the Origins of the First World War* (1985)

J.B. Kelly, *Britain and the Persian Gulf 1785–1880* (Oxford, 1991 edn)

P.M. Kennedy, *The Samoan Tangle: A Study in Anglo-German-American Relations 1878–1900* (Dublin, 1974)

P.M. Kennedy, *The Rise of the Anglo-German Antagonism* (1981)

P.M. Kennedy (ed.), *The War Plans of the Great Powers 1880–1914* (1985)

Paul Knaplund, *Gladstone's Foreign Policy* (1970 edn)

H.W. Koch (ed.), *The Origins of the First World War* (1984 edn)

A. Lamb, *Britain and Chinese Central Asia: The Road to Lhasa 1767–1905* (1960)

William L. Langer, *European Alliances and Alignments* (NY, 1956 revised edn)

D.E. Lee, *Great Britain and the Cyprus Convention* (Cambridge, 1934)

Walter LeFeber, *The Cambridge History of American Foreign Relations, vol. II: The American Search for Opportunity 1865–1913* (1993)

K.A. Lerman, *The Chancellor as Courtier* (Cambridge, 1990)

D. Levering Lewis, *The Race to Fashoda* (1988)

C.J. Lowe, *Salisbury and The Mediterranean 1886–1896* (1965)

David MacLean, *Britain and her Buffer State* (1979)

A.J. Marder, *The Anatomy of British Sea Power, 1880–1905* (NY, 1940)

J.A.R. Marriott, *The Eastern Question* (1917)

A. Marsden, *British Diplomacy and Tunis 1875–1902* (Edinburgh, 1971)
G. Martel, *Imperial Diplomacy: Rosebery and the Failure of Foreign Policy* (1986)
W.N. Medlicott, *Bismarck, Gladstone and the Concert of Europe* (1956)
W.N. Medlicott, *The Congress of Berlin* (1965 edn)
W.N. Medlicott, *Bismarck and Modern Germany* (1965)
R. Millman, *British Foreign Policy and the Coming of the Franco-Prussian War* (Oxford, 1965)
R. Millman, *Britain and the Eastern Question 1875–1878* (Oxford, 1979)
G. Monger, *The End of Isolation* (1965)
A.J.A. Morris, *The Scaremongers* (1984)
L.B. Namier, *In the Margin of History* (1939)
Sir Lewis Namier, *Vanished Supremacies* (1958)
Keith Neilson, *Britain and the Last Tsar* (1996)
I. Nish, *The Anglo-Japanese Alliance* (1967)
R. Oliver and T. Matthew, *History of East Africa, vol. I* (Oxford, 1963)
Otto Pflanze, *Bismarck and the Development of Germany, vol. II* (Princeton, 1990)
Otto Pflanze, *Bismarck and the Development of Germany, vol. III* (Princeton, 1990)
A. Porter, *Origins of the South African War* (1975)
A.F. Pribram, *England and the International Policy of the European Great Powers 1871–1914* (Oxford, 1931)
A.F. Pribram, *Austria-Hungary and Great Britain 1908–1914* (Oxford, 1951)
Felix Rachfahl, *Deutschland und die Weltpolitik, 1871–1914* (Stuggart, 1923)
H. Ragsdale (ed.), *Imperial Russian Foreign Policy* (Cambridge, 1993)
James Ratallack, *Germany in the Age of Kaiser Wilhelm II* (1996)
G.J. Renier, *Great Britain and the Netherlands 1813–1815* (1930)
J.C.G. Röhl, *Germany without Bismarck* (1967)
J.C.G. Röhl, *Kaiser Wilhelm II: New Interpretations* (1982)
J.C.G. Röhl, *The Kaiser and His Court* (1994 transl.)
P.J.V. Rolo, *Entente Cordiale* (1969)
G.H. Rupp, *A Wavering Friendship: Russia and Austria 1876–1878* (Cambridge, Mass., 1941)
Jeremy Salt, *Imperialism: Evangelism and the Ottoman Armenians 1878–1896* (1993)

G.N. Sanderson, *England, Europe and the Upper Nile 1882–1899* (Edinburgh, 1965)
Bernadotte E. Schmitt, *The Annexation of Bosnia* (Cambridge, 1937)
Paul Schroeder, *The Transformation of European Politics 1763–1848* (Oxford, 1994)
Hugh Seton-Watson, *The Russian Empire 1801–1917* (Oxford, 1967)
R.W. Seton-Watson, *Disraeli, Gladstone and the Eastern Question* (1935)
R.T. Shannon, *Gladstone and the Bulgarian Agitation* (1963)
R.T. Shannon, *The Age of Disraeli 1868–1881* (1992)
R.T. Shannon, *The Age of Salisbury 1881–1902* (1995)
G. Shöllgen (ed.), *Escape into War* (Oxford, 1990)
Alan Sked, *The Decline and Fall of the Habsburg Empire 1814–1918* (1989)
Colin L. Smith, *The Embassy of Sir William White at Constantinople 1886–1891* (Oxford, 1957)
Paul Smith (ed.), *Lord Salisbury on Politics* (Cambridge, 1982)
E.D. Steele, *Palmerston and Liberalism 1855–1865* (Cambridge, 1991)
Zara Steiner, *The Foreign Office and Foreign Policy 1898–1914* (Cambridge, 1969)
M.D. Stojanovic, *The Great Powers and the Balkans 1875–1878* (Cambridge, 1939)
Jon Tetsuro Sumida, *In Defence of Naval Supremacy: Finance, Technology and British Naval Policy 1889–1914* (1989)
B.H. Sumner, *Russia and the Balkans 1870–1880* (Oxford, 1937)
M. Swartz, *The Politics of British Foreign Policy in the Era of Disraeli and Gladstone* (1985)
A.J.P. Taylor, *Germany's First Bid for Colonies 1884–1885* (1938)
A.J.P. Taylor, *The Struggle for Mastery in Europe 1848–1918* (1954)
A.J.P. Taylor, *The Trouble Makers* (1956)
A.J.P. Taylor, *Essays in English History* (1976)
F.M.L. Thompson, *English Landed Society in the Nineteenth Century* (1963)
G.C. Thompson, *Public Opinion and Lord Beaconsfield*, 2 vols (1886)
A.P. Thornton, *The Imperial Idea and its Enemies* (1985 edn)
J.E. Thorold Rogers, *Speeches on Questions of Public Policy by John Bright* (1869)
L.C.F. Turner, *Origins of the First World War* (1970)

Bruce Waller, *Bismarck at the Crossroads* (1974)

J.A. White, *Transition to Global Rivalry: Alliance Diplomacy and the Quadruple Entente 1898–1907* (Cambridge, 1995)

R. Williams, *Defending the Empire* (1991)

S.R. Williamson, *The Politics of Grand Strategy* (1967)

S.R. Williamson, *Austria-Hungary and the Origins of the First World War* (1991)

K. Wilson, *The Policy of the Entente* (Cambridge, 1985)

Peter Winzen, *Bülows Weltmachtkonzept: Untersuchungen zur Führphase seiner Aussenpolitik 1897–1901* (Boppard-an-Rhein, 1977)

Walter G. Wirthwein, *Britain and the Balkan Crisis 1875–1878* (NY, 1935)

5. ARTICLES/THESES

F.R. Bridge, 'Izvolski, Aehrenthal, and the End of the Austro-Russian Entente, 1906–1908', in *Mitteilungen des österreichischen Staatsarchivs*, vol. 29, 1976

A.E. Campbell, 'Great Britain and the United States in the Far East, 1895–1903', *Historical Journal*, 1958

M. Cowling, 'Lytton, the Cabinet, and the Russians, August to November 1878', *English History Review*, 1961

M.L. Dockrill, 'David Lloyd George and Foreign Policy', in A.J.P Taylor (ed.), *Lloyd George: Twelve Essays* (1971)

M.L. Dockrill, 'British Policy during the Agadir Crisis', in F.H. Hinsley (ed.), *British Foreign Policy under Sir Edward Grey* (Cambridge, 1977)

F. Dwyer, 'R.A. Cross and the Eastern Crisis of 1875–8', *Slavonic Review* vol. XXXIX, June 1961

Richard B. Elrod, 'The Concert of Europe', in *World Politics*, vol. XXVIII, 1976

Niall Fergusson, 'Germany and the Origins of the First World War: New Perspectives', in *Historial Journal*, 1992

Niall Fergusson, 'Public Finance and National Security: The Domestic Origins of the First World War Revisited', in *Past & Present*, February 1994

W.A. Gauld, 'The *Dreikaiserbündnis* and the Eastern Question, 1877–8', in *English Historical Review*, October 1927

D.R. Gillard, 'Salisbury's African policy and the Heligoland Offer of 1890', in *English Historical Review*, 1960

A. Gollin, 'Asquith: a new view', in M. Gilbert (ed.), *A Century of Conflict, 1850–1950. Essays for A.J.P. Taylor* (1966)

J.A.S. Grenville, 'Lansdowne's abortive project of 12 March 1901 for a secret agreement with Germany', in *Bulletin of the Institute of Historical Research*, 1954

J.D. Hargreaves, 'The Origin of the Anglo-French military conversations in 1905', *History*, 1951

J.D. Hargreaves, '*Entente Manquée*, Anglo-French Relations, 1895–1896', *Cambridge Historical Journal*, 1953

J.D. Hargreaves, 'Lord Salisbury, British Isolation and the Yangtze Valley, June–September 1900', in *Bulletin of the Institute of Historical Research*, 1957

D. Harris, 'Bismarck's Advance to England, January 1876', in *Journal of Modern History*, vol. III, no. 4, December 1931

F.H. Hinsley, 'Bismarck, Salisbury and the Mediterranean Agreements of 1887', in *Historial Journal*, 1958

A.V. Ignat'ev, 'Foreign Policy of Russia in the Far East', in H. Ragsdale (ed.), *Imperial Russian Foreign Policy* (Cambridge, 1993)

J. Joll, 'The Ideal and the Real: changing concepts of the international system, 1815–1982', in *International Affairs*, vol. 58, no. 2

R.A. Kann, 'Wilhelm II and Francis Ferdinand', in *American Historical Review*, 1952

D.E. Lee, 'The Proposed Mediterranean League of 1878', in *Journal of Modern History* 1931

S.L. Mayer, 'Anglo-German Rivalry at the Algeçiras Conference', in P. Gifford and W.R. Louis (eds), *Britain and Germany in Africa* (New Haven, 1967)

J. McDermott, 'The Revolution in British Military Thinking from the Boer War to the Moroccan Crisis', in P. Kennedy (ed.), *The War Plans of the Great Powers 1880–1914* (1985)

D.M. McDonald, 'A Lever without a fulcrum: domestic factors and Russia Foreign Policy, 1905–1914', in H. Ragsdale (ed.), *Imperial Russian Foreign Policy* (Cambridge, 1993)

W.N. Medlicott, 'The Powers and the Unification of the Two Bulgarias, 1885', in *English Historical Review*, 1939

Ralph R. Menning, 'Origins of a Political Friendship', in *Austrian History Yearbook*, 1993

Ian F.D. Morrow, 'The Foreign Policy of Prince von Bülow', in *Cambridge Historical Journal*, 1932

L.M.Penson, 'The new course in British Foreign Policy, 1892–1902', in *Transactions of the Royal Historical Society*, 1943

Otto Pflanze, 'Bismarck's Gedanken und Erinnerungen', in G. Egerton (ed.), *Political Memoir: Essays on the Politics of Memory* (1994)

H. Pogge von Strandman, 'Domestic origins of Germany's colonial expansion under Bismarck', in *Past and Present*, 1969

A.N.Porter, 'Lord Salisbury, Foreign Policy and Domestic Finance, 1860-1900', in Lord Blake and H.Cecil (eds), *Salisbury: The Man and his Policies* (1987)

K.Robbins, 'Foreign Secretaries, Cabinet, Parliament and Parties', in K. Robbins (ed.), *Politicians, Diplomacy and War in Modern British History* (1994)

R.Robinson and J. Gallagher, 'The Imperialism of Free Trade', in *Economic History Review*, 1953

F.S.. Rodkey, 'Lord Palmerston's Policy for the Rejuvenation of Turkey, 1839–1842', in *Transactions of the Royal Historical Society*, 1929

P.J.V. Rolo, 'Landsdowne', in K. Wilson (ed.), *British Foreign Secretaries and Foreign Policy* (1987)

P.W. Schroeder, 'World War One as Galloping Gertie', in H.W. Koch (ed.), *The Origins of the First World War* (1984 edn)

Zara Steiner, 'The Foreign Office under Sir Edward Grey', in F.H. Hinsley (ed.), *British Foreign Policy under Sir Edward Grey* (Cambridge, 1977)

Zara Steiner, 'Elitism and Foreign Policy: the Foreign Office before the Great War', in B.J.C. McKercher and D.J. Moss (eds.), *Shadow & Substance in British Foreign Policy 1895–1939* (Alberta, 1984)

Eric Stokes, 'Milnerism', in *Historical Journal*, 1962

N. Stone, 'Moltke and Conrad Plan their War', in P.Kennedy (ed.), *The War Plans of the Great Powers 1880–1914* (1985 edn)

B.H. Sumner, 'Ignatyev at Constantinople 1846–1874', *Slavonic and East European Review*, vol XI, 1937

Jürgen Theiner, *The Foreign Policy of the 5th Marquis of Lansdowne*, unpublished M.A. dissertation, University of East Anglia, 1990

F. Thimme, 'Die Krüger-Depesche', in *Europäische Gespräche*, Jahrgang 2, 1924

H.A. Turner, 'Bismarck's imperialist venture: anti-British in origin?', in P. Gifford and W.R. Louis (eds), *Britian and Germany in Africa* (New Haven, 1967)

Bruce Waller, 'Bismarck and Gorchakov in 1879: "The Two Chancellors' War" ', in K. Bourne and D.C. Watt (eds). *Studies in International History* (1967)

E. Walters, 'Franco-Russian Discussions on the partition of Austria-Hungary, 1899', in *Slavonic and East European Review*, vol. XXVIII, no. 70, December 1949

E. Walters, 'Aehrenthal's attempt in 1907 to Re-Group the European Powers', in *Slavonic and East European Review*, vol. XXX, no. 74, December 1951

S. Wank, 'Foreign Policy and the Nationality Problem in Austria-Hungary, 1867–1914', in *Austrian History Yearbook*, 1967

O. H. Wedel, 'Austro-Hungarian Diplomatic Documents 1908–1914', in *Journal of Modern History*, vol. 3, no. 1, March 1931

S. Williamson, 'Influence, Power and the Policy Process: The case of Franz Ferdinand', in *Historical Journal* 1974

K. Wilson, 'Constantinople or Cairo: Lord Salisbury and the Partition of the Ottoman Empire 1886–97', in K. Wilson (ed.), *Empire and Continent*, (1987)

K. Wilson, 'Isolating the Isolator: Cartwright, Grey and the Seduction of Austria-Hungary 1908–1912', in Wilson (ed), *Empire and Continent* (1987)

Index

Abdülhamid II 21–2, 65–6, 113–4, 122, 132, 136–7, 147, 178, 186, 203, 229, 233
Aberdeen, 4th earl of 23, 101, 192
Addison, Christopher 394
Aehrental, Count L. von
  and *Dreikaiserbund* 351–2
  Bosnian crisis 352–3
  British hypocrisy 353–4, 356
  keeps Germany in dark 353–355
  opposes preventative wars 355
  firmness over Bosnia 355–7, 359–60, 371
  supported by Germany 358
  Britain 'has Germany on the brain' 359
  and Tripoli 372–3
Albrecht, Archduke 35
Alexander II, Tsar of Russia 20, 32, 74, 95, 97, 105, 122, 132, 128
  and Russian foreign policy 33–4, 46, 48, 50–1
  and Reichstadt 36–7
  and Britain 49
  and Russian honour 70
  British warnings to 89–90
  rude to Queen Victoria 116
  feels insulted by Britain 139
  and San Stefano 148
  and Berlin Congress 154–5
  and German alliance 176
  his own foreign minister 201
Alexander III, Tsar of Russia 203
Alexander of Battenberg, 202–3, 207–8
Andrassy, Julius (Guyla) 21, 23–4, 31, 47, 58, 66, 177
  comparison with Disraeli 35
  and Habsburg policy 35–6, 50

  and Reichstadt 67, 96
  and Bismarck 46
  lies about Reichstadt 67, 96
  might act with Britain 118–9, 120
  unwilling to act with Britain 133, 142
  and conference 141
  as possible ally for Britain 147
  at Berlin 159
Arabi, Colonel 184, 185, 187
Asquith, Herbert Henry
  and Relugas 325
  unscrupulous ambition of 326
  lacks interest in diplomacy 331
  and naval programmes 349
  and crisis over 350–1
  supports Grey 366–9
  and Britain's 'free hand' 376
  Churchill's complaints to 377
  mobilizes fleet 392
  crisis in 1914 392–3

Balance of Power 2–3
  definitions of 3–4
  'foul idol' 4
  influence on Disraeli 4–5, 59
  and Eastern Question 18–19, 20–1, 31 and *passim*
  and Second Mediterranean Agreement 221
  influence on Grey 338–9, 361, 364
  and Balkans 351–2 and *passim*
  and Grey on 3 August 1914 393–4
Balfour, A.J. (1st Earl)
  and Derby at Foreign Office 126

and pressure on Salisbury 240–1
occupation of Wei-hai-Wei 254
wants German alliance 256, 257–8, 288, 301–3
suspects Eckardstein 258
and German blackmail 264
Portuguese agreement 265–6
opposes Japanese alliance 301–2, 303
implications of Ententes 304–5
and Anglo-French Entente 307, 310, 311
and Persia 308
gloomy about Russia 308–9
and Austria 314
not Germanophobic 315, 323,
and Moroccan Crisis 1905 320
and contacts with French 324
weakness of Government 324–5
resignation of 325–6
Bannerman, Sir H. Campbell-forms Liberal Government 325–6
unable to avoid Grey at FO 326
defeats Relugas plot 331
talks with French are concealed from him 333, 334, 335–6
dislikes contact with France 337
need for disarmament 349
mentioned 391
Bax-Ironside, Sir H. 371
Benckendorff, Count 355
Berchtold, Leopold von 384, 387, 388
Bertie, (Lord) Francis
advantages of Japanese 296, 301
first Moroccan crisis 319–20, 321
and contacts with France 334
Grey's commitment to
Paul Cambon and France 335–6
and balance of power 339
need to support France 366
naval agreement with France 376–7
Bethmann-Hollweg, T. von 360, 363
and balance of power 364
and German weakness 379–80
wants to abstain in Balkans 382
wants better relations with Great Britain 383
and 'War Council' of 1912 384
and Balkan crisis 384
assurances to Grey in 1914 391
Beauchamp, Lord 393, 394
Blake, Lord 126, 131
Bismarck, Herbert von 190–1, 192, 200–2, 223, 225
Bismarck, Prince Otto von 2, 4, 385
Derby mistrusts 19
and *Dreikaiserbund* 19–20, 31, 34, 46
view of diplomacy 20–1
fails to understand Derby 22
and cooperation with Britain 22, 24
impressed by Disraeli 31
and monarchical diplomacy 32, 36. 46, 49, 51–2

contest with Gorchakov 20, 34, 49, 58
fears British plots 45
and relations with Austria 46, 50
trapped by Russians 49–50
'silent and impenetrable' 51
Realpolitik of 52, 57–8, 66–7
meets Salisbury 57–8
Constantinople Conference 66–7
distrusted by all 66–8, 96, 134
conference proposed to 141
cooperates with Salisbury 154
at Berlin Congress 155–60
and Disraeli at Berlin 156–158
and Anglo-German alliance 170–3
hates Gladstone and Liberals 174, 190, 200
principles of his diplomacy 174–7
alliance with Russia 175–6
alliance with Austria 177
renews *Dreikaiserbund* 177–8
and conservative triumph 179
ill-will towards Britain 182
encourages France against 182–3
need to cooperate with 184
unites Europe against Britain 184–5
no interest in Europe 185
and 'Egyptian baton' 188–9, 190–2
imperialism of 189–90
blackmails Britain 190–3
distrusts democracy 198–9
Salisbury asks for help 199–200
no cooperations against Russia 201
Bulgarian crisis 1887 203
favours Salisbury 203–4
Churchill wants to align with 209
Salisbury exploits difficuties 212–3
Mediterranean Agreements 214–6, 220–2
pushes his luck 217
dislikes Anglo-Russian rapprochement 218–9
puzzled by Salisbury 219–20
seeks Salisbury's help 222
proposes alliance to 223
agreement over Heligoland 225–6
effects of downfall of 226–7
Wilhelm II calls 'pygmy' 228
superior to his successors 250, 399
Boulanger, General 214
Bradford, Lady 17
Bright, John 23
denounces balance of power 3–4
Gladstone's policy in Egypt 185
resigns over 186
wants end to wars 223
British foreign policy
and balance of power 1, 3–4, 6, 400–1
no single tradition 1–2, 400
Disraeli's influence on 2–3, 153
and the Eastern Question 16–19, 98 and *passim*
Tory traditions 23–4

rejection of Berlin Memo. 24–5
Bulgarian atrocities and 38–9
jingoism and 98–9
proposed new departure 147–8, 152–3
and Berlin Congress 155
and German alliance 170–3
and 'splendid isolation' 211, 228–9, 232, 295–6
Salisbury/Chamberlain 230–1
and Jingo public opinion 245
no change under Lansdowne 280
Salisbury's principles 290
dilemmas of 297–8
'hand to mouth' nature of 313–4
flexibility and success 314
not anti-German 315–6
favourable position (1905) 315–7
and traditions of 400–1
Buchanan, Sir G. 382
Bülow, Prince B. von
and Disraeli at Berlin 156
and World Policy 249
feebleness of diplomacy of 249–50
gap between intention/action 250–1
wants force Britain into alliance with Germany 250–1, 257–8
Chamberlain and alliance 255–6, 258–9, 264–5, 274–5
thinks Britain desperate
for German alliance 258–60, 262–3, 273–3, 280–5, 288
does not listen to Hatzfeldt 262–3
blackmail over Portuguese colonies with Britain 263
opposes British alliance 266
no help for France in 1898 267
and Samoan crisis 270–1
and Continental League 274
offended by Chamberlain 275–6, 300
and China 277
England 'must come to us' 281
time on Germany's side 282
and the Far East and Britain 283
frustrated by British 285
on Kaiser and Edward VII 292
threatens to aign with Russia 315
Lansdowne fails to take this threat seriously 316
and Anglo-French Entente 317
failure of World Policy 317–8
failure in Morocco 318–9, 323–4
and Anglo-French alliance 322, 337
failure of Björkö 323
still distrusts Britain 337
naval programme 350
Bosnian crisis 354–5
weakness of German position 360
and Jules Cambon 371
failure of 399
Burns, John 393

Butler, R.A. 400–1

Cairns, 1st Earl 40, 43–5, 55, 74, 82, 88, 95, 97, 99, 102, 104–5, 111, 114, 126–7, 129, 146, 149, 151
Cambon, Jules 371–2
Cambon, Paul
and new French policy 269
on Salisbury 305
and French policy 305–6
links Morocco and Egypt 306–7
exceeds instructions 306–7
and Entente 311
misrepresents Lansdowne 320–1
asks Grey for commitment 333–4, 335–6
Anglo-French cooperation 375–5
expects British support 390–1
'ils vont nous lâcher' 391
Grey reassures 393
Cambridge, Duke of 23, 146
Canning, George
and balance of power 3
and Eastern Question 18, 32, 55
and British policy 23
invoked by Gladstone 173
and British isolation 182
Carnarvon, 4th Earl of 15, 40, 43, 55, 62, 80, 168
distrusts Disraeli 63, 71, 91, 93
rallies Salisbury against D 71–2
on Salisbury's ambitions 77–8, 87, 106, 110, 130–1
lack of unity with Derby 83
Disraeli's dislike of 85, 95
alliance with Derby and Salisbury 92–3
dissents from Cabinet policy 97
opposes Jingo policy 99–100
opposes Disraeli 100, 103–4, 111, 119
insulted by Disraeli 109–110
relations with Salisbury 110
joins Derby against the PM 114
offers resignation 115–6
resigns and unresigns 117–8
resignation antcipated 120–1
resigns 121–2
place offered to Derby 124
does not withdraw 125
'coward' (Queen Victoria) 135
in Salisbury's Government 197
Cartwright, Sir F. 356, 387, 389
Cassell, Sir E. 374
Castlereagh, Viscount 64
Cawdor, Lord 316, 348–9, 350
Cecil, Lady Georgiana 89
Cecil, Lady Gwendolen 106
Cecil, Lord Robert see Salisbury, 3rd Marquis of
Chamberlain (Arthur) Neville 1, 400, 401
Chamberlain (Joseph) Austen 315, 324

Chamberlain, Joseph
  attacks Disraeli 169
  Jingoism over Egypt 185
  resigns over Ireland 204
  leads disident Liberals 205–6
  Colonial Secretary 229–30
  struggle with Salisbury 230–2, 248–9, 253–4
  and public opinion 230, 239
  and Jameson Raid 238–9
  alarmed by isolation 239–40
  benefits from Jongoism 245–6
  short-sighted policy of 247–8
  impatience with Salisbury 248–9, 266
  seeks German alliance 249–51, 254–5
  abhors drift 252–3
  seems desperate to Germans 256–7, 264
  Eckardstein misrepresents 257–9
  warned by Salisbury 259
  not easily squashed 260
  repudiates isolation 261–2
  pays German blackmail 264
  won't concede to Germans 265
  critical of Salsbury 266–7, 277–8
  Samoan crisis 269–70
  Boer War 273
  German alliance, again 274–6
  offends Bülow 275–6, 300
  German alliance, yet again 280–3, 288
  limitations of foreign policy 296
  Joe's war and diplomacy 299
  critical of Germany 300
  opposes Japanese alliance 303
  Anglo-French Entente and 306
  Tariff Reform and 324–5
  as Disraeli's heir 397
Chateaubriand, Vicomte 279
Chirol, Sir V. 300
Churchill, Lord Randolph
  makes himself a nuisance 197–8
  opposes Salisbury 203, 207–8
  makes a bigger nuisance 206–7
  crudeness of ideas 209, 212
  resigns 209
  forerunner of Chamberlain 230
Churchill (Sir) Winston S.
  critical of Salisbury 246
  Anglo-German war is not inevitable 350
  and firm action against G. 367–8, 369–70
  move to Admiralty 369
  and talks with Germany 374
  French naval agreement and 375–7, 394–5
  and 1914 crisis 391–2
  and Lloyd George in 1914 392
  critical of N. Chamberlain 400–1
Clarendon, 4th Earl of 3, 13, 16
Clark, Sir G. 332–3
Clemenceau, G. 371
Cleveland, President G. 236–7, 239
Cobden, R. 4, 23, 223

Conservative Party
  and foreign policy 2–3, 17, 41–2
  and balance of power 4–5, 295–6
  pacific tradition of 23, 173–4 (see also Derby, 15th earl of)
  Disraelian Jingoism and 102, 114, 161–2, 165
  and public opinion 120–3
  old versus new policy 153
  self-destructive tendencies 324–5
Corry, Monty (Lord Rowton) 96, 108, 118
Courcel, G. de 232, 248, 261, 262
Cowley, 2nd Earl of 61, 89
Cromer, 1st Earl of 309, 317, 326
Cross, R.A. (Lord) 68, 73, 82, 86, 91, 95, 99, 111, 123, 197, 279
Crowe (Sir) E.
  conflicting views on Germany 250
  no differences with G 338–9
  dim view of G aims 341
  different view of G aims 342, 347
  'Crowe's fork' 348, 360, 375
  and Ententes 363
  support for France 366
  traditions of foreign policy 400
Currie, (Sir) P. (Lord) 22, 24
  Derby 'a traitor' 146
  overtures to Bismarck 200–1, 213
  and Salisbury and public 231
  and S and British power 297
Curzon, G.N. (1st Marquess)
  critical of Salisbury 245–6, 247, 254, 264, 266, 277, 298, 307
  Salisbury criticises 297, 299
  Anglo-Russian Entente 343

Delcassé, T.
  and Fashoda 267–8
  and Continental League 274
  French foreign policy and 305
  and Morocco 305–6
  suspicious of British 306–7
  opens talks for Entente 309
  and 1st Moroccan crisis 318–9
  misrepresents Lansdowne 320–1
  resigns 321
  relations with Germany 371
Derby, 14th Earl of
  Tories not bellicose 5
  character 12–13
  Toryism of 13
  stop-gap Prime Minister 196
Derby, 15h Earl of
  and balance of power 4–5
  Disraeli's Foreign Sec. 4–5, 12 (see also Disraeli, B.)
  duel with Disraeli 6
  Eastern Question 11 and *passim*
  and Lady Derby 13–14
  Salisbury wants as PM 15
  opposed to policy of prestige 17, 63, 71, 88,

90, 98, 103–5, 110, 114–5, 137, 148, 152–3
differences with Disraeli 19–20, 21, 53–4, 96, 134, 171, 178,
cooperation with 'Concert' 21–2, 31
prevaricates 22
and Tory tradition 22–4, 53, 79, 84, 90, 105, 137, 145, 398–9
disdains public opinion 24, 40, 80–1, 88, 90, 152–3
and Berlin Memorandum 25, 26, 27
fears isolation 30–1
Bulgarian massacres 37–41, 64
resists pressure for action 43
negotiates with Russia, 47, 48, 54
cheered by mob 49
distrusts Bismarck 51–2, 57–8, 67–8
Salisbury and conference 54–5
and Turkish policy 58–9, 65
poor opinion of Ignatyev 61–2
will not coerce Porte 62–3
will not 'desert Disraeli' 63–4
failure of conference 66–7
pledges Britain to nothing 68
Eastern Question 1877 71–2
growing differences with D 71–5, 78–82, 85–6, 89–91, 97–8, 101–6, 114–5
Britain's vital interests 74
relations with D and S 77–9
dislikes S's politics 77, 83
'black legend' about 79
no seizure of Turkish land 80
resists D and the Queen 81–2, 83
D appeals to for support 82
willingness to resign 83–4
reliance on middle classes 84, 87–8, 91–2
and Cabinet 'leaks' 85–6, 95–6
tries to avert war 86–8
isolated in Cabinet 87–8
Disraeli conspires against 89–91
opposes 'prestige' policy 90
worried by D's attitude 91–2
unity with Carnarvon and S 92–3, 103–4
undermined by Disraeli 95–6
and Andrassy's lies 96
possible resignation of 96–7
and need for secrecy 99
focus for opposition to D 100–101
will not lead opposition to D 101–2, 113–4
misses opportunity against D 103
'frank' discussion with D 104–5
crux of disagreement with D 104–5
relations with Shuvalov 108
D as source of 'leaks' 108
traduced by historians 109, 115, 139
keeps Carnarvon in Cabinet 109–110
relations with Carnarvon
and Salisbury deteriorate 110–11
attacks Queen's speech 111
no alternative policy to D 113–4, 130
verge of resignation 114–5

assumes has resigned 115
falls ill 115–6
objections to sending fleet 117
against Austrian alliance 119
resignation anticipated 119
decides to resign 121
effect on relations with D 121–2, 129
resignation not publicised 122
alarm at resignation 123
mediation by Northcote 123–4
a 'check' on D 124–7
'black legend' about return 126–7
personal versus public life 129–130
altered relations with D 129
not 'cosmopolitan' 131
Russians fails to help 132–4
swamped by Jingo tide 133–5
lone voice against war 134–5
'a coward' (Queen Victoria) 135
slander and libels against 136, 138–9
disgust at Disraeli 137–8
cool nerve of 137–9
abused by press and clubland 138–9, 151
no British base in Med. 138, 142–3, 145–8
Shuvalov praises coolness of 139
and British policy 139–40
and risk of war with Russia 139–41
Bismarck a 'cynic' 141
refuses to go to Berlin 141–2
cautious diplomacy triumphs 142–3
divided from colleagues 143, 145–6, 147
Beaconsfieldism outflanks 145
prepares for resignation 147
S wants Foreign Office 148
will not go over hypotheses 149
protests about Cabinet 'leak' 150
final resignation 151
resignation speech 151–2
offered and declines Garter 152
antipathetic to D's policy 152–3
critical of Berlin 161, 223
represents centre ground 161–2
suspicions of Lytton 167
and cost of 'prestige' 169
adheres to Liberals 174
German colonial claims 191–2
continuity with S's policy 195–6, 199
Bismarckian animus against 199–200
dangers of democracy 224
and a new diplomatic world 297
and Sanderson 342
and Country Party Toryism 398
contingent nature of defeat 398–9
Derby, 16th Earl of, 123, 197
Derby, Mary, Countess of 6, 15
character 13–14
critical of Salisbury 15
on Derby and colleagues 22
Shuvalov correspondence 55, 65, 70
encourages Salisbury's

cooperation with Russia 70
and Cabinet unity 73
and Disraeli and Derby 77
relations with Shuvalov 77
supposed treachery of 79, 86, 89, 95, 98–9, 104–7, 136
helps Fred Wellesley 89
lives to regret this 89
Carnarvon warns her 91
Derby/S/Carnarvon alliance 92
worried by Disraeli 93
D divulges Cabinet secrets 95
on Derby 96
'far from pleasant' situation 97
blamed by Disraeli 98–9
'Derby holds the key' 100
a pawn in Disraeli's game 104–7
no reliable evidence against 107–9
reacts to allegations 107–8
tells Shuvalov about fleet 122
Cross speaks to 123
on Derby's return 125
scurrilous rumours about 136
Halifax on Derby to 162
Deym, Count 241
Disraeli, B. (1st and last Earl of Beaconsfield)
and British foreign policy 2–3, 4–5, 12, 16, 27, 29–30, 32, 58, 84, 102, 153–3, 245, 298–9, 397
mastery of image 2
'political acrobat' 3
leaders of Conservatives 11–12
and Derby 13–14 (see also Derby, 15th Earl of)
and Salisbury 14–5 (see also Salisbury, 3rd Marquis of)
and Lady Derby 15
Realpolitik of 15–16, 19, 26, 37–8, 43–4
Britain's world position 16
elections and diplomacy 17, 199
and Eastern Question 17–161 *passim*
and Berlin Memorandum 19–20, 24–7, 37–9
and Massacres 19–20
opposes Russian expansion 19–20, 32–3
differs from Derby over EQ 19, 21–22
and agreement with Bismarck 22
rearmament and prestige 23
prestige and public opinion 24, 27, 30–1
excitement of high politics 29
not Palmerstonian 29–30, 32, 47
S thinks policy myopic 30
Bismarck impressed by 31
amorality of policies 30–32
and cooperation with Russia 32–3, 47–8, 56–7, 69
comparison with Andrassy 35
and geopolitics 37–39
'coffee-house babble' 38–9
Real and Ideal politik 39–41
goes to Lords 39–40

and Cabinet's views 40–1
Gladstone critical of 41–2
critical of Gladstone 42–3
dislike of moralising 43, 68
and Bismarck's help 45–6, 51
radical solution to EQ 47–8
Russia must not occupy Constantinople 50–52
differences with Derby 53–4, 63–4, 71–2, 74–5, 78–80
wooing of Salisbury 54–8, 86–7
'critical moment' 58
and Cabinet divisions 58–61, 70–2, 75, 80–1, 82–3, 85–6, 88, 91–2, 95–6, 96–7, 101–2, 114–5
refuses coerce Porte 62–3
position on Eastern Question 63–4
hostile to Salisbury's ideas 65–6
suspicious of Bismarck 67–8
resourcefulness of 68–9
ill-health of 68, 82
'golden bridge' for Russia 69–70
'courage' of 72–3, 79–80, 101
Britain's vital interests 73–4
relations with Salisbury 77–9
changing relations Derby 78–9
carcases of dead policies 78
and public opinion 80, 84, 120–1
manouevres of 81–3
willing to see S go 82, 85
steering against Russia 83–7
enlists Queen's support 83–4
difficult maintaining Cabinet 83
Toryism and diplomacy 84–5
Cabinet 'leaks' 85–6
divisions between Derby and S 86–7
die is cast for war 87
conspires against Derby 88–90
and Fred Wellesley 89–90
and policy of prestige 90–2
trouble in Cabinet 91–2
divulges divisions 95–6
no 'second campaign' 96–7
flatters the Queen 96
tries win Derby over 96–7
wants support of mob 98
blamed by Derby 98–99
Jingo tide helps 99–100
further wooing of S 99
'be firm' (the Queen) 99–100
Derby wins support against 100–1
Queen supports D 101
tries rally Cabinet 101–3
importance of public opinion 102
fears conspiracy against him 103
uncertain future of Cabinet 103–4
frank discussion with Derby 104–5
uses Lady Derby as pawn 104–9
and 'prestige' (Derby) 105
woos S yet again 105–6

source of Cabinet 'leaks' 108–9
divide and rule 109–110
quarrels with Carnarvon 109–110
defeated by Derby 111
won't be restrained 113–4
further Cabinet disputes 114–5
offers to resign 115
Queen support him 115–7
Derby and Carnarvon 117–9
won't let Carnarvon go 118
Queen offers him the Garter 118
wants action 119–20
events help him 120–1
invokes public opinion 120–1
and Derby's resignation 121–2
has to let Derby return 122
alarm at Derby's resignation 123–4
relations with Derby 125–6
and foreign policy direction 126, 129–30
Derby's return a mistake 129
position after Derby's return 130–1
bellicosity of 132–3
Gladstone 'a vindictive fiend' 132
Jingoism behind him 133–6
Salisbury behind him 134
Queen behind him 135–6
renewed bellicosity of 137–8, 140
Jingoism outflanks Derby 145–6
leakeage of Cabinet secrets 146, 150
and Cyprus 147–8
prepared for Derby to go 148–9
'time for action' 150
and Derby's resignation 151–2
new direction of policy 152–3
prelude to Berlin 154–5
and Bismarck at Berlin 156–7
dominating figure at Berlin 156–9
'fluent Jingo' 159
triumph of 160–2
need to feed Jingoism 165–6
consequences of failure 166–9
and German alliance 170–3
and new foreign policy 172–3
Gladstone attacks 173–4, 179, 181
advantages compared to S 196
S on as head of Cabinet 197
S as successor 204
Chamberlain and opinion 230
price of imperialism 298–9, 397
contingent nature of victory 398–9
Dyke, Sir W. Hart- 120–1, 123, 130

Eckardstein, Baron
misrepresentations of 257–9
misleads Berlin and London 258–60, 263
and Chamberlain 274–5
further lies of 281–4
told not to raise alliance 286
raises alliance 283–4
web of lies 284–6

misleads Berlin 287, 292
yet more lies of 289–90
blames Hatzfeldt 291
failure of 293
and Entente 306
Edward VII. King 276, 283, 291–2, 309, 356
Elgin, Earl of 326
Elliot, Sir H. 38, 39, 55, 63, 64–5
Esher, Lord 332

Fischer, Fritz 250, 384
Fisher, Admiral 319
Flourens, E-L 214
Forster, W.E. 131–2, 134
Franz Ferdinand 384, 387, 389
Franz Joseph 35–6, 50, 194, 384
Freeman, E.A. 42, 101
Frere, Sir B. 168
Freycinet, M. 214

Gambetta, L. 184
Garvin, J.L. 350
Geoffrey, M. 267
George V, King 386, 388, 389
Giers, N. 202
Gladstone. William E. 11
and loss of prestige 2, 17
and old Tory party 5, 41–2, 53
Berlin Memorandum 25
critical of Disraeli 41–3, 114, 399
Bulgarian massacres 43
jeered by mob 49
approves of Salisbury 54–5
moralism of 118
'a vindictive fiend' 132
windows smashed by mob 143
condemns Government 169
attacks Beaconsfieldism 173–4
Disraeli hates 174, 200
limitations of liberalism 174–7, 179
'Concert' a myth 176–9
Bismarck out-manouevres 177–8
difficulties of ethical policy 181, 190–1, 194
difficulties in S. Africa 181–2
isolates Britain 182, 193–4
ruins relations with France 182–8, 190, 193, 207
and Egypt 183–90
fails to understand Bismarck 190
German colonial claims 191–2
liberalism/pacifism 192–4
crisis with Russia 193–4
failure of policy of 194
legacy to Salisbury 195–6, 199
resigns 196–7
abandons Midlothianism 204–5
declines office in 1886 205
new German foreign policy 228
death of 262
noble ideals of 397–8

Goblet, R. 214
Goluchowski, Count A. 352
Gorchakov, A. 19, 26–7, 31, 32, 107, 122, 174
  and Russian policy 33–4, 48
  and Reichstadt 36–7
  and cooperation with Britain 47–8, 54, 56
  cooperation with Germany 49–50
  Constantinople conference 66–7
  'golden bridge' 69–70
  British warnings to 89, 132
  and feelings against Derby 136
  warned by Shuvalov 138, 140, 150
  restrains Tsar Alexander 139
  and Berlin Congress 141, 154, 158–9
  and San Stefano 148
  and Bismarck at Berlin 156–7
  blames others for Berlin 157
  policy towards India 201
Gordon, General C. 194
Goschen, Sir E.
  German policy is 'chaos' 342
  Bosnian crisis and 353–4
  Germany/balance of power 364
  Grey's support for France 369
  mediation in Balkans 382–3
  will Britain go to war? 389
Goschen, George J. (Lord) 217–8, 277–8
Granville, 2nd Earl 41, 42, 43
  Concert of Europe 174, 176
  Whiggsh instincts of 176
  and Ottoman Empire 178
  'barking without biting' 182
  and Egypt 183–90
  hopes crisis will pass 184
  criticised by Lyons 185
  Egyptian diplomacy of 186–8
  fails to understand Bismarck 190
  German colonial claims 191–2
  'wild and irrational spirit' 193
  and crisis with Russia 193–4
  critical of Salisbury 198
  not reappointed to FO 204–5
Grey, Sir E. (Viscount)
  alleged continuity with Lansdowne 6–7, 279, 321, 323, 326–7, 334, 337
  and Relugas plot 325–6
  Bannerman does not want to appoint him to FO 326
  fears Germany 326–7, 340–1
  character 331–2
  primacy of French Entente 332–3, 338, 339, 341, 345, 365, 395
  conceals military talks 333–5
  commitment to Cambon 334–5
  authorises military talks 336
  casuistry of 336–7
  views of German policy 337–8
  and German hegemony 338, 345, 355, 361
  and balance of power 338–9, 340–1, 345, 356, 364
  relations with Germany 338–9
  different to Lansdowne 339–40
  lacks flexibility 340–1, 347, 356, 369, 379
  lack of dissent from 341
  helps create German danger 342–3, 356–7
  and Russian Entente 342–3
  failure of German talks 347–8
  risk of war 348–9
  cuts Cawdor programme 349
  ignores German weaknesses 349, 355
  naval scare 350–1
  not anti-German 350
  and Austria 351–2, 357–8
  Bosnian crisis 353–5
  need to guard Russian Entente 354–6
  and balance of power 356
  blank cheque for Russia
  and for France 357
  unbalances Europe 359–60, 364–5
  mistrusts Germany 360–1, 364
  warned of German isolation 360
  denies Triple Entente 363
  no German agreement 363–4
  policy of the Ententes 363–4
  assumes German bad faith 364
  trusts France and Russia 365–6, 372
  second Moroccan crisis 366–8
  need to support France 369–70
  mechanistic diplomacy of 369
  'free hand' 370, 376, 394
  and Tripoli 372–3
  depends on France and Russia 373, 382
  Haldane mission 374–5
  French naval agreement 375–6
  responsibility without power 377
  Balkan crisis 382, 385–7
  better relations with G 383, 385–6
  no counter to Russia 386
  Scutari 387–9
  assassination in Sarajevo 390
  France on her own 391
  and 1914 crisis 391–2
  assures Cambon 393
  3 August speech 393
  danger from Germany 394–5
  danger of isolation 399
  traditions of foreign policy 400
Grierson, General 334–5

Haldane, R.B. 325–6, 331, 335, 369–70, 374–5, 389
Halifax, 1st Viscount 107, 162
Halifax, 3rd Viscount 400
Hamilton, Sir E. 194
Hamilton Lord G. 240, 273, 303, 307
Harcourt, Lewis
  and Triple Entente 364
  dangers of backing France 368

opposes Grey 370
agreement with Germany 374–5
opposes French agreement 376
and war in 1914 391, 393, 394
Hardinge, Sir C. 324, 344, 354, 356–60, 363
Gathorne Hardy 45, 48, 67, 82, 86, 88, 91, 92, 95, 99, 102, 111, 115–6, 119, 132, 140, 148, 150–1, 166–8, 197, 206, 209, 215
Hartington, Marquess of 43, 85, 194, 204–6, 209, 229, 240, 287–8
Hartwig, N. 370–1
Hatzfeldt, Count P. von
 Salisbury and Russia 218
 puzzled by Salisbury 219
 Mediterranean Agreement 220
 British alliance 224
 Salisbury on Turkey 235–6, 300
 Kruger telegram 239
 on isolation's dangers 240
 Salisbury's pragmatism 246
 Salisbury's strength 248
 Chamberlain's alliance 254–7
 cautions Berlin 258, 262
 acts on instructions 258–9
 alliance proposals 259, 270
 concessions for Germany 259–60
 Berlins deaf to advice of 262–3
 and Nicholas II 263
 teased by Salisbury 264
 Salisbury not declining 266
 Samoan crisis 271
 folly of Berlin's policy 272–3
 another alliance proposal 275–6
 Chamberlain's impatience 278
 alliance revisited 280–1
 agreement with Russia 287–8
 negotiations with Lansdowne 288–9, 291
 Eckardstein's lies 289, 291
 and British 'politique' 313
Hayashi, Count 281–2, 286–7, 295–6, 296–7, 300–2
Haymerle, Baron H. 177
Henry, Prince of Prussia 386, 389
Hicks-Beach, Sir M. 82, 95, 197–8, 288, 299, 303
Hitler, A. 398, 400
Hohenloe, Prince C. 234, 241
Holstein, Baron F. von
 incompatible alliances and 227
 suspicion of Britain 234
 Britain needs Germany 235, 257–8, 259–60, 266–7, 272–3, 280–5, 287–9
 Continental League 238, 251
 Hatzfeldt's reports 248
 Bülow and Britain 255–6
 blackmail the Tsar 263
 pressure on Britain 270
 shocked by Bülow 275
 Britain's options limited 281, 300
 'we can wait' 282
 suspicious of Salisbury 284–5
 believes Eckardstein 287–9
 blackmails Britain 288
 let Britain come to us 290–1
 suspicious of King Edward 291–2
 suspicious of Salisbury again 299–300
 Salisbury on 304
 Lansdowne on 316
 suspicious of Entente 317, 322
 failures of German policy 317–8
 relations with Britain 337, 350
Hotzendorff, Conrad von 353–4, 355, 384, 387
Hunt, W. 82
Hornby, Admiral 116, 122, 136–7, 139, 142
Huguet, Col. 334–5

Ignatyev, N.P. 26–7, 32, 34, 59, 61–2, 64–5, 69–70, 82, 148, 154
Ignatyev, Mme. 57, 61
Ito, Count 301–2
Izvolsky, A. 343–4, 352–9, 370–1, 373–4, 381, 384–8

Jameson, L.S. 238–9
Jagow, G. von 385, 386
Jomini, Baron A. 33

Kiderlen-Wächter, A. von 385
Kimberley, Earl of 34, 228, 233–4, 262
Kitchener, F.M. Lord H. 267
Kokotsev, V. 384
Kruger, Paul 238–9, 273
Kühlmann, R. von 383

Lamsdorff, Count 286
Lansdowne, 5th Marquess of
 continuity with Grey? 6–7, 321, 323, 332–3, 334, 337, 339–40
 character and policy 279
 and Germany 279–80, 290–1
 and Salisbury 280
 German alliance 281–5
 talks with Japan 281–2
 talks Japan and Germany 282–3, 287
 draft German alliance 283–4
 dubious about this 284–5, 288
 Japanese alliance 286
 agreement with Russia 287–8, 293, 295–6
 events in Far East 288
 and Hatzfeldt 288–9
 asks for German text 289
 text of alliance 290–1
 Salisbury on alliance 290–1
 no German text 291
 favours German alliance? 292
 too high a hurdle 293
 Japanese negotiations 295–7
 limits of British power 298–9
 Japanese alliance terms 300–2
 agreement with Germany? 302–3

opposition to Jap alliance 303–4
Russia and France 304–5
origins of French Entente 306–7
agreement with Russia? 308–10
talks with France 309
future of Jap alliance 310
possible failure of Entente 310–11
Entente signed 311
not anti-German 313, 317, 324–5
success of his policy 314–5
weakness of Germany 315–6, 338, 399
Moroccan crisis 319–20
supports Delcass_ 320–
misrepresentations of this 320–1
compared with Grey 321, 323, 339–40
insular concerns of 322
no French alliance 322–3
continuity with Salisbury 324, 326–7
Entente a means to an end 332
and military talks 332–3
and Sanderson on 342
and Austria and Macedonia 352
Lascelles, Sir. F. 238–9, 263–4, 264–5, 271, 275, 279–80, 281–2, 283–4, 290–2, 322, 332, 340, 342
Layard, Sir. H. 81, 99, 113, 115, 120, 122–3, 137–8, 146
Leopold, King of Belgium 228
Law, A. Bonar 390
Lichnowsky, Prince M. 387, 388
Lloyd George, D. 331, 350–1, 366–7, 369–70, 390, 392–3, 400
Loftus, Lord A. 142, 146, 148
Loreburn, Lord 366–8, 370
Lowe, R. 49
Lüderitz, A. 191
Lyons, 1st Earl 83, 95–6, 149, 182–5, 199, 206, 215, 217
Lytton, 1st Earl 53, 72, 78, 87, 166–9, 206

Malet, Sir E. 238
Malietoa, King 270
Mallet, L. 319, 334, 356–7, 359, 373
Malmesbury, 3rd Earl 39
Manners, Lord J. 85–6, 95, 99, 102, 111, 135, 197
Manteuffel, General 46
Maple, Sir B. 257
Marchand, Captain 267–8
Mataafa, King 270–1
Milner, Sir A. (Lord) 266, 273
Marder, Professor A. 224
Marschall, Baron 229, 238–9
McKenna, R. (Lord) 367–8, 376
Mensdorff, A. 356–7
Metternich. Count P. von 291, 300, 302–3, 306, 322, 333, 337–8, 360, 366, 370
Moltke, General H. von 379
Monson, Sir E. 268, 306–7
Montagu, E. 392

Morier, Sir R. 201–2
Morley, John (Lord) 295–6, 331, 347, 367, 369–70, 376, 392–3
Munch, Count 50
Münster, Count 108, 170–3, 191–2, 199–200
Muraviev, Count M. 273–4, 276

Namier, Sir Lewis 383
Nekliudov, Count A.V. 370–1
Nicholas II, Tsar 242–3, 246–7, 263, 285, 308, 323, 349, 359, 384
Nicolson, Sir A. 332, 344
  and Russian Entente 354
  danger of Bosnian crisis 356
  support for Russia 358, 363
  defeat for Entente 359
  Triple Entente 363
  support for France 366
  change of policy 370
  Russian intentions benign 373–4
  naval agreement with France 375
  support France and Russia 386–7
  1914 crisis 389–91
Nikita, King of Montenegro 387–8
Noailles, G, de 274
Nomura, Marquis 301
Northcote, Sir S. (Iddesliegh, Earl of)
  mentioned 40, 49, 55, 62, 82
  and Bulgarian Atrocities 41, 43
  trepidation of 45, 88
  and Turkey 65
  wants 'a policy' 72–3, 74, 91
  against isolation 92
  lampooned by Disraeli 95–6
  agrees with Disraeli 99
  support for Derby 100
  checks Disraeli 102–3
  appeals for unity 104, 109–111
  and the fleet 117, 122
  and Derby's resignation 123–4, 125
  moderate Derby's return 129–30
  need for action 134–5
  Cabinet 'leaks' 146
  on Cyprus 148
  Derby's final resignation 151–2
  and Berlin 159–60
  and Randolph Churchill 197–8
  Salisbury writes to 205
  becmes Foreign Secretary 206–7
  supports Salisbury 208
  dies 209
  on Bismarck 212

O'Conor, Sir N. 253
Olney, R. 237, 241
Oubril, Count P. 157

Paget, Sir A, 194

Palmerston, 2nd Viscount

and balance of power 4
offers post to Stanley 13
success of foreign policy 17, 29–30, 86, 153, 182
Eastern Question and 18, 30, 32
criticised by Gladstone 41–2
invoked by Gladstone 173
Peel, Sir Robert 11, 130
Peters, K. 225
Poincaré, R. 375–6, 380–1, 384, 388
Ponsonby, A. 391–2
Ponsonby, Sir H. 89

Repington, Col. 332–3, 334, 335
Rhodes, C. 270
Ribot, A. 371
Richmond, Duke of 82, 99, 102, 197
Richtoften, Baron O. von 283
Ripon, Lord 335
Ritchie, C. 303
Rosebery, 5th Earl of 205, 228–9, 325
Roosevelt, F.D. 398
Rouvier, M. 318, 321
Runciman, W. (Lord) 368
Russell, Lord J. (1st Earl) 3, 173
Russell, Lord Odo, (Ampthill) 22, 24, 30, 31, 66–7, 81, 95–6, 157, 174–5, 178–9, 183–6, 188, 190–2

Saburov, Count 174–5, 178
Salisbury, James, 2nd Marquis of 13, 14
Salisbury, Robert, 3rd Marquis of
  continuity with Lansdowne 6
  mentioned 12
  and Disraeli's Cabinet 1874 14–15
  Russian expansion 18–9, 55
  critical of Disraeli 29–30 and *passim* (see also Disraeli, B.)
  on foreign policy 30, 64
  blames Elliot 38
  wants agreement with Russia 47
  mistrusts Bismarck 51–2, 67–8
  Disraeli woos him 53–6, 86–7, 104–6
  Constantinople Conference 54–7, 63–7
  Disraeli's policy is dubious 55–6
  meets Bismarck 57–8
  Disraeli distrusts 59, 65–6, 82
  distrusts Disraeli 61–65, 78–9, 103
  and Lady Derby 70, 92–3, 98–9
  and Eastern Question 70–2, 80–1
  and British policy 72
  and Derby and Disraeli 77–9 (see also Derby, 15th Earl of)
  ambition of 77–8
  and Queen Victoria 83
  succumbs to war fever? 87–8
  and a 'clear policy' 91
  a 'party by himself' 95
  popular opinion and war 98, 101
  as frondeur 100
  and the 'three nobles' 103–4
  Derby appeals to him 105
  and Carnarvon 109–11
  joins Derby for last time 111
  will resign with Derby 114–5
  resolute 116
  supports Disraeli 118, 120–1
Salisbury, 3rd Marquis,
  possible Foreign Secretary 118–9, 121
  and Derby's return 124–5
  shadow Foreign Secretary? 126, 129
  opportunism of? 130–1
  need for action 134–5
  'critical moment' 137
  balance of power 145
  and Cyprus 148–9
  and Realpolitik 148–50
  and Disraeli 151–3
  Bismarck's cooperation 154, 155
  at Berlin 155–61
  and Jingo opinion 165–6
  Anglo-German alliance 170–3
  and Gladstone 173–4
  Bismarck's blackmail 189, 213
  foreign policy of 195–7
  similar to Derby's policy 195, 199, 217–8, 230
  and public opinion 195–6, 212–3, 216–7, 225, 234, 252
  politics and foreign policy 196–8, 207–8, 211–2, 219, 223–4
  at Foreign Office 197
  forms first Government 197–8
  PM and Foreign Secretary 198
  casus belli 198–9
  and isolation 199–200, 211–12
  needs German help 199–200
  Russia the real menace 201–2, 212–13
  Bulgarian crisis 202–3, 205, 207–9
  and Churchill 203, 206–7, 209
  acquires prestige 203–4
  and Rosebery 205
  will serve under Hartington 205
  forms Government 206–7
  assumes Foreign Office 209
  and policy of 209–212
  not isolationist 211–2
  and Bismarck 212–4
  and France 215–7
  Mediterranean Agreement 216–7
  never a Jingo 217–18
  and Russia 218–9
  puzzles Bismarck 219–20
  problems of democracy 220, 223–4, 231–2, 259, 313
  2nd Mediterranean Agr. 220–2
  possible German alliance 222–4
  naval building 224–5
  Britain not isolated 225
  Heligoland/Zanzibar 226

517

effects of fall of Bismarck 227–8
return to power 229–30
struggle with Chamberlain 230–2, 247–9, 253, 261–2
contempt for democracy 231–2, 239
differences in Cabinet 231–2, 240–1, 243, 269, 277–8, 290
cooperation with all 232–3
Armenian question 232–5, 242
Future of Turkey 233–6
crises 236–41
pragmatic diplomacy of 241–2, 246, 256
hampered by Jingoism 245–6
and Russia 246–7
and France 247–8
and Germany 249–53
'apathy' of 254
Chamberlain and Germany 256–9
'dying nations' 259
'jargon about isolation' 259, 290
and German blackmail 260–5
not in decline 266–70
refuses German alliance 270, 272–3, 278–80, 284, 288–9, 290–1, 302
Samoa 271–2
Kaiser complains about 271–2
unruffled 273–6, 324
criticised 277–8
leaves FO 279
continuing influence of 280–1, 282–3
magisterial paper of 290
nature of isolationism of 295–6
and Japanese alliance 297–9, 300–4
and Turkey 300
Cambon on 305
retirement 305
Sanderson on 342
and Austria 351
comparison with D and Derby 399
Salisbury, Lady 64, 106, 107
Salisbury, 4th Marquis 324
San Guilino, Marquess 372
Sanderson, Sir Thomas (Lord) 86, 108, 117, 236, 289–90, 300, 313, 315–7, 333–4, 335–7, 338, 340–1, 342, 344, 399
Sandon, Lord 16, 145
Sazonov, S. 371, 371, 382, 384, 386–7
Scott, Sir C. 286
Scott, C.P. 367
Sefton, Lord 174
Selborne, 2nd Earl 297, 299, 303, 348
Selves, J. de 373
Seymour, Sir E. 5
Shannon, Prof. R.T. 38–9
Shuvalov, Count P. 6, 29, 37, 47–8, 50–1, 56, 69–70, 71, 114, 131
and Lady Derby 55, 65, 98, 106–7, 122, 129, 135, 138
Anglo-Russian relations 73–4, 77, 85–6, 89, 91, 96, 98, 107–9, 122, 132–4, 136–7,
138–40, 139–41, 142, 146–8, 149–53, 154–5, 157–60
Simon, Sir J. 393–4
Smith W.H. 95, 99, 103, 117, 122, 139, 197
Sophie, Queen of Holland 14
Soveral, Marquess de 314–5
Spencer, Earl 229
Spender, J.A. 335
Spring-Rice, C. 237, 343–4
Staal, Baron G.G. de 262
Stalin, J. 398
Stanley, Venetia 390
Sukhomilinov, General 383
Swaine, Colonel 236, 238

Taylor, A.J.P. 176, 336, 382
Tenterden, Lord 38, 108, 148
Temperley, Prof. H. 398
Tewfiq, Khedive 183–7
Tirpitz, Admiral 248, 270, 374, 380, 399
Trevelyan, G.O. 132
Trevelyan, G.M. 332, 340
Tweedmouth, Lord 349
Tyrrell, W. 365–6, 383

Vansittart, R. 250
Victoria, Queen[tab]
mentioned 2, 6, 17, 24–5, 30, 48, 51, 72, 74, 150, 155
supports Disraeli 81, 82–4, 86, 89–91, 95–7, 101, 111, 120, 130, 147–8, 160
blames Derby 98–9, 108, 115–116, 118–25, 152
hereditary loopiness 114, 133–6
and Gladstone 174, 186, 188, 203–8
and Salisbury 216, 220–1, 226, 240, 265, 291–2
Victoria, Crown Princess 133–4, 141, 160, 265, 291

Wellesley, Fred 88–90, 91, 105–6, 107
Wellesley (see Cowley)
Wellesley, Gerald 107–8
Wellington, 1st Duke of 13, 89
White, H. 237
Wickham-Steed, H. 391
Wilhelm I, Kaiser 32, 46, 49–51, 221, 228
Wilhelm II, Kaiser 221
and foreign policy 227, 228–9, 249–52, 317–9, 323, 337–8, 349, 355, 364, 370–2, 384–5, 387–8, 399
and Britain 227–9, 235–9, 240, 251, 255, 257–60, 262–5, 270–6, 280–5, 286, 289, 291–2, 249–50, 374–5, 385–6
character 228
William III, King 3
Wilson. Sir H. 398, 400
Witte, S. 251, 301, 323
Wolff, Sir H. Drummond- 207, 214, 216–7
Wolseley, Sir G. 187

518